Octavius Ogle, W. H. Bliss

Calendar of the Clarendon State Papers

Octavius Ogle, W. H. Bliss

Calendar of the Clarendon State Papers

ISBN/EAN: 9783741172854

Manufactured in Europe, USA, Canada, Australia, Japa

Cover: Foto ©Andreas Hilbeck / pixelio.de

Manufactured and distributed by brebook publishing software (www.brebook.com)

Octavius Ogle, W. H. Bliss

Calendar of the Clarendon State Papers

CALENDAR

OF THE

CLARENDON STATE PAPERS

PRESERVED IN THE BODLEIAN LIBRARY

VOL. I

To January, 1649

EDITED BY

THE REV. O. OGLE, M.A.

AND

W. H. BLISS, B.C.L.

UNDER THE DIRECTION OF THE

REV. H. O. COXE, M.A.

BODLEY'S LIBRARIAN

Oxford

AT THE CLARENDON PRESS

NOTE.

The Clarendon Papers preserved in the Bodleian Library have been placed there at different times, and have come from various quarters.

An account of those that were in the Library in 1786, when the third volume of a considerable number of selected letters was published by the University of Oxford, is to be found in the prefaces to the three volumes of that collection, from which the following particulars are gathered.

In 1759 a large number, consisting partly of original State Papers, partly of authentic copies, was given to the University of Oxford by the descendants of the Earl of Clarendon; and in 1767, on the publication of the first volume, several papers, which had come into the possession of Richard Powney, LL.D., were presented by his executors.

Subsequently, a third portion of State Documents purchased of Mr. Joseph Radcliffe, one of the executors of the third Earl of Clarendon, was presented by Dr. Radcliffe's Trustees, and further additions were made by John Douglas, D.D., canon of Windsor, afterwards Bishop of Salisbury, who bought several letters from William Guthrie, author of the new Geographical History, and obtained the gift of others from Viscountess Midleton, from the custody of Mr. Richards (from whose father Dr. Powney had at an earlier period obtained a portion of his collection), and almost immediately afterwards original letters of Lord Clarendon, in the possession of William Man Godschall, Esq., of Albury, Surrey, to the number of 220 were transmitted through Dr. Douglas in the course of the year 1781.

With these materials, Mr. Thomas Monkhouse, Fellow of Queen's College, Oxford, the editor of the third volume, completed the selection of papers published in 1786. In these three folio volumes, which have been long out of print, is contained a very large portion of the collection of Clarendon State Papers which had up to that time become the property of the University.

A further acquisition, however, and one of great interest and value, was made so lately as 1860, when, a century after the reception of the first instalment of the collection, other papers enclosed in boxes and in Lord Clarendon's private writing chest, were sent by the trustees of the bequest made to the University by Henry Hyde, Earl of Clarendon and Rochester, in 1753.

It may be worth observing that in this *escritoire* are the writing materials used by Lord Clarendon himself— pens, silk, wax, pounce-box, and scissors, just as he left them.

Of the 3000 papers calendared in this volume, a large number were sent to Lord Clarendon for his use while he was writing his *History*, and are all, together with public and private letters addressed to himself, endorsed by his own hand. Copies of his own letters, and the correspondence of his secretary, Edgeman, form a portion of the remainder. And of these, an interesting series, written during the Chancellor's stay at Jersey, has afforded materials to Dr. Hoskins for his carefully compiled account of " Charles II. in the Channel Islands." Numerous holo-

PREFACE. vii

graph drafts and letters of the King and Queen form the most valuable part of the collection.

Above three hundred copies of letters of State, addressed by Queen Elizabeth to foreign princes in the early years of her reign, are calendared as Addenda. Of these, many are of considerable interest, relating, as they do, to the mercantile and religious affairs of the kingdom; and should be read in conjunction with the foreign series of State Papers edited by Mr. Stevenson for the Master of the Rolls.

Queen Elizabeth's letters, the papers that passed between the King and Parliament connected with the Treaty of the Isle of Wight, and those calendared in the two Appendices, have been selected from the mass, and are bound in separate volumes. All the other papers are arranged in chronological order, except the holographs of Charles I. and Henrietta Maria, the greater number of which have been also bound by themselves.

The first portion of the present volume, including nearly all the papers anterior to 1646, has been edited by the Rev. Octavius Ogle, M.A., formerly Fellow of Lincoln College, who was unable to continue the work; for the remainder one of the assistants in the Bodleian Library is responsible. He begs to express his acknowledgements to those who have kindly assisted him in a task to which he has been able to give only a portion of his time, and which has therefore been extended over four years.

The third and fourth volumes of Papers are being prepared for the press.

OXFORD, 1872.

Calendar

OF

CLARENDON PAPERS.

1. *Constitutions* of Henry VIII and eleven Knights of the Garter, settling the rights of Garter Principal King of Arms. *Translation written and endorsed in a later hand**. — 1523. Richmond, April 23.

2. "*Several Memorials* among Lord Cecil's, transcribed out of a book of his, being sent unto me by Richard King, Minister and Dean of Tuam." A letter, addressed "Most worthy Sir," mentioning the rising of Wiat; Sir Rd. Southwell; Sir Edwd. Hastings; Sir Tho. Cornwallis; the French King and the "Romish parties" of Scotland, Ireland, and England; William Walsh, and others. Begs a place for the bearer in Her Majesty's fleet. Reports speeches of the Spanish ambassador, and the French and Scottish agents. *Superscribed as above and signed Ed. Dunne. Mutilated.* — [1563]. Naples, Aug. 3.

3. *Orders* to be observed concerning Garter, Clarence, and Norroy Kings of Arms, and the other Officers of Arms, made by the Earl Marshal, the Duke of Norfolk. *Copy.* — 1568. July 18.

4. *A Circular Letter* of the Earl of Leicester, enclosing a copy of the next to the nobility and magistrates of the realm. *Copy.* — 1584. Whitney. Oct. 4.

5. *The Instrument of an Association* for the preservation of Her Majesty's royal person. *Copy.* *See Rapin, vol. ii. p. 119.* — Hampton Court, Oct. 19.

6. *Commission* to Sir R. Cross, in command of the Swiftsure and the Crane, to attend Sir F. Drake and Sir J. Hawkins. *Imperfect draught.* — No date.

7. i. *Act of the States General* granting privileges to English merchant-adventurers, dated Jan. 9, 1587. ii. *Confirmation* of the above Act, dated July 14, 1598. iii. *Safe* — 1587.

---
* See Ashmole's History of the Order of the Garter, p. 194.

1587.	*Conduct* to English merchants, of same date as the last. iv. *A Resolution of the States General* to the same effect, dated June 3, 1599. *Copies.*
1590. Deptford, May 7.	8. *The Lord High Admiral (Howard of Effingham) to the Lord Treasurer (Burghley),* about some extra victuals in hand, and a quarrel of Mr. Douglas, the Scottish Ambassador, with an Italian merchant. Endorsed by Mr. Aylesbury *.
June 11.	9. *The same to the same.* There is continued intelligence of the great preparations of the King of Spain, who is reported to have been ready to put to sea fourteen days.
1593. St. James's, March 31.	10. *Warrant* of the same to deliver to the Earl of Cumberland the two ships, the Elizabeth Bonaventure and the Lion. *Copy.*
1598. March 30.	11. *Table* of the comparative gravities of the river and the fountains in Madrid.—Spanish. *Printed.*
1600. No date.	12. *Commission from the Lord High Admiral (Nottingham)* to Capt. John Troughton to the Spanish coast and the Levant, to suppress piracy. *Rough draught.* Year endorsed on the back.
1604. No date.	13. "*A Discourse* of the present practises of the Papists against Protestants throughout Europe." (Three pages.)
1605. No date.	14. *A Discourse written by the Earl of Devonshire in defence of his Marriage (after a divorce).*† (Fifteen pages.)
1608. St. George's Channel, July 6.	15. *Capt. Williams to the Lord High Admiral (Nottingham).* Has delivered his prisoners at Dublin Castle, and encloses a copy of his instructions from the Lord Deputy to cruise off the Irish coast, in his ship the Tremontana.
London, July 15.	16. *Mr. J. Yonge to the same,* about the exchange of the ordnance of the forts.
July 20.	17. *J. Hankin and T. Thompson to the same,* making complaint of one John Allott (or Elliott) for absence from duty.
Exeter, July 28.	18. *Mr. Ferdinand Gorge and others to the Lords of the Privy Council,* pointing out defects in the commissions issued by the Admiralty Court. *Copy.* Without signature. Name of writer endorsed by Mr. Aylesbury.

* These Admiralty papers probably came into Lord Clarendon's hands from his father-in-law, Mr., afterwards Sir Thos., Aylesbury, sometime Secretary to Lord High Admiral Buckingham.
† He married Lady Penelope Devereux, the divorced wife of Robert, Lord Rich, in 1605, and died April 3, 1606.

19. *Mr. Alex. Lowther to Mr. Harriott*; a private letter, desiring to make his personal acquaintance. This summer is said to be hotter than any known in England. Mention is made of Mr. Aylesbury, resident in Oxford.—Latin.
1608. Gloucester Hall, Oxford, July 27.

20. *Mr. Richard Gifford to Mr. Lumley.* Requests him to make endeavours to procure his release from prison in Florence.
Florence, July 31.

21. *The same to the Lord Treasurer (Buckhurst).* Sets forth his case as an English subject imprisoned by a foreign Duke.
Florence, July 31.

22. *Warrant* of Lord Nottingham for the appearance of William Goringe and William Goodcare before him.
Hallinge, (Croydon) Aug. 17.

23. *Letter of the same*, concerning the same men, being disorderly keepers of ale-houses in Cholsea.
Hallinge, Aug. 20.

24. *Sir W. Monson to the same*, announcing the recovery of a French barque from the pirates.
Plymouth, Aug. 30.

25. *Capt. Wood to the same*, on receiving an acquaintance from Capt. Button.
Portsmouth, Sept. 9.

26. *Sir W. Monson to the same*, on the restoration of the French barque to its owners, and his receiving a fly-boat laden with sugars from Capt. Button. Don Lewis Fachados has left Lisbon with twenty galleys.
Portsmouth, Sept. 9.

27. *The same to the same*, on the expected arrival of the ambassador, and with details of naval movements.
Endorsed with Post memoranda.
'The Vanguard,' Sept. 27.

28. *Geo. Giustiniani to the same*, requesting him to allow the new Venetian Ambassador to be conveyed to England in one of His Majesty's ships.—Italian.
London, Oct. 4.

29. (*William Bourchier*) *Earl of Bath to the same*, concerning the making up of his account for the Vice-Admiralty of Barnstaple.
Tavistock, Nov. 9.

30. *Sir R. Hawkins to Sir T. Crompton*, in behalf of one Peter Peterson.
Nov. 14.

31, 32, 33. *Five Blank Pardons* for Ireland, signed and sealed by the Lord High Admiral.
No date.

34. *A Farrier's Bill*, headed "The Ld. Hamberalls byll."
1608–9. Jan. 10.

1608-9. Westminster, Feb. 19.	35. *Mr. Jobson to the Lord High Admiral (Nottingham)*, about the adjudgment of some sugars, the right to which is disputed by the Spanish Ambassador.
Feb. 22.	36. *Sir W. Monson to the same.* He intends to pursue his search for the pirates upon the West coast.
March 2.	37. *A Note* of a chest of tobacco left at Scilly by Henry Collenor and William Longcashell.
Plymouth, March 4.	38. *Capt. Wood to the Lord High Admiral (Nottingham)*, announcing the capture of the pirate Jennings at Limerick.
Chichester, March 5.	39. *The Mayor of Chichester to the same*, touching the seizure of some tobacco.
London, March 13.	40. *Sir D. Dun to the same*, on the business of the sugars, previously mentioned.
March 14.	41. *Mr. Rosearrock to the same*, announcing the seizure of 1000 lbs. of tobacco.
March 18.	42. *Sir D. Dun to the same*, narrating the trial at Chester of the captured pirates.
March 20.	43. *Mr. Rosearrock to the same.* Complains of one Randall for breaking open the house in which the captured tobacco was deposited.
March 24.	44. *Sir W. Monson to the same.* Has brought the captured ship Ulysses into Stokes Bay, and intends to come into the Downs.
March 24.	45. *Mr. Hall to the same*, concerning the tobacco seized at Chichester.
1609. Oatlands, Aug. 25.	46. *Sir John Trevor to the same*, returning a warrant for signature.
1610. Dublin, Aug. 10.	47. *Sir Oliver St. John to the same*, thanking him for Capt. Owen Wynne's kindness to his wife at Chester.
Holyrood, Aug. 25.	48. *(George Hume) Earl of Dunbar to the same*, praising Sir William St. John's service on the Scottish coast.
Holford, Aug. 25.	49. *Capt. Fludd (of the Advantage) to the same*, about the Penelope, suspected to have piratically seized a Spanish ship, laden with hides and tallow.

50. *Mr. Rich. Hall to the Lord High Admiral* (Nottingham), detailing the history of his ship the Penelope, and the army of sorrows which have followed him throughout the business. — 1610. Plymouth, Aug. 17.

51. *Sir Rich. Cooper to the same*, on the same business. — Plymouth, Aug. 28.

52. *Sir W. St. John (of the Adventure) to the same*, of his voyage from Leith to Yarmouth. — Yarmouth, Aug. 26.

53. *Sir Rich. Cooper to the same*, of the matter of the Penelope. He is going to Ireland on information of two rich pirates. — Plymouth, Sept. 12.

54. *(Henry Wriothesley) Earl of Southampton to the same*, in behalf of the bearer, a Mr. Leigh. — Carisbrook Castle, Sept. 15.

55. *(Thomas Howard) Viscount Bindon to the same.* A letter of compliments. — Nov. 14.

56. *Sir Peter Buck to the same.* Two men have been caught sounding the river between Rochester and Chatham. — Dec. 3.

57. *Sir Thomas Sherley to the same.* Petitions to be kept in Sir Giles Wroughton's house, instead of in prison, for his debts. — Sarum Gaol, Dec. 4.

58. *Capt. Owen Wynne to the same*, sending a pirate whom he has captured off Ireland. — 'The Lion's Whelp,' Dec. 26.

59. *A Circular Letter* from the Lord Treasurer to the stewards and bailiffs of the King's manors in the midland counties, announcing an approaching sale of lands to pay the King's debts. — 1610-11. Whitehall, Jan. 15.

60. *To the Lord Deputy* (Chichester). Places the Speedwell at his disposal for the suppression of piracy. *Draught.* Without signature. — 1612. May 10.

61. *A Note* of the collection and disposal of the ploughing fines in Tyrone and Armagh in 1612. — No date.

62. *A Note* of the money collected in Ulster in 1612 by the ploughing fines (870*l.*), and its disposal in building churches and bridges, and in other public works. Two copies, one imperfect. — No date.

63. *The Lord Deputy* (Chichester's) *answer* to the charge of undue grants to his servants of forfeitures of concealment in the matter of the King's lands. *Draught.* — No date, probably 1612.

1612. No date.	64. *Warrant* from His Majesty to the Lord Deputy to examine the title of the Crown to O'Carroll's country, and to make grants of the same to such British and Irish as he thinks fit. *Draught.*
No date.	65. *A Blank Draught* of grants of the O'Carroll country.
1612-13. Feb.	66. *The Lord Deputy (to Sir H. May?).* Explains the danger of granting the ploughing fines to individuals, who would incline to compromise them. *Draught and Copy.*
March 3.	67. *The same to the same.* Defends his conduct in the plantin of Wexford, and exposes the mischievous conduct of Mr. Walsh and the Commissioners. Extracts, dated as above, and signed A. C. Endorsed, "A branch or two of a letter written to Mr. May in Feb. 1612, to be imparted to my Lord Treasurer."
1613. London, May 7.	68. *Sir H. May to Mr. Annesley.* Sir Randall McDonnell is to have an act of parliament to settle his lands on his wife's children. The Lord Deputy may do as he will about Sir Randall's claim to the plough-money on his own lands, so his outward behaviour be smooth to him. Parliament should be prorogued, if not disposed to the King's ends.
June.	69. *The Lord Deputy (Chichester) to Sir H. May.* Narrates some disputes of precedence between the Viscount of Buttevant (who has hitherto ranked next to the Earls) and the Viscount of Gormanstown; and between the Baron of Killeene and the Baron of Dolvyn. Does 'baro' imply the title of Baron or of Baronet? and does 'Dominus' infer more than the lordship of the manor? Desires a warrant to be got for some skilful person to search the records in the Tower. Two copies, somewhat differently worded.
June 19.	70. *Sir H. May to Mr. Annesley.* Sir Thomas Overbury is still a close prisoner. His Majesty growing daily more infected towards him. Sir Oliver St. John is pressing his suit for the government (of Ireland), but will fail *.
July 14.	71. *(Thomas Howard) Earl of Suffolk to the same.* His Majesty intends to repair Mr. Arthur Mill's losses by the fines imposed on the jury empanelled on Sir T. Loftus and others.
Sept. 13.	72. *Sir H. May to the Lord Deputy (Chichester),* concerning some lands in dispute between Mr. Andrews and the Bishop of Dromore.

* Sir Oliver St. John, afterwards Viscount Grandison, was appointed Lord Deputy in 1616.

73. *Sir Thomas Loftus to the Lord Deputy (Chichester)*, asking permission to redeem his cows and garrans seized by the sheriff, Sir Richard Græme. 1613. Sept. 21.

74. *The Lord Deputy (Chichester) to (Robert Carr) Earl of Somerset.* Complains of the insolent conduct of the Irish recusant lords, and asks the support of the Council against the ill-will of the papists. *Copy.* Dublin, Nov. 13.

75. *Sir H. May to Mr. Annesley.* The Lord Deputy is to name five or six for a new creation of Barons, special regard being had to the point of religion. Sir Garrett Moore and Sir Thomas Cocle are contemplated. M^r. Treasurer of Ireland has offered Lord Burleigh 3000*l*. for a Barony, but failed in obtaining it. Nov. 17.

76. *The Lord Deputy (Chichester) to (Thomas Howard) Earl of Suffolk* in Mr. Annesley's behalf; and in the matter of the forfeitures of Sir Thomas Loftus and others for the murder of Mr. Danylls (or Danielle), which are to be made over to Mr. Arthur Mills. *Draught.* Dublin, November.

77. *(Thomas Howard) Earl of Suffolk to the Lord Deputy (Chichester).* The jury have gone directly against the evidence in finding Sir T. Loftus and the others guilty only of manslaughter, and will hear more about it. All the goods of the prisoners are to be seized, and no favour shewn them. Signed T. S. No date.

78. *The names of such as were in company with Sir Thomas Loftus when Mr. Danielle was murdered* (fifteen in all). No date.

79. *Sir Humphrey May to Mr. Francis Annesley.* Recommends the bearer for some small holding in the new plantation of Wexford. Whitehall, Dec. 73.

No year given, but endorsed as "Received Jan. 20, 1613."

80. *Account* by the Lord Deputy (Chichester) of the drawing of ploughs by the rumps of beasts, and the pulling the wool off the sheep twice a year with cloven sticks in Ulster; and the steps he had taken since 1606 to abolish these customs by fines granted to individuals, and this year to Sir William Uvedale. *Draught.* 1613.

81. *Plan of a Sham Fight* on the Thames at the marriage of the Princess Elizabeth (of Bohemia). 1613.

CALENDAR OF

1613.
No date.
82. *A Letter* proposed to be sent from His Majesty to the Lord Deputy concerning the settlement of Mr. Andrews' claims to the lands in Dromore. *Draught.*

No date.
83. *Sir H. May to Mr. Annesley.* To thank the Lord Deputy for his kindness to Capt. Russell and Sir Randall M'Donnell. Mr. Netterville will fail in his suit, notwithstanding his bribes. The Lord Deputy should answer to the complaints about the plough fines, that he marvels they do not likewise complain that they have to cut their glibbes and wear English clothes. Clanricarde is not likely to recover.
Endorsed, "Rec^d Aug. 8, 1613."

No date.
84. *Draught of a Schedule* sent by Mr. F. Annesley to Sir H. May, stating the sums to be charged various Englishmen for grants of Forts in Ireland.

1614.
Whitehall,
March.
85. *Warrant* from Lord Nottingham for commissions to Mr. Spruson and certain ships trading to the West Indies and Brazil to apprehend pirates; addressed to Sir Daniel Dun.

May 31.
86. *Message from the Commons to the Lords* by Sir Roger Owen, touching language used by the Bishop of Lincoln in apparent disrespect of the Commons. The Lords answer that the Bishop has excused himself satisfactorily, and that no members of their house ought to be called in question by the Commons on public rumour only.
The substance of this paper is given in Carte's Hist. Regl. vol. iv. p. 37.

Monaghan,
Aug. 10.
87. *Sir Edward Blaney to Mr. F. Annesley*, offering 600*l*. for a grant in Monaghan.

Newstead,
Aug. 16.
88. *Sir H. May to the same.* Sir John Græme's suit is by no means to be furthered: the cause of this at present a secret.

Leicester,
Aug. 16.
89. *The same to the same*, concerning the grant of leases to Mr. Netterville.

Aug. 16.
90. *Memoranda of Sir Humphrey May for the Lord Deputy of Ireland.* Every man should cast about to relieve the King's revenue, other services being undervalued in respect of this. The country contributions are to be advanced, and the Lord Deputy to consider of a new and abated establishment, and what payments may be transferred to the treasury. To write (for the King's view) concerning the grant of mountain lands. The King will write for the pardon of M'Guire and his son.
Imperfect at the beginning.

91. *Sir H. May to Mr. Annesley.* Further explanation of Mr. Netterville's business, and about the settling of O'Carroll's country. How is the contribution in Ireland going on? Concerning Annesley's unlucky money affairs, and the progress of the Mount-Norris business. Sir Foulke Conway's letter is signed and sealed for a counsellor's place, but stayed on the false information that he is a papist. The Lord Deputy must write to clear this. — 1614. Windsor, Sept. 17.

92. *The Lord Treasurer (Suffolk) to the Lord Deputy (Chichester).* Declaring the King's pardon to Sir Thomas Loftus and others in the matter of the murder of Mr. Davylls. The jury are to be summoned before the Star Chamber. — Northampton House, Nov. 6.

93. *Sir H. May to Mr. Annesley.* The Lord Deputy is in high favour at court for the prosperous beginning of the Irish parliament. Concerning Netterville's and Sir John Græme's suits. A lease is to be made out for Sir Edward Blaney. — Nov. 8.

94. *Mr. Dudley Norton to the same,* about his coming to Ireland. To send back my Lord Treasurer's first letters about Sir Thomas Loftus and the rest, and to hasten the money for Mr. Mills. — Westminster, Nov. 9.

95. *Sir H. May to the same.* Some letters have not been received. Nothing must be done in Sir J. Græme's business to his advantage. The Lord Deputy to write accordingly to my Lord Chamberlain to say that the King has not executed the grant because it is harsh to the country, (this reason to be omitted if the Lord Deputy think fit): and that a proclamation has been signed to give liberty of free trade, without payment of licence money, for all commodities except wool and linen yarns, and to desire therefore that the grant be called in. Netterville's business has wearied him much, but will be settled. — London, "from my bed in scribbling haste," Dec. 21.

96. *Memoranda to be imparted to my Lord (Deputy) by Sir H. May's advice.* 1. Some Acts to be propounded in Parliament for the reformation of the extortions committed by sheriffs and their officers. The Lord Deputy to send his advice on the matter by Sir Josias Bodley. 2. The undertakers have been quickened by the King's letters, and more buildings are likely to be effected this summer. 3. What Protestant voices will be in the higher House? And will the Papists agree? My Lord to advise the King to create three or four Barons to strengthen the House. 4—7. To thank the Privy Seal and Chancellor, and to ask concerning the settlement of O'Carroll's and O'Rourke's countries. — No date.

1614.		8. The cost of the soldiers is much complained of, and the King is much displeased at it.
No date.		97. *Memoranda.* My Lord (Deputy) to transmit forward intelligence to the King immediately, and in his next to Lord Rochester to thank the King for his late favours.
1614–15. Jan. 13.		98. *Sir H. May to Mr. Annesley.* Encloses the King's letter for a lease to Edmund Midhope, in the matter of Netterville's business. The bargain may be Annesley's if he will, but not to his loss.
Jan. 14.		99. *The same to the same.* Will use due circumspection, but they that think he is limping in his fortune perchance hereafter will know that he hath legs to go upon when they have no eyes to see them. A letter enclosed to Sir Toby Calefield concerning his plough-tail business. The Lord Deputy had written to have Mr. Blundell sent over to attend in Parliament.

Endorsed, "About the noise of Mr. Chambers' grant."

Westminster, Feb. 26.		100. *Sir Dudley Norton to the same*, announcing the payment of Mr. Mills' money.
1615. April 7.		101. *Sir H. May to the same.* Concerning Mr. Netterville's leases, and Sir William Uvedale's business of the ploughtails. He will be glad of any lawful favour shewn by the Lord Deputy to Mr. Gild, but not to any one's prejudice. Annesley should not listen to rumours, and should himself be sparing of speech. Knows the malignity which attends his actions, but trusts His Majesty's favour and justice. Believes the Treasurer's place is safe, but will write again. The Mount-Norris business is not forgotten. Concerning the plantation of Longford and Wexford. For other matters refers to Sir Toby Calefield and the Lord Deputy.
April 25.		102. *The same to the same.* Has sent to the Lord Deputy two grants by the King of life-pensions of 100*l.* and 80*l.* a-year to the Ladies McGuire and O'Kelly in lieu of their jointures.
May 17.		103. *The same to the same.* Is sorry anything in his letter to the Lord Deputy should seem to Annesley's prejudice, but is ready if needful to testify to his faithful services and friendship.
May 27.		104. *The Magistrates of Hamburg to the Lord High Admiral* (*Nottingham*), requesting the restitution of a ship taken by pirates, retaken by the English, and brought into Cardiff. —Latin.

105. *Sir H. May to Mr. Annesley.* Has sent him what he promised. 1615. June 17.

106. *The Lord Deputy (Chichester) to Capt. Edw. Trevor and Marm. Whitchurch, Esq.* Warns them of the penalties they incur in abetting the custom of ploughing with horses' tails. They ought to set a good example to the natives, and aid the execution of the directions in the printed book for the rules of plantation in the escheated northern counties. Dublin, June 15.
Copy.

107. *Sir H. May to Mr. Annesley*, recommending Mr. Barham. London, Sept. 15.

108. *The same to the same.* His cousin Norton is to be sent home as soon as possible, as ruining himself by his constant doting on some unworthy wench or other. Is unwilling at present to move in the matter of the Northern Forts, especially Mountjoy, the proposed residence of a President of a provincial government of Ulster. London, Sept. 15.

109. *The same to the same.* If Annesley will not pay Lady Morrison he is to let him know, that he may repay Sir Richard Morrison. The Lords have made abatements of above 10,000*l.* a-year in His Majesty's Irish charges, and have discharged the ward at Mount-Norris, without its being in his power to help Annesley in the matter. Dec. 11.

110. *The same to the same.* Sir Dominick Sarsfield has quite cleared himself to His Majesty and the Lords of the charges made by enemies in Ireland. Ignorance in England of persons in Ireland is the high misfortune of Irish employments. Dec. 19.

111. *The Lord Deputy (Chichester) to the Council.* Concerning the grant by the King to private persons of the benefits arising from the fine of 10*s.* ordained for the barbarous custom of ploughing with horses drawing by their tails. No date.
Imperfect at the end.

112. *His Majesty to the Lord Deputy (Chichester).* The fines for ploughing with horses' tails are to be strictly enforced. The obstinacy of the natives on this point. All pretences of necessity from the rocky nature of the ground are to be transmitted to the King and Council. No date.
Draught.

113. *Sir H. May to Mr. Annesley.* Encloses a letter to the Lords Justices* in Annesley's favour, requesting leave for him 1616. April 12.

---

* Thomas Jones, Archbishop of Dublin, and Sir John Denham, Chief Justice of the King's Bench, were appointed Lords Justices of Ireland in 1615.

1616.	to come to England, to repair the wrongs which he conceives hath been done him; a course, however, which May neither advises nor discourages. The Lord Deputy is in great favour with His Majesty and the Lords.
1616–17. Jan. 21.	114. *Sir H. May to Sir F. Annesley, Knt.* To send him a copy of Sir Foulke Conway's letter. To learn what the customs in Ireland yielded the first year they were established, before they were farmed. Whether custom was then paid by the fishermen.
March 17.	115. *The same to the same.* Acknowledges the receipt of money through Lord Ridgeway and Captain Pinner. Has written to the Lord Deputy in Annesley's favour, and trusts he will turn toward him each day more than other. Sir Dudley Norton will be troubled to hear that by my Lord of Buckingham's favour, Mr. Holcroft has obtained the reversion of the Chancellor of the Exchequer's place. The King went yesterday towards Scotland, and he is to follow; so that he will not be able to help Annesley in the Wexford business. Sir Francis Bacon has been promoted to be Lord Keeper*, and he may thereby get his place in the Star Chamber.
1617. London, Dec. 14.	116. *The same to the same.* If Annesley will come speedily to England, he will get a direct answer from the Lord Keeper, which now he suspends with delays.
1618. The Hague, Dec. 12.	117. *Propositions of the French Ambassadors to the Magistrates of the Low Countries.* It pertains to the honour and security of the new Magistrates to treat their prisoners kindly, though accused of most treasonable offences. Wise princes have often pardoned such; and it is a principal mark of freedom in a republic to spare the lives of citizens. Especially is this true in the case of Barnevelt, who has rendered such great services to the State. The French King therefore entreats a favourable trial for him.—French. *Copy.*
The Hague, Dec. 19.	118. *The Magistrates of the Low Countries to the French Ambassadors*, in answer to the last. The Low Countries have given the French King no cause to suspect their friendship. The prisoners have aspired to change the religion and laws of the country, but nothing hasty or informal will be done in a matter of such importance. The King shall have no reason to complain, so far as the requirements of justice admit of clemency.—French. *Copy.*

* Sir Francis Bacon was appointed Lord Keeper on March 7.

119. *The Prince (Maurice) of Orange to the King of France (Louis XIII).* Is sorry to find that umbrage has been given to the King by his administration of the principalities of Orange. He cannot believe that his Governor, the Sieur Vosbergen, has done anything to the disadvantage of the King. The garrison of his fortress is a matter which all his predecessors have had acknowledged as their undoubted right, and he can find no mention in his brother* (the late Prince)'s papers or will, of a promise that the garrison should be entirely composed of Catholics: at all events, such promise could only be personal. But he is conscious that the prosperity of his Principalities entirely depends upon the favours of his Majesty.—French. *Copy.* — 1618-19. The Hague, Jan. 17.

120. *The French Ambassadors to the Magistrates of the Low Countries.* Pressing the necessity of having fair judges, the prisoners being such high and hitherto meritorious officers. The King, actuated solely by the consideration of the welfare of the States, prays them, by the memory of the late King and his own friendship, to be merciful.—French. *Copy.* — The Hague, Jan. 24.

121. *The Lord High Admiral (Nottingham) to my Lords,* resigning his office from age and inability, thanking His Majesty for his favours, and expressing his happiness to see so worthy a successor (Buckingham†) in his place. — Hampton Court, Jan. 17.

122. *(Lord Danvers) to the Lord High Admiral.* Sets forth the true political reasons for the expedition ostensibly prepared against the Algerine pirates, its object being chiefly to watch the Spaniards' motions and check their growing power by sea, while protecting the interests of allies in Germany, Venice, and Bohemia. Intends to accompany the expedition in person. *Rough draught.* — Feb. 3.

123. *List* of twenty serviceable ships in the Thames, with their tonnage, and an estimate of the charge for six months of sixteen of them. (The estimate to cover seven months.) *Date endorsed.* — Feb. 4.

124. *Details of the above Estimate,* the crews in all being 1440 men, and the total charge for six months (to last with good husbandry for seven months) being 21,926*l*. 10*s*.

125. *The Commissioners to my Lords.* About making ready the ships; and recommending one Cadman as purser for the Destiny. — Feb. 5.

* Prince Maurice, the Stadtholder, succeeded his half-brother, Philip William, as Prince of Orange in 1618.
† The Marquis of Buckingham was appointed Lord High Admiral Jan. 16, 1618-19.

1618–19.
Hampton
Court,
Feb. 13.

126. *Lord Nottingham to my Lords*, recommending Captain Ryman to their service.

Doctors'
Commons,
Feb. 13.

127. *Sir Henry Marten* to the Lord High Admiral (Buckingham).* Concerning certain prohibitions taking from him the power of Thames, and of the sea about Harwich; and enclosing the two next.

128. *His Reasons* in brief why his Lordship should oppose these prohibitions.

129. *Further Suggestions* for my Lord Admiral in the case of Blake's prohibition against Violett.

Feb. 14.

130. *The Commissioners to my Lords*, for money to victual the first six ships.

Feb. 16.

131. *The same to the same*, about graving and grounding the ships and removing the cook-rooms.

Feb. 15.

132. *Capt. Hewes to the same.* Asks for some employment. He has seven years ago received his Majesty's pardon for piracy.

New-market,
Feb. 16.

133. *The Lord High Admiral (Buckingham) to the Surveyor of the Victualling (Sir Allen Apsley).* To be careful of the victualling of the ships. The bread to be well baked and the beer sufficiently boiled.   *Copy.*

Chester,
Feb. 16.

134. *(William Stanley) Earl of Derby to my Lords*, to continue his Patent as Vice-Admiral of Lancashire and Cheshire.

London,
Feb. 16.

135. *The Commissioners to the same*, concerning a fire at Deptford.

London,
Feb. 10.
(sic)

136. *Sir Thomas Smyth to the same*, enclosing an abstract of a letter of Sept. 28, 1618, from the English Agent at Spahan in Persia. The Persians have defeated the Turks, with many thousands slain on both sides. By the late grant of a firman to have the refusal of all silk, they will have a settled trade with Persia, if supply come currently this year, maugre all their enemies, pope, Turk, or devil.

---

* Sir H. Marten, afterwards Dean of Arches, was appointed Judge of the Admiralty Court in 1617.

137. *Mr. Chancellor (Fulke Greville) to the Lord High Admiral (Buckingham),* about pressing men, and victualling the ships *.
1618–19. London, March 1.

138. *The Commissioners to my Lords,* complaining of the absence of Captains from their ships.
March 6.

139. *Sir W. Courtenay to the same,* recommending Sir Edward Seymour as Vice-Admiral of Devon in the place of Sir Lewes Stuckley.
Powderham, March 11.

140. *Sir W. Courtenay, Sir E. Seymour, and others to the same,* about the embargo on ships in South Devon.
Powderham, March 12.

141. *(William Stanley) Earl of Derby to the same,* recommending Captain Salisbury.
Chester, March 11.

142. *Mr. Chancellor (Greville) to the Lord High Admiral (Buckingham),* touching the exportation of lead.
Austen Friars, March 11.

143. *Capt. Mervyn to my Lords,* about the powder and shot carried by the Indian fleet.
Drury Lane, March 14.

144. *A Note* of the Merchants' estimate for ten ships against the pirates.
March 16.

145. *List* of a committee to meet the Lords about the merchant shipping.
March 18.

146. *Sir H. Marten to my Lords,* touching the Admiralty jurisdiction and attacks on it in a book of Anthony Munday.
Aldersgate Street, March 20.

147. *Sir Allen Apsley to the same,* requiring money for the victualling. Beef will be dearer at Easter than in Lent by 2d. a-day in a man's allowance.
The Tower, March 24.

148. *Sir H. May to Sir F. Annesley,* hoping to see him soon, and that he will come to England prepared with matters of his profit and his Baronetcy.
1619. April 15.

149. *Sir Thomas Smythe to my Lords,* forwarding a complaint of the English merchants in the East India trade, that the Dutch possess all the forts.
London, April 21.

---

* Sir Fulke Greville, afterwards Lord Brook, was promoted from the Treasurership of the Navy to the Chancellorship of the Exchequer in 1603. This and his next letters are addressed, "Rt. hon. Grandfather," and signed by him as "Your loving Grandchild."

1619.
Canterbury,
May 9.

150. (*James Hay*) *Lord Doncaster* to —, asking for blank letters from His Majesty to the German Princes, to be taken by him on his mission.

No date.

151. *List* of the thirteen German Princes to whom letters are desired, with their proper titles of address.

Trinity House, Ratcliffe.
Aug. 28.

152. *The Brethren of the Trinity House to the Lord High Admiral* (*Buckingham*), requesting leave for Peter Richards and Ambrose Jennens, merchants of London, to arm their ship Frances of 160 tons, now at Plymouth, with six mynions and 2 sackers of cast-iron ordnance.

1619!*
Frankfort,
Oct. 17.

153. *A Journal of Foreign News*. The sickness increases mightily at Frankfort. The enemy has somewhat retreated from the city. It is hoped that Minden will be ours shortly. Our forces are much discontented for want of payment. The French forces on the Rhine are doing nothing, and will not prosecute the war offensively against Austria. In brief, *Gallus tergiversatur, Succi suspicantur, hostes non cunctantur, Danus pacificationem renovet*. The Spaniards are coming with 18,000 men to restore the Elector of Mentz and the Bishop of Wirtzburgh. The enmity between the Admiral and Chancellor (who is at Mentz) continues. Saxony and Brandenburgh have made peace with the Emperor, who is said to have annulled the Edict of Religion made at Passau. If so, the Calvinists will all come over to France.

Without signature.

Nov. 7.

154. (*Mr. Coke*) *to the Lord High Admiral* (*Buckingham*), with hints for his first entrance upon office. The last paragraph is as follows: " Lastly, where no stranger was permitted heretofore to sail up the Medway or to come amongst the ships, the Low Country men now daily haunting that way both know the channels and the state of the navy, and bringing with them a few trifling commodities carry thence fuller's earth for the dressing of our cloths, and store of gold and silver, as generally men complain. This your Lordship may be pleased to consider as a service long neglected, and worthy to be reformed at the entrance of your office, especially for that from Ulissing to the ships at Chatham one with good wind and tide may come to do mischief in less than 10 hours."

Draught.

In Mr. Coke's hand.

---

* This summary probably relates to the period of 1619-20. The Elector of Saxony withdrew from the Protestant cause at that time. Mansfeldt, who is mentioned in it, died in 1626.

155. *Decision* in a suit for 1000 marks to be paid for procuring the defendant the Knighthood of the Bath. Judgement for the plaintiff. Signed Henry Devenish.
1619. Nov. 16.

156. *Lord Nottingham to the Lord High Admiral (Buckingham).* Desires to know to whom belongs Sir Walter Raleigh's ship, now at Plymouth, and said to be worth 7000*l*. Hitherto he was never questioned withal in the teke of traitor's good, but had carried it without contention.
Hampton Court, Nov. 29.

157. *The Brethren of the Trinity House to the same*, requesting leave for William Samuel to arm his ship Priscilla of Dartmouth, of 160 tons, with ten mynions and four sackers.
Trinity House, Ratcliffe, Dec. 18.

158. *Instructions to Vice-Admiral Sir Robert Mansell, in command of the fleet to be sent against the pirates.* To act in courtesy and harmony with the ships of Spain and the States fitted for the same purpose. The ports of Spain will be open to him; Gibraltar to be the rendezvous. The service without the Straits to be left to the Spaniards. The chief nest of the pirates and armadores is Algiers, where they are to be demanded of the magistrates, or attacked if within the mole. The town must not be assaulted, as belonging to the Grand Signior. Turks or Moors of note to be exchanged, if possible, for Christian captives. Not to go eastward of Sparta Verita. Rewards of 40*l.* and under may be given on the spot. A council of war appointed to advise; (Sir Richard Hawkins and six others). Provision for cleaning the ships, and appointing a successor if needful.
No date.*

159. *Mr. Henry Dade (Deputy Vice-Admiral for Suffolk) to Mr. Aylesbury.* Concerning the conduct of Admiralty suits in the county of Suffolk.
1620. Malsford, May 22.

160. *Lord Nottingham to my Lords*, recommending the bearer, a Mr. Norton.
May 30.

161. *The Brethren of the Trinity House to the Lord High Admiral (Buckingham)*, requesting leave for Edward Wilde of Limehouse to arm his ship the John, of 160 tons, with two sackers and eight mynions.
Trinity House, June 23.

162. *Mr. Phineas Pett to Mr. Aylesbury*, recommending his kinsman Peter Pett as royal shipwright in the place of the late Mr. Brighte.
Ratcliffe, July 3.

* Buckingham is mentioned in this as Lord High Admiral.

1620. Trinity House, July 6.	163. *The Brethren of the Trinity House to the Lord High Admiral (Buckingham)*, requesting leave for Robert Sluce of Leith to arm his ship the Mary Rose, of 180 tons, with four mynions and two falcons.
Trinity House, July 12.	164. *The same to the same.* A similar application for four sackers and eight mynions for the Grace of London, of 120 tons, belonging to Humfry Slaney.
Deptford, July 14.	165. *Mr. Edgebury to the same*, recommending two men for cooks' places on board.
Marquis House, Aug. 3.	166. *Sir Robert Mansell to Mr. Aylesbury*, recommending Peter Pett for the building of the new pinnace. His family have had the employment since Henry the Seventh's time.
The Hague, Aug. 9.	167. *Sir Dudley Carleton to Secretary Naunton**. Recommends the joining together of the two fleets now preparing in England and the States. *Extract.* In Secretary Calvert's hand, and endorsed by him, as sent to His Majesty, which he "having read and imparted the contents to my Lord Admiral first, and then to myself, commanded me to make such an answer as I sent to Secretary Naunton, 12 August, and afterwards His Majesty gave me the letter itself of Sir Dudley Carleton to take away with me and to read."
Aug. 13.	168. *Minutes of a Conversation (of Secretary Calvert?) with His Majesty.* Sir Dudley Carleton is to remain at the Hague and not follow the Prince of Orange, unless necessary. Mr. Trumbull's warnings of dangerous persons about His Majesty are too general to be serviceable. If the French King proceed with his expedition against Bearn, he is to be earnestly remonstrated with. In Secretary Calvert's hand, and endorsed by him as the "minute of a letter to be sent to Secretary Naunton."
Aug. 26.	169. *Mr. Robert Pye to Mr. Aylesbury.* The Privy Seal for 1452*l.*, whereof 452*l.* is intended for Sir Thomas Sutton, is improperly directed, nor is there so much money in the Exchequer.
St. Martin's Lane, Sept. 5.	170. *Secretary Calvert to the same*, forwarding a new commission for Sir R. Mansell, with the title of Captain-General omitted.
Yarmouth, Sept. 24.	171. *Sir William St. John to my Lords*, requesting payment of 100*l.* for extra victualling his ship. With a copy of the Admiralty order for payment attached, dated Oct. 2.

* Sir R. Naunton was appointed Secretary of State in 1618, and Sir George Calvert, afterwards Lord Baltimore, in 1619.

172. *The Lord High Admiral (Buckingham) to the Vice-Admiral of North Wales.* An order for the restitution of the goods of Henry Stone, cast away at Holyhead. *Copy.* 1620. Nov. 7.

173. *Mr. Aylesbury to Sir Henry Marten,* with memoranda for the examination of Captain King and others, who had brought some tons of iron into Devonshire. Newmarket, Nov. 24.

174. *The same to the same.* The Spanish Ambassador has complained of Captain King. The news of the overthrow in Bohemia is confirmed, but is too bad to repeat. Newmarket, Nov. 28.

175. *Bill of Charges* from Captain Christian for bringing the ship Lord Thomas from Dartmouth to the Thames, amounting in all to 21*l*. 12*s.* 10*d.* Dec. 27.

176. *Sir Henry Marten to Mr. Aylesbury.* Has taken sufficient caution of Captain North's ship. Aldersgate Street, Dec. 27.

177. *Lord Nottingham to the same,* asking for the arrears of his pension. If he gets them not, he will take a lodging by Mr. Chancellor, and live with him till he has eaten out his money. *Date endorsed by Aylesbury.* 1620.

178. *Report* in favour of a petition of the East Country merchants, shewing how their trade is decayed by reason of the exorbitant raising of the standard of money in Germany, Prussia, Poland, and the Eastern countries. The only remedy is a royal proclamation to forbid importations thence except in native shipping, as has already been done in the case of the Levant Company. No date.

179. *Extracts from the Journals of the House of Lords,* on various subjects. No date.
Endorsed, "In the hand of the third Lord Clarendon." Printed in the Parliamentary Journals, vol. iii. pp. 33, 41, 51, 54, 63, 141.

180. *An Address of the Presbytery of Aberdeen to the Bishop of Aberdeen*,* shewing the danger to the Protestant religion from the proposed relaxation of the penal laws against Papists. No date.

181. *Minutes* relating to the supply of saltpetre to his Majesty's stores, and proposed improvements in the working of the mines. *Endorsed by Mr. Aylesbury.* No date.

* Alexander Forbes: translated from Caithness to Aberdeen in 1615.

1620-1.
Dublin,
Feb. 21.

182. *The Lord Deputy (Grandison) to Mr. Aylesbury.* Reminds Buckingham to secure Viscount Thurles' wardship, in case the Earl of Ormond die. Sir Francis Blundell has urged the matter of the Lady Elizabeth's aid, for which however he thinks the present time unfit.

Brussels,
March 14.

183. *Lord Digby to the Marquis of Buckingham.* Has had audience of the Archduke and the Infanta. If the King of Spain is to send his daughter to England, with a portion of two millions, and cause the restoration of the Palatinate, a close alliance will be expected, and the Hollanders not to be preferred to the Spaniards. The Archduke's confessor has informed him that the reason of Chancellor Pecthius being sent into Holland, is to endeavour to persuade them to return to allegiance, the truce being now about to expire. *Copy.*

Cl. S. P. vol. I. App. p. L

1621.
Harkney,
April 5.

184. *Mr. Edward Misseldean to Mr. Aylesbury.* Sir Albertus Morton is set upon what he imparted to him. *Exitus acta probat.* 'Tis said of Pyramus and Thisbe *Ex æquo captis ardebant mentibus ambo,* and so it is with him and Aylesbury.

July 1/5.

185. *Count Mansfeldt to the Forces of the Bishop of Bamberg.* Letter sent by a trumpet, requiring their immediate withdrawal from Bohemia, and threatening to lay waste the country with fire and sword, if they follow the example of the Bishop of Wurtzburg in interfering.—French. *Copy.*

Endorsed in the King's hand, "12 Agust, 1621."

Straubing,
July 12.

186. *(Maximilian Emmanuel) Duke of Bavaria to the Emperor (Ferdinand II).* He cannot at present aid Don Balthazar de Maradas in the conquest of Tabor, being reluctant to diminish his forces in the presence of Mansfeldt, who has attacked the Landgrave of Lechtenberg, and committed other overt acts of hostility.—French. *Copy.*

Endorsed in the King's hand, "12 Agust, 1621."

Vienna,
July 16.

187. *Lord Digby to the Prince of Wales.* Encloses the three next papers. Desires that no alteration be made in the resolutions taken at his departure.

Cl. S. P. vol. I. App. p. viii.

Vienna,
July 16.

188. *The same to the Lords Commissioners for the affairs of Germany.* Had his first audience of the Emperor on the 5th, the day after his arrival, and made his propositions *(as below).* The Commissioners appointed to treat with him are the Count of Mecaw, Lord Chamberlain to the late Emperor Matthias,

and Baron Stralendorff, Vice-President of the Council of the Empire, who have asked for particulars, which he has declined to give till the Emperor assent to the general propositions; and gives reasons for this course. Has received the answer which he encloses. They are attempting to amuse him till the return of a messenger sent to the Duke of Bavaria, who is said to favour a general peace, before the Prince Palatine be restored; as also do the Electors of Treves and Mentz, and the Bishop of Spires. The Duke of Bavaria desires to be assured of the payment of his expenses. Requests punctuality of payment in his own salary, and that no new resolutions be taken. *Copy.*

1621.

Cl. S. P. vol. I. App. p. ii.

189. *Lord Digby to the Lords Commissioners for the affairs of Germany.* Has endeavoured to dissuade the Emperor from re-commencing the war in the Lower Palatinate, but he will only consent to a general cessation. Is afraid, if once the Duke of Bavaria obtains the Upper Palatinate, he will never give it up, holding Donawert, as he does, in the same way on the execution of a ban of the Emperor Radolphus, and still retaining Upper Austria in payment of his expenses in the wars of Bohemia, which he reckons at 1,200,000*l.* The Emperor has consented to write to Marquis Spinola, leaving it to his discretion to suspend the execution of the ban and continue the truce, and that all acts of the Duke of Bavaria against Mansfeldt shall be without prejudice to the Count Palatine. The effectual restitution must come from Spain, whither he intends to go, and thence to Ratisbon. Desires that despatches to that effect be sent to the Ambassador in Spain and Mr. Cottington, and that preparation be made for war, Sir Robert Mansell's fleet being still continued on the coast of Spain. *Copy.*

Vienna, July 16.

Cl. S. P. vol. I. App. p. vi.

190. *Propositiones Baronis Digby, Serenissimi Magnæ Britanniæ Regis Legati, ad Sacram Cæsaream Majestatem, and Responsio Cæsareæ Majestatis ad Propositiones dicti Legati* (arranged in parallel columns). i. The restoration of the Prince Palatine. *Answered.* The Emperor can take no final resolution till after the Diet summoned at Ratisbon. ii. A suspension of the execution of the ban, and of hostilities in the Lower Palatinate. *Answered.* The Emperor cannot consent to this while Mansfeldt is invading Bohemia, and Brandenburg exciting revolt in Silesia and Moravia.—Latin.
Endorsed by the King. Cl. S. P. vol. I. App. p. v.

No date.

191. *Don Gonzalo Fernandez de Cordova to the Landgrave of Darmstadt (Louis V).* A short note concerning Mansfeldt's

Creutznach, Aug. 4.

1621. proceedings, and the suspension of arms in the Lower Palatinate.—Spanish.   *Copy, enclosed in N°. 193.*
Endorsed in the King's hand, "11 August, 1621."

Vienna, Aug. 5.
192. *Lord Digby to the Prince of Wales.* Letters from Rome announce that the young King of Spain has dealt very effectually with the Pope, who has named a Congregation of well-disposed Cardinals for the despatch of the business, Cardinal Bellarmine being left out, as averse to it. Desires that his wife meet him in France.
Cl. S. P. vol. I. App. p. viii.

Aug. 12.
193. *The same to Secretary Calvert.* The Duke of Bavaria is much discontented at the prospect of entire restitution, and has used high language to the Emperor, being backed by the Nuncio and Father Jacintho, a Capuchin sent by the Pope to solicit the Electorate for the Duke of Bavaria. The Jesuits also are strongly in his favour, and the danger from Mansfeldt renders it hazardous to offend him. Encloses a letter from Don Fernandez de Cordova to the Landgrave of Darmstadt, promising to remain quiet unless provoked. *Copy.*
Cl. S. P. vol. I. App. p. xvii.

Vienna, Aug. 12.
194. *The same to the Prince of Wales.* Intends to go to Spain in September. The rumour of *Burgos** not being able to get children is widely spread in Germany. Father Maestro, writing from Rome, gives good hopes of success in his business, if moderation be observed in England. The new embroilments of the Marquis of Jagendorf and Count Mansfeldt have overturned all things here for the present.
Principally in cypher.
Cl. S. P. vol. I. App. p. xvi.

Vienna, Sept. 5.
195. *The same to the Lord High Admiral* (Buckingham). The Emperor has promised, now that the Diet cannot hold, to settle matters as speedily as possible, and has sent Ambassadors to all the Princes, especially his brother the Archduke Charles to the Duke of Saxe. The Duke of Bavaria complains of the suspension of arms in the Lower Palatinate as a violation of the agreement that no peace should be made without the knowledge of the Princes. The Marquis Spinola has however ordered his Lieutenant-General Don Fernandez de Cordova to do nothing unless provoked. This provocation has been given by Sir Horace Vere lodging his troops in Spires against the wish of the Bishop. The business of the match appears to be in a fair way. Wishes his wife to meet him in France on his way to Spain.   *Copy.*
Cl. S. P. vol. I. App. p. ix.

* Probably the Prince himself is meant.

196. *Lord Digby to the Lords Commissioners for the affairs of Germany.* The Diet having been hindered, principally by the difficulties of the Duke of Saxe, to whom Nosticks had been sent in vain, Baron Echemburg, President of the Council, has given him, by the Emperor's authority, good hopes of a final settlement, but the Condé d'Onate has advised him to leave for Spain, the Emperor being greatly incensed at the proceedings in the Palatinate and at Spires. Vice-Chancellor Stralendorff has since intimated the same to him, and after much negotiation, the Emperor declares himself unable to command a cessation of arms, except on condition that Mansfeldt discontinue hostilities, the Prince Palatine's commission to Jagendorf be revoked, and Tabor and Wittingau restored. Has promised the first, declared that Jagendorf has no commission, and will apply to His Majesty about Tabor and Wittingau. Leaves his cousin Digby as Agent, and Mons. Rusdorf in behalf of the Prince Palatine. *Copy.*
Cl. S. P. vol. I. App. p. x

1621. Vienna, Sept. 5.

197. *The same to the Prince of Wales.* Explains the grounds for his promises to the Emperor mentioned in the last.

No date.

198. *The Emperor's Answer to Lord Digby.* Though the hostilities of Mansfeldt have hindered the assembling of the Diet, and Sir Horace Vere's invasion of Spires has broken the truce, he will still recommend a suspension of arms if Jagendorf be disowned, Tabor and Wittingau restored, and Mansfeldt disarm in case of suspension of the ban.—Latin. *Copy.*
Cl. S. P. vol. I. App. p. xv.

Sept. 13.

199. *Captain Stewart to Mr. Aylesbury.* Has received information from Cornelius Biggin, Captain of the Brownfish, Dutch man-of-war, that he and others are commissioned by the States to intercept 4000 English on the seas for the Spanish service. This is confirmed also by Robert Sluce of the Mary Rose.

1621-2. Aboard the Nonsuch, Feb. 23.

200. *The Moorish Governor of Tetuan to (Mr. John Duppa),* giving permission, in the name of his Sovereign, Muley Abdallah, to the English to trade to that port.—Spanish. *Copy.*

1622. June 26.

201. *Mr. John Duppa to Lord —,* on his return from Tangier; giving account of his proceedings with the Moriscoes, having been left by Sir Robert Mansell to ransom the English slaves at Tetuan. Has arranged with the Muccaden of that place for the exchange of eight English, and that no more

Cadiz, July 10.

1622. British subjects shall be sold, he engaging that Muley Abdallah, King of Fez, shall make like proclamation throughout Barbary. Desires to be sent on this employment. Muley Sedan commands from Fez to Morocco, but Muley Mahomet has usurped the command of Alcassar.

Endorsed by Windebank, "Mr. John Dupps to my Lord on his return from Barbary." Cl. S. P. vol. i. p. 1.

Madrid, Aug. 1⁵/₁₅.
202. *Lord Digby to Secretary Calvert*, requesting him to pay the bearer, John Alegre, the proper courier's allowance, being usually one-half the expenses on the return voyage.

Magd. Coll. Oxford, Sept. 2.
203. *Mr. John Oliver (junior Fellow of Magd. Coll.) to Mr. (Henry) Hyde*, about the entry of his son (Edward) at Magdalen College.

Sept. 9.
204. *His Majesty to Lord Digby*. Instructs him to complain of the delay in the negotiations, the conduct of the Infanta and of the Emperor, and the siege of Heidelberg, and encloses a paper of his offers on the points demanded by the Pope in return for granting the dispensation. *Copy.*

Printed in Wilson, p. 209, with a few unimportant variations, and in Rapin, vol. ii. pp. 216–219, with the omission of one page of manuscript.

Madrid, Sept. 11.
205. *Sir Walter Aston to Secretary Calvert*. Recommends Mr. Cottington on his return, as the realest and worthiest friend he has met.

Hampton Court, Oct. 3.
206. *His Majesty to Lord Digby*. Instructs him to demand the immediate restitution of Heidelberg, a cessation of hostilities for seventy days in the Lower Palatinate, and the carrying out of the general Treaty; and in case of refusal to intimate his withdrawal from the Spanish Court. *Copy.*

Printed in Wilson, p. 207, with a few slight variations, and partly in Rapin, vol. ii. p. 217.

Oct. 4.
207. *Minute* of the Private Instructions sent to Lord Digby, not to withdraw without private information from England, but publicly and outwardly to give out to the contrary, that the King may make use thereof in Parliament.

Printed in Wilson, p. 210, and partly in Rapin, vol. ii. p. 217.

Oct. 9.
208. *Mr. John Oliver (junior Fellow of Magd. Coll.) to Mr. (Henry) Hyde.* A further communication about the entry of his son (Edward) at Magdalen College.

Oct. 12.
209. *Secretary Calvert to the Lord High Admiral (Buckingham),* that the Prince of Orange may be treated with to entertain Count Mansfeldt for one month more, he having

made overture of a new descent into Germany. Sir Dudley Carleton writes that Bethlem Gabor is taking up arms against the Emperor. *Copy.*

By Windebank. Cl. S. P. vol. i. p. 2.

1622.

210. *Secretary Calvert to (John Digby) Earl of Bristol*.* His Majesty will consent to yield that the children of the proposed marriage shall be brought up *sub regimine matris* till the age of nine instead of seven years. *Two Copies.*

Cl. S. P. vol. i. p. 3.

St. Martin's Lane, Oct. 14.

211. *His Majesty to Sir Thomas Roe.* Thanks him for his services in diverting the Turks from the invasion of Germany. *Copy.*

By Windebank. Cl. S. P. vol. i. p. 3.

Newmarket, Nov. 14.

212. *The same to (John Digby) Earl of Bristol.* He is to press the King of Spain to a final resolution on the marriage treaty. Will permit the children to be under government of the mother for nine or if necessary ten years, and that the ecclesiastical jurisdiction shall first take notice of offences and then either banish or deliver to secular justice. *Copy.*

By Windebank. In the margin are the following words: "This letter was drawn and written for His Majesty's signature by Mr. Cottington the Prince's Secretary." Cl. S. P. vol. i. p. 4.

Newmarket, Nov. 14.

213. *Petition of Sir Giles Mompesson to His Majesty,* to be recalled from banishment, and answering the charges alleged against him by the Commons, about his Patents for the exclusive Licensing of Innkeepers, and Assessment of the price of Horse meat: a case which, as he complains, Sir E. Coke has in the Commons frequently likened to that of Dudley and Empson. *Copy.*

See Rapin, vol. ii. p. 203.

No date.

214. *(William Bourchier) Earl of Bath to the Lord High Admiral (Buckingham).* The ship Sampson of Plymouth, suspected of piracy about Newfoundland, has come into Clovelly harbour, and been arrested by him.

Tavistock, Jan. 1.

1622-3.

215. *His Majesty to Mr. George Gage.* He is to deliver the articles now agreed upon, if he finds that the dispensation will be granted. *Copy.*

Endorsed by Windebank as sent by Mr. Lawson, Jan. 7. Cl. S. P. vol. i. p. 5.

Westminster, Jan. 5.

216. *Secretary Calvert to the same.* His Majesty and the Prince have signed all the Articles sent by the Earl of Bristol, and have written to the King of Spain engaging to observe

Whitehall, Jan. 5.

* John, Lord Digby, was created Earl of Bristol Sept. 15, 1622.

1622-3. *verbatim* the last article, which promises full toleration of Roman Catholics. Mr. S. Digby has returned from Germany and will be sent to-morrow to Spain. Sends a token to *Aristides* which he hopes he deserves. He will probably be found at Alexandria. *Æneas* again recommends secrecy, and that the letter shall not be delivered to Father Maestro, till there is certainty of success. *Copy.*

Endorsed by Windebank as sent by Mr. Lawson, Jan. 7. Cl. S. P. vol. I. p. 5.

Whitehall, Jan. 7.
217. *His Majesty to the Earl of Bristol.* Announces his signature of the Articles. The reason of his last peremptory instructions was that Heidelberg was meantime taken, and Manheim beleaguered, while the gross delay at Brussels went on, and that Gage had brought nothing from Rome but exceptions to the dispensation. The Infanta (Isabella) at Brussels has fallen away from her promise of restoring Frankendale, if put into her hands. Desires to know particulars of the letter of the King of Spain to the Emperor in behalf of the Prince Palatine. *Copy.*

By Windebank. Cl. S. P. vol. I. p. 6.

Whitehall, Jan. 7.
218. *Secretary Calvert to the same.* Recommends Mr. Digby, the bearer. Frankendale is beleaguered by 12 companies of horse and some foot under Pappenheim, and 2 regiments of the Dukes of Saxe and Holsten. Capt. Burgh the Governor writes that they have only 4 months' bread and wine, dating from November 24th. Desires him to divert the translation of the Electorate at the Diet, and to send word when it is time for the Prince to send love-letters and tokens to his mistress. *Copy.*

Cl. S. P. vol. I. p. 6.

Whitehall, Jan. 14.
219. *The same to the same.* In the matter of *Ormus*, His Majesty is very sensible of the accident, and will proceed as a just Prince and a faithful friend to the King of Spain. Two of the Prince's musicians, Angelo and Drew, have been dismissed for assisting at mass, but restored at the intercession of the Spanish Ambassador. A Committee of Council has been appointed to examine complaints of depredations made by English East Indian merchants upon the Portuguese, but annulled on representation of the Lord Admiral that it is derogatory to his Court. *Copy.*

Endorsed by Windebank, "My master's letter to the Earl of Bristol."

Cl. S. P. vol. I. p. 9.

No date.
220. *Protestation of His Majesty*, that he will not enforce the existing laws nor exact new laws against the Roman Catholics, unless when absolutely necessary to the safety of the

State; but that it is impossible for him to procure the abrogation by Parliament of the present penal laws, or to promise to refuse his assent to such new laws as may be made. The whole promise however to depend upon the marriage of the Prince and the Infanta. *Copy.* — 1622–3.

<small>The preamble and the last paragraph are crossed out. Endorsed by Windebank.
(? S. P. vol. I. p. 10.</small>

221. *Mr. Gage to His Majesty.* The dispensation was finally resolved upon in a Congregation held March 22. Defends the Cardinals from suspicions of vexatious delay. Encloses letters from Cardinals Llandino and Lodovisio. — 1623. Rome, April 14.

<small>Cl. S. P. vol. i. p. 11.</small>

222. *A Proclamation for registering of Knights,* with intent to clear all controversies touching precedence. *Printed.* — Windsor, April 15.

223. *Sir F. Cottington to Secretary Calvert.* The Prince wishes the fleet to be brought to the Groyne, instead of to St. Andero. The ordinary allowance for a post between Madrid and London is 3000 reals, or 75*l.* — Madrid, April 17.

<small>Endorsed by Windebank, "Sir Francis Cottington to my master."
Cl. S. P. vol. i. p. 12.</small>

224. *Instructions received by Sir F. Cottington from the Prince of Wales,* to make several applications to His Majesty with a view to the conclusion of the marriage treaty. — June 7.

<small>Cl. S. P. vol. i. App. p. xviii.</small>

225. (*John Digby*) *Earl of Bristol to Sir F. Cottington,* forwarding papers. — Madrid, June 1⁸⁄₃.

<small>Cl. S. P. vol. i. p. 12.</small>

226. *A Proclamation of the King of Spain (Philip IV),* deferring the betrothal of the Prince of Wales and the Infanta to Christmas, at the Prince's request.—Latin. *Copy.* — August.

<small>Cl. S. P. vol. i. App. p. xxix.</small>

227. (*John Digby*) *Earl of Bristol to the Prince of Wales.* Suspicions of his real affection have been hinted to the Infanta, who rejects them completely. There is no foundation for the fear of her entering into religion after her betrothal. — Madrid, Sept. 21.

<small>Cl. S. P. vol. i. App. p. xix.</small>

228. *The same to the same.* Has means of deferring the *desposorios* if necessary, but shows the inconveniences of such a course, and urges on the Prince the fulfilment of the match. — Madrid, Sept. 24.

<small>Cl. S. P. vol. i. App. p. xx.</small>

<small>* For a series of letters of the date of this and subsequent years see the Appendix, at the end of this volume.</small>

1623. Madrid, Oct. 14.	229. *(John Digby) Earl of Bristol to His Majesty*, pointing out the effects of the proposed deferment of the *desposorios* till after Christmas. *Copy.* Printed in Rymer, xvii. 572, with some immaterial omissions.
Westminster, Nov. 13.	230. *His Majesty to (John Digby) Earl of Bristol.* Is astonished that the Berk Strott in the Palatinate (the prime flower of his son-in-law's revenue, and the main cause of his eagerness for satisfaction) is in possession of a Spanish garrison, the country being freshly delivered into the hands of the Bishop of Mentz, contrary to the agreement with the Infanta at Brussels. Desires, before farther steps in the marriage are taken, that a letter be procured from the King of Spain promising to help in the restitution of the Palatinate. *Copy.* Endorsed, "This agreeth with the original of His Majesty's letter, sent by Mr. Grimley."—Edw. Conway. Cl. S. P. vol. i. p. 13.
Madrid, Nov. 14.	231. *The Earl of Bristol to Secretary Calvert*, to pay the bearer, a Spanish courier, something beyond the usual allowance of 50*l.*
Dec. 11.	232. *Questions* to be asked of Captain Sallinue, relative to some silver money exported. Signed "Falkland."
Dec. 13.	233. *The Answers* of Capt. Sallinue to the Articles, whereon he was examined.
Madrid, Dec. 16.	234. *Sir Walter Aston to the Prince of Wales.* Has with difficulty procured an answer in the matter of the Palatinate. Wishes to know whether the Prince intends to break off the match or not. The Condessa d' Olivarez appears to consider it a dead business, though revived by the Prince's late letters. Cl. S. P. vol. I. App. p. xxi.
No date.	235. *The Answer which the most Serene Prince of Wales has ordered to be given to the paper which the Conde d' Olivares presented to him on June 3ᵈ, 1623.* Argues against the proposal of the Divines, whereby the consummation of the marriage would be deferred till spring, and engages his honour that, if the Infanta return with him to England, all that they require shall be punctually fulfilled.—Spanish. *Copy.* Cl. S. P. vol. I. App. p. xxii.
No date.	236. *His Catholic Majesty's Answer with regard to the Dowry and times of payment.* Is willing to pay a Dowry of two million crowns of twelve reals each, in consideration of the great clemency shewn to Roman Catholics in England.

Though the sum far exceeds what has been usual, will pay 300,000 ducats in specie, and the same in jewels, before the Infanta's departure. The remainder to be a fund for an annuity at 20,000 per 1,000,000, to be remitted to Antwerp. —Spanish. *Copy.* 1623.

Cl. S. P. vol. I. App. p. xxx.

237. *The secret discovery which Don Fennyn, a Spanish Secretary, made to the Duke of Buckingham in the year 1623 at Madrid.* A long account, accompanied with a rude map, of the existence of gold mines and jewels in Hispaniola, Jamaica, and Florida; of the method of capturing the Spanish plate fleet; of a secret treaty between Gustavus Adolphus and the Duke to secure him his intended conquests in those parts; of a plan to seize the cargoes of indigo from Portobello: and of a means of defending the miners from the vapour of the quicksilver employed. (The author is said in the paper to have been poisoned by the King of Spain's favourite for conferring with the Duke.) No date.

Endorsed, "Presented, and the design attempted and in some measure attained by Cromwell." Cl. S. P. vol. I. p. 14.

238. *Nath. Brooke to Capt. Bost*, touching the repairs of a pump at Haselworth Castle, which will cost 10*l*. 1624. June 12.

239. *Traité entre Jacques Roi de la Grande Bretagne et les Etats Generaux des Provinces Unies.* A defensive alliance, with leave for the Dutch to levy 6000 men in England, to be paid by His Majesty. The Dutch in return to supply His Majesty, if called on, with 4000 men or their pay yearly. The alliance to be for at least two years. With copies of the commissions, on the one side to the Duke of Buckingham (Lord High Admiral), Marquis of Hamilton (Grand Maitre d' Hotel), Earl of Pembroke (Chamberlain), Sir Edw. Conway (Secr. of State), and Sir Rich. Weston (Ch. of Exchequer); on the other side to Sieurs François d'Aersen, Albert Joachimi, and Noel de Caron.—French. *Copy.* June 15.

Cl. S. P. vol. I. p. 21.

240. *A sheet of Figures and Private Accounts.* No date.

241. *Patent* of Sir F. Annesley to the post of Vice-Treasurer and Receiver-General in Ireland. *Copy.* 1625. May 20.

242. *Speeches* of the Lord Keeper (Bp. of Lincoln), and the Lord Admiral (Buckingham), introductory of the answer of the latter on the whole matter of the Spanish negotiations. Aug. 9.

Cl. S. P. vol. I. p. 26.

1625.
Southampton,
Sept. 7.

243. *Traité entre Charles Roi de la Grande Bretagne, et les Etats Generaux des Provinces Unies des Pays Bas.* A league offensive and defensive against the King of Spain, the Commissioners being Baron Ley (Lord High Treasurer), Duke of Buckingham (Lord High Admiral), Earl of Pembroke (Chamberlain), Earl of Holland, Earl of Carlisle, Lord Conway (First Secretary of State), Baron Brooke, Sir Robert Naunton (Master of Gardes Nobles), Sir Albert Morton (First Secretary of State), and Sir Richard Weston (Chancellor of the Exchequer) on the one side; Sieurs François d'Aersen, Albert Joachimi, and Rienck de Burmanio a Fervert Grierman de Feuveradeel on the other. Consists of forty Articles, the principal provisions of which are: The Alliance to last for fifteen years. Spain and Flanders to be blockaded. The Dutch to furnish one-quarter of a fleet under His Majesty's command. All contraband of war, "comme sont munitions de bouche et de guerres, navires, armes, voiles, cordage, or, argent, cuivre, fer, plomb, et semblables," to be fair prize. Each party to furnish 25,000 to 30,000 men. All prizes to be the property of the capturer.—French. *Copy.*

Cl. S. P. vol. I. p. 27.

Hampton Court,
Dec. 27.

244. *Order from the Lord High Admiral (Buckingham)* to the Custom Officers in the port of London, to re-ship certain potashes and seize some lead, wax, and pipe-staves brought in by a ship of one Hans Smith (a Dunkirker) & Co., in violation of the rights of the Eastland Company of Merchants. *Copy.*

No date.

245. *His Majesty's Answer to the Petition concerning Religion presented unto His Highness, the 8 of July 1625, by the Lords and Commons of this present Parliament.* *Copy.*

Printed in Rapin, vol. ii. p. 241, with some variations, the principal being that in Art. 3 the words in this copy "above 4 miles distant" are printed in Rapin "above 10 miles distant," and in the same line the word "hath" is printed "is allowed."

1626.
Pirton,
April 20.

246. *Mr. Henry Hyde to Mr. Nicholas Hyde (his brother),* urging that a Statute be passed to compel the destruction of rooks—"the wildest and most unprofitable vermin that is, in my opinion, and easiest to be destroyed." He would have the use of guns allowed for this purpose. An account of his dispute with a neighbour about the division of some lands at Trowbridge.

Rome,
May 30.

247. *Pope Urban VIII to the King of France (Louis XIII).* Implores his help for the orthodox religion, endangered in England by the enforcement of the Oath of Allegiance. The Cardinal Spada will unfold his meaning to the King.

A translated Copy.

Cl. S. P. vol. I. p. 33.

CLARENDON PAPERS. 31

248. *A Letter*, supposed to be written by certain Jesuits in England to their Rector in Brussels, its object being to shew that they had stirred the dissension between Parliament and the Duke of Buckingham. *Copy.*
Endorsed, "This was counterfeited by a friend of the Lord Duke's, purposely to get him off."
1626. No date.

249. *The Lord Privy Seal (Manchester) to the Lord Chief Justice (Sir Nicholas Hyde)*, applying for the examinations taken in the case of Mr. Hugh Pyne. Cl. S. P. vol. l. p. 33.
1627. June 16.

250. *Sir Dudley Carleton to Sir Thos. Aylesbury*, his neighbour. He thinks soon to return home, and writes concerning some buildings which adjoin Sir Thomas's ground.
The Hague, July 31.

251. *Mr. Walond to Sir John Stawell*, of Mr. Pyne's concluding words, confessed by George Morley, "and therefore before God, he is no fitter to be a King than Hirke Wright," who is Mr. Pyne's shepherd and a natural fool.
Cl. S. P. vol. l. p. 33.
Nov. 14.

252. *Warrant to Mr. Attorney General and Mr. Solicitor* to summon Mr. Pyne, and examine George Morley and William Collier, witnesses.
Signed, "Tho. Coventry, C. S.; H. Manchester; Pembroke; Conway."
Cl. S. P. vol. l. p. 34.
Whitehall, Nov. 18.

253. *The Lord Privy Seal (Manchester) to the Lord Chief Justice (Hyde)*. Bail is not to be taken for Mr. Pyne at present. Cl. S. P. vol. l. p. 34.
Whitehall, Nov. 22.

254. *Questions* to be asked of the two witnesses, Collier and Morley, in Mr. Hugh Pyne's behalf, to invalidate their testimony.
No date.

255. *Further Questions* to be asked of Collier in the same matter.
No date.

256. *A Copy of the Treasonable Words* alleged to have been uttered by Mr. Pyne to Collier and Morley.
No date.

257. *The Evidence* of two witnesses, Richard Frackpitt and Hugh Manne(?), in Mr. Pyne's behalf, against Collier and Morley.
No date.

258. *Orders to be observed in Assemblies of Council.* Twenty-two orders regulating the method of debate and the order of business. *Two Copies.* Cl. S. P. vol. l. p. 34.
1627-8. Whitehall, Feb. 10.

1627-8.
March 17.

259. *The King's Speech in Parliament.*

Printed in Rushworth, vol. I. p. 476, and Rapin, vol. ii. p. 261, with great variations of expression, but no difference of meaning. Specially, at the end of the fourth paragraph this copy has "for the preservation of that which others is falling out for particular ends hazard to lose." In the last paragraph the words of the printed copy. "which is to remember a thing to the end we may forget it," are here omitted.

1628.
April 4.

260. *The Duke (of Buckingham)'s Speech at the Council Table*, on the acceptance by the King of the five subsidies.
Copy.

Printed in Rushworth, vol. I. p. 535, with some very small variations.

April 15.

261. *Bill of Sale* by (James Hay) Earl of Carlisle, to Richard Hopper, Esq., of his jewels and plate.

No date.

262. *Petition of the Governor and Fellowship of Merchants of the Muscovia Company* to the King, to intercede in their behalf with the Emperor of Russia (through the expected Russian Ambassador) for a restoration of their privileges, as set forth in the next paper. *Copy.*

June 11.

263. *Charter of Privileges* formerly granted by the Emperor of Russia to the above Company. *Copy.*

No date.

264. *A Relation of Sir D. Cotton's Embassy into Persia.* A detailed account of the Embassy and journey through Persia of my Lord —, accompanied by Lord Shirley, from his arrival on Jan. 6, 1627, to conclude a new treaty; the late Noghte Beg having disavowed that made by Lord Shirley; and the continuance by the writer since the death of the Ambassador. The allowance for the whole company, fourteen in number, was not 6s. 8d. a-day, less than in England we allow the vilest labourer. Cl. S. P. vol. I. p. 36.

No date.

265. *A Sermon*, "Of doing reverence, and particularly of bowing the knee at the name of Jesus."

1629.
Whitehall,
May 6.

266. *Minute of the Privy Council.* That the Judges certify their opinion to the Board, what coercive process from the Courts of Star-Chamber, Chancery, and other Courts of Equity, ought to be awarded against a Peer of the realm for breach of decree, or other contempt. Cl. S. P. vol. I. p. 46.

Westminster, May 8.

267. *Grant* by His Majesty of a Pension of 300l. per ann. for life to his niece, the Princess Elizabeth of Bohemia. *Copy.*

No date.

268. *Petition of the Low Country Merchants*, being subjects to the House of Burgundy, to be exempted from the payment of the City Ship-money. *Copy.*

269. *His Majesty's Privy Seal Warrant*, granting the prayer of the petitioners. *Copy.* — 1629. July 14.

270. *Minute of the Privy Council*, embodying the report of the Judges on the question submitted to them, with precedents, and confirming the right of the Courts to attach Peers. Cl. S. P. vol. i. p. 47. — Whitehall, July 29.

271. *Mr. Lawrence Hyde to Mr. Henry Hyde* (his brother), of his son Edward's good behaviour, and advising him to increase his allowance at College from 40l. to 50l. a-year, and to get him a new suit of satin to enable him to join the Revellers in College. — Temple, Nov. 17.

272. *The Lord Treasurer (Weston) to the Lord Chief Justice (Hyde) and Sir Francis Harvey*, requiring the names of residents in the several counties of their circuit, qualified to be appointed Escheators. — 1629.

273. *A Schedule* of the grants made in the Duchy of Lancaster during the reign of James I. and the first five years of Charles I. — No date.

274. *Warrant* of the Lord Treasurer (Weston), granting to Mr. John Norwood the place of Under Searcher in the Port of London. — 1629-30. March 9.

275. *Hugonis Savilii (?) Scoto Britanni Observationes in Nativitatem Principis Walliæ Londini nati anno 1630, die 8 Jun. H. 5.45 P. M. Colligebat Kal. Julii 1630.* A horoscope of Charles II. predicting him to be fair, handsome, with hair and eyes somewhere between auburn and black, thin beard, shrill voice, mincing gait. He will live either 108 or at least 66 years, be very fortunate, and with every good quality; gain wealth by marriage and war, and be particularly fond of mathematicians, sailors, merchants, learned men, painters, and sculptors.—Latin. — 1630. Madrid, July 1.

276. *A Schedule* of the debts of Sir Allan Apsloy, amounting to 8964l. 2s. 0d. (due on account of victualling the fleet). — July 6.

277. *Pacificatio Ratisbonensis, inter Sacram Cæsaream Majestatem, et Regem Franciæ Christianissimum, die 13 mensis Octobris, Anno 1630, Conclusa atque Firmata*, relative to the settlement of the Dukedoms of Mantua and Montserrat in Italy. *Printed.* — Oct. 13.

278. *The Lord Treasurer (Weston) to Lord Chief Justice (Hyde) and Sir F. Harvey*, requiring the names of residents in the several counties of their circuit, qualified to be appointed Escheators. — Wallingford House, Nov. 9.

1630.
Drayton,
Nov. 9.
279. *(John Mordaunt) Earl of Peterborough to Lord Chief Justice (Hyde).* Requests that a warrant be granted for the apprehension of one Godfrey Bertram for beating his servant, and hunting in his grounds.

Whet-
ham (?),
Nov. 19.
280. *Sir John Erule to the same.* Thanks him for having procured his exemption from the Sheriffwick that year.
Endorsed by Lord Clarendon "Sir John Earnley."

Dec. 15.
281. *Sir F. Cottington to his Majesty.* Thanks him for kindness. Is leaving for Cadiz. Has begged heads of Brutus and Cassius from the King's house at Carthagena, which are to meet him at Sevillo. *Copy.*
Endorsed by himself. Cl. S. P. vol. I. p. 48.

No date.
282. *A List of Indentures* from the King, leasing the different Customs to several persons, and extending from 1625 to 1630.

No date.
283. *Cardinal Pasman to Cardinal Barberini.* The Pope having refused to receive him as Ambassador from the Emperor, under pretence that the office was beneath the dignity of a Cardinal, he endeavours to answer the objection by adducing precedents and other arguments.—Latin. *Copy.*

No date.
284. *A List of the principal Piedmontese Nobility and Gentry*, classified under twelve heads according to their political attachment to Madame or Prince Thomas of Savoy.—Italian.

1631.
No date.
285. *List of the Jury of Peers* in the trial of Mervyn Lord Awdley (Earl of Castlehaven)*.
Printed in Rushworth, vol. II. p. 95.

No date.
286. *An Account of the formal Proceedings in the Trial of Lord Awdley* for Rape, and the speech of the Lord High Steward (Lord Keeper Sir Thomas Coventry) in sentencing him to death.
See Rushworth, vol. II. p. 96.

Greenwich,
May 5.
287. *Mr. Endymion Porter to Lord Chief Justice (Hyde),* requesting him to accept bail for an Irish gentleman, Mr. Brady, arrested for a debt.

Whitehall,
May 6.
288. *Mr. E. Taverner to ———.* A love-letter, excusing his delaying marriage till he can maintain a wife properly.

Whitehall,
May 11.
289. *Minute of the Privy Council,* ordering, on petition from the University and Aldermen of Cambridge, that with the surplus of the money collected for the relief of 4000 poor in

* The Earl of Castlehaven's trial commenced April 25, 1631.

the late visitation, Jesus Common be enclosed for the maintenance of the new workhouse, built at the cost of 500*l*. And that no inhabitant of the town shall exercise more trades than one, nor any one to which he has not been apprenticed. *Copy.* 1631

Endorsed by Lord Clarendon.   Cl. S. P. vol. I. p. 51.

290. *His Majesty to the Master and Council of the Court of Wards*, ordering an allowance to be made to Ann, Marie, and Elizabeth, the three daughters of Viscountess Dorchester and the late Viscount Danning. Encloses a report thereon, dated June 10, fixing the allowance at 500*l*. per annum for maintenance and 100 marks per annum for lodging. *Copies.* Greenwich, June 12.

Signed, "Arundel and Surrey; Pembroke and Montgomery; Dorset; Holland."

291. *Mr. Welles to Sir. Thos. Aylesbury (Navy Surveyor)*, concerning shipping stores at Portsmouth. Aug. 29.

292. *Extract from the Queen's Charter of Liberties*, with reference to her right to prosecute by her Attorney, or otherwise.—Latin. *Copy.* No date.

293. *An Account* of moneys received by the late Sir Allen Apsley for the sale of the King's lands during the years 1630–31. No date.

294. *Articles of a Treaty* agreed upon by Don Gaspar de Guzman, Condé Duke of San Lucar, and Lord * Cottington. An offensive and defensive alliance against the Hollanders. Commissioners on both sides to reside in England or Flanders. The King of Spain to resign such lands as shall be agreed upon, and to pay his Majesty 100,000 crowns monthly. Free toleration for Roman Catholics in all the lands resigned. His Majesty to hold the island of Zealand, but a free passage to Antwerp to be guaranteed. Also, *A Proposition* between the same parties, that if Zealand be conquered within a year, his Majesty shall deposit Walcheren and Tergus in the hands of the King of Spain as security, till the war be ended.—Spanish. *Two Copies.* 1631-2. Madrid, Jan. 11.

One by Windebank, with a translation. A translation occurs also in a Paper printed Cl. S. P. vol. ii. App. p. xxvi.   Cl. S. P. vol. I. p. 49.

295. *Heads of the Secret Articles* in the Treaty between Lord Cottington and the Condé Duke. *Copy.* No date.

In Lord Cottington's hand.   See Cl. S. P. v. I. p. 49, and vol. ii. App. p. xxxii, where they are reduced to form.

* Sir Francis Cottington was created Lord Cottington July 10, 1631.

1631-2.
Bervoaldi,
Jan. 13.

290. *Capita Fœderis inter Sueciæ et Galliæ Reges initi.* A Treaty between Gustavus Adolphus and Louis XIII against the Duke of Bavaria and the Catholic League, to last five years.—Latin. *Printed.*

297. *A Minute of several Letters and Warrants relating to Ireland, upon the Earl of Strafford's going to that government,* entered in the Signed Office.

These all bear dates 1631-2, except a warrant for use of martial law, which is dated January 1639.

Whitehall,
Feb. 19.

298. *Copy of Propositions presented to His Majesty by the Lord Viscount Wentworth, Lord Deputy of Ireland,* concerning the government of that Kingdom,* and are entered in the Council Book by His Majesty's express command.

Two copies, one with several additional propositions. Printed in the Earl of Strafford's Letters, vol. ii. p. 63.

Whitehall,
Feb. 22.

299. *Order of Council* to enter the propositions as above, with the names of the Lords who were present. *Copy.*

Endorsed, " Propositions concerning the government of Ireland allowed by His Majesty, 22 Feb. 1631."

Whitehall,
March 2.

300. *Directions to the Masters of Requests, and a Caveat entered in the Signet Office,* in accordance with the above propositions. *Copy.*

This paper has an endorsement to the effect that all these Papers relating to the Government of Ireland were enclosed in a letter of the Lord Deputy to Secretary Windebank, dated Dublin, March 3, 1639, and printed in the Earl of Strafford's Collection, vol. ii. p. 292.

West-
minster,
March 18.

301. *Letters of His Majesty,* giving orders to the Lord Deputy for the appointment of a Commission, on the petition of Lewis (Jones), Bishop of Killaloe, to inquire into the property alleged by him to belong to that Bishopric, but to have been leased away. *Copy.*

Endorsed by Lord Clarendon. Cl. S. P. vol. i. p. 52.

1632.
March 25.

302. *Petition* to (Francis Annesley) Lord Mount-Norris to attach the person of the late Sub-Sheriff of Mayo in satisfaction of a debt to the Crown.

Worlam,
April 29.

303. *Mr. Bernard Lee to Sir John Backhouse,* a short letter concerning the ownership and rating of some land.

July 4.

304. *Lady (Barbara) Villiers to Mr. Edward Hyde,* her nephew, condoling with him on the loss of his wife†.

---

* Lord Wentworth was appointed Lord Deputy of Ireland Jan. 12, 1631-2.
† This was his first wife, the daughter of Sir George Ayliffe. She died six months after her marriage. See Clarendon's Life, Part i. p. 918.

305. *Copies of Papers relating to the negotiation of a Treaty* 1632.
*with Gustavus Adolphus, King of Sweden (extending over the
years* 1631-32), *for the restoration of the King of Bohemia
(Frederic, Count Palatine) to his Electoral Dominions,* and
comprising—

    Westminster, Sept. 20, 1631. *Powers to Sir Henry Vane,*
    Ambassador Extraordinary from England to Sweden.
    —Latin.

    1632. *Preliminary Articles* (five in number) on the part of
    Sweden.—Latin.

    1632. *Preliminary Articles* (nine in number) on the part
    of England.—Latin.

    Nuremberg, June 29, 1632. *The Acceptance of the King
    of Bohemia.*—French.

    Sir H. Vane to His Majesty. A relation of his Embassy
    to the King of Sweden, in which the duplicity of that
    King in the matter is clearly shewn.

    Hampton Court, Sept. 28, 1632. *Secretary Coke to Sir
    H. Vane,* recapitulating the different steps taken in
    the negotiation, and desiring him to leave the Swedish
    Court.

    1632. *His Majesty to the King of Sweden,* formally re-
    voking the powers given to Sir H. Vane, and recalling
    him.—Latin.

    1632. *Instructions* to Mr. William Curtins, sent as Agent
    to the King of Sweden.

                       All these are transcribed in the same hand.

306. *Summary of Foreign News.* In a terrible inundation   Leyden,
of the Elbe 24 villages, 5000 men, and 10,000 cattle have   Nov. 6.
been destroyed. There is great noise of a fleet from Sicily to
invade France at Marseilles. Mansfield is 7000 strong, but
yet undertakes nothing. The Turkish Emperor will make   Paris,
peace with Poland. The differences between the Pope and   Nov. 8.
the Venetians are not yet composed. The English Ambassador has had audience, and is to go hence in a few days,
the following terms having been agreed on. The King of
France to maintain 12,000 men. *Acta Suecorum* to remain
integra. Duke Bernard to be Generalissimo. Saxony to be
admonished not to separate himself. The Duke of Rohan is
gone to Alsatia.

                                Partly unintelligible from mutilation.

1632. No date.	307. *Statistics* concerning the smuggling of gold and silver thread, and reasons for bringing the offenders before the Star-Chamber rather than the Court of Exchequer. The duty is mentioned as 6s. 8d. upon every pound weight. Within 7 years 22,000 papers have been imported, whereof 600 only have paid duty.
No date.	308. *A Computation of the values of Flemish money in English.* The Rix-Dollar = 4s. 10d. The Lion-Dollar or 2 Gulden piece = 3s. 11d. The Spread Eagle piece = 2s. 10d. The Flemish Shilling = 6d. The Gold Rider = 21s. 6d. The Jacobus passes there as = 11 Guilders 6 Stivers, or 22s. 6d.
No date.	309. *The Dean of Hereford to Lord* ——. Details some grievances which he alleges against the Bishop of Hereford in respect of money matters. <small>Imperfect, with no signature. Endorsed as "found among the papers of 1631."</small>
1633. London, May 17.	310. *Secretary Windebank to His Majesty.* Has informed the Deputy of the States that, whereas His Majesty's resolution concerning the ship had been in his favour, it would now be in favour of the Spanish Resident, in consequence of his own passion and menace of a truce with Spain in case of delay. He has endeavoured to excuse himself, but Windebank has also demanded reparation for the outrages upon the Dunkirkers, and will write to Mr. Boswell, Agent in Holland, on the matter. *Original, and also an unfinished Copy.* Cl. S. P. vol. L. p. 53.
Doncaster, May 23.	311. *Order of His Majesty*, to the Clerk of the Signet, that letters be drawn up in conformity with the above memorial. Signed by the King. Cl. S. P. vol. L. p. 56.
May 25.	312. *Minutes by Secretary Windebank*, of an interview with Necolalde, to entreat him to continue his good offices with the Emperor, notwithstanding the agreement made with the Swedes for restitution of the towns of the Palatinate held by them, on payment of 15,6ccl. Necolalde answers by narrating the hindrances to his intervention caused by Sir Robert Anstruther's embassy, and other ill offices. Cl. S. P. vol. L p. 61.
No date.	313. *Memorial to His Majesty,* by Sir Francis Nethersole, in behalf of the Queen of Bohemia, for keeping up the contribution intended by His Majesty in her behalf. That he will be pleased to spur on the matter by declaring that

the money shall not be diverted to any other than the specified use, and that the contribution shall not be made a precedent. *Copy.*
Cl. S. P. vol. I. p. 55.

1633.

314. *His Majesty to Secretary Windebank,* informing the Privy Council of the issue of the subjoined instructions.
Cl. S. P. vol. I. p. 56.

Westminster, June 17.

315. *Instructions* to be sent to all Justices of the Peace, to urge the people to the contribution. *Draught.*

No date.

> The following passage is scored out by His Majesty, as not judged 'fit to pass:'—"After our having so long forborn to demand any (supply) of them for foreign affairs, assuring them that as the largeness of their free gift will be a clear evidence to us of the measure of their affections towards us, which we esteem our great happiness, so their forwardness to assist us in this kind shall not make us more backward to require their aid in another way, no less agreeable to us than to them, when the season shall be proper for it."
> Cl. S. P. vol. i. p. 57.

316. *A Memorial from Sir Francis Nethersole to Secretary Windebank.* Wishes the lines struck out in the Instructions to stand. Petitions that he should be made receiver of the whole contribution and not only of the 30,000*l.* advanced thereon. That Sir Abraham Williams' name be subscribed to the letters, as known to be a servant of the Queen of Bohemia.
Cl. S. P. vol. I. p. 58.

No date.

317. *His Majesty to the same.* Takes exception to the clause in the Proclamation for the contribution, which says that his Ambassador has compounded in his name for those parts of the Palatinate which the Swedes possess. This would interest his honour too much in the contribution, as if demanded by him and not by his sister with his permission. *Copy.*
Cl. S. P. vol. I. App. p. xxxi.

Holyrood, June 22.

318. *Report of the Privy Council to His Majesty,* of their examination into a charge made by Sir F. Nethersole (though he denies it) against Lord Goring, that he had divulged the secret of the proposed contribution. They find Lord Goring completely guiltless, and recommend exemplary punishment upon so insolent an offender as Nethersole.
Date endorsed by Windebank. Cl. S. P. vol. I. p. 63.

June 22.

319. *Secretary Windebank to the same.* Approves of the exception taken by him. Sir Francis Nethersole is confined to his house, according to His Majesty's command.
Two Copies.
Cl. S. P. vol. I. App. p. xxxi.

London, July 9.

1633.
Aug. 11.

320. *Secretary Windebank to His Majesty.* Encloses the following memorial, and states his wish not to appear personally in the matter. *Cl. S. P. vol. l. p. 59.*

321. *Memorial touching the Contribution.* That in consequence of the objections raised by His Majesty on one side, and the people on the other, to the present form, the business be cast in a new mould: that a narrative of the circumstances be prefixed, and that the letter be read in all churches, the proceeds being made known to His Majesty only upon oath of Receivers-General. *Cl. S. P. vol. l. p. 60.*

Aug. 18.

322. *Necolalde to Secretary Windebank.* Professes in general terms the good-will of the Condé Duke and himself, but declines an audience until satisfaction be given to his complaints. Encloses a list of a case of religious books, value 500*l.* 4*s.*, which had been carried to the library of the late Archbishop of Canterbury*, as contraband, and which he desires to have restored to him.—Spanish.
With two Copies of an English Translation, one endorsed by Windebank. *Cl. S. P. vol. l. p. 64.*

Sept. 30.

323. *Account* of money due to Lord Viscount Powerscourt† for his personal entertainment from April 1 to Sept. 30, 1633, amounting to 317*l.* 17*s.* 9*d.* Irish, or 239*l.* 3*s.* 2*d.* English money, with an order from Lord Mount-Norris on George Hull for the payment.

Hafnia,
Oct. 14.

324. *The King of Denmark (Christian IV) to His Majesty.* Recommends Caspar Heigen, Secretary of the Hanseatic Society in Bergen, seeking satisfaction for the poisoning of his brother Gerard Poleman by the sailors of the ship 'Discovery,' on his return from Peru.—Latin. *Cl. S. P. vol. l. p. 68.*

Smolensk,
Oct. 15.

325. *The King of Poland (Uladislaus VI) to the same.* Requests leave for Alexander Stuart to enlist 500 men in England against the Muscovites.—Latin. *Cl. S. P. vol. l. p. 69.*

Lubeck,
Nov. 10.

326. *The Senate of the Hanse Towns to the same,* requesting restitution of the goods of the murdered Gerard Poleman to his brother.—Latin. *Cl. S. P. vol. l. p. 70.*

London,
Nov. 15.

327. *Necolalde to Secretary Windebank,* enclosing the next paper for His Majesty's consideration.—Spanish. *Cl. S. P. vol. l. p. 69.*

* Archbishop Abbot died Aug. 4, 1633.
† Lord Powerscourt was one of the Commissioners for the plantation of Leinster and Ulster. See Archdall's Irish Peerage, v. 271.

London, Nov. 13. *Representation by Necolalde of the intentions of the Emperor and King of Spain* relative to the peace of the Empire and the affairs of the Palatinate. The object of the Duke of Feria's army in Germany being solely to drive the foreigners from the Empire, His Majesty is invited to join in alliance with them, the proposed restoration of the Prince Palatine being likely to be much facilitated thereby. Has no express orders at present to present this invitation, the Condé d'Oñate having not yet arrived at Vienna to conclude the treaty between the two Powers themselves.—Spanish.
1633.
Cl. S. P. vol. I. p. 77.

328. *Secretary Windebank to Mr. B. Leander,* alim John Skidmore, alias Jones, formerly Fellow of St. John's College, Oxford, now a Benedictine monk, giving him His Majesty's leave to return to England.
Whitehall, Dec. 1.
Three Copies, one a Rough Draught by Windebank, stating that leave is given by the Archbishop of Canterbury's intercession.
Cl. S. P. vol. I. p. 72.

329. *Proclamation* against proselytizing and attending mass publicly by Roman Catholics.
No date.
Rough Draught by Windebank. Cl. S. P. vol. I. p. 71.

330. *Father Philip (the Queen's Confessor) to Secretary Windebank.* Has spoken to the Queen in the matter of Mr. Fisher's Patent.
No date.

331. *A Petition* of the Resident of Spain to His Majesty, that justice may be done in the case of Powell and Newman, alleged by him to be guilty of piracy in the West Indies.
No date.
Copy without signature.

332. *Two Rent-Rolls* of Little Marlow and Medmenham Rents due (to the Crown?) Ladyday and Michaelmas 1633.
1633.

333. *Answer by Secretary Windebank to Necolalde's Paper of Nov. 13th,* requiring as the conditions of His Majesty's entering the proposed league that the Prince Palatine be publicly pronounced free of the ban issued against his father, that the Lower Palatinate be at once restored, and means thought of for the future restitution of the Upper Palatinate and the Electoral dignity.
1633–4. Jan. 31.
Copy.
Endorsed by Windebank. Cl. S. P. vol. I. p. 79.

334. *Secretary Windebank to Mr. Hopton.* Excuses his blurred manner of writing. Directs him how to answer the Spanish objections to the recruiting allowed in England for
Feb. 16.

1633-4. the service of the States. It is a custom as old as Elizabeth's time, and open to the Spaniards equally with the Hollanders. Forwards 1000*l*. of arrears. If the Infant Cardinal be recalled from Milan, His Majesty will be willing, on request, to convoy him, in his fleet, to Flanders. *Draught*.
By Windebank.   Cl. S. P. vol. L p. 72.

Feb. 16.   335. *Secretary Windebank to Mr. Hopton.* Narrates the progress of events from the Embassy of the Abbot de Scaglia to propose a league with Spain against the States. Though the Swedes have taken from Spain and Bavaria the whole of the Lower Palatinate, Necolalde has constantly protested against any treaty with them, notwithstanding His Majesty's declaration that he will not prejudice the Emperor thereby. Necolalde has also a grievance about the ship of sugar brought by the Hollanders as a prize into Plymouth, and adjudged to them by the Admiralty. He is now however grown wiser and desires to renew the assurance given to Lord Cottington of the restitution of the Palatinate. His Majesty desires to check the success of the Hollanders by assisting Spain with a large fleet, under pretext of the violation of his harbours by the hostilities of the Hollanders and Dunkirkers. The motion however must come from Necolalde, and Hopton must shape his course accordingly, representing the great offers made by France, on condition of relinquishing the Spanish Alliance. Encloses a copy of Necolalde's paper of Nov. 13th.   *Copy*.
By Windebank.   Cl. S. P. vol. L p. 74.

1634.
Madrid,
April 6.   336. *Mr. Hopton to Secretary Windebank.* Congratulates him on his promotion to his present place*, and thanks him for the money sent.   Cl. S. P. vol. I. p. 80.

April 7.   337. *The same to the same.* Has endeavoured to force from the Condé Duke an acknowledgment of the news communicated in Windebank's last despatch, and has complained of the interruption of trade by Spanish men-of-war in the Channel. In an audience of the King has urged the seizing the present opportunity. Has delivered the enclosed paper, and thinks they will accept the offer. It is bootless to tell them of remote conveniences; they will always consider the interests of the Duke of Bavaria, and will greatly presume upon any partnership. Advises therefore that the fleet be fitted at His Majesty's sole cost. Necolalde is more moderate in his letters than his words, and the Spaniards cannot be accused of want of justice.   *In Cypher*.
Cl. S. P. vol. L p. 80.

---

* It does not appear what this alludes to. Windebank was made Secretary of State on June 15, 1632. See Laud's Diary, and Rushworth, vol. ii. p. 139.

March 18. *Mr. Hopton to the Condé Duke*, proposing to station a fleet in the Channel, to be paid in part by the King of Spain, and then to propose a peace to the Hollanders.—Spanish. *In Cypher.* 1634.

Three Copies, one endorsed by Mr. Hopton, and two endorsed by Windebank. Cl. S. P. vol. i. p. 85, date not printed.

338. *The same to Lord Cottington.* Refers him to his despatch to Windebank. The business is in danger to miscarry by the humours of two Spanish ministers who will hardly mend, though ground, as they are, in the mortar of misfortunes. There is little speech now of the Infant Cardinal's return. There will be 20,000 men in Milan this year under command of the Marquis de Leganes. April 7.

Cl. S. P. vol. i. p. 87, date wrongly printed.

339. *An Extract* from the last, in Windebank's hand, with an immaterial sentence which does not occur in the former copy. No date.

340. *Motives and Reasons to be offered to His Majesty for a distinction between such Recusants as voluntarily take the Oath of Allegiance with a resolved conscience of the lawfulness thereof, and such other as either oppose the same, or take the same with a scruple of conscience*, making distinction between religion and loyalty, and contending that the laws against Recusants are only to punish disloyalty. May 12.

Endorsed by Windebank as delivered by Mr. Howard. Cl. S. P. vol. i. p. 89.

341. *Necolalde to His Majesty*, entreating his attention to his arguments in the matter of the Caravel laden with sugar. —Spanish. London, May 16.

Cl. S. P. vol. i. p. 91.

342. *Mr. Hopton to Secretary Windebank.* Has nothing to communicate but the good-will of the Spanish people to His Majesty. Madrid, May 21.

Cl. S. P. vol. i. p. 93.

343. *The same to Lord Cottington.* Condoles with him on his great loss. Will account for the pictures which have miscarried. Wishes an allowance of 100*l*. a quarter for secret service. Madrid, May 21.

Cl. S. P. vol. i. p. 94.

344. *The same to Secretary Windebank.* The galleons of Terra Firma under Don Antonio Oquendo are gone. Great forces are collecting at Biscay and Navarre, and there is some probability of a rupture with France. The Marquis of Leganes is arrived at Milan. The Genoese disavow the peace made for them by the Cardinal Infant with the Duke of Madrid, May.

1634.

Savoy.   Savoy. The King of Denmark's son is to marry the Elector of Saxony's daughter. The Duke of Arscot is still imprisoned. The English prisoners at Cadiz and seventeen at Seville have been set at liberty. Don Juan de Benavides, General of the Armada which the Hollanders took five years since, has been beheaded at Seville. *Copy.*

Endorsed by himself.   Cl. S. P. vol. i, App. p. xxxii.

Westminster.   345. *Secretary Windebank to the Lord Treasurer (Portland*).* His Majesty desires that the whole business be communicated to the Council next Sunday, and that Lord Cottington, the Lord Treasurer, and Windebank, meet Necolalde at once and enter into treaty with him.

No date, endorsed by the Earl of Portland as received June 6th.
Cl. S. P. vol. i. p. 94.

Dublin, June 17.   346. *The Lord Deputy (Wentworth) to Lord Mount-Norris, Christopher Wandesford, Esq. (Master of the Rolls), and Sir George Radcliffe, Knt.*, appointing them a Commission to examine into the amount of the fees taken by his Secretaries.

Cl. S. P. vol. i. p. 95.

Brussels, June 18.   347. *Prince Thomas (of Savoy) to His Majesty.* Sends assurances of his gratitude and respect by Capt. Fulvio Pergamo, his private Secretary.—French.   Cl. S. P. vol. i. p. 96.

Madrid.   348. *Mr. Hopton to Secretary Coke.* Two taxes have been imposed—one-eighth of all wine used in the town, and one-twenty-fourth of all that is sold in the kingdom of Castile by the yard. It has been the most plentiful year ever known. The revenues of the Crown have been nearly doubled in four years, and expenses lessened by one-quarter of all salaries paid by the Crown. The Duke of Ciudad Real has reduced Bilboa to order by putting six of the chief malcontents to death. The French Ambassador has not yet received satisfaction, and abstains from visiting the palace. Don Antonio Muscoso has gone as Ambassador from the King to the Infant Cardinal, who has concluded a peace between the Duke of Savoy and Genoa. Levies continued to be shipped to Barcelona.

No date. Endorsed by Windebank as delivered to him by Lord Cottington on June 27th.   Cl. S. P. vol. i. p. 98.

Greenwich, June 29.   349. *Petition of Sir John St. John and Sir Edward Hungerford to the King*, in behalf of their nephews and nieces, children of the late Sir Allen Apsley, begging for them a reversion which had been promised to their father. With the King's pleasure thereon, annexed.   In Windebank's hand.

* Sir R. Weston was created Earl of Portland in 1633.

350. *Mr. Plunkett to Mr. Courtney.* Has delivered to Mr. Howard Courtney's answer to that gentleman, who desires to confer with Mr. Preston, from whom and from Mr. Withrington he had chiefly drawn his book. 1634. July 5.
Cl. S. P. vol. I. p. 102.

351. *Mr. Anthony Fletcher to Alderman Venn,* concerning the ship Thomas belonging to the Merchant Adventurers, which has been seized by a Hollander man-of-war. *Copy.* Rotterdam, July 9.
Endorsed by Windebank.

352. *Secretary Windebank to Mr. Hopton.* The question of the sugar-ship has been decided in favour of the Hollanders, but costs awarded to the Portuguese, as a favour to the King of Spain. He is to represent the justice of this course, and the unfriendly behaviour of Necolalde in this and other matters. Also to hint at the offers of Prince Thomas, the league between France and Sweden, the powerful fleet of the Hollanders, (being twenty sail in the Channel, of which the Admiral is of 1000 tons with fifty-five brass ordnance,) and the consequent importance of His Majesty's friendship. Has received from Necolalde copies of intercepted letters between Richelieu, the Prince of Orange, and the States Ambassador, with propositions to surprise Dunkirk and Gravelin without the knowledge of England and Spain. Gerbier writes from Brussels that the Abbot Scaglia has made overtures similar to those of Prince Thomas, but holds Necolalde unfit to be employed in such treaty. The Hollanders have taken English ships trading to Dunkirk, and profess their determination to confiscate all traders with Spanish subjects. July 11.
Also a rough draught of the same. Cl. S. P. vol. I. p. 103.

353. *Extract of a Letter from Sir John Pennington,* mentioning that some French gentlemen from the French Ambassador have been suspiciously observing the English shipping, having come from London to Dover in light horsemen, and his anxiety as to their intentions. The Downs, July 14.

354. *A Paper* of the Forms of Address proper to the different foreign Princes. No date.

355. *Minute* by Secretary Windebank of an interview with Necolalde held at Roehampton. His Majesty is content to defer farther treaties of restitution if the ban be taken off. Necolalde's answer that it is not in his master's power, but that the Condé d'Oñate has been sent to solicit it. He has power to contract for the money requisite to furnish the proposed fleet. July 16.
Cl. S. P. vol. I. p. 106.

1634.
Madrid,
July 17.

356. *Mr. Hopton to Secretary Windebank.* The Spaniards are backward in accepting His Majesty's offer either because the league between France and Holland has destroyed their hope of success, or because they have not money enough. Necolalde's claim of interference in the affair of the sugar-ship is extravagant. Cl. S. P. vol. I. p. 102.

Madrid,
July 17.

357. *The same to the same.* Defends his conduct in having delivered to the Condé Duke his paper of March 18th, which expressed nothing more than a proposition between the Lords of the Council and the Spanish Resident. Cl. S. P. vol. I. p. 103.

July 21.

358. *A Minute of Council,* authorizing a writ to be issued to Sheriffs and Mayors, to divide the six months' payment (of the contribution for the Queen of Bohemia?) into two quarterly payments. *Copy.*

Madrid,
July 23.

359. *Mr. Hopton to Secretary Windebank.* The Condé Duke has informed him of the intercepted letter of the Prince of Orange, and has conversed with him on the decision in the matter of the sugar-ship. Cl. S. P. vol. I. App. p. xxxiv.

Dublin
Castle,
July 13.

360. *Petition of Sir Charles Coote to the Lord Deputy (Wentworth),* against Sir Rowland de la Hoyde (?), who has usurped the office of Collector of Compositions in the county of Clare.

Berry
Castle,
July 27.

361. *(Old) Articles, by which the Agreement or secret Capitulation concerning the arming of the Fleet by His Majesty of Great Britain may be equally settled.* When the ban is taken off, twenty ships to be armed by England, of 400 tons at the least, five to be at the charge of the King of Spain. The Spanish King to make reparation for depredations by Biscayners, Dunkirkers, and other his subjects on the coast of England; and to provide a loan of 200,000 crowns towards the expenses of England. The ships to put to sea by the beginning of September, and again in the beginning of April.

Four Copies, two in Spanish, "as they were delivered by Mr. Hopton to the King of Spain," one with an article omitted, and one signed by the King, with the prefix of the word "Old" in his hand. Also four rough draughts by Windebank of parts of the Articles, one in Spanish and English. Cl. S. P. vol. I. p. 109.

July 28.

362. *Necolalde to Lord Cottington.* Requests in menacing language the 4000*l.* promised towards the costs of the Portuguese in the suit about the sugar-ship.—*Spanish.*
Cl. S. P. vol. I. p. 111.

363. *A Paper* of Nocolalde, containing the points insisted on by him in the Secret Treaty (all which are mentioned in Secretary Windebank's subsequent letter to the King of Aug. 8.)—Spanish. — 1634. July 28.

364. *Minutes* relating to the same Articles.—Spanish. — No date.

365. *Mr. Hopton to Secretary Coke.* The Queen is with child. Nothing is spoken of but the Infant Cardinal's journey. He will march with 24,000 men. The Duke of Bavaria refuses to join his forces with the King of Hungary, and is suspected of a league with France. The attempt to make the war a war of religion has offended the Protestant forces of the Emperor so much that the pretence is withdrawn. A fleet is preparing at Lisbon for Pernambuco, with Don Frederick de Toledo as General, much against his will, Don Philip de Silva being declined by the Portuguese. The Duke of Arscott is still under restraint. Satisfaction has been given to the French Ambassador. *Copy.* — July.

<small>Endorsed by himself, and the date "July" by Windebank.
Cl. S. P. vol. I. p. 107.</small>

366. *The same to Secretary Windebank.* Taylor has arrived. Has conversed with Secretary Carnero about the sugar-ship, and pointed out the impossibility of His Majesty's interfering with the sentence of a Court of Law. — Madrid, Aug. 7.

<small>Cl. S. P. vol. I. p. 115.</small>

367. *Secretary Windebank to His Majesty.* Forwards a copy of the new Articles, the alterations having been required by Nocolalde, who has refused to be screwed higher than 200,000 crowns. Comments upon the alterations, to which he is inclined to agree. — Aug. 8.

<small>Cl. S. P. vol. I. p. 113.</small>

368. (*New*) *Articles by which may be settled the arming of a Fleet of twenty Ships by His Majesty of Great Britain with the assistance of the King of Spain.* The important differences between these and the last Articles are the omissions of the condition of the removal of the ban, the charge of five ships upon Spain, and the claim for reparation of depredations. — Tulbury, Aug. 11.

<small>Two Copies, signed by the King, one with the prefix of the word "New" in his hand. Also a draught, and two copies in Spanish, cypher, in Windebank's hand, with his own and Nocolalde's alterations.
Cl. S. P. vol. I. p. 112.</small>

369. *Mr. Hopton to Secretary Windebank.* The Condé Duke will not be drawn to speak of the sugar-ship business, — Madrid, Aug. 13.

1634. but he does not think it is much taken to heart. Prince Thomas's Secretary has arrived, but neither he nor his papers are much esteemed.

Two Copies, one in cypher. Cl. S. P. vol. i. p. 117.

Madrid, Aug. 13. 370. *Mr. Hopton to Secretary Windebank.* Praises Mr. Taylor. Necolalde having concealed his orders from Spain has put all things at a dead fault. If Windebank's son come abroad, he will furnish him with a servant, and assist him in his travels.

Aug. 19. 371. *Minutes of a Despatch of Secretary Windebank to His Majesty.* He has communicated to the Resident the King's alterations in the Articles, at which he seemed much troubled, and said he durst not agree to them. His objections are detailed at length, and are in substance exactly the same as those expressed in Necolalde's subsequent paper of Aug. 26.

Endorsed by Windebank.

No date. 372. (*Newest*) *Articles*, including

Madrid, Oct. 18, 1632. *Necolalde's Powers from the King of Spain* to conclude the treaty.—Spanish. *Copy.*

Certified by Necolalde, and dated Aug. 18, 1634.

Powers to Lords Portland and Cottington and Sir F. Windebank from His Majesty to treat with Necolalde.

Draught by Windebank.

And differing from the former Articles in the wording of some passages, in requiring the loan to be paid in two or three months' time, and in delaying the sailing of the ships till the next year.

Draught by Windebank, corrected by the King, and endorsed, "Newest Articles," with the prefix of the words, "I hold no preamble fittest," in his hand. Cl. S. P. vol. i. p. 122.

Aug. 21. 373. *Necolalde to Secretary Windebank,* forwarding a copy of a speech made by the French Ambassador in the Assembly at Frankfort.—Spanish.

Endorsed by Windebank, "The French Amb. speech at the Assembly at Ratisbon."

Madrid, Aug. 23. 374. *Mr. Hopton to the same.* There is no alteration in the main business, but they will name a successor to Necolalde. Mr. Taylor will return by sea in a few days.

Cl. S. P. vol. i. p. 126.

375. *Mr. Taylor to Secretary Windebank.* Don Francisco de Melo is spoken of as the Ambassador to England. Mr. Hopton has provided for Mr. Windebank's journey from St. Sebastian to Madrid.
Cl. S. P. vol. l. p. 127.
1634. Madrid, Aug. 22.

376. *The same to Lord Cottington.* Has spoken with the Condé Duke on matters of the English trade to Brazil.
Cl. S. P. vol. l. p. 127.
Madrid, Aug. 22.

377. *Necolalde to Secretary Windebank.* Contains his objections to the alterations in the last Articles. Desires that all prizes brought into English ports by either side should be restored. Objects to any definite sum of money being fixed as yet.—Spanish.
Cl. S. P. vol. l. p. 228.
Aug. 26.

378. *Copy of the Alterations in the Articles* as proposed by Necolalde.—Spanish.
In cypher, partly decyphered by Windebank.
No date.

379. *Father Leander to Secretary Windebank.* Bespeaks his favour for the bearer, and the continuance of his protection to himself. Encloses the next paper, with the directions of Father Reade, Procurator at Rome of the English Benedictine monks.
Cl. S. P. vol. l. p. 128.
Aug. 26.

380. London, July 12. *Father Leander to Cardinal Bentivoglio*, of ecclesiastical affairs in England. Explains the controversy about the Oath of Allegiance, justifying His Majesty's intentions, and quoting passages from the book against the oath, offensive to the Puritans. Why should not the Pope, who writes to the Pagans of India and the schismatics of Abyssinia, write to His Majesty, expressing his interest in him, and regretting that the doctrine of the deposition of princes should have been promulgated in England? Advises that the Bishop of Chalcedon* be not sent back to England, and that it will be dangerous to send hither any Bishops with foreign jurisdiction, the Irish and Scotch being sufficient for Confirmation.—Latin. *Copy.*
Cl. S. P. vol. l. p. 129.

381. *Thomas Williams to the Archbishop of Canterbury (Laud).* Narrates two notable controversies debated at Rome, one between the English and Seminary Priests about the Bishop of Chalcedon, and the other between English and French Capuchins about missions to England and Scotland. The Seminary Priests contend that a Bishop is neces-
Paris, Aug. 30.

* Richard Smith. He was apprehended and imprisoned at Wisbeach in 1628. See Rapin, vol. ii. p. 276.

1634. ary for Confirmation, for protecting moneys left to poor Catholics but appropriated by the Jesuits, and generally to restrain the abuses of Jesuit confessors. The Jesuits deny the necessity, and object personally to the Bishop of Chalcedon. There is now a good opportunity to drive the Jesuits out of the realm. They have grown to such power in forty years, that they have daily in their college 550 young students of the best Papist families in England, each paying 30*l.* or 40*l.* yearly. They have also 200,000*l.* or 300,000*l.* yearly in rents; they number 360 of their order, with Rectors in each county, and a Provincial over them; they raise persecutions against the priests while they escape themselves; and are deadly enemies to the state and religion. Friar Joseph is the chief mainspring, endeavouring to get a French Capuchin appointed Queen's confessor, filling the country with French friars, and having obtained that no English or Scotch Capuchins be allowed to visit the country. They intend to educate the Queen's children as Papists.

Abstract, endorsed by Windebank. Cl. S. P. vol. i. p. 138.

Madrid, Sept. 11.

382. *Mr. Hopton to Secretary Windebank.* Don Francisco de Irasso, Condé de Humanes, is the new Ambassador to England. Though he is of good understanding and has sufficient knowledge, there is nothing whereof we need be afraid.

Cl. S. P. vol. i. p. 143.

Madrid, Sept. 11.

383. *Mr. Taylor to the same.* Of the recall of Necolalde, and the new Ambassador. Cl. S. P. vol. i. p. 144.

Madrid, Oct. 9.

384. *Powers* from the King of Spain to Necolalde to act in the Secret Treaty.—Spanish. *Copy.*

In Windebank's hand, and endorsed by him. In substance this is the same as those printed in Cl. S. P. vol. i. p. 131.

Madrid, Oct. 11.

385. *Mr. Taylor to the Lord Treasurer (Portland).* Has represented to the Condé Duke that the Infant Cardinal must not in his passage to Flanders disturb the Count Palatine in the possession of his country, to which the Condé has agreed. Has pressed thereupon that the King of Hungary and the Duke of Lorraine observe the same respect. The Duchess of Mantua, Ursino Duke of Brachiano, the Prince of Subruc nephew to Paul V., and the Cardinal of Polonia are expected. Humanes is to leave on the 15th.

Abstract by Windebank. Cl. S. P. vol. i. p. 145.

Madrid, Oct. 11.

386. *Mr. Hopton to Secretary Windebank.* Gives reasons for the request with reference to the Infant Cardinal's march through the Palatinate. Cl. S. P. vol. i. p. 147.

387. *Mr. Hopton to the Lord Treasurer (Portland).* The French Ambassador and the Nuntio continue their secret negotiations with the Condé Duke, but the treaty is not likely to come to anything. Eight thousand horse are to be levied, and the king will take the field himself, but with what intention is not yet clear.   Cl. S. P. vol. I. p. 148.

1634. Madrid, Oct. 11.

388. *The Archbishop of York (Neile) to the Archbishop of Canterbury (Laud).* John Hilton, (whose wife and children are recusants,) being candidate for the mayoralty of Appleby, and objected to on that ground, is alleged to have said that some Privy Councillors and the King himself had their wives recusants, and yet kept their places, and why might not he do the like? Has bound him in 1000l. to appear before the Council, and desires His Majesty's directions.

Copy.
Endorsed by himself, with a notice that the King pardoned Hilton.
Cl. S. P. vol. I. p. 153.

Winchester House, Oct. 15.

389. *Mr. Hopton to Secretary Windebank.* Count Schomberg, the Emperor's Ambassador, has arrived, and is to be styled Excelencia instead of the usual Señoria illustrissima, a matter which has heretofore caused great disgusts between Austrian and Venetian Ambassadors. The preparations still go on, and the House of Austria appears to prosper.
Cl. S. P. vol. I. p. 149.

Madrid, Oct. 16.

390. *Mr. Taylor to the same.* England may have all that Spain can restore of the Palatinate, if they will oblige them in the business of the Duke of Lorrain, and lend assistance against the Hollanders. But they will not break with the Duke of Bavaria. Will leave at the beginning of next month.
Cl. S. P. vol. I. p. 150.

Madrid, Oct. 16.

391. *The same to Lord Cottington.* The disposition of the times is very favourable for the Prince Palatine's business. Likes the Condé de Humanes the better the more he sees of him. The King is reported likely to go to Perpignan next spring, and there is prospect of a war with France.
Cl. S. P. vol. I. p. 151.

Madrid, Oct. 16.

392. *Secretary Windebank to Mr. Hopton.* Sends the Articles, with comments on Necolalde's exceptions to them. He should hint to the Condé Duke the great offers made by the French Ambassador of a league with France and the Protestant Princes of Germany, and use this as an argument of His Majesty's good-will to Spain. If the Prince Elector goes into the Palatinate it will be without His Majesty's advice or assistance, and then, if the ban be taken off, His Majesty

Oct. 16.

1834. will leave him to his own counsels. Is contented now that Necolalde should remain. His Majesty, rather than Spain, is aggrieved by ill-usage upon the seas. Gerbier writes that the Marquis of Aytona has order from Spain to treat for a league, but His Majesty prefers keeping this negotiation secret at present. A proposition has just arrived, earnestly pressing for assistance to the Prince Palatine on passing into the Palatinate, to which His Majesty is resolved not to hearken. *Draught.*
                In his own hand.   CL. S. P. vol. L p. 134.

Hampton Court, Oct. 11.

393. *A Copy of the Paper, with the King's hand to it, of such moneys as he allowed the Lord Treasurer Portland to receive to his own use*, amounting to 44,000*l*. Among other items are, A gift from His Majesty, 10,000*l*.; Sir William Wittipoole for pardoning his burning in the hand, 500*l*.; the third part of the Imposition on Coals, 4000*l*.
    Signed, dated, and certified by the King at 44,500*l*.   CL. S. P. vol. L p. 158.

Rome, Oct. 23.

394. *Father Wilford (alias Reade, alias Selbys), to Father Leander.* Has delivered to Cardinal Barberini, as governing all, his letter to Cardinal Bentivoglio. Did what he could to hinder the publication of Father Francis Clare's book.
                                                  CL. S. P. vol. L p. 152.

Oct. 19.

395. *Secretary Windebank to His Majesty.* Mr. Courtney, the author of the book against the Oath of Allegiance, is apprehended and committed to the Gatehouse in Westminster. *Rough Draught.*
                In his own hand.   CL. S. P. vol. L p. 159.

Madrid, Nov. 9.

396. *Mr. Hopton to Secretary Windebank.* The Condé Duke has had advice that a league has been concluded between England, France, and the States, which he has denied.
                                                     CL. S. P. vol. i. p. 160.

Madrid, Nov. 9.

397. *The same to Lord Cottington.* Asks for more information on State affairs. There is great joy at the Infant Cardinal's arrival in Flanders. The last picture of the Labrador has been sent back to London. Requests money. Recommends mercy to one Christian de Chevery, Armador of the St. Sebastian squadron, apprehended by the Lord Deputy of Ireland. CL. S. P. vol. l. p. 161.

Madrid, Nov. 9.

398. *Mr. Taylor to Secretary Windebank*, concerning the report of the French alliance. Mr. Windebank has arrived at Court. CL. S. P. vol. L p. 161.

399. *Mr. Taylor to Lord Cottington,* of the same report, which if true will hinder the departure of the Condé de Humanes. Cl. S. P. vol. I. p. 163.
1634. Madrid, Nov. 9.

400. *A Paper of Memoranda* on some of the Articles of the Secret Treaty with Spain.
Wallingford House, Nov. 9.

401. *Mr. Hopton to Secretary Windebank,* announcing his son's safe arrival, and promising him his best assistance.
Madrid, Nov. 9.

402. *Secret Instructions for our trusty and well-beloved servant Endymion Porter, Esq., one of the Grooms of our Bedchamber, employed by us to the Infant Cardinal in the Low Countries.* To compliment the Infant Cardinal, and, if occasion offers, communicate with the Marquis of Aytona or Abbot of Scaglia concerning the proposed league, which the King desires should be treated of in England. *Draught.*
By Windebank, with a parenthesis inserted by the King. Cl. S. P. vol. I. p. 166.
Nov. 11.

403. *Father Leander to Secretary Windebank.* Desires that the information he gives may not be prejudicial to his credit. Two English and two Scotch Capuchins have been allowed to come to England at the intercession of Cardinal Osupbrius, the Pope's brother, but complain that they are greatly opposed by Père Joseph and the French Capuchins. Desires leave to go to Doway and return. Encloses the next.
Date endorsed by Windebank. Cl. S. P. vol. I. p. 167.
Nov. 13.

Father Selbye to Father Leander. Father Clare's book will be forbidden, but, as a favour to His Majesty, they will not proceed against his person. Leander's actions are closely scanned there. Cl. S. P. vol. I. p. 168.

404. *Father Leander to Secretary Windebank,* with directions how to address his letters to Father Selbye, alias Wilfrid, alias Iloade. Desires his favour for Humphry Turberville, confined in the Gatehouse for religion.
Date endorsed by Windebank. Cl. S. P. vol. I. p. 169.
Nov. 15.

405. *The same to the Pope* (Urban VIII). Quotes six propositions from the book against the Oath of Allegiance, which he condemns as offensive and seditious.—Latin. *Copy.*
In his own hand, with date endorsed by Windebank. Cl. S. P. vol. I. p. 169.
Nov. 15.

406. *Father Selbye to Father Leander.* The request to suspend the Pope's brief in a matter of faith cannot be complied with. (Explained in the margin by Leander that such
Rome, Nov. 18.

1634. was not his meaning.) The Cardinal of Lyons, Bishops, and Sorbonne Doctors are to meet to procure that Monsieur d'Orleans' marriage be declared invalid. *In Cypher.*
Cl. S. P. vol. i. p. 164. with the exception of an immaterial postscript.

Madrid, Nov. 18. 407. *Mr. Hopton to Secretary Windebank.* Has told the Condé Duke that, if Spain will not assist him, there is danger of the Prince Palatine putting himself under the protection of France. Cl. S. P. vol. i. p. 165.

Nov. 22. 408. *A Letter* (signature illegible, and addressed "To my master"). Has attempted to stop the condemnation of Father Clare's book. Persuades his correspondent to various measures to further his ends. Writes in cypher of places to be filled up by persons whom he names. Cl. S. P. vol. i. p. 171.

Dec. 1. 409. *Mr. Phillips to Secretary Windebank.* Will not come to him lest exception be taken. Has spoken to the Queen, who is pleased with what Windebank has done. Encloses the next, to be shown to the Archbishop of Canterbury.
Date endorsed by Windebank. Cl. S. P. vol. i. p. 172.

A Paper of conditions to be observed in choosing one or more Catholic Bishops for England.
Cl. S. P. vol. i. p. 173.

Dec. 6. 410. *An Abstract of the Will of the Right Hon. Paul, Lord Viscount Bayninge, son of Paul, Lord Viscount Bayninge, deceased.*

No date. 411. *Propositions to be made on my Lord Herbert's part unto Sir Thomas Clemham touching my Lord Bayninge's estate.* (Sir T. Clemham being one of the executors.)

No date. 412. *A Relation of such ships of Dunkirk as have been taken by the Hollanders out of His Majesty of Great Britain's ports since the year 1632 to 1634.* A paper presented by Neoolaldo detailing eight distinct cases of seizure in the eastern ports from Aberdeen to London. *Copy.*

Madrid, Dec. 7. 413. *Mr. Hopton to Secretary Windebank.* Has commended to the King the maritime alliance and the protection of English merchants. The Condé Duke has discussed the Articles with him, wishing that the protection to Spanish ships be extended to the whole of the Channel, and objecting to the 8th Article, whereby the approbation of His Majesty is necessary to the English ships fighting in defence of the Spanish. Has proposed that the King of Spain grant to the Prince Palatine the usufruition of that part of the Palatinate which he holds, during the negotiations for the restitution of the whole. The Condé Duke advises that an English Ambassador be sent to the Emperor: and dwells still upon the rumoured league with France. *In Cypher.*

1634.

Also a decyphered copy in Windebank's hand. Cl. S. P. vol. i. p. 173.

414. *Father Leander to Cardinal Barberino.* Urges him earnestly to take some steps for the advancement of the Roman Catholic Church in England. Defends himself against the accusation of favouring the Oath of Allegiance, and justifies the middle course he is charged with taking. Deprecates harsh measures, and sees the restoration of England to orthodoxy in the rose, which forms part of the emblem of the Rose and Lily prophetically applied by Archbishop Malachy to the present Pope.—Latin.

Dec. 8.

Two Copies to the same purport, but differing considerably in the wording, one as sent to Windebank for his approval, the other a corrected copy with Windebank's suggestions. Both copies are printed in (?. S. P. vol. i. pp. 180 and 185.

415. *Mr. Hopton to Secretary Windebank.* Great preparations are being made of men and money. Don Fedrique de Toledo is dead, but the King was so offended with him that he would not allow him to be buried except as a private man. Mr. Windebank is well.

Madrid, Dec. 15.

Cl. S. P. vol. i. p. 177.

416. *The same to the same.* The Secretary of War has asked him to intercede for some Spanish ships detained in England.

Madrid, Dec. 16.

Cl. S. P. vol. i. p. 178.

417. *The same to Lord Cottington.* The Condé has had such jealousies of the English, as make him unfit to be spoken to. Congratulates him on the place of Master of the Wards which he hears he has been presented to.

Madrid, Dec. 16.

Cl. S. P. vol. i. p. 179.

418. *Father Leander to Secretary Windebank.* Defends his arguments in his letter to Cardinal Barberino, but submits the amended copy in deference to Windebank.

Dec. 16.

Date endorsed by Windebank. Cl. S. P. vol. i. p. 184.

419. *Secret Articles agreed upon between England and Spain,* being supplementary to Art. 3 of the Treaty. *Copies.*

London, Dec. 16.

In Spanish and English, endorsed by Windebank. Cl. S. P. vol. i. pp. 214, 215.

420. *The Oath of Allegiance,* as taken by Father Leander, with an appended declaration that the Pope has no dispensing power in this Oath. *Copy.*

Dec. 17.

Endorsed by Windebank. Cl. S. P. vol. i. p. 210.

1634.
Rome,
Dec. 19.

421. *Father Selbye to Secretary Windebank.* The Duke of Lorrain arrived a fortnight back, and has been well received by the Pope, who is reported to be favourable to him in the matter of his sister's marriage with the Duke of Orleans. The Bishop of Grenoble is arrived to plead against the marriage as without the consent of the parents, and desires to have the case heard in France, which the Pope will not allow. He is said to have granted the Duke a pension of 20,000 gold crowns per annum. *Cl. S. P. vol. I. p. 182.*

Madrid,
Dec. 31.

422. *Mr. Hopton to the same,* giving good hopes of the Palatine negotiation. A new defensive league between the Emperor and Spain, to which the King is to be invited; also between the Duke of Bavaria, Electors of Cologne and Mentz, and the Duke of Newburg. *Cl. S. P. vol. L. p. 216.*

No date.

423. *A Minute* on the same in Spanish and English.
In Windebank's hand.

No date.

424. *The Oath of Allegiance.*
A copy by Windebank. Cl. S. P. vol. I. p. 88.

No date.

425. *A Comparison* in nine heads of the Powers of the King in Temporal matters, the Pope in Spiritual, and God in both, with eight cases wherein the temporal sword must be subordinate to the spiritual.—Latin.
Endorsed by Windebank, "Mr. Damport." Cl. S. P. vol. L. p. 90.

No date.

426. *A Paper,* concerning the act *primo Elizabethæ* abrogating mass. Questions its legality as without the concurrence of the Lords Spiritual, and passed by a House of Commons not freely elected, but nominated by the Sheriffs. This is on supposition that Parliament has *vota decisiva* in making laws; if only *consultores,* the King's right to abrogate is unquestionable. *Cl. S. P. vol. I. p. 91.*

No date.

427. *The Representation of Prince Thomas (of Savoy).* France by her alliance with the Protestant Princes designs entirely to ruin the House of Austria, as an obstacle to her own greatness. Hence it is important to prevent them gaining Lorrain, after which they may gain Geneva and Savoy, holding already Pignerola and Cassel, then become masters of Flanders and Burgundy, subdue the Hollanders, and finally break with the English. His Majesty should join Austria in checking this, stir up the Huguenots, bring the King of Denmark and the Princes of Italy into this alliance, and procure peace with the Dukes of Saxony and Brandenburg. The interests of

religion accord with this, the Prince Palatine may be restored, and the Electorate follow after the death of the Duke of Bavaria.—Italian.   1634.

Also a translation by Windebank, from which this summary is taken, the original having become unintelligible by mutilation.
Cl. S. P. vol. I. p. 96.

428. *Father Leander to Secretary Windebank.* Asks a protection from molestation for his friend Mr. William Price.   No date.
Cl. S. P. vol. I. p. 106.

429. *Reasons for creating an English Cardinal.* King James, judging from the history of the reigns of Henry IV, Henry VIII, and Elizabeth, thought it expedient in temporal respects to have a national Cardinal. But this cannot be done without His Majesty's approbation. The difficulty of obtaining the honour shewn by the cases of Père Joseph and Prince Peretti, great-nephew to Sextus V. He must be truly national, have his maintenance from England, be nobly born, learned, and prudent. All these requisites are in —— to whom the only objection is his youth. The man most spoken of for the place wants all the requisites, is the known creature of another, has no means, and no birth.   No date.

In the hand of Mr. Price; also a copy by Windebank.
Cl. S. P. vol. I. p. 133.

430. *Mr. Price to Secretary Windebank,* giving a summary of his arguments in the last paper, and urging the defects of the person spoken of.   No date.
Cl. S. P. vol. I. p. 137.

431. *Verax et humilis Informatio de Juramento Fidelitatis, ab Eminentissimis Dominis Cardinalibus perpendenda.* An elaborate defence by Leander of his former letter to the Cardinal Barberino, and a minute examination of the Oath of Allegiance (the wording of which is very different to that given in a former paper), which is divided into eight heads, and considered in parallel columns in reference to the *sensus præsumptus* and the *sensus verè intentus*.—Latin.   *Copy.*   No date.

In his own hand.   Cl. S. P. vol. I. p. 168.

432. *Apostolicæ Missionis Status in Anglià.* A lengthy description of the state of the English Protestant Church, with a detailed account of the Roman Catholic Clergy in the country, viz. 500 Secular Priests, 250 Jesuits, about 100 Benedictines, 20 Dominicans, 20 Carmelites, 30 Franciscans, 4 English and Scotch Capuchins, and 4 Minimes. This number is too great, and moreover distracted by the controversy concerning a Bishop. Recommends methods of making the   No date.

1634. Clergy more select, and that no Bishop be sent, with many reasons for this advice. Considers other defects in the Catholic discipline, and suggests remedies.—Latin.

In Leander's hand, endorsed by Windebank.   Cl. S. P. vol. L p. 197.

No date.   433. *A Letter to be written by the Pope (Urban VIII) to His Majesty*, with congratulations on his marriage, and declaring that the Brief does not apply to the sense in which His Majesty understands the Oath of Allegiance.—Latin.

Rough Draught.
By Leander, endorsed by Windebank.   Cl. S. P. vol. L p. 205.

No date.   434. *Instructions relating to the Reconciliation of moderate Papists and Protestants.* A paper, directing an agent how to point out the particulars in which the two Churches agree and disagree, and proposing a qualified form of the Oath of Allegiance. As to the appointment of a Bishop, he is to take directions from His Majesty and the State.

In Leander's hand, endorsed by Windebank.   Cl. S. P. vol. L p. 207.

No date.   435. *Censura de quibusdam capitibus in libro inscripto Collectiones Theologicarum quarundam conclusionum, etc., quæ quibusdam suspecta videbantur*, on the position of St. Peter with relation to the rest of the Apostles, and other theological topics.

In the same hand as the paper printed in Cl. S. P. vol. L p. 90.

436. *Copy of the Oath of a Privy Councillor.*

No date.   437. *A Paper* (in Leander's hand) vindicating moderate Catholics from the charge of disloyalty to the King.
Cl. S. P. vol. L p. 209.

No date.   438. *Father Leander to Cardinal Barberino*, of the good treatment of Catholics in England.   *Copy.*
In Leander's hand, endorsed by Windebank.   Cl. S. P. vol. L p. 211.

1634-5.
Jan. 9.
439. *Projet de Traité entre le Roi d'Angleterre, le Roi très Chrétien, et les Provinces Unies des Pays Bas*, on the basis of the restitution of the Prince Palatine, and defensive against Spain and the Empire.   *Copy.*
In Windebank's hand.   Cl. S. P. vol. L p. 230.

Madrid,
Jan. 11.
440. *Mr. Hopton to Secretary Windebank.* The show of preparation in Spain does not really betoken a rupture with the French, but is meant only to induce them to treat.
Cl. S. P. vol. L p. 217.

441. *Mr. Hopton to Lord Cottington*, of the goodwill of the Condé Duke and Don Francisco de Silva to his Lordship.
Cl. S. P. vol. l. p. 218.
1634–5. Madrid, Jan. 11.

442. *The same to the Lord Treasurer (Portland)*, of the jealousy in Spain of the reported league between England and France.
Cl. S. P. vol. l. p. 219.
Madrid, Jan. 11.

443. *The same to Secretary Windebank*. The Queen was delivered of a daughter on the 16th, and by the advice of the Condé Duke, he has been to congratulate the King, though fearful to anticipate his orders from home.
Cl. S. P. vol. l. p. 219.
Madrid, Jan. 18.

444. *The King of Spain (Philip IV) to His Majesty*, acquainting him with the birth of the Princess.—Latin.
Cl. S. P. vol. l. p. 220.
Madrid, Jan. 18.

445. *Father Leander to Secretary Windebank*, asking permission to leave England for a short time, to make arrangements with Abbot Cavarell, founder of the College and Convent of Douay, about the completion of those foundations.
Cl. S. P. vol. l. p. 221.
No date.

446. *Secretary Windebank to Abbot Cavarell*, excusing the delay of Leander's journey to Douay for a few weeks, on the ground of the good he can do by remaining in England.—Latin. *Copy.*
In Windebank's hand. Also two rough draughts in Leander's hand.
Cl. S. P. vol. l. p. 222.
Jan. 11.

447. *Mr. Hopton to Secretary Windebank*. An account of a conversation with the Condé de Schomberg, Ambassador at Madrid for the Emperor, concerning the prospects of the Prince Palatine.
Cl. S. P. vol. l. p. 222.
Madrid, Jan. 27.

448. *Secretary Windebank to Mr. Hopton*, of Necolalde's objections to the third and tenth Articles of the Treaty: of the Elector Palatine's business, and the false rumour of the conjunction of France and England. *Rough Draught.*
In Windebank's hand. Cl. S. P. vol. l. p. 226.
Jan. 14.

449. *The same to the same*, enclosing his powers to conclude the Treaty, subject to his previous reservation of the third, eighth, and tenth Articles. *Draught.*
In Windebank's hand. Cl. S. P. vol. l. p. 229.
Jan. 14.

1634-5. Jan. 24.	450. *Powers* to *Mr. Hopton* to treat as above. *Rough Draught.* In Windebank's hand. Cl. S. P. vol. l. p. 230.	
No date.	451. *Alterations* in several of the Articles sent to Mr. Hopton subsequently to the last despatch. *Rough Draught.* In Windebank's hand. Cl. S. P. vol. l. p. 231.	
Feb. 9.	452. *Mr. Matthew Wilson to Dr. More*, requesting medical advice for his ailments.	
Atrebatum, Feb. 22.	453. *The Abbot Cavarell to Secretary Windebank*, consenting to Leander's further stay in England.—Latin. Cl. S. P. vol. l. p. 233.	
Brussels, Feb. 23.	454. *A. Kieffel to the same*, proffering his services, and enclosing the next.—French. Cl. S. P. vol. l. p. 234.	
Brussels, Feb. 23.	455. *The same to His Majesty*, urging an immediate invasion of France, a league with the King of Spain, and the recall of all English subjects from the Low Countries.—French. Cl. S. P. vol. l. p. 234.	
Madrid, Feb. 24.	456. *Mr. Taylor to Secretary Windebank.* Is only waiting till the news of the conclusion of the Treaty comes from England. The Condé d' Humanes is to set out about Easter. Mr. Windebank is well, and progressing in his Spanish studies. Cl. S. P. vol. l. p. 236.	
Madrid, Feb. 24.	457. *The same to the Lord Treasurer (Portland)*, of an interview with the Condé Duke, and the desire in Spain to see the Treaty concluded. Cl. S. P. vol. l. p. 237.	
Madrid, Feb. 24.	458. *The same to Lord Cottington*, forwarding friendly messages from the Condé Duke. Cl. S. P. vol. l. p. 238.	
Madrid, Feb. 25.	459. *Mr. Hopton to Secretary Windebank.* Great preparations for war, but the Spaniards would be glad to treat with the French on good conditions. The death of Don Federique de Toledo and Don Gonsalvo de Cordova, the two best men the King had. Lord Carnarvon has arrived. Mr. Christopher Windebank is well. Cl. S. P. vol. l. p. 238.	
Madrid, Feb. 25.	460. *The same to Lord Cottington.* Of the dangerous disposition of the Condé Duke. He has sent the Labrador painting to England. Cl. S. P. vol. l. p. 240.	

461. *Mr. Hopton to the Lord Treasurer (Portland)*, urging despatch in the present crisis, to prevent the Spaniards cooling. — Cl. S. P. vol. I. p. 241. — 1634-5. Madrid, Feb. 25.

462. *Dr. More to Mr. Wilson*, in answer to his letter of Feb. 9, recommending him to return to his native air. — Feb. 27.

463. *Five Petitions from Recusants*, viz. from Mr. Wilson to be restored from banishment on the medical advice above given (endorsed by Windebank, "Sent by the Queen 18 of April by Mr. Dorrington, with an earnest recommendation"): from Mr. Carleton of Norwich (endorsed by Windebank), Mr. Cobb of Sandringham, and Messrs. Weedon (endorsed by Windebank), for protection against informers: and from John Folliott, imprisoned in Warwick Castle on suspicion of being a priest. — No date.

464. *Prince Thomas (of Savoy) to the King*, recommending the Baron de Pupols.—French. — No date.
Endorsed by Windebank as delivered to him Feb. 28. Cl. S. P. vol. I. p. 242.

465. *Father Barlowe to Secretary Windebank*. An extravagant eulogium of Windebank and Father Leander.—Latin. — Douay, Feb. 28.
Cl. S. P. vol. I. p. 242.

466. *The Duke of Savoy (Victor Amadeus) to His Majesty*, recommending Mr. Daler on his return to England.—French. — Turin, March 11.
Cl. S. P. vol. I. p. 244.

467. *Duke Bernard (of Saxony) to the same.* A short letter of compliment to accompany Col. Leslie.—French. — Spire, March 14.
Cl. S. P. vol. I. p. 244.

468. *Mr. Hopton to Secretary Windebank.* An account of debates with the King and Condé about the Articles which they have resolved to send back to England. The probability. The King of Poland's marriage discussed. A fleet of eighteen ships is bound to Fernambuco, and an effort is to be made to recover Brazil. — 1635. Madrid, April 7.
Cl. S. P. vol. I. p. 245.

469. *Duke Bernard (of Saxony) to His Majesty.* A short letter of compliment.—French. — Spire, April 10.
Cl. S. P. vol. I. p. 245.

470. *Father Leander to Don Gregorio de Panzana.* An earnest exhortation through him to the Pope to seize the opportunity of advancing Catholic interests in England by cultivating friendly relations with the King.—Latin. — April 12.
Cl. S. P. vol. I. p. 249.

1635.
Rome,
April 13.

471. *Mr. Wilford to Father Leander*, entreating him to keep aloof in the controversy about the oath of allegiance. If you get the chesnuts, give others (i. e. the Jesuits) leave to burn their toes. Cardinal Borgia is ordered by the Pope to return to Spain, notwithstanding the protests of the other Spanish Ambassadors, of whom it may be said *turba medicorum occidit Cæsarem*. False rumour spread by Richelieu of the Turks' coming to Malta. *Copy.*
By Windebank. Cl. S. P. vol. L p. 250.

Rome,
April 15.

472. *The same to the same*, desiring an answer to the Cardinal Duccabella's accusations of him, as having written against Mr. Courtenay, the champion of the Catholic cause. *Copy.*
By Windebank. Cl. S. P. vol. L p. 251.

April 16.

473. *Father Leander to Secretary Windebank.* An answer to certain questions propounded by him as to the essentials and functions belonging to a Bishop. Cl. S. P. vol. L p. 252.

No date.

474. *Positions delivered by a Catholic Roman Divine concerning the Ordination of a Bishop.*
In Windebank's hand, the whole being extracted from Leander's previous letter.

No date.

475. *Father Leander to Secretary Windebank*, averring that there is no priest at present in England who can be properly said to be endowed with Episcopal functions; with special reference to his own order of Benedictines.
Cl. S. P. vol. L p. 255.

No date.

476. *A Paper of Propositions*, whereby to check the opposers in Rome of the English religious orders, Sir Toby Matthews and Mr. Gage being the two principally complained of. The method suggested is that Mr. Courtenay's proposition concerning the independence of Princes be laid before a convention of the religious orders, and their declaration concerning it published. Endorsed by Windebank, "Leander."

Madrid,
April 20.

477. *The Condé Duke d'Olivarez to the Lord Treasurer (Portland).* A short letter of compliment.—Spanish.
Cl. S. P. vol. L p. 267.

Madrid,
April 22.

478. *The same to Lord Cottington.* A letter of compliment and praise of Mr. Taylor.—Spanish. Cl. S. P. vol. L p. 268.

April 25.

479. *Mr. Courtenay to Secretary Windebank*, professing his ignorance of the charges made against him.
Cl. S. P. vol. L p. 259.

No date.

480. *Extracts* from Mr. Courtenay's book against the Oath of Allegiance. Endorsed by Windebank. Cl. S. P. vol. L p. 258.

481. *The humble Remonstrance of Edward Courtenay, prisoner,* addressed to Windebank, asserting his innocence, and promising to write no more if he may be set at liberty.   1635. No date.
Cl. S. P. vol. I. p. 260.

482. *Mr. Hopton to Secretary Windebank.* Mr. Taylor is resolved to leave at once for England, either with or without the Condé's order.   Madrid, April 15.
Cl. S. P. vol. I. p. 262.

483. *The same to the same.* Great preparations for war; Don Philip de Silva is to command the army for the present, but it is very doubtful whether after all they will come to a rupture with France.   April 16.
Cl. S. P. vol. I. p. 263.

484. *The same to Lord Cottington.* No new resolution concerning the league. The best advised judgments think that no rupture with France will take place.   April 16.
Cl. S. P. vol. I. p. 265.

485. *The Condé Duke d'Olivarez to the same.* Condolences on the death of the Lord Treasurer (Portland).—Spanish.   Madrid, April 18.
Cl. S. P. vol. I. p. 269.

486. *Mr. Hopton to Secretary Windebank.* The poverty of Spain will probably render it disinclined for war this year. The Duke of Maqueda has requested the restoration of one Captain Fiton's ship, taken in piracy off Ireland.   Madrid, May 4.
Cl. S. P. vol. I. p. 265.

487. *Don Geronimo de Salcedo to Lord Cottington.* A short letter of compliment.—Spanish.   Madrid, May 4.
Cl. S. P. vol. I. p. 270.

488. *Mr. Francis Hyde to (Edw. Hyde?).* Their cousin Laurence Hyde (a merchant), who was never a wit, has been wrongfully used, but is not likely to get much redress in Venice. Has tried with little success to move the College to punish the villain Greek who betrayed Val. Hyde. Has been much cheered by the news of a calm from Lambeth, as one so weatherbeaten may well be fearful of more storms. Has as much employment as his ignorance of Italian will allow. The Duke yesterday married the Sea. The news of the taking and loss again of Rochelle has been posted on the Rialto.   Venice, May 8.

489. *Mr. Wilford to Father Leander.* Advice concerning the course he should adopt in defence of his book against Mr. Courtenay. Above all he should take heed in future of meddling with deponibility of princes, for that article will never pass here. Cardinal Borgia is gone to Naples. A report that the English have taken Rochelle. *Copy.*   Rome, May 9.
In Windebank's hand.   Cl. S. P. vol. I. p. 271.

1635.
May 18.

490. *An Estimate for a Building to be erected for Her Majesty* (by Christopher Wren), being a two-storied building occupying the whole south side of the Privy Garden, estimated at 13,305*l*.
Cl. S. P. vol. I. p. 270.

Madrid,
May 31.

491. *Mr. Hopton to Secretary Windebank.* The war preparations will all be employed for Italy. He is of opinion that France is too strong for Spain to venture on a rupture. The Condé d'Humanes has not yet set out.
Cl. S. P. vol. I. p. 274.

Madrid,
May 31.

492. *The same to Lord Cottington.* An interview with the Condé when the rupture with France was discussed. The Spaniards see better than they did the profit of the friendship of England, but they are like ill husbands that will not lay out their money in one season for the use of another. Their hope is that England will not agree with France. A discourse with the Emperor's Ambassador about the rumour of the King of Poland's marriage with the Prince Palatine's sister, to which he expressed himself greatly averse.
Cl. S. P. vol. I. p. 276.

June 6.

493. *Mr. Wilford to Father Leander*, desiring a copy of what he has written against Mr. Courtenay, and repeating his advice to him to make his peace at Rome, and write no more on the subject.
Cl. S. P. vol. I. p. 277.

Madrid,
June 10.

494. *Mr. Hopton to Secretary Windebank.* The French invasion of Luxemburg has altered the position of affairs, and the King is now to go in person to Barcelona to the army. Of the frequent and unnecessary complaints of the English merchants forwarded to him from the Council. *Two Copies.*
Cl. S. P. vol. I. p. 278.

Madrid,
June 10.

495. *The same to Lord Cottington.* The breach between France and Spain widens. Repetition of his complaint of the trouble which English merchants cause him.
Cl. S. P. vol. I. p. 280.

Madrid,
June 13.

496. *The same to Secretary Windebank.* The French Resident has announced to the King that, in consequence of the imprisonment of the Elector of Treves and other causes of complaint, his master is purposed to declare war. The King is inclined to go to the army, but if the Condé Duke can prevent him he will.
Cl. S. P. vol. I. p. 281.

Madrid,
June 13.

497. *The same to Secretary Coke:* of the declaration of war by France. The plate fleet has arrived, and the Spaniards are better provided with money than was thought. Has

delivered a memorial concerning the complaints of the merchants of Lisbon, though he does not think their case a good one. *Copy.* 1638.

In his own hand. Cl. S. P. vol. I. p. 282.

498. *Mr. Hopton to Lord Cottington.* The Condé Duke is very confident, and thinks the opportunity a good one for the King to procure the restitution of his nephews. The Condé d'Humanes is a great lover of *arbitrios.* The King is to go to the army in person, and perhaps before Lord Aston arrives. Madrid, June 1.

Cl. S. P. vol. I. p. 284.

499. *The same to Secretary Windebank.* The rupture goes on. Loss of the armada from Italy on Cape Corso. The Condé d'Humanes is to leave in twelve days. The road through France is still open to the Ordinaries of Flanders. Madrid, June 19.

Cl. S. P. vol. I. p. 286.

500. *The same to Lord Cottington.* Though the preparations go on, the Spaniards are not without hope that the Pope will interfere to prevent war. The Condé d'Humanes wishes to go back in the ship which brings Lord Aston. Madrid, June 19.

Cl. S. P. vol. I. p. 287.

501. *Don Juan de Necolalde to Secretary Windebank.* Encloses a complaint from Dunkirk of the behaviour of the English ships there.—Spanish. June 21.

Cl. S. P. vol. I. p. 288.

502. *Mr. Hopton to the same;* of the Condé d'Humanes journey. If money be remitted him instead of bills of exchange he can make a profit of twenty per cent. All Hidalgos are to accompany the King on pain of losing their privileges. Three millions a-year during the war to be laid upon meal. The holy men of Carien to be tried for cozenage and witchcraft. Madrid, June 27.

Cl. S. P. vol. I. p. 289.

503. *The same to the same.* The Condé Duke's excuses for the remissness in concluding the Treaty, which, he promises, shall now go on well. Galasso with 30,000 men has parted from the King of Hungary to succour the Infanta in Flanders. Has gathered from the Condé de Schomberg a suspicion that the perpetuity of the Electorate is settled in the Duke of Bavaria's house. The Condé Duke thinks the Pope has shewn too much partiality for France for his mediation to be accepted. *Two Copies.* Madrid, June 31.

Cl. S. P. vol. I. p. 291.

504. *The same to Lord Cottington.* The army will probably enter France by way of Navarre. Little good is likely to be done unless the King go in person. Madrid, June 31.

Cl. S. P. vol. I. p. 293.

1635.
July 3.

505. *B. Be*(....) *to Father Leander*, concerning their agents in Brittany and elsewhere. The Marshal de la Force is dead of a hurt in Lorraine. The Cardinal la Vallette is gone thither with an order for an army of 240,000 to oppose the King of Hungary, Gallas, and the other generals.

Signature Illegible. Addressed "A Mons. Monsieur Scudamore, Londres."
Cl. S. P. vol. l. p. 294.

Antwerp,
July 6.

506. *Mr. T. Talbot to R. Hunt*: describes the atrocities committed by the French at Tirlemont, and their subsequent movements about Brussels and Antwerp.

Endorsed by Windebank. See Lord Strafford's Collection, vol. l. pp. 440-445.

Madrid,
July 19.

507. *Mr. Hopton to Secretary Windebank*. Great anxiety is felt in Spain for the safety of the Infant Cardinal. The Condé d'Humanes is to start at once. The present state of things is likely to bring the business of the Prince Palatine to some certainty. The English coast should be protected by ships, for the action of 1588 is still in men's minds, and the danger which England then run. The probable cause of the Spaniards' coldness in the Treaty is the fear to offend the Duke of Bavaria. A proposal has been mentioned in the Council that the Prince Palatine should renounce all his rights in Germany, and Spain should give him in Limburg and thereabouts the full value of the Palatinate.

Cl. S. P. vol. l. p. 295.

Madrid,
July 19.

508. *The same to Lord Cottington*. The Condé Duke will try to prevent the King going in person to the war. The Spaniards feel so unfit for war, that the French King, if he would treat, might have what he would. Don Suero de Quinones wishes to send two pictures to the King, a Tintoretto, and a Venus and Adonis of Luquotto. Cl. S. P. vol. l. p. 297.

Madrid,
July 25.

509. *The same to Secretary Windebank*: of the Treaty of peace made in the East Indies between the English and Portuguese. Some experienced man of the East India Company should be in Madrid to help the conclusion of it there. Has begun a negotiation for Sir Henry Colt's liberty.

Cl. S. P. vol. l. p. 299.

Madrid,
July 25.

510. *The same to Lord Cottington*. The landscape-painter is dead, and his pictures, of which he has a few, are much prized. Cl. S. P. vol. l. p. 300.

Madrid,
July 28.

511. *The same to Secretary Windebank*. The Condé Duke has asked him for a messenger to England, to carry instructions, as he thinks, to engage England against France. The quarrel between France and Spain should administer an occasion to

the King for the matters of Germany. The heft of the war 1635.
lying on Flanders and at sea, His Majesty may now be as
much sought to as the Duke of Bavaria has been.

Cl. S. P. vol. I. p. 301.

512. *Mr. Hopton to Lord Cottington.* There have been in- Madrid,
roads about Perpignan on both sides. The Condé d'Humanes July 28.
is to start directly. Cl. S. P. vol. I. p. 301.

513. *His Majesty to Secretary Windebank.* Has given Lord Salisbury,
Holland the least important of Mr. Hopton's letters, to Aug. 6.
prevent jealousies. Cl. S. P. vol. I. p. 302.

514. *Mr. Hopton to the same.* The King's journey to Madrid,
Barcelona is fixed for Oct. 8. Of the Peace with Saxony, Aug. 8.
and the East India business. *Two Copies.*
Cl. S. P. vol. I. p. 313.

515. *Mr. Hopton's Paper concerning the East India business,* No date.
a short statement delivered to the King of Spain.—Spanish.
Copy.
Endorsed by himself. Cl. S. P. vol. I. p. 314.

516. *His Majesty to Secretary Windebank,* enclosing some Salisbury,
letters directed to *Wakerlin,* which *Wilkerius** had given him. Aug. 9.
Cl. S. P. vol. I. p. 301.

517. *Mr. Preston to Mr. William Haywood* (Chaplain to Aug. 10.
the Archbishop of Canterbury), enclosing for His Grace's (Mislaid
perusal papers in answer to Mr. Courtenay's declaration. Is 1634.)
afraid he will be thought to be persecuting Mr. Courtenay,
who, as a prisoner, cannot answer for himself; and that his
book may hinder a good understanding between the King
and the Pope. Cl. S. P. vol. I. p. 303.

518. *Remarks upon Mr. Courtenay's Declaration relative to* No date.
the Doctrine taught in his Book, particularly with reference to
the deponibility of Princes.
In Preston's hand. Cl. S. P. vol. I. p. 305.

519. *Mr. Hopton to Secretary Windebank.* A conversation Madrid,
with the Condé Duke about the treatment of the Prince Aug. 11.
Palatine in the Treaty with the Duke of Saxony. A proposition that the Palatine's house shall, by way of recompense,
have the Electoral voice of the Crown of Bohemia as a loan,
so long as the Empire remains in the House of Austria. The
Limburg proposition, mentioned before, came from the Emperor. There is great anxiety in Spain how the King of

* Probably these are feigned names.

1635. England will act, but an evident determination to secure the peace of Germany to the exclusion of the Prince Palatine. Hence arises all the coldness and delay in the Treaty.

Original, with a duplicate, and also a decyphered copy.
Cl. S. P. vol. i. p. 315.

Madrid, Aug. 11.

520. *Mr. Hopton to Lord Cottington.* The Spaniards are merely trifling with the King of England in the matter of the Treaty: "to what purpose serves *cantar mal porfiar* (an ill singer and always singing)." The business never had God's blessing upon it, and there are very few Princes and Commonwealths in Europe who would not be glad to see a bone between England and Spain, which reason of state has been the destruction of the Prince Palatine's House.

Original, and also two decyphered copies, one by Windebank.
Cl. S. P. vol. i. p. 317.

Lindhurst, Aug. 11.

521. *His Majesty to Secretary Windebank*, returning the secret instructions which follow. Taylor must not address the Emperor too much in the *precario* style.

Cl. S. P. vol. i. p. 306.

Lindhurst, Aug. 15.

522. *Secret Instructions for the Lord Aston, sent Ambassador to the King of Spain.* To press the Prince Palatine's business and the unsatisfactory conduct of the Emperor in his late Treaty with the Duke of Saxony. To complain of Necolalde's carriage. To take notice of a proposition, said to have been made by the Condé de la Roca at Venice to Lord Fielding, that the Prince Palatine should marry a Princess of the House of Austria, and the claims of the Duke of Bavaria be satisfied by the Electorate of Bohemia.

Four Copies.
One signed and dated by the King, and one headed C. R., apparently in the King's hand. Cl. S. P. vol. i. p. 306.

Lindhurst, Aug. 15.

523. *Secret Instructions for John Taylor, Esq., employed to the Emperor*, being of exactly the same purport as those for Lord Aston. To remind the Emperor that next January the Prince Palatine will be eighteen years old, and then by the Constitutions of the Empire will demand investiture of his hereditary rights. *Two Draughts.*

Both by Windebank. Cl. S. P. vol. i. p. 310.

Madrid, Aug. 25.

524. *Mr. Hopton to Secretary Windebank.* The propositions for the accommodation of the Prince Palatine are only meant to trifle away the time, but if they shall see the King of England lay his hand upon his sword they will find out some issue for this business. The delay of the Condé d'Humanes is merely to gain time to see what the King means to do. Has infor-

uation, but on slight grounds, that the Earl of Tyrone has been secretly in Madrid to arrange a sedition in Ireland, in case of a rupture between the Crowns. The East India business is transmitted to Lisbon. 1635.

Original, also a decyphered copy by Windebank of the part in cypher.
C. S. P. vol. i. p. 320.

525. *Mr. Hopton to Lord Cottington.* No answer has yet come about Don Suero de Quinones, who is selling his pictures, and has already sold the Venus and Adonis of Luquette. Madrid, Aug. 25.
Cl. S. P. vol. i. p. 322.

526. *Secretary Windebank to His Majesty*, asking for instructions in the matter of Mr. Hopton's late despatches. Advises that in the present low condition of the Palatine House, the proposition of the loan of the Electoral voice be entertained, quoting the precedent of the loan of the Dukedom of Austria by Spain to the Empire. [The King's answer in the margin is, "It may be a little listened to, to bring better conditions, not otherwise."] This proposition implies taking off the Imperial Ban. [The King remarks, "It is a poor pill that has not some gold."] Mr. Hopton should be continued in Spain after Lord Aston's arrival. *Two Copies.* Westminster, Aug. 27.

One endorsed by the King, "I have answered your letter in the margin. Woodstock, Aug. 28."
Cl. S. P. vol. i. p. 316.

527. *Lord Aston to Secretary Windebank.* Requests, through him, of His Majesty, the remission of a bond for 150*l.*, the grant of twenty-one years' reversion of the Mulberry garden, and appointment to some post at home. Sept. 1.

No signature. Date endorsed by Windebank.

528. *Secretary Windebank to Mr. Hopton.* An answer to his previous despatches in accordance with the King's instructions; particularly demonstrating that the offers of Limburg and an Electoral voice are mere rodomontades. The King moreover has been advertised, that the Emperor declares that he glories in nothing more than in exclusion of a heretic from the Empire. Hopton is to remain in Madrid to assist Lord Aston. Don Suero de Quinones' pictures are to be conveyed to England. *Copy.* Sept. 3.

In Windebank's hand. Cl. S. P. vol. i. p. 324.

529. *Mr. Hopton to Secretary Windebank.* The French and Hollanders have retired from Brabant. Peace with France still treated of, but there is little likelihood of it. Don Philip de Silva is appointed General of the Horse and Governor of the Army in Catalonia, till the Marquis de Leganes arrive. Madrid, Sept. 4.
Cl. S. P. vol. i. p. 313.

1635.
Venice,
Sept. 8.

530. *Lord Fielding to Mr. Edward Hyde.* Assuring him of his affection.
Endorsed by Lord Clarendon.

Ostend,
Sept. 11.

531. *Mr. John Taylor to Secretary Windebank,* announcing his safe arrival there, (on his way to the Imperial Court,) and the courtesy of Captain Smith and the Baron of Passeaux.
Endorsed by Windebank as " Received from Captain Smith, who wafted him in one of His Majesty's ships."

On board the Henrietta Maria,
Sept. 15.

532. *Lord Aston to the same.* Recommends the suit of Capt. Towerson. Complains of the discourtesy shewn him at Portsmouth by Lord Wimbleton.

Sept. 20.

533. *The Condé Duke d'Olivarez to Lord Aston.* A letter of compliment, with friendly professions to His Majesty.—Spanish.
Copy.
Endorsed by Lord Aston.

Sept. 20.

534. *Secretary Roças to the same.* A similar letter.—Spanish.
Copy.
Endorsed by Lord Aston. These two are mentioned in his subsequent letter of Oct. 10.

The Henr. Maria,
Sept. 22.

535. *Lord Aston to Secretary Windebank.* Has been detained at Cowes by stress of weather, and compelled to take a fortnight's extra provision from the "St. Andrew," the "Lion's" provisions being too bad for use.

Madrid,
Sept. 25.

536. *Mr. Hopton to the same.* The Condé d'Humanes is not likely to recover. Don Christoval de Benavides has been named in his place.
Cl. S. P. vol. I. p. 328.

Madrid,
Sept. 29.

537. *The same to the same.* The Prince Palatine must lose no time, for the resolution of the Emperor to exclude him is manifest. Propositions for peace between France and Spain are made both by the Emperor and the Pope; and if it is prevented, it will be for some private object of Richelieu. The Condé d'Humanes is dead.
Cl. S. P. vol. I. p. 329.

Antwerp,
Sept. 29.

538. *Mr. Taylor to the same.* Has visited the Abbot Senglie. The Cardinal Infant is reported to have crossed the Mosel at Genep, and the French to have retired in disorder from Mayence. The Imperialists have crossed the Rhine at Oppenheim in pursuit. The lines of the Hollanders and Spaniards are very close to each other, with hot service on both sides. The army in Artois under the Baron de Balançon is still about St. Paul.

539. *Father Leander to Secretary Windebank*, begging His Majesty's protection for himself and his brother Benedictines against the influence of his enemies in Rome. — 1635. Oct. 1.
Cl. S. P. vol. l. p. 331.

540. *Mr. Taylor to the same.* The French have been defeated in their retreat, and Creutznach taken. The Cardinal Infant's army is at Genep. The Hollanders have not yet been able to take Skink's-sconce. — Diest, Oct. 5.

541. *Secretary Windebank to His Majesty.* The Cardinal de la Valetta has retreated to Sarbruck after a battle with Gallas. The Protestants in France complain much of an altar set up by Lord Scudamore in his chapel. Strongly dissuades His Majesty from the employment of Captain Brett on the Romish business, as recommended by Father Philips, on whose good faith he casts some doubt. *Draught.* — Oct. 6.
In his own hand. Cl. S. P. vol. l. p. 337.

542. *Lord Aston to Secretary Coke,* of his arrival in the Groyne and the extraordinary honours paid him by the Governor. — Oct. 9.
Cl. S. P. vol. l. p. 332.

543. *The same to Secretary Windebank,* of the compliments paid him on his arrival. Some English mariners in the service of Spain have sought the protection of Captain Porter's ship, which may cause some difficulty. — Betanzos, Oct. 10.
Cl. S. P. vol. l. p. 334.

544. *Mr. Selbys to Father Leander.* Has spoken in his defence at Rome. Unsuccessful assaults on Valenza sul Po by the French. The Marquis de Leganes has not yet arrived at Milan. — Rome, Oct. 10.
Cl. S. P. vol. l. p. 336.

545. *A Rent-Roll* for Michaelmas 1635, of (Crown ?) lands at Little Marlow, Medmenham, and elsewhere.

546. *Captain Shaw (to Secretary Windebank!).* Piccolomini's reception of Mr. Taylor evidences his good intentions. The Emperor intends that His Majesty shall be obliged to him alone for the Palatinate. One conference with Piccolomini would advance the treaty more than 5000*l.* spent in embassies. Balançon is besieging Limburg. — Genep, Oct. 13.

547. *Mr. Taylor to Secretary Windebank.* The Cardinal Infant conceives well of his business and will write to the King of Hungary, whom the Condé Piccolomini assures him he will find well disposed. The Emperor will keep the decision about the Prince Palatine in his own hands. The Bavarians — Camp at Genep, Oct. 16.

1638.

are much dissatisfied with the King of Hungary for holding the towns he had taken in the Palatinate. There is talk of a treaty between France and Spain, as also between Spain and Holland. *Partly in Cypher.*

Genap, Oct. 18.

548. *Captain Shaw (to Secretary Windebank.)* Enlarges upon Piccolomini's good feeling. The Emperor's intentions are to the same purport as described in his last.

Genap, Oct. 18.

549. *Exemplar literarum Cardinalis Infantis ad Imperatorem*, recommending the business of Taylor to him.—Latin.
Copy.
Also two copies to the same effect addressed to the King of Hungary.
Cl. S. P. vol. i. p. 398.

Genap, Oct. 18.

550. *The King of Hungary (Ferdinand) to His Majesty*, promising his good offices in the same business.—French.
Copy.
Cl. S. P. vol. i. p. 399.

Genap, Oct. 20.

551. *Mr. Taylor to Secretary Windebank.* Has had an interview with the Cardinal Infanta, wherein he pressed the business of the Prince Palatine, hinting that His Majesty will help to bring the French and Hollanders to an agreement with Spain, if he receives satisfaction therein. Also a conversation with Piccolomini on the disposition of the Duke of Bavaria, and the general state of the Palatinate.
Cl. S. P. vol. i. p. 339.

Madrid, Oct. 20.

552. *Mr. Hopton to the same.* The Condé d'Oñate is named English Ambassador. His character is that of a very gallant gentleman, but somewhat hasty. The Pope has named Cardinal Zaneti Legate for the meeting of Plenipotentiaries to be held at Constance to negotiate a peace. The Spaniards are more inclined to peace, because they hear that the Treaty with the Duke of Saxony is not very sure. The complaints of the *armadores* in Spain are unreasonable and breed much mischief. The East India peace is well received in Spain and Portugal, so far as it can be without knowledge of the conditions. Cl. S. P. vol. i. p. 343.

Madrid, Oct. 20.

553. *The same to Lord Cottington.* Has written at large to Windebank concerning the new Spanish Ambassador. Nothing as yet has been heard of Lord Aston. Encloses the next.

554. Seville, Oct. 9. *Mr. Talbot (Consul at Seville) to Mr. Hopton.* Will try to find a remedy for the evil complained of, that British ships stay so long in harbour after their moneys are aboard.

555. *Secretary Windebank to His Majesty*, enclosing the draught of a letter to the Lord Deputy concerning the Earl of Cork, and Sir Robert Gordon's claim to the Clerkship of the Warrants in the Common Pleas. Again dissuades the employment of Captain Brett; (to which the King's answer is, " If I may trust oaths, he is mine as much as I can expect any Papist to be.") *Original.*

1635. Westminster, Oct. 21.

With the King's answers on each point written in the margin.
Cl. S. P. vol. l. p. 348.

556. *Mr. Taylor to Lord Cottington.* The Cardinal Infant is leaving for Antwerp. Balançon has arrived with forces before Limburg. The French retreat from Mayence was not so disastrous as reported, and Creutznach is not yet yielded. The Hollanders are parleying with the Spaniards, and are thought to be willing to make truce.

Genap, Oct. 21.

557. *Captain Shaw to Secretary Windebank.* Piccolomini has sent Mr. Taylor to the King of Hungary. *Two Copies.*

Genap, Oct. 22.

Apparently sent by different routes.

558. *Mr. Hopton to the same.* The Condé d'Oñate will not start till March. Mr. (Christopher) Windebank is well, but apprehensive lest the troubles in Italy should prevent his passing through that country. Cl. S. P. vol. l. p. 346.

Madrid, Oct. 24.

559. *Secretary Windebank to His Majesty*, with Captain Brett's instructions, and requesting for himself a safe warrant under the King's hand in the matter, as being so full of peril. Has freed on bail sundry Roman Catholic Priests at the Queen's intercession and the King's verbal warrant, which he now asks should be written. Forwards the Lord Tunbridge's complaint of the Lord Deputy, and entreats His Majesty to interfere in his favour; (which, in answer, he expresses himself unwilling to do). Taylor's statements about Piccolomini's good-will to England are confirmed by Captain Shaw. The Treasury is extremely low, and the Commissioners* take no steps to replenish it, which he conceives to be the main duty of a Treasurer. *Original.*

Westminster, Oct. 28.

With the King's answers in the margin. Cl. S. P. vol. l. p. 352.

560. *Secret Instructions for Captain Arthur Brett, sent to Rome by our dearest Consort the Queen.* Not to meddle with religious matters. Only to style himself the Queen's servant. To represent the leniency shewn to Roman Catholics in

Hampton Court, Oct. 28.

---

* After Lord Portland's death in 1634, the office of Treasurer was for the first time put in commission, Laud being Chief Commissioner.

1635. England. To clear all misunderstandings concerning the Oath of Allegiance, and to make them understand that the English Roman Catholics groan under the burden laid on their consciences by the Pope's briefs and censures against it. To press for exemplary punishment of Courtenay, otherwise the King will execute the rigour of the law against him. The King will never have a Roman Bishop in England, as a foreign jurisdiction within the jurisdiction of the Church of England. To get the Jesuits recalled from England, or the King must put the penalties of the law in force against them. To make overtures concerning the restitution of the Prince Palatine. To find out about the King of Poland's rumoured marriage with an Italian Princess. To advise with Father Wilford Read, Procurator of the Benedictines.

Signed and dated by the King. Cl. S. P. vol. I. p. 334.

Cologne, Oct. 29. 561. *Mr. Taylor to Secretary Windebank.* The King of Hungary is going towards Vienna. Piccolomini has shewn him very great courtesy. The Imperialists have taken Siburg. Frankendale cannot hold out long. Uncertain rumours about a Treaty between the Duke of Saxony and Oxenstiern.

Cl. S. P. vol. i. p. 346.

Madrid, Nov. 1. 562. *Mr. Hopton to the same.* The Spaniards have nominated their Commissioners and have a good inclination for peace, which the Emperor also desires. The Condé de Sobre has been sent on an Embassy to conciliate the King of Poland.

Cl. S. P. vol. i. p. 349.

Madrid, Nov. 1. 563. *The same to Lord Cottington.* The King of Hungary has been dangerously ill, but is said to have recovered.

Cl. S. P. vol. i. p. 350.

Frankfort, Nov. 3. 564. *Mr. Taylor to Secretary Windebank.* The plague has made dreadful ravages throughout the Palatinate. In Heidelberg there are said to be not fifty burghers left. The Treaty between the Duke of Saxony and the Swedes broken off.

Cl. S. P. vol. i. p. 351.

Madrid, Nov. 9. 565. *Mr. Hopton to the same.* The Marquis de Legunes has embarked at Barcelona. The Nuncio has had an interview with the King about the treaty of peace, which goes on fairly, but great preparations are being made for a sharp war next year.

Cl. S. P. vol. i. p. 357.

Nov. 9. 566. *Father Leander to the same.* Being so near death, he recommends his brother Benedictines to His Majesty's favour, and requests protection for Mr. Price.

Cl. S. P. vol. i. p. 360.

567. *Instructions to the Lord Scudamore, our Ambassador residing with our good Brother the French King.* To represent that the restitution of the Palatinate concerns France more than England. To remind him of his oath at the confederation of Heilbronn not to make peace until the liberties of Germany were re-established. To induce him to restore Lorrain to the Duke, on condition that the Emperor restores the Prince Palatine. If the Emperor refuse this, England will join France in the war. To declare to the King the strange conduct of his Ambassador Extraordinary in refusing to receive this proposition. *Two Copies.*
One by Windebank. Cl. S. P. vol. i. p. 392.
1635. Whitehall, Nov. 9.

568. *Mr. Hopton to Lord Cottington.* The Condé is well pleased with the state of the war in Germany and Italy, but would not refuse a good peace. Cl. S. P. vol. L p. 358.
Madrid, Nov. 10.

569. *Mr. Taylor to Secretary Windebank.* Has had an audience with the King of Hungary. The affairs of the Palatinate are likely to be put in the same state as before the wars with Sweden. The French are reported to have retired to winter quarters. Cl. S. P. vol. i. p. 358.
Norlingen, Nov. 11.

570. *Lord Aston to the same.* Has had audiences of compliment with the King, Queen, Prince, and Condé, which latter told him often that Wat Aston was very welcome, speaking it like an Englishman. Windebank's sons are well.
Cl. S. P. vol. i. p. 364.
Madrid, Nov. 12/22.

571. *Lord Mount-Norris to the King*, entreating an audience to submit certain propositions concerning the Customs in Ireland, and enclosing the next paper. Cl. S. P. vol. L p. 361.
Dublin, Nov. 26.

572. *A Note of the clear Profits of the Customs of Ireland to the Farmers for the three years from Lady-day 1632 to Lady-day 1635*, being respectively 4951*l*. 2*s*. 6*d*., 8373*l*. 13*s*. 10*d*., and 20,019*l*. 15*s*. 2*d*.
Cl. S. P. vol. L p. 362.

573. *A Proposal to His Majesty concerning the Customs of Ireland*, offering 6000*l*. a-year more rent than the Duchess of Buckingham pays, or, if no further restraint be made than now, 8000*l*. a-year more.
Endorsed by Windebank, "Sir James Gallaway." Cl. S. P. vol. L p. 360.
No date.

574. *Mr. Darcy's Proposals to His Majesty about the Customs of Ireland*, that the farmers be required to give up their leases, and make returns of the goods exported and imported since Lady-day 1632.
Endorsed by Windebank. Cl. H. P. vol. i. p. 440.
No date.

1635.
No date.
575. *Reasons humbly offered to His Most Excellent Majesty for to re-assume the Customs and Licences of Ireland into His royal hand;* setting forth the profits and probable increase of trade. *Two Copies.*

One in Windebank's hand.　　Cl. S. P. vol. l. p. 440.

No date.
576. *Remembrances touching the Revenue of Ireland;* putting the subsidies at 308,946*l*.: the King's revenue for 1627 at 42,000*l*.: the King's whole charge at 62,000*l*.; and his debts in Ireland at 72,000*l*. Proposes that the debts be paid, 200,000*l*. of the subsidies be appropriated, and the revenue raised at least 10,000*l*. per annum.

Partly in Mr. Darcy's hand.　　Cl. S. P. vol. l. p. 442.

No date.
577. *Improvements to be made in Ireland;* setting the sum to be gained by re-assumption of the Customs at 38,000*l*. per annum.　　*Two Copies.*

In Darcy's and Windebank's hands.　　Cl. S. P. vol. L p. 443.

No date.
578. *Mr. Darcy's Proposals:* to farm the revenues of Ireland at an increase of 12,000*l*. per annum on the present rent, and to make yearly returns of profits.

Endorsed by Windebank.　　Cl. S. P. vol. L p. 444.

Whitehall, Nov. 16.
579. *Warrant* to Sir Robert Aiton (Secretary of the Court of Requests) to use the Privy Seal *pro tempore* on the death of the Chancellor, Viscount Savage.　　*Copy.*

Madrid, Nov. 28.
580. *Mr. Hopton to Secretary Windebank.* Praises Lord Aston greatly. Don Suero de Quinones has "played the jade" with him, and sold the picture of Luguotto, which however may be re-bought for 75*l*. Mr. Windebank is well, and will set out to Italy in March.

Cl. S. P. vol. l. p. 366.

Madrid, Nov. 28.
581. *The same to Lord Cottington,* praising Lord Aston and begging for money due to himself.　　Cl. S. P. vol. L p. 368.

Madrid.
582. *Lord Aston to Secretary Coke,* with an account of his first formal audience of the King.　　*Copy.*

No date, probably enclosed in Hopton's previous letter to Windebank.

Madrid.
583. *The same to Lord Cottington,* of his audience of the Conde Duke.

No date, probably accompanying the previous letter.

584. *Mr. Taylor to Secretary Windebank.* The Emperor is out of town. There is a rumour that the Swedes and the Duke of Saxony are agreed. Cl. S. P. vol. I. p. 368. — Vienna, Nov. 28. 1635.

585. *Lord Aston to the same*, promising a detailed account of his second audience with the King. — Madrid, Dec. 1/6.
No address, but endorsed by Windebank.

586. *Mr. Taylor to the same.* Has had an audience with the Emperor. Pressed him on the subject of the Treaty with the Duke of Saxony, and informed him that the King was ready to enter into the propounded league with Spain and himself for the defence of the hereditary countries and restitution of the Duke of Lorraine. Presses for money. — Vienna, Dec. 6.
Original, and also a duplicate copy of the principal part.
Cl. S. P. vol. I. p. 369.

587. *The same to the same.* The news that the Prince Palatine is in England has shewn them that the King is determined to take a party. They neither hope nor apprehend much from the King of Poland. The proposition of a general Treaty is now a game grown cold, nor does the Pope much incline to it. Again presses for money. Has heard from Secretary Coke that His Majesty expected his return before this, which was impossible. — Vienna, Dec. 11.
Cl. S. P. vol. I. p. 371.
With the exception of the paragraph concerning money and the postscript about Secretary Coke's letter.

588. *Lord Aston to the same.* Has had an audience with the King and delivered the next paper to him; also with the Condé. Has found in the Marquis de Mirabel particular good affections towards His Majesty. The Condé affirms that the proposition which passed between Lord Fielding and the Condé de Roca at Venice, concerning the satisfying of the Duke of Bavaria with the Electorate of Bohemia, originated with the former. Has complained to the Condé of the untoward carriage of Necolalde in England. Has delivered also a paper on the East Indian business. — Madrid, Dec. 11/21.
Cl. S. P. vol. I. p. 379.

589. Madrid, Dec. 6. *Paper delivered by Lord Aston to the King of Spain.* If through his intercession the Imperial ban be taken off, and the Prince Palatine restored, His Majesty will enter into any confederacy with Spain and Austria as shall be reasonable.— Spanish. *Copy.*
Cl. S. P. vol. I. p. 381.

1635.
Madrid.
Dec. 11.

590. *Lord Aston to Secretary Coke.* The French King has consented to the Treaty, and named his Plenipotentiaries, but there is not much likelihood that Spain will do the same.

Cl. S. P. vol. I. p. 383.

Madrid.
Dec. 11.

591. *The same to Secretary Windebank.* The Spaniards neglect the maritime Treaty, because they have their hearts so set upon a league of greater importance, that they hope to include the one in the other. A Mr. Lindsay has been there from Sir Thomas Dishington with a project for the King's service, but is referred to Necolalde.

Cl. S. P. vol. I. p. 384.

Vienna,
Dec. 13.

592. *Mr. Taylor to the same.* A review of the miserable state of Germany. The King of Spain and the Condé Duke have with great duplicity brought about the Treaty with the Duke of Saxony, who was supposed to be firm in the matter of the Palatinate. The Duke is now ready to make peace with the Swedes, who will not however so easily quit the footing they have gotten in Germany. The German princes have no great mind to the war with France. Spain is too weak to help, the Pope watching to play them a trick for Naples, Poland not well inclined, Denmark likely to be angered by the loss of the bishopric of Bremen, Holland at war with them, the Turk threatening the border. All their hope is in the King of England. Has been told by a chief minister that the Electorate is still in the power of the Emperor to dispose of. The Duke of Bavaria since his marriage feeds on nothing but capons and chickens fed with the flesh of vipers. What a child would he beget to infect the world!

Two Copies.
One without the last two paragraphs of the printed copy.
Cl. S. P. vol. I. p. 372.

London,
Dec. 18.

593. *Don Juan de Necolalde to Lord Aston.* A letter of compliment on his arrival in Spain.—Spanish.

Cl. S. P. vol. I. p. 417.

Vienna,
Dec. 19.

594. *Mr. Taylor to Secretary Windebank.* Has had an audience with the Emperor, and delivered the next paper. His Majesty's power is the greatest this day in the whole world, and he is able, with his only authority, to settle the affairs of Christendom. Has taken a resolved tone and let it be known that unless the whole Lower Palatinate be brought together again, nothing can be done. An Ambassador should be sent to the Duke of Saxony, who is not likely to oppose the business. The Empress so much resents the King's denying her, from inadvertence as he assured her, the title of

"Majesty," that she had much ado to hold from tears. Presses again for money. *Two Copies.* 1635.

Cl. S. P. vol. i. p. 375; the date being there misprinted.

595. Vienna, Dec. 16. *Memoriale eorum, quæ ex Majestatis serenissimi Magnæ Britanniæ Regis Cæsareæ suæ Majestati Joannes Taylorus exposuit.* A repetition of the arguments used by him in his audience as narrated in his despatch of Dec. 6.—Latin. *Three Copies.*

One partly in cypher. Endorsed by Windebank.
Cl. S. P. vol. i. p. 377.

596. *Secretary Windebank to Lord Aston*, enclosing letters from the Queen to the Queen of Spain about a daughter of the Lady of Falkland. Captain Porter has returned from Dunkirk. The King is pleased to recall Mr. Hopton. Westminster, Dec. 10.

Cl. S. P. vol. i. p. 388.

597. *The same to Mr. Hopton.* A recapitulation of and answer to his despatches from Oct. 20 to Nov. 9. His Majesty recalls him in order to employ him next spring at the Diet in Germany. Sends a proposition of His Majesty to the French King, which Seneterre the French Ambassador has refused to receive. The Prince Elector is lodged at Whitehall with an allowance of 50*l.* per diem. The French Ambassadors refuse to give him the title of Elector, but only *Altesse Palatine.* Necolalde has given him his full title. Thanks him for his care of his son. *Draught.* Westminster, Dec. 10.

In Windebank's hand. Cl. S. P. vol. i. p. 389.

598. *Mr. Hopton to Secretary Windebank.* Character of the Condé d'Oñate, who has always been an opposer to the ambition of the Duke of Bavaria. By the Spanish ministers generally the abatement of the Duke is more studied than his advancement by the Emperor. The journey of the Prince Palatine to England has made much noise there. Madrid, Dec. 21.

Cl. S. P. vol. i. p. 385.

599. *The same to Lord Cottington.* Though he sees a good inclination in those of power, he is in great fear lest passion, distrust, and want of time bring all to nought. Madrid, Dec. 21.

Cl. S. P. vol. i. p. 386.

600. *Letters Patent* from His Majesty, annexing a Prebend of Ch. Ch. to the Public Oratorship of the University of Oxford.—Latin. *Two Copies.* Westminster, Dec. 11.

See Laud's History of his Chancellorship, p. 3.

601. *Mr. Hopton to Lord Cottington,* giving good hopes of a satisfactory progress of the business in Lord Aston's hands. Madrid, Dec. 11.

Endorsed as an "Abstract."

1635.
Dec. 16.

602. *The Duke of Medina to Lord Cottington.* A brief letter of compliment.—Spanish. *Endorsed by Windebank.*

Vienna,
Dec. 16.

603. *Mr. Taylor to Secretary Windebank.* Stralendorf, Vice-Chancellor of the Empire, sent for him to show his commission, which he told him was *ad referendum* not *plenipotentia.* They mightily apprehend the Duke of Bavaria by reason of the election of the King of the Romans. "We are certain of three voices, the Bishop of Treves they have in their hands, Brandenberg is so near to the Palatine house we may assure ourselves of him, the Duke of Saxony will not oppose it, the Bishop of Mentz owes them many obligations." He is told that so as the Electorate remain in the house of the Duke of Bavaria, he will be willing to elect a King of the Romans. *Cl. S. P. vol. i. p. 387.*

St. James',
Dec. 30.

604. *Instructions for our trusty and well-beloved John Taylor, Esq., our Agent with the Emperor.* To deliver the demand for Investiture, and desire an authentic attestation of such delivery. Not necessarily to insist upon the restoration of the Upper Palatinate, but to press earnestly for that of the Lower, or at least that it be temporarily sequestored to some neutral Prince; and to endeavour to win the Spanish representatives to favour this sequestration. To press for the reservation of the jointure of the Queen of Bohemia, which is the best piece of the Lower Palatinate. *Two Copies.* *Cl. S. P. vol. i. p. 403.*

No date.

605. *His Majesty to the Emperor (Ferdinand).* A letter to accompany the demand for investiture.—Latin. *Draught.* By Windebank. *Cl. S. P. vol. i. p. 402.*

No date.

606. *The Prince Elector Palatine to the same.* A demand for investiture of his rights, being now of full age.—Latin. *Copy.* By Windebank. *Cl. S. P. vol. i. p. 402.*

[1635.]

607. *Mr. Chillingworth to Mr. Lewyer*, giving his reasons for being unable to join the Church of Rome, or allow her claim to supremacy. *Copy.* *See Chillingworth's Works, p. 301.*

No date.

608. *Propositions humbly tendered to His Majesty by Sir Roger O'Shaugnessy, Knt., Patrick Darcy, and Richard Martin, Esqrs., Agents for the Freeholders of His Highness' County of Galway in Ireland,* praying that their titles may be secured to them, and their tenures be according to the compositions made with the late Queen Elizabeth.

See Strafford's Letters, vol. i. pp. 454, 476, 493. *Cl. S. P. vol. i. p. 362.*

609. *Reasons and Motives presented to His Majesty's gracious consideration by the Agents for the Freeholders of the County of Galway, whereby he may be graciously inclined to hear and determine their cause here in England, and not to remand the same into Ireland,* alleging many precedents of appeal from the Lord Deputy to the King and Privy Council. 1635.
 Endorsed by Windebank. Cl. S. P. vol. i. p. 363. No date.

610. *Warrant* from His Majesty, reducing the composition for recusancy paid by Richard Forster, Esq., from 20*l.* to 5*l.* per annum, in consideration of his poverty. *Copy.* No date.

611. *Petition* from Mr. Walter Williams, a compounded recusant to His Majesty, to have the accusations against him, of proselytizing and harbouring a priest, examined by the Justices of the Peace for Monmouthshire. *Copy.* No date.
 Endorsed by Windebank, "S*r*. Gregorio."

612. *A Letter* concerning some cyphers entrusted to the writer. No date.

613. *Mr. Hopton to Secretary Windebank.* The rupture between France and Spain goes on. The Spanish fleet under the Marquis de St. Cruz has suffered great loss in a storm. The Condé d'Humanes is leaving for England. *Copy.* No date.
 Without signature; endorsed, "Copy of mine to Mr. Sec. Windebank."

614. *A Valuation* of the cargo of the Plate Fleet.—Spanish. No date.
 Endorsed by Mr. Hopton (?), "The Cargaçon of the Fleet that came this year, 1635."

615. *Petition* of Francis Fana, ship-carpenter, a native of Angola, and Spanish subject, to His Majesty against Captain Peters, a Dutchman, alleged to have used him hardly and detained him in England for two and a half years without giving him wages. *Copy.* No date.

616. *A Declaration of such things as have happened to John le Drue and his company, since his arrival at Timby.* A narrative of the wrongs alleged by a Dunkirker to have been done him by the Mayor, and Sir John Parrott, the Vice-Admiral. No date.

617. *Memorandum* concerning a proposed sale of land to pay a bequest of 500*l.* of the late Sir Harry Shirley to the College of Douay, which Lord Essex, guardian to his son and heir, will not allow. No date.

M

1635–6.
Vienna,
Jan. 2.

618. *Mr. Taylor to Secretary Windebank.* The Emperor at the King's request has set open the gates of his full mercy to the Count Palatine, promising to do *quicquid secundum justitiam et dignitatem Imperii fieri potest.* The Commissioners in return have pressed him to unfold himself, and he has given them the accompanying paper. He hopes to get the ban taken off and the Lower Palatinate restored. The Electorate and Upper Palatinate must be treated of afterwards. The Spanish ministers hang back. The Prince Palatine must come to this court when the ban is taken off, but the proposed marriage must be treated of warily, else the Duke of Bavaria will move heaven and earth against them. The Great Cham of Tartary has sent an Ambassador to the Emperor with protestations of friendship. The Emperor has graced Taylor with a wild boar killed by himself. Encloses the three next papers. *Two Copies.*

Partly in cypher, decyphered by Windebank. Cl. S. P. vol. I. p. 394.

619. *Vienna, Dec. 28, 1635. The Emperor (Ferdinand) to His Majesty.* A more general declaration of friendly feeling.—Latin. *Copy.*

Cl. S. P. vol. I. p. 396.

620. *Responsum Joannis Tayleri 2 Jan. ad ea quæ 28 Decembr. ipsi a Dominis Consiliariis Cæsareæ suæ Majestatis fuerunt proposita,* requesting the Emperor, as an earnest of his good-will, to remove the ban from the Prince Palatine.—Latin. *Three Copies.*

Cl. S. P. vol. I. p. 397.

621. *Responsum Cæsareæ Majestatis ad ea quæ 16 Decembris Joannes Taylerus exhibuit.* Notwithstanding the conduct of the late Palatine and his uncle in making war and fostering the hostilities of Sweden, he has determined, at the intercession of the King and the Cardinal Infant, to appoint commissioners to treat with Taylor concerning the Prince.—Latin. *Copy.*

Cl. S. P. vol. I. p. 398.

Jan. 2.

622. *Secretary Windebank to Mr. Taylor.* Answer to his despatches from Sept. 11 to Dec. 11. The proposition which he made of a league should not be ventured too far, unless on very sure grounds of the entire restitution of the Prince Palatine. He need not be troubled at Secretary Coke's mention of his return, and if he has acted on it, must go back to Vienna. Sends copies of the demand for investiture, and the proposition made to the French King. *Draught.*

In his own hand. Cl. S. P. vol. I. p. 400.

623. *Captain Shaw to (Secretary Windebank?).* Piccolomini has arrived at Brussels. If the Spaniards do not hinder the treaty, there will be no difficulty from the Emperor. Renews his application for a sergeant-majorship, which Necolalde had before asked for him.
1635–6. Brussels, Jan. 3.

624. *Secretary Windebank to Lord Aston,* forwarding copies of the demand for investiture, and the instructions sent to Taylor. Thanks him for his care of his son. *Two Copies.*
In his own hand. Cl. S. P. vol. I. p. 424.
Jan. 4.

625. *Mr. Taylor to Secretary Windebank.* Has been told by Stralendorff that the ban will be taken off, and the question of the Electorate deferred. Will not speak of the match with the Emperor's daughter till he has more certainty of their allowing it. It would entail a complete restitution, to which he sees many hindrances. The Duke of Saxony has retired to Brandenburg. Banier has entered the French service.
Cl. S. P. vol. I. p. 405.
Vienna, Jan. 9.

626. *Lord Aston to the same,* requesting, at the instance of the King of Spain, a ship for the voyage of the Condé d'Oñate.
Cl. S. P. vol. I. p. 406.
Madrid, Jan. 9.

627. *The same to Secretary Coke.* The negotiations for a general peace are understood to be in no great forwardness. The Cardinal Borgia, dismissed by the Pope, and Don Carlos de Colonia, superseded by the Marquis de Leganes, are expected in Madrid.
Cl. S. P. vol. I. p. 407.
Madrid, Jan. 9.

628. *Mr. Hopton to Lord Cottington.* Has no small hope that if they once begin to treat in earnest they will find cloth for every man's coat. Wishes to have a share in the benefit of the transportation of the *asientistas'* money to England.
Cl. S. P. vol. I. p. 408.
Madrid, Jan. 9.

629. *The same to Secretary Windebank,* commending a private suit to him. Both Windebank's sons are well, and very good brothers.
Madrid, Jan. 11.

630. *Lord Aston to the same,* enclosing the following notes, which have passed between himself and the Condé Duke. The Spaniards seem well inclined to a treaty, but are in awe of the Duke of Bavaria. Has not delivered to Mr. Hopton his letters of revocation, as he finds him so useful.
Cl. S. P. vol. I. p. 409.
With the exception of an immaterial postscript referring to the bearer.
Madrid, Jan. 12.

1635-6.

631. Madrid, Dec. 19, 1635. *The Condé Duke d'Olivarez to Lord Aston*, asking for an explanation of the words "by all possible means" and "such a confederacy as shall be reasonable" in his paper of Dec. 6.—Spanish.

Cl. S. P. vol. I. p. 411.

632. Dec. 21. *Lord Aston to the Condé Duke d'Olivarez*, giving the explanation required.—Spanish. *Copy.*

In Lord Aston's hand. Cl. S. P. vol. I. p. 412.

633. Dec. 27. *The Condé Duke d'Olivarez to Lord Aston*, asking for an explanation of the words "to the uttermost of his power" used in his last communication.—Spanish.

Cl. S. P. vol. I. p. 414.

634. Dec. 27. *Lord Aston to the Condé Duke d'Olivarez.* Had not meant by those words that the Spanish King should be obliged to engage in a war against the Emperor or Duke of Bavaria.—Spanish. *Copy.*

In Lord Aston's hand. Cl. S. P. vol. I. p. 415.

635. Jan. 10, 1635-6. *Secretary Roça to Lord Aston*, being the King's answer to his paper of Dec. 6, consenting in general terms to assist the cause of the Prince Palatine with the Emperor and to conclude the alliance with England. Asking for a ship to convey the Condé d'Oñate to England.—Spanish.

Cl. S. P. vol. I. p. 416.

Madrid,
Jan. 12.

636. *Mr. Hopton to Lord Cottington.* The Condé Duke affects secret meetings with him to the exclusion of Lord Aston, from whom however he conceals nothing. They seem desirous of His Majesty's friendship for their own ends against Holland and France, and suspect some secret treaty between the Emperor and Bavaria. Is confident they have no secret agreement with the Emperor concerning the Prince Palatine. They dare not openly displease the Duke of Bavaria, in respect of the coming election. Has mentioned to the Condé a proposition of a secret league, the basis of which should be the restitution of the Prince Palatine, to be demanded by Spain as an equivalent for the restoration of Wirtemberg, and the marriage of the Prince with a Princess of the House of Austria.

Cl. S. P. vol. I. p. 418.

Madrid,
Jan. 12.

637. *Lord Aston to the same* enclosing the next papers. The King's answer is not to be despised, though not so

plain as could be wished. The hostilities of Mansfeldt and other adherents of the Prince Palatine have hitherto been great hindrances to a business which may now go on smoothly enough. Cl. S. P. vol. l. p. 421. 1635–6.

638. Madrid, Jan. 11. *The Condé Duke d'Olivarez to Lord Aston.* Two brief notes of compliment.—Spanish.
Two Copies.
Cl. S. P. vol. l. pp. 422, 423.

639. *Mr. Taylor to Secretary Windebank.* The Duke of Newburgh has obtained of the Emperor that the claim which either he or the *Agnati* have to the Electorate should remain as it was at the Diet of Ratisbon in 1627. This includes the children of the Palatine Frederick, and therefore is a great point gained, being against the late peace with Saxony and the wishes of Bavaria. The late loss of six regiments by the Duke of Saxony has caused a great panic. They have also great fears of a treaty between France and Denmark. Great praise of Colonel Leslie. Cl. S. P. vol. l. p. 425. Vienna, Jan. 16.

640. *Secretary Windebank to Mr. Taylor.* His Majesty is not satisfied with his letters to Secretary Coke, as having used arguments to the Emperor of mercy rather than of justice. He is also too positive in offering a league with the House of Austria. He is to shew great impatience for an answer, threatening to depart if it is not given at once. Desires an explanation of a passage in his despatch of Dec. 26th. If he speaks in the name of the Imperialists when he says " *We* are certain of 3 voices," His Majesty likes it not.
Three Copies.
In Windebank's hand, one imperfect. Cl. S. P. vol. l. p. 428. Jan. 16.

641. *Lord Aston to Secretary Windebank.* Praises the Condé d'Oñate highly. Windebank's sons are both well.
Cl. S. P. vol. l. p. 431. Madrid, Jan. 1⅔.

642. *The same to Secretary Coke,* promising diligence in observation and writing. *Copy.*
Endorsed by himself and Windebank. Madrid, Jan. 1⅔.

643. *Mr. Taylor to Secretary Windebank.* The Spanish Ambassador, the Condé d'Oñate, is inclined to put some impediment in the way by referring the business to Spain. Ought the Count Palatine to sign himself Elector? Piccolomini, it is thought, will command the Duke of Saxony's army. The Imperialist army against France is said to consist of 10,000 Vienna, Jan. 23.

1635-6. light horse under Bassompierre, 6000 cuirassiers under the Count de Rithberg, 8000 foot and 4000 horse under Coloredo. The Duke of Lorraine is to come to Vienna.

(T. S. P. vol. I. p. 427.

Vienna, Jan. 14.
644. *The Emperor (Ferdinand)'s Answer to Mr. Taylor.* He only waits for somebody properly commissioned from England to conclude the treaty.—Latin.   *Two Copies.*

Cl. S. P. vol. I. p. 434.

Westminster, Jan. 19.
645. *Secretary Windebank to His Majesty.* Encloses the despatches from Spain, and calls special attention to Mr. Hopton's of the 12th. (The King notes his approval of the proposition made therein to the Condé Duke.) Advises His Majesty to grant a ship to convey the Spanish Ambassador to England. Captain Brett has not reached Rome, having been ill at Weymouth. Apologises for having brought Mr. Darcy's proposals before him. (The King notes that he thinks them unimportant.)

Apostiled in the King's hand, dated Jan. 31st.   Cl. S. P. vol. I. p. 445.

Vienna, Jan. 30.
646. *Mr. Taylor to Lord Cottington.* The Duke of Bavaria is content to restore the Lower Palatinate, and that the Prince Elector should be allowed to plead fairly his right to the Electorate. The Emperor is very joyful thereat, and has determined to receive the Prince at Vienna, and likes well the idea of giving him his daughter. They will send a messenger to His Majesty in a few days to inform him of this.   (T. S. P. vol. I. p. 432.

Weymouth, Jan. 30.
647. *Captain Arthur Brett to Secretary Windebank.* Has been driven back hither and detained by weather.

Endorsed by W'indebank.

Madrid, Feb. 1.
648. *Lord Aston to the same.* The merchants' complaints are generally of that nature that he conceives it improper for him to stir in. There is much delay in the establishment of a peace between the subjects of the two Crowns in the East Indies, but the Indian merchants may rely on this, that the Spaniards profess to like the treaty as well as the English, and instructions accordingly are being sent to the Vice-Roy of Goa. Will deliver Mr. Hopton's letters of revocation about Easter.   Cl. S. P. vol. I. p. 436.

Madrid, Feb. 1.
649. *The same to Secretary Coke.* The merchants' complaints are very numerous, but little matter in them. The

case of Sir Henry Colt, supposed to be a prisoner in Havannah, has been carefully inquired into, and the statement appears unfounded. *Copy.* — 1635-6.

Endorsed by himself. Cl. S. P. vol. I. p. 437.

650. *Mr. Hopton to Secretary Windebank.* Thanks him for past favours, and gives him intelligence of his son. — Madrid, Feb. 1.

Cl. S. P. vol. I. p. 439.

651. *Letters from His Majesty to Sir Ralph Freeman and Sir Thomas Aylesbury* (Masters of Requests), ordering new dies to be cast with a view to uniformity in the coinage. — Newmarket, Feb. 1.

Signed by the King.

652. *Secretary Windebank to Mr. Taylor.* His Majesty is still dissatisfied at his pressing the restitution of the Count Palatine as an act of grace instead of justice. He should manage that the ban should be declared not to touch the present Palatine, rather than that it should be taken off. He should also foment the jealousies between the Imperialists and Spaniards in the matter, and try to prevent the Duke of Bavaria's concurrence in the election of a King of the Romans. — Westminster, Feb. 5.

Cl. S. P. vol. I. p. 447.

653. *Mr. Taylor to Secretary Windebank.* The Emperor is willing to yield the whole Palatinate, take off the ban, and restore the Electorate to the Prince Elector, after the Duke of Bavaria's death. *Copy.* — Vienna, Feb. 13.

Endorsed by Windebank. Cl. S. P. vol. I. p. 446.

654. *A Copy of the Lady Mount-Norris's letter to the Earl of Strafford, when her husband was in prison under the sentence of death by martial law, and he was so hard-hearted that he gave her no relief.* So endorsed. Cl. S. P. vol. I. p. 449. — Feb. 13.

655. *Don Juan de Necolalde to Lord Aston,* acknowledging the receipt of his letter of Jan. 12.—Spanish. — London, Feb. 14°(?).

Cl. S. P. vol. I. p. 471.

656. *The King of Hungary (Ferdinand) to His Majesty.* General expressions of good-will, and commiseration of the state of the Palatinate.—Latin. *Copy.* — Vienna, Feb. 17.

Endorsed by Windebank.

---

* The date of the month here is illegible. It is printed in Cl. S. P. as Jan. 14, which it evidently cannot be.

1635-6.
Vienna,
Feb. 29.

657. *Colonel Leslie to Secretary Windebank*; commending Mr. Taylor's services, and hinting at the poverty of his own allowance.
             Cl. S. P. vol. I. p. 450.

Vienna,
Feb. 29.

658. *The same to Lord Cottington*; offering his services at the Imperial Court.
             Cl. S. P. vol. I. p. 450.

Vienna,
March 3.

659. *Mr. Taylor to Secretary Windebank*. A note of the different papers enclosed in his packet.   Endorsed by Windebank.

Vienna,
March 3.

660. *The same to the same.* Requires money. Mons. Rusdorf must not come hither by any means.
          Postscript in cypher, and partly illegible.

Vienna,
March 3.

661. *Mr. Taylor to Secretary Windebank.* A long account of his negotiations with the Emperor and the King of Hungary. Encloses the following papers. Defends himself against accusations in Windebank's last despatch, and is confident of full success in the business. A great astronomer has fixed the Duke of Bavaria's death between the 15th and 25th of August next. Verdeman, the Ablegate commissioned to England, is to refuse the title of Alteaa Electorale to the Prince Palatine, but if insisted on, to give it as if of himself. Has hinted to the Empress the match between the Prince Palatine and the Archduchess. Colonel Leslie has been of great service. Sets forth at length the state of affairs in Germany.   *Two Copies.*
   Principally in cypher, decyphered by Windebank.   Cl. S. P. vol. I. p. 451.

662. Vienna, Feb. 16. *Mr. Taylor's Propositions to the Emperor, after the arrival of the first Courier,* urging a speedy answer as to the requirements of the Emperor, and the reception of the Prince Palatine.—Latin.
                 Two Copies.
              Cl. S. P. vol. I. p. 459.

663. Vienna, Feb. 20. *Mr. Taylor's Propositions to the Emperor (Ferdinand), after the arrival of the second Courier:* pressing still more strongly for an answer, and threatening departure if it is not given.—Latin.
                 Two Copies.
              Cl. S. P. vol I. p. 460.

664. Vienna, Feb. 24. *The Emperor (Ferdinand)'s Answer to the Demand of Investiture.* If the Count Palatine make humble submission, and renounce all treaties made by himself and his father, he will remove the ban, restore part of the Palatinate, and grant investiture.

He only waits for Taylor's plenipotentiary powers from 1635-6.
England.—Latin. *Four Copies.*
Cl. S. P. vol. I. p. 461.

665. Vienna, March 2. *Responsio Joannis Tayleri ad ea, quæ a Dominis Consiliariis Cæsareæ suæ Majestatis 24 Februarii accepit;* pressing for a specific answer to the questions before urged; What part of the Palatinate will he restore? Will he grant him the Electorate? and whon?—Latin. *Four Copies.*
Cl. S. P. vol. I. p. 462.

666. *Mr. Taylor to Lord Cottington.* Assures him of the good feeling of the Imperial Court to England. It is in His Majesty's power to make the Prince Elector's House greater than ever by obliging Austria and by the match with the Archduchess. Vienna, March 3.
Cl. S. P. vol. I. p. 463.

667. *The Lord Deputy (Wentworth) to Secretary Windebank.* Excuses himself from gratifying Lord Newburgh by acting in Dr. Medcalf's business as an interested party rather than a judge. Dublin, March 3.

668. *Secretary Windebank to Mr. Taylor.* He must rectify his forwardness in offering a league, and his appeals to the Emperor's grace in behalf of the Prince Palatine. Fears he is too sanguine, as Mr. Hopton writes very coldly of the business. Must expect no *plenipotentias* till the Emperor makes his answer. Westminster, March 4.
 Copy.
In his own hand. Cl. S. P. vol. I. p. 478.

669. *Lord Aston to Secretary Windebank.* Relates a conversation with the Condé Duke apropos of the fitting out of the English fleet, reported by the Condé to consist of forty-five "navios de autoridad," and of which he appears to be in some apprehension. The Condé d' Oñate is to be sent with all expedition. They are well disposed to England, but their real object is to see what they can get, and they will be fearful to piece heartily with us till after the election of a King of the Romans. Touching the complaint of Mr. Humphrey Slanie and Mr. Nicholas Crisp of a pinnace confiscated at the island of St. Thomas, desires to know how far he may use His Majesty's name to justify the letters patent of traders on the coast of Africa. Encloses the next paper, received from the East India Company, and remarks upon the introduction of the demand for liberty of trade in money of what prince's stamp soever. Mr. Hopton will return at once. Furnishing Madrid, March 5.

1635-3. and his coach have cost near 2000*l*., and therefore he desires payment of money due. Windebank's sons are both well.
Cl. S. P. vol. I. p. 464.

670. *What I have received orders to represent concerning the Treaty of Peace now on foot between the Crowns of England and Spain in the East Indies.* The Viceroy of the Indies and the Governor of the English trade having met at Goa, Jan. 25, 1635, and agreed to friendship on the basis of the Treaty of 1630, wherein no mention is made of the East India trade, it is proposed that this be authentically confirmed, for as by it the English may lose the friendship of the Persians and the Dutch, it is reasonable they should be secure of that of Spain.—Spanish. *Copy.*
Cl. S. P. vol. I. p. 468.

Madrid, March 5.
671. *Lord Aston to Secretary Coke.* The Cardinal Borgia has arrived. The treaty between France and Spain progresses very slowly. The Hollanders are said to be negotiating a peace with Spain, making great offers out of their conquests in Brazil. Has delivered a memorial representing the great charge and vexation to English traders from the constant boarding of their ships by ministers of the Inquisition, the Almirantazzo, the Ahnojaritazzo, and the Alcades de Sacas. Many of the merchants' complaints, however, are unfit to be stirred, of which he gives instances. *Copy.*
Endorsed by himself. *Cl. S. P. vol. I. p. 470.*

Madrid, March 5.
672. *Mr. Hopton to Secretary Windebank.* Will return immediately, but hopes for money. Windebank's sons are well: one goes to Italy shortly.
Cl. S. P. vol. I. p. 473.

Madrid, March 8.
673. *The same to Lord Cottington.* Has observed some dryness in the Condé Duke when informed of his departure.
Cl. S. P. vol. I. p. 474.

Madrid, March 11.
674. *Lord Aston to Secretary Windebank.* Commends the Condé d'Oñate, who is about to start for England. Finds in the Emperor's Ambassador and the Cardinal Borgia an extraordinary desire to preserve His Majesty's friendship.
Cl. S. P. vol. I. p. 474.

Vienna, March 12.
675. *Mr. Taylor to the same.* Curtius has been sent to the Duke of Bavaria to gain his consent to the restitution of the Prince Elector to the Palatinate, since there is no

way under heaven for the accommodation of affairs but by the intervention of the King of England. Has urged the point on Curtius, whose answer is, "Well, well, we must do it for you, but we must see what you will do for us; and are resolved to come up roundly to you." The Infant Cardinal has written to express to the Emperor his satisfaction at his resolution. They would fain His Majesty would break from crown to crown with France and set his ancient title on foot, for their blood is up and they think of nothing but perpetuating the war. It would suffice them if His Majesty would league with them to maintain peace in Germany, recover Lorrain, make a grant for the defence of Flanders, and force the Hollanders to agreement with Spain. Great display of power should be made at home. Nothing should be said of this to the Spanish ministers. *Two Copies*.

1635-6.

Partly in cypher, decyphered by Windebank.   Cl. S. P. vol. l. p. 475.

676. *Mr. Hopton to (Secretary Windebank).* Will return to England as speedily as possible. Mr. Thomas Windebank is about to leave for Italy.

Madrid, March 18.

Endorsed by Windebank.

677. *Mr. Taylor to Secretary Windebank.* Has pressed anew for an answer to his paper of Feb. 16th, and urged on the King of Hungary the importance of His Majesty's friendship, without whom the House of Austria could not be assured of one confederate in the world. Has likewise engaged the good services of the Danish Ambassador. These Princes will come home to you and grant all you desire, but withal will demand great matters of you, to which it will be to His Majesty's glory to engage himself. Raises his voice and tells them we must have all and more than all, for all is not enough for what we must do for them. Renews his recommendation of a great display of power.

Vienna, March 19.

Partly in cypher.   Cl. S. P. vol. l. p. 479.

678. *Lord Aston to the same.* Encloses his reply to Her Majesty's letter, giving reasons for his suspending her letter to the Queen of Spain. Has announced to the King the demand of investiture, and entreated his good offices. Has gathered from conversations with the Cardinal Borgia, the Emperor's Ambassador, and the Condé d'Oñate, that upon equal conditions they will be content to take off the ban, and restore to the Prince Palatine what the Emperor and the King possess, but if entire restitution be pressed, they would be obliged to break with His Majesty rather than Bavaria. The preparations at home have been of great use, but should not proceed to action, or they will undo all the good done.

Madrid, March 19.

Cl. S. P. vol. l. p. 481.

1635-6.
March 20.

679. *Letters of Thanks* from the University of Oxford to the King and Archbishop of Canterbury for the annexation of a Prebend in Christ Church to the Public Oratorship.—Latin. *Copy.*

Printed in Laud's History of his Chancellorship, p. 5.

Madrid,
March 19.

680. *Mr. Hopton to (Secretary Windebank).* Of precisely the same purport as his last. Endorsed by Windebank.

March 23.

681. *Signor Gregorio Panzani to Secretary Windebank.* Hears that oaths are required of Catholic gentlemen who serve in the fleet, and fears that disturbances may thereby be created.—Spanish. Cl. S. P. vol. i. p. 485.

1636.
Vienna,
March 26.

682. *Mr. Taylor to the same,* commending Germain to him. Cl. S. P. vol. i. p. 487.

Vienna,
March 27.

683. *The same to the same.* Radolt, the Emperor's Ablegate, has departed. Is confident that all desired satisfaction will be given when the *plenipotentias* arrive. The King of Denmark offers to league with the Emperor against the Swedes. They cannot give the title of "Elector" till the investiture be conferred. This party is not so low as is believed, and cannot be overthrown without the very frame of Christendom going near to break. Wishes a picture by Vandyke of the Prince Elector for the Archduchess. Lord Cottington, if his health permitted, and next to him Windebank, would be very welcome at this Court (where the Italian language will serve), and his stay need not be long.

Two Copies.

Partly in cypher, decyphered by Windebank. Cl. S. P. vol. i. p. 448.

Vienna,
March 27.

684. *Colonel Leslie to Lord Cottington.* If His Majesty would succeed at this Court, Ambassadors should at once be sent to all Princes in Christendom, especially the King of Denmark, and the Sea Towns. Cl. S. P. vol. i. p. 490.

Westminster,
March 31.

685. *Secretary Windebank to Mr. Taylor.* The Earl Marshal (Arundell and Surrey) is appointed Ambassador Extraordinary to the Emperor, and the Earl of Leicester is to be sent to France, but only to do good offices in favour of the Duke of Lorrain and to further general peace.

Cl. S. P. vol. i. p. 502.

Vienna,
April 2.

686. *Mr. Taylor to Secretary Windebank.* Is still pressing for full restitution, but letters from Necolalde persuade them that the English Court will be content with less.

Cl. S. P. vol. i. p. 491.

687. *The King of Spain (Philip IV) to His Majesty*, in commendation of Mr. Hopton.—Latin.
Cl. S. P. vol. L p. 504.
1636. Madrid, April 2.

688. *Lord Aston to Secretary Windebank*. According to what has been already capitulated, the East India merchants may safely resort thither, but his paper has given new matter for consideration, which they will probably confer upon with their Vice-King before answering. A letter from the Queen to Her Majesty has been sent by mistake through Necolalde.
Cl. S. P. vol. I. p. 491.
Madrid, April 3.

689. *The same to Secretary Coke*. Has obtained that no guards from any Tribunal shall be put aboard English ships without sufficient cause, and then with very moderate fees. There are rumours of a peace with France and a truce with Holland. The death of the Duke of Medina Sidonia will be a great loss to the English residents at St. Lucar de Baremeda. The coins of "bollon" minted in the time of Ferdinand and Isabella, Charles V, and Philip II, are to be restamped and issued at thrice their present value. The Condé d'Oñate only waits for a passage. *Copy.*
Endorsed by himself. Cl. S. P. vol. L p. 493.
Madrid, April 3.

690. *The Duke (Charles) of Lorrain to His Majesty.* A short note of civility, accompanying the Sieur de Ragecourt. —French.
Brussels, April 4.

691. *Letters Patent* of His Majesty, granting the office of Vice-Treasurer of Ireland to Sir Adam Loftus.
Westminster, April 4.

692. *Lord Aston to Mr. Hopton*. Doubts of the Condé d'Oñate's recovery, and will move the Condé Duke to appoint the Marquis de Mirabel in his place as Ambassador.
Madrid, April 5.

693. *The same to Secretary Windebank*. The Condé d'Oñate is very ill, but expected to be soon well enough to sail. The favour of a ship to convey him is greatly desired here. Yesterday being the King's birthday, the Condé Duke was made Camerero Mayor, a dignity of late years esteemed too great for any subject.
Cl. S. P. vol. L p. 494.
Madrid, April 9.

694. *Mr. Taylor to the same.* Curtius has returned from Bavaria, and the Vice-Chancellor Stralendorff has announced that no further answer can be given without the *plenipotentias*. This is owing to the Condé d'Oñate, who has
Vienna, April 9.

1636. been instructed by Necolalde. The Duchess of Bavaria is reported with child. The Duke has with great difficulty been persuaded by Curtius to profess contentment at the proposed restitution of the Prince Elector after his death, on condition of retaining the Upper Palatinate or Upper Austria. A Diet is to be held at Ratisbon on June 7th. The King of Hungary intends to lie with 30,000 men between the Neckar and Rhine, the rest of the forces to be divided, and 10,000 to be sent to Italy. The King of Denmark is concluding his treaty with the Emperor. The title of "King" should be given to the King of Hungary, who professes great friendship to England: hitherto His Majesty has only styled him "Serenitas" or "Serenissime Princeps;" so also with his Queen.

Partly in cypher. Cl. S. P. vol. l. p. 496.

Vienna, April 9. 695. *Mr. Taylor to Lord Cottington.* Repeats assurances of the good intentions of the Emperor. Colonel Leslie should be corresponded with, as accompanying the King of Hungary to the army.

Partly in cypher. Cl. S. P. vol. l. p. 500.

Brussels, April 10. 696. *The Princess (Henriette) of Lorrain to His Majesty.* A letter of compliment.

Endorsed by Windebank. "Princess Palsburg."

Westminster, April 11. 697. *Secretary Windebank to Lord Aston.* In answer to his despatches since that of Jan. 12th approves of all that he has done. Explains the state of the negotiations with the Emperor, that he may inform the King of Spain thereof. His Majesty has informed all foreign ministers that he will have no foreigners fish in his seas except by special licence, and all merchant ships shall be safely conducted through his waters. Both French and Hollanders mislike this. The French daily insult His Majesty's subjects between Dover and Dunkirk, and rob the letter-boats. The Bishop of London (Juxon) is made Lord Treasurer. *Rough Draught.*

By himself. Cl. S. P. vol. l. p. 506.

Madrid, April 12. 698. *Lord Aston to Mr. Hopton.* Of the recovery of the Condé d'Oñate and the sickness of the King.

San Sebastian, April 13. 699. *Mr. Hopton to Secretary Windebank.* Is about to sail in the "Elizabeth and Francis" of London. Windebank's son is started for Barcelona. Cl. S. P. vol. l. p. 503.

Hague, April 14. 700. *The Earl Marshal (Arundell and Surrey) to the same.* Has been kindly received by the Queen of Bohemia.

701. *Mr. Taylor to Secretary Windebank.* The Diet holds for June 7th, and will before all other business elect a King of the Romans, a course which disgusts the Princes. His *plenipotentiæ* are important, that something may be done before the Diet, which however is likely to be got together with difficulty. The Emperor decays apace, and dropsy is feared.
Partly in cypher.   Cl. S. P. vol. I. p. 505.
1636. Vienna, April 16.

702. *The Earl Marshal (Arundell and Surrey) to the same.* Has written from the Hague to Denmark, the Cardinal Infant, and the Condé Piccolomini. Windebank's son has been unwell.
Cl. S. P. vol. I. p. 514.
Utrecht, April 18/8.

703. *Mr. Howard to the same.* Has had an interview about Mr. Damport's book with Mr. Smith, who has entreated him to intercede with Windebank to procure Mr. Courtenay his liberty.
Cl. S. P. vol. i. p. 513.
The Hague, April 22.

704. *Mr. Taylor to the same.* Excuses himself in the matters touched on in Windebank's despatch of March 5th. The Prince Palatine had better not visit this Court till the ban is taken off. The Electors are likely to find impediments in the way of the Diet. The sincerity of Denmark in the treaty is now suspected. His Majesty by protecting the interests of others may make a strong party in Germany, and should secure the King of Hungary, as not likely to be led by the Spaniards.
Partly in cypher.   Cl. S. P. vol. I. p. 511.
Vienna, April 23.

705. *Lord Aston to the same.* The King's illness has given excuse for not answering the Paper concerning the Investiture. The Condé d'Oñate has recovered. Has been informed through Necolalde that His Majesty will lend the ship desired. Windebank's son has had a fever but is well again.
Cl. S. P. vol. I. p. 514.
Madrid, April 26.

706. *Chancellor Oxenstierne to His Majesty.* Asks permission for Captain Robert Stewart to enlist troops in England to serve in Germany.—Latin.
Cl. S. P. vol. I. p. 516.
Stralsund, April 26.

707. *Lord Aston to Secretary Coke.* The King and Condé d'Oñate are both recovered. The reported peace between France and Spain is not likely to come to anything, France being unwilling to part with any possessions in Italy. Copy.
Endorsed by himself and Windebank.
Madrid, April 26.

1636.
Vienna,
April 30.

708. *Mr. Taylor to Secretary Windebank.* The Condé d'Oñate has persuaded the Emperor to do nothing till his son arrive in England. The Diet will assemble, and His Majesty should send an Ambassador, and likewise write to all the Princes. Spain will do nothing except for its own ends. Complains (in a postscript) of the infrequency of Windebank's letters.

Partly in cypher. Cl. S. P. vol. I. p. 517, (with the omission of the postscript).

Cologne,
May 6.

709. *The Earl Marshal (Arundell and Surrey) to the same.* The Elector of Mentz promises all good offices. Requests copies of Lord Leicester's commission, and other papers.

Cl. S. P. vol. I. p. 519.

Cologne,
May 6.

710. *The same to Secretary Coke.* The Spanish Court continues to profess friendship, but with what reality he does not presume to judge. Has heard nothing of the report of a match between the Cardinal Infant and the Princess Elizabeth. Dissuades the Prince Elector from going as yet to Vienna. The Spanish commanders in Frankendale and the Duke of Bavaria's forces in Heidelberg consider themselves freed by the last war from all engagements as to their behaviour. It is difficult to prevent the merchants' cases being tried by the provincial laws and *prematicas*. Captain Ryder of the "Prosper" of London has made complaint of the conduct of the Veedor of Malaga. *Copy.*

Endorsed by himself. Date endorsed by Windebank. Cl. S. P. vol. I. p. 522.

Madrid,
May 7.

711. *Lord Aston to Secretary Windebank.* Has had an interview with the Condé Duke, and been informed by him of the Emperor's answer to Mr. Taylor. The Emperor's Ambassador is friendly, but vague in his promises. Encloses a petition to His Majesty for payment of moneys due to him.

Cl. S. P. vol. I. p. 520.

Vienna,
May 7.

712. *Mr. Taylor to the same.* Liege has declared against the Emperor, as also the Duke of Newburg. This favours His Majesty's cause, and he has reason to think they mean to propose that the restitution be granted, but be kept secret till the Duke of Bavaria's death: which proposition he is determined to reject. Has obtained satisfaction for Denmark in the matter of the bishopric of Bremen. The Prince Elector should not leave his uncle's protection.

Partly in cypher. Cl. S. P. vol. I. p. 524.

Vienna,
May 14.

713. *Mr. Taylor to the same.* The King of Hungary is much pleased with the appointment of the Earl Marshal.

and with Lord Leicester's ambassage to France. Has told
him that this is not owing to the intervention of Spain.
The Emperor leaves for Lintz on the 19th. Denmark is to
treat with the Swedes, but not in the Emperor's name. The
mighty counterpoise of the peace of Christendom put by His
Majesty to the restitution of the Prince Elector will doubtless
sway the balance at the Diet in spite of the Duke of Bavaria.

Partly in cypher.   Cl. S. P. vol. i. p. 527.

1636.

714. *Mr. Hopton to the Lord Treasurer (Portland?)* [*].
Has had an unsatisfactory interview with the Condé Duke,
which makes him doubt of the peace. Has seen also the
Secretary Carnejo, who is hot upon a league.

Imperfect and mutilated copy, endorsed by himself.

No date.

715. *Mémoirs pour le Roi de la Grande Bretaigne et le
Prince Electeur Palatin touchant la Diete de Ratisbon.* Recommends that letters be written to the Electoral College
giving the Earl Marshal full authority to represent England
in pleno consessu, that the Prince write to plead his cause and
inform each of the Electors, except the Duke of Bavaria, of
his demand of Investiture.—French.   Cl. S. P. vol. i. p. 519.

No date.

716. *The Earl Marshal (Arundell and Surrey) to Secretary
Windebank.* Requests weekly letters to be sent to him. Has
met Taylor. Recommends Mr. John Pors of Frankfort to
the service of His Majesty to give weekly intelligence.

Cl. S. P. vol. I. p. 529.

Nurem-
berg,
May 14.

717. *Secretary Windebank to Mr. George Conn* at Rome,
recommending to him Sir William Hamilton sent on Her
Majesty's special service.   Cl. S. P. vol. i. p. 525.

West-
minster,
May 14.

718. *Lord Aston to Secretary Windebank.* The Condé
d'Oñate's health will not permit him to leave before the
24th at earliest.   Cl. S. P. vol. i. p. 530.

Madrid,
May 15.

719. *Secretary Windebank to His Majesty,* concerning an
application from the Resident of Savoy to be allowed to levy
troops in England. For a privy seal for 1500*l.* due for laces
and out-work for Her Majesty. And for Lord Maltravers to
examine a complaint of the heralds arising from the absence
of Sir John Borough, Garter. *Answer by His Majesty.* Allows
all the applications, and orders one Gritton to be appointed
messenger of the Court of Wards.

Apostilled by the King.   Cl. S. P. vol. i. p. 546.

London,
May 18.

---

[*] Probably this paper belongs to the early part of 1635; but it was discovered too late to be inserted in the entries of that year. Portland died
March 14, 1634, and his office was administered by a Commission till Bp. Juxon's
appointment, dated March 5, 1635.

1636.
Nuremberg,
May 11.

720. *Sir John Borough to Secretary Windebank.* Recommends Mr. Pors of Frankfort for the employment he desires. Great expense attends the ambassage of the Earl Marshal, who has left for Ratisbon.   *Cl. S. P. vol. I. p. 537.*

May 13.

721. *Don Juan de Necolalde to the same.* Complains of Spanish silver stayed at Dover for a custom of 1½ per cent. beyond the third part payable under agreement with Lord Cottington. Also of a ship unjustly arrested at Falmouth by the Lord Chamberlain. Also of the conduct of Cole, mayor of Newcastle, and of a levy of 300 men for Sir William Treasam's regiment, promised six months since.—Spanish.
   With an English translation.   *Cl. S. P. vol. I. p. 531.*

London,
May 13.

722. *Secretary Windebank to His Majesty.* Forwards letters concerning the redemption of his jewels; a certificate of the bishop of Durham; and anonymous attacks upon himself (Windebank) from Ireland. *Answer by His Majesty.* He need not be troubled with these threats. Orders a grant of a lunatic to David Ramsay, his father having granted many, and himself some.
   Apostiled by the King.   *Cl. S. P. vol. I. p. 547.*

Nuremberg,
May 14.

723. *Mr. Taylor to Secretary Windebank.* Has urged upon the King of Hungary the importance of the friendship of England. The Diet cannot begin on June 7th, and probably not at all that month.   *Cl. S. P. vol. I. p. 534.*

May 15.

724. *Observations on the Order of the Court of Castle Chamber against the Lord Mountnorris,* setting forth at great length the conduct of the Lord Deputy and the Council to him while lying under sentence of death pronounced by the Council of War of Dec. 12th, and daily expecting death from sickness.   *Cl. S. P. vol. I. p. 543.*

Madrid,
May 19.

725. *Lord Aston to Secretary Windebank.* Captain Stewart has arrived with a ship at the Groyne, but the Condé d'Oñate is not yet well enough to leave. Has had audience of the King, who uses friendly language. There is some suspicion, which he has attempted to remove, that His Majesty intends to preserve his neutrality when he has obtained the restitution of the Prince Desires, as a present for the King, who has expressed a wish for them, three brace of Irish greyhounds, six brace of English mastiffs, and some river hawks which would fly but in a reasonable place and cover fowl in the river.   *Cl. S. P. vol. I. p. 538.*

726. *The Earl Marshal (Arundell and Surrey) to Secretary Windebank.* Has determined to go to the Emperor at Lintz. No appearance as yet of the Diet's meeting. — 1636. Ratisbon, May 29. June 8.
Cl. S. P. vol. I. p. 538.

727. *Lord Aston to the same*, in renewed commendation of the Condé d'Oñate, who has started for England. — Madrid, May 31.
Cl. S. P. vol. I. p. 541.

728. *The Earl Marshal (Arundell and Surrey) to the same.* Commends Mr. Taylor's services. Has complained to the Spanish Ambassador of the conduct of Contieras, Spanish Governor of Frankendale, to the inhabitants. — Nuremberg, May.
Cl. S. P. vol. I. p. 536.

729. *His Majesty to the Earl of Pembroke*, recommending Mrs. Dorothy Savage, daughter of Lady Savage, as a wife for his son Lord Herbert, lately become a widower. *Draught.* — May.
Partly in Windebank's, and partly in the King's hand. Date of month endorsed by Windebank. Cl. S. P. vol. I. p. 547.

730. *Secretary Windebank to His Majesty.* Forwards a letter of Lord Scudamore's concerning a difference between him and Lord Leicester, on the latter not communicating with him. *Answer by His Majesty,* that Lord Leicester has mistaken his instructions. — London, June 1.
Apostiled by the King. Cl. S. P. vol. I. p. 548.

731. *Memorial, delivered by Lord Aston to the King of Spain (Philip IV),* thanking him for his good offices, and informing him of the missions of the Earl Marshal and the Earl of Leicester. — Spanish. *Copy.* — Madrid, June 9.
Endorsed by himself. Cl. S. P. vol. I. p. 556.

732. *Don Juan de Necolalde to Secretary Windebank.* Requests a convoy for a ship at Dunkirk to Corunna, with some coach harness for the King of Spain, and renews the request for permission to levy men. — Spanish. — June 13.
Cl. S. P. vol. I. p. 549.

733. *The Earl Marshal (Arundell and Surrey) to the same.* The Emperor is in perplexity, whether he can get even one Elector to come to Ratisbon. The King of Hungary is afraid to see him, lest he should offend the Duke of Bavaria. No Spanish minister has yet appeared. The Duke of Tuscany has done friendly service with the Emperor. — Lintz, June 18/28.
Cl. S. P. vol. I. p. 561.

1636.
Lietz,
June 15.

734. *Mr. Howard to Secretary Windebank.* Has met with Bedinfield, alias Salisden, who, through Father Lammerman, the Emperor's confessor, has attempted to do some service. Doubts the good intentions of the Imperialists.

Cl. S. P. vol. I. p. 567.

Linz,
June 16.

735. *Mr. Taylor to the same.* The King of Hungary has been entertained at Munich by the Duke of Bavaria, but has been refused his request of the command of 10,000 men. The Diet is yet very uncertain. Requires money.

Cl. S. P. vol. I. p. 550.

Madrid,
June 17.

736. *Lord Aston to the same.* Mr. Taylor's account of his first reception at Vienna, and the subsequent change in his favour agrees with his own experience. Has been favourably received by the King, and delivered a paper with reluctance, being forced thereto by the Condé Duke, who is put out of humour by a malicious despatch of Necolalde concerning His Majesty's claim of sovereignty of the seas, and by the appointment of Lord Leicester. Has appeased him, and shewn what mischief Necolalde does. Earnestly entreats that his pension be not taken away. Desires instructions with regard to the expenses and employment of Windebank's son. Excuses himself for not having claimed precedence of Cardinal Borgia.

Cl. S. P. vol. I. p. 551.

Madrid,
June 17.

737. *The same to Secretary Coke.* The Almirante de Castella has been appointed Captain General on the coasts of the Bay of Biscay. The Nuntio is pressing for a suspension of arms. The Venetian Ambassadors are henceforth to be treated on terms of equality by those of Austria and Spain. The Condé de Monterey has been superseded in Naples by the Duke de Medina de las Torres, but is now reinstated.

Cl. S. P. vol. I. p. 558.

Linz,
June 18.

738. *The Earl Marshal (Arundell and Surrey) to Secretary Windebank.* Has pressed for an answer from the Emperor on the two points of the restitution of the Prince Palatine to lands and dignities. The commissioners appointed to treat with him are the Bishop of Vienna, Vice-chancellor Stralendorff, and Doctor Gebhard. Encloses a copy of their *plenipotentias*, in which Mr. Taylor is declared to have promised "an offensive and defensive league." Cannot yet discover whether this important error is Taylor's or the Secretary's.

Cl. S. P. vol. I. p. 572.

Lintz, June 26. *The Emperor's Plenipotency to the Three Commissioners*, containing the clause complained of by the Earl Marshal.—Latin. *Copy.* 1636.
Endorsed by Sir J. Borough and Windebank. Cl. S. P. vol. I. p. 574.

739. *Colonel Leslie to Secretary Windebank.* Advises on the conduct of the Earl Marshal's negotiations, to take possession of all he can get, but not to be content till all is restored, and to make a party in Germany and Italy to counterpoise the Duke of Bavaria. Cl. S. P. vol. I. p. 559. Donauwert, June 11.

740. *The Earl Marshal (Arundell and Surrey) to the same*, giving a journal of his proceedings from the commencement of the business. Mr. Taylor only allows having used the phrase "arctissimum fœdus," and Stralendorff confesses the error to be that of a Secretary: but they are evidently trifling with him. Cl. S. P. vol. i. p. 573. (with the exception of an immaterial postscript). Lintz, June 22. July 2.

741. *Secretary Windebank to the Earl Marshal (Arundell and Surrey)*; an answer to the foregoing. He will receive particular directions in Secretary Coke's despatch. Informs him of the application to Lord Aston to conclude the maritime treaty. Fears that little will be done by the fleet this year. *Draught.* No date.
In his own hand. Cl. S. P. vol. I. p. 578.

742. *Lord Aston to Secretary Windebank.* The Condé Duke has informed him that they are now ready to conclude the maritime treaty which was dropped last year. This he thinks to be caused by their alarm of a French attempt on Flanders, and has not engaged His Majesty to anything. Madrid, June 25.
Principally in cypher; also a decyphered copy by Windebank. Cl. S. P. vol. I. p. 566.

743. *Mr. Henry Tayller to the same.* Desires an order touching the Marquis of Mirabel's passage to Dunkirk. Cl. S. P. vol. I. p. 563. London, June 28.

744. *Don Juan de Necolalde to the same.* Of the Irish recruits, the Lord Lieutenant having received orders to let no troops go out of the kingdom.—Spanish. Cl. S. P. vol. I. p. 564. London, June 28.

745. *The same to the same.* Of the recruits for Colonel Tresham's regiment, which he proposes to divide into two battalions.—Spanish. Cl. S. P. vol. I. p. 564. London, June 28.

1636.
London,
June 24.

746. *Don Juan de Necolalde to Secretary Windebank.* Of the order for the Marquis of Mirabel's passage.—Spanish.

Cl. S. P. vol. I. p. 565.

Madrid,
June 29.

747. *Lord Aston to Secretary Coke.* Has been much delighted with a midsummer's night *fiesta* of the King and Queen at Buen Retiro. The Nuntio continues his solicitations to peace with small account. The Calais fleet has joined the Dunkirk fleet at the Groyne, where the Condé d'Oñate lies, still very weak. The Cardinal Borgia, in order to remain at Madrid, has renounced his Archbishopric (of Seville) for a pension of 20,000 ducats per annum, and the reversion of the Bishopric of Toledo, in case the Cardinal Infant marry. The Archbishopric of Seville has been conferred on the Patriarch. *Copy.*

Endorsed by himself. Cl. S. P. vol. I. p. 569.

Madrid,
June 30.

748. *The same to Secretary Windebank.* Has been visited by Secretary Roças on the business of the maritime treaty. Makes suit to the King for a share with Captain Stewart of the profit made by carriage to Dunkirk of some 500 chests of plate for the Spanish merchants, and shows his industry in the matter.

Cl. S. P. vol. I. p. 568.

Madrid,
June 30.

749. *The same to His Majesty.* Explains the whole business of the carriage of Spanish plate in Captain Stewart's ship, and petitions for a share in the profits.

Cl. S. P. vol. I. p. 572.

Lintz,
July 3.

750. *Mr. Taylor to Secretary Windebank.* The Earl Marshal is starting for Vienna. Denies the offer of "an offensive and defensive league."

Cl. S. P. vol. I. p. 580.

Lintz,
July 3.

751. *Mr. Howard to the same.* Fears the Earl Marshal is too impatient of delay. Is confidently assured by Father Lammerman that the Emperor intends to give satisfaction.

Cl. S. P. vol. I. p. 581.

Lintz,
July 9.

752. *Mr. Taylor to the same.* The Bishop (of Vienna) has attempted to explain away the phrase, "fœdus tam offensivum quam defensivum contra communes hostes." Has yet good hopes of the conclusion of the business. The Diet will not be so soon as expected.

Partly in cypher. Cl. S. P. vol. I. p. 581.

Vienna,
July 9.

753. *The Earl Marshal (Arundell and Surrey) to the same.* Father Chiroga, the Queen of Hungary's confessor, promises his best offices. If we get anything, it must be by degrees, not by leaps.

Cl. S. P. vol. I. p. 583.

CLARENDON PAPERS. 103

754. *Don Juan de Necolalde to Secretary Windebank.* Renews his former applications, and recommends the claim which a negro makes for wages on a Hollander.—Spanish.

1636.
London,
July 12.

Cl. S. P. vol. I. p. 584.

755. *The same to the same.* Undertakes that all due satisfaction shall be given to the Company of Fishery in the matter of Captain Peter Viclart, if the arrest be taken off the ship "St. Ambrosio" detained at Falmouth.—Spanish.

London,
July 12.

Cl. S. P. vol. I. p. 585.

756. *Secretary Windebank to the Lord Treasurer (Juxon) and Lord Cottington.* An order to forward the plate brought by Capt. Stewart according to consignment, after payment of duties. *Copy.*

Bagshot,
July 12.

In Windebank's hand, and endorsed by him with notice of Capt. Stewart's committal to the Fleet at Reading, and subsequent enlargement.

Cl. S. P. vol. I. p. 588.

757. *Mr. Howard to Secretary Windebank.* Has good hopes that the Jesuits are well affected to the business in hand. Has borrowed 50*l.* of Windebank's son.

Ratisbon,
July 13.

Cl. S. P. vol. I. p. 594.

758. *Mr. Taylor to the same.* The Spanish Ambassador interprets the disputed words in the same way as the Bishop of Vienna. The Diet will perhaps not meet this year. Is anxious for the Earl Marshal's return.

Lintz,
July 14.

Cl. S. P. vol. I. p. 586.

759. *Petition of Lady Mount-Norris to His Majesty,* for her husband's return to England, with His Majesty's answer in consent, dated July 18. *Copy.*

No date.

Cl. S. P. vol. I. p. 594.

760. *Don Juan de Necolalde to Lord Aston.* Is preparing to leave on the arrival of the Condé d'Oñate.—Spanish.

London,
July 19.

Cl. S. P. vol. I. p. 606.

761. *Sir John Borough to Secretary Windebank.* Encloses the subject of an interlude presented at Prague to the Earl Marshal by the Jesuits, shewing that Peace being banished from all other countries is expected to be restored from England. The loss of Zabern opens a passage to the heart of Germany, and if Saxe Weimar defeat Galasso, the Emperor's affairs will be in desperate case.

Ratisbon,
July ⅞.

Cl. S. P. vol. I. p. 595.

1638.
Ratisbon,
July 28.

762. *The Earl Marshal (Arundell and Surrey) to Secretary Windebank.* The Jesuits' play is looked upon as a good omen, that they who are so powerful admit so much. Objects indignantly to Mr. Comptroller's plan of a powder-mill at his cottage at Aldbury, his only recreation.

Cl. S. P. vol. i. p. 597.

Linz,
July 21.

763. *Mr. Taylor to the same.* The Emperor intends to set out for Ratisbon on the 23rd, where the Earl Marshal will join him. Galasso is very near the French before Zabern, and a battle is expected. The Cardinal Infant is said to have entered France. One Tod has revolted in Sweden, with the country of Finland, for the King of Polonia.

Cl. S. P. vol. i. p. 587.

(From which the substance is here taken, the original having become almost entirely illegible.)

Madrid,
July 24.

764. *Lord Aston to the same.* Gives a summary of the despatches sent by Mr. Fanshawe's hands. The Spanish King offers to conclude a maritime treaty, which His Majesty has opportunity to make on his own terms, if he thinks the French and Hollanders growing too powerful. Presses his suit for a share in Captain Stewart's profits on the carriage of the silver. Desires warrant for the continuance of a payment of 50l. per annum to Geronimo Salzedo, Agent to the Ambassador in Spain. *Partly in cypher.*

Madrid,
July 24.

765. *The same to Secretary Coke.* A new *premática* has been issued, limiting the profit on exchange of plate for *bellon* (the only current money) to 25 per cent., and great gains have accrued to the King thereby. The Cortes is dissolved, and henceforth the Council Real is to signify to the cities which have *votes* the supplies that are needed, instead of a Parliament being summoned. The Nuntio will not accept the Cardinal Borgia's resignation of his Archbishopric, and requires him to return to Seville. The Pope expects to be informed of the summoning of a Diet, intimating that his consent is necessary to give validity to the summons. The Cardinal Infant has been ordered to invade France with his whole army of 60,000 men. Their great fear of the French fleet has induced them to put all their moneys, in 500 chests of 20,000 rials a-piece, into His Majesty's ship. This King is endeavouring to strengthen himself at sea. Has complained of the conduct of the Marquis of Villa-Franca at Barcelona to a ship of London. *Copy.*

Endorsed by himself. Cl. S. P. vol. i. p. 589.

Ratisbon,
July 27.
Aug. 6.

766. *Sir John Borough to Secretary Windebank.* The Emperor is at Straubing. No Elector has yet arrived. The

cold entertainment of the Emperor in passing through the Duke of Bavaria's country has made men think the Duke ill-affected to the election of the King of Hungary. Oscrlinsky, a Polonian Ambassador, has arrived to offer mediation between Austria and France, and to negotiate a match between his King and the Emperor's daughter. Mr. Taylor has arrived and is confident of success.

Cl. S. P. vol. i. p. 598.

1636.

767. *Mr. Taylor to Secretary Windebank.* News has arrived of the loss of Zabern. Has conversed with the Bishop of Vienna on the disputed clause, whence he conceives good hopes. The various news from the different seats of the war has raised their hopes to great height.   Cl. S. P. vol. L p. 592.

Lintz, July 28.

768. *A Note what money is levied and paid for shipping business,* estimating the whole paid at 175,447*l*., and the arrears at 26,253*l*.*

In Windebank's hand.   Cl. S. P. vol. L p. 600.

July 28.

769. *Settlement* by William Earl of Morton of an additional 400*l*. per annum on his daughter-in-law, Lady Dalkeith.

Draught.

In Mr. Hyde's hand.

July 28.

770. *Mr. Porter to Secretary Windebank.* Forwards a letter of His Majesty on business.   Cl. S. P. vol. L p. 607.

Rover, July 30.

771. *Sir John Borough to the same.* The Emperor is here, and there are great murmurs at the non-arrival of the Elector of Mentz and the others. Galasso has left all the other side of the Rhine to the enemy. The Earl Marshal has not yet returned.   Cl. S. P. vol. i. p. 607.

Ratisbon, Aug. 4.

772. *Secretary Coke to the same.* Of the victualling of some ships, and 500 trees required from the New Forest for tree-nails, which His Majesty cannot spare.

Cl. S. P. vol. i. p. 608.

Rufford, Aug. 3.

773. *Secretary Windebank to His Majesty.* Encloses despatches from the Earl Marshal and Mr. Taylor, with an answer from His Majesty.

Apostiled by the King.   Cl. S. P. vol. L p. 609.

Croydon, Aug. 4.

* The total sum for 1636 is reckoned in Rushworth, vol. ii. p. 344, at 207,140*l*. 2*s*. 3*d*.

1636.
Augusta.
Aug. 7.

774. *The Earl Marshal (Arundell and Surrey) to Secretary Windebank.* Is waiting apart till the Emperor has entered Ratisbon.
Cl. S. P. vol. I. p. 599.

Rufford,
Aug. 7.

775. *The Duke of Lenox to the same.* Of a false rumour that His Majesty was displeased with Windebank about the ship-money, and had confined him to his house; and also that he had had ventures of merchandise in company with Necolalde.
Cl. S. P. vol. I. p. 610.

Madrid,
Aug. 9.

776. *Lord Aston to the same.* Has had conversation with the Emperor's Ambassador on the subject of the Palatinate. One Richard Green has attempted to extort money from this Court and been banished.
Cl. S. P. vol. I. p. 600.

Madrid,
Aug. 9.

777. *The same to Secretary Coke.* The Ambassador of Modena is departing, having settled the maintenance of 10,000 men under his Duke's command. The French fleet is expected to attack Genoa. This King has 50 ships of war at sea, 40 more at Naples, and 40 galleys in Barcelona. Examines at length Sir Henry Martin's opinion on the case submitted to him concerning the seizure of Spanish moneys on board English ships.
Copy.
Endorsed by himself. Cl. S. P. vol. I. p. 602.

Ratisbon,
Aug. 18.

778. *The Earl Marshal (Arundell and Surrey) to Secretary Windebank.* Has had audiences of the Emperor, and a visit from the Condé d'Oñate, wherein the whole matter of the Palatinate was argued. Mr. Avery seems to have used very indiscreet language of the Duke of Saxony. The Duke of Bavaria has arrived with a train of 1000 attendants. The Elector of Mentz is expected to-morrow. The rest only send plenipotentiaries, except the Elector of Treves, who neither comes nor sends.
Cl. S. P. vol. I. p. 611.

Ratisbon,
Aug. 18.

779. *Mr. Taylor to the same.* Has hopes of a good disposition in the Emperor and the Electors. General Butler with 10,000 men is advanced to Nuremberg. Requires money.
Cl. S. P. vol. I. p. 616.

Ratisbon,
Aug. 18.

780. *Mr. Howard to the same.* Has written to the Archbishop of Canterbury to let him know what opinion Churchmen here have of the Church of England. The Earl Marshal is too impatient of delay, and therefore not well fitted for a German treaty. Suspects some of those who are about him.
Cl. S. P. vol. I. p. 617.

781. *Secretary Windebank to His Majesty.* Encloses despatches from Mr. Taylor and Colonel Leslie, and the epitome of the Jesuits' play at Prague. Recommends a Mr. Morton of Turin for employment at that Court.
Hainers Hill, Aug. 14.
With the King's acknowledgment of receipt. Cl. S. P. vol. I. p. 617.

782. *The Earl Marshal (Arundell and Surrey) to Secretary Windebank.* Cannot make out the cypher of his despatches. The Bishop of Vienna professes all reality.
Ratisbon, Aug. 12/2.
Cl. S. P. vol. I, p. 618.

783. *Sir John Borough to the same.* The King of Hungary has marched into Burgundy, the Prince of Condé retiring, and the Duke of Lorraine attacking his rear with the slaughter of 800 men. Piccolomini has crossed the Soame, and a way now lies open for the Cardinal Infant's army to march to Paris.
Ratisbon, Aug. 12/2.
Cl. S. P. vol. I. p. 619.

784. *Mr. Taylor to the same.* Has still better hopes of success, if only the King will join the Emperor in promoting a general peace.
Ratisbon, Aug. 12/2.
Cl. S. P. vol. I. p. 620.

785. *Mr. Howard to the same.* The affair is in a better way now than ever. Commends Mr. Taylor's zeal.
Ratisbon, Aug. 12/2.
Cl. S. P. vol. I. p. 621.

786. *Paper delivered by the Earl Marshal (Arundell and Surrey) to the Emperor (Ferdinand).* Denies that any such treaty, as has been pretended, has been offered by the King, and states on what basis he is willing to treat. Insists, as before, on the principle of total restitution as a preliminary. Points out the deficiency in the offers made to Taylor, and refuses to negotiate on the ground of mercy instead of justice. Repeats the promise of the King's friendship and desires an explicit answer.—Latin.
Ratisbon, Aug. 18.
Copy.

787. *Instructions* (to Mr. Morton), to invite the Duke of Savoy and the other Princes of Italy to the proposed Confederacy.
Aug. 23.
In Windebank's hand. Cl. S. P. vol. I. p. 623.

788. *Lord Aston to Secretary Windebank.* Has had large conferences with the Condé Duke, but dare not press him to specify particulars, for fear an answer to them should be required. The Duke of Bavaria will not assist the Imperialists in the election of King of the Romans, but they think themselves sure of Saxe, Mentz, and Brandenburg. Encloses the next papers.
Madrid, Aug. 30.
Cl. S. P. vol. I. p. 621.

1636.

789. Madrid, Aug. 22. *Secretary Roças to Lord Aston.* Declares the King's satisfaction at the progress of the Palatinate negotiations, and promises his good services. —Spanish.
Cl. S. P. vol. L p. 613.

790. Madrid, Aug. 27. *The same to the same.* Announces the appointment of the Marquis de Fuentes to the command-in-chief of the naval forces in Flanders.— Spanish.
Cl. S. P. vol. L p. 614.

Ratisbon, Aug. 30. Sept. 9.

791. *The Earl Marshal (Arundell and Surrey) to Secretary Windebank.* The difficulty which precludes the hope of agreement is the Condé d'Oñate's insisting on his master's *convenientias*, referring for an explanation to the paper given to Lord Cottington by the Condé Duke, and evidently meaning a rupture with France and Holland. He likewise declares that Spain and Bavaria alone have power to restore the Palatinate, the Electorate only being in the Emperor's hands. The proscription of the Landgrave of Hesse is delayed, to give him time to come in, under promise of full restitution. *Copy.*
In Windebank's hand.

Ratisbon, Aug. 31. Sept. 10.

792. *Sir John Borough to the same.* Repeats the contents of his last. The Ambassadors are assembling at Cologne for the Treaty, and the King should be represented there.
Cl. S. P. vol. L p. 633.

Madrid, Aug.

793. *Lord Aston to Secretary Coke.* Waits for further information in the merchants' business. The French fleet is before Marseilles, with above 2000 dead of the plague. Peace is thought to be near: the Duke of Lorraine to be restored, the French to quit all Italy except Pinavola, and the Valteline to be a free passage. News has come of the safe arrival of the New Spain and Brazil fleets. *Copy.*
Endorsed by himself. Cl. S. P. vol. L p. 605.

Ratisbon, Sept. 5.

794. *The Earl Marshal (Arundell and Surrey) to Secretary Windebank.* Has received the enclosed paper, which he has told them might very well have passed the Duke of Bavaria's file. They are in high spirits here in consequence of their late successes.
Cl. S. P. vol. I. p. 616.

795. Ratisbon, Aug. 29. *Answer of the Emperor.* He cannot admit that he ever promised full restitution of the Prince Palatine, and refuses to entertain the matter

as a question of justice. Requests the Earl Marshal 1636.
to state specifically what he offers.—Latin. *Copy.*
Cl. S. P. vol. I. p. 627.

796. *Mr. Taylor to Secretary Windebank.* Lord Aston Ratisbon,
writes, that unless something be done by the King against Sept. 1.
the Hollanders, Spain will do nothing to help him in the
Palatinate business. Cl. S. P. vol. I. p. 629.

797. *Secretary Windebank to His Majesty.* Earnestly de- Hainesthill,
nies the accusation made against him of visiting the Spanish Sept. 2.
Ambassador Extraordinary, and apologises for his conduct
in the matter of the transportation of the Spanish silver.
The Foreign Committee recommends that either both or
neither of the French Agents be recalled, Angier being the
chief fomenter of the differences between the two Ambassadors.
Apostilled with the King's answers on the several points.
Cl. S. P. vol. I. p. 634.

798. *Lord Aston to Secretary Windebank,* forwarding a Madrid,
despatch of the Condé Duke to the Condé d'Oñato. Sept. 3.

799. *Mr. Thomas Windebank to the Earl Marshal (Arundell* Rome,
and Surrey). Requests to be re-admitted into his service. Sept. 6.

800. *Mr. Taylor to Secretary Windebank.* For the present Ratisbon,
they are willing to restore the Lower Palatinate. The diffi- Sept. 9.
culty is about the Electorate and the Upper Palatinate. A
treaty is to be made at Cologne between France, Spain, and
the Empire. Windebank's son has started for Italy.
Cl. S. P. vol. I. p. 630.

801. *Sir John Borough to the same.* Of his son's journey Ratisbon,
to Italy. He cannot pass through Venice because of the Sept. 9.
quarantine, but is gone by way of Vienna, Gratz, and Triesto.
Has little hope of success in the negotiations. Gives the
details of the waylaying and assassination of the Earl
Marshal's two servants near Nuremberg.
Cl. S. P. vol. I. p. 631.

802. *The Earl Marshal (Arundell and Surrey) to the same.* Ratisbon,
Desires his revocation, as having no hope of a successful Sept. 13.
issue. *Copy.*
In Windebank's hand.

1636.
Madrid,
Sept. 13.

803. *Lord Aston to Secretary Windebank.* Has been startled by the Condé Duke's news from Germany that the Earl Marshal has refused to treat of any leagues whatever. Everything expected from Spain must be in a manner bought of them. Has received from Secretary Coke a letter from the Prince Palatine to be delivered to the King of Spain, being the first letter he has ever had from a public minister without being informed of the contents. Repeats his request for a continuance of his pension. *Cl. S. P. vol. i. p. 636.*

Madrid,
Sept. 13.

804. *The same to Secretary Coke.* Would have been glad of a copy of the Prince Palatine's letter. Has no cause to complain of the Spanish ministers in the merchants' business. Affairs in Milan are now perfectly quiet. The French fleet is still off Toulon, and the Marquis of Villa-Franca watching it. *Copy.*
Endorsed by himself. *Cl. S. P. vol. i. p. 638.*

Ratisbon,
Sept. 14.

805. *The Earl Marshal (Arundell and Surrey) to Secretary Windebank.* Has little hopes of a good issue unless the King satisfy them in all they ask. Would even concur with the Duke of Bavaria to stop the current of the house of Austria. The Emperor grows weaker daily. The Agent for the Grand Duke of Tuscany deserves some diamond ring, and the Duke's secretary some chain, for their zealous services. The Elector of Treves is said to have offered to vote for the King of Hungary, and surrender the Electorate to the Archduke Leopold. *Cl. S. P. vol. i. p. 640.*

Ratisbon,
Sept. 14.

806. *The same to the same.* Has received a resolute answer at last from the Commissioners. The Emperor cannot transfer the Electoral dignity nor the Upper Palatinate from the Duke of Bavaria during the line of William late Duke. He will restore the Lower Palatinate on compensation being made, and will take off the ban *ex merá gratiá*. Has answered that this is much short of the plenary restitution which he had been led to expect, and to which he still holds, declining to enter into any legal argument with Doctor Gebherd on the effects of the peace of Prague, against which at the time Mr. Taylor was sent to protest. Gives many reasons for thinking it improper to treat with the Electors. May be of some use if employed at the Congress of Cologne. Recapitulates the history of the assembling of the Diet. The Duke of Bavaria is much suspected of hindering its progress. Despairs of any good issue to his mission, and advises that all efforts be directed to keeping France and Austria asunder. Enumerates the five males of William of Bavaria's line. Repeats the rumour concerning the Elector of Treves.
Cl. S. P. vol. i. p. 647.

807. *Mr. Taylor to Secretary Windebank.* Hopes that His Majesty will accept the terms offered, and that a way to further restitution may be found hereafter.
Cl. S. P. vol. l. p. 647.
1636. Ratisbon, Sept. 14.

808. *Mr. Howard to the same.* Gives the substance of a desultory conversation with the Pope's Nuncio, who advises that an Ambassador be sent to Cologne and promises to write to the Pope to induce him to urge the restitution of the Prince Palatine.
Cl. S. P. vol. l. p. 650.
Ratisbon, Sept. 17.

809. *The same to the same.* Mr. Francis Windebank is on his way to Florence avoiding Venice and all conversation with Englishmen. Mr. Thomas Windebank is at Sienna. The Diet incline to begin with the election of King of the Romans.
Cl. S. P. vol. l. p. 651.
Ratisbon, Sept. 17.

810. *Mr. Taylor to the same.* Repeats at length the arguments of his last letter.
Cl. S. P. vol. l. p. 652.
Ratisbon, Sept. 17.

811. *Mr. Howard to the same.* Has again seen the Nuntio, who professes great friendship. Thinks Cardinal Richelieu will not further the peace. The case of the Elector of Treves is to be waived at the Diet. The Earl Marshal should not depart yet.
Cl. S. P. vol. l. p. 654.
Ratisbon, Sept. 17.

812. *The Earl Marshal (Arundell and Surrey) to the same.* Father Lammerman has been to congratulate him on the glorious issue of the negotiations. Has told him plainly his opinion of the matter, and hinted his return to the Condé d'Oñate.
Cl. S. P. vol. l. p. 649.
Ratisbon, Sept. 18.

813. *The same to the same.* The Turks have entered Transylvania with sixty or seventy thousand men to secure it for Gabor's nephew. Is much censured as ill-affected, because he will not call the Emperor's answer satisfactory.
Cl. S. P. vol. l. p. 658.
Ratisbon, Sept. 18.

814. *Mr. Taylor to the same.* Believes they will not press the point of the Prince Elector's renouncing the Electorate to William's line. They do not make much account of the movement of the Turks.
Cl. S. P. vol. l. p. 659.
Ratisbon, Sept. 18.

815. *Lord Aston to the same.* Cannot understand the difference which, from the Condé Duke's information (given in his last despatch), there seems to be between his instruc-
Madrid, Sept. 24.

1636. — tions and those of the Earl Marshal. The Spaniards declare plainly they will not break with Bavaria except for an equal advantage from England.

Partly in cypher. Cl. S. P. vol. l. p. 645.

Madrid, Sept. 14. — 816. *Lord Aston to Secretary Coke.* They are in great joy here at the good news of the raising of the siege of Doll, and the retreat of the French from Italy. The Cardinal Infant is said to be advancing on Paris. The Duke of Modena has consented to receive a garrison of 1400 Spaniards into the Castle of Modena. The two fleets are still in sight of each other. Two armies are to invade France by way of Perpignan and Biscay. Genoa has attempted to excuse its conduct in allowing the passage of Crequi's forces, but is looked on with suspicion, as a cold friend. *Copy.*

Endorsed by himself. Cl. S. P. vol. l. p. 656.

Venice, Sept. 16. — 817. *Mr. Francis Windebank to ——.* Announces his safe arrival at Venice and pleads necessity for having taken that route.

Ratisbon, Sept. 17. (sic.) — 818. *Mr. Howard to Secretary Windebank.* Has been told by the Nuntio that the Emperor is much troubled at the naming by the French of the Cardinal of Lyons, Plenipotentiary for Cologne. It is thought that Richelieu means to hinder the treaty. Has heard from Mr. (Francis) Windebank at Venice.

Cl. S. P. vol. l. p. 658.

Sept. 19. — 819. *Secretary Windebank to Mr. Taylor.* He is to remain notwithstanding the Earl Marshal's recall, in order to discover their final resolutions and to keep the negotiations open. *Copy.*

In Windebank's hand, and endorsed by him. Cl. S. P. vol. l. p. 662.

Metsham? Oct. 5. — 820. *Clement Radolt (the Emperor's Agent) to (Secretary Windebank),* requesting an early audience of His Majesty.— Italian. *Copy.*

In Windebank's hand, and endorsed by him.

Haines Hill, Oct. 7. — 821. *Secretary Windebank to His Majesty.* Forwards a letter from Mons. de Vic. Apostiled with an answer of His Majesty to Sir William Hamilton's letters: promising that there should be no persecution of Roman Catholics in the Palatinate, in case of restitution. Cl. S. P. vol. i. p. 665.

Ratisbon, Oct. 7. — 822. *Mr. Taylor to Secretary Windebank.* If Austria and England join in strait friendship the Palatinate business will be satisfactorily settled. The appointment of the Cardinal of Lyons will stop the Austrians from proceeding with the treaty. Mr. Francis Windebank is at Florence, and Mr. Thomas at Rome. Requests more money.

1636.

Cl. S. P. vol. 1. p. 660.

823. *The Earl Marshal (Arundell and Surrey) to Secretary Windebank.* Of the welfare of his two sons. Will have some difficulty to know how to conduct himself to the King of Hungary, who has so much neglected His Majesty.

Ratisbon, Oct. 8.

Cl. S. P. vol. l. p. 661.

824. *The same to the same.* Wonders that he has not heard of the Spanish Ambassador's arrival in England. Is at a stand in his business, but will justify all he has done. Hopes to bring back with him both Mr. Francis and Mr. Thomas Windebank.

Ratisbon, Oct. 1/11.

Cl. S. P. vol. l. p. 662.

825. *Mr. Taylor to the same.* Builds his hopes principally on His Majesty's satisfying the *convenientias* of Spain. The Duke of Saxe stands on a general amnesty, in which the Prince Elector must be included. The difficulty is how to satisfy the Duke of Bavaria for his expenses. Christendom cannot exist without peace, which depends on His Majesty. Requests more money.

Ratisbon, Oct. 13.

Partly in cypher.   Cl. S. P. vol. l. p. 663.

826. *Lord Aston to the same*, enclosing the next paper.

Madrid, Oct. 16.

Cl. S. P. vol. l. p. 664.

827. *The Secretary of the Duke of Archot to Lord Aston.* Requests him to forward a letter of his King to the Condé d'Oñate, with orders to entreat a passage for the Duchess of Archot in a ship of His Majesty from Flanders to Spain.—Spanish.   *Copy.*

Cl. S. P. vol. l. p. 664.

828. *The Earl Marshal (Arundell and Surrey) to Secretary Windebank.* The Spanish Ambassador reports that Sir Robert Anstruther is to replace him. Has had audience of the King of Hungary, and explained his grounds of dissatisfaction.

Ratisbon, Oct. 1/11.

Cl. S. P. vol. l. p. 671.

829. *Mr. Taylor to the same.* Hopes for speedy success, the glory of which will be due to the King of Hungary, whose election is now certain. The whole Lower Palatinate will be restored and a fair way still open to the remainder of the lands and the Electorate. The Emperor inclines to pardon all the rebellious princes and unite all the forces of Germany. If His Majesty will join in this, the treaty of Cologne will be needless.

Ratisbon, Oct. 1/11.

Cl. S. P. vol. l. p. 673.

1636.
Ratisbon,
Oct. 18.

830. *The Earl Marshal (Arundell and Surrey) to Secretary Windebank.* Is much put out at having received Lord Leicester's letters of revocation instead of his own. Repeats at length the substance of his conversation with the King of Hungary, whom he thinks inclined to try and find means to satisfy his demands. Father Magno, confessor to the King of Polonia (Ladislaus), has arrived to conclude his match with the Emperor's daughter, but the Pope is not thought likely to grant a dispensation. The Turks have been defeated with great loss by the Hungarians. Requests money. *Copy.*

In Windebank's hand. Cl. S. P. vol. i. p. 677.

Ratisbon,
Oct. 18.

831. *Mr. Howard to the same.* Thinks the Earl Marshal's high carriage has done good, but could wish he had more confidence in Mr. Taylor. Has had conference with the Nuntio, who thinks the treaty of Cologne will not hold yet for some months. Has written frequently to Mr. F. Windebank, and by Dr. Harvey to Mr. Wilford, but fears the answers miscarry. Cl. S. P. vol. i. p. 680.

Madrid,
Oct. 15.

832. *Lord Aston to the same.* Understands now the conduct of the Earl Marshal, and is convinced that the Spaniards will do nothing at present to discontent those whom they expect to assist them in the election of the King of Hungary. The Duke of Bavaria is said to be still standing off. Declines to undertake a complaint against Captain Stowart concerning some moneys of the Conde d'Oñate. Cl. S. P. vol. i. p. 666.

Madrid,
Oct. 25.

833. *The same to the same.* Would not have made suit to His Majesty in the matter of the conveyance of the Spanish plate, if he had not understood that Mr. Hopton had abandoned the affair. Repeats his request for Windebank's good services in the continuance of his pension.

Cl. S. P. vol. i. p. 667.

Madrid,
Oct. 25.

834. *The same to Secretary Coke.* The arrangement at Modena is not yet settled. They are much irritated with the Duke of Parma for deserting them, after having been held as high in their estimation as the Cardinal Infant. Biscay and Navarre are full of soldiers ready for the proposed invasion of France, but they are probably only intended to occupy the Duke of Espernon and Mons. Grammont, who are there to resist them. The French fleet has had encounter with Villa-Franca, and some 300 great shot have passed between them. Has pressed for an answer to the letter of the Prince Elector. *Copy.*

Endorsed by himself. Cl. S. P. vol. i. p. 668.

835. *Mr. Walker (Blanch Lyon) to Lord Maltravers.* They have been detained from their proposed return to England by the favourable reception of the Ambassador by the King of Hungary.
1638. Ratisbon, Oct. 18.

Endorsed by Windebank, "Mr. Walker alias Blanlyon to the Lord Maltravers."

836. *Lord Aston to Secretary Windebank.* Has pressed again for an answer to the Prince Elector's letter. Excuses himself for carrying on the business by the delivery of papers, as compelled thereto by the request of the Condé Duke. The *Asientistas* will not be eager to send their moneys to Dunkirk by His Majesty's ships, if more than 1 per cent. be demanded for the Captain, being able to make better bargains by merchant ships. Again requests his aid in the continuance of his pension.
Madrid, Oct. 19.
Cl. S. P. vol. L p. 674.

837. *The same to Secretary Coke.* Has received from Sec. Roças the King's reply, which he has desired him to put into writing, and which he encloses. *Copy.*
Madrid, Oct. 19.

Endorsed by himself. Cl. S. P. vol. L p. 675.

838. Madrid, Oct. 27. *Secretary Roças to Lord Aston.* The King cannot treat separately with the Prince Palatine, and therefore thinks it proper to defer answering his letter till affairs are settled.—Spanish. *Copy.*
Cl. S. P. vol. L p. 676.

839. *Mr. Jean Pers to Secretary Windebank,* forwarding some letters of the Earl Marshal, and promising to write every week.—French.
Frankfort, Oct. 30. Nov. 10. (sic)

840. *Don Juan Mir to Don Carlos.* A complaint of one Juan de la Barra for having cheated him in certain shipments of oils, almonds, and salt-fish.—Spanish.
Nov. 3.

Endorsed by Windebank, "Joan Mir to Don Carlos."

841. *The Earl Marshal (Arundell and Surrey) to Secretary Windebank.* The Imperialists are now very desirous of His Majesty's friendship. Thinks *linea Galielmi* may be brought to *linea Maximiliani,* who had a son born last Thursday. Tells them they had better let him go home than trifle with him. Mr. F. Windebank is gone to join his brother Thomas at Rome.
Ratisbon, Nov. 4.
Cl. S. P. vol. L p. 681.

1636.
Ratisbon,
Nov. 4.

842. *Mr. Taylor to Lord Cottington.* The satisfaction given by the King of Hungary to the Earl Marshal (as advised by him in an audience), has bred a great change for the better, and all are now paying court to the Earl Marshal. Col. Leslie carries himself bravely in the matter. The Emperor has taken the votes of the electors, and they support the course of restoring the Lower Palatinate, and finding some means of satisfying the difficulty of the Electorate. The King of Hungary will be elected, and a general amnesty granted. One army will then be formed under the command of the King of Hungary. The late defeat by the Swedes, though great, was of such a nature "quod si fleat Italia, Africa non ridet."
Cl. S. P. vol. i. p. 68s.

Hampton Court, Nov. 9.

843. *The Duke of Lenox to Secretary Windebank*, commending Mr. Wallace to him from His Majesty.
Cl. S. P. vol. i. p. 697.

Hampton Court, Nov. 9.

844. *Mr. Stenart to the same*, commending Mr. Wallace.
Cl. S. P. vol. i. p. 697.

Essex, Nov. 11.

845. *Don Juan de Necolalde to Lord Aston.* Is driven from London with the rest of the Court by the Plague, and is preparing for his departure.—Spanish.
Cl. S. P. vol. i. p. 690.

Madrid, Nov. 11.

846. *Lord Aston to Secretary Coke.* Don Diego de Isarza with 3000 men, joined by the Marquis de Valparaiso, have entered France, taken San Juan de Luce, and are before Bayonne, where Don Alonso Idiaques is to meet them by sea with 6000 more. Prince Thomas' wife is expected at Court. Roças has been with him to arrange means by which infection of the Plague from London may be prevented. *Copy.*
Endorsed by himself.   Cl. S. P. vol. i. p. 690.

Ratisbon, Nov. 12.

847. *The Earl Marshal (Arundell and Surrey) to Secretary Windebank.* The Emperor was nearly dead last Friday. The Duke of Bavaria's son is christened Ferdinand. The Elector of Treves has been carried to Lintz. The King of Hungary wishes him to stay; but he intends to leave on Saturday. Windebank's sons are at Naples.
Cl. S. P. vol. i. p. 691.

Ratisbon, Nov. 11.

848. *Mr. Howard to the same.* Finds his letters have been intercepted. Has hopes of the Electorate if the Treaty of Prague can be squashed. Dr. Harvey is returning from Venice.
Cl. S. P. vol. i. p. 691.

849. *Lord Aston to Secretary Windebank.* Has had conference with Roças and the Condé Duke concerning the alleged detention of Spanish moneys, and desires information on the subject. Madre Luyza, the nun whom His Majesty saw at Casion, is dead at Valladolid; the Inquisition having, after strict enquiry, discovered nothing to her disgrace. She has been buried in haste to avoid the crowds of those who believe her to be a saint. Desires pictures of the Queen, Prince, Duke, and Princesses, for the Condessa Duquesa. The King has sent him a stag of his own killing, much to his contentment. Encloses a letter from the Condé Duke, who appears dissatisfied with the Earl Marshal's proceedings.
Two Copies.

Cl. S. P. vol. L p. 684.

1636. Madrid, Nov. 11.

850. Madrid, Nov. 11. *The Condé Duke d'Olivares to Lord Aston.* Of the complaints of the merchants concerning the detention of their moneys; and of the extravagant conduct of the Earl Marshal, in denying the propositions made by Mr. Taylor and Lord Aston.—Spanish.
Two Copies.

Cl. S. P. vol. L p. 687.

851. *Mr. Wallace to His Majesty.* The Cardinal has offered him 10,000 crowns by Mons. de Punguy for the papers of Fanquan, which contain the history of his amours, and the instructions of Mons. de Sainterre for the accusation of Windebank, Lord Cottington, Strafford and others. Offers important information to His Majesty.—French.

Date endorsed by Windebank. Cl. S. P. vol. L p. 698.

Nov. 12.

852. *Sir W. Hamilton to Secretary Windebank.* Has learnt that the Spanish Ambassador has menaced the Pope for not declaring against the proposed marriage of the King of Poland with the Prince Palatine's sister, and for not undertaking the defence of Piacenza, for the weal of the Catholic religion. *Cypher.*

Cl. S. P. vol. l. p. 693.

[Rome.] Nov. 13.

853. *The Earl Marshal (Arundell and Surrey) to the same.* Gives his reasons for determining at last to leave the Emperor's Court, being convinced of their dissimulation.
Copy.

By Windebank.

Nurenbergh, Nov. 13.

854. *The same to the same,* announcing his departure from Ratisbon and arrival here.

Cl. S. P. vol. l. p. 701.

Nurenbergh, Nov. 13.

1636.
Nuremberg.
Nov. 13/23.

855. *Mr. Howard to Secretary Windebank.* Thinks the Earl Marshal has done well in leaving, and there are other reasons why he should not return. Has taken leave of the Nuntio. The Cardinal of Lyons is to be the Protector of France, and the Cardinal of Savoy removed to be Protector of Germany with a pension of 50,000 crowns from Spain. Carolus Panlutius is to be Secretary to the Treaty of Cologne. Galasso is said to have been defeated in Burgundy.

(S. P. vol. L p. 701.)

No date.

856. *Remembrances left by the Earl Marshal (Arundell and Surrey) with Mr. Taylor at his departure from Ratisbon.* If the Electors do any public act to the prejudice of the Prince Elector, he is to protest against it; and not in any case to depart till an absolute and positive answer be given. *Copy.*

Endorsed by Windebank. *(S. P. vol. L p. 701.)*

Madrid,
Nov. 15.

857. *Lord Aston to Secretary Windebank.* Encloses his answer to the Condé Duke. Finds them desirous to secure friendship, but preparing to lay the blame of any failure upon His Majesty.

(S. P. vol. L p. 693.)

858. Nov. 13. *Lord Aston to the Condé Duke d'Olivares.* Acknowledges his note, and begs him to suspend his judgment of the Earl Marshal's conduct till farther information.—Spanish. *Copy.*

In his own hand. *(S. P. vol. L p. 695.)*

Hernau,
Nov. 19.

859. *Mr. Taylor to Secretary Windebank.* The Earl Marshal has left for England, but has been promised that good news shall overtake him. They promise the restitution of the Lower Palatinate for the present, and the Upper may be treated of hereafter, with an alternation of the Electorate to commence after the death of the Duke of Bavaria's son.

(S. P. vol. L p. 699.)

Ratisbon,
Nov. 21.

860. *Col. Leslie to the same.* Praises the Earl Marshal and Mr. Taylor. The Emperor has too little resolution, but will submit the question of the Electorate to the Electors before they part. The Upper Palatinate may be restored hereafter.

(S. P. vol. L p. 700.)

Ratisbon,
Nov. 21.

861. *The same to Lord Cottington.* The Earl Marshal is unjustly blamed for not waiting for a more positive answer. Will write more when the Electors have given their answer to the Emperor.

862. *Mr. Taylor to Secretary Windebank.* The King of Hungary promises his best services. Has conferred with the Count of Swartzenburg, the Ambassador of Brandenburg, and is to have audience of the Bishops of Osnaburg and Mentz. 1636. Ratisbon, Nov. 25.
Cl. S. P. vol. I. p. 704.

863. *Mr. Wallace to the same.* Entreats pardon for failing in his promises. Has not the papers, but promises to obtain them.—French. Nov. 26.
Cl. S. P. vol. I. p. 705.

864. *Lord Aston to the same.* Has heard from the Earl Marshal, and had conversation subsequently with the Condé Duke, refusing to balance a private treaty with satisfaction to the Prince Palatine. Thinks the only way is to take what is to be had, and get more as they can. Madrid, Dec. 3.
Cl. S. P. vol. I. p. 706.

865. *The same to Secretary Coke.* The Princess de Carignan, Prince Thomas' wife, has arrived at Court. Describes the proposed etiquette of the Ambassador's reception by her, which she refuses to allow. The forces are to be recalled from Navarre and Biscay. The French fleet has retired, and the Duke of Maqueda is to remain at Cadiz; the Duke of Fernandino being thought strong enough to divert all attempts. Peace between France and Spain is much talked of. Madrid, Dec. 3.
Copy.
Cl. S. P. vol. I. p. 707.

866. *The same to the same.* A *prematica* has been issued, requiring all legal instruments of writing to be sealed; the prices of the sealing being from one to four reals. The rent of this tax is estimated at two million ducats per annum. News has arrived of the election of the King of Hungary as King of the Romans. The Duke of Florence's Ambassador is attempting to reconcile Spain to the Duke of Parma. Madrid, Dec. 17.
Copy.
Corrected by himself. Cl. S. P. vol. I. p. 709.

867. *Mémoire pour être donné a Mons. le Comte d'Arondell de la part de la Reine de Boheme.* Thanks His Majesty for what he has already done, and entreats a loan of ships, and his farther exertions in behalf of the Prince Palatine, and that no peace be agreed to till satisfaction be had. Asks advice how to style the King of Hungary, if elected King of the Romans by the vote of the Duke of Bavaria.—French. The Hague, Dec. 31.
Two Copies.
Cl. S. P. vol. I. p. 710.

1636.
No date.

868. *Questiones a Sacrâ Regiâ Majestate Legato Hispanico Comiti de Oñate propositæ, quibus responsum expectat.* i. Is it in his power to alter the Emperor's answer to the Earl Marshal? ii. Will the King of Spain give up his share of the Lower Palatinate? iii. What are the *convenientias* spoken of? iv. Can His Majesty hope for full satisfaction of the promises made to Lord Aston?—Latin. *Copy.*

In Windebank's hand. Cl. S. P. vol. l. p. 669.

No date.

869. *Answer of the Condé d'Oñate.* i. Cannot undertake in the beginning of a treaty to say what will be its conclusion. It depends upon the part His Majesty undertakes. ii. Cannot treat severally of the different heads of the Palatinate negotiation. The discussion ought to be carried on in Germany. iii. The interpreters will understand the meaning and the propriety of the word "*convenientias.*" iv. This should be expressed more clearly before he can answer it.—Spanish.
Copy.

With a translation, both in Windebank's hand. Cl. S. P. vol. l. p. 670.

No date.

870. *Mr. Wallace to His Majesty.* Has learnt from his friend Capt. Renolledo, confidential Secretary to the Spanish Ambassador, that restitution of the whole Palatinate, and if possible of the Electorate, was resolved upon in Spain before the Ambassador left; but they are temporizing to see how matters go with France this winter.—French.

Cl. S. P. vol. l. p. 696.

No date.

871. *A Paper,* informing His Majesty that Father Leander, two days before his death, did, in the presence of Signor Gregorio (Con?), retract what he had taught or held concerning the Oath (of Allegiance).

Cl. S. P. vol. l. p. 711.

No date.

872. *Instructions* to Mr. Curtius, employed in Germany on a mission to the Landgravine of Hesse, the Elector of Mentz, and other Princes in behalf of the Prince Palatine. *Draught.*

In Windebank's hand.

No date.

873. *A Complaint* by Don Juan de Necolalde of the seizure in May and June of some Dunkirkers by Dutch frigates.—Spanish. Endorsed by Windebank.

No date.

874. *A Despatch* of some Ambassador (at Venice?), complaining at great length of the French Ambassador, as having violated etiquette in the matter of visiting.—French. *Copy.*

875. *Memorial of Lord Aston to the King of Spain (Philip IV),* concerning the wrongs of some private merchants.—Spanish.   *Copy.*   1636. No date.

876. *A Paper,* giving the character of Mr. Charles Walgrave of Norfolk, and recommending him as successor to Capt. Brett.—Italian.   No date.
Endorsed, & Panzani*.   Cl. S. P. vol. I. App. p. xxxiv.

877. *Secretary Windebank to Lord Aston.* The delay of Mr. Fanshawe's return has been the cause of his long silence. Recapitulates at length the contents of the despatches which he has received since his last, with comments on each. Thinks that an error was committed in so large offers of a league, but that all promises, being founded on entire restitution, now fall to the ground, unless that condition be fulfilled. No moneys have been detained, except legitimately, for the purposes of coinage. Explains Capt. Stewart's affair, the state of the Palatine negotiation, and the treachery of Necolalde, which under pretence of a friendly interposition, set the Treaty of Prague on foot. Excuses the reception of the Condé d'Oñate on the plea of the Plague raging in London at the time. Six ships are to be equipped to suppress the pirates of Sallee. Encloses extracts from the Earl Marshal's despatches.   *Two Copies.*
Cl. S. P. vol. I. p. 715.   1636–7. Hampton Court, Jan. 15.

878. *Lord Aston to Secretary Windebank.* The Condé de Linhares, late Vice-Roy of the East Indies, has returned with a large fortune. Two members of the Council of Portugal have waited on him to conclude the Treaty begun last year. Desires supplies of money.   Cl. S. P. vol. I. p. 718.   Madrid, Jan. 17.

879. *The same to the same.* There is much stir here about the detention of Spanish moneys by His Majesty, and it is reported that in England a breach with Spain is expected.
Cl. S. P. vol. I. p. 713.   Madrid, Jan. 22.

880. *The same to the same.* Recommends the complaint of Don Carlos de Coloma, a Spaniard of Majorca, against a London merchant.   Madrid, Feb. 1.

881. *Warrant* of Secretary Coke, granting permission to John Veruge, serjeant of Capt. Griffin's company in Col. Morgan's regiment, to levy and transport thirty men for service in the Low Countries.   *Draught.*
In Coke's hand.   Whitehall, Feb. 7.

---

* Panzani ceased to be Nuntio in England, and Major Brett to be Queen's Agent at Rome, at the end of 1636, being succeeded by Gregorio Con and Sir W. Hamilton. See Rushworth, vol. II. p. 376.

1636-7.
Madrid,
Feb. 7.

882. *Lord Aston to Secretary Windebank.* Has expressed his great dissatisfaction to the Condé Duke, who offers the restitution of their portion of the Palatinate if the Secret Treaty, settled with Lord Cottington, be carried out, and the Duke of Bavaria's portion and the Electorate may then be farther treated of. Has received no answer in the East India business. Cl. S. P. vol. l. p. 721.

Madrid,
Feb. 7.

883. *The same to Secretary Coke.* They are better inclined than heretofore to an accommodation with the Duke of Parma, the Nuntio having announced that the Pope will otherwise declare war in his defence. Has obtained licence for Benjamin Wright to import into Spain 200,000 ducats' worth of French linen on payment of 5 per cent. above the ordinary customs. *Copy.*

Endorsed by himself. Cl. S. P. vol. l. p. 722.

Westminster,
Feb. 14.

884. *Secretary Windebank to His Majesty.* Desires to know whether Lord Goring's directions to him to deliver the grant of the farming of the customs are correct. *Answer by His Majesty.* He is not to do so till farther notice.

Apostilled by the King. Cl. S. P. vol. L p. 724.

Lyons,
Feb. 16.

885. *Mr. Thomas Manbye to Mr. Arthur Annesley.* Mr. Hyde, Secretary to the Embassy at Venice, is dead. Mantua has been assaulted by soldiers from the Franche-Comté, but delivered by the peasants.

Feb. 21.

886. *Don Juan de Necolalde to Lord Cottington.* Entreats his favourable consideration of the case of one Garçia de Yllan, Licentiate of Law, in trouble about the non-payment of duty upon some jewels imported, not, as he alleged, for trade, but for the use of his wife and daughters.—Spanish.

No date.

887. *The same to His Majesty,* in behalf of the same Garçia de Yllan.—Spanish.

Feb. 21.

888. *The same to Secretary Windebank.* Forwards a memorial for His Majesty through Mr. Fis, and complains generally of the treatment of Spaniards in England.—Spanish.

Cl. S. P. vol. l. p. 724.

Madrid,
Feb. 25.

889. *Lord Aston to the same.* Repeats his request for the pictures and dogs previously desired.

Cl. S. P. vol. L p. 725.

890. *Lord Aston to Secretary Coke.* Describes the festivals and bull-fights in honour of the election of the King of the Romans. Of the complaints of the Aldermen of Yarmouth and others. In consequence of the Plague, no ship from London is to enter Spanish harbours. The Marquis de Valparaiso is dismissed from his government in Navarre. The Almirante de Castilia is replaced by the Duke of Nothera, and the Marquis de Castil Rodrigo sent to Seville to demand a donative of 800,000 ducats. The Pope has sent a brief in behalf of the Duke of Parma, but has obtained no satisfaction as yet. The Venetian Ambassador is to go to England, being replaced by the Venetian Ambassador in Holland. The order prohibiting the embarkation of Spanish moneys in English bottoms is revoked. Cl. S. P. vol. i. p. 716.
1636–7. Madrid, Feb. 15.

891. *The same to Mr. Thomas Windebank,* of the conduct of his brother (Christopher), with whom his father is inclined to be too severe, complaining bitterly of his having wasted his time. Defends himself from the charge of neglect, and promises to do his best to keep him out of mischief.
March 15.

892. *Don Juan de Necolalde to Secretary Windebank.* Has forwarded to the Cardinal Infant the complaints against Col. Andres de Contreras, Governor of Frankendale, who has accordingly been dismissed and indicted. Desires the fulfilment of the promise of the levy of 300 men.—Spanish. *Copy.*
Cl. S. P. vol. i. p. 741.
March 16.

893. *Lord Aston to the same,* of the conduct of his son (Christopher), and the allowance fit for him. The worst he can accuse him of is a little negligence.
Madrid, March 18.

894. *The same to the same.* Acknowledges his despatch of Jan. 15, and answers it in detail, defending his offer of "any league that shall be reasonable" by the wording of his instructions. It is suspected here that His Majesty is settling leagues with France and Holland to the prejudice of the House of Austria.
Cl. S. P. vol. i. p. 728.
Madrid, March 18.

895. March 18. *Lord Aston to the Condé Duke d' Olivares.* Gives explanations in accordance with Windebank's despatch on the matters of the Spanish moneys and the Earl Marshal's behaviour in Germany.—Spanish. *Copy.*
Cl. S. P. vol. i. p. 731.

1636-7.

896. No date. *Lord Aston to the King of Spain (Philip IV).* Requests his good services and assistance in putting down the Sallee pirates.—Spanish. *Two Copies.*

Cl. S. P. vol. l. p. 736.

Madrid, March 18.

897. *The same to Secretary Coke.* It is rumoured that the French intend to invade Spain and attack Madrid, and great preparations for defence are being made, with large levies of horse and foot and money. The Duke of Valette has been defeated near San Juan de Luce, by Paulo Denso, the Duke of Nothera's lieutenant. The Dunkirk fleet in the Groyne is to escort the Princess de Cariñan to Flanders. The Duke of Parma is reconciled to the King. The Condé de Linhares has arrived at court and presented valuable jewels to the King and Queen. Has received no answer in the matter of the Sallee pirates. *Copy.*

Cl. S. P. vol. L p. 734.

Madrid, March 18.

898. *The same to Secretary Windebank,* pressing for money.

Cl. S. P. vol. l. p. 737.

Madrid, March 18.

899. *The same to Lord Cottington.* Asks his assistance in his requests for money. Fears that he is afflicted with stone, but it has not yet destroyed his health.

Cl. S. P. vol. L. p. 737.

Madrid, March 12.

900. *The same to Secretary Windebank.* Has been advertised by the Condé Duke that His Majesty has refused to admit the messenger sent to announce the election of the King of the Romans, and that the Prince Palatine has protested, the election having taken place without his vote and that of Treves.

Cl. S. P. vol. l. p. 738.

901. No date. *Lord Aston to the Condé Duke d'Olivarez.* Recapitulates a conversation with him on the subject of the gentleman sent to England with news of the election of the King of the Romans, and declares his ignorance of his alleged reception.—Spanish. *Copy.*

902. Madrid, March 19. *Secretary Roças to Lord Aston,* in answer to his request of assistance against the pirates, allowing four galleons and two tenders to enter the Spanish ports.—Spanish. *Two Copies.*

Cl. S. P. vol. l. p. 739.

903. No date. *Lord Aston to the Condé Duke d'Olivarez.* 1637.
Acknowledges the receipt of the preceding, and shows
how unsatisfactory the answer is.—Spanish.   *Copy.*

Cl. S. P. vol. I. p. 740.

904. *Gazette Extraordinary,* containing an account of the   Paris,
capture by the French of St. Ursane, and the defeat of the   March 20.
Spanish garrisons of Hesdin and St. Pol.—French.   *Printed.*

905. *Lord Aston to Secretary Windebank.* Wishes for in-   Madrid,
formation in the matter of the Prince Palatine's protest and   April 1.
other public measures. Thinks the Spanish Court has some
jealousy of His Majesty's views in fitting out the fleet against
the Sallee pirates.

Cl. S. P. vol. i. p. 743.

906. *The same to Secretary Coke.* The Commissioners for   Madrid,
a general peace have met, and there is much hope of an   April 1.
accommodation with France, the Spanish ministers professing that they only wish to recover their own. The Duke of
Parma has given up Savioneta, and a strong garrison of
Italians has been placed there. The French have landed
10,000 foot and 600 horse in Sardinia, and taken Oristan,
but have since been defeated by the islanders.   *Copy.*

Endorsed by himself.   Cl. S. P. vol. i. p. 744.

907. *Lord Scudamore to (Secretary Windebank ?)* The   Paris,
Comte de Brion and Père Hilarien have returned to Creil,   April 3.
where they are to deliver to Mad. la Comtesse her revocation, and to Sedan, where they carry permission to Mons.
le Comte to continue, if he will not return to France. The
tax upon the Villes Franches is vigorously enforced, but there
is great complaint of the non-payment of troops. The French
fleet is before the islands, which however are reported im-
pregnable. Marshal Vitry is at Aix. The Duke de Longueville has taken St. Amour in the Franche-Comté, and the
Duke of Lorraine Fontaine-Francoise in Burgundy. Piccolomini is reported about to invade Champagne. Bigle, the
Marshal d'Estré's Secretary, has arrived with the confirmation and continuation of the passports. Has heard nothing
new from Père Joseph about the Treaty.

Cl. S. P. vol. i. p. 745.

908. *The Condé d'Oñate and Villa-Mediana to Lord Aston.*   Chelsea,
A complimentary acknowledgment of a letter received from   April 6.
him.—Spanish.

1637.
York,
April 11.

909. *Affidavit* of the service of a summons upon Sir Edward Loftus (second son to the Lord Chancellor of Ireland), to answer the complaint of Sir John Gifford.

Madrid,
April 13/23.

910. *Lord Aston to Secretary Windebank.* Will not acknowledge the Prince Palatine's protest as an act or counsel of His Majesty without farther directions. The Emperor's Ambassador professes much sorrow for the harm it will do; but he defends the Prince, and advises that the protest be made good, and that His Majesty persevere, lest his threats lose credit.
Cl. S. P. vol. I. p. 747.

Madrid,
April 13/23.

911. *The same to Secretary Coke.* Sec. Roças has given him general promises of assistance to the fleet against the pirates. The news of the death of the Emperor is confirmed. The Turks are reported to have put to sea with 80 sail, taken one ship of London, and sunk another. The Hercules has been repaired in Lisbon. The Pope has consented to the raising of 600,000 ducats among the clergy for the King, but they are henceforth to be free from all innovation, and the Nuntio has refused to require sealed paper in his tribunal. The Hollanders are reported to have taken Arica in Peru from the Spaniards. Has many complaints from the merchants, especially one from Malaga of an enforced donative, but has no cause to complain of want of justice.
Copy.
Endorsed by himself. Cl. S. P. vol. I. p. 748.

912. Madrid, April 19. *Secretary Roças to Lord Aston.* The restriction of his offer to four galleons and two tenders was in accordance with the number mentioned in Lord Aston's request.—Spanish.
Copy.
Cl. S. P. vol. I. p. 750.

Venice,
April 17.

913. *Lord Fielding to Mr. Edward Hyde.* Promises his assistance to his kinsman, Mr. Hyde, in his present unhappy condition, occasioned by the oppressions inflicted on the English by this state.
Cl. S. P. vol. I. p. 747.

Paris,
April 22.

914. *The Duke of Orleans to His Majesty.* A congratulation on the accouchement of the Queen*.—French.
Cl. S. P. vol. I. p. 746.

Madrid,
April 29.

915. *Lord Aston to Secretary Windebank.* The Condé Duke has declared that any act of the English fleet in the Spanish

---

* The Princess Anne was born Friday, March 17.

dominions, if lent to the Prince Palatine, will be considered 1637.
a breach of the peace. Conceives little fear of what they can
do in such case; but all chance of satisfaction would then be
desperate. Desires precautions to be taken for the merchants,
and requests his own recall. Cl. S. P. vol. i. p. 752.
(with the exception of an immaterial postscript.)

916. *Secretary Windebank to Lord Aston.* Apologises for Westminster, his continued neglect. Acknowledges and answers in detail April 19. the despatches received since that of Jan. 17. The explanation given by the Condé d'Oñate of the required *convenientia* agrees with the language of the Conde Duke, as implying direct war with the Hollanders, and little less with Franco. The French grow very cold in the matter of the Treaty, which makes him think their accommodation with Spain is near conclusion. The pictures and the dogs shall not be forgotten. His Majesty has not treated with the Hollanders at all, nor with France to the prejudice of the House of Austria. The letters announcing the election of the King of the Romans were duly delivered to His Majesty by Radolt, the Emperor's Agent. The protest of the Prince Palatine is his own act, for which His Majesty is not responsible.
Two copies, one in cypher. Cl. S. P. vol. i. p. 752.

917. *Lord Aston to Secretary Windebank.* Sends his Secretary Madrid, to represent the state of affairs. The Spaniards believe May 9. that a large fleet has been lent to the Prince Palatine with designs against them, and are resolved to declare war on the first act of his. Cl. S. P. vol. i. p. 756.

918. *The same to Secretary Coke.* Since the death of the Madrid, Duke of Alcala, his colleague, Don Francisco de Melo, is to May 9. act alone at the general meeting for peace. The Marquis de Mirabel is expected to be appointed his colleague. A Friar Dashili of the order of the Minimes has arrived from France under pretence of a devotion of the French Queen to St. Isidor, but really as agent from Richelieu to the Condé Duke, offering a suspension of arms, and restoration of commerce, which they are not likely to agree to. The King is gone to Aranjuez. Great preparations go on still in Navarre. *Copy.*
Endorsed by himself. Cl. S. P. vol. i. p. 757.

919. *The same to Lord Cottington.* The peace between Madrid, Spain and France is much laboured at. Its success much May 9. depends on His Majesty, though the Condé Duke seems in no fear of the clouds which threaten.
Cl. S. P. vol. i. p. 758.

1637.
May 11.

920. *Don Juan de Necolalde to Lord Aston.* A complimentary notice of his approaching departure.—Spanish.

Madrid,
May 15.

921. *Lord Aston to Secretary Windebank.* Forwards a letter from the Condé Duke to the Condé d'Oñate. Has received no directions and therefore retires as much as possible. The Friar has long audiences with the Condé Duke, and there is a great opinion of a present peace.

Cl. S. P. vol. I. p. 759.
(with the exception of an immaterial postscript).

May 11,
and
April 5.

922. *Two Forms of the Oath of Allegiance.*

The first copy (in Windebank's hand, and signed and dated by the King) is *verbatim* the same as that printed in Cl. S. P. vol. i. p. 88, the words "either do" in the 6th line of the 3rd paragraph being inserted by the King. The second copy (in Windebank's hand, and also signed by the King) differs in this respect; the words "Effects of Excommunication" are inserted after the word "Leagues" in the 3rd line of the 2nd paragraph; "effects of" being in the King's hand, as is also the word "whatsoever" in the 1st line of the 3rd paragraph, which last word is substituted for "though it be under Confession," crossed out by the King. An endorsement by Windebank certifies that the King signed on the 5th and these amendments were made by him on the 27th of April.

Madrid,
May 27.

923. *Lord Aston to Secretary Coke.* The King and Queen have returned from Aranjuez in consequence of the heat. The Hercules, one of the fleet against Sallee, has been repaired and put out from Lisbon. The fleets under the Duke of Fernandino, Don Antonio de Oquendo, and the Duke of Maqueda are greatly in want of provisions. The sealed paper and the forced donative have brought in great sums, and they are making vigorous efforts to repair their former neglect at sea. The Cardinal Borgia, on returning from Seville, has been reported dead, but is recovering. Great levies are being made throughout the kingdom, Valencia supplying 6000 horse. Has represented the complaint of Mr. Pettiplace of Carthagena, who being rated at 2000 reals for the forced donative, and having refused to pay, has had his goods embargoed. *Copy.*

Cl. S. P. vol. i. p. 760.

Madrid,
May 27.

924. *The same to Secretary Windebank.* Of his son's expenses, and the arrears of his own pension.

Madrid,
May 27.

925. *The same to the same.* Of the donative exacted by Spanish ministers from English subjects resident in Spain.

May 27.

926. *An Examination* of the case of Mr. Morse, arrested by Newton and Cooke, on suspicion of being a Romish Priest.

Signed, apparently, by two Justices.

927. *Certificate of the Barons of the Exchequer to the Prince Palatine*, of the due appointment of Clerks, and the taking and recording of depositions in the Court of Exchequer.

Signed by Humfrey Davenport, Tho. Trevor, and Ric. Weston.

Cl. S. P. vol. I. p. 766.

1637.
May 17.

928. *Secretary Windebank to Lord Aston.* Justifies the Prince Palatine's protest, and the King's conduct in the matter. The King is greatly displeased with the Condé d'Oñate, but hopes not to be driven to the extremity of helping the Prince with forces by sea. The fleet is not yet gone and no answer from France.

Principally in cypher.

Westminster, May 29.

929. *Projet de Ligue offensive et defensive entre le Roi Tres-Chrétien, et le Roi de la Grand Bretagne, leurs royaumes subjets et pays de leur obeissance, pour leur conservation et santé, contre la maison d'Autriche, Duc de Baviere, et leur adherans : pour parvenir a une bonne paix et retablir tous leur allies spoliez par l'Empereur et les Espagnols, et leur adherans, en leurs biens et dignites, sans nul excepter, meme le Prince Electeur Palatin.* An army to be raised, in May at the latest, of 24,000 foot and 4500 horse, the French King to pay two-thirds. An English fleet of at least 30 ships of 400 tons apiece to act especially against the convoys to Flanders, and 30 French ships to be stationed in the Mediterranean. Neither to treat without the other. All prizes to be shared. Commerce between England and France to be free. To be signed June 1, 1637.—French. *Copy.*

Cl. S. P. vol. I. p. 761.

No date.

930. *Lord Aston to Secretary Windebank.* Has had an interview with the Condé de Linhares, whose commission gives him full power of war and peace in the Indies, and who requests freightage in English ships for the Spanish supplies going to Brazil. Has received no satisfaction as yet in Mr. Pettiplace's case.

Cl. S. P. vol. I. p. 763.

Madrid, June 2.

931. *The same to Secretary Coke.* The Condé de Lernos, late Vice-King of Naples, but now a Benedictine monk, has been imprisoned for leaving the kingdom. The Cardinal Borgia is returned. Many but unavailing complaints are made against the Duke of Fernandino, especially one of cutting the cables of Captain Dreadcake's ship at Barcelona. The Hollanders have taken El Puerto Calvo, a port in the Indies belonging to the Portuguese. The Condé d'Oñate is

Madrid, June 2.

1637. reported as likely to take the place of the Duke of Alcala. The Condé de Linhares is to take a great fleet from Lisbon, and 24,000 soldiers to Brazil. The news is confirmed of the capture of the islands S⁂. Margarita and S. Honorato by the French. Forwards a letter of Captain Rainsborough* from before Sallee. *Copy.*

C. S. P. vol. l. p. 764.

Madrid, June 3.

932. *A letter*, signed Rochas, and endorsed by His Majesty, " Rochas' letter to Champaign that discovered the Spaniards' intentions towards (the) Queen Mother."—French.

C. S. P. vol. l. p. 765.

June 11 and 15.

933. *Three Law-Papers and Affidavits* in the case of a disputed debt for lodgings.

Madrid, June 17.

934. *Lord Aston to Secretary Windebank.* Has urged on the Condé Duke the exorbitance of his conditions. The Condé de Linhares asks leave to take 100 English gunners with him to Brazil in October. C. S. P. vol. l. p. 767.

Madrid, June 17.

935. *The same to Secretary Coke.* The Duke of Fernandino has left for Italy in high favour, as is the late Governor of S⁂. Margarita and S. Honorato. The Minime Friar has with great solemnity been presented, for the French Queen, with a thumb of S. Isidiro, Patron Saint of Madrid. Don Melchor de Borja has taken nine rich Holland ships. There has been great alarm from Malaga of the Plague, arising from illness caused by some spoilt corn from an English ship, and very strict precautions have been taken in Madrid; all entrances except the four principal gates having been walled up. Don Diego de Luxan has been banished, and a young Labrador imprisoned for accusing the government of the Condé Duke. The Condé d'Oñate has arrived at Barcelona, pleading age as an excuse for not going to Germany. *Copy.*

Endorsed by himself. C. S. P. vol. l. p. 768, (but date misprinted).

Madrid, June 17.

936. *Mr. Christopher Windebank to Secretary Windebank.* A letter of respect, and apology for his past misconduct.—Spanish.

This letter is headed with the ⁂ customary to Roman Catholics, which seems to indicate that the son was a Papist.

* See Carte's Hist. of Engl., vol. iv. p. 231.

937. *Mr. Taylor to Secretary Windebank.* Fears his weekly letters miscarry. The Emperor professes that, though willing, he can do nothing till His Majesty answer his letters. The Count of Sleek, the second, if not the first, man in this Court, makes like protestations. Galasso, with 11,000 foot and 29,000 horse, is attempting to drive Bannier, who has only 12,000 men, from Torgau. Piccolomini is to command 22,000 men and 50 pieces of artillery, and to be independent of the Infant Cardinal. The Duke of Lorraine has 18,000 in Burgundy, and in all, the Emperor, Electors, and the League have 90,000 men in the field. The Tartars are in Moldavia, above 100,000 strong. The Turks also are moving towards Christendom. Caramirus is to come from Cracovia for the Queen of Poland, the marriage being fixed for August. The Treaty at Cologne is thought impossible.

1637. Prague, June 10.

Partly in cypher. Cl. S. P. vol. I. p. 769.

938. *Secretary Windebank to Lord Aston.* Desires him to call the King's special attention to the Spanish Ambassador's answer of $\frac{May\ 25}{June\ 4}$, and his impertinent and insufferable behaviour. Lord Cottington's Secret Treaty was based entirely on the restitution of the Prince Palatine. His Majesty will give no leave for recruits till he obtain hope of satisfaction. The Treaty with the French is agreed upon, and the merchants should be cautiously prepared for a possible rupture with Spain.

Westminster, June 24.

Cl. S. P. vol. I. p. 779.

939. *The same to the same.* Acknowledges his despatches, and encloses eight papers, numbered as below*.

Westminster, June 24.

Imperfect draught in his own hand, ending with the words, "The rest was about Kit." Cl. S. P. vol. I. p. 778.

i. Chelsea, March 30. *The Condé d'Oñate and Villa-Mediana's Answer.* Has power from the Emperor to settle the terms of the Palatinate negotiation.—Spanish.

Cl. S. P. vol. I. p. 781.

Chelsea, April 8. *A Note to the same effect as the last.*—Spanish. Copy.

In Windebank's hand. Cl. S. P. vol. I. p. 781.

* Of the eight papers enclosed six follow. Nos. 4 and 7 are noted in the Cl. S. P. as missing at the time of their publication.

ii. April ⅓. *Commencement du Traité entre l'Ambassadeur d'Espagne et François Windebank a Chelsea:* proposing, on the part of the Spanish Ambassador, to join in quieting France, and either to adopt the Secret Treaty, or to agree on the consideration, in lands or money, to be given for the restitution of the Lower Palatinate.—French. *Copy.*

In Windebank's hand. Cl. S. P. vol. I. p. 780.

iii. April 1/1. *Réponse de sa Majesté au Papier de l'Ambassadeur d'Espagne, daté ⅖ du present:* consenting, if satisfaction be given, to join in putting down Richelieu, but refusing as yet to enter into the details of the proposed Treaty.—French. *Copy.*

In Windebank's hand. Cl. S. P. vol. I. p. 784.

v. May 4/8. *Réponse de sa Majesté au Papier de l'Ambassadeur d'Espagne du 18/8 d'Avril 1637;* giving reasons for refusing to enter into the details of the proposed Treaty, as against Holland.—French. *Copy.*

Cl. S. P. vol. I. p. 784.

vi. May 22. *Annotations sur le Papier de sa Majesté du 11/22 de Mai.* His Majesty, instead of delaying the Treaty, has consented to almost all of the six Articles submitted to him.—French. *Draught.*

In Windebank's hand. Cl. S. P. vol. I. p. 785.

[There is a minute endorsed, that the Spanish Ambassador had audience between the delivery of the last Paper and the delivery of this.]

viii. May 13. *The Spanish Ambassador's Paper of Articles, collected out of his audiences and conferences with the Earl of Buchan,* being the six Articles referred to in the last. (1) No assistance to be given to the enemies of Spain. (2) Spanish and Dutch to be admitted equally to the fisheries. (3) Levies to be allowed Spain, but not the Dutch or French; and all in their service at present to be recalled, if possible, by proclamations and all other means. (4) All possible succours to be granted to Spain. (5) Ships to be supplied on payment by Spain. (6) The Dutch to be reduced in eighteen months to a truce or peace, otherwise war to be declared against them.—Spanish.

Two copies, one in Windebank's hand, and one endorsed by him. Cl. S. P. vol. I. p. 786.

940. *Mr. Taylor to Secretary Windebank.* Letters from England should be sent by way of Cologne, to avoid the Hollanders. Has complained of the extravagant proceedings of Villa-Mediana; and the King's refusal to answer the Emperor's letters is alleged as the chief difficulty in the way of sending Count Leslie to England in his stead. The latter grows in favour every day. The Emperor has proposed, through Curtius, a meeting of English, Austrian, and Bavarian Ambassadors at Brussels. Count Sleek agrees with him in his opinion of the Spanish demands, but the Emperor will not rely on Spain so much as his father did. Bannier is on the point of retiring before Galasso, avoiding Geleine, who threatens him from Thuringia with 11,000 men. Desires instructions and fresh credentials.

1637. Prague, June 27.

Partly in cypher. Cl. S. P. vol. l. p. 771.

941. *Secretary Windebank to Lord Aston,* asking him to undertake a suit of Father Antony de Quivoga, Reader of Divinity at Salamanca, to be made Commissary in Peru to the General of the Franciscans.

Westminster, June 29.

942. *Lord Aston to Secretary Windebank.* The Condé Duke holds to the Secret Treaty of Lord Cottington as the basis of negotiations. Was perplexed for an answer in the matter of the Prince Palatine's protest by Windebank's former declaration, that the Prince had wholly submitted to His Majesty's counsels.

Madrid, July 1.

Partly in cypher. Cl. S. P. vol. l. p. 774.

943. *The same to the same.* Of the progress of Windebank's son, and the continuance of his own pension. The Spanish Ambassador in England has advertised this Court that His Majesty has consented to treat at Brussels.

Westminster, July 1.

The last paragraph, being a postscript, is in cypher
Cl. S. P. vol. l. p. 775.

944. *Mr. Taylor to the same.* The Emperor and Count Trautsmandorff continue the same assurances. They will not act against Spain, but will endeavour to temper the Spanish demands. Bannier has retired towards Lusatia to avoid Wrangle. The Spaniards desire an agreement between Austria and Sweden, proposing to keep Pomerland themselves, and in its stead to take Juliers from Newburg and give it to Brandenburg.

Prague, July 3.

Partly in cypher. Cl. S. P. vol. l. p. 777.

1637.
Vienna,
July 8.

945. *Mr. Taylor to Secretary Windebank.* Till His Majesty side with one party or the other, he will get nothing but shows, and there is no party safe but the House of Austria. Quotes, as against Villa-Mediana, the Emperor's words "stante lineâ Guilihelmianâ" (sic), and his offer of the whole Lower Palatinate. Thinks some good use might be made of the Duke of Bavaria, with whom he has spoken. The Emperor disapproves of Villa-Mediana's exorbitant demands of a war with the Hollanders. Would not by any means have the Emperor offended. An instrument of divers strings must be warily handled; and it is more easy to tune one string than when they should all disagree. The Spanish *convenientias* are now the only *remora* to the business. The Swedes are a declining party and should not be meddled with. Desires new credentials. The villain that would have killed the Emperor is arrested. Thanks him for the privy seal for 1000*l.*, and desires his letters not to be sent by merchants, but under cover to Mons. Roclans, Postmaster at Antwerp.

Cl. S. P. vol. l. p. 787.

Madrid,
July 10.

946. *Lord Aston to the same.* Has made farther efforts to divert the Condé Duke from the Secret Treaty. Suspects that the peace with France is not so forward as is reported. Desires to be recalled and nominated to some place at home. The King has been ill for a week with fever.

Cl. S. P. vol. l. p. 789.

Westminster,
July 12.

947. *Secretary Windebank to His Majesty.* Desires to know his pleasure as to the detention of certain Spanish merchants in consequence of the advice of Mr. Gerbier to intercept the Abbot d'Escaglia, and Monsignt, Monsieur's Secretary. Also whether the embargo laid for the same reason upon transporting the French hither from Flanders is to continue. *Answer by his Majesty.* No, and the merchants may be released.

Apostiled by the King.   Cl. S. P. vol. l. p. 794.

Westminster,
July 14.

948. *The same to Lord Aston.* Villa-Mediana has been very ill, of the *mal francese*, as the joke goes. The King has granted licences to the Holland fishermen, much to the distemperature of the Spanish Ambassador. The French ambassador, Seneterre, is leaving for France. The Prince Elector and his brother have returned to Holland, (having been nearly lost on their voyage,) with pensions of 12,000*l.* and 2000*l.* or 3000*l.* per ann. The Bp. of Lincoln is sentenced to be suspended and pay 10,000*l.* to the King, and 1000 marks to John Mounson. Expresses his dissatisfaction at his son not keeping within his allowance of 80*l.*

949. *Mr. Taylor to Secretary Windebank.* The Nuntio 1637.
agrees with him in his views of the Emperor and the Duke Vienna,
of Bavaria. They do not desire the ruin of Holland, but are July 15.
jealous of its great growth, and would have it reduced. There
are only two questions which need answer: Will you be content with the resolutions of Ratisbon? and will Spain be
content with less than a war with Holland? Neither Swedes
nor French, nor the Cologne Treaty, are to be trusted.
France demands passports for Cologne for its own Ambassadors, and the German Princes its allies, else they refuse to
treat. Urges that the Emperor should be recognized and
new credentials sent to himself. The Empress is to-day
brought to bed of a son. Bannier and Wrangle are said to
have joined forces. The Prince Elector is not one of those
for whom the French have interposed.

Cl. S. P. vol. i. p. 790.

950. *Count Leslie to the same.* They must not be cozened Vienna.
by Richelieu. The Prince Elector cannot be restored but by July 15.
treaty with the House of Austria. Petitions for his brother
to be appointed Groom of the Bedchamber to the Prince.

Cl. S. P. vol. l. p. 793.

951. *Mr. Taylor to the same.* Gives details of Bannier's Vienna,
retreat and defeat by Galasso. The Emperor has refused July 22.
passports to the German adherents of France. It is reported
that the Prince Elector is to be sent into France, a course
which Count Leslie regrets. Casamirus, Prince of Polonia,
is coming here with an allowance of 600l. a day. A diet is
to be held in Hungary, and the Empress crowned there.

Cl. S. P. vol. L p. 795.

952. *The same to the same.* The Prince Casamirus comes Vienna,
to-day, and will be received with great honour. Banier July 26.
has lost all his foot, baggage, and artillery, and has joined
Wrangle, their united forces being 12,000 strong. Earnestly
discourages the league with France, as not conducive to the
interests of the Prince Palatino, who will become a subject
of France instead of *magnus Vicarius Imperii.* Enumerates
the gains of the French by the war, which they desire to
continue, and exhorts him to trust to the Emperor. Encloses
the next two papers.

Endorsed by Windebank as sent to His Majesty on Aug. 15, and received
back from Lindhurst Aug. 17.

1637.

953. *List* of the Protestant allies of the French King for whom passports to Cologne were demanded. (The Prince Palatine is not included.)—Italian.
Two Copies.
In Taylor's and Windebank's hands.

954. Vienna, July 17. *The Emperor's Answer to the Venetian Ambassador's request for the Passports.* Refuses to grant them, inasmuch as the request does not come from the Princes themselves, and is calculated to disturb the constitutions settled at Prague and Ratisbon.—Latin.
Original and copy in Taylor's hand, and endorsed by Windebank.

Madrid, July 19
955. *Lord Aston to Secretary Coke.* The Pope is reported dead. The Duke of Albuquerque died on the 19th. The Cardinal Borgia is to remain in Spain, being appointed President of the Council of Arragon. Large levies of troops are still being made. Colarte, the Flemish general, lies in the Groyne with the Dunkirk fleet of eight sail and two millions of plate for Flanders, waiting to be strengthened by the Duke of Maquedn's fleet. Genoa lays claim to the prize captured in the Mediterranean, but the vessels and crews being Hollanders it will be held a good prize, and the doctrine of restitution, though much preached, is little practised here. The plague still rages at Malaga, but the private and public charities there are very noble. Peace with France is sincerely desired. The Condé d'Oñate is still at Barcelona. Sallee is reported to be taken, and the expedition has won His Majesty much credit.
Copy.
Endorsed by Windebank.

Madrid, July 19.
956. *The same to Secretary Windebank.* The Condé Duke has a project of raising twelve million ducats by sealing (stamping) and raising the value of all *bellon* and silver plate, or by seizing all the *plata labrada* in Spain at a fixed valuation.

Dublin Castle, Aug. 1.
957. *The Lord Deputy (Wentworth) and Council of Ireland to Lord Mount-Norris,* forwarding a petition to them from one Walter Peppard, concerning the lands and towns of Bannock; which complaint Lord Mount-Norris is to answer at the Board by a certain day.

Vienna, Aug. 5.
958. *Mr. Taylor to Secretary Windebank.* Banier is before Stettin, and Wrangle is reported to have gone to Stralsund. Believes that all hope is in the Emperor alone, but a restitution *in integrum* can hardly be expected.

959. *Lord Aston to Secretary Coke.* The Infant Cardinal, as Abbot of Alcobaça, a rich monastery in Portugal, is under Cardinal Richelieu, as having been made General of the *Bernardines*, which gives much offence here. The Condé d'Oñate is still under displeasure at Barcelona. The plague has ceased at Malaga. The King has recovered and is attempting to compel the clergy to use the *papel selada* in their tribunals. The Nuntio threatens to leave in consequence of a servant of his being whipped. The Dukes of Cardona, Ciudad Real, and Nuthera, and the Condé de Cerbellon are about to invade France with large forces. *Copy.*

1637.
Madrid.
Aug. 11.

Endorsed by Windebank.

960. *The same to Secretary Windebank.* The Spaniards shew, by their reception of the news of the French treaty, and by their putting forward the secret treaty, that they never intended really to come to terms with His Majesty.

Madrid,
Aug. 11.

961. *Mr. Taylor to the same.* The Imperialists' army is in great disorder. Banier and Wrangle are both at Stettin. The Marquis of Brandenburgh is returned to Berlin. The Queen of Polonia was married on Sunday. There is much discontent with Spain here. The Bishop of Treves is to be set at liberty.

Vienna,
Aug. 13.

Partly in cypher, decyphered by Windebank.

962. *Secretary Windebank to His Majesty.* Encloses despatches concerning the Bishop of Lincoln, the Spanish and French negotiations, the Protestant Princes for whom passports are demanded, and Mr. Gerbier's difficulty in preventing the Queen Mother (Mary de Medici) coming to England.

Hampton,
Aug. 15.

Apostiled by the King, "Lindhurst, Aug. 16."
Cl. S. P. vol. ii. p. 1.

963. *Mr. Taylor to Secretary Windebank.* Duke Bernard Weimar's passage of the Rhine, the disorder of Galasso's army, and the rumours of help given by England to Flanders, cause great anxiety here. They consider the league with France to have put an end to any hope of success with England.

Vienna,
Aug. 19.

964. *Count Leslie to the same.* Urges His Majesty to write to the Emperor, as the only way to obtain his desires for the Prince Palatine.

Vienna,
Aug. 19.

1637.
Chirbma,
Aug. 11.

965. *The Condé d'Oñate and Villa-Mediana to Secretary Windebank*, concerning the meeting of Plenipotentiaries from Austria, England, Spain, and Bavaria at Brussels, to settle the business of the Palatinate. (See C. S. P. vol. ii. p. 1.)

Original, and copy endorsed by Windebank as "received from Don Alonço de Cardenas Nov. 17."

Holme Hill,
Aug. 15.

966. *Secretary Windebank to Lord Aston.* The King is not likely to grant the Condé de Linhares the 100 gunners he requires, nor to proceed with the secret treaty after the conduct of the Spaniards, nor to send to Brussels, as requested. The Spanish Ambassador is much exasperated at having lost his suit with Capt. Steward. Necolalde is leaving, the King having granted him a ship, but refuses to take the present usual for an Agent, requiring that of a Resident. The treaty with France is near conclusion.

Vienna,
Aug. 16.

967. *Mr. Taylor to Secretary Windebank.* Relates a conversation with Count Sleek, in which he shewed the slavishness of the Emperor's submission to Spain. Duke Bernard has lost 1000 out of 5000 since the passage of the Rhine. Fifteen French regiments from Basle are to join him and march to Frankfort on Maine, Sir James Ramsay being at Hanau with 4000 men. The Spaniards have surprised Nimeguen. The Bishop of Treves has arrived. The King of Polonia has deferred solemnizing his marriage for a month. The Condés d'Oñate, father and son, are greatly blamed.

Vienna,
Aug. 16.

968. *The same to the same.* The Emperor has invited him, through Leslie, to an audience, from which he anticipates important satisfaction.

Both three partly in cypher, decyphered by Windebank.

Madrid,
Aug. 17.

969. *Lord Aston to the same.* An embargo has been laid on all shipping, under pretence of keeping secret the sailing of the plate-fleet for Flanders, but really, as he thinks, in fear of hostility with England. Also a short note enclosing the two next papers.

970. Aug. 19. *Memorial from Lord Aston to the King of Spain (Philip IV)*, representing the rude behaviour of the Condé d'Oñate to His Majesty, and desiring him to shew a due resentment of it.—Spanish. *Copy.*

In Lord Aston's hand.

971. Aug. 25. *Answer of the King of Spain (Philip IV).* He is much displeased with his Ambassador's behaviour. The offence taken against the Condé was chiefly because in his personal treating with His Majesty he had proposed only restitution of the Lower Palatinate, as being all which was in the hands of Spain. This however the King justifies, and concludes by expressing his good disposition in favour of His Majesty and the Prince Elector, and his readiness to treat at Brussels by his brother, the Infant Cardinal.—Spanish. — 1637.

<small>Original, and copy in Lord Aston's hand. Also translations of both papers in Windebank's hand.</small>

972. *The Condé d'Oñate to Lord Aston.* A letter of compliment.—Spanish. — Aug. 17.

973. *Mr. Taylor to Secretary Windebank.* Has spoken very high to the Emperor on the conduct of Spain in denying the resolution of Ratisbon. Count Sleek is reported likely to supersede Galasso. Hanau is said to have been delivered over by Sir J. Ramsay. The report of the capture of Nimeguen seems unfounded. — Vienna, Sept. 1.

<small>In cypher, decyphered by Windebank.</small>

974. *Lord Aston to the same.* Relates at length his conferences with the King and Condé Duke concerning the conduct of the Condé d'Oñate. — Madrid, Sept. 3.

975. *The same to Secretary Coke.* Asks for explanation of a passage in his despatch, directing his conduct in the event of hostilities. — Madrid, Sept. 3.
Copy.

<small>Endorsed by himself and Windebank.</small>

976. *The same to Lord Cottington.* Not clearly understanding what satisfaction is expected from Spain, he is unable to discover the Condé Duke's real intentions, but believes they would consent to the removal of the ban, the restitution of the Princes' possessions held by them, and some other retribution. Dissuades violent measures, as unlikely to gain any good, though doing much to the Spaniards' prejudice. — Madrid, Sept. 3.

<small>Cl. S. P. vol. ii. p 2, (with the exception of an immaterial postscript).</small>

977. *Mr. Taylor to Secretary Windebank.* Mons. Pius, the Danish Ambassador, has arrived, about the tolls of the Elbe. The league with France is thought to be more show than substance. Duke Weimar is fortified on the Rhine. Contreras has arrived from Frankendale, being much blamed for his cruelties there. — Vienna, Sept. 9.

1637.
Madrid,
Sept. 14.

978. *Lord Aston to Secretary Windebank.* Has hinted to the leading merchants the possibility of a breach, and has remonstrated with the Condé Duke concerning the embargo.

Madrid,
Sept. 14.

979. *The same to Secretary Coke.* Has fears for the merchants' safety. A Genoese Ambassador has arrived to claim the prize taken in the Mediterranean. News of the movements of the Dukes of Nothera, Cardona, and Fernandino. The Duke of Maqueda has been superseded. The Condé de Lernos is dead.

Vienna,
Sept. 16.

980. *Mr. Taylor to Secretary Windebank*, pressing for credentials to treat with the Emperor, and containing various immaterial news from the Continent.

Madrid,
Sept. 25.

981. *Lord Aston to the same;* of interviews with the Condé Duke concerning the opening of the ports, and taking the embargo off the ships.

Vienna,
Sept. 13.

982. *Mr. Taylor to the same.* The Emperor is desirous that the business (of the Palatinate) should be settled, but has no thought of a complete restitution to the Prince Palatine.

Vienna,
Sept. 30.

983. *The same to the same,* with news of the Imperialist armies, and again pressing for credentials.

Sept. 30.

984. *The Condé Duke d'Olivarez to Lord Aston,* concerning the taking off the embargo.—Spanish. *Original and Copy.*

Vienna,
Oct. 7.

985. *Mr. Taylor to Secretary Windebank.* Gives news of the armies of Galasso and Getz. Duke Weimar has recrossed the Rhine. Count Curtius is gone to Berlin to treat with the Swedes. Presses for fresh credentials and acknowledgment of the Emperor.

Westminster,
Oct. 11.

986. *Secretary Windebank to Lord Aston.* His Majesty is ill-pleased with the King of Spain's offer of advice as to the Hollanders, and much suspects the renewing of the treaty, which however he will be willing to discuss at Brussels, when the Infant Cardinal has received powers from Austria and Bavaria. The Condé d'Oñate has given further offence by visiting a Polish Ambassador, sent to invite His Majesty to his King's marriage, whom His Majesty has refused to receive, in consequence of that King's false behaviour in his proposed marriage with the Princess Palatine. Desires a watchful eye to be kept on the Irish resident abroad, especially O'Donnell, the so-called Earl of Tyrconnel, as they are

said to be stirring dissensions for their own ends. Advices economy in sending extraordinary couriers, the present arrangement saving 5000*l.* to 6000*l.* a-year. *Two Copies.*
             Both in Windebank's hand.

1637.

987. *Secretary Windebank to Lord Aston.* Expresses his indignation at the disgraceful conduct of his worthless son. Utterly renounces him, will have no intercourse with him, nor allow him one groat as long as he lives with his wife. If he leave her and go to France or Italy, he will allow him 80*l.* per annum, and will pay the expense, if not great, of a dissolution of the marriage.

Westminster, Oct. 11.

988. *Count Leslie to Secretary Windebank.* England should join itself more to the party of the Emperor, for without Austria the Palsgrave will never be restored, and they are in danger of falling between two stools by their present policy.

Ebersdorfe, Oct. 14.

989. *Mr. Taylor to the same.* Discourses at great length concerning the present disposition of the Powers at war, all being inclined to peace with the Emperor except France, and repeats the advice frequently before given.

Vienna, Oct. 14.

990. *The City of Dantzick to His Majesty.* Desires his intercession with the King of Poland to desist from a demand of customs for two years imposed upon them in a late peace between that King and Sweden, of which peace His Majesty was the mediator.—Latin.

Dantzick, Oct. 15.

991. *Lord Aston to Secretary Windebank.* The embargo has been taken off all ports except those of Portugal, Cadiz, and San Lucar, against the shutting of which he has remonstrated as a breach of the peace. The Nuntio urges a suspension of arms, and the Venetian Ambassador that Holland be admitted to the general peace. It is rumoured that the Hollanders have refused to pay His Majesty for liberty of fishing in his seas.

Madrid, Oct. 17.

992. *The same to Secretary Coke,* chiefly concerning a dispute of the merchants of Jersey about their trade to Spain in certain articles not mentioned.   *Copy.*

Madrid, Oct. 17.

993. *The same to Secretary Windebank.* Has heard from Necolalde at San Sebastian, who complains, (as is his usual custom,) that he has been disappointed in the promise of conveyance to Spain by a ship of His Majesty. Is dissatisfied with Windebank's son.

Madrid, Oct. 19.

1637.
Vienna,
Oct. 21.

994. *Mr. Taylor to Secretary Windebank.* There is not much chance of the proposed peace with Sweden, now that a league has been made between Sweden and France, but still Curtius is to go to Berlin. The general amnesty would only include those who had been with the Duke of Saxony in the late disturbances, excluding therefore the Prince Palatine and many others. The Danish Ambassador's opinion is that the mistake of England is in demanding entire restitution and taking part with France, Sweden, and Holland.

Paris,
Oct. 25.

995. *Count Egmont to His Majesty,* recalling a Mr. Seton whom he had sent to negotiate an affair with him, and substituting the bearer, a Mr. Sanderson.—French.

Vienna,
Oct. 28.

996. *Mr. Taylor to Secretary Windebank.* They will not send powers to the Infant Cardinal at Brussels, nor entrust the business to the Spaniards. Trautmansdorf urges a match between England and Austria. The Duke of Savoy is dead, not without suspicion of poison, and the Landgrave (of Cassel) is also reported dead. The Duchess of Mantua and the Venetians are said to have come to an agreement. Don Francisco de Melo is expected from Flanders and the Duke of Monteleone from Spain. The Prince of Eckenburg goes Ambassador to Rome.

Vienna,
Nov. 4.

997. *The same to the same.* The Landgrave's widow has applied to the Emperor for pardon and restitution of the lands given to Darmstadt. The reports of the Duke of Savoy's death prove false. The ministers here profess readiness for partial restitution and the alternation of the Electorate, and advise a match between the Prince of Wales and the Emperor's daughter.

Westminster,
Nov. 5.

998. *Secretary Windebank to Lord Aston.* The meeting for the proposed Confederacy of England, France, and other Powers will be held either at Hamburg or the Hague; but more will be known when M. Dellievre (Ambassador Extraordinary from France) has entered into negotiation. The Treaty proposed by the Spanish Ambassador at Brussels is broken off. The death of the Duke of Savoy is likely to cause trouble in Italy, and new differences between France and Spain. His ungracious son is to be hastened away to France or Italy.

The Hague,
Nov. 6.

999. *Letters of Credence* of the United States to their Ambassador, the Chevalier Joachimi.—French.

Endorsed by Windebank.

CLARENDON PAPERS.   143

1000. *A Letter of Thanks to the Lord Deputy (Wentworth)* 1637.
of Ireland from the master and others of the Dutch ship Nov. 8.
Zutphen, for protecting her when in danger.   *Copy.*

1001. *Lord Aston to Secretary Windebank.* A private letter Madrid,
concerning an application made to him by Windebank (for Nov. 11.
the Queen, apparently) in behalf of the Confessor to the
Spanish Ambassador in England; also informing him of the
unfortunate marriage of his son Christopher, and his own wish
to be recalled; with a statement of his present poverty.

1002. *The same to Secretary Coke.* The ports are now Madrid,
entirely opened. The elder Condé d'Oñate is gradually being Nov. 11.
received into favour again. The commotions in Portugal increase, and Eçixa in Granada has revolted. A donative, fixed
at the King's pleasure in each case, is to be collected in
Castile. The judge who sentenced the Nuntio's servant has
been banished. The Duchesses of Chevreuse and Arscot have
arrived. The Condé de Linhares has had great honours be-
stowed on him, and will set out for Brazil in the spring.
Grison Ambassadors have arrived to confirm the capitulation.
The Duke of Albuquerque, the Condé de la Puebla, and Don
Carlos Coloma are all dead of calentures.   *Copy.*
                                   Endorsed by himself and Windebank.

1003. *The same to Secretary Windebank.* The passports de- Madrid,
manded for the Protestant Princes are not likely to be Nov. 11.
granted. Desires leave to nominate the English Consuls in
the ports of Spain, the King of Spain having hitherto nominated them, contrary to the custom with all other nations who
trade there.

1004. *Mr. Taylor to the same;* of the approaching Treaty Vienna,
between the Imperialists and Swedes, with the news of Nov. 18.
Galasso's army at Suet, near Stettin. The Imperialists,
though greatly injured by the war, have yet vast powers,
but are much alarmed by the success of the French and the
States in Narbonne and Breda. He has used this news in
pressing on the Imperialist Court their bad treatment of
England, and has told them that "if they were cunning
musicians, they might sing a most melodious counterpoint to
this," by aiding the King's views in the matter of the Palatinate. The Spaniards are now the only hindrance to the
restitution of the whole Lower Palatinate.

1005. *Sir F. Willoughby to the Lord Deputy (Wentworth)* Galway,
and Council of Ireland, concerning the provision of biscuit, Nov. 19.
and the victualling of a Dutch ship.   *Copy.*

1637.
Vienna,
Nov. 25.

1006. *Mr. Taylor to Secretary Windebank*, with news of the Imperialist army in Pomerland. His opinion of the Treaty with the Emperor, and the disposition of the Swedes. Don Francisco de Melo has arrived as Ambassador from Spain.

Vienna,
Dec. 2.

1007. *The same to the same.* Account of a conversation with Don Francisco de Melo, wherein he lays all the blame of the continuance of the war on the Spaniards, and the duplicity of their former Ambassador, Villa-Mediana.

Madrid,
Dec. 7.

1008. *Lord Aston to Secretary Coke.* Severe proceedings of a Spanish Commissary at Seville and Cadiz against English and other merchants for trading in silver and plate without licence. Report of a journey to be made by the King of Spain to Portugal on pretence of quelling insurrection. Particulars of a Treaty about to be made between the Grisons and Spaniards. *Copy.*

Madrid,
Dec. 7.

1009. *The same to Secretary Windebank;* of the embargo, which by his efforts has at last been taken off the Spanish ports. Account of the Irish of quality now resident in Madrid, viz. the Condé de Bishaven, the (so-called) Marquis de Mayo, and Don Gulielmo Burgh. Capt. R. Noble has lately left the Asturias to attempt the levy of 3000 men in Ireland for the Spanish service.

Madrid,
Dec. 9.

1010. *The same to the same*, enclosing the next two letters; with comments on them.

1011. Nov. 23. *Benjamin Wollnode (master of an English ship) to Lord Aston.* A complaint of the seizure of his ship by the Spanish Fleet, when on a voyage to Virginia, on pretence that Virginia was not included in the Articles of Peace.

1012. St. Lucas, Nov. 29. *William Rous to Lord Aston*, entreating his interference to procure his release, having been captured by the Spaniards at Carthagena, while engaged in privateering.

Vienna,
Dec. 9.

1013. *Mr. Taylor to Secretary Windebank*, concerning the probabilities of the Treaty between Sweden and the Emperor being concluded.

Dec. 10.

1014. *Lord Aston to the same*, enclosing a letter from the Duchess of Chevreuse to a Mr. Montague.

1015. *Lord Aston to Secretary Windebank.* Full exposition of the state of affairs in Germany, with his reasons for thinking that all the German Powers will soon give in their adherence to the Emperor, and the Swedish Treaty will be concluded, the Spaniards' desire to keep part of the Palatinate being now the sole hindrance. Now therefore is the time for the King to acknowledge the Emperor, and to come to an understanding with him, if he wishes to benefit the Prince Elector.

1637.
Vienna,
Dec. 16.

1016. *The same to the same,* containing a complaint of the King of Spain against a decision of the English Admiralty Court, adverse to the Conde d'Oñato, in the matter of some goods seized by him on board an English ship, on pretence of their being confiscate.

Madrid,
Dec. 19.

1017. *Mr. Taylor to the Emperor (Ferdinand III),* accepting, in the name of the King, the invitation to send an Ambassador to the Conference at Brussels, but desiring to know what terms will be offered the King, and what will be required of him; recommending also that the Emperor send some one in a public capacity to England.—Latin. *Copy.*
Endorsed by Windebank.

Posonii,
Dec. 11.

1018. *Lord Aston to Secretary Windebank,* relating a conversation with Carneio, Secretary to the Condé Duke, and the Duke's jealousy of the rumoured league between England and France.

Dec. 18.

1019. *The same to His Majesty,* asking leave to return to England on account of the state of his health.

Dec. 18.

1020. *Mr. Taylor to Secretary Windebank.* Has had audience of the Emperor, who assures him of his goodwill to England in the business of the Prince Palatine. All Germany is now united to the Emperor, and the King should at once acknowledge him, and send a representative to the Conference at Brussels. Desirability of a match between the King's and Emperor's children. Encloses the next.

Presburg,
Dec. 19.

1021. *A Paper,* containing particulars of the success of the Imperialists under Galasso in storming the castle of Wolgast.—Dutch.
With a translation by Windebank.

1022. *Secretary Windebank to Lord Aston.* Is unwilling that the Nuntio's negotiation for a suspension of arms should cease, it being manifestly to the King's advantage that the rupture between the Emperor and France should continue.

Westminster,
Dec. 19.

1637.	The King is willing to license the Holland fishermen, but will maintain his sovereignty of the seas, being one of the fairest flowers of his crown and his undoubted right of inheritance, of which sovereignty the fishing is a principal branch. Requests him to demand punishment of one Daly, a disguised Irish friar, who has been attempting to foment a Spanish party in Ireland. The King refuses Necolalde a ship, who persists in declining his present. Mons. de Belliovre, the French Ambassador, is in great credit at court.

(Original, with a rough draught, partly printed in Cl. S. P. vol. ii. p. 3.

No date.	1023. "*Relation* de la plata quo viene en los Galeones este anno de 1637."—Spanish.

Endorsed by Lord Aston.

No date.	1024. An *Account* of the Polish Ambassadors in England from the year 1620 to 1637, with a long list of presents made by one of them, amongst others "to Jeofferie the Queen's dwarf, 10 pieces, which he enclosed and gave him in a peare from his table."
No date.	1025. *Statement* of a suit for debt, Nowell *v.* Nelson, upon writ of error returnable in Parliament.
No date.	1026. *Paper* concerning the affairs of a Hamburg Company, for argument at the bar of the House of Lords. *Printed.*
No date.	1027. *Abstract* of the case of Laurence Lownes, Esq., concerning Manors in the County of York. *Printed.*
No date.	1028. A *Note* (for a speech?) of the great happiness of the English government, in the constitution and mutual checks of the two Houses of Parliament.
No date.	1029. *Statement* of the case of the Attorney-General *v.* John Hampden, Esq., and Baron Weston's argument in the same.
No date.	1030. *Report* of the answers of Mr. Prynne, Dr. Bastwick, and Mr. Burton before the Lords.
No date.	1031. *Minutes* of the settlement of the monopoly of wines, and the disputes between the vintners and merchants. The vintners to take of the English merchants 4000 tons of Spanish, and 5000 tons of French wine (paying a duty of 40s. a ton), and to have licence of selling cooked victuals, except venison, pheasants, and partridges. *Much mutilated.*

1032. *Petition* to His Majesty of John Wentworth, prisoner in the Gate-house, Westminster, for removal to some other prison in consequence of his infirmities.

Endorsed by Windebank, "Wentworth, R(oman) Ca(tholic)."

1637.
No date.

1033. *Petition* to His Majesty of John Southworth for discharge, being imprisoned in the Gate-house for visiting a house infected with the plague.

No date.

1034. *Petition to the King and Privy Council.* "The case of several Protestant Dissenters, called Quakers, within the County of Hereford, stated in relation to their late and present sufferings upon old Statutes made against popish Recusants," with a list of the names of the petitioners, and the fines levied yearly upon them. *Copy.*

No date.

1035. *Mr. Taylor to Secretary Windebank*, of the same tenour as his former letters concerning the prospects of peace, and a good understanding between the Empire and England.

1637-8.
Vienna,
Jan. 6.

1036. *Lord Aston to Secretary Coke.* The league with the Grisons is not yet completed. Court news of the Duchess of Chevreuse and the Cardinal of Savoy. The mutineers in Portugal remain still on foot. *Copy.*

Endorsed by himself.

Madrid,
Jan. 9 (?)

1037. *The same to Secretary Windebank;* of the arrival of a galleon in the Groyne with secret intelligence for the King of Spain, which the Marquis de Mancera hopes to discover for him.

Madrid,
Jan. 11.

1038. *Mr. Taylor to the same.* The Baron de Reck, President of the Aulic Council, has given his vote decidedly in favour of the Emperor's siding with England. A great feeling against Spain is apparent in the Empire.

Vienna,
Jan. 13.

1039. *Lord Aston to the same.* Complains of the great coldness of the Condé Duke to him, and attributes it to the Spaniard's jealousy of the English King looking out for new friends. Despairs of ever being able to do anything with them.

Madrid,
Jan. 17.

1040. *The same to Secretary Coke.* Has obtained redress for Mr. Leechland, the owner of a ship. There is talk of a suspension of arms between France and Spain, as proposed by the Nuntio. The tumults in Portugal lessen. *Copy.*

Endorsed by himself.

Madrid,
Jan. 17.

1637-8.
Presburg,
Jan. 19.

1041. *Mr. Taylor to Secretary Windebank.* The Swedes have proposed terms to the Emperor. A rumour has reached him that Lord Leicester has left Paris, the proposed league with France being broken off, which he hopes to be true.

Presburg,
Jan. 26.

1042. *The same to the same.* The Swedes are said to be divided on the question of making peace with the Emperor, without the concurrence of France and their other allies.

Presburg,
Feb. 2.

1043. *The same to the same,* on the probability of the Swedes treating. The Aulic Council is much divided on matters of religion, demanding to be styled by the Emperor " Evangelici." A conversation with Count Trautmansdorf, in which much apprehension is expressed of the Prince Elector's ill-will (should he be restored), as surmised from his previous behaviour.

Presburg,
Feb. 9.

1044. *The same to the same.* The Council and Emperor are at better accord. Sir K. Digby and Mr. Porter are reported to be at the conference of Brussels, where the jealousy of Bavaria must be guarded against. The Empress is to be crowned Queen of Hungary on Sunday.

Madrid,
Feb. 10.

1045. *Lord Aston to the same.* Has been informed by the Condé Duke that the business of the Palatinate on the part of the Spaniards was put into the hands of the Cardinal Infanta at Brussels with full powers to act. An account of the *fiestas* held in honour of the Duchess of Chevreuse. Further mention of the cases of Ross and Wollnode.

Madrid,
Feb. 10.

1046. *The same to Secretary Coke.* Of the raising of large forces in Spain and Germany for Italy. No suspension of arms is intended at present by Spain. The Condé d'Oñate is recalled, and Don Jasper de Bracamonte is to be Ambassador to England. Don Martin de Axpe is to set out with the Duchess of Chevreux as Resident till his arrival. The Prior of the Convent of the Escurial has been raised to the rank of Grandee; a privilege enjoyed hitherto by no clergymen, except Cardinals and the General of the Franciscans. *Copy.*

Presburg,
Feb. 23.

1047. *Mr. Taylor to Secretary Windebank.* Has received no answer yet to his paper to the Emperor. Count Curtius is appointed Vice-Chancellor of the Empire. The Diet goes on with more conformity than formerly.

Westminster,
Feb. 14.

1048. *Secretary Windebank to His Majesty.* Asks instructions concerning the reference of the Irish Customs business to the Archbishop of Canterbury, Sir A. Hopton's private instructions, and a suit of Sir Richard Strode's in the Star Chamber. Apostiled by the King. C. S. P. vol. ii. p. 5.

1049. *Lord Aston to Secretary Windebank.* Don Martin de Aspe having fallen ill, Don Alonso de Cardeñas is to go to England "como gentilhombre," there existing in Spain four degrees of foreign ministers in lieu of the two English degrees of Agent and Ambassador, viz. Secretary, Agent, Resident, Gentilhombre. — 1637-8. Madrid, Feb. 28.

> Endorsed by Windebank, "Brought by Capt. Stradling, who landed the Duchess of Chevreux at Portsmouth, April 14."

1050. *Secretary Windebank to His Majesty.* Asks instructions concerning the congratulations to be offered by Lord Leicester on the French Queen (Anne of Austria) being with child[a], and Sir A. Hopton's voyage. — Whitehall, March 1.

> Apostiled by the King, "March 2." Cl. S. P. vol. ii. p. 6.

1051. *Mr. Taylor to Secretary Windebank.* Count Leslie has been very ill. — Vienna, March 1.

1052. *Secretary Windebank to His Majesty,* enclosing despatches of Gerbier and Taylor. — Westminster, March 5.

> Apostiled by the King, "March 7th." Cl. S. P. vol. ii. p. 7.

1053. *The same to Lord Aston.* Gives him notice of his recall, in consideration of his infirmity, Sir Arthur Hopton to succeed him, and instructions respecting his taking leave: with answers to previous despatches. The Spanish Ambassador shall receive proper satisfaction in the matter of Capt. Stoward. *Copy and Rough Draught.* — Westminster, March 6.

1054. *The King of Spain (Philip IV) to His Majesty.* Letters of credence to accompany Don Alonso de Cardeñas. —Latin. — Madrid, March 7.

1055. *Mr. Taylor to Secretary Windebank;* detailing an audience with the Emperor (the substance of which is embodied in the next paper). Count Curtius goes to Hamburg with full powers to treat with Sweden. Necessity of fresh credentials to himself, and acknowledgment of the Emperor by His Majesty. Encloses the next. — Presburg, March 9.

1056. *Possonii, March 11. Mr. Taylor to the Emperor (Ferdinand III).* A memorial of his last audience delivered at the Emperor's request, wherein he excuses His Majesty for not having answered the Emperor's letters, and avows his willingness to join in the defence of Flanders, if the business of the Palatinate be settled,

---

[a] Louis XIV. was born Sept. 5, 1638.

1637-8. and to send a Plenipotentiary to Brussels, in case the proposed treaty takes place. Complains of the delay on the part of the Spanish and Imperial Courts. *Copy.*

Madrid, March 10. 1057. *Lord Aston to Secretary Windebank.* A short account of Don Alonso de Cardeñas, whose appointment is caused by dissatisfaction with the Condé d'Oñate. The Spaniards are confident of success in Germany, their chief anxiety being for Italy and the recovery of Brazil.

Madrid, March 10. 1058. *The same to Secretary Coke,* repeating the news of former letters. The tumults in Portugal have ceased. The treaty with the Grisons does not advance, nor the proposed suspension of arms, there being no inclination for peace, except on the restitution of all losses in the last war with France. *Copy.*

Madrid, March 13. 1059. *The same to Secretary Windebank,* correcting an immaterial error in his last.

Madrid, March 13. 1060. *The same to Secretary Coke,* with immaterial Court news. *Copy.*

Presburg, March 16. 1061. *Mr. Taylor to Secretary Windebank.* Great consternation among the Imperialists at the news of a defeat by Duke Weimar.

Presburg, March 16. 1062. *The same to the same.* Application for a pass to England for a Mrs. Margaret Tenyson, a lady in attendance on the Empress Dowager.

Westminster, March 19. 1063. *Secretary Windebank to Lord Aston.* Capt. Steward's business is not yet settled, owing to Lord Cottington's late indisposition.

Whitehall, March 19. 1064. *The same to (William Cavendish) Earl of Newcastle,* announcing his appointment as Gentleman of the Bedchamber to the Prince of Wales.
Rough draught by himself. Cl. S. P. vol. 5. p. 7.

Welbeck, March 21. 1065. *(William Cavendish) Earl of Newcastle to Secretary Windebank.* A letter of thanks. Cl. S. P. vol. 5. p. 8.

Paris, March 22. 1066. *(James Erskine) Earl of Buchan to the same,* urging reward to those who are capable of serving his Majesty; and instancing particularly the case of Sir Thos. Dishington.

Madrid, March 22. 1067. *Lord Aston to the same,* on the progress of some private business of a Mr. Richaut.

1068. *Mr. Taylor to Secretary Windebank.* Has delivered a second paper to the Emperor in accordance with the first. Affairs have been delayed in consequence of the recent disasters in Alsatia.
1637-8. Vienna. March 24.

1069. *Secretary Windebank to Mr. Taylor.* Censures him severely for assuming His Majesty's sanction of the paper delivered to the King of Hungary, and the title of Emperor therein accorded. *Copy.*
In Windebank's hand.
1638. Westminster, March 30.

1070. *The same to the same,* ordering him to give an account of his conduct in assuring a Danish Secretary that he had given the title of Emperor by His Majesty's command, and that His Majesty disavowed the manifesto of the Prince Elector. *Copy.*
In Windebank's hand.
Westminster, March 30.

1071. *(James Erskine) Earl of Buchan to Secretary Windebank,* recommending to his favour some business of the bearer.
Paris, March 31.

1072. *Mr. Taylor to the same.* An account of an audience with the Emperor, and a conversation with Count Trautmansdorff, in both which he urges the necessity of a good foundation to be laid for the Conference at Brussels. Review of the state of Germany, and the prospect of peace with Sweden. There is no inclination to peace on the part of Spain.
Vienna, March 31.

1073. *Lord Aston to the same,* expressing his hope of the King's favour on his return, and his wish that Sir Arthur Hopton's embassy had been delayed a few months, to confirm the apprehensions he has excited in the Spanish Court of the loss of the friendship of England.
Madrid, April 3.

1074. *(James Erskine) Earl of Buchan to the same,* desiring directions to guide his intercourse with the French Court, and recommending that Captain Alexander Erskine should be permitted to raise some regiments of Scotch guards for the French King.
Paris, April 1/11.

1075. *Lord Aston to the same.* Has taken leave of the Spanish King and Queen.
Madrid, April 1/11.

1076. *Secretary Windebank to Mr. Taylor,* censuring him for the delivery of his second paper to the Emperor.
Rough Draught.
In Windebank's hand.
April 6.

1638.
Vienna,
April 6.

1077. *Mr. Taylor to Secretary Windebank*, with news of the army. "Mars seems common, giving good and bad success to both parties."

Vienna,
April 14.

1078. *The same to the same.* The Swedes will treat with the Emperor alone without England, France, or Holland. The young Duke of Newburg is ingratiating himself with the Emperor, and said to be likely, should the Duke of Bavaria die, to marry his widow, with a view to the Electorate. The Duke of Wirtemberg has made submission, and his country divided into fourteen Amts or Governments. His views on the English negotiations with the Emperor repeated at length.

Whitehall,
April 21.

1079. *Secret, and Formal, Instructions* to Sir A. Hopton on his embassy to Spain. *Copy.*

Whitehall,
April 21.

1080. *Secret Instructions for our trusty and well-beloved Sir Arthur Hopton, Knt., our Ambassador Resident with the King of Spain.* To avoid giving the title of Emperor. How to conduct himself with reference to the French and Swedish treaties, and the interference of Spain with the fisheries on the English coast. *Copy.*

Cl. S. P. vol. II. p. 8.

Vienna,
April 21.

1081. *Mr. Taylor to Secretary Windebank.* He hears that Spain is well disposed to a treaty.

Vienna,
April 28.

1082. *The same to the same.* There is a rumour that the Prince Elector is with Melander, but, as is believed, without his uncle's sanction.

Madrid,
May 3.

1083. *Lord Aston to the same.* Has taken leave of the Condé Duke.

Vienna,
May 5.

1084. *Mr. Taylor to the same.* The state of affairs with Spain demands that something should at once be done by England: can do little himself, being now only "Joannes sine nomine." A minute account of the contributions of the several German States to the war, and of the state of affairs in Italy.

Westminster,
May 7.

1085. *Letters of Credence* for Sir Arthur Hopton.—Latin. *Copy.*

May 10.

1086. (*Charles IV.*) *Duke of Lorraine to His Majesty*, to introduce the Abbé le Moleur, and to offer his services in some business in Flanders.—French.

1087. *Mr. Taylor to Secretary Windebank*, answering at great length and with much vehemence the charges made against him. *Two Copies.*
Vienna, May 12. 1638.

1088. *The same to the same.* An account of the war, and his views on the assumption of arms by the Prince Elector.
Vienna, May 12.

1089. *(James Erskine) Earl of Buchan to the same.* The misery in France caused by the war is so great that "in most pearts of the contray the pour peiple doeth ette on another." Encloses the next.
Paris, May 12.

1090. *Count Egmont to His Majesty*, asking permission to visit England.—French.
Paris, May 13.

1091. *Memorial of Count Egmont to His Majesty*, to the same purport, but fuller than the last. He has not till now been able to avail himself of his permission to come to England, and desires letters to the Cardinal Infant to shew that he is under the King's protection, and has no prejudicial motive in coming.—French. *Copy.*
Endorsed by Windebank, with the date.
May 13.

1092. *Sir Arthur Hopton to Secretary Windebank*, announcing his immediate departure.
Plymouth, May 17.

1093. *Mr. Taylor to the same.* Of the apprehension excited by the arming of the Prince Elector. The Danish Ambassador has suddenly taken leave.
Vienna, May 19.

1094. *(James Erskine) Earl of Buchan to the same*, pressing for an answer to Capt. Alex. Erskine's proposition.
Paris, May 20.

1095. *The same to the same*, of Count Egmont's visit to England.
Paris, May 26.

1096. *Mr. Taylor to the same.* The King of Denmark has been requested by the King of Hungary to induce the Prince Elector not to be precipitate in taking up arms, holding out hopes of the Lower Palatinate. News has come of the loss of Meppin, which he thinks will prove of great importance to the Prince Elector, and to Holland, the neutrality of Friesland being now broken by Gallas. A review of the power of the Empire from the Adriatic to the Baltic. There is an excellent intelligence between Holstein and Denmark, which it is hoped will daily increase. Guetz is retiring before Duke Weimar.
Vienna, June 2.

1638.
Paris,
June 15.
1097. *(James Erskine) Earl of Buchan to Secretary Windebank*, recommending his brother, the bearer, to his kindness. Is leaving this place, in which there is nothing but perfidy and treason.

Corunna,
June 15.
1098. *Sir A. Hopton to the same.* The Condé Duke is sending one Ilabthorpe, a Jesuit, into England. Desires information concerning Scotch and other affairs, and how he is to behave to Mr. Christopher Windebank if he returns with his wife to Madrid.

June ?.
1099. *Notes* of a Suit in Chancery, between Lady Ashley and the Dowager Countess of Clare, the latter being accused of fraudulently preventing a settlement by the late Earl of 1000*l*. per annum on his son Denzil Hollis, with a view to his marriage with Lady Ashley's daughter.

In Lord Clarendon's hand.

Rehnen,
June 15.
1100. *The Prince Palatine (Charles Lewis) to His Majesty*, referring to the bearer for news of his undertakings.

Cl. S. P. vol. ii. p. 10.

Vienna,
June 16.
1101. *Mr. Taylor to Secretary Windebank.* A minute account of Gallas' forces in Lower Saxe and Westphalia. On the Rhine, a convoy from the Swiss to Duke Weimar has been intercepted by the garrison of Brisach. The strength and position of Guetz' forces. Position of the Spaniards and French in Italy, the Spaniards having broken the neutrality with the Duchess of Savoy.

Vienna,
June 1?.
1102. *The same to the same.* Unimportant news of the siege of Brisach. The journey holds for Prague the 1st of July.

Vienna,
June 29.
1103. *The same to the same.* War news; of Brisach, the arming of Denmark, the complaints against Gallas, and the movements of the Margrave of Brandenburgh. Renews his arguments about his want of credentials, and the King's refusal to answer the King of Hungary's letter. Is going to Prague.

Vienna,
July 7.
1104. *The same to the same.* Brisach is relieved, and Duke Weimar retired. The Hollanders have been defeated near Antwerp, and the French near St. Omer's, and Chatillon taken prisoner. Great war preparations in men and money. The Prince Elector is said to be levying forces at Emden. Nothing can be done for England till the King makes approaches. Cannot go to Prague for want of money.

1105. *Sir A. Hopton to Secretary Windebank.* Has been courteously received, and has answered only in general terms about the Emperor's title. The Condé Duke complains that Richelieu gives out that his personal hatred of him is the cause of the war, whereas he has everything to gain by peace. The Palatinate business stands much as it did.
Partly in cypher, decyphered by Windebank.
1639. Madrid, July 1/7.

1106. *Mr. Taylor to the same.* Brandenburgh is marching with 20,000 men on the Swedes at Stettin. Desires some recompense to his wife and children in consideration of his ten years' service.
Vienna, July 15.

1107. *Paper of Memoranda,* of business transacted at a Privy Council, consisting principally of notes about money to be obtained, and preparations for war at Hull and other places.
In Secretary Windebank's hand.
Whitehall, July 18.

1108. *Sir A. Hopton to Secretary Windebank.* The Condé Duke continues his professions of good-will. Believes the general wish of Spain is to give the King satisfaction in Germany, but the Condé Duko and the old Condé d'Oñate oppose it. Has not opened the fisheries question, having waited to see what they would do in a parallel case with the Genoese.
Madrid, July 1/3.

1109. *Mr. Taylor to the same.* Acknowledges that he has spoken, but only in general terms, of the King's willingness to assist in the defence of Flanders, if satisfied in the Palatinate business. Unimportant war news. Earnestly repeats his application for money, and some reward to his family.
Vienna, July 21.

1110. *Sir A. Hopton to the same.* Of the bad success of the Spaniards at Biscay. The Condé Duke shuffles about the fisheries business, and desires the King to supply some Irish levies for the service of Spain, to which he has objected, that all the Irish who enter the Spanish service become traitors to the King.
Madrid, Aug. 1/3.

1111. *Mr. Taylor to the same.* Recounts the good effects in Germany and Spain which the King's recognition of the Emperor would have. The Duke of Saxe and Margrave of Brandenburgh have received investiture of all they hold in the Empire, and the King of Denmark is to receive the same of Holstein and Bremen. Deputies from Lunenburgh, Oldenburgh, and Wirtzburgh on the same business. Spain is to receive investiture for Milan and Sienna, and
Prague, Aug. 7.

1639. a time is to be fixed for the Duchess of Savoy to demand the same. Curtius is near Hamburgh, with passports for the Swedish and French Commissioners to the treaty at Lubeck. Guetz has retired into Wirtemburgh. Desires money or his recall. It will not do to trust to a coming peace for the accommodation of the Palatinate. Philosophers have long talked "de anno Platonico," when all the astres should return to their first aspects, and we may wait as long before things return to the state of the year '18. Encloses the next.

    1112. Luxemburg, May 25. *Passport* from the Emperor to the Swedish Plenipotentiaries for the conference at Lubeck.—Latin.   *Copy.*

Madrid, Aug. 15.
    1113. *Sir A. Hopton to Secretary Windebank.* The Condé Duke is exceedingly importunate to get the Irish levies some secret way, that the French may not ask the like. Fuentarabia still holds out, though growing every day more desperate.

Aug. 12.
    1114. *The Condé Duke d'Olivarez to Sir A. Hopton.* A note requesting 6000 or at the least 4000 infantry.—Spanish.
   Copy.
   By Sir A. Hopton, endorsed "The 3rd Billet."

Westminster, Aug. 11.
    1115. *Secretary Windebank to His Majesty*, enclosing despatches, and representing a saving of 1400*l.* a-year, by appointing the two Secretaries of State as postmasters for foreign parts.
   Apostiled by the King.   Cl. S. P. vol. ii. p. 11.

Prague, Aug. 14.
    1116. *Mr. Taylor to Secretary Windebank.* News of the movements of Gallas, who has marched to meet Banner.

Prague, Aug. 21.
    1117. *The same to the same.* Guetz and the Duke of Saxe have been defeated in a bloody engagement by Duke Bernard. The King of Polonia is on his way to Vienna, on pretext of taking hot baths. Repeats his request to have credentials sent him or to be recalled.

Westminster, Aug. 24.
    1118. *Secretary Windebank to His Majesty.* Asks advice concerning the return of the Marquis de la Vieuville to the Princess Phalsburgh.
   Apostiled by the King.   Cl. S. P. vol. ii. p. 12.

Prague, Aug. 28.
    1119. *Mr. Taylor to Secretary Windebank.* Gallas and Banner each shun the other. Guetz is collecting troops

again. There are evil reports of Scotland, and rumours of 1638.
the failure of Sir Thomas Roe's negotiation, which do much
hurt. Repeats his request to be recalled. The King of Denmark offers a league offensive and defensive to the Emperor,
but on mighty conditions. Bavaria has received investiture.

<small>The last part in cypher, decyphered by Windebank, but partially obliterated.</small>

1120. *Mr. Taylor to Secretary Windebank.* The Empire's Prague,
policy is one of defence, Sweden being nearly exhausted, and Sept. 4.
likely to receive but little help from France. All Germany
is united and desirous of peace. Has little hopes of the
Palatinate business receiving help from the King of Denmark.
Suggests that the King should offer to mediate between the
Empire and Sweden. Duke Weimar is still about Brisach.
The expense which the King of Polonia causes at Vienna
by his train of 1000 attendants makes them curse his coming.
The plague is said to be exceeding hot among the Swedes.

1121. *Secretary Windebank to His Majesty.* Desires in- Drury
structions for Lord Leicester concerning Madame de Rohan's Lane,
business, suggesting that Mons. de Soubize be advised with. Sept. 8.

1122. *His Majesty to the Infant Cardinal*, recommending Oatlands,
the Marquis de la Vieuville to his favour.   *Copy.* Sept. 9.
<small>Endorsed by Windebank as sent by Sir Balthazar Gerbier.</small>

1123. *Mr. Taylor to Secretary Windebank.* Of Curtius' suc- Prague,
cess with the King of Denmark, and Sir Thos. Roe's failure. Sept. 11.

1124. *Sir A. Hopton to the same.* News of the war in Madrid,
Fuenterabia. Has learnt that his brother is dead, and de- Sept. 15.
sires the King's protection during his absence to the estate
to which he succeeds thereby. The knave priest who made
Mr. Christopher Windebank's match is dismissed all his
offices for it.

1125. *Secretary Windebank to His Majesty,* forwarding Sir Drury
A. Hopton's despatches concerning recruiting in Ireland for Lane,
Spain and the fisheries question. Sept. 17.
<small>Apostiled by the King.   Cl. S. P. vol. II. p. 12.</small>

1126. *The same to the same.* Asks the warrant of his Drury
handwriting on the margin of a letter to the Princess Phals- Lane,
burgh, and suggests the conferring of knighthood upon Sept. 18.
Gerbier.
<small>Apostiled by the King.   Cl. S. P. vol. II. p. 14.</small>

1638.
Hampton Court,
Sept. 18.

1127. *Instructions for Captain William Legg concerning the Ordnance, Arms, and Provisions sent to Kingston-upon-Hull.* Among others 8000 muskets and 2000 pikes are mentioned, to be brought out of the Low Countries by Sir Jacob Ashley. He is to sell powder and shot only on production of authorized certificates. To go thence to Newcastle, leaving six diculverings of iron with their field carriages and upon unshod wheels, with their ladles and sponges, for the fortification of the town. The prices are to be as follows: powder 1s. 6d. the lb.; English match 45s. the cwt.; Dutch match 30s. do.; musket shot 18s. do.

> An order of Privy Council, signed by the Archbishop of Canterbury and nine other Privy Councillors.

Hampton Court,
Sept. 18.

1128. *Instructions for Thomas Heath, Storekeeper at Newcastle*, to the same purport as the last. The following additional prices are annexed: muskets 18s. 6d.; bandaleers 3s.; rests for muskets 10d.; long pikes 3s. 2d.; coralets, consisting of back, breast, gorget, and headpiece, 22s.; swords 7s. 6d.; girdles and hangers 2s.

> Signed as before, and countersigned by Secretary Nicholas.

Prague,
Sept. 18.

1129. *Mr. Taylor to Secretary Windebank.* They are confident of being able to relieve Brisach. The King of Polonia is still at the bath, but receives no benefit.

London,
Sept. 21.

1130. *Mr. Gerbier to the same*, enclosing copies of the Princess Phalsburgh's propositions, and asking the warrant of his own hand.

Drury Lane,
Sept. 21.

1131. *Secretary Windebank to His Majesty.* Encloses an amended copy of the answer to the Princess Phalsburgh's propositions, and asks directions thereon.

> Apostiled by the King. Cl. S. P. vol. II. p. 15.

Hampton Court,
Sept. 23.

1132. *The Archbishop of Canterbury (Laud) to Secretary Windebank.* Approves of the refusal to allow a Bishop* to go abroad. Desires Sir W. Hamilton to be instructed to prevent the creation of English titular Bishops at Rome, and to disavow the King's wish that Mr. Conn should be created Cardinal.

> Cl. S. P. vol. II. p. 17.

Hampton Court,
Sept. 24.

1133. *A Memorial for (Mountjoy Blount) Earl of Newport, Master of the Ordnance.* To order Capt. Legg to survey the Holy Islands.

> Signed by Nicholas.

---

* Godfrey Goodman, Bishop of Gloucester, lately converted to Popery, who applied for leave to go abroad for the benefit of his health.

1134. *Mr. Gerbier to Secretary Windebank.* Mr. Barkley will visit him for instructions to Sir William Boswell concerning the Queen-Mother. — Kingston, Sept. 15. 1638.

1135. *Mr. Taylor to the same.* Details at great length a conversation with Baron de Rock, President of the Council of the Empire, and Count Sleek, President of the Council of War, wherein he has complained vehemently to them of their indifference to the great services done them by the King, notably in Flanders, and their enormous demand. They excuse themselves by laying the blame upon the abominable conduct of Spain, assuring him that Bavaria is gained over to their own views. They in turn complain of the conduct of the Prince Elector, his own want of credentials, and the refusal of the title of "Emperor." His own conclusion thereon is, that they are sincere but tied by Spain. News from Brisach and the seat of war. Curtius is gone to Lubeck to meet the Swedish Plenipotentiaries. The King of Polonia is better. — Prague, Sept. 15.

1136. *Secretary Windebank to Sir A. Hopton.* An account of his family troubles. His nephew Rob. Reade and his son Tom have both had small-pox badly, and himself a fever, the new disease of the time, whereof few families in England are free. Approves of his conduct in the fisheries business and the matter of the Irish levies. If pressed, he is to say that the King will not grant levies to any, having refused the French, but will allow recruiting for old companies indifferently to all. Sir Thos. Roe does not advance much in his negotiations. The Queen-Mother, he hopes, is lodged in Holland for some time. — London, Sept. 30.

Rough draught in his own hand, and endorsed by himself.

1137. *Declaration* of Mr. Gerbier to the two Secretaries of State, the Lord Treasurer, and the Earl Marshal, that he has discovered during his stay at Brussels a plot of President Cogneux Faboroni and Monsigot to induce the Queen-Mother to come to England.—French. *Copy.* — Oct. 2.

In his own hand.

1138. *Propositions de la part de Madame la Princesse de Phalsbourgh, et la Response de sa Majesté de la Grande Bretagne.* The propositions are for a league between England, Spain, and the Emperor, against France, on the basis of a complete restitution of the Prince Elector, and the creation — Brussels, July 13. London, Oct. 6.

1638. (if necessary) of an eighth Electorate for the Duke of Bavaria. The answer expresses a modified assent.—French.

> The propositions are in the hand of Gerbier, the answer in that of Windebank. Another copy, dated Sept. 15, is in Gerbier's hand throughout, but the marginal answers signed "C. R." in the King's hand. This is endorsed by Windebank, "as the Copy sent to the King in his despatch of Sept. 18." An amended copy, somewhat different, also occurs, being that sent by Windebank to the King in his despatch of Sept. 22, which was not signed by the King.
>
> Cl. S. P. vol. II, p. 16.

Oct. 6. 1139. *Secretary Windebank to Mr. Gerbier.* He is not to deliver out of his own hands the King's answer to the propositions.—French.   *Rough Draught.*

> In his own hand, and endorsed by him.

Prague, Oct. 9. 1140. *Mr. Taylor to Secretary Windebank.* The King of Polonia has obtained a pass for the Duke of Simeren (the Prince Elector's uncle) to this court, of which he has complained, as being a slight to the King's request, but is met by the old argument of non-acknowledgment. Fuentarabia and Brisach are relieved. Debates the question of the King's mediation between the Emperor and Sweden.

Venice, Oct. 15/5. 1141. *Mr. Francis Hyde to Mr. Edward Hyde*, thanking him for his care in the business of their cousins Laurence and Valentine. Valenza still holds out, though besieged by the united forces of France, Savoy, Parma, and Mantona.

> This letter is endorsed by Lord Clarendon "H. Hyde;" but the signature is plainly "Fran."

Oct. 20. 1142. *Proposition of (Charles IV) Duke of Lorraine to His Majesty, and His Majesty's Answer.* The proposition is to the effect that if the King will induce France to restore the Duchy of Lorraine, the Duke of Bavaria will restore the Electorate to the Prince Palatine; on the failure of either party, the Prince and Duke to join forces to compel compliance. The King answers courteously, declining to take any steps till he has the signature of the Duke of Bavaria to the proposition. —French.

> Copies by Windebank. Two copies of the answer, slightly differing from each other; one endorsed by Windebank, with the date.

Vienna, Nov. 3. 1143. *Mr. Taylor to Secretary Windebank.* There is rumour of the total defeat of the Prince Elector.

Vienna, Nov. 3. 1144. *The same to the same.* The defeat of the Prince Elector is attributed to the cavalry, which ran away. The Prince is said to be dead of his wounds, as also General King. Hartsfeld will not deliver Prince Rupert to the Bavarians, but bring him hither with all respect.

1145. *Sir A. Hopton to Lord Cottington.* Complains of the coolness of the Condé Duke in the affair of the Palatinate, and gives his opinion that neither the French nor Spaniards in any treaty will give any satisfaction, farther than mere promises will go. 1638. Madrid, Nov. 7.
Endorsed by Windebank.

1146. *The same to Secretary Windebank.* Further details of the design in behalf of the Prince Elector. Spain to retain part of the Palatinate for the present, and to pay the Prince 100,000, or 200,000 crowns per annum, he to reside there, hold a city or two, and refrain from all hostilities. The Electorate not to be despaired of. A Scottish Jesuit, named Semple, an ambitious and vain man, will be employed in the business. Madrid, Nov. 7/17.
In cypher, decyphered by Windebank.

1147. *The same to the same.* Has heard from the Secretary to the German Embassage that the Emperor is anxious to settle the Palatinate business. Recommends the young Count Trautmansdorff, who is going to England. Madrid, Nov. 9.
Principally in cypher, decyphered by Windebank.

1148. *The same to the same.* Has seen Father Semple, who confirms the account in his last. The Emperor's Ambassador at Madrid is anxious for the settlement, his whole patrimony of 60,000 francs per annum lying within six leagues of Heidelberg, and now yielding nothing. Is assured by him that the whole Palatine, if restored, would not yield 100,000 crowns in the lifetime of the Prince Elector. Madrid, Nov. 12/22.
Two copies in cypher, one decyphered by Windebank.

1149. *Mr. Taylor to the same.* Of the confinement of Prince Rupert at Neustadt, and the movements of the Duke of Lorrain's forces at Brisach. Vienna, Nov. 10.
Cl. S. P. vol. ii. p. 16, (with the exception of a postscript).

1150. *Minutes* of the Committee, relative to the preparation of forces for Scotland. Whitehall, Nov. 11.
In the hands of Lord Cottington and Windebank.

1151. *Capt. Legge to Secretary Windebank.* The arms are not yet arrived. Kingston-on-Hull, Nov. 16.

1152. *Sir A. Hopton to the same.* The Condé Duke has inquired whether there be any thing in the news about the Princess Phalsburgh's treaty, complaining that negotiations Madrid, Nov. 15.

1638.   should be carried on through a third party. He has given an evasive answer, and pressed him afresh about the Palatinate, wherein he makes professions, whereof he can form no judgment, because of his closeness, wilfulness, and hard-heartedness.
Two copies in cypher, one decyphered by Windebank.

Whitehall, Nov. 18.   1153. *Minutes* of the Committee for Scotland on two occasions, appointing Sir Jacob Ashley Commissary General with Lord Clifford at York.
In Windebank's hand.

Nov. 27. Dec. 7.   1154. *Don Alonso de Cardeñas to Secretary Windebank*, defending his conduct in the proposition of the treaty conference to Flanders, and enclosing a letter of the Condé d'Oñate, which he considers sufficient to justify him.—Spanish.

Dec. 3.   1155. *Minutes* concerning the raising 2000 horse and 10,400 foot, and the fixing a rendezvous.
In Windebank's hand.

Drury Lane, Dec. 4.   1156. *Secretary Windebank to Sir A. Hopton.* Informs him of Cardeñas having offended the King by a letter sent into Germany, and discovered by Sir Thomas Roe, and declaring him no fit minister for this Court. He is to press the King of Spain to give satisfaction to Mr. Ricaut, in whose debt he is. His son Christopher writes from Italy and promises to remain there and in France. The Queen-Mother is here, and receives an allowance from the King of 100l. a-day.
Duplicate by himself, principally in cypher.

Vienna, Dec. 8.   1157. *Mr. Taylor to Secretary Windebank.* The bad news from Brisach, the suspicion that Bavaria has a secret understanding with France, and the threatened invasion of Polonia by the Turks, make them eager to come to terms with Sweden. Prince Rupert will be taken to Neustadt next week.

Dec. 12.   1158. *Address* of Anthony Champeney, Dean of the Secular Catholic Clergy in England, exhorting them to pray for the King's success against the Scots. *Copy.*
Endorsed and dated by Windebank.

Vienna, Dec. 15.   1159. *Mr. Taylor to Secretary Windebank.* News from Brisach. The great zeal and affection of the Duke of Lorraine.

Vienna, Dec. 22.   1160. *The same to the same.* An account of the jealousies between the commanders before Brisach. A lengthy narrative of interviews with Trautmandorf, and the Duke of Lor-

raine, of the same import as former conversations. Points
out in detail the growing power of the French, whose aim is,
in his opinion, to regain the Empire. They would serve the
Prince Elector even worse than the Swedes served his father.
Earnestly presses however that one course or the other be
taken.

1639.

1161. *Secretary Windebank to Sir A. Hopton.* Gives a full
account of the negotiations with the Princess Phalsburg, and
minute instructions how he is to treat with Father Semple in
the matter. The King is willing to treat with Spain for a
league on the ground of those propositions, if a fit person
be sent in the room of Cardeñas. The letter of Cardeñas
which gave offence was addressed to the Marquis of Castaneda
in Germany.

Dec. 17.

Draught in his own hand, in two parts, the latter endorsed, "This was added to the despatch of Dec. 17."

1162. *Mr. Taylor to Secretary Windebank.* Brisach is at its
last gasp. The French King is marching on Burgundy with
a large army. They are very solicitous that the King of Denmark should mediate for them with the Swedes. Despairs of
any good issue to the King of the present state of affairs.

Vienna, Dec. 19.

1163. *Reasons* against the design of the Pope to send a
Prepositus into England over the secular clergy, without
defining his jurisdiction, and hoping that the King will
effectually remonstrate with the Pope's Agent.

No date.

Endorsed "Mr. Gage," but not in his hand.

1164. *A Design to extricate His Majesty out of these present
troubles with the Scots, and at once to render him free from the
Minors of His Majesty's Royal Prerogative in England.* Suggests the raising of 10,000 men in Flanders, employing Col.
Gage to gain the consent of the Infant Cardinal, and Dr.
Holden to bribe the Pope by promise of abrogating the laws
against Recusants, to persuade the English Catholics to
maintain the army.

No date.

In Mr. Gage's hand.   Cl. S. P. vol. II. p. 19.

1165. *List of Addresses* of the following agents: Sir William
Boswell at the Hague, Sir Henry de Vic at Brussels, Mr.
Richard Brown at Paris, Sir Thomas Roe Ambassador Extraordinary at Vienna, Sir Arthur Hopton at Madrid, Mr.
John Talbot at Venice.

No date.

1166. *A List of the Trainbands, both horse and foot*, in the
counties of Cumberland, Northumberland, Westmoreland,

No date.

1638. York, Durham, Lancaster, Cheshire, Nottingham, Stafford, Derby, Lincoln, Leicester, Rutland, and the town of Newcastle, with the Lord Lieutenants of each: the whole amounting to 19,579 foot and 1363 horse.

In Windebank's hand.

No date. 1167. *Minutes* concerning provisions, and other necessaries.

In Lord Cottington's hand.

1638–9.
Vienna,
Jan. 4.

1168. *Mr. Taylor to Secretary Windebank,* strongly recommending for the King's service the bearer, the Earl of Crawford, who has lately come into the title by the death of his brother.

Brussels,
Jan. 8.

1169. *Col. Henry Gage to the same.* Answers two complaints brought against him by Sir William Tresham, relative to the regiments under their several command, serving with Prince Thomas; and accuses him in turn of, having aggregated the remains of his (English) regiment to the disaffected (Irish) regiment of Don Eugenio O'Neale. Capt. Pavier has also a complaint against Sir William, with reference to the raising some levies for the King of Spain.

Drury
Lane,
Jan. 11.

1170. *Secretary Windebank to Mr. Taylor,* ordering him to return at once to England. *Copy.*

By himself.

Vienna,
Jan. 12.

1171. *Mr. Taylor to Secretary Windebank.* Count Piccolomini has arrived, and reports that England is treating very hotly at Brussels. Renews his assurances of the good intentions of this Court. Prince Rupert is daily expected, and will be well treated, being likely to be liberated on parole. Hartsfeld praises him for ripeness of judgment far beyond his years. Proposes to meet him on his way and instruct him in the state of affairs. The character of Baron de Reck, who is entirely on our side, and a story of Trautmandorf at a Court sermon, in which Father Gaus reflected strongly on him, likening the loss of the Saviour by his parents to the loss of Drisach, and the ignorant doctors in the Temple to the Emperor's ministers. Lord Craven has paid his ransom and comes with Prince Rupert.

Principally in cypher, decyphered by Windebank.

Jan. 11.

1172. *A Letter* (probably from some official to Secretary Windebank), desiring from the King that plaster moulds be procured for him of the marble heads of Julius Cæsar, Marcus Marcellus, and Hannibal, at Aranjuez. *Copy.*

By Windebank.

1173. *Sir A. Hopton to Secretary Windebank.* A Franciscan Friar, named Murtagh O'Grady, has advertised this King of a colony of 2000 Irish in the island of St Christopher, which he offers to bring away and enlist in the service of Spain, intending himself to embark at Bristol. Father Semple tells him that Lord Buchan has orders to deal in the Palatinate business, and he fears that he may introduce some impracticable conditions from the Prince Elector and the Queen of Bohemia, in whose confidence he is. — 1638–9. Madrid, Jan. 14.

1174. *Mr. Taylor to the same.* The report of treaties at Brussels is a device of the Spaniards to prevent this Court coming to any final resolution; at which he has expressed strong indignation at Court. The Condé Duke is cursed here by all men. The Spanish Ambassador has taken investiture of Milan, Burgundy, and the provinces of the Low Countries. Warns him that Bavaria and France have a secret understanding. — Vienna, Jan. 19.

Principally in cypher, decyphered by Windebank.

1175. *Secretary Windebank to Sir A. Hopton.* Instructs him to clear the Queen-Mother from the imputation of being the author of a manifesto reflecting upon the Infant Cardinal's treatment of her while residing at Brussels, and to procure the restitution of her Resident, who, on account of this forgery, had been disgraced. An account of the loss of his despatch concerning the Condé Duke's letters, through the laziness of a postboy. The Queen after a dangerous labour was delivered last Sunday the 20th of a daughter, who lived only long enough to be christened Catherine. The Lord Deputy has been informed of the Irish Colonels Tyrone and Tyrconnell levying men for Spain without the King's leave. One thousand recruits have been sent to Flanders to the English regiments, though the quarrels between Col. Gage and Sir W. Tresham do much to lessen the value of the favour. — Jan. 22.

Rough Draught.
By himself.

1176. *Sir A. Hopton to Secretary Windebank.* Relates the specious professions of the Condé Duke, who appears desirous to treat secretly and confidentially with him, whereby he is induced to believe that the business of the Palatinate is now resolved on both here and in Germany, but it must begin here. The Condé Duke hints at a marriage between the children of the two Crowns. — Madrid, Jan. 22.

1177. *The same to the same.* A general loan is to be made. — Madrid, Jan. 26.

1638-9. and 3000 men embarked for Flanders, with 1000 for Lisbon, a sign that kingdom is not yet settled. The Marquis of Villena goes as Viceroy to Mexico, the Marquis of Mancera to Peru. Lord Huchan is getting 4000 ducats of this King through Father Semple, which is suspicious. Mr. Christopher Windebank writes to say he is coming at once.

Madrid, Jan. 16.
1178. *Sir A. Hopton to Lord Cottington.* Spain begins to find how powerful France is since the taking of Brisach, and to prepare accordingly. Has a good opinion of the Condé Duke, as a man who expects no more from others than he is willing to give himself. Has sent the box of seeds, but cannot get a skin of Alcala wine good enough to send.

Vienna, Jan. 16.
1179. *Mr. Taylor to Secretary Windebank.* Recounts proofs of the duplicity of the Infant Cardinal, and hopes that the Emperor is now shaking off the bondage of Spain. Lesly and Piccolomini are very zealous in our behalf. The armies of the Empire are greatly weakened.

Principally in cypher, decyphered by Windebank.

Vienna, Jan. 19.
1180. *The same to the same.* The Marquis de Gonzaga has been sent express to Spain to represent the dangerous state of affairs in Germany, and that the Emperor is absolutely resolved to restore the Prince Elector; since, without it, there can be no peace in Germany. Dilates on the way in which the Infant Cardinal has played false with Piccolomini, pretending to have power to treat at Brussels, while he acknowledged to the Emperor that he had none. The jealousies between the Empire, Spain, and Bavaria increase. Dislikes the leave given to levy 6000 Scotch for the French service. The Emperor and his brother will take the field in person.

Principally in cypher, decyphered by Windebank.

Madrid, Jan. 19.
1181. *Sir A. Hopton to the same.* The Condé Duke delays settling the fishing business, being unwilling to secure to the Hollanders their herring-fishery, which supports their land actions by its profits, and their maritime by the mariners it breeds. He is still very eager for the secret conference, and appears to think Don Alonso de Cardeñas indiscreet.

Feb. 1.
1182. *Memorandum* by Secretary Windebank, recommending that Mr. Gage be employed to his brother, on pretence of a devotion of the Queen, to propose to the Infant Cardinal an exchange of 6000 troops, in consideration of new levies for the English and Irish regiments in Flanders.

1183. *Mr. Taylor to Sir William Howard.* The disposition of this Court is better than ever. Prince Rupert is to go to Lintz.
1638-9. Vienna, Feb. 1.

1184. *The same to Secretary Windebank.* The Empire is driven to desire foreign friendships through the treachery of Bavaria, who is *baculus arundineus, Rex Ægypti*. The marquis de Grani has received orders to seize the land of Cleves, the Court being much offended with the Duke of Newburgh. Rumours that the Prince Elector is to marry the Duke of Florence's sister, and his sister the Duke's brother, and that he has requested the King of Denmark to mediate for him with the Emperor.
Vienna, Feb. 2.
Principally in cypher, decyphered by Windebank.

1185. *Col. Gage to Mr. George Gage.* The French and Hollanders are full of ambitious designs upon Scotland. He finds Prince Thomas and the Spaniards well inclined to his suggestion of an exchange of 4400 soldiers with 10,000 Irish and English. Defends himself and Capt. Pavier against a complaint of Sir W. Tresham.
Brussels, Feb. 5.
Cl. S. P. vol. II. p. 21.

1186. *Instructions for our trusty and well-beloved Colonel Henry Gage, now in the service of the Infant Cardinal in Flanders.* To negotiate the proposed exchange of 6400 troops with Irish and English unarmed recruits.
Feb. 5.
Rough Draught.
By Windebank. Cl. S. P. vol. II. p. 23.

1187. *Mr. Taylor to Secretary Windebank.* The Empire looks to the King as the one from whom their defence must come, and by whom they must subsist. Hopes they will send Lesly to England. At present they will communicate through the Duke of Lorraine and the Princess Phalsburgh. The King and the Prince Elector must forget past ill-usage.
Vienna, Feb. 9.
Partly in cypher, decyphered by Windebank.

1188. *The same to the same.* The Court holds to its resolution of sending to England. The Pope in vain urges a cessation of arms. Since the taking of Babilau by the Turks it is more feared he will break with the Venetians.
Vienna, Feb. 16.

1189. *Col. Gage to the same.* The Infant Cardinal seems willing to make the exchange, but fears weakening himself too much, and the difficulty of raising so many men in England and Ireland. Suggests some difficulties about the payment of the men.
Brussels, Feb. 18.
Cl. S. P. vol. II. p. 24.

1638-9.
Madrid,
Feb. 16.

1190. *Sir A. Hopton to Secretary Windebank.* The Condé Duke entirely disavows the propounder of the proposition (Father Semple), who is probably prompted by the Condé de Schomberg; though he seems not to dislike the substance of it.
Partly in cypher.

Brussels,
Feb. 19.

1191. *Mr. George Gage to the same.* Gives an account of the defeat of the Spanish fleet by the Dutch yesterday in the roads of Dunkirk. The Spaniards are compelled to wait for convoy from England. Sends messages to Father Philips (the Queen's Confessor) that he is engaged upon the Queen's business.

Madrid,
Feb. 24.

1192. *Sir A. Hopton to the same.* Expresses his doubts whether they will entertain the proposition, though inclined to believe the Condé Duke sincere in the matter.
Partly in cypher, decyphered by Windebank.

Madrid,
Feb. 25.

1193. *Don Juan de Necolalde to the same.* A complimentary letter, offering his services in Flanders, whither he is about to be sent.—Spanish.
Endorsed by Windebank.

Madrid,
Feb. 28.

1194. *Sir A. Hopton to the same.* A minute account of conversations with Father Semple and the Condé Duke, whence he gathers that the propositions will come to nothing. The Nuntio and Venetian Ambassador are attempting to negotiate a peace, the great difficulty being the restitution of Lorraine, to which Spain is strictly engaged, though if great advantage offered they would find, he thinks, a dispensation for their promises. The Condé Duke still dwells upon the secret conference. Has spoken of the conduct of Cardeñas to the King and Condé Duke.

Madrid,
Feb. 28.

1195. *The same to Lord Cottington.* They will probably remove Cardeñas, if they can supply his place. Discusses the Scotch troubles, and advises that the disease be searched to the bottom and cured with a gentle hand, otherwise it will hereafter break out more violently. Sends some Calabaça seeds and Oregones wine.

Dublin,
March 2.

1196. *The Lord Deputy (Wentworth) to Secretary Windebank.* Demurs to the grant of lands worth 30,000*l.* to Lord St. Albans without further orders, and complains of the many requests contrary to his instructions, which he is obliged to undergo ill-will by refusing, arguing at length against the remittance of Mr. Smith's fine of 1000 marks for a conspiracy against Sir A. Blundell, as calculated to make the decrees of his Court *bruta fulmina*. With great earnestness he demurs to the appointment of the young Earl of Desmond, nephew to the Duke of Buckingham, to the command of a troop, as an infringement of his privileges, complaining bitterly of the Earl of Holland, and shewing the ill consequence of such an example. Points out that Lord Chichester had lands to the value of 10,000*l.* a-year at one gift, and Lord Falkland 10,000*l.* in money at once. Strongly distrusts the Earl of Antrim's ability to do anything against the Earl of Argyle, and objects to supplying his force of 6000 men with arms at the King's expense, much more to place the men under Col. Neale, understood to be a traitor. Thinks the Scotch are conscious they have gone beyond all terms of reconciliation, and advises that Newcastle be protected by an army, and strong garrisons placed in Berwick and Carlisle. The King should put himself confidently in the hands of his English subjects. It would be impossible to raise even 5000*l.* in Ireland. The troops for St. Bees shall be on board by the 20th.

1638-9.

Partly in his own hand. Printed in Strafford's Letters, vol. ii. p. 292.

1197. *Col. Henry Gage to Secretary Windebank.* The Infant Cardinal is obliged unwillingly, for the present, to refuse the levies required. They fear a great invasion, this spring, of the French, who are impetuous at first, but their impetuosity being broken, are the easiest men under heaven to be dealt with. Piccolomini is coming to Brussels with power to treat of the Palatinate. The Lord Marshal should answer his letters more punctually, as he is inclined to resent the slight.

Brussels, March 1/3.

1198. *Mr. George Gage to the same.* His extreme grief for the failure of his business has thrown him into an illness. Gives his brother's opinion, dissuading the King from using the Irish for any sudden assaults, no raw troops of any nation being equal to the English, when led by resolute commanders.

Brussels, March 1/3.

No signature ; endorsed by Windebank.

1199. *Mr. Taylor to the same.* Has never had better hopes of the business than now, when all agree to advance it. Duke John of Nassau of Adenar is to go plenipotentiary to Brussels. Is very indignant with the Scots.

Vienna, March 2.

1200. *Colonel Gage to the same.* Gives reasons at length why the levies cannot be granted at present, and suggests that the English troops in Flanders be employed, as being excellent troops if well commanded, with peculiar powers of enduring hardships.

Brussels, March 5.

1638-9.
Brussels,
March 5.

1201. *Mr. George Gage to Secretary Windebank.* The Infant Cardinal will not, though desirous, be able to make the proposed exchange. News of the Spaniards' repulse at Bouzy, Cambray, and Dunkirk. Suggests the recall of his brother, and Lieut.-General Dowridge, an eminent artillery officer and engineer.
Cl. S. P. vol. ii. p. 16.

Madrid,
March 7.

1202. *The King of Spain (Philip IV) to His Majesty.* Letters of revocation of the Condé d'Oñate and Villa-Mediana.—Latin.

Endorsed by Windebank, as presented by the Condé at his leavetaking on May 13.

Madrid,
March 9.

1203. *Sir A. Hopton to Secretary Windebank.* The Condé Duke and the King of Hungary's Ambassador disavow the proposition, as coming through Semple. Recapitulates his opinion on the prospects of the proposed treaty, and a peace with France. A loan has been taken up at 8 per cent., payable on the arrival of the plate fleet in May. Is not sufficiently informed concerning some merchants' complaints forwarded to him by the Board.
Principally in cypher, decyphered by Windebank.

Vienna,
March 9.

1204. *Mr. Taylor to the same.* Is starting immediately for England.

Vienna,
March 11.

1205. *Count Leslie to the same.* Hopes the King will receive reasonable satisfaction in the business of the Palatinate. Is much grieved at Taylor's recal.

March 15.

1206. *Secretary Windebank to Sir Arthur Hopton.* Explains Gage's negotiation for the exchange of troops, wherewith to surprise Edinburgh Castle, and its failure. The King will be at York with 7000 troops by April 1st. No Irish troops can be spared to Spain except in exchange. Accuses Lord Buchan of forging credentials to treat with Spain in the Palatinate business.
Rough Draught.
By himself. Cl. S. P. vol. ii. p. 19, (with immaterial omissions).

Madrid,
March 19.

1207. *Sir A. Hopton to Secretary Windebank.* The Condé Duke has informed him of what he has heard from the Infant Cardinal of the Princess Phalsburgh's propositions, and another offer made in Germany to the Emperor. He gathers that they will only be willing to restore what they have in their own power, and will expect the King to do something against France. The Condé Duke is very bitter against the German nation. Does not hope much from the Emperor, or Schomberg, who, he hears, is a pensioner of the Duke of Bavaria. *Two Copies.* 1638-9.

Principally in cypher, one decyphered by Windebank.

1208. *Sir A. Hopton to Lord Cottington.* Repeats the opinions he has expressed to Windebank. The Duke of Bavaria's present policy is to weaken the House of Austria, by falling off from it, so that a peace may be made with France, without his being compelled to any restitution. Has heard that the French are helping the Scotch with commanders, and the Duke of Longueville is to be their General. The Duke of la Vallette is condemned to lose his head for treason at Fuentarabia, though the Condé protests his innocence. Madrid, March 19.

1209. *Col. Henry Gage to Secretary Windebank.* A letter of compliment, thanking the King for accepting his fruitless services. Brussels, March 19.

1210. *A Memorial of Don Alonzo de Cardeñas,* requesting protection in the English harbours for some frigates bearing Spanish despatches from Flanders. March 20.

In English. Apparently a copy or translation. Date endorsed by Windebank.

1211. *Mr. H. Tayller to Secretary Windebank,* offering his services at that Court. 1639. Brussels, March 26.

1212. *Instructions to Sir A. Hopton.* Empowering him to act in private conference with the Condé Duke, but only unofficially. The basis of the negotiation to be the Princess Phalsburgh's proposition. Informs him, under the seal of the most profound secrecy, that the King and Queen will not be unwilling to listen to proposals for a match between the children of the two Crowns. The fishery and recruiting questions to be dependent upon the main business. *Draught.* March 26.

By Windebank.

1213. *Sir Arthur Hopton to Secretary Windebank.* The Condé Duke is willing to let the King have 5000 troops, if he will take the coast of Flanders and the Low Countries under his protection. Desires information concerning the fisheries. Cl. S. P. vol. ii. p. 31. Madrid, March 30.

1639.
March 31.

1214. *Secretary Windebank to His Majesty.* Encloses despatches from the Lord Deputy (that of March 2), the Earl of Antrim, and the Infant Cardinal to the Princess Phalsburgh. Desires instructions concerning the Lord General (Earl of Arundell)'s guard; the revocation of patents, especially those on transportation of butter, and cards, and dice; the arrest of thirteen Scotch ships in the port of London, and other minor matters.

Apostiled by the King. "April 2." Ch. S. P. vol. II. p. 31.

No date.

1215. *Minute to the House of Lords.* The King's summons of the Lords to York by April 1st. Rough Draught.
By Windebank.

Brussels, April 2.

1216. *Mr. J. Taylor to Secretary Windebank,* announcing his arrival there.

Brussels, April 2.

1217. *The Cardinal Infant to the Princess Phalsburg,* informing her that he has powers to treat in the matter of the Palatinate, and requesting her to inform the King, that he may send a plenipotentiary to act in his behalf.—French.
Copy.
By Windebank.

April 4.

1218. *A Relation of John Taylor, his Negotiation in Germ-[any, from] the time of the Earl Marshal's departure thenc[e, to the] present 1639, April 4, that by his Majesty's order he [sent] home, wherein will appear his care, zeal, and [diligence] towards his Majesty's service.* A long, minute, and interesting account of the whole of his negotiation at the Court of Vienna for the restitution of the Palatinate, concluding with a summary review of the chief persons and powers with whom he has treated.

Entitled as above, but imperfect.

Madrid, April 7/8.

1219. *Sir A. Hopton to Secretary Windebank.* Doubts the sincerity alike of the Empire and Spain, and attributes their conduct to a slavish fear of the Duke of Bavaria. Lord Huchan has gone to England. Mr. Richaut is likely to be defrauded of his money; but it would be a dangerous reprisal to meddle with the *assentistas* money.

Partly in cypher, decyphered by Windebank.

Madrid, April 7/8.

1220. *The same to Lord Cottington.* The success of all negotiations must depend upon the issue of the tumults in Scotland.

1221. *Secretary Windebank to His Majesty.* Complaint of the unfitness of the Kentish levies for service, both in arms and men. The French Ambassador complains that English merchants contract to take Spanish forces to and from the Low Countries, to which he has answered that the State cannot interfere, and that the merchants do it at their own peril, France being at liberty to treat them as enemies. He is assured by Sir A. Hopton that the transport of men is as justifiable as that of money, and that if not allowed, the King of Spain will seize the merchants' ships for the service. The Ambassador also complains of not being able to procure the promised Scotch levies in consequence of the detention of the Scotch ships.
1639. April 9.

Apostiled by the King, " Good Friday."

1222. *Sir A. Hopton to Lord Cottington.* News of the war preparations for the coming summer. They have levied 20,000 men for the defence of the kingdom, 10,000 for Flanders, 8000 for Italy, now armies in Guipuscoa under the Marquis de los Velez, in Catalonia under the Marquis de Teracusa, in Alsatia under Don Francisco de Melo, and in Burgundy under the Duke of Lorraine. A rumoured league between the Pope, Venice, and the Duke of Florence for clearing Italy of strangers. The characters of the principal Ministers at the Court of Madrid.
Madrid, April 9.

1223. *Secretary Windebank to His Majesty.* Has difficulty in obtaining money. Suggests the suspension of Scottish merchants' privileges in the Dutch States. Of the Lord St. Alban's complaint of the Lord Deputy's delay in confirming his grants from the Crown.
Drury Lane, April 13.

Apostiled by the King. " York, April 16th." Cl. S. P. vol. ii. p. 35.

1224. *Cardinal Genetti to Mons. d'Avaux,* (French Ambassador at Vienna). Curtius writes that he has heard from D'Avaux that the Catholic King has given the Dutch Princes passports to the Conference at Cologne. The King of England has consented to the overtures of the Emperor in the Palatinate affair, as his Resident at Vienna (Mr. Taylor) has declared to the Count of Nassau, the Emperor's Plenipotentiary at Brussels. The Ambassadors from England and Bavaria are expected shortly at Brussels.—Italian.
Cologne, April 14.

Extract by Windebank, with the writer's name endorsed by him. These words are added in his hand: " If this be true and sincere, Mr. Taylor is a brave man, and I shall have no more to do here. But if it be false or feigned, only to propose a specious excuse to exclude us the general treaty, I leave it to my Mr. (Master). Never was greater impudence on Taylor's part, nor more suffering of mine, that protest here the contrary. I hope you will resent it."

1639.
April 19.

1223. *Secretary Windebank to Sir A. Hopton.* The King has no confidence in Semple, and both the Infant Cardinal and the Marquis de Seralbo in Flanders have disavowed the Princess Phalsburgh's propositions, so that that negotiation is at an end. Distrusts the Condé Duke's sincerity in his desire for a private conference, but has nevertheless persuaded the King to send Hopton instructions, as desired. The chief end of the treaty at Brussels is to separate the Prince Elector from his confederates and gain time. The merchants must take heed that they do nothing in transporting men to Flanders in violation of the peace with France, and must not expect any protection. The French King threatens to retaliate by laying an embargo on all English ships and goods. Encloses papers about Ricaut's business. The Scotch affairs are in no good condition; but the King is going from York with 3000 horse and near 10,000 infantry. The Marquis of Hamilton commands eight ships and 5000 men, to attack Scotland on the other side, and a reward is proclaimed for the heads of Argyle and the other chief rebels. Taylor is revoked from Vienna and returned. He has been too busy in delivering papers there in the King's name, which Sir Thomas Roe alleges to be to the prejudice of the treaty with France; and then Hopton may judge in what condition the poor creature is likely to be. *Rough draught.*
In his own hand.

Madrid,
April 19/29.

1226. *Sir A. Hopton to Secretary Windebank.* The extraordinary Ambassador from Germany is on his return, having propounded an accommodation of the Palatinate business, and offered satisfaction to the Duke of Bavaria from his master's own estate, but having obtained no positive answer. Expresses his opinion of the great prosperity of Spain, and its power by land and sea; their only weak point being Burgundy. The Turks' descent upon Christendom is held to be certain.

Madrid,
April 19/29.

1227. *The same to Secretary Coke.* Treats of the claim made by the King to Virginia, and the treatment of English with letters of marque on that coast, which he thinks a very serious matter, and likely to lead to war. Details the great forces and preparations of Spain. The business of the merchants in the Terçeras has been favourably settled.

Madrid,
April 19/29.

1228. *The same to Lord Cottington,* to the same purport as that to Coke. There seems to be this fatality about the Palatinate business, that each side attempts to force an advantage from the other. Advises that they be taken while they are in good humour, for Spain will always be able to prop up the Imperial Crown.

1639.

1229. *His Majesty to Secretary Windebank.* Orders the suppression of the Proclamation for Scotland, and the printing a new form, which he encloses.

York, April 20.

Cl. S. P. vol. ii. p. 37.

1230. *The same to the same.* Announces the attachment of Lords Say and Brook, and desires information from his Attorney and Solicitor (Sir John Banks and Sir Edward Lyttleton) whether a Lord is not censurable who refuses to serve him in wars out of the kingdom, when offered sufficient pay.

York, April 21.

Cl. S. P. vol. ii. p. 38.

1231. *Petition to the Queen from the Recusants in Berkshire,* that proceedings at Abingdon against Mr. Anthony Englefield* and others may be stopped.

No date.

Endorsed by Windebank as delivered by the Queen, April 21, 1639.
Cl. S. P. vol. ii. p. 38.

1232. *Secretary Windebank to His Majesty.* Complains that he is not sufficiently informed by his brother Secretary. Has used the King's name to gain the Lord Keeper's assistance with the country gentry.

Drury Lane, April 24.

Apostiled by the King, "York, April 27." Cl. S. P. vol. ii. p. 39, (with the omission of a postscript).

1233. *The same to the same.* Of the attachment of the two Lords; the supply of money; and a plot of Capt. Napier and one Farloe against the Archbishop of Canterbury.

Drury Lane, April 30.

Apostiled by the King, "Durham, May 4." Cl. S. P. vol. ii. p. 40.

1234. *Sir A. Hopton to Secretary Windebank.* The German Ambassador's proposition is that a pass be granted to the Prince Elector, as to the other Princes, to treat at Cologne. This is thought derogatory, and it is proposed that he should treat apart through the King at Brussels.

Madrid, May 1/11.

In cypher, decyphered by Windebank.

1235. *The same to Lord Cottington.* Of the state of the Spanish shipping, and the little likelihood of peace. The glimmering of hope in the Palatinate business has died out again.

Madrid, May 1/11.

* He was Collector for gathering the Recusants' contributions under the Queen's letter. See Rushworth, vol. ii. p. 834.

1639.
May 8.

1236. *Secretary Windebank to Sir A. Hopton.* Recapitulates the substance of his former despatches, fearing they may have miscarried, and earnestly recommends to him the reconciliation of the Queen-Mother to that Crown, which has been offended by the manner of her departure from Brussels and the forged manifesto. Any offer of forces from the Infant Cardinal will now come too late, the crisis being past, and others supplied. Cardeñas has tried to obtain audience of the King, but in vain. Desires to know the truth concerning Mr. Wheeler's murder, wherein the Earl of Buchan is implicated. The state of Scotch affairs. The proclamation against Argyle and others by name was not published, another being substituted. The Earl of Leicester has been in England nearly two months; is lately sworn a Privy Councillor, and about to return to France. *Draught.*
By himself.

Newcastle,
May 17.

1237. *His Majesty to Secretary Windebank.* Has reinforced his army with 4000 foot and 300 horse, which will cause 6000*l.* a month increase of charge.
Cl. S. P. vol. ii. p. 42.

Drury
Lane,
May 18.

1238. *Secretary Windebank to His Majesty.* Of a conversation with the French Ambassador concerning the English merchants' complaints of taxation in France, and the French suspicions of a treaty made with Spain, which he has denied.
Apostiled by the King, "Newcastle, May 11." Cl. S. P. vol. ii. p. 42.

Vienna,
May 18.

1239. *Count Leslie to Mr. Taylor,* giving him news of the forces.

Vienna,
May 18.

1240. *Mr. W. Gibbs to the same* (his brother-in-law). Of Banier's position at Leitmeritz, and Gallas's in front of Prague, the forces on each side being about 21,000 men.

Madrid,
May 1⁄2?.

1241. *Sir A. Hopton to Secretary Windebank.* There is a rumour of a rupture between England and Holland. Of the Irish lords, Tyrone is still here, and the other with his regiment in Navarre; both unlikely to cause trouble, though it is said they have been dealt with to do something in Ireland.

Drury
Lane,
May 21.

1242. *Secretary Windebank to His Majesty.* The Attorney and Solicitor's advice on a method of fining Lords Say and Brook, as they escape under the present indictment.
Apostiled by the King, "Alnwick, May 24." Cl. S. P. vol. ii. p. 45.

1243. *Secretary Windebank to His Majesty.* Of the difficulty in raising money from the citizens, and the refusal of Sir Francis Seymour to pay the shipping money.
1639. Drury Lane, May 14.

Apostilled by the King, "Berwick, May 19." Cl. S. P. vol. II. p. 46.

1244. *Col. Gage to Mr. George Gage.* The Spaniards having offered to supply the troops formerly requested, wishes to know whether the offer will be acceptable. *Extract.*
Brussels, May 18.

In Windebank's hand. Cl. S. P. vol. II. p. 50.

1245. *Memoranda* by Windebank chiefly of an interview with Cardeñas concerning the protection of ships driven hither by stress of weather.
May 30.

1246. *Don Alonso de Cardeñas to His Majesty*, complaining that 1000 Spaniards had been forcibly taken by the Hollanders out of English ships, and demanding protection and a safe convoy to Dunkirk for 360 who had taken refuge in the Isle of Wight.—Spanish.
No date.

With an English translation by Windebank.

1247. *Extracts out of a Proclamation given at Thetford in the second year of the reign of King James*, A.D. 1604, respecting the reception of Spanish and Holland ships of war in the English ports.
No date.

Endorsed by Windebank.

Probably presented by Cardeñas about this date.

1248. *Secretary Windebank to His Majesty.* Encloses an important paper received from Cardeñas, whereby he proposes to bring the Venetian Ambassador on the stage to mediate in the Palatinate business. Explains the policy which he advises, of giving an evasive answer, neither accepting nor refusing the treaty at Brussels, but striving to obtain a treaty apart, wherein only his own interests shall be involved. The States Ambassador is directed to request the King to take the treaty concerning the East India Company out of Sir William Boswell's hands, which he hopes will not be done.
Drury Lane, May 31.

Original, apostilled by the King, "Camp, near Berwick, June 4th," who assents to Windebank's advice. Also a rough draught in Windebank's hand.

1249. *A Memorial from Don Alonso de Cardeñas*, desiring to be informed whether the proposition, which the Cardinal Infant has been informed has been made to the Emperor by the Venetian Ambassador at his Court, that the affair of the
May.

1639.	Palatinate be referred to the general conference at Brussels or Lubeck, and that the Prince Palatine be invited to attend there, be made by the order and consent of the King of England.—Spanish.	*Copy.*

With an English translation.
This is a copy of the paper referred to in the last.

Vienna, June 1.
1250. *Count Leslie to Mr. Taylor.* Condoles with him on the injustice done him. Banier does nothing; and they are in hopes yet to resist him successfully.

Madrid, June 4.
1251. *Sir A. Hopton to Secretary Windebank.* Will serve the Queen-Mother as best he can; but the Court is very averse to her, and refuses to receive her Ambassador. Great preparations are made to compel Richelieu, by the war in Italy, to make a peace on the basis of the restitution of the Duke of Lorraine, of Brazil, and the Malaccas. The plate-fleet is daily expected. Recounts the circumstances of Mr. Wheeler's death in a street squabble, and acquits Lord Buchan entirely of any complicity therein.

Prague, June 4.
1252. *Mr. W. Gibbs to Mr. Taylor.* An account of Banier's attack upon Prague and retirement to Melnick.

Drury Lane, June 4.
1253. *Secretary Windebank to His Majesty.* The Queen complains of the strict orders in France not to suffer any French to come to England.

Apostilled by the King. " Camp, near Berwick, June 9."
Cl. S. P. vol. ii. p. 51.

Gant, June 5.
1254. *Mr. H. Tayller to Mr. J. Taylor.* News from the camp. Banier is still at Leitmeritz, preparing to retreat.

June 6.
1255. *Secretary Windebank to Sir A. Hopton.* Presses him in the name of the King and Queen to attempt a reconciliation between the Spanish Court and the Queen-Mother, and the re-establishment of her Ambassador Martelli, and the bestowal of a promised benefice upon his brother. The news of the King's camp at Berwick, the gallant service of the Marquis of Hamilton by sea, and the symptoms of the return of the rebels to obedience. Desires his continued efforts in behalf of his unfortunate son, now at Rome.	*Draught.*

By himself.

Madrid, June 12.
1256. *Sir A. Hopton to Secretary Windebank.* His efforts in the Queen-Mother's behalf, and their partial success, notwithstanding the great coldness of the King and Condé Duke.

The business of the secret conference has not advanced. 1639.
Inclines to believe that Tyrone and Tyrconnel have been
invited by the Scotch covenanters to raise troubles in Ireland,
but at present there is no danger from them, one being here,
the other with his regiment in Navarre. The moulds from
the heads at Aranjuez shall be sent when dry. Richaut's
business advances but slowly.
> Partly in cypher, decyphered by Windebank.
> There is also a French translation of that part of this which refers to the Queen-Mother, in Windebank's hand, evidently meant for her perusal; a sentence of the original likely to be distasteful to her being omitted.

1257. *Count Leslie to Mr. J. Taylor.* An account of Vienna,
Hanier's advance upon Prague, and subsequent retreat to June 8.
Brandeis.

1258. *The Marquis of Brandenburg to His Majesty*, re- Regio-
commending Capt. Richard Mackmoiler to his service.— montana
Latin. Bordeaux-
 ram,
 June 8.

1259. *Secretary Windebank to the same.* An account of Drury
an interview between the Lords of the Committee and the Lane,
Lord Mayor concerning seditious papers by one Lilburne. June 8.
The French Ambassador disavows the orders mentioned
in his last. 20,000*l.* is ready to be sent.
> Apostilled by the King. "Camp, June 12." Cl. S. P. vol. ii. p. 53.

1260. *The same to the same.* Interview of the Lords with June 11th.
the Lord Mayor and Aldermen, who refuse the required loan.
Rough Draught.
> In Windebank's hand, without date, which is learnt from the contents.
> Cl. S. P. vol. ii. p. 54.

1261. *Sir A. Hopton to Secretary Windebank.* Has conversed Madrid,
with the Condé Duke on the Queen-Mother's business, and June 4/14.
obtains no definite answer. On Cardeñas' offence also, which
they desire to be passed over quietly. A minute account of
the opening of the secret conference, and the Condé Duke's
earnest protestations that nothing can be done in the Palatinate business by any power except Spain.
> Original and duplicate in Windebank's hand of the part which concerns the Queen-Mother.

1262. *Sir A. Hopton to Lord Cottington.* Desires that the Madrid,
quarrel with Cardeñas be terminated in some way. The June 4/14.
Spanish war policy is defensive, hoping to wear out the
French. The French Armada is off the Groyne, under command of the Archbishop of Bordeaux, and looking out for the
plate-fleet.

1639. The leaguer by Prague, June 18.	1263. *Mr. W. Gibbs to Mr. Taylor.* Of the bad condition of their army, almost all their chief officers being prisoners, and Banier with 14,000 men closely beleaguering them.
June 17.	1264. *The Infant Cardinal to His Majesty*, recommending Capt. Maurice Macdonnel to his favour.—French.
June.	1265. *Secretary Windebank to the same*, dissuading him from venturing in person into Scotland. *Rough Draught.* In Windebank's hand, without date, but the negotiations for peace are alluded to in it, and the pacification was made June 17. Cl. S. P. vol. ii. p. 56.
No date.	1266. *The same to the same*, conveying the request of the Queen and Lords of the Council that he will not venture in person into Scotland. *Rough draught.* By himself.
Whitehall, June 19.	1267. *The same to the same.* A humorous account of the physical effects of the demand of a loan upon the Mayor and Aldermen. Apostiled by the King. " Berwick, July 7." Cl. S. P. vol. ii. p. 57.
No date.	1268. *The same to the Lord Mayor*, rebuking him severely from the Lords of the Committee for his neglect in not answering the King's letter, and requiring an answer by next Wednesday. *Rough draught.* By himself.
No date.	1269. *The same to His Majesty*, complaining bitterly of the refusal of the City to grant the loan, on pretence that the accommodation with the Scots renders it unnecessary. *Rough draught.* By himself.
Drury Lane, July 1.	1270. *The same to the same.* In expectation of his return, they have not of late pressed the City. Apostiled by the King. Cl. S. P. vol. ii. p. 58.
Drury Lane, July 5.	1271. *The same to Sir A. Hopton*, informing him of the accommodation with the Scots. The Spaniards who escaped from the Hollanders' visitation of the English ships have been landed at Portsmouth and kindly received. *Copy.* By himself.

1272. *Secretary Windebank to His Majesty*, forwarding Gerbier's letters concerning the Queen-Mother, and the Marquis of Ceralvo's, concerning a treaty at Brussels, from which he dissuades the King. Of the indignities put upon merchants by the Dutch fleet.

1639. Drury Lane, July 6.

Apostiled by the King, "Berwick, July 10." Cl. S. P. vol. ii. p. 59.

1273. *The same to the same.* Recommends a successor to be appointed to Lord Chaworth, Sheriff of Notts, lately dead; the re-admission of Don Alonzo de Cardeñas to Court as Spanish Minister; and the negotiation of a Spanish treaty at Madrid in preference to Brussels.

Drury Lane, July 9.

Apostiled by the King, "Berwick, July 13." Cl. S. P. vol. ii. p. 61.

1274. *The same to the same.* Encloses a draught of a circular letter to the gentry. The Mayor is such a beast, and his brethren the Aldermen such cattle, as they will be neither driven nor go of themselves.

Drury Lane, July 12.

Apostiled by the King, "Berwick, July 14." Cl. S. P. vol. ii. p. 63.

1275. *His Majesty to Secretary Windebank*, requesting the Queen to write.

Berwick, July 12.

Cl. S. P. vol. ii. p. 64.

1276. *Secretary Windebank to Sir A. Hopton.* The Queen-Mother, through one Bonnefont, has made overtures to the Infant Cardinal of a marriage between the Princess Mary and the Prince of Spain. There is still some restiveness in the Covenanters, though the Castle of Edinburgh is given up. His son Christopher has promised to leave Italy and write no more to his wife. *Rough Draught.*

July 15.

By himself. Cl. S. P. vol. ii. p. 65,
(with the exception of an unimportant introduction and a postscript).

1277. *Sir A. Hopton to Secretary Windebank.* Of the arrival of the plate-fleet. The Archbishop of Bordeaux has challenged the Spanish fleet, who are to go out to meet him under Don Antonio de Oquendo. Salsen is taken by the French. Perpignan he expects will be besieged, and taken. The Condé Duke suspects that the Queen-Mother intends to return to them again, but they are resolved not to receive her, and to break with her entirely, refusing also the benefice requested for the Abbot Fabroni. A proposition said to be made by Col. Gage to the Infant Cardinal of a loan of money to the King.

Madrid, July ⅙.

Partly in cypher, decyphered by Windebank.

1639.
Aug. 1.

1278. *Secretary Windebank to Sir A. Hopton.* Contradicts the report of a rupture between the King and the Hollanders. Thanks him for his efforts in the Queen-Mother's behalf; the King being willing to re-admit Cardeñas (on confession of his offence) in return for the grace done to her minister. Discusses at length the progress of the secret conference, wherein he wonders to find no mention of the children of the two Crowns, and desires him to test the Condé's sincerity by proposing his mediation with the Emperor. The Prince Elector is arrived since Duke Bernard's death, and gone to the King in the North, who is expected to return immediately.
Rough draught.
By himself.

Drury Lane,
Aug. 2.

1279. *The same to His Majesty,* congratulating him on his safe return, and informing him of the Lord Chamberlain's (Lord Pembroke) vehement disavowal of the glosses on the Articles of Pacification.

Madrid,
Aug. 5.

1280. *Sir A. Hopton to Secretary Windebank.* Of the Queen-Mother's business and the proposition of Cardeñas. There are complaints of French trading to Spain in English ships.

Madrid,
Aug. 5.

1281. *The same to the same.* A private letter concerning Mr. Christopher Windebank, his wife and child; and the proposition that the wife be placed in a convent.

Madrid,
Aug. 1⅔.

1282. *The same to the same,* advising that the Queen-Mother's ambassador be retained at Madrid, even though they refuse to restore his entertainment.
Extract in Windebank's hand. The rest of the despatch does not occur. There is also on the same paper an extract from the subsequent despatch of Aug. 1⅔.

Aug. 16.

1283. *Secretary Windebank to Sir A. Hopton.* Of the complaint of the Hollanders concerning the transportation of Spanish troops in English merchant ships, and the King's answer, retaliating with a complaint of the searching of English ships by the Hollanders, which he will not longer endure, and has given instructions to Sir John Pennington accordingly. Cardeñas has consented to avow that the King never gave him reason to assert that he had given way to a treaty at Brussels. Wishes him to contrive secretly that the King may be rid of the heavy expense of the Queen-Mother's stay, by her return to France or Flanders. Gage's proposition to the Infant Cardinal for a loan was entirely unauthorized; but if it could be done, on the condition of the 1639. protection of Spanish traders to Flanders, the King might entertain it, in hopes of opening thereby the fisheries business. The Earl of Traquaire is to be Commissioner at the Scots Parliament. Lord Aston is dead of the stone.

Draught.
By himself.

1284. *The Submission of Don Alonso de Cardeñas*, disavow- No date. ing that he had any authority from His Majesty to justify him in writing to the Marquis de Castaneda, that His Majesty approved of the treaty for restitution of the Palatinate being remitted to Brussels.

Translation, in Windebank's hand.

1285. *Sir A. Hopton to Secretary Windebank.* A proposi- Madrid, tion of the Condé Duke to be allowed to levy 6000 Irish Aug. 2/11. soldiers for service in Spain, paying the King ten ducats, or a loan of twenty ducats, a man. The French in Catalonia are fortifying Salses, and neglecting Italy, Richelieu's wisdom having died, it is said, with Père Joseph. The Council will not receive the Queen-Mother's Resident, though the Queen of Spain would be glad that he should remain.

In cypher, decyphered by Windebank.

1286. *The same to the same.* The French, having burnt Madrid, Laredo, have retired to their ships. Spinola is with the Aug. 2/11. Spanish army, which is 14,000 strong, and in good heart.

1287. *The substance of what is humbly desired of His Majesty* August. *in behalf of Recusants, with the reasons thereof.* That the prosecution of Mr. Pulford and all extraordinary prosecutions of the penal laws be remitted.

In an unknown hand. Cl. S. P. vol. ii. p. 66.

1288. *A Brief Discourse concerning the provision of Catholic* Sept. 3. *Bishops in Ireland*, urging their nomination by the Queen in preference to the Pope, on the ground of the necessity of appointing loyal persons.

In an unknown hand; date and endorsement by Windebank.
Cl. S. P. vol. ii. p. 66.

1289. *Sir A. Hopton to Secretary Windebank.* An applica- Madrid, tion from the Condé Duke for leave for the Spanish fleet, Sept. 3/13. now in the Groyne, to put into English ports in case of necessity. Represents that if the unjust practice of the Hollanders in searching English ships be permitted, the Spaniards will probably adopt the same course. *Two Copies.*

1639.
Madrid,
Sept. 7/17.

1290. *Sir A. Hopton to Secretary Windebank.* Discovery of a plot between some Irish Bishops and the Irish resident in Spain for an insurrection in Ireland, giving the names and description of the conspirators.

In cypher, and a copy decyphered by Windebank.
Cl. S. P. vol. II. p. 69.

Madrid,
Sept. 7/17.

1291. *The same to the same.* Further details of the conspiracy mentioned in the last.

In cypher, and a copy decyphered by Windebank.
Cl. S. P. vol. II. p. 70.

Westminster,
Sept. 19.

1292. *Grant* from the King to Mr. George Kirke, Gentleman of the Bedchamber, of 2000 acres in lieu of a former grant of the Holland Fen in Lincolnshire, which is hereby revoked. *Copy.*

Stickhem
(Stockholm?),
Sept. 18.

1293. *Count Leslie to Mr. Taylor.* There never was a better conjunction than now, the Emperor's intentions being real, and the Germans more tractable. The Duke of Lorraine has arrived.

Madrid,
Sept. 24/
Oct. 4.

1294. *Sir A. Hopton to Secretary Windebank.* The Condé Duke is still very wary and jealous in the matter of the secret conference. They will have nothing to with the Queen-Mother, who might have lived comfortably at Brussels, but for the busy and dangerous character of her ministers. The Venetians have made peace with the Turks, with whom the French are said to be earnestly negotiating a descent into Hungary. The Spaniards have laid siege to Salses.

Partly in cypher, decyphered by Windebank.

Antwerp,
Sept. 15.

1295. *Count Leslie to Mr. Taylor.* Has been sent to recall Piccolomini to supersede Gallas, much against the will of the Infant Cardinal. Expresses strongly his opinion of the favourable opportunity for England, who might have of Spain, as the Infant Cardinal assures him, what they pleased if they only knew how to negotiate. If time be lost, a peace will be made without mention of the Prince Elector.

Partly in cypher, decyphered by Taylor.

Drury
Lane,
Sept. 18.
Oct. 8.

1296. *Secretary Windebank to Col. Gage.* Authorizes him to offer to the Infant Cardinal the King's protection for the Spanish fleet, on payment of 150,000*l.* sterling, and promise of better treatment in the Palatinate business. *Copy.*

By himself.

1297. *Secretary Windebank to Count Leslie*, to the same effect as that to Gage, adding the condition that Prince Rupert be better treated, great complaint being made of his rigorous imprisonment and hard usage. — *Copy.*
By himself.

1639. Drury Lane, Sept. 18. Oct. 8.

1298. *Don Alonso de Cardeñas (to Secretary Windebank)*, requesting him to give orders that the requisite stores may be put on board the fleet before they are all spoiled. — Spanish.
Endorsed by Windebank.

Sept. 18. Oct. 8.

1299. *Secretary Windebank to Sir A. Hopton.* The King cannot spare Irish levies for Spain. The report of the Queen-Mother's desire to return to Flanders is a false and malicious scandal. The arrival of the Spanish fleet of near seventy ships in the Downs before the delivery of any message is disrespectful, and their conduct in refusing to strike to the King's ships equally so. Fourteen or fifteen have escaped to Dunkirk, Van Tromp declaring that "having his hands full of flies it was impossible but some of them would escape through his fingers." The King will demand 150,000*l.* for their protection. Taylor has been committed to the Tower for his conduct at Vienna. The Prince Elector is about to depart for Germany. The Lord Deputy is returned to England to hear the great suit of Chancellor Loftus.

Rough Draught.
In his own hand. Cl. S. P. vol. ii. p. 71, (with unimportant omissions. The date $\frac{7}{17}$ in the first line should be $\frac{9}{19}$.)

Sept. 19.

1300. *The Infant Cardinal to His Majesty*, desiring his protection for the Spanish fleet in the Downs. — French.

Dunkirk, Oct. 3.

1301. *Count Leslie to the Earl Marshal (Arundell).* Urges that the House of Austria be obliged by assisting the Spanish fleet. The Spanish intentions are much changed, and the Emperor is determined to give the King satisfaction, but his letters must first be answered.

Dunkirk, Oct. 3.

1302. *Sir A. Hopton to Secretary Windebank.* The business of the conference and that of the Queen-Mother remain as they were. The siege of Salsas is hotly pressed. In detaining the moulds of the heads to send some pictures for the Queen with them.
Partly in cypher, decyphered by Windebank.

Madrid, Oct. $\frac{7}{17}$.

B b

1639. Madrid, Oct. 7/17.	1303. *Sir A. Hopton to Lord Cottington.* Particulars of the siege of Salsas. The quarrel between the Pope and this Crown has reached a great height; great tumults have arisen in Portugal, and the Nuntio's tribunal is likely to be abolished throughout the kingdom. The only obstacle to the conference at Cologne is the refusal of the States to accept passports for "Commissaries," demanding the style of "Ambassadors." The interests of the Prince Elector must be provided for at such conference, if ever.
Madrid, Oct. 7/17.	1304. *Secretary Windebank to Sir A. Hopton,* answering Cardeñas' complaints on the same subject respecting his audience and that of the Holland Ambassador.
Dunkirk, No date.	1305. *Count Leslie to Secretary Windebank.* Presses earnestly that the Emperor's letters be answered, the occasion being so favourable. Vehemently asserts the innocence of honest John Taylor, who, he hears, is imprisoned*.
Weteren † (? Wesseem), Oct. 6.	1306. *Col. Gage to the same,* of Mr. Grimsditch, his nephew, who has just joined the Colonel's regiment.
Dunkirk, Oct. 10.	1307. *Capt. Shaw to the same.* Of his nephew in Gage's regiment, who promises to reform.
Dunkirk, Oct. 11, 9 A. M.	1308. *Count Leslie to the same.* Is very sorry the King is driven to want so small a sum as 150,000l., which alters his view of coming to England.
Dunkirk, Oct. 11, 6 P. M.	1309. *The same to the same.* The Infant Cardinal cannot entertain the proposition of such an unreasonable sum, considering it the King's own interest to protect the fleet, and not believing the possibility of a rupture with France or Holland. The whole affair is remitted to Cardeñas. The Spaniards disavow any interest in Prince Rupert, who is the Emperor's prisoner, but the Infant Cardinal promises to intercede in his behalf, the good effects whereof will soon be seen.
Werchten, Oct. 11/21.	1310. *Col. Gage to the same.* Has been disabled by illness from undertaking the negotiation with the Infant Cardinal. Mr. H. Tayller and another were to have gone as Ambassadors to the King but for Cardeñas boasting of the favour shewn him at Court.

* That concerning Taylor is written on a separate slip of paper which appears to have been inclosed as a postscript in this or some other letter.
† This place, whatever it be, appears from the letter to be near Vealo on the Maas.

1311. *Sir A. Hopton to Secretary Windebank.* Complaint has been made that the Spanish ships were compelled to lower their colours when entering the English ports, and were not allowed to land their sick. There is no progress in the conference or the Queen-Mother's negotiation. Tyrone lately told a friend, that the Scottish business was not ended yet, for Argyle had some Irish blood in him.

1639.
Madrid,
Oct. 1¾.

Partly in cypher, decyphered by Windebank.

1312. *Secretary Windebank to Sir A. Hopton.* Directions for his guidance in the matter of the defeat of the Spanish fleet in English waters, how he is to meet complaints on the subject. *Copy.*

Oct. 18.

In his own hand. Cl. S. P. vol. ii. p. 76.

1313. *Col. Gage to Secretary Windebank.* The 150,000*l.* demanded will not be given till they see how the King resents the injury done to Spain. Relates the arrogance of the States, who decided to attack the fleet, "though it were placed upon His Majesty's beard," and advises retaliation by closing the ports, stopping the herring-fishery (which is to them another India), and recalling English subjects.

Brussels,
Oct. 18.

Cl. S. P. vol. ii. p. 79.

1314. *Count Leslie to the same.* Explains the apparent inconsistency of his two last letters, and his reason for altering his resolution of coming into England. The loss of the Spanish fleet has injured the King's reputation extremely, even among neutrals and wellwishers, which is principally owing to the insolent language and pamphlets of the Hollanders. If they wished restitution of the Palatinate as the price of the fleet's safety, they should have said so at first, but they have deceived throughout the whole business. Prince Rupert has been excellently treated throughout. Wishes Taylor not only at liberty, but back at Vienna.

Brussels,
Oct. 28.

1315. *Petition* of Mr. William Murray, Groom of the Bedchamber, for the Examiner's and Affidavit's Office in the Court of Exchequer. Referred to the Lords Keeper, Treasurer, and Privy Seal.

Whitehall,
Nov. 1.

The note of reference by Windebank.

1316. *Sir A. Hopton to Secretary Windebank.* Further details of the Irish conspiracy. *Two Copies.*

Madrid,
Nov. 1.

In cypher, one decyphered by Windebank.
Cl. S. P. vol. ii. p. 80, (the date misprinted).

1639.
Madrid,
Nov. 4.

1317. *Sir A. Hopton to Secretary Windebank.* Notwithstanding the Lord Deputy's opinion of the Irish business, he will watch it carefully, for often great flames rise out of small sparks. Discusses the question of Cardeñas' disparity in rank, as Resident, with himself, as Ambassador. The decay of Spanish navigation encourages the hope that this is the time when the commerce of the Indies shall be opened to other nations. Believes Spain will pay the 150,000*l.*, but points out the great danger of a rupture with France and Holland. *Partly in cypher, decyphered by Windebank.*

Madrid,
Nov. 4/14.

1318. *The same to the same.* Of the business of some merchants. The siege of Salses continues and is likely to be successful. The Queen-Mother's minister is about to leave. A report of some disaster to the Armada which would be ruinous to Spain. No news concerning the Irish business. Encloses the next.

1319. *Proposition* of the Condé Duke for the transportation of soldiers in English ships between Spain and Flanders; offering ten crowns a man to the King for all safely landed.—Spanish. *Copy.*
With English translation by Windebank.

Madrid,
Nov. 9.

1320. *Sir A. Hopton to Secretary Windebank.* Conversations with the Condé Duke about the proposed transportation of troops, and the right of searching neutral ships. Points out the necessity of great care lest anything happen to the Spanish fleet, there being an immense quantity of English shipping in the Spanish ports, upon which they might retaliate any supposed injury. The Condé Duke's insincerity in the matter of the conference. Suggests that he might be authorized to offer help in the recovery of Brazil. It is believed that Richelieu will be the only impediment to the conference at Cologne this winter. *Two Copies.*
Partly in cypher, decyphered by Windebank.

Brussels,
Nov. 1/11.

1321. *Col. Gage to the same,* detailing conversation with Spanish ministers concerning the late disaster in the Downs, in which they suggest among other things an invasion of Normandy by the King (as rightly his own, and most open to attack), to be joined by a Spanish invasion by way of Artois. Gage suggests the seizure of the property of the Hollanders in their many rich, and he fears dangerous, settlements on the English coast. An army could be raised and maintained without Parliament as easily as ship-money, if there were proper ministers in the shires.

1322. *Sir A. Hopton to Secretary Windebank.* The Spanish King's and Condé Duke's civil reception of his condolences, their design being to exasperate the King against the Hollanders.
    1639. Madrid, Nov. ½¼.

1323. *The same to the same.* A fuller account of the audiences mentioned in the last. The Condé Duke seems on the whole well satisfied, but suspects encouragement to the Hollanders from some of the King's ministers, and says that Pennington fired in the air (though not making this a complaint). The secret conference is for the present suspended. Of the detention of the Prince Elector at Moulins, which they hold to be the sign of a secret agreement between France and Bavaria. Their hopes of recovering Brazil, the loss of which the Condé Duke represents as the only hindrance to a general peace. Salses is still besieged and will soon be assaulted, after which the troops will be employed to quell the disaffection which is growing throughout Catalonia. The Queen-Mother's Resident has taken leave of the King, but there is a difficulty in the way of his audience of the Queen, who is unwilling to refuse her mother's present, and is in very ill condition of body, in consequence of her grief. There has been no meeting about the Irish business for three months, the time being judged inopportune, and Tyrone and Tyrconnel receiving overtures from France. O'Driscol, now made Bishop of Brindisi, is the Irish agent at Rome. Tyrone is made Major-domo to the King; he is not in favour with the intelligent Irish, though a favourite with the simpler class, and can do nothing. Tyrconnel is utterly lost by drunkenness. Has sent the moulds of the heads, but the pictures of the King and Queen are not finished. Encloses the next.
    Madrid, Nov. ⅔⁸.

1324. Madrid, Nov. 24. *Paper* delivered by Sir A. Hopton to the King of Spain, assuring him of the care had for the good treatment of the fleet in the Downs, and the King's resolution to resent the behaviour of the Hollanders in attacking it.—Spanish.   *Copy.*
    With two copies of English translation in Windebank's hand.

1325. *Sir A. Hopton to Lord Cottington.* A repetition of the account of the way in which the King and Condé Duke received the news. Notified that he has sent a box of seeds, especially calabash, onion, and melons.
    Madrid, Nov. ⅔⁸.

1326. *Extractum ex Prothocollo Celsissimorum ac Præpotentium Dominorum Statuum Generalium Provinciarum Confœderatarum.* An ordinance, concerning the style in which they
    Nov. 26.

1639. are to be addressed by foreign Powers, and the ceremonial of the reception of foreign Ambassadors.—Latin. *Copy.*

Madrid, Nov. 29.
1327. *The King of Spain (Philip IV) to His Majesty.* A letter of credence for the Marquis de Velada.—Latin.

Brussels, Dec. 3.
1328. *Col. Gage to Secretary Windebank.* Of the honour done his nephew by the Infant Cardinal in a special increase of pay, to the amount of 50l. Encloses the next.

1329. Brussels, Nov. 26. *Don Miguel de Salamanca to Col. Gage,* notifying the above-mentioned gift of the Infant Cardinal.—Spanish.

Brussels, Dec. 3.
1330. *Col. Gage to Mr. George Gage* (his brother), explaining a misunderstanding that had arisen between Count Leslie and Sir Balthazar Gerbier on a punctilio of visiting, and some words said to have been spoken at Piccolomini's table in disrespect of the King.

Madrid, Dec. 6.
1331. *Sir A. Hopton to Secretary Windebank.* Expresses his fears that the Condé Duke is about to put an embargo on all foreign ships, with intention of injuring the English trade. The Hollanders are said to be in doubt whether to excuse themselves to, or complain of, the King. The success of the siege of Salses seems doubtful. Encloses the next.

Original, with a duplicate of the part concerning the embargo.

1332. Madrid, Dec. 6. *Secretary Roças to Sir A. Hopton.* The King's answer to his paper of Nov. 1¼. He professes himself satisfied with what His Majesty has undertaken to do to rebuke the insolence of the Hollanders.—Spanish. *Two Copies.*

With two English translations in Windebank's hand.

Dec. 13.
1333. *Secretary Windebank to Sir A. Hopton.* Gives the reasons, at length, which have determined the King to summon a Parliament on April 13th. The King will listen to no propositions from France till the Prince Elector be set at liberty. The Infant Cardinal is much displeased with Gerbier's carriage, and will hear him no more. *Draught.*

In his own hand. (Cl. S. P. vol. II. p. 81, (with unimportant omissions ; "Arvens" on p. 82 should be "Arsens.")

Madrid, Dec. 15. Jan. 4.
1334. *Sir A. Hopton to Secretary Windebank.* The Spaniards are greatly dissatisfied with the English, and the embargo

would have been issued ere now, but that the Duke of Medina Sidonia is engaged in a bargain for two ships. They have sent 50,000 ducats to England to purchase ships. May he give licence to English merchants to freight as Spanish men of war at their own peril? 1639.

1335. *Secretary Windebank to the Princess Phalsburg.* Expresses the King's gratitude for her efforts in his behalf.—French.   *Rough draught.* No date.
By himself.

1336. *Instructions from the Pope (Urban VIII) to his Nuntio (Count Rozetti?) in England.* The Catholics are not to assist willingly in the Northern expedition either with men or money. The clergy are to desist from that foolish, nay rather illiterate and childish, custom of distinction in the Protestant and Puritan doctrine, as if Protestantism were a degree nearer to the Catholic faith, both being without the verge of the Church*.   *Copy.* No date.
Endorsed by Windebank. Cl. S. P. vol. II. p. 44.

1337. *Reasons* against allowing Father Edward Dillon, a disaffected Franciscan, styled the Cardinal Protector of Ireland, to be made Bishop of Athenry in Connaught; the Archbishop of Tuam, in that province, already receiving a pension of 1000 ducats from Spain. No date.
Endorsed by Windebank. Written in the same hand as the paper of Sept. 3, concerning Titular Irish Bishops.

1338. *An Apportionment* of a rate of 70,000*l.* among the several counties, calculated on a basis of the payments to the three rates of the Ship-money of 1639, the 400,000*l.* Bill, and the 1,260,000*l.* monthly assessment. Of these, London, Westminster, and Middlesex are together rated at something more than one-tenth of the whole. Many counties are marked as "eased" in their apportionments. No date.

1339. *Minutes,* in Windebank's hand, of letters written and business transacted by him during the months of April—July, while the King was absent in the North. No date.

1340. *A Letter,* offering the services of the writer to effect an accommodation of disputes between the Ambassadors of Venice and Savoy at some Italian Court respecting title and precedence.—Italian.   *Rough Draught.* No date.
Endorsed by Windebank, "Lord Fielding."

---

* This paper is printed also in Rushworth, vol. II. p. 811, who doubts its authenticity, and says it is badly translated. See Rapin, vol. ii. p. 311.

1639.
No date.

1341. *A Paper*, discussing at some length the position of the Palatinate negotiations, and the interests of the several Powers concerned in it.—Spanish. *Copy.*
Endorsed as delivered by order of the King (of Spain?) to Lord Cottington.

No date.

1342. *Papers*, relating to the case of Andrea Pellegrino, Count of Peglia, Conservator General of the English in Italy, and comprising,—

    i. *Count Pellegrino to (the Duke of Savoy)*, deprecating the slanders which have been heaped upon him, and entreating restoration to favour.—Italian.

    ii. Sept. 20, 1638. *The same to the same*, giving explanations of his reasons for proposing to leave Turin for Venice or elsewhere in Italy.—Italian.

    iii. *The same to the same.* An application for the continuance of his salary at Venice.—Italian.

    iv. *Letters of Recommendation* from His Majesty (Charles II.) to the Republic of Venice in favour of Count Pellegrino as his Consul in that city.—Italian.

    v. *Letters Patent* of Count Pellegrino to the English Consulship at Venice.—Italian. *Copies.*
These are all without date, except the second. The last three seem to belong to this year.

1639-40.
Madrid,
Jan. 10.

1343. *Sir A. Hopton to Secretary Windebank.* A quarrel between the commanders before Salses has much weakened the Spanish army. On Twelfth-day the King made six Grandees, the largest number ever known; the Condé d'Oñate being one, but for life only, his son not being in favour. They are buying ships everywhere. An exorbitant new imposition has been laid on Malaga wine. Three Irish are here, a brother of Lord Westmeath, Serg.-Major Byrne (a creature of Tyrone's), and Father Gerard, negotiating to bring over Irish forces to Spain. Thinks there is nothing to be feared from these men while Spain has war with France, but there will be afterwards.

Vienna,
Jan. 12.

1344. *Count Leslie to the same*, giving his account of the misunderstanding at Brussels with Gerbier. Prince Rupert is still at Lintz, well treated.

Madrid,
Jan. 11.

1345. *Sir A. Hopton to the same.* The Spaniards are impatient to know the King's resolution concerning the insult in the Downs, alleging it to amount to a matter of *fœ publica*. Exorbitant impositions have been laid on the

merchants, contrary to the articles of peace, particularly 1639-40.
that of 30 per cent on Malaga wine. Salces is recovered.
The Portuguese nobility have engaged to raise 2500 men.
The King is to hold a Cortes in Catalonia in the spring.
150 ships are to be built, besides those they are buying.
Brass money to be abolished, no silver or gold to be exported,
and all trade is at a stand.

1346. *Sir A. Hopton to Secretary Windebank.* Their ex- Madrid,
pedients for raising money. A report that the Turks will Feb. 1.
invade Hungary, which may hasten the conference at Cologne,
the obstacle being the States' refusing passports in other
terms than the Princes have them. Tyrone has applied to be
received into favour, and if he were settled in England it
might extinguish the turbulence in Ireland, of which nation
he is the north star. He sees that he can effect nothing
through the help of Spain.

1347. *Proclamation of the Duke of Lorraine (Charles IV)* Madrid,
against a libellous publication falsely imputed to the Duchess Feb. 1.
of Lorraine, and tending to cause dissensions between them.
Forbids the reading of it on penalty of treason, and orders
it to be publicly burnt.—French. *Copy.*

Endorsed by Windebank.

1348. *Mr. H. Tayller to Secretary Windebank,* announcing Brussels,
his return to England in the employment of the Marquis de Feb. 4.
Velada.

1349. *Sir A. Hopton to the same.* Details of the various Madrid,
preparations for war. Spain will never want money however Feb. 7.
long the war last. In the indictment of the Duke of Arscot,
Sir Balth. Gerbier is mentioned as suggesting to him an application to France for assistance. The dislike of Gerbier,
arising from this, prejudices the negotiations with the House
of Austria. Wishes that affairs could be kept more secret
in England than they are. Expeditions are preparing for
Brazil, the East Indies, and Ceylon, where the Hollanders are
negotiating to expel the Portuguese and obtain a monopoly
of the cinnamon trade.

Original, with a translation in Gerbier's hand of the passage in the Duke
of Arscot's indictment, which Hopton writes in the original Spanish.

1350. *The same to Lord Cottington.* Congratulates him on Madrid,
being called to the Junta of eight on foreign affairs. Court Feb. 7.
news, and of the preparations for war. Troops go daily to
Catalonia.

1639-40.
Feb. 7.

1351. *Secretary Windebank to Sir A. Hopton.* Explains the King's great perplexity as to the proper treatment of the Hollanders at such an inopportune time. He has determined to delay his answer to them till the arrival of the Marquis de Velada. Hopton is to draw the King and Condé Duke from the subject by the suggestion of a marriage between the Princess Mary (the King's eldest daughter) and the Prince of Spain. He is not however to put it in writing unless greatly pressed.
Draught.
By himself.

Feb. 7.

1352. *The same to the same.* Enlarges upon the accompanying despatch, and forwards the Hollanders' memorials, wherein they justify their conduct by the Treaty of Southampton in 1625, when the King was at open war with Spain. Coke has retired and is succeeded by Sir H. Vane, who is to take charge of the affairs of France, Germany, and Holland; and Windebank those of Spain, Italy, Flanders, and Switzerland, but duplicates are to be sent to both, except in cases of secrecy. The Lord Keeper (Coventry) is dead, and succeeded by Sir John Finch, Littleton being made Chief Justice of the Common Pleas. Great preparations are being made for the north next summer.
Copy.
By himself.

Madrid,
Feb. 18.

1353. *Sir A. Hopton to Secretary Windebank.* The Condé Duke will be satisfied with nothing less than a rupture with Holland, offering in that case money and men from Flanders, and satisfaction in the secret treaty. Hopton quotes the Spaniards' own conduct on previous occasions as justification of the King's neutrality. All the Knights of the three military orders are summoned for the Cortes in Catalonia. Desires instructions whether he is to accompany the Court.
Two Copies.
Partly in cypher, decyphered by Windebank.

Madrid,
Feb. 18.

1354. *The same to Lord Cottington.* Of the preparations for war. Hopes much good from the coming Parliament, of which the Condé Duke has no good opinion. Notwithstanding their dissembling, the loss in the Downs is rooted in their hearts.

Brussels,
Feb. 15.

1355. (*Charles IV*) *Duke of Lorraine to His Majesty,* asking permission to employ Mr. George de Fortescue, an English subject, as his Resident at Rome.—French.

Madrid,
Feb. 27.

1356. *Sir A. Hopton to Secretary Windebank.* They are

pressing for the King's answer, in order, as he thinks, to put 1639-40.
him off on the subject of his complaints of the impositions on
the merchants. Some disturbances in Catalonia between the
soldiers and inhabitants. A narrow escape of the King and
Queen from fire. Strange hatred in the common people of
the Condé Duke, the nobles however being his servile flat-
terers. The Condé de Castro is appointed Major-domo in the
room of the late Duke of Alva.

1357. *Secretary Windebank to Sir A. Hopton.* English   Feb. 28.
merchants may take freight as men of war at their own peril,
but without warrant from the King. Hopton's Secretary is
not to correspond with Mr. Nicholls, the Prince Elector's
agent here. The Lord Lieutenant concurs in his opinion
concerning the Irish serving in Spain and France. Tyrone
is to be answered on fair but general terms and sounded as
to what conditions he requires. Gerbier is to be removed
from Brussels, and sent to France in place of Angier. Writs
are issued for the Parliament, which is fixed for April 13th.
No answer is as yet given to the States' Ambassador.
Rough draught.
By himself, partly in cypher.

1358. *Jean de Perriet to Lord Cottington.* A complaint   Brussels,
from a Brussels bookseller, enclosing a petition to the King,   March 1.
that he has been defrauded of a reward offered in King James's
time for the discovery of the author of a book entitled
"*Corona Regia,*" and falsely attributed to Casaubon.—French.

1359. *The Condé Duke d' Olivares to the same,* recommending   Madrid,
to him the Marquis Virgilio Maluezzi, the new Ambassador   March 6.
Extraordinary.

1360. *The King of Spain (Philip IV) to His Majesty.*   Madrid,
Letters of credence for the Marquis de Maluezzi, Ambassador   March 7.
Extraordinary to England, containing heavy complaints of
the Hollanders' insolence, and demands for a speedy show
of resentment.—Latin.

1361. *The Infant Cardinal to the same.* A note of civility   Brussels,
to accompany the Marquis de Velada.—French.   March 9.

1362. *Sir A. Hopton to Secretary Windebank.* Relates a   Madrid,
conference with the Condé Duke, wherein he has explained   March 4/14.
the difficulty of the King's neutral position, and suggested the
proposition by Spain of a marriage between the Prince of
Spain and the Princess Mary, but could not gather the inclinations of the Condé Duke or King thereon.
Principally in cypher, decyphered by Windebank.

1639-40.
Madrid,
March ¾.

1363. *Sir A. Hopton to Secretary Windebank.* Repeats the substance of his last despatch.

In cypher, decyphered by Windebank.

Brussels,
March 18.

1364. *The Duke of Lorraine (Charles IV) to His Majesty,* introducing to him his envoy, the Marquis de Villa.—French.

Brussels,
March 18.

1365. *The same to Secretary Windebank,* thanking him for his support, and desiring him to assist his envoy, the Marquis de Ville, in his negotiation.—French.

Brussels,
March 24.

1366. *Capt. Shaw to the same,* answering the complaint of Gerbier concerning the words spoken at Piccolomini's table. Encloses the next.

1367. Feb. 20. *Count Piccolomini to Capt. Shaw,* giving news from the Imperial army of the assault and capture of the fortress of Clumnitz(?) and the city of Kinigratz(?)—Italian.

1640.
Drury Lane,
March 27.

1368. *Secretary Windebank to Sir A. Hopton.* Desires him to entertain them with fair answers, and so gain time. The Holland Ambassador has gone without taking leave. Hopton is to clear Gerbier of the imputation laid on him in the Duke of Arscot's indictment. The elections for Parliament have been very tumultuary. The Prince Elector is set free in France on conditions to which England is not privy. This will probably put the Marquis de Villada somewhat out of his fence. The Duchess of Chevreux, being threatened by a visit from her husband, is meditating a retreat into Flanders, a result he thinks too good to be true. The Duke of Lorraine was coming to her, but that has been stopped. *Copy.*

By himself, partly in cypher.

Madrid,
April 7/17.

1369. *Sir A. Hopton to Secretary Windebank.* A conference with the Condé Duke on the subject of the marriage. They profess to like it very well, but he thinks they will entangle it with other matters, and only want to sell their Prince. One comfort is, the negotiation cannot be long, for the Condé Duke says plainly that they think the Princess has been bred up a Protestant long enough. *Two Copies.*

Partly in cypher, decyphered by Windebank.

Madrid,
April 7/17.

1370. *The same to Lord Cottington.* The redress of the merchants' wrongs in the matter of the new impositions must be the first demand in answer to any requirement of Spain.

1371. *Col. Gage to Secretary Windebank.* Desires him to complain to the Marquis de Velada of the insolence of the Irish serving in Spanish pay, who pretend to precedence of the English in marching, as being descended from Hiscny, and so originally Spaniards. This he thinks too much to be borne from a nation so often conquered, who first received from England civilization and Christianity, and for 500 years laws and governors.
Brussels, April 1¼. *1640.*

1372. *The same to Sir Balthazar Gerbier,* to the same effect and nearly in the same words as the last.
Brussels, April 1¼.

1373. *Count Leslie to Sir William Howard.* Has no hope of any settlement of the business so long treated, the fault being entirely with England, who will find a peace at last made without any consideration of them. The recall of Taylor is stranger than anything he ever saw or read.
Vienna, April 11.

1374. *Speeches of His Majesty and the Lord Keeper (Finch) at the opening of Parliament.*
April 13.
    Printed in Nalson, vol. I. p. 307, Rushworth, vol. ii. p. 1114, and Rapin, vol. II. p. 314, with some verbal differences, the most important being that in the 2nd paragraph the words of this copy are " made his entry here by blood, not by bloodshed," and in the 16th paragraph after the words " as soon as may be" follow " with this promise in the Act, that His Majesty's royal assent shall not determine the sessions."

1375. *Speeches of Mr. Sergeant Glanville, on being presented to His Majesty as Speaker, and Reply of the Lord Keeper.*
April 15.
    Printed in Nalson, vol. I. p. 312, and Rushworth, vol. ii. p. 1118, with some unimportant variations. In both there is a misprint towards the end of Glanville's second speech of " so considerable mines" for " two considerable mines."

1376. *Speech of Sir Benjamin Rudiard in Parliament. Two Copies.*
April 16.
    Endorsed by Lord Clarendon. One is verbatim as printed in Nalson, vol. I. p. 310, and Rushworth, vol. ii. p. 1129. The other differs very considerably in expression, being much longer and more diffuse, but to the same purport throughout.

1377. *Speech of Mr. Hyde* against the Earl Marshal's Court.
April 19.
    In his own hand. A summary of this speech is given in his Life, p. 934.

1378. *Secretary Windebank to Sir A. Hopton.* Neither Veluda nor Maluezzi have as yet made any intimation of their business. Fears there will be no better success from this Parliament than the last. His son has returned from France
Drury Lane, April 24.

1640. with much honour. The Marquis de Ville is returning unsatisfied, the King having absolutely refused to meddle with the Duke's marriage with Mad^m. Canterone, or to allow him levies. The Duchess of Chevreux is not yet gone. Copy.
By himself.

May 8. 1379. *Speech of His Majesty on the dissolution of Parliament.*
Printed in Nalson, vol. I. p. 342, Rushworth, vol. II. p. 1154, and Rapin, vol. ii. p. 318, with many verbal differences.

Madrid, May 8. 1380. *Sir A. Hopton to Secretary Windebank.* Has suspicions of a secret treaty in negotiation between Spain and France. Progress of the disturbances in Catalonia, where the people are so stubborn that the word "force" must not be used with them. Weakness and preparations of the Spaniards at sea.

May 9. 1381. *Mr. Edmund Attwood to ———.* Apparently to some Bishop, stating briefly reasons why Roman Catholics refuse communion with the Church of England.
Endorsed by Windebank.

Drury Lane, May 11. 1382. *Secretary Windebank to Sir A. Hopton.* The Lord Admiral, Lord Deputy, Marquis of Hamilton, and himself, are to treat with the Spanish Ambassadors. Parliament is dissolved, without granting the King any supply. Copy.
In his own hand, partly in cypher. Cl. S. P. vol. II. p. 83, (with unimportant omissions).

Whitehall, May 25. 1383. *Result of that which hath been treated between the Ministers of their Majesties the Kings of Great Britany and Spain in the year 1640.* A league offensive and defensive, the King to break with the Dutch after Scotland is reduced. Three thousand Irish to be levied for Spain. Convoy to be given between Spain and Flanders, and Dunkirk to be succoured if attacked. Twenty additional British ships to be placed in the Channel. Spain to lend 1,200,000 crowns, and to pay 100,000 crowns a month for the twenty ships. Secrecy much urged.
In Windebank's hand, signed and dated by the King. Cl. S. P. vol. II. p. 84.

St. George's, near Brussels, May 25. 1384. *Col. Gage to Mr. George Gage.* Relation of a defeat of the Hollanders in their attempt to besiege Bruges, and an irrecoverable disaster in Chatillon's French army caused by the explosion of all his powder.

1385. *The Infant Cardinal to His Majesty.* A letter of civility, thanking him for his courtesy to the Duchess of Chevreux during her stay at his Court.—French. — 1640. Ghent. May 26.

1386. *Secretary Windebank to Sir A. Hopton.* The result of the conference with the Spanish Ambassadors. The King to enter into a league offensive and defensive with Spain, as soon as Scotland is reduced, on condition of receiving 1,200,000 crowns as loan, half at once, and half at next Michaelmas. *Rough Draught.* — May 27.

By himself. Also a copy of the agreement in his hand.

1387. *The same to the same.* A full detail of the conference, the results of which are stated in the last. Dr. Eden to treat with a Spanish Doctor of Civil Law concerning the complaints of the merchants. *Draught.* — No date.

Endorsed by Windebank, "This was intended to have been sent, but it was not."

1388. *Sir A. Hopton to Secretary Windebank.* Wishes to know whether the proposed marriage has been discussed, for he has learnt from the Venetian Ambassador that the Prince of Spain is promised to the King of Hungary's daughter, though this report may be invented by him to break off the alliance. The Condé Duke disavows all knowledge of the application to Sir B. Gerbier of the charge in the Duke of Arscot's indictment, and this should be enough to satisfy Gerbier. *Two Copies.* — Madrid, June 8.

Partly in cypher, decyphered by Windebank.

1389. *Affidavit* of Mr. Morgan, Deputy-surveyor of that port, of the receipt of a pass to Dunkirk for Aaron Gerrard, a Dutchman. — Dover, June 9.

1390. *Sir A. Hopton to Secretary Windebank.* Dislikes the new treaty, as throwing all the weight, if there be war, upon us, and doubts the sincerity of Spain. Expresses fears for Ireland if the Lord Deputy leave to command the army against Scotland. Complaints of English merchants concerning illegal impositions which should be represented to the Spanish Ambassador. News of a great destruction made by the Hollanders on the Spanish sugar-works in Brazil. *Two Copies.* — Madrid, June $\frac{1}{2}\frac{3}{3}$.

In cypher, decyphered by Windebank. Cl. S. P. vol. ii. p. 86, (with some omissions).

1640.
Ratisbon,
June 19.

1391. *Count Leslie to Secretary Windebank.* Prince Rupert, who is still at Lintz, beloved by all, is allowed to send closed letters to the King and Queen. The Imperial Diet begins on July 26th, when the Palatinate business will doubtless be settled. Urges that Taylor be sent to it, and the friendship of Spain gained, as the conjuncture is good and there is no time to be lost.

June 17.

1392. *Secretary Windebank to Sir A. Hopton.* A long account of the delays and evasive dealings of the Spanish Ambassadors, who evidently do not intend to furnish any money, unless the league be immediately made, which is of course impossible. They deny that they have any instructions to treat about the marriage. He is to make instance to the King of Spain for Prince Rupert's liberty. The King will give the title of Emperor, and send an Ambassador to the Diet. Dangerous illness of the Lord Lieutenant. The army for Scotland will amount to 30,000 foot and 4000 horse. Repulse of the Covenanters by Lord Ettrick at Edinburgh Castle. Capture of Scotch ships with arms from Holland, and Colvil on board, who has confessed to the treasonable letter from the Covenanters to France. The moulds sent from Aranjuez are the wrong heads, Francis 1st instead of Hannibal, and Caracalla instead of Marcellus. Sir Thos. Roe is sworn Privy Councillor, and Lord Lowden liberated and allowed to return to Scotland. *Two Copies.*
By himself.

Lille,
June 30.

1393. *Capt. Shaw to Lord Cottington.* Details of the military operations of the French and Spaniards in the Netherlands. Complains bitterly of the ingratitude of the Hollanders in furnishing the Scotch rebels with arms, and accuses Sir B. Gabier of complicity.

Lille,
June 30.

1394. *Complaint of Mr. George Popham,* in the employment of the Spanish Ambassadors, that he has been arrested by Mr. Gray, an Officer of the High Commission Court.

No date.

1395. *His Majesty to the Duke of Lorraine (Charles IV),* in answer to his letter of June 20th, condoling with him on his defeat by the King of France, and regretting that he has not suggested any other method of assisting him than that of actual force, but expressing confidence that the French King will see the justice of restoring him to his Duchy.—French.
Rough copy, endorsed by Windebank

1396. *An Account* of moneys due to Lady Cave (who died March 4. 1632), on the decease of her husband Sir Thomas Cave, with a release to Mr. Hyde, signed Mary Cave, and dated as in the margin.
1640. July 7.
In Mr. Hyde's hand.

1397. *Sir A. Hopton to Secretary Windebank.* The evasive language of the Condé Duke concerning the proposed loan and marriage. Prince Rupert probably will not be set at liberty as long as the Empire is in danger, being esteemed an active prince. Thinks nothing will be agreed to unless the King consent to defend the coast of Flanders. News of the capture and dispersion by the French of the galloons, which will lessen the probability of a loan. Velasquez, the King's painter, certifies that the heads sent are correct, that of Hannibal only being doubtful, there being so few statues of him existing.
Madrid, July 14/24.
Two Copies.
Partly in cypher, decyphered by Windebank.

1398. *Secretary Windebank to Sir A. Hopton.* The Spanish Ambassadors, to avoid the suspicion of doing nothing, promise a loan of 100,000 crowns. The proposition of seizing moneys in the Mint has been abandoned. Don Alonço de Cardeñas is commissioned Ambassador Resident, and the King is like to retaliate by commissioning Gerbier in the same way at Brussels. Dr. Eden is appointed to treat with a Spanish civilian about the merchants' complaints. Cardeñas has complained of ships fitted by the Earls of Warwick and Marlborough for the West Indies, as privateers under pretence of trading, which Windebank defends as being customary. The young Prince is christened Henry. A proposition is on foot for the coining of brass money.
July 24.
Copy.
In his own hand. Cl. S. P. vol. ii. p. 87.
(with unimportant omissions).

1399. *Sir A. Hopton to Secretary Windebank.* Another conference with the Condé Duke, wherein the same duplicity was exhibited, and he has no hopes of any settlement. Desires to know whether he may give the title of Emperor.
Madrid, Aug. 1st.
Two Copies.
Partly in cypher, decyphered by Windebank.

1400. *The same to the same.* The Condé Duke's great coolness and incivility in a conference, wherein he declared that all the treaties were at an end. Father Semplo tells him, as a secret, that he is to be sent into England to negotiate. Encloses the next.
Madrid, Aug. 11.
Two Copies.

1640.

1401. No date. *Memorial* presented by Sir A. Hopton to the King of Spain, entreating his good offices for the restoration of Prince Rupert to liberty*.—Spanish.
Copy.

Madrid,
Aug. 12/22.

1402. *Sir A. Hopton to Secretary Windebank.* Thinks they are willing to do something in the way of a loan, if they can possibly afford it. Urges great caution in the seizure of the moneys at the Mint. Cardeñas, now that he is appointed Ambassador, had better be obliged than offended. Thinks nothing can be done by the Doctors for reparation of the past wrongs of the merchants, whose eagerness to buy is the chief cause of their sufferings. Thinks nothing will come of Semple's secret.
Two Copies.

Madrid,
Aug. 12/22.

1403. *The same to Lord Cottington.* The difficulty in the way of a loan arises from the disturbances among the Catalans, who are struck wild, and must be dealt with like wild beasts. The people throughout the country are greatly discontented with the exorbitant taxes, especially on wine. The Dukes of Marqueda and Ciudad Real have fought a duel in a quarrel about their jurisdictions, and are both seriously wounded. A fleet for Dunkirk is ready in the Groyne.

Drury Lane,
Aug. 20.

1404. *Secretary Windebank to His Majesty.* The Marquis of Hamilton's troops are to be disbanded for want of money to pay them. Mr. Percy desires to raise a troop of Cuirassiers at his own charge, and under his own command. The Lord Lieutenant is to leave on Monday.
Apostiled by the King, "Newarke, Aug. 23."
Cl. S. P. vol. ii. p. 89, (date misprinted).

Newark,
Aug. 21.

1405. *His Majesty to Secretary Windebank.* If he can get money, doubts not a happy end to the expedition, and has no fears for Newcastle.
Copy.
By Mr. Loveday†. Cl. S. P. vol. ii. p. 91,
(with the omission of an unimportant postscript).

York,
Aug. 23.

1406. *The same to the same.* Urges haste in sending money, and in the raising the coin.
Original, and a copy by Mr. Loveday. Cl. S. P. vol. ii. p. 91.

---

* The difficulty of the title of the Emperor is carefully avoided by omitting all mention of him.
† The MSS. of this letter, with those of Aug. 23, 24, 27, 29, and Sept. 8 and 11, are on one sheet of 2 fol., and endorsed as copies by Mr. John Loveday, Magd. Coll., Oxon. (1728), of originals in the possession of Mr. Richards of Mattingley, near Heckfield, Hants, and of Sir W. Backhouse of Swallowfield.

1407. *His Majesty to Secretary Windebank*, enclosing one to the Queen. *Copy.*
By Mr. Loveday. Cl. S. P. vol. ii. p. 91.
1640. York, Aug. 24.

1408. *Sir A. Hopton to the same.* The Condé Duke promises a speedy settlement. The Catalans are reported as beginning to relent. Great apprehensions are entertained for the safety of the fleet of galleons, which is to leave Spain this month. Ill news from all quarters, which greatly disturbs the Condé Duke, who, in his excessive diligence and uncorruption, is a pattern to all favourites and ministers. Semple says his mission to England is about the restitution of the Palatinate.
Madrid, Aug. 26. Sept. 4.

1409. *His Majesty to the same*, for money. *Copy.*
By Mr. Loveday. Cl. S. P. vol. ii. p. 91.
York, Aug. 27.

1410. *Secretary Windebank to His Majesty.* The Lord General is better. Lord Cottington is hastening the pepper business, and will send 20,000l. to-morrow by Sir W. Uvedall.
Apostiled by the King. "York, Aug. 30." Cl. S. P. vol. ii. p. 91.
Drury Lane, Aug. 28.

1411. *His Majesty to Secretary Windebank.* Thanks him for the good news sent in his letter of the 26th *. *Copy.*
By Mr. Loveday. Cl. S. P. vol. ii. p. 93.
Northallerton, Aug. 29.

1412. *Secretary Windebank to His Majesty.* Condoles with him on the disastrous news. Expresses fears arising from the meetings held by Lords Essex, Warwick, Bedford, Say, Russel and Brooke, Pym, and Hambden, and advises that Essex be employed with the army. The Lords are to confer with the Mayor and Aldermen, on the defence of the city, but are averse to allowing a general muster. Uvedall will leave to-morrow with the 20,000l.
Apostiled by the King, "York, Sept. 2," who desires all unsatisfied Lord Lieutenants to return at once to their counties.
Cl. S. P. vol. ii. p. 94.
Drury Lane, Aug. 31.

1413. *The same to the same.* Urging again that Essex be sent for in an obliging way. The Earl Marshal is doing his best to raise forces. I pray God we find money and commanders.
Apostiled by the King, "York, Sept. 2," who desires the Earl Marshal to know that here we preach the doctrine of serving the King, every one upon his charge for the defence of the realm, which is taken as canonical in Yorkshire, and may well be so in London.
Cl. S. P. vol. ii. p. 96.
Arundel House, Sept. 1.

* This letter does not occur. It probably had reference to money.

1640.
No date.

1414. *Lord Tyrone to Sir A. Hopton.* A paper setting forth the terms on which he will return to the King's allegiance: viz. freedom from molestation in his religion, restitution of all his estates, and the annulling in the Irish Parliament of the sentence against his father.—*Spanish.*

Endorsed by Windebank as received from Hopton Aug. 14th.

Madrid,
Sept. 1¾.

1415. *Sir A. Hopton to Secretary Windebank.* They wait the issue of the Scotch troubles. The King is to go to Saragossa in person against the Catalans. Will do as the other Ambassadors do in respect of accompanying him. They are buying large quantities of shipping, but are greatly deficient in mariners. *Two Copies.*

Drury Lane,
Sept. 3.

1416. *Secretary Windebank to His Majesty.* Urges the policy of conciliation of the disaffected Lords, and redress of grievances. Portsmouth should be prepared as a place of retreat, in case of the worst. *Copy.*

By himself. Cl. S. P. vol. ii. p. 57.

York,
Sept. 3.

1417. *Sir H. Vane to Secretary Windebank.* Leslie has occupied Newcastle and Tynemouth, and is making works on the hill at Gateside. The King has sent for Essex. Expresses doubts as to the result of the war. Cl. S. P. vol. ii. p. 98.

Drury Lane,
Sept. 5.

1418. *Secretary Windebank to Sir A. Hopton.* The King's ill success against the Scots, who have taken Newcastle, and defeated his forces, Serg.-Maj. O'Neale, Charles Porter, and 100 soldiers being slain, and Mr. Willmott and Sir John Digby taken prisoners. On their side the loss is reported about the same, with the Earl of Montrose. The King's forces are about York, amounting with the Train-bands to about 30,000. The danger is greater than any since the Conquest. The design of the copper money is abandoned. The Lord Lieutenant and Lord Cottington, Constable of the Tower, wish him, in case of necessity, to send over two skilled workmen in making walls and houses of earth in moulds. *Copy.*

By himself, partly in cypher.

No date.

1419. *Petition* of English lords to His Majesty for the summoning of a Parliament for the redress of grievances, with the King's answer thereto. *Copy.*

The petition is printed in Nalson, vol. I. p. 437. Rushworth, vol. iii. p. 1260, and Rapin, vol. ii. p. 393, in all of which the names of the Earl of Bristol and Lord Paget are added to the names given here. The answer is printed in Whitelocke's Mem. p. 36.

1420. *Petition* of the Scotch to His Majesty, justifying the passage at Newburn on Tyne, and desiring redress, with the King's answer thereto, signed "Lanerick." *Two Copies.* 1640. Sept. 5.

<small>Printed in Nalson, vol. I. p. 432, and Rushworth, vol. III. p. 1255, with some variations.</small>

1421. *Secretary Windebank to His Majesty.* An account of the hearing of Lords Bedford and Hertford by the Council on the subject of the petition presented by them, and their somewhat evasive answers. The powder promised to the City should be supplied. The Lords are of opinion that the Mint business should not yet be set on foot. Encloses a list of those who voted in Council for a Parliament. Proclamations have been issued, inviting the apprentices to rise. Suggests that the Queen be written to, that Rozetti should retire into France, and the Capuchins disperse. Drury Lane, Sept. 7.

<small>Apostiled by the King, "York, Sept. 9," who says, "I see ye are all so frighted, ye can resolve on nothing." Cl. S. P. vol. ii. p. 110. (On p. 111, l. 35, "unreasonableness" should be "unseasonableness.")</small>

1422. *His Majesty to Secretary Windebank*, acknowledging his letter of the 6th. *Copy.* York, Sept. 8.

<small>By Mr. Loveday. Cl. S. P. vol. ii. p. 113.</small>

1423. *Secretary Windebank to His Majesty.* The Lord Constable is strengthening the Tower, and will provide thirty horses if the King will pay the men. Is the army which is to be raised here to make a stand in these parts to guard the Queen and furnish a retreat? (Yes.) The Earl of Bristol will not meddle with the Lords' petition. Drury Lane, Sept. 9.

<small>Apostiled by the King, "York, Sept. 11," who puts the expense of the army at 40,000l. a month. The first part is lost.
Cl. S. P. vol. ii. p. 114.</small>

1424. *The same to the same.* Further explanations on the interview with Essex and Hertford. A like petition is to be presented by the City, if not prevented. Lord Bath and the gentry of Devonshire have presented one against the new Canons and the Oath. One O'Connor, chaplain to the Queen-Mother, has been committed by him for seditious words. Advises that great ships be forbidden to enter the port of Newcastle. Sir R. Mansel has some deep imaginings for beating the rebels out of that haven. Alderman Abdy is dead. The Committee approve the plan for strengthening Portsmouth. Drury Lane, Sept. 11.

<small>Apostiled by the King, "York, Sept. 13." Cl. S. P. vol. ii. p. 115.</small>

1640.
Drury
Lane,
Sept. 18.

1425. *Secretary Windebank to His Majesty.* Of the City petition, which the Aldermen are unwilling to disavow. Advises that Dr. Burgess, who has left for York to present a petition, be committed to prison; and that the privilege granted to York, of wardship of heirs to those who perish in the service, be extended to the south. Cottington has sent 10,000l. to-day, and will send like sums at intervals of four or five days. The Bishop of Lincoln's being in the Tower is a great inconvenience, he should be moved to another prison. No likelihood of a creation of Cardinals soon, but the Queen's nomination of W. Montagu might hasten it.

Apostiled by the King, " York, Sept. 20." Cl. S. P. vol. ii. p. 117.

Drury
Lane,
Sept. 20.

1426. *The same to the same.* Desires instructions as to the sale of Scotch ships which have been arrested. Mr. Percy's troop is formed, and waits only for pay. Is the Captain to have the same pay as that of the only other troop of Cuirassiers, i. e. 20s. a day more than any other Captain of horse? (Yes.) Sir W. Berkeley has some plan for discovering what English lords have intelligence with Leslie*.

Apostiled by the King. Cl. S. P. vol. ii. p. 119.

York,
Sept. 21.

1427. *His Majesty to Secretary Windebank,* for copies of all Acts of Council concerning the Scotch business. The ordinary winter-guard of ships must be kept at sea. Wishes to revise George Kirke's discharge of his jewels, before registered. *Copy.*

By Mr. Loveday. Cl. S. P. vol. ii. p. 120.

Drury
Lane,
Sept. 23.

1428. *Secretary Windebank to His Majesty.* Lord Herbert wishes to join his father at York, Somersetshire, whereof he is Lieutenant, being in very good order. The Lord Constable representing the inconveniences which would arise from having the Mint in the Tower, the Board advises that it be moved to Leadenhall. Cottington proposes a plan of prolonging the loans which will come due soon: 12,000l. is sent to-day.

Apostiled by the King, " York, Sept. 25." Cl. S. P. vol. ii. p. 120.

Sept.

1429. *Petition* of the gentry of York, to His Majesty, complaining of the heavy sums which they are compelled to pay for the billeting of soldiers. *Copy.*

Endorsed by Lord Clarendon.

* In this letter there is allusion to a letter of Windebank's of the 16th, which does not occur.

1430. *Secretary Windebank to Sir A. Hopton.* The purpose of sending to the Emperor is now at a stand. Of the success of the Scots, and their intention to conquer England. The vulgar look on them as redeemers and dote on them, especially in London. Edinburgh Castle is yielded to the rebels, after a gallant defence by Lord Ettrick. The rebels make vast profits of the Newcastle collieries, and intend by manning the colliers to grow powerful at sea. Success of Lieut. South in surprising Sir Arch. Douglas, when making an incursion into Yorkshire. *Draught. By himself.*
1640. Sept. 24.

1431. *List* of the Peers assembled for the great Council at York, with a letter from the Scots to Lord Lanerick, pressing their previous petition and the King's Speech at the first meeting. *Copy.*
Sept. 24.

<small>Also two duplicates of the Speech, one in Windebank's hand, with a list of the Peers appointed to meet at Rippon. Printed in Nals. vol. I. p. 443, Rush. vol. III. p. 1275, and Rap. vol. ii, p. 324.</small>

1432. *Instructions* for the Commissioners (apparently at Rippon), with reference to the payment of the Scotch and English forces. *Copy.*
No date.

1433. *Secretary Windebank to His Majesty.* Encloses the Acts of Council required. Of means to get money. The Lord Chamberlain and others who have places in Parliament at their disposal should be treated with to reserve them for the King, if a Parliament be summoned.
Drury Lane, Sept. 25.

<small>Apostiled by the King, "York, Sept. 27." The Mayor and City are to be flattered, not threatened. The Queen-Mother's Frenchman in the Tower is to be at the Queen's disposal.
Cl. S. P. vol. ii. p. 112.</small>

1434. *The same to the same.* A design to put by Ald. Acton from being chosen Lord Mayor, as being a friend to the King. Twenty-five Scotch officers who have served in Sweden (among them Col. Lumsden, Col. David Lesly, and Col. Sinclair) will leave Gottenburg for Scotland on Nov. 1, and should be intercepted. Hull should be strengthened.
Drury Lane, Sept. 28.

<small>Apostiled by the King, "York, Oct. 1." Cl. S. P. vol. ii. p. 114.
(On p. 124, l. 10, "Aston" should be "Acton.")</small>

1435. *The same to the same.* Of Taylor's (the paymaster at Berwick) requirement of money to pay the garrison there. The election of Lord Mayor has been very disorderly: Ald. Soame, a disaffected man, being put up over seven or eight
Drury Lane, Sept. 30.

1640. seniors to supersede Acton. Advises that if Acton cannot be chosen, the present Mayor be continued for a year. Forwards a letter from Rome concerning the red hat, which should be communicated to the Duke of Lennox.

Apostiled by the King, " York, Oct. 3." Cl. S. P. vol. II. p. 125.

Sept. 1436. *Mr. Hyde to Lady ———*.* A letter of civility, thanking her for her good opinion of him. *Rough Draught.*
By himself.

Oct. 1. 1437. *Secretary Windebank to Sir A. Hopton.* Good effect of the King's Speech at York and promise of a Parliament for Nov. 3. Hopes that the negotiation at Rippon and the proposed loan of 200,000*l.* will disperse the black storm.
Copy.
By himself.

York, Oct. 3. 1438. *Treasurer Vane to Secretary Windebank.* Forwards information of what took place yesterday at the first meeting at Rippon. The Scots know that they are on vantage-ground. God send the King once out of these straits. His sorrow at the tumults on the election of Lord Mayor.

Drury Lane, Oct. 4. 1439. *Secretary Windebank to His Majesty.* Announces the success of the money treaty with the City.

Apostiled by the King, "York, Oct. 6." Cl. S. P. vol. II. p. 127.

Drury Lane, Oct. 6. 1440. *The same to the same.* The City have rejected Acton, and chosen Ald. Wright, who is next in order. Is he to be admitted when he comes to take oath in the Exchequer? (Yes). Advises that a proclamation be published declaring the falseness of a report that the Queen-Mother has procured the grant of an imposition on leather, which injures the Queen extremely in public opinion. Sir Toby Mathew was yesterday apprehended.

Apostiled by the King, " York, Oct. 9." Cl. S. P. vol. II. p. 128.

Drury Lane, Oct. 9. 1441. *The same to Sir A. Hopton,* directing him to further Capt. Steward's business with the Spanish King. *Copy.*
By himself.

Drury lane, Oct. 14. 1442. *The same to His Majesty.* A detailed account of the management of the loan of 200,000*l.* from the City, whereof there is much difficulty in getting more than 50,000*l.* The

---

* The name is endorsed by him, and appears something like Carnarvon.

Lord Privy Seal's conduct in the matter. The writs for the Parliament are out, and Windebank not being elected for Oxford, Mr. Henry Jermyn will resign to him his seat for Corfe Castle.

1640.

Apostiled by the King, "York, Oct. 16." Cl. S. P. vol. ii. p. 129.

1443. *Secretary Windebank to His Majesty.* Of the money business, and the writs for Parliament, which have been delayed. Is one Ogle, of the Bishopric of Northumberland (suspected of holding intelligence with the Covenanters), to be discharged? (Yes.) And Cunningham, who has been so long in prison for refusing the oath? (Yes.)

Drury lane, Oct. 16.

Apostiled by the King, "York, Oct. 18." The Lords there will write a very effectual letter to the City for the rest of the 100,000*l*.
Cl. S. P. vol. ii. p. 132

1444. *Sir Giles Mompesson to Mr. Hyde.* Is glad that he still retains his friendship, which his long silence had made him fear was forfeited. Hopes that he will be returned to Parliament.

Oct. 18.

1445. *Sir G. Ayliffe** *to the same*, forwarding some books. Lord Andover has written to him not to go to Wilton to vote for him, as he will not stand against Sir Henry Ludlow and Sir James Thinn for the shire.

Rubson, Oct. 19.

1446. *Speech of His Majesty* at the opening of the Parliament. *Three Copies.*

Nov. 3.

Printed in Nalson, vol. I. p. 481, Rush. vol. iii. p. 1335, and Rap. vol. II. p. 350, with some variations.

1447. *Dr. Gilbert Sheldon*† *to Mr. Hyde.* If any good success happen in Parliament, they must thank men of Hyde's prudence and temper for it.

All Souls, Oxford, Nov. 6.

1448. *Speeches* of Mr. Pym, Lord Digby, Sir E. Doring, Mr. Grimston, and Sir J. Colepepper, in the debate upon Grievances.

Nov. 7.9.

These speeches are printed in Parl. Hist. vol. II. p. 640, &c., Nalson, and Rushworth, but with great variations of wording, as from different reports, and with some difference of substance also.

1449. *Sir A. Hopton to Secretary Windebank.* All business

Madrid, Nov. 7/17.

---

* Lord Clarendon's father-in-law.
† Warden of All Souls, Oxford; described by Lord Clarendon in his Life, p. 918.

1640.   with that Court is at a standstill. Sends the two workmen
of earthworks as requested. Nothing is concluded in Catalonia, the Catalans waiting to see the acceptance of their
terms, before they invite the French into their country.
Their conditions are reasonable, through dislike, as he thinks,
of the French. There is a mysterious jealousy of the Infant
Cardinal, whom they wish to recall from Flanders, on pretence of service in Portugal. The dislike of the Condé Duke
is supposed to be the cause, and the Infant Cardinal also
complains of his love affairs being interfered with, his mistress
having been ordered from Brussels. They are offering Prince
Thomas the command of the army against the Catalans or
the French, but both he and his brother are weary of their
service; all strangers being sure to be badly treated as long
as the Condé Duke rules. The Princess of Carignan wishes
to go to her husband, but they are unwilling to lose her as a
hostage. The Danish Ambassador is negotiating for a closer
alliance with Spain and England against Holland and Sweden.
Copy.

Partly in cypher.

Lambeth, Nov. 7.   1450. *The Archbishop of Canterbury to the University of Oxford,* accompanying a gift of eighty-one Hebrew, Arabic, Persian, Greek, Latin, Italian, and English manuscripts to the Bodleian Library, under the same conditions as his former gifts: giving as a reason that they are not safe in his own house during these perilous times.—Latin.   *Copy.*

Printed in Laud's Remains, vol. II. p. 213.

Oxford, Nov. 9.   1451. *The University of Oxford to the Archbishop of Canterbury,* expressing gratitude to him and loyal attachment to the Church.—Latin.   *Copy.*

Printed as the last.

Westbury, Nov. 10.   1452. *William Fauconer (the elder) to Mr. Hyde,* concerning a money arrangement for his grandson.

Nov. 24.   1453. *Articles of the House of Commons assembled in Parliament against Thomas Earl of Strafford in maintenance of their accusation, whereby he stands charged with High Treason*.*
Copy.

Printed in Rush. Trial, p. 6.

* These are not the final Articles of the Indictment, (which were not prepared till Jan. 30, 1640-1.) but preliminary Articles of Impeachment. See Whitelock's Memorials, vol. I. pp. 111, 131.

1454. *Petition of the Earl of Strafford to the Lords*, that no witness be examined till he has put in his answer to the indictment, and that then the names of all witnesses be submitted to him before examination, for his exception or cross-examination. *Copy.* — 1640. Nov. 17.

1455. *Petition of the same to the same*, to be heard by counsel against the request of the Commons, that the depositions taken in his case should be delivered to the Committee appointed to draw up the Articles of indictment. *Copy.* — No date.

1456. *Sir John St. John to Mr. Hyde*, for his opinion on some papers. — Battemore, Nov. 30.

1457. *Lady Lee* to the same.* Thinks the Parliament will hold, because of the King's necessities. The Papists in Oxfordshire begin to look blank. Sends a venison pie. Wishes to know if Mr. Pledwell has made any learned speech in Parliament yet. He had done well to have been chosen Speaker. — Nov.

1458. *The Remonstrance of the House of Commons in Ireland to the Right Hon. the Lord Deputy.* The principal grievances are illegal taxation, arbitrary determination of cases, monopoly of tobacco, the destruction of the plantation of Londonderry, the exorbitant power of the High Commission, and the prohibition to go to England without purchasing a licence. *Copy.* — Nov.

Printed in Rush., Trial of Strafford, p. 17.

1459. *Sir Giles Mompesson to Mr. Hyde.* Requests a meeting at Christmas concerning a Chancery suit in which he is engaged. — Dec. 1.

1460. *Archdeacon Marler to the same*, lamenting the violent feeling in Parliament against the clergy. Of Mr. Hyde's rents at Pyrton. — Dec. 2.

1461. *Minute* of the appointment of Commissioners to treat with the Scotch Commissioners in London. [Also some notes (in Lord Clarendon's hand) of a much later date, concerning the dissolutions of Parliament in this reign.] — Dec. 3.

1462. *Sir Giles Mompesson to Mr. Hyde*, concerning the same business as his last. — Dec. 5.

---

* Of Ditchley, afterwards Countess of Rochester; Sir J. Wolstenholme's daughter. See Lord Clarendon's Life, p. 948.

1640.
Durham,
Dec. 5.

1463. *William Tomlinson to Mr. Triplett*, informing him that he has been summoned to London as his clerk, to give evidence before the Grand Committee of Religion, on the informations laid against him by Lilburne. With a copy of the summons.

Dec. 7.

1464. *Resolutions of the House of Commons against Ship-money.* Also *Speech of Lord Falkland* on that occasion, severely censuring the Judges for their extrajudicial opinion published in the Star-Chamber. *Copies.*

The Resolutions are printed in Parl. Hist. vol. II. p. 672.

Bishopston,
Dec. 9.

1465. *Mr. John Earles* to Mr. Hyde*, rallying him on the reserve and scantiness of his letters, and mentioning familiar topics on which he may write, even though the Earl Marshal himself intercept his letters.

Paris,
Dec. 1½.

1466. *Mr. William Aylesbury to the same.* Though Hyde said it was not in the wit of man to save Windebank, he has reached Calais in safety. He in the Tower (Strafford) must be better looked to.

Cl. S. P. vol. II. p. 133.

Dec. 11.

1467. *Petition of the City of London to the Commons,* against Bishops. *Copy.*

Printed in Nals. vol. i. p. 666, Rush. vol. iv. p. 93. Parl. Hist. vol. II. p. 673, with some verbal differences. The words printed "Barnes' poems" are here "Carew's poems."

Dec. 14.

1468. *Mr. Laurence St. Loe to Mr. Hyde,* concerning an executorship account, and other money matters.

Lydiard,
Dec. 15.

1469. *Sir John St. John to the same,* complimenting him on his efforts to abolish ship-money, as the greatest patriarch of the kingdom.

Lydiard,
Dec. 16.

1470. *Archdeacon Marler to the same.* God bless the Parliament and him from their clutches. The Canons by this time are subject to more damnation than the ship-money.

Bruton,
Dec. 18.

1471. *Sir John Berkeley to the same,* to engage his assistance in a case concerning the fens.

Dec. 18.

1472. *Mr. Thomas Triplett to the same.* A story of a mad parson who has summoned Lesley to appear before the

* Fellow of Merton College, Oxford; described by Lord Clarendon in his Life, p. 918.

CLARENDON PAPERS. 213

Council at York. Entreats him to get rid of the Scots, who, 1640.
though they receive pay from Parliament, take grass, hay,
and straw without payment, so that the farmers are ruined
through want of fodder for their beasts.

1473. *Mr. William Aylesbury* to Mr. Hyde*, desiring him Paris,
to send money. Dec. 1/7.

1474. *Sir Giles Mompesson to Mr. Philip Basnett*, about the Dec. 22.
carriage of some marmalade and preserved quinces.

1475. *Minutes* of the adjournments of the Committee ap- Dec. 23.
pointed to enquire into the jurisdictions of the County of
York, and the Council of the Marches of Wales.
In the hand of Mr. Hyde, Chairman of the Committee.

1476. *Mr. W. Aylesbury to Mr. Hyde*, desiring Parliament Paris,
news. Rumour says Lord Holland is to be Lord Deputy, Dec. 14.
and Lord Bedford Treasurer. The Aldermen's petition has Jan. 4.
troubled him much.

1477. *Minute* of a Committee to examine into the com- Dec. 30.
plaints against Mr. Witherings concerning the management
of the Post-Office arrangements.

1478. *Speech of Mr. Pym* on the Articles against Sir George Dec. 31.
Ratcliffe for conspiring with the Earl of Strafford.
Printed in Nals., vol. L p. 702, Parl. Hist. vol. ii. p. 699.

1479. *The Lord Conway's narrative of his Conduct in the* No date.
Action at Newburn. A long and interesting account of the
preparations for the battle, and the causes of defeat, comprising his correspondence with the Lord Lieutenant, and
defending himself against the various charges brought against
him. Cl. S. P. vol. ii. p. 99†.
(On p. 104, l. 35, "Coring" should be "Conway;" on p. 108, l. 5, "800"
should be "8000," and L 17, "order" should be "Oratory.")

1480. *Mr. John Flügel to His Majesty.* A letter from the No date.
Ablegate of the Duke of Courland, thanking His Majesty for
inducing the King of Poland to confirm the resignation of the

---

* Son of Sir Thos. Aylesbury, and brother to Lord Clarendon's first wife.
† This paper is described in the Preface to 2nd vol. of Cl. S. P. as having been
printed in a volume by Sir David Dalrymple. (Mem. on the Reign of Charles I,
p. 81.) It is the Editor's opinion that it goes far to vindicate Lord Conway
from the censures of Lord Clarendon, who had probably not seen the paper when
he wrote that part of his History. There is another copy in the Harleian MSS.

1640. late Duke Frederic, in favour of his nephew, the present Duke James, and asking him to continue to him the same allowance as King James had made to Duke William.—Latin. *Two Copies.*

No date. 1481. *Complaint of Don Alonso de Cardeñas* concerning the Letters of Marque granted to Lords Warwick, Say, Brook, Mr. Pym and others, and their abuse of the privilege.—Spanish and English. *Copies.*

No date. 1482. *Lady Dalkeith to Mr. Hyde,* lamenting the position she is in as a Scotchman's wife.

The year endorsed by Lord Clarendon.

No date. 1483. *Reasons why the Oath in the Canons made 1640 may not safely be sworn in the plain and common sense of the words in which it is penned.* The objections taken are to the statement that the established doctrine and *discipline* contain all things necessary to salvation, to the obligation against any future alteration, and to the assertion that they *ought of right* to stand as they are*.

No date. 1484. *The effect of three Arguments of the King's Solicitor, Sir Francis Bacon, to maintain the jurisdiction of the Council of the Marches over the four Shires* of Salop, Worcester, Gloucester, and Hereford. *Copy.*

In Windebank's hand.

No date. 1485. *Reasons why the four English Counties ought to be under the jurisdiction of the Council of the Marches of Wales.* To this are annexed answers to certain objections to the view maintained†. In Windebank's hand.

No date. 1486. *Keys to various Cyphers,* principally those used by the Ambassadors resident abroad, comprising

1. *Cypher with the R. Hon. Lo. High Tres. of England,* 30 *July,* 1632, *and J. Boswell, Agent Resident with the States General.*

2. *Lord Aston's cypher.* A modern copy.

---

* The Oath itself and various objections to it are printed in Nalson, vol. i. pp. 373, 396, Rushworth, vol. ii. p. 1186, and Rapin, vol. ii. p. 321.
† These papers are evidently prepared with a view to a Committee of this Parliament, of which Lord Clarendon (Life, p. 936) mentions that he was Chairman, the object of which was to determine whether Salop, Worcester, Gloucester, and Hereford were under the jurisdiction referred to.

3. *Leander's cypher.* Endorsed by Windebank. 1640.

4. *Mr. Hopton's cypher.*
   Three distinct cyphers, one endorsed as "Oct. 1638."

5. *Mr. Curtius' cypher.* End. by Windebank.

6. *Cypher with Mr. Morton, Resident at Turin, sent to him 23 April, 1635. Also another sent 16 Nov. 1635.*
   End. by Windebank.

7. *Father Welford's cypher.* End. by Windebank.

8. *John Taylor's cypher.* Two distinct.

9. *Cypher of Mr. Avery, received June 28, 1638.*
   End. by Windebank.

10. *Mr. Gerbier's cypher.* End. by Windebank.

11. *Cypher with the Earl of Leicester, sent to him into France, 26 Oct. 1637.* End. by Windebank.

12. *Lord Deputy's cypher.* End. by Windebank.

13. *Sir W. Hamilton's cypher.* End. by Windebank.

14. *Sir Thos. Roe's cypher.* End. by Windebank.

15. *Sir Oliver Fleming's cypher.* End. by Windebank.

16. *Cypher between my Lord Treasurer (?) and Lord Fielding.*

17. *Cypher to correspond with Mr. Dawson.*

18. *Cypher with Mr. Elson.*
   Written and endorsed by Lord Clarendon.

19. *Cypher of the Lord Hatton.*

20. *Five Anonymous cyphers.* One written by Windebank.

1640-1.
1487. *Mr. Triplett to Mr. Hyde.* Entreats him to prevent Jan. 1. his Parliament journey, for what can they have of a cat but her skin! and he is already ruined, having neither horse nor money.

1488. *Dr. Hodson[*] to the same*, stating the hardships of York. Triplett's case. Jan. 2.

---

[*] Prebendary of York. See Lord Clarendon's Life, p. 957.

1640-1. Jan. 1.	1489. *Answer to a message from the Parliament to the Scots*, that while they consider their demands for losses, the Scots will consider the Articles of Peace. They excuse themselves till they are informed what proportion of their losses will be made good. *Copy.*
Paris, Jan. 1/12.	1490. *Mr. W. Aylesbury to Mr. Hyde.* Windebank's carriage is very strange; he is as merry as if he were the contentedest man living; and avows the King and Queen both knew of his coming away, and that he had the King's order for all he over did concerning the Papists. He never could be a good Privy Councillor, for he tells all he ever knew or did. Cl. S. P. vol. ii. p. 134.
Lydiard, Jan. 9.	1491. *Sir John St. John to the same.* Desires his help to persuade his daughter Lee to accept an offer of marriage. Thinks Parliament undertakes too much at once. Hopes the great offenders will not escape.
Lambeth. Jan. 12.	1492. *Dr. John Oliver to the same*, requesting him to protect his interests during his absence at his parsonage in Kent.
Lydiard, Jan. 13.	1493. *Archdeacon Marler to the same.* Is sorry to hear his business engages him so much.
Covent Garden, Jan. 14.	1494. *Dr. Donne to the same*, desiring his advice concerning a petition to the Commons, which he copies, and in which he represents that he has been cozened out of the living of Tillingham in Essex, by Thos. Nicholson and the Rev. Michael Hudson, by means of a pretended exchange to the living of Ufford in Northampton, the title to which presentation is now disputed by the Crown.
Hydon Lane, Jan. 15.	1495. *Sir John Wolstenholme to the same*, recommending the petition of the bearer, John Burnett.
York, Jan. 15.	1496. *Mr. Triplett to the same.* Humourously describes his great pleasure on receiving Hyde's letter with the news that he need not appear before Parliament. Recapitulates the evidence of Lilburne and Grey's complicity in the plunder of his house by the Scots; and narrates stories at length to show how little title they have to the character of Saints.
Bishopston, Jan. 15.	1497. *Mr. John Earles to the same.* Hopes that he and Lord Falkland will bestir themselves in Mr. Triplett's behalf.

1498. *Mr. Triplett to Mr. Hyde*, recommending to him the bearer, Mr. Johnson, parson of Bishop's Wearmouth, another of Lilburne's victims.
1640-1. York, Jan. 16.

1499. *The same to the same*, with a present of liquorice cakes. Jokes of the comfort Seneca affords him in his troubles.
York, Jan. 18.

1500. *The same to the same.* Lilburne's consternation at the testimonial given to his integrity by his parishioners.
Jan. 21.

1501. *Mr. W. Aylesbury to the same.* Urges him to be cautious in his proceedings against the judges, which he cannot think the King likes.
Paris, Jan. 21. Feb. 1.

1502. *Sir Giles Mompesson to the same*, apologizing for having accused him of neglecting his law business.
Jan. 24.

1503. *Archdeacon Marler to the same.* Ironical admiration of the new great statesman of Hakeney (!), whose abilities are so transcendent as to direct both King and Parliament. All the clergy look for a doom as well as the Metropolitan. Too many rabbits at Pyrton. Wishes to be advised how to get out of the commission before being turned out with the rest of the clergy.
Lydiard, Jan. 27.

1504. *Mr. Laurence St. Loe to the same*, concerning the same matters as his last.
Jan. 30.

1505. *Sir Simon Harcourt to the same.* Desires to be remembered in the contemplated changes in places of judicature. Thinks they proceed but slowly with the Lord Keeper and Lord Lieutenant.
Jan.

1506. *Archdeacon Marler to the same*, concerning the encouragement given by Parliament to persecute and inform against orthodox clergy.
Lydiard, Feb. 5.

1507. *Resolutions* of the Post-Office Committee, to restore Mr. Witherings to the management of the foreign posts.
Feb. 3.

1508. *Mr. Triplett to Mr. Hyde.* Entreats further assurance that he need not go to London. Yorkshire suffers incredibly from both armies.
York, Feb. 5.

1509. *Dr. Hodson to the same.* Triplett's joy at the receipt of his letters.
Feb. 5.

1640–1. Feb. 8.	1510. *Petition of Lady Purbeck to the House of Lords*, complaining of grievous wrongs from the late Duke of Buckingham and others, who by force confined her husband* as of weak intellect, separated her from him, seized her dowry, and obtained, through the connivance of the Archbishop of Canterbury, a sentence against her in the High Commission Court on a charge of adultery.
No date.	1511. *Minute* of proofs that a patent was passed for John, Viscount Purbeck, in the 17th of James I.
Feb. 10.	1512. *Minute* of the reconstitution of the Post-Office Committee to examine witnesses, &c., and report on abuses.
Feb. 10.	1513. *Archdeacon Marler to Mr. Hyde.* Of a lease of a house and lands. Are the Scots to be maintained here as executioners of the papists and prelates, or have we agreed with them as Hezekiah with the Assyrian?
York, Feb. 11.	1514. *Mr. Triplett to the same.* Puts his losses at 65*l*. Hopes Alderman Abell's fine will help pay the Scots army, then Abel will pay Cain. Fears to be proceeded against in his absence. Encloses the next.
No date.	1515. *Petition of Mr. Triplett to the Lords at Rippon*, stating particulars of his losses in the plunder of his house by the Scots. *Copy.*
Paris, Feb 12/22.	1516. *Mr. W. Aylesbury to Mr. Hyde.* Who is to be Lord Lieutenant? We† have but little hopes of it. Hears that Nicholas is to succeed Windebank. Thinks it strange his father gets nothing in these changes. Wishes a handsomely-bound copy of Dr. Donne's Sermons sent him, to present to Lady Leicester.
Paris, Feb. 19. March 2.	1517. *The same to the same.* Is grieved to hear Lord Holland is to be Lord Lieutenant, there being in that case no possibility of providing for us†. Urges Hyde to find some place for him. Sends, for Lord Falkland, an edict lately issued, to shew him the absolute power of the French King. The conduct of the English Parliament is said to be the cause of its issue.
Lydiard, Feb. 21.	1518. *Archdeacon Marler to the same*, about his lands, and money matters.

* Lord Purbeck was brother of the Duke of Buckingham, Lady Purbeck was daughter of Sir Edw. Coke.
† I. e. Lord Leicester.

1519. *The Landgravine of Hesse to His Majesty*, thanking him for his exertions in behalf of the Palatine House.— French. — 1640-1. Lipstat, Feb. 24. March 4.

1520. *The Earl of Strafford's Answers to the fifth and sixth Articles* of the indictment, being those concerning his treatment of Lord Mountnorris. *Copy.* — Feb. 24*.

    Printed in an abridged form in Rush., Trial, p. 23.

1521. *Archdeacon Marler to Mr. Hyde.* Advises a lease of twenty-one years, which is reckoned worth ten years' purchase; as also a lease for three lives. — Lydiard, Feb. 24.

1522. *Mr. Francis Kibblewhite to the same*, concerning the sale of some of his wood, for which 70*l.* is offered. — Feb. 27.

1523. *Mr. Triplett to the same*, of his new fears. Is dining with Col. Lunsford, Capts. Washington, Chudley, Vaughan, and others. Encloses the next. — York, Feb. 27.

1524. *Summons* to Mr. Triplett to appear before the Grand Committee of Religion on the 29th of May next. — No date.

1525. *Secretary Vane to the Lord Justices of Ireland (Lord Dillon and Sir W. Parsons)*, giving notice of the passage of Irish from Spain under pretext of raising men for Spain. But among the Irish friars there is a whisper as if they expected some rebellion in Ireland, and particularly in Conagh (Connaught).   Cl. S. P. vol. ii. p. 134 †. — Whitehall, March 16.

1641.

1526. *Speech* of Mr. Hyde, on bringing up the Report of the Committee, recommending the abolition of the Court at York. *Copy.* — April 26.

    Printed in Parl. Hist. vol. ii. p. 766.

1527. *The Earl of Strafford to His Majesty.* The famous letter in which he absolves the King from his promise to him, and begs him to give his assent to the Bill for his execution. *Copy.* — Tower, May 4.

  Endorsed by Lord Clarendon, "My Lord Strafford's last letter to the King‡." Printed in most histories.

---

* This date is from Rushworth.
† To the printed copy is attached a note to the effect that this letter is printed in the "History of the Execrable Irish Rebellion," &c., folio; printed in London for Robert Clavel, 1680. Some doubts are said to have been cast upon its authenticity; but the signature is undoubtedly in Vane's hand, and it is endorsed by the Lord Justice Parsons.
‡ As some doubt has been thrown on the authenticity of this celebrated letter,

1641.
York,
May 7.

1528. *Mr. Triplett to Mr. Hyde.* The abolition of the Court of York will be the utter ruin of that city. Humourously laments his double ruin, by the Scots and as a member of Convocation, and wishes he had stuck to the profession of medicine.

May 11.

1529. *Lord Mountnorris to the Earl of Strafford.* A pathetic letter, enumerating the wrongs done him by the Lord Lieutenant, and desiring a reconciliation, and his intercession with the King in behalf of his wife and seven children.

Apparently an original, though endorsed as a copy; it is directed as an original would be. Cl. S. P. vol. ii. p. 135.

Lydiard,
May 16.

1530. *Archdeacon Marler to Mr. Hyde.* News of his cellar and garden. Ironical hopes of peace when the Archbishop and Judges go the same way as the Lord Lieutenant.

May 24.

1531. *The Declaration and Protestation of the Lords Spiritual and Temporal and Commons in Parliament assembled* (of Ireland) on the occasion of the Impeachment of the Lord Chancellor (Sir Richard Bolton), and Lord Chief Justice of the Common Pleas (Sir Gerard Louther), affirming the supreme right of Parliament to decide all cases civil and criminal. To which is annexed a petition to the King to the same effect. *Copy.*

See Carte's Life of Ormond, vol. I. p. 149, where an extract from this is printed.

June 8.

1532. *Note* of the state of affairs in Parliament at this date, especially the question of the Bishops' seats.

June 12.

1533. *Dr. Morley to Mr. Hyde.* His fears that he cannot exchange livings with Dr. ——, on account of the Oath of Simony.

Sydon Lane,
June 28.

1534. *Sir John Woldenholme to the same,* desiring certain steps may be taken in the passing of the farmers' bill of oblivion to exempt his name, inserted for a debt as heir and executor to his father.

March 13
to June 28.

1535. *Five Papers of Minutes* of the sittings and resolutions of the Committee on the Court of York, and the Council of the Marches. *In Lord Clarendon's hand.*

and Carte (Hist. of Engl. vol. iv. p. 352) openly asserts it to have been a forgery, on the evidence of the Earl's son, and imputes it to the Bishop of Lincoln, this endorsement of Lord Clarendon may be noted of some importance, as implying his belief in its authenticity.

1536. *Dr. Walter Raleigh to Mr. Hyde.* Hopes to alter the opinions of Hyde's cousin. Begs him not to be too wise nor reserved to an old friend.
                                                                    1641. Chedzoy, July 12.

1537. *Mr. Triplett to the same.* A humourous expression of gratitude for being allowed to keep his living, though not a groat is paid him by the parishioners.
                                                                    July 12.

1538. *Resolutions* of the Committee of Jurisdictions, that the jurisdiction of the Council of the Marches of Wales is a grievance and fit to be abolished by Bill.
                                                                    July 19.
                    In Mr. Hyde's handwriting.

1539. *A Calculation of His Majesty's ordinary yearly Revenue,* by a medium of five years, made by warrant from the Lords Commissioners of the Treasury. It is reckoned under three heads, the totals of each being, by Customs and Impositions of that nature, 482,305*l.* 0*s.* 1*d.*; by Revenues esteemed legal, 277,774*l.*; by several ways and means held illegal, 139,403*l.* 5*s.* 11*d.*
                                                                    Aug. 16.

1540. *The Confession of the Duke of Medina Sidona, and the King of Spain's Answer.* Explaining his share in the rebellion of the Duke of Braganza, who wished him to proclaim himself King of Galicia. The King pardons him by decree.—Spanish. *Copy.*
                                                                    Sept. 21.

1541. *Five Papers of Accounts* relative to the Almshouses and the renting of the poor's ground at Pyrton.
                                                                    Oct. 6.
        Signed by Mr. Hyde, Nevill Maskelyne, Rickards, and Skillinge.

1542. *A Note of Evidence* against Capt. Venn for endeavouring to raise an armed mob in Westminster to coerce Parliament when Mr. Palmer was sent to the Tower*.
                                                                    No date.
            Endorsed by Lord Clarendon. Apparently imperfect.

1543. *The Council of Ireland to the Lord Keeper* (Lyttleton), requesting a Commission to examine in Dublin Sir James Ware, Sir Paul Davis, and Sir Philip Percival, (witnesses in the case of Lord Mountnorris against the late Earl of Strafford and other members of the Council,) on the ground that their presence is required in Ireland, as officers of the Parliament.   *Copy.*
                                                                    Dublin, Nov. 29.

---

* Mr. Palmer was sent to the Tower Nov. 14, 1641. See Clar. Hist. Rebell. bk. iv. p. 116.

1641.
Nov. 30
to Dec. 11.

1544. *Minutes of the Conference between the two Houses* about the tumults, and proceedings of the Commissioners against the officers and constables placed to secure the passages to the House. *Copy.*

Endorsed by Lord Clarendon.

Dec. 18.

1545. *Message sent by His Majesty to the House of Peers by the Lord Chamberlain,* offering to raise 10,000 English Volunteers for the suppression of the Irish rebellion, if the Parliament will pay them. To which is subjoined *His Majesty's Proclamation* declaring the Irish to be rebels. *Copies.*

Endorsed by Secretary Nicholas.
See Carte's Life of Ormond, vol. i. p. 208; Rap. vol. ii. p. 401.

Dec. 19.

1546. *Minute* of the rescue of two apprentices from the Sheriffs, when committed to Newgate for threatening to pull down the Lord Mayor's house.

No date.

1547. *Robert Read to Mr. Hyde,* offering to let him some land. The arable land is reckoned at 10s., the pasture at 1l. per acre.

No date.

1548. *Petition* of the poor of London to the House of Commons. *Copy.*

Printed in Clar. Hist. Rebell. bk. iv. p. 165.

No date.

1549. *Petition* of the Brewers of London to Parliament, complaining of a tax of 4d. upon every quarter of malt imposed for the King's use, and which had been voted illegal in a former Parliament.—Printed.

1641-2.
Jan. 2.

1550. *Warrant* from Secretary Nicholas for printing forty copies of the Proclamation of Dec. 28th.

Printed in Rush. vol. iv. p. 473. and Rap. vol. ii. p. 401. To the original is subjoined this minute (in Lord Clarendon's(?) hand), "The Justices in Ireland desired but forty Proclamations, which occasioned the direction, and a hurry of business only hindered the stop of more from being printed off."

Jan. 6.

1551. *Warrant* of His Majesty, appointing Sir John Colepepper Chancellor of the Exchequer.—Latin. *Copy.*

Paris,
Jan. 3/13.

1552. *Mr. Richard Brown (English Minister at Paris) to* ———.* Col. Gray, Serg.-Maj. Wagstaff, and other Protestant officers of the cashiered Irish regiment, were dismissed without pay or passport, but having obtained both by his inter-

* Probably to one of the Secretaries of State.

vention, are coming to serve against the rebels. Col. Pinot has accepted a company in Col. Colon's regiment. The rest of the officers are gone to St. Malo's, avowedly to join the Irish rebels, and should be intercepted by one of the King's whelps. Great complaints from the factors of French merchants in London, of the indignities they are compelled to submit to. 1641-2.

<small>An extract, (the writer's name being endorsed); to which is subjoined an extract from a letter of Feb. 7, recommending Col. Gray to the King's service. Cl. S. P. vol. ii. p. 136. (with the omission of the second extract, and some unimportant parts of the first).</small>

1553. *Mr. Roger Lort to Mr. Arthur Annesley* (his brother-in-law), requesting him to furnish him with an answer to the calumny which is bruited in Wexford, that Annesley has deserted his duty in leaving Ireland. Blackpool, Jan. 26.

1554. *Remonstrance* prepared by the Committee of both Houses sitting at Grocers' Hall. *Copy.* Jan.
<small>The substance of this is printed in Clar. Hist. Rebell. bk. iv. p. 167.</small>

1555. *Sir Henry de Vic to Lord Falkland*, congratulating him on his appointment as Secretary of State. Venice, Feb. 1.

1556. *Order* of the House of Commons to the Lord Lieutenant to remove from their commands all except Lord Clanricarde who will not receive the Communion and take the oaths of allegiance and supremacy, especially Sir John Nettersfield and Sir George Hambleton, and recommending Lord Ffolliot in Nettersfield's place. *Copy.* Feb. 5.
<small>In Lord Mountnorris' hand.</small>

1557. *The Marquis of Ormond to (Mr. Hyde).* That there is still much tampering with the Irish officers to contradict wth [sic] they have done; but to little purpose. He conceives it may much conduce to the King's service to take notice of the right inclinations of the Earl of Kildare, Sir Fulke Hunks, Col. Gibson, and Sir Richard Grenville, and to assure them of His Majesty's favour. Mentions a Proclamation whereof much use may be made. The army like to be in great distress for victual. Dublin, Feb. 8.
<small>Endorsed by Lord Clarendon as in the text.</small>

1558. *Lord Wilmot to Mr. Hyde,* asking to be excused, on the ground of infirm health, from obeying the recent order of Parliament, that all officers should repair to their commands in Ireland. Feb. 9.

1641-2.
Paris,
Feb. 11.

1559. [*Mr. R. Brown*] *to* ———. It is impossible for him to stop the Irish from leaving the ports of France. Two regiments of 4000 men are to embark; some say for Portugal or Holland, others for England or Ireland, probably for Holland. The King goes to Lyons this day, accompanied by the Cardinal, and it is said will proceed to Roussillon, where the French affairs are in a better state. Letters of Marshal de Breze, from the camp at Elne, state that he has defeated the Spaniards in Perpignan and is master of the field. Duke Doria has been taken prisoner and sent to Narbonne, having previously thrown a million of gold into the sea. Cardinal Mazarin with the Cardinal of Lyons go to Rome to strengthen the French party in the Conclave, the Pope not being likely to outlive March.

Cl. S. P. vol. ii. p. 137.
(with large omissions.)

Feb. 12.

1560. *List of Lieutenants nominated and recommended by the House of Commons to His Majesty* as persons to be entrusted with the Militia of the kingdom.—Printed.

Endorsed by Lord Clarendon.

Brussels,
Feb. 15.

1561. [*Sir Henry de Vic*] *to* [*Lord Falkland*]. Details of the military preparations there for the ensuing campaign.

Apparently a duplicate, being without signature or address.

Venice,
Feb. 21.

1562. *Sir Gilbert Talbot to Lord Falkland*, to open an official correspondence with him, by Sec. Nicholas' directions.

Dublin,
Feb. 27.

1563. *The Marquis of Ormond to His Majesty*, signifying of a letter coming from the principal officers of the army in Ireland. Of the frivolous cavils of the rebels, which have caused him to march out with 2500 foot and 500 horse. And of Mr. Durgh's (Burke's) death.

Endorsed by Lord Clarendon as in the text.

[Brussels,]
March 6.

1564. [*Sir Henry de Vic*] *to* [*Lord Falkland*]. Information obtained by a spy concerning the designs of Plunket and O'Neile upon Ireland, the latter using a Spanish proverb, that "In time medlars grow ripe." Cl. S. P. vol. ii. p. 137.

On p. 139, l. 5, "4 tons" should be "40 tuns."

March 7.

1565. *Declaration of Parliament presented to His Majesty at Newmarket the 9th of March*, 1641, *by the Earls of Pembroke and Holland, the Lord Dunsmore, Lord Seymour, and eight of the Members of the House of Commons.* Copy.

Printed in Clar. Hist. Rebell. bk. iv. p. 177.

1566. *Mr. Henry Warren to Dr. Henry Jones**, concerning the distribution of the rebels' lands among the plundered Protestants, and the appointment of a Commission for that purpose. News of the military success in various parts of Ireland.
1641-2. Dublin, March 7.

1567. *Sir G. Talbot to Lord Falkland.* The maxim of the House of Savoy to divide their affections between France and Spain seems likely to be overruled in favour of France by the necessities of the Spaniards. Prince Thomas is swerving in his allegiance now that his wife and children have escaped and he finds he can get nothing from Spain or the Emperor. The French King is on his way to Catalonia. Details of news from the Italian states.
Venice, March 7.

1568. *The same to the same.* Detail of preparations for war in Milan and throughout Italy. The King of Spain is said to have forbidden Monsignor Panzasoli, the new Nuntio, to come to Madrid.
Without signature or address.
No date.

1569. *Sir A. Hopton to the same.* Details of the preparations to reduce Catalonia and Portugal. The armies are in a very bad state through dissensions of the commanders and desertions of the soldiers. The people in general seem to have lost their love for their country. The plate-fleet has arrived in safety.
Madrid, March 7/₅.

1570. *Mr. Edward Hyde to His Majesty.* Expects a warm debate to-morrow on the King's last message. Encloses a paper to be sent from Huntingdon to the Lord Keeper. There are great suspicions of the King's designs in going to York; and his best strength will be in giving no ground for suspicion of violation of the laws.
Rough draught, endorsed by himself, "Mine to the King to Newmarket."
Cl. S. P. vol. ii. p. 138.
No date †.

1571. *Mr. R. Brown to* ———. Has endeavoured to persuade Mons. le Prince to prevent the Irish officers leaving St. Malo. 1500 out of the 5000 Bretons are now at St. Malo, but nobody knows whither they are designed. The fleet at Brest will soon be ready to sail, and probably will be able to enter the Mediterranean, the French being much weaker there than the Spaniards, and able to man fifteen sail
Paris, March 14/4.

---

* Jones seems to have been a London agent for the Protestants.
† The message from Newmarket was sent March 9th, and that from Huntingdon reckoned herein, March 15th. This letter therefore was written between those dates.

1641-2. at most. A Scotch regiment of Guards, 4500 strong, all Protestants, is to be formed under command of Lord Kantyre. News of the revolt of Arragon. The French are successful in the war about Perpignan. Will complain to the Ministers of the Gazetteer making Admiral Trump a Knight of the Garter. Cl. S. P. vol. ii. p. 140.
(with large and important omissions).

York, March 18.
1572. *Mr. Hardinge to Mr. Hyde*, describing his journey, and lamenting his absence from London, entreating him to get some friends to come and see him.

St. Johnston's, March 11.
1573. *Mr. Nicholas West to Mr. Huly* (Draper). A letter from Scotland apprising him of the rumour of the death of Sir Phelim O'Neale and 2000 of his best men near Dublin. Also that 12,000 Scots are coming to England under Leslie. To which is annexed the examination of Huly concerning the above before Lord Falconberg and Nicholas. *Copy.*

Venice, March 21.
1574. *Sir Gilbert Talbot to Lord Falkland.* The quarrel between the Pope and the Duke of Parma is not beyond a hope of settlement, though, the Duke having declared the excommunication illegal, the pride of Rome will not be satisfied without recantation and submission. The present difficulty is, who is to pay the Pope's garrisons in Castro and Montalto.

York, March 21.
1575. *His Majesty to the Lord Keeper* (Lyttleton*). Has signed a Commission for passing a Bill for raising 400,000*l.*, and will consent to one for the clearing of Lord Kimbolton, Mr. Hollis, and the rest, if worded so as not to reflect upon him. *Copy.*
Endorsed by Sec. Nicholas. Cl. S. P. vol. ii. p. 140.

Brussels, March 22.
1576. [*Sir Henry de Vic*] to [*Lord Falkland*]. Is endeavouring to obtain justice on the printer of the pretended Irish Manifest. The Governor has sent Don Diego de la Torre to forbid O'Neile going into Ireland. Cl. S. P. vol. ii. p. 139.
(with an unimportant omission).

March 23.
1577. *Lord Falkland to Mr. Hyde.* Hyde has been named one of those to proceed against the Archbishop and the Judges, especially Judge Beckly. Has tried to excuse him on account of his infirmities; but great exceptions have been taken to his non-attendance at the House, while well enough

* Sir Edward Lyttleton was created Lord Lyttleton in Feb. 1641.

to attend the Dover Committee, and he has been ordered to 1641–2.
be in his place to-morrow morning.

C. S. P. vol. ii. p. 141.

1578. *Commission from His Majesty to Lord Falkland*, to York,
sign the Bill of Tonnage and Poundage, if it be in substance March 23.
the same as the last. Signed by the King.

1579. *Eleven Papers of Grants* entitled Docquetts, and No date.
endorsed by Lord Clarendon; comprising, among others,
grants of the keepership of Hartleton Lodge in Richmond
Park to Humfrey Rogers, licences to travel beyond seas,
appointment of Sir John Conyers as Lieutenant of the Tower,
grant of baronetcies to Mr. St. Quintin and Mr. James Enyon,
deanery of St. Paul's to Dr. Stewart, an almshouse in Peterborough, presentations to benefices, allowance of 4*l.* per
diem to Lord Howard of Charleton on his embassy to Venice.

Some are signed Edw. Norgate, some J. Williams, and one Phil. Warwick.

1580. *A Breviary of Matters about Drogheda since the 3rd* No date.
Dec. 1641 (to March 26, 1642), being a diary of the siege of
that town, of which Sir Henry Tichborne was Governor, by
the rebels under Hugh Boy O'Neale. Also another shorter
account of the same events.

 1642.
1581. *Petition* of the Kentish gentry to the House of Com- March 27.
mons in favour of Episcopacy, a national Synod to settle
religious differences, a definite settlement of the Militia
question, consideration of the civil lawyers, and assent to the
King's message of Jan. 20. *Two Copies.*

A summary is printed in Parl. Hist. vol. II. p. 1147.

1582. *Mr. Morton to [Lord Falkland]*. Complains grievously La Torre,
of having been left in his employment (at Turin) for three March 28.
years without any pay. Endorsed by Lord Clarendon.

1583. *Mr. W. Aylesbury to Mr. Hyde*. Has met with a Rome,
Franciscan, Father Morton, at Naples, who threatens to go March 29.
to England to accuse Windebank of greater matters than
the Parliament ever laid to his charge. Has had audience
of Cardinal Francisco Barberino, who tries to persuade Sir
Walter Pye that the English and Irish troubles have never
been fomented by the Pope's ministers.

C. S. P. vol. II. p. 141.

1642.
No date.

1584. *An Account of the Services done about Dublin.* A long and minute history of military operations in Ireland from the 27th of November to the end of March.

Venice,
April 4.

1585. *Sir G. Talbot to [Lord Falkland].* The Princes of Savoy have received 20,000 crowns from the Spaniards. The accommodation between Rome and Parma is suspended. The Venetians are preparing against an invasion by the French.
Without address.

Paris,
April 5.

1586. [*Mr. Browne**] *to [Lord Falkland].* Doubts as to the destination of the 5000 Bretons which have been raised, but concludes they are either for Holland or Picardy. Success of the French in Catalonia, but they are at present checked by the siege of Colivure, the walls whereof are thirty-six feet thick. The various positions of the French in Piedmont and elsewhere. Later news that the Bretons are for Middleborough, and that Colivure has surrendered.
Without signature or address.

York,
April 10.

1587. *Secretary Nicholas to Lord Falkland.* The King wishes the Parliament to confer upon the widow and children of Sir Simon Harcourt the lands belonging to the person before whose castle in Ireland he was slain.
Cl. S. P. vol. II. p. 142.

York,
April 12.

1588. *Lord Grandison to Mr. Hyde.* His dissatisfaction at the King's resolutions concerning Ireland, and his unwillingness to accept any post till he has Hyde's opinion. The King is determined to take the Prince with him to Ireland.
Without signature. The name endorsed by Lord Clarendon.

Dantzick,
April 13/23.

1589. *Mr. Francis Gordon to [Lord Falkland].* The troubles in England encourage exorbitant impositions on the Eastland trade by the Powers of the Baltic. The Duke of Nieuburg is to marry the King of Polonia's sister. The new order of Knighthood, "Sodales Beatæ Virginis," founded in Polonia (where religious toleration is professed) for the extirpation of all who do not believe in the Immaculate Conception, is likely to do much mischief, the people enduring no dignities but senators and gentlemen. Rumour that the Muscovite Emperor will resign in favour of his son, and retire into a monastery, which will bring on a war with the Poles,

---

* Mr. Browne was Envoy at Paris at this time, and this letter, endorsed "Duplicate," seems a copy sent to Hyde of his despatch to one of the Secretaries of State.

from their repeated outrages on the Muscovite frontiers. 1642.
Demands his recall, the spite of the Chancellor of Poland
against all heretics having caused him to be cast in a suit
for 4000 thalers.

1590. *Sir G. Talbot to Lord Falkland.* Alarm of the   Venice,
Spaniards as to the loyalty of the Princes of Savoy. The   April 18.
war between the Pope and the Duke of Parma is like to shed
more ink than blood. Defeat of the Spaniards by the French
at Rossiglione.

1591. *Opinion of the Scots Privy Council* against the King's   Edinburgh,
hazarding his person by visiting Ireland, and persuading him   April 12.
to return to his Parliament. (Signed "Arch. Primrose, Clerk
of the Council.")   *Copy.*
Printed in Parl. Hist. vol. ii. p. 1117.

1592. [*Lord Loudon*] *to* [*the Lords of the Privy Council*].   Edinburgh,
A letter to accompany the last, urging the same arguments   April 12.
as are therein contained.   *Copy.*
Without signature or address.

1593. *The Lords Justices and Privy Council of Ireland to*   Dublin,
His Majesty, thanking him, in terms of great loyalty, for his   April 23.
gracious intention of visiting Ireland in person.   *Copy.*
Thirteen signatures are annexed to this letter.

1594. *Sir H. de Vic to* [*Lord Falkland*]. Col. O'Neale is   Brussels,
in Brussels, and, he suspects, intends to go to Ireland. The   May 1/11.
expected success of the siege of La Bassée, and the good
management of Don Francisco de Melo, Governor of Brussels,
has much raised the spirits of the Spaniards.
Without signature or address. Endorsed by Lord Clarendon.

1595. [*Sir H. de Vic*] *to* [*Lord Falkland*]. Surrender of La   Brussels,
Bassée. Beck is now about to proceed to the siege of Lan-   May 1/11.
drecy. Rumours of a negotiation with the Hollanders,
through the Bishop of Bois-le-duc. Rumours of a new army
for Alsatia, to be furnished by the Emperor and Duke of
Bavaria. Movements of the Duke of Lorraine at Liege.
O'Neale is looking for a house at Louvain or Diest, being in
disgrace for not returning to his regiment.
Without signature or address. Endorsed by Lord Clarendon.

1596. *Minute* of a grant to Mr. Thomas Pott of the office   May 8.
of Master of the Harriers and Beagles to the Prince, with a
salary of 26*l.* per annum, to commence from Midsummer
1641.   Date endorsed.

1642. Venice, May 9.	1597. *Sir G. Talbot to Lord Falkland.* Alarm arising from the muster of the Spanish forces of Milan, and doubt as to their destination. Confidence of the French, who threaten Nice, and are urging the Duchess of Mantua and other Italian Princes to their assistance or neutrality. The treaty between Parma and the Pope is dead. Bologna is putting itself in a state of defence. Civil war among the Pope's forces in Rome. The Pope much suspected by the Spaniards for his leaning to France; the Duke of Lorraine also having been lately excommunicated.
May 11.	1598. *Petition of the County of Cornwall to His Majesty,* returning thanks for the general pardon, beseeching him not to admit of arbitrary government or any change in religion, condoling with him on the distress occasioned him by pamphlets and sermons, desiring him to be reconciled to Parliament, and offering their lives and fortunes in his defence. Endorsed with the names of four gentlemen commissioned to deliver it. *Copy.* Endorsed by Lord Clarendon.
Dublin, May 13.	1599. *The Earl of Ormond to Sir Robert Poyntz.* An account of his late victory (at Kilrush*). The rebels are not cowardly, but want only arms, ammunition, and order. If they got these and despair of pardon, the war will be indefinitely prolonged. *Copy.* Cl. S. P. vol. ii. p. 143.
May 17.	1600. *Order* of Parliament, that the King's removal of the next Term to York is illegal.—Printed. See also Parl. Hist. vol. ii. p. 1335.
May 17.	1601. *Order* of the same against the King's demanding the attendance of any subject on his person, unless bound by special service.—Printed. See also as the last.
No date.	1602. *A Paper of Observations* on the form of the general pardon for Devonshire. Also two Papers, being an extract apparently, in law Latin, from the words of the pardon, and an English translation of the same. Endorsed by Lord Clarendon.
No date.	1603. *Minutes* by the Earl of Dover of occurrences in Parliament between the dates of Aug. 1641 and May 19th, 1642. There is nothing here of importance that does not occur in Parl. Hist., but in some cases the divisions of the Lords are given. Endorsed by Lord Clarendon.

* See Carte's Life of Ormond, vol. i. p. 303.

CLARENDON PAPERS. 231

1604. *Resolutions of the Parliament* that the King intends to make war upon them, and declaring all who assist him traitors. To which is annexed their *Petition* to the King to disband; threatening ulterior steps in case of refusal. *Copies.*

1642. May 20.

Printed in Clar. Hist. Rebell. bk. v. p. 214, and elsewhere.

1605. *His Majesty to Mr. Hyde*, commanding him to repair to York.

York. May 21.

1606. [*Sir H. de Vic*] *to* [*Lord Falkland*]. Account of a signal victory gained by the Spaniards over the French near Cambray. The consequent festivities were sobered by the late death of the Infant Cardinal. Has not been able to extract from Don Miguel de Salamanca any explanation of the preparations at Dunkirk. O'Neile is in great disfavour with this government, and will probably go to Ireland, if not stopped. He is not bald, but has a high forehead, and wears long hair.

Brussels, May 2⅟.

C. S. P. vol. II. p. 143.

1607. *Sir G. Talbot to Lord Falkland*. Prince Thomas and the Governor of Milan are about to march together to attack Rossignano. Distracted state of Spanish affairs and their fears for Italy. News of the Duchess of Mantua, Duke of Modena, and the quarrel between Rome and Parma. The Pope has summoned the Grand Duke of Florence to Rome, to shew his title to Castelleone; but really, as it is thought, to enlist him against the Spaniards.

Venice, May 13.

1608. *Warrant* to their Gentleman Usher to bring Lord Keeper Lyttleton before the House of Lords*. Also *Appointment of a Committee* of that House for consideration of an accommodation with the King.   *Copy.*

May 13.

Endorsed by Lord Clarendon.

1609. *Paper* by Mr. Hyde, and endorsed by him, "At York, advices not pursued." It is the rough draught of an answer by the King to the Parliament's Declaration of May 26. It is very sharp and precise in its demands, as, that the contrivers of the Declaration be expelled Parliament, that the Parliament be adjourned to York or Oxford, and that all matters of treason, felony, or breach of peace be out of protection of Parliament. Much of its substance is embodied in the King's answer to the Petition of July 15, which is printed in Clar. Hist. Rebell. bk. v. p. 275.

No date.

---

* He had fled the day before to the King at York. See Clar. Hist. Rebell. bk. v. p. 230.

1642.
Hamburg,
May 27.
June 6.

1610. *Mr. John Averie (the Resident at Hamburgh) to Lord Falkland.* The movements of the Swedes and Imperialists in Silesia. Efforts of the latter at Hamburg to raise levies. News of a Swedish fleet of thirty sail and 10,000 men at Stockholm. The Elector of Brandenburgh is likely to break off the treaty with Sweden for a cessation of arms. The match between the Archbishop of Bremen and the sister of the Duke of Brunswick is concluded. The King of Denmark will visit Holstein at Whitsuntide.

June 1.

1611. *Order of Parliament* against the King's disposing of the jewels of the Crown.
Printed in Clar. Hist. Rebell. bk. v. p. 256.

Paris,
June 13.

1612. [*Mr. Browne*] *to* [*Lord Falkland*]. The French preparations to resist Don F. de Melo, and carry on the war in Arragon. Richelieu's retreat, on pretence of health, to the neighbourhood of Avignon, has caused much dejection to his friends.

No date.

1613. *Petition* from two soldiers of the Train-bands at Hull to be admitted into the King's service.

June 4.

1614. *Affidavits* of William Launsdale and Richard Yeddon, the above soldiers, that Sir John Hotham had represented that the King had issued proclamations to commit to York gaol any soldiers caught out of Hull.

June 3 & 4.

1615. *Affidavits* of Thomas and William Rand of a conversation of Mr. Alured, M.P., about drawing the Train-bands in to garrison Hull.
Two papers, endorsed by Lord Clarendon.

Brussels,
June 7.

1616. [*Sir H. de Vic*] *to Lord Falkland.* Military news of the Imperialist forces under Beck and Don Francisco de Melo on the Rhine, acting against Count Guebriant.
Endorsed by Lord Clarendon.

June 17.

1617. *Lord Paget to the Honourable House of Parliament,* announcing his resolution to join the King's cause[*]. *Copy.*
Endorsed as written during his journey to York. To which is appended "The Declaration of the Lords now at York to maintain His Majesty's lawful right against the new ordinance of the Militia." The Declaration of which this is an abstract is printed in Cl. Hist. Reb. bk. v. p. 562.   Cl. S. P. vol. ii. p. 144, (with the exception of the Declaration).

[*] See Clar. Hist. Reb. bk. v. p. 261.

1618. *Order* of His Majesty to Sir J. Stradling, of the ship Bonaventure, to repair speedily and privately to Newcastle on important business. *Copy.* — 1642. York, June 23.

1619. *Lord Herbert to Mr. Hyde.* Offering his father's excuses to the King, and promise to prefer Mansfield or Fell to his Vice-Chancellorship.   Cl. S. P. vol. II. p. 144. — June 25.

1620. *Lord Pembroke to the same*, to the same purport as his son's previous letter.   Cl. S. P. vol. II. p. 145. — The Cockpit, June 30.

1621. *Sir G. Talbot to Lord Falkland.* The heads of the accord between the Duchess and Princes of Savoy. — Venice, July 11.

1622. *Order of Parliament* against carrying away the plate belonging to the Colleges at Oxford, with warrants to the Serjeant-at-Arms and his deputies to see to the execution of the Order.   *Copies.* — July 12.

Endorsed by Hyde. The order is printed in Wood's Ath. Oxon. vol. L p. 352.

1623. *Sir G. Talbot to Lord Falkland.* Efforts of the Venetians against the Barbary pirates in the Adriatic. Three thousand Spanish troops admitted into Rome. The Pope has suspended the excommunication of the Duke of Lorraine, to gratify the Emperor. — Venice, July 18.

1624. *Warrant* from Lord Henry Grey of Ruthin and Sir Arthur Haselrig, the Parliamentary Commissioners, for calling out the Militia of the hundred of Gartrie. — July 18.

1625. *The Houses of Parliament to the National Assembly of the Church of Scotland,* accompanying a copy of their petition of July 15, and containing the general protestations of a desire for peace.   *Copy.* — July 22.

Endorsed by Hyde. See Burnet's Memoirs of the Dukes of Hamilton, p. 196.

1626. *Lord Mandeville (Speaker pro tempore of the House of Lords) to Lord Falkland,* enclosing the next, and desiring its transmission to the King. — July 26.

1627. July 26. *Reply of both Houses of Parliament to His Majesty's demands, brought by Rushworth to Beverley, 28th July.*   Printed in Clar. Hist. Rebell. bk. v. p. 280.

1628. *Sir H. de Vic to Lord Falkland.* Military news. Encloses a letter of O'Neale to the Governor. — Brussels, July 26.

234   CALENDAR OF

1642.   1629. *A Petition to His Majesty in the name of the Catholics
July 31.   of Ireland, which petition was sent enclosed in a letter from the
           Lord Gormanstown &c., directed to the Earl of Ormond and
           dated the last of July*, 1642, desiring some way to be found
           by which they may be able to plead their cause before him,
           their former agent, Lieut.-Col. Reade, having been seized and
           put to the torture of the rack.   *Copy.*
                                                       Endorsed as headed.

London.   1630. *Lord Herbert to Mr. Hyde*, making general profes-
Aug. 4.   sions of his father's good-will to the King.
                                                   Cl. S. P. vol. ii. p. 146.
               The words at the end of the printed copy of the letter, "able to appear in
               this service," should be " capable of appearing in His Majesty's service."

The   1631. *Mr. Bulstrode Whitelocke to the same*, asking that his
Temple,   uncle, Mr. Bulstrode, may succeed Mr. Platt as one of the
Aug. 4.   Judges of circuit in South Wales.
                                                   Cl. S. P. vol. ii. p. 147.

London,   1632. *Lord Herbert to the same;* containing the same
Aug. 5.   general professions from his father, guarded by the condition
           that he have some security of the King's intentions. He
           wishes to make Pinke, or anybody but Fell, Vice-Chancellor.
           If the King come to Portsmouth, the Parliament say they
           will meet him with their army.   Cl. S. P. vol. ii. p. 147.

Bradford(?)   1633. *Mr. St. Leger to Lord Falkland*, announcing his in-
Aug. 11.   tention to desert the Parliament, and offering his service and
           his troop to the King.

No date.   1634. *A Declaration* by the King, after setting up his
           standard at Nottingham (Aug. 25), containing his reasons for
           taking up arms, and enumerating the provocations received
           since the commencement of the Parliament.
                                                       In Mr. Edgeman's hand.

Wellington,   1635. *His Majesty's Protestation made at the head of his
Sept. 19. army.*   Printed in Clar. Hist. Rebell. bk. vi. p. 195.

Dublin,   1636. *The Lords Justices of Ireland to Secretary Nicholas*,
Oct. 12.   forwarding the original of the rebels' petition of July 31,
           asking for supplies, and accusing Sir John Dungan, Henry
           Talbot, and Dr. Dermot O'Meara, of complicity with the rebels.
                           Signed by the Lords Justices and the Marquis of Ormond.

Maiden-   1637. *His Majesty to Mr. Hyde*, commanding him to desire
head,   Sir William Waller and David Waller, esq. to be his sureties
Nov. 9.   for sums to be raised in Oxfordshire.

CLARENDON PAPERS.   235

1638. *Particulars,* whereof Sir Hardress Waller is desired to make relation. An account sent to the King of the state in which the Lord Lieutenant found Irish affairs on his arrival. — 1642. No date.*

1639. *Warrant* to Mr. Hyde for payment of 30*l.* on account of powder supplied at Oxford, and receipt for the same. — Dec. 5 & 6.

1640. *Proclamation* by the King for adjournment of part of Hilary Term to Oxford. *Printed.* — Oxford, Dec. 27.

1641. *Answer* by the King to the reasons urged by Parliament against the adjournment of the Term to Oxford.
Rough draught.
In Hyde's hand. — No date.

1642. *Petition* of Sir Nicholas Byron to the King for payment of 3*l.* per diem, due to him when Governor of Carlisle. With allowance of the same, signed by Lord Falkland. — Dec. 30.

1643. *Lord Herbert* to *Mr. Hyde,* with his confident assurances of his father's professions. He hopes he will speedily come to the King, but cannot assure him of it.
Cl. S. P. vol. ii. p. 148. — No date.

1644. *The same to the same.* His father is settling his estate upon him, which will give him a fortune as well as a life to lay at the King's feet. Deprecates resentment of his father's conduct.
Cl. S. P. vol. ii. p. 149. — No date.

1645. *A List of the names of the Commanders, Captains, Lieutenants, Cornets, and Ensigns of the Horse and Foot now in force in this Kingdom* (Ireland), *as well the old standing army, as that lately raised in and since October* 1641. — No date.

1646. *Instructions sent with the Commission of Array,* for organizing the Militia throughout the kingdom, and immediately summoning the Train-bands. *Copy.*
Endorsed by Hyde. — No date.

1647. *A Calculation* of the Property in Ireland belonging to the Protestants, and that forfeited in the late Rebellion. The total is reckoned at 10,868,949 (acres), of which 4,758,657 have been forfeited. — No date.

1648. *Minutes* of Public Letters, Petitions, &c., relative to the affairs of Ireland during the years 1641–2.
In Hyde's hand. — No date.

---

* The date of this is fixed at the end of November by a passage in Clar. Hist. Rebell. bk. vi. p. 154.

1642. No date.	1649. *His Majesty to the Parliament*, consenting to levy men for Ireland, on condition the levies be made in the old way, under such officers as he shall appoint, and Parliament shall not have cause to disapprove. *Copy.*
1642-3.	1650. *Extracts of letters of intelligence.* Particulars of the Petition for Peace. The claim made on Edw. Shipton. *Copy.* Endorsed by Hyde, "Shipton's memoranda." In part Cl. S. P. vol. ii. App.
London, Jan. 6.	1651. *A Treatise or Argument in law, upon the late Orders and Ordinances made by both or either of the Houses of Parliament without the King's consent.* Published for the use of those who profess not the study or practice of the Law; with a prefatory letter to a friend at Oxford.
Jan. 9.	1652. *Declaration of the Officers in Ireland*, addressed to the Lords Justices and Council, setting forth their grievances, being principally the want of pay, and the absence of martial law; and complaining that the moneys sent for them are otherwise applied. *Copy.* Printed in Carte's Life of Ormond, iii. 127.
Oxford, Jan. 11.	1653. *The King to Ormond.* Has had no answer to Serj.-Major Warren's message; fears the delay may render the business fruitless. Sends a memorial for his guidance; and has given full instructions to the bearer. *Memorial.* There is danger that the Irish rebels in their propositions for peace may desire— 1. An abrogation of the penal Statutes concerning religion. 2. Confirmation by their Parliament of all laws affecting Ireland. 3. The Repeal of Poyning's Law and other Statutes. 4. That the Irish Parliament should have a proposing power without the approbation of the King and Privy Council. 5. That the native Irish may be restored to their plantation-lands. 6. That they may be governed by Irish officers and ministers of State. With instructions under each head how to handle it. *Original.*

1654. *The King to Ormond.* Has received his of Jan. 18, in answer to the King's sent by Serj.-Major Warren; assuring him the service shall not be hindered by the arrival of a more powerful head. Begs him to send particulars; and to tell him what use he will make of Mr. Burke's despatch. Accommodation is much spoken of. Has received propositions from both houses of Parliament; but no peace can be drawn out of the Articles propounded. There is no hope of sending supplies to Ireland. *Original.*
1642-3. Oxford, Feb. 2.

Endorsed, "Sent by Geo. Lane."

1655. *The same to the same.* Sends an account of affairs by the bearer*. Begs for a speedy answer to his letter written on Candlemas-day. *Original.*
Oxford, Feb. 7.

1656. *The same to the Earl of Forth.* Promises him, for his many services, the making of an English baron, or something instead of it. *Original.*
Feb. 7.

Printed in the Ruthven Correspondence; Roxburghe Club, 1868. Preface, p. xxix.

1657. *The same to Ormond.* Keeps Col. Gardiner to take this letter in answer to his of Jan. 31. Commands him not to slacken in the business of the King's letter of Jan. 12. Bids him hinder the concurrence of the Protestants in the request of the Justices to stay the execution of the commission. Begs him to send Warren over with full instructions. *Original.*
Oxford. Feb. 8.

Endorsed, "Rec. Feb. 19."

1658. *Proclamation* of His Majesty for the strict observance and execution of the laws and statutes made against carrying or sending of gold or silver out of the kingdom. *Printed.*
Oxford, Feb. 10.

1659. *Minute* of Mr. Hyde's being sworn a Privy-Councillor.
Oxford, Feb. 12.

1660. *The King to Ormond.* Sends the bearer, who has made a proposition of consequence, to Ormond for his counsel. Hints that the proposition may be made to concur with some already sent by the King. Thanks him for his letter of Feb. 2. Mr. Burgh † was sent, having been named upon a commission by Lord Justice Parsons. *Original.*
Oxford, Feb. 11.

Endorsed, "By Sir Wllm. St. Leger. Approving of the shewing of the Comm. brought by Mr. Thomas Burke for receiving the Irish remonstrance to the Lds. Justices, &c."

* Col. Gardiner. † i. e. "Burke."

238   CALENDAR OF

1642-3.   1661. *Mr. Norton to Sir John Colepepper.* Has been driven
York,   from his house by Sir J. Hotham. A memorandum of his
March 7.   accounts as Receiver, acknowledging the receipt of about
           3000*l.*

March 17. 1662. *Receipts* of Thomas Jay and Leonard Pinckney for
           44*l.* 16*s.* for cheese (at 1*l.* 12*s.* per cwt.) and bread for the
           forces under Prince Rupert.

March 17. 1663. *Mr. Thomas Hughes to Sir Edward Hyde.* His
           efforts, which he hopes will be successful, to compose differences
           and raise forces in Monmouthshire, and win Lord Herbert and
           Mr. Morgan to the cause.

Oxford,   1664. *The King to Ormond.* Adds this to the answer to
St. Pa-   Ormond's last despatch. Desires him to send speedily to
trick's Day, Chester as many muskets and barrels of powder as he can
[March 17.] spare.   *Original.*
                         In cypher. Endorsed, "Recd. Ap. 23, 1643."

Oxford,   1665. *The same to the same.* Has fully instructed the bearer,
March 23. and only adds that Lord Forbes' fleet is to be seized whether
           there is peace with the Irish rebels or not, if it can be under-
           taken with certainty of success. If there be peace in Ireland
           then the Irish army is to come over with all speed. *Original.*
                         In cypher. Endorsed, "Recd. 23 Ap."

Cornhill, 1666. *Mr. Philip Willoughby to Mr. William Lane* of some
March 25. business of Sir Rowland Egerton and Lord Northampton.
                                              Endorsed by Lord Clarendon.

No date.   1667. *Petition of Lord Mountnorris* to the House of Com-
           mons, setting forth his losses by the rebellion, amounting to
           4500*l.* per ann., and 10,000*l.* personal estate; and begging
           restitution of his offices.   Endorsed by himself.

1643.   1668. *Notice,* by Sir Edward Hungerford to tenants, of his
March 29. warrant from Parliament to receive the rents of Papists,
           Bishops, Deans, Chapter and Prebendaries of Sarum. *Copy.*
                                                Endorsed by Sir E. Hyde.

March. *   1669. *Memorials touching Scarborough.* An account of the
           surrender of that town by Sir Hugh Cholmeley to the Queen.
                   In the same hand as that paper printed in Cl. S. P. vol. II. p. 161 which is
                   endorsed by Hyde, "Sir Hugh Cholmeley's memorials."

           * The Queen arrived in York from Holland Feb. 23, and Scarborough was
           surrendered shortly afterwards. See Hist. Rebell. bk. vi. p. 547.

1670. *Receipt* of William Barber to Sir E. Hyde of 100l. — 1643. April 8.

1671. *Mr. W. Beauvais to Col. N. Fiennes*, Governor of Bristol, desiring promotion of his brother. — London, April 8.

1672. *Warrant* to Capt. Thomas Counsoll to seize the cattle and goods of Sir Robert Poyntz of Acton, Mr. Chester, and Capt. Veale of Alvaston, and bring them to Bristol. — Bristol, April 10.
Signed, "Cle. Walker."

1673. *Sir William Waller to the same*, complaining of Capt. Rawlins' contempt of his warrant, and desiring a commission for Capt. Bowen. — Gloucester, April 20.

1674. *Letter to the same, signed "Jo. Seymour, Edw. Stephens, and John Codrington,"* complaining of a burglary at Mr. Pullie's house at Wootton, and a theft of hay from Sir Walter Whitmore's at Pucklechurch, committed by the forces; and pointing out that no contributions for the defence of Bristol can be expected if such treatment be permitted. — Winterborne, April 24.

1675. *The same to the same.* Sends four men, captured on their way to Oxford, for examination. — April 24.

1676. *Capt. Edw. Scotten to Col. Fiennes.* Account of an interview with the Lord General, at Reading, and his enquiries about Bristol, why the town was not fired, and martial law was not executed on the conspirators. — London, April 26.

1677. *Mr. Henry Olande to the same.* The deputy-lieutenants are very backward with papists and malignants; affinity and consanguinity mars all. Loves action, and longs to be employed with him or Capt. Fiennes. — Dorchester, April 28.

1678. *Major Hercules Langrishe to the same.* Account of the taking of Reading, and his going thence to besiege the island of Portland. — Dorchester, April 29.

1679. *Alexander Popham to Col. N. Fiennes.* Intends an attack upon the island. Finds difficulty in raising money, but cannot leave that country now that it is so deeply engaged. — Dorchester, May 1.

1680. *Summons* from the Parliamentary Officers to the Castle and island of Portland to surrender.   *Copy.* — Weymouth, May 4.

1681. *Col. Langrishe to Col. N. Fiennes.* Has taken Portland, and will join him at Bristol in three days. — Weymouth, May 7.

1643. Oxford, May 13.	1682. *His Majesty to the Earl of Newcastle*, commanding the release of Lord Savile. *Copy.* In Nicholas' hand, and endorsed by him.
Bath, May 21.	1683. *Col. Alex. Popham and other Officers to the same.* The enemy is moving on Shaftesbury. Sir W. Waller is drawing his forces to Bath, whither they desire him to send troops to join him.
May 26.	1684. *Col. John Fiennes to the same.* Movements of Col. Popham, Sir E. Hungerford, and Sir W. Waller on the enemy.
Lackham, May 27.	1685. *Mr. J. Montagu to the same*, desiring the restoration of two geldings and two fowling pieces taken from his house by Capt. Rawlins.
May 29.	1686. *Messrs. Thos. Wrathe, John Pym, and Edw. Popham to Col. Fiennes and Alex. Popham.* They are delighted at the capture of Warminster, and will hold out till their arrival.
Bath, May 30.	1687. *Sir E. Hungerford to the same*, desiring him to send 200 muskets. Is going to Malmesbury to settle a disorder occasioned by Col. Strode's sending for 100 men thence.
May.	1688. *Informations against the Lord Viscount Savile**, for correspondence with the rebels, while Governor of York. Appended to this is the next. *Copy.* Date endorsed by Nicholas.
	1689. Gray's Inn, Dec. 24. *W. Risley to Lord Savile.* A letter concerning a suit in chancery, and mentioning a report that he had compounded with Parliament for 2000*l.*
[May.]	1690. *The Lord Viscount Savile's Answer to the charges sent by the Earl of Newcastle*, satisfactorily justifying all he has done, as with a view to the King's service, or to save his property at Howley. *Copy.* Endorsed by Nicholas.
[May.]†	1691. *The Message which the Lords would have sent to the King, if the Commons would have joined, and the City suffered.* This was contemplated as an answer to the King's message of April 12th. (Printed in Clar. Hist. Reb. bk. vii. p. 379.) It assents to the King's propositions and petitions for a disbanding of armies, an establishment of Church government

---

* By the Earl of Newcastle. See Clar. Hist. Rebell. bk. vi. p. 371.

† It seems probable, from the tenor of this, that it was framed after the King's subsequent message of May 20th (Cl. S. P. vol. ii. p. 386), to which Clarendon says the Peers were inclined to return a favourable answer.

by an assembly of divines, a settlement of the Militia by Act 1643.
of Parliament, trial of recusants, and those accused by
Parliament before Jan. 1, 1641, and a general pardon.
Cl. S. P. vol. ii. p. 149.

1692. *The Prince Elector to Mr. John Pym*, thanking him The Hague,
for his good offices. *Copy.* June 7/17.
Cl. S. P. vol. ii. p. 151.

1693. *The Earl of Essex to the Deputy Lieutenants of Gloucestershire and others*, inviting them to rise and meet him about Malmesbury or Gloucester. Caversham, June 2.

1694. *Schedule* of Receipts and Expenditure in the King's Exchequer at Oxford from Easter Eve to the present date. June 3.

1695. *His Majesty to the Earl of Newcastle*, declaring himself satisfied with Lord Savile's reply, and requesting the Earl's opinion thereon. *Copy.* Oxford, June 5.
In Nicholas' hand, and endorsed by him.

1696. *Col. Edw. Popham to Col. N. Fiennes.* Has endeavoured without success to unite their forces against the enemy. Relates the loss of Taunton through a mutiny of the townsmen against the garrison on their being about to depart, and the probable loss of Bridgewater from the same cause, the garrison having there forced their way out. Glastonbury, June 5.

1697. *Mr. J. Ashe to the same*, recommending to him a kinsman, one Capt. Sampson. Freshford, June 5.

1698. *Mr. A. Forbes to the same*, complaining of the seizure of a horse. Bath, June 5.

1699. *Capt. H. Archbould to the same*, requesting employment under him, instead of under Sir E. Hungerford, where Capt. Franklin is the only good soldier. Malmesbury, June 6.

1700. *Major Langrishe to the same.* Their horse is only 1000 strong, though reported at 2000. Will return to Bristol, if it is to be besieged, as rumour says. Wells, June 6.

1701. *Anth. Nicoll and W. Gould to the same.* Expect to join Sir W. Waller. Desire 500 foot and 500l. to be sent. Bath, June 7.

1702. *Joshua Lloyd to the same.* Notice of consignment of sixty-three barrels of gunpowder on account of the Parliament, the price being 572l. 14s. Rochelle, June 9.

1643. Arundel House, June 13.	1703. *Mr. John Fiennes to Col. N. Fiennes* (his brother). Has got his propositions shaped into an ordinance, but the House has been so busy with the discovery of a plot that he has as yet been able to do nothing more. Has endeavoured in vain to get from the clerks, who are all malignant, a copy of the Order whereby Col. N. Fiennes is joined to the committees of Gloucestershire and Somersetshire. My Lord will do what he can, but Stroud, Stephens, and Hodges are against them. Goes to-morrow to the Lord General's army at Wheatley Bridge, and thence will join his brother. Advises him to give up his command unless he gets an allowance of money for arms and the defence of Bristol.
Bath, June 18.	1704. *Mr. John Ashe to Col. Fiennes*, of the difficulty of getting in contributions from Keynsham and other hundreds.
Bath, June 24.	1705. *Edw. Cooke to the same*, requesting him from Sir W. Waller to send 500 men as soon as possible, the enemy being on the march to Oxford, and delay the greatest danger. Also to issue a proclamation to all officers, noting specially Capt. Geezcley, to return to their colours.
Bristol Castle, June 26.	1706. *Th. Throckmorton and Charles Haynes to the same*, desiring release for a fortnight on parole, before they leave for France, promising not to return during the war.
No date.	1707. *Col. Aldworth to the same*, of a like difficulty.
No date.	1708. *Col. Edw. Massie* to the same*, explaining the delay of some trows laden with wine which he had desired to be sent.
No date.	1709. *Rich. Aldworth to the same*, concerning the appointment of a day of public humiliation, and preachers to preach before the Aldermen and himself.
No date.	1710. *The same to the same*, on a report of the enemy's troops crossing the Severn at Aust.
No date.	1711. *C. Walker to the same*, concerning Mr. Fabian's and Mr. Roynon's political opinions.
No date.	1712. *Sir W. Waller to the same*, desiring money to be sent.

* He was Governor of Gloucester for the Parliament. See Clar. Hist. Rebell. bk. vii. p. 415.

1713. *Warrant to the Attorney General (Sir E. Herbert)* for a discharge to Mr. John Ashburnham for all moneys received by him for the King's use. *Copy.*
1643. Oxford, July 9.

1714. *Edict of the French King* giving the rights of belligerents to the ships of His Majesty and those of the Parliament which shall put into French ports, as of two formed parties at war with each other.—French. *Copy.*
Paris, July 10.

With translation, both in the handwriting of the late Sec. Windebank.

1715. *The Commissioners of Sussex to Mr. Hugh Peters*, desiring him to raise the county in behalf of the Parliament.
Lewes, July 15.

1716. *Warrant* of the Committee to Sir Edmund Sawyer (Auditor) to certify to the Star Chamber the King's revenue for the year commencing Sept. 29th, 1642. *Copy.*
Westminster, July 16.

Endorsed by Hyde.

1717. *Assignations upon His Majesty's ordinary revenue for the year* 1643. Two sheets of charges, in detailed items, the principal headings being as follows—
July 17.

	£	s.	d.
Court of Wards	61,817	16	4
Duchy of Cornwall	12,541	0	7
Duchy of Lancaster	10,438	0	9
Receiver General	69,508	15	4
Hanaper	4,005	14	7
Alienations	3,921	0	0
The Mint	12,253	0	0 (ultra wast)
The ancient Revenue of the Pipe	7,316	3	4
Recusants	895	0	0
And the whole of the charges amounting to	227,900	6	4

1718. *Receipt* for 50*l.* from Sir Edward Hyde for the use of Mrs. Katharine Scot. Signed, "Clement Thynne."
July 31.

1719. *Letters of —— to ——.* Copies of six letters (without date) on one sheet, evidently addressed to different persons, but endorsed with the name of Sir Ralph Hopton*, treating of the exchange of Col. Lansford for Col. Carr and other prisoners.
No date.

The last is printed in Cl. S. P. vol. ii. p. 155, and attributed by the editor to Sir William Waller or the Earl of Essex. See also pref. to vol. ii. p. 5.

* Sir Ralph Hopton was created a Peer in August 1643. The endorsement therefore proves these letters to be of an earlier date. They were probably written during the Western campaign of that year.

1648. Exeter, Aug. 4.	1720. *Lord Stamford to His Majesty.* Professes to be holding the town for the King, and preservation of peace. Entreats the King to put away from his counsels the Earl of Bristol, the Archbishop of York, and the rest of their cabal. <div align="right">Cl. S. P. vol. II. p. 130.</div>
Aug. 7.	1721. *Notes of the Proceedings in the House of Commons* on this day, with a copy of the Petition of the City to the Commons against the propositions of the House of Peers for peace. <div align="right">The book is mentioned in Hist. Rebell. bk. vii. p. 418, and is printed at large in Parl. Hist. vol. xii. p. 367.</div>
Newport, Aug. 26	1722. *Sir Edw. Bayston to Sir E. Hyde,* desiring him to join with Lord Hertford in procuring from the King his pardon and that of his son Rogers.
Aug. 28.	1723. *Mr. Francis Kibblewhite to the same,* concerning some money transactions with the late Archdeacon Master, and an account of a trunk of Hyde's which he had charge of and saved from the plunder of his house. <div align="right">No year given in the date. Endorsed by Hyde.</div>
Dublin, Sept. 9.	1724. *The Lords Justices and Council of Ireland to Secretary Nicholas,* desiring a speedy supply of powder and match, there not being a month's supply left, and that some course be taken to protect the ships bringing provisions from Chester, otherwise Sir Abraham Shippman will send no more.
Sept. 13.	1725. *Bond* of Sir E. Hyde to Sir Giles Mounpesson for 104*l.*
Sept. 27.	1726. *Instructions for Mr. Hugh Peters appointed to be sent into Holland upon special services by the Committee of Lords and Commons for the safety of the Kingdom,* the object being to act with Mr. Samuel Glover, already sent, and Mr. Walter Strickland, resident at the Hague, in borrowing money. <div align="right">Signed by Lord Say and Seale, Nath. Fiennes, Gilbert Gerard, Jo. Pym, and Anth. Nicoll.</div>
Dublin, Sept. 28.	1727. *The Marquis of Ormond to Secretary Nicholas.* A cessation of arms is concluded. Urges that use be made of the time thereby gained in gathering strength and provisions. It is most requisite that the Parliament in Ireland be continued. <div align="right">Cl. S. P. vol. II. p. 155.</div>
Oxford, Oct. 10.	1728. *Order of His Majesty* that no warrant shall be valid unless signed by a Secretary of State. <div align="right">*Copy.*</div>

1729. *Articles of Covenant and Agreement* made and concluded between Henry Lord Percy, Henry Lord Jermyn, Sir John Culpeper, Master of the Rolls, and John Ashburnham esq., of the one part, and John van Haesdonck, gent, of the other. Van Haesdonck to deliver at Weymouth the following arms and ammunition, 4000 muskets with bandoleers at 24s. a-piece, 1200 pairs of pistols with holsters and spanners at 56s. the pair, 600 carbines with bolts and swivels at 32s. a-piece, 20 tons of match at 40s. the cwt., 400 barrels of powder at 5l. 15s. the cwt., the arms to be proved by double charges. If Haesdonck's profit be more than 500l. his troop is to be increased by him. *Copy.*

1643. Oct. 16.

    Annexed is a Copy of a *Bond* for 14,000l. of the above parties to Haesdonck.

1730. *Petition of Thos. Cholwick to Sir Edward Hyde,* setting forth that he purchased the ship St. George of Dartmouth, in conjunction with Capt. John Smith, for 1300l. to fit her for the King's service, and being unable to fulfil his engagements desires to be discharged from his liability.

Nov. 1.

1731. *Warrant* to certain named persons to go on board the St. George and take inventory and make valuation; and the valuation made accordingly.   Signed, " Fra. Seymour."

Nov. 17.

1732. *The Marquis of Ormond to Lord Inchiquin.* Has sent an answer to his letter by Lieut.-Col. Power.
    Endorsed, " A Copy," but apparently Original.

Dublin. Nov. 30.

1733. *Articles of Agreement* between His Majesty of Great Britain on the one part, and Mr. John van Haesdonck of the other part; being letters of marque to Haesdonck.

Dec. 10.

1734. *Sir A. A. Cooper to Sir Edward Hyde,* asking for a licence to leave his county. The King's forces are weak and ill-paid there, Lord Hopton commanding away the profits of delinquents' estates for the pay of his army; and the demand for 600 men driving the people to the nearest Parliament garrison.   Endorsed by Lord Clarendon.

Weymouth, Dec. 29.

1735. *Propositions* for the better applying of the several extraordinary revenues arising from the counties and cities within the King's quarters to all necessary uses for the support of His Majesty in this war, in an uniform way.—These suggestions, made at Oxford, embody provisions of standing Committees of Finance in the several counties; a plan for the establishment in every garrison of " Ghest-houses as large as they can, with physicians, chirurgians, and tenders belonging

[No date.]

1643.   to them;" and a plan for payment of the soldiers by a fourth part in money, and the other three parts thus: "That the trooper receive once every year a new suit of clothes, with a long cloak, a new montero with a steel cap in it, a new saddle and bridle, two shirts, a new pair of boots, and a pair of stockings, and every fourth month a new pair of boots and a pair of stockings, and every week a convenient proportion of provisions for himself and his horse. The footsoldier once a year a new suit of clothes with stockings and shoes, and a montero with a steel cap in it, and two shirts, and every three months a new pair of shoes and stockings and convenient provision weekly for himself."   No signature; headed as above.

No date.   1736. *Resolutions* of the well-affected in Cornwall, with their letter to the High Sheriff, complaining of the dishonesty of Sir Francis Bassett and others, commissioners and collectors of taxes, in perverting them to their own uses, and refusing accounts.

1737. *Account* of the negotiations during this year for a cessation of arms, and the overtures made by the King for peace.
    In Lord Clarendon's hand.   See Rapin, vol. ii. p. 471 et seqq.

1738. *Eight papers, containing relations of military affairs*, drawn up for the most part by the respective commanders, and communicated to Sir E. Hyde, in order to be made use of, as for the most part they are, in his History of the Rebellion.

(1) Lord Hopton's account of the affairs of the West, from Sept. 1642 to June 1643.   *Copy.*

(2) Col. Slingsby's relation of the battle of Lansdown, fought July 5, and that of Roundway, fought July 13, 1643.

(3) Col. Slingsby's relation of the siege of Bristol, taken by Prince Rupert, July 26, 1643.

(4) Lord Hopton's account of the affairs of the West; continued from his last to the taking of Bristol. *Copy.*

(5) Lord Byron's account of the first battle of Newbury, fought Sept. 20, 1643.

(6) Lord Hopton's relation of the battle of Alresford, fought March 29, 1644.   *Copy.*

(7) Col. Slingsby's relation of the same.

(8) Skipton's relation of the siege of Lyme.

All these are endorsed by Sir E. Hyde.

CLARENDON PAPERS. 247

1739. *An Abstract, or the frame or heads of a Grant and Conveyance proposed to be made by His Majesty for the securing of the payment and discharge of divers debts and sums of money lent, and which hereafter shall be lent to His Majesty, or secured, or which hereafter shall be secured for His Majesty's use and service:* assigning New Forest, Sherwood Forest and Park, Beskwood Park, Clarendon Park, and Bowood Park to commissioners for payment of the King's debts. To which is attached a schedule of the debts, amounting to 11,199*l.* 1*s.* 6*d.*, with the names of the debtors, the greater number of whom are inhabitants of Oxford, Abingdon, and Wallingford.

1643.

Cl. S. P. vol. ii. p. 158 (with the exception of the schedule).

1740. *The sum of the business delivered to Mons. d'Harcourt at his first coming to Oxford.* An elaborate history of the whole dispute between the King and Parliament from the time of the publication of the Liturgy for Scotland to the present time; with an enumeration of the grievances of the King.

[No date.*]

Corrected in several places by the King, who has subjoined the words, "There must be added a short account of the last treaty, how and why it broke off."

Cl. S. P. vol. ii. p. 157.

1741. *Notes* concerning duration of Parliaments, freedom of elections, and some other points; in two columns, one headed "Cons^{tt}," the other "Diss^{ts}." (Apparently the heads of some propositions made or intended to be made to the King.)

No date.

1742. *Statement of a case of homicide* by a prisoner attempting to escape in St. James's Park, and rough notes on the course to be adopted in prosecution, with description of witnesses.

No date.

Five papers, without signature.

1743. *Warrant of His Majesty to the Marquis of Ormond,* ordering account to be made of arrears due from the Lord-Lieutenancy to his predecessor (the Earl of Leicester), and meanwhile 1000*l.* to be paid to his assignees in advance.

1643-4. Oxford, Jan 14.

Copy.

1744. *Lord Goring to Her Majesty.* Recommends that the Count d'Harcourt be treated well. The French pretend a disinclination in the King to a defensive and offensive league, but really they consider his demands too high. The points to be pressed are the loan of moneys, and immediate declaration

Paris, Jan. 15.

---

* There are no doubt the instructions mentioned in Clarendon's Life, pt. II. p. 987, as given to the Count d'Harcourt at Oxford, and communicated by him to the King's opponents.

1643-4. against the Parliament and Scotland. Of the preparations of arms at Dunkirk, and the sale of the Queen's jewels. *Copy.*

Endorsed by Hyde, "Lord Norwich's* letter to the Queen, intercepted and made the argument of the quarrel to him."

Cl. S. P. vol. ii. p. 163. (On p. 163, l. 23, "his" should be "her.")

Oxford, Jan. 20. 1745. *Instructions to Randal, Earl of Antrim, given at our Court at Oxford.* To persuade the Catholics in Ireland to send 10,000 men to England, ammunition, artillery, and ships. If the conditions offered are too high, to do the best he can to get 2000 men for Scotland, to join Lord Seaforth and Sir James M'Donald in falling on the Marquis of Argyle's country. To correspond with the Earl of Montrose, and to attempt to draw General Monro and his forces into the King's service, by promise to him of an Earldom of Scotland, with 2000*l.* per annum. *Copy.*

Cl. S. P. vol. ii. p. 163.

Oxford, Jan. 21. 1746. *His Majesty to Mr. Chancellor of the Exchequer (Sir E. Hyde).* The Processes of the Court of Exchequer are to be sealed with the usual seal at Oxford. *Signed by the King.*

Oxford, Jan. 22. 1747. *The King to the Earl of Forth.* Promises to make him Master of the Ordnance. *Original.*

March 3. 1748. *[Lady Ranelagh] to Sir Edward Hyde.* Urges, in the name of his dear friend, the late Lord Falkland, the sending of a message by the King to Parliament, their late disappointments with the Scots having put them into an hearkening temper. Argues the futility and danger of treating them as no Parliament. *Two Copies.*

Without signature. One endorsed by Hyde, "Lady Ranllee to me after the death of my Lord Falkland."

Cl. S. P. vol. ii. p. 167.

March 10. 1749. *Certificate of the Lord Chancellor and Judges* concerning the disputed right to the customs of Waterford, the point mooted being in whose power the passage to Waterford haven lay at the time of the cessation of hostilities. *Copy.*

March 16. 1750. *Account of moneys* paid into the Exchequer from the Diocese of Oxford, from July 16, 1641, to the present date, the total being 773*l.* 1*s.* 3½*d.*

Endorsed by Sir E. Hyde, "What are we the better for this? By this I suppose the Bishop is 100*l.* in arrear."

---

* He was created Lord Norwich Nov. 28, 1644.

1751. *Account* in detail of the battle of Hopton-heath, near Stafford, (fought March 19, 1643-4,) in which the Earl of Northampton was killed. 1643-4. [March 19.]
   The account is fuller than, but adds no material details to, that given in Hist. Rebell. bk. vi. p. 349.

1752. *Questions* addressed by Prince Rupert's command to the Sheriff of Anglesea, for information necessary to steps being taken for the protection of the island, and requiring a contribution of 1200*l.* a month, by a rate of 6*d.* in the £ per month on all estates.   *Copy.* 1644. March 26.

1753. *Warrant* of His Majesty to John van Haesdonck, giving him power to release or take ransom for prisoners.   *Copy.* Oxford. April 20.

1754. *Account* of the Earl of Marlborough for victualling the King's fleet at Dartmouth, the amount being 755*l.* 9*s.* 8*d.* April.

1755. *The Accompt of Abraham Biggs,* his disbursement for arms, ammunition, and other necessaries for His Majesty's garrisons and armies in Cornwall since this Rebellion. The total is 2010*l.* 2*s.* 2*d.* Fowey. May 26.

1756. *The Accompt of Abraham Biggs,* his collection of His Majesty's customs in the ports of Cornwall to June 6, 1664, amounting to 2005*l.* 8*s.* 7*d.*, with his expenditure thereof. No date.

1757. *The Propositions of the Roman Catholics of Ireland* humbly presented to His Sacred Majesty in pursuance of their remonstrance of grievances, and to be annexed to the said remonstrance.*   *Copy.* [May.]

1758. *The humble Answer* of the agents for the Protestants of Ireland to the said Propositions, made in pursuance of "Your Majesty's directions of the 9th of May, 1644, requiring the same."*   *Copy.*

1759. *A Summary* of the seventeen Irish Propositions.   No date.

1760. *Other Answers* to the seventeen Propositions.   *Copy.* No date.
   Two papers.

1761. *Examinations* of Mr. Geo. Fawley and Robert Bickerstaffe, his servant, suspected to be in correspondence with the rebels in Abingdon.   Partly in secretary Nicholas' hand. June 2-4.

1762. *The King to Ormond.* Recommends the bearer, Mr. Brent. Begs a supply of powder. Will shortly send full instructions to make the Irish peace, by Brian O'Neale. Bewdley, June 13.
   Original.
   Endorsed, "Rec'd. 9 July."

* These two papers are printed in "The History of the execrable Irish Rebellion." Append. No. xII. See also Life of Ormond, I. 500.

K k

1644.
Dublin,
June 21.

1763. *The Marquis of Ormond to Lord Inchiquin*, touching a charge made against him by Lord Muskerry, and advising him not to leave his command and go to England at present, lest it should prejudice his defence. *Copy.*

[July 1.]

1764. *Memorials* touching the battle of York. A minute and interesting account of this battle, better known as that of Marston Moor.
In the same hand as the paper printed in Cl. S. P. S. p. 181, which is endorsed by Hyde, "Sir Hugh Cholmeley's Memorials."

July 6.

1765. *The Ambassadors of the States to the Parliament*, desiring to mediate between the King and them.
Imperfect Copy.
Endorsed by Sec. Nicholas. See Rapin, vol. ii. p. 506; Whitelock, p. 90.

July 9.

1766. *Receipt* given by Smith to Sir N. Crisp for the 40*l.* mentioned in his complaint. *Copy.*

July 9.

1767. *Agreement* originally made between Capt. Smith and Sir N. Crisp for the use of the St. George.

No date.

1768. *Complaint* of Capt. John Smith to the Lords of the Admiralty against Sir Nicholas Crisp, alleging that whereas Crisp had received 400*l.* for the expenses of the ship St. George of Dartmouth, in conveying Her Majesty to France, he has only paid Smith 40*l.*

No date.

1769. *Answer* of Sir Nicholas Crisp and Mr. Andrew King to the above complaint, denying that the money received was for the expenses of Capt. Smith.

No date.

1770. *Account* of sums expended, as between Capt. Smith and Sir Nich. Crisp, shewing Smith to be indebted to him 506*l.* 15*s.* 3½*d.*

Edinburgh,
July 16.

1771. *Appointment of Scotch Commissioners* (the Earl of Loudon, Marquis of Argyle, Lord Balmerino, and others) to make a treaty in England.

Bath,
July 17.

1772. *The King to Ormond.* Has commanded Digby to inform him of the necessity the King had to put on him in concluding the Irish peace. Trusts he will not be deterred by difficulties from easing the King of the treaty. Is confident that if he joins his fortunes to the King's, he will have a good part. *Original.*
Endorsed, "Recd. Aug. 14 by Sir Brian O'Neil."

1773. *Sir Thomas Wharton to the Marquis of Ormond*, to the same purport as his next letter.
Cl. S. P. vol. II. p. 169; date July 19.
1644. Cork, July 18.

1774. *The same to the same.* Beseeches him not to join with the rebels against the Irish Protestants, but rather advise the King to an accommodation with the Parliament against the rebels. Is now employed to the Parliament with this view.
Cl. S. P. vol. II. p. 169.
Cork, July 19.

1775. *Lord Inchiquin to the same.* Details the designs of the rebels as a justification of his determination to assume a posture of defence, and remove such as are accounted dangerous; and desires Ormond to take the same resolution throughout Ireland.
Cl. S. P. vol. II. p. 170, where the name Dwyer is printed Droyer.
Cork, July 25.

1776. *Sir Hardress Waller to the same*, touching the condition of the Protestants in Munster, as agent for whom he is gone to England.
Bristol, July 29.

1777. *Mr. Robert Moulton to the same*, with news of the Earl of Essex's success at Plymouth, Plimpton, and in the West.
Milford Haven, July 31.

1778. *Lord Inchiquin to Col. Barry.* Justifies his conduct in expelling the people from the town, detailing the complaints against them, and illustrating the bad faith of Papists by the conduct of his own brother in a money transaction.
Cl. S. P. vol. II. p. 171.
Cork, July 31.

1779. *The same to the Marquis of Ormond.* Denies the charge made by Lord Cork, that there has been any communication till now between him and the Parliament. Now that there is no living in Ireland for any but Papists, will decline any employment in common with them, and rather serve for his bread in the Low Countries, and is therefore sending letters to the Parliament by Sir T. Wharton.
Without date, but endorsed as received Aug. 4.
Cl. S. P. vol. II. p. 168.
No date.

1780. *His Majesty to the Lords Commissioners at Oxford*, ordering an examination by them of alleged abuses in the non-payment of the garrison at Wallingford, and giving permission for trade between Oxford and London.
Signed by the King and Lord Digby, and endorsed by Hyde.
Lenhard, Aug. 5.

K k 2

1644. Dublin Castle, Aug. 10.	1781. *Mr. G[eo.] C[arr] to Mr. Gerrard Booth*, requesting to know for His Excellency's information, whether assurance will be given by Capt. Seaman for the safe return of hostages, if given to secure Mr. Brook's safe return. *Copy.* Endorsed as such by himself.
From aboard Capt. Seaman, Aug. 10.	1782. *Mr. Gerrard Booth to the Marquis of Ormond*, requesting safe conduct for the delivery of dispatches from Lord Inchiquin.
From aboard Capt. Seaman, Aug. 12.	1783. *Capt. Gerrard Booth to Mr. George Carr*, forwarding a packet of letters for the perusal of His Excellency. Endorsed. "Enclosing my lo. Inchiquin's pacqt. to his Exc."
Dublin, Aug. 15.	1784. *Mr. Carr to Capt. Booth*, acknowledging the receipt of the preceding.
From on board the London, Aug. 15.	1785. *Capt. Seaman to the Lord Lieutenant (Ormond)*, offering to send Capt. Booth on shore, on receipt of a hostage.
Lanreth, Aug. 19.	1786. *Lord Digby to Secretary Nicholas*, at Oxford. The opening of the trade between Oxford and London has been referred to the Lords there. Cannot at present give hopes of sparing any horse for Oxford, but hopes the whole army will soon turn that way, for they intend to attack Essex in his quarters. They have not of late made the least attempt upon one another. *Partly in cypher.*
Cork, Aug. 25.	1787. *Lord Inchiquin (Murrough O'Brien) to the Lord Lieutenant (Ormond.)* A Parliament ship has arrived, and persuaded the town of Youghal to join the Covenant. Will be compelled to do the same himself, unless means be taken to relieve the distress of the Irish Protestants, and re-establish religion as it was before the rebellion. Earnestly entreats Ormond to put himself at the head of the Protestant movement.
Cork, Sept. 14.	1788. *The same to the same*, explaining that the oath taken in Ireland is simply for the Protestant against the Romish religion, and begging him to join them as commander.
Cork, Sept. 19.	1789. *The same to the same.* Justifies his interleaguing with the Parliament fleet, and his advice to Capt. Booth not to trust himself on shore without a hostage. Insists upon his view of the rebels' designs, and that the most zealous embracers of the Covenant have no intention of lifting a hand against the King. Is only pledged to desist from hostilities till the 1st of next month, and hopes for assurance that no further cessation is intended. Cl. S. P. vol. II. p. 173.

CLARENDON PAPERS.   253

1790. *His Majesty to the Earl of Antrim,* thanking him for his services in landing forces in the Scotch Highlands. May find it requisite to send him there in person. *Copy.*
Cl. S. P. vol. ii. p. 175.
1644. Chard, Sept. 27.

1791. *Lord Peterborough to Sir Edward Hyde.* A letter of thanks (extravagantly worded) for some favours received in the matter of a wardship.
Sherborne, Oct. 4.

1792. *Dr. Col. Brockett to the Marquis of Ormond,* commending Lord Inchiquin's zeal and devotion to the Protestant religion. A ship from Middleborough has arrived at Cork, laden with provisions, as a benevolence for the distressed Protestants there.
From His Matie fort at Castle Park, Oct. 29.

1793. *Affidavit* of Sir John Backhouse of the assessment of 400l. as the twentieth part of his property at the time of the making of the ordinance of Nov. 29, 1642, for assessment.
Printed form, filled up.
Nov. 8.

1794. *Father O'Hartegan to the Lords and Confederate Council of Catholics in Ireland.* Relates the particulars of several conferences with the ministers there, touching the Queen going to Ireland, and with the Nuncio and leading English Roman Catholics there. The Queen's opinion of Ormond, Inchiquin, and Clanricard. Thinks God reserves the rethroning of the King to the Irish nation. *Copy.*
Endorsed by Hyde. Cl. S. P. vol. B. p. 176.
Paris, Nov. 27.

1795. *His Majesty to the Members of the Houses* in London, desiring a safe conduct for the Duke of Richmond and the Earl of Southampton. *Original.*
Signed by the King, with the names of the Duke of Richmond and Earl of Southampton inserted in his own hand, but not directed to any person. See Rapin, vol. ii. p. 508. Printed in Parl. Hist. vol. xiii. p. 336.
Oxford, Nov. 17.

1796. *Notes* of abuses in the administration of the ordnance department, apparently drawn up to be laid before the Council.
No signature.
Oxford, Dec. 2.

1797. *Order of Council,* in which the Earl of Essex's answer to the application of a pass for the Duke of Richmond to London is quoted, and Prince Rupert's rejoinder thereto, it being unanimously agreed that such answer would not be any acknowledgment of the Parliament. *Two Copies.*
One endorsed as follows: "Order at Council Board concerning the message sent to the two Houses at Westminster, wherein he stiled the two Houses a Parliament; also with a mem^{dum} that the King and the writer were the only persons who concurred not in the opinion that it was fit to call those sitting at Westminster a Parliament, Prince Rupert not voting." The other copy is thus endorsed by Nicholas: "Order of the Council Board, drawn by His Majesty's special directions, when in compliance with his Council, he gave way (against his own opinion and only one Counsellor) to stile the two Houses a Parliament in his letters, after himself by Proclamation not long before, and likewise the members of both Houses at Oxon, had declared they were no Parliament." See Rapin, vol. ii. p. 508.
Oxford, Dec. 5.

254   CALENDAR OF

1644.
Oxford,
Dec. 13.

1798. *Instructions* from His Majesty to the Duke of Richmond and Earl of Southampton on their mission to the Parliament, as to the manner of treating for a peace or cessation of arms: the securities to be demanded if the King come to London to treat in person. Offers of pardon and favour to be made to the Independents: arguments to be used to the Scotch Commissioners: information on the affections of the city: and visits to prisoners of quality.   *Original.*

<small>In Sec. Nicholas' hand, and signed by the King: also a Rough Draught in Hyde's hand.</small>

<small>Cl. S. P. vol. II. p. 179.</small>

Dec. 13.

1799. *Commencement of the King's instructions to the Commissioners,* sent with his reply to the Propositions of Parliament.   <small>In Hyde's hand.   Cl. S. P. vol. II. pp. 179, 180.</small>

Oxford,
Dec. 13.

1800. *Answer of His Majesty to the Propositions of the Parliament sent to him by the Earl of Denbigh,* desiring that Commissioners be appointed on both sides to treat for a peace.
Copy.

<small>Endorsed by Sec. Nicholas.   Printed in Parl. Hist. vol. xiii. p. 349, and in King Charles's Works, part I. p. 216.</small>

Oxford,
Dec. 15.

1801. *Minute* of Privy Council, admitting Edward Pierce, Doctor of Laws, to the office of Master of Requests Extraordinary, on the King's warrant, therein recited in full, with a notice of his knighting by the King.   *Copy.*

Westminster,
Dec. 10.

1802. *Reply of the Parliament to His Majesty's Letter,* agreeing to his desire for peace, but desiring time for consideration, and sending back the Duke of Richmond and Lord Southampton.   *Copy.*

<small>Signed by Grey of Warke, and Lenthall.   Endorsed by Nicholas.
Printed in Parl. Hist. vol. xiii. p. 351.</small>

Dec. 14.

1803. *Extract from a Despatch* sent from Paris to Sec. Nicholas, informing him that Mr. Augier, who had come thither commissioned by the Parliament, had, at the writer's request, been refused audience and ordered to leave Paris.
Copy.

<small>Endorsed by Nicholas.</small>

Oxford,
Dec. 17.

1804. *The King to Ormond.* Recommends Lord Herbert to him as one to be used and trusted in the matter of the treaty, or any other, but will not answer for his judgment.
Original.

<small>In cypher.   Endorsed. "Recd. June 29, '45, by the E. of Glamorgan."</small>

1805. *Account* of the movements of the Marquis of Newcastle, Sir Thomas Glemham, and the Scots army during part of the year 1644 down to the surrender of York by Sir Thomas Glemham. 1644. No date.

<small>A sheet of notes, in Hyde's hand, apparently prepared for his History.</small>

1806. *A copy of Latin verses*, entitled "In Causidicum nostrum," qui spontanea pietate motus, (ut prædicabat) et pro Charitativo se venditans, ad Defensionem nostram se accinxit: postquam vero ob impressionem Libelli sui mille quadringentosque Reales pauperibus Clientibus suis expressit: et nunc ducentos Ducatos (quos Rex Pius nobis miseria Proseucticis erogavit) extorquere etiam voluit. No date.

1807. *Petition* to be employed as His Majesty's Resident in Turkey, or for a letter of recommendation to the ambassador at Constantinople.—French. No date. Without signature.

1808. *Case in Chancery* between the estate of Sir Charles Egerton and his sister Lacy, wife of Richard Wise, esq. No date.

1809. *Some Observations and Memorials touching the Hothams*,[*] relating particulars of the intrigue of Sir John Hotham and his son with the Earl of Newcastle, and giving an account of their capture and execution. 1644–5. No date.

<small>Endorsed by Hyde, "Sir Hugh Cholmeley's Memorials." Cl. S. P. vol. ii. p. 181.</small>

1810. *Preparations to be made at Oxford for the King's service.*—"The things that fell in our discourse were these." Oxford to be protected by my Lord of Danby and my Lord of Dorks. The scholars to be trained in martial discipline. Sir Nathan Brent, Warden of Merton, Dr. Ratcliff, Principal of Brasenose, Dr. Clayton, Master of Pembroke, Dr. Hood, Rector of Lincoln, to be "quickened" in the matter. *Draught.* No date.

1811. *Certificate of Receipts and Issues* (in the expenses of the King's household, apparently) extending from Sept. 28, 1644, to Jan. 4. Oxford, Jan. 4.

1812. *His Majesty to the Earl of Antrim*, thanking him for his services in the Scotch business. Sends Col. Steward to negotiate further supplies for Scotland. *Copy.* Oxford, Jan. 4.

<small>Cl. S. P. vol. ii. p. 186.</small>

---

[*] Sir J. Hotham and his son were executed on the 1st and 2nd of Jan. 1645.

1644-5.
Oxford,
Jan. 9.

1813. *The King to Ormond.* Thinks it necessary, upon the rumours of a peace, to tell him the true sense of it. The rebels have agreed to treat, and will insist on the continuance of the Irish war. Gives Ormond grounds for him to persuade the Irish to despatch a peace on reasonable terms, and to press them for their speedy assistance to the King and their friends in Scotland; the King's intention being to unite the Scotch and Irish forces in Wales and Cumberland; to which end ships must be provided before the end of March.

Postscript.—In order to bring the Irish to a peace, Ormond is to promise to join them against the Scots and Lord Inchiquin. *Original.*

In cypher, decyphered by Ormond.
Endorsed by Col. Barry, "Recd. Mar. 6."

Jan. 14.

1814. *Declaration* by His Majesty of the reasons which induced him to commit to prison Lords Sussex, Andover, and Percy, for correspondence with the rebels. *Copy.*

Endorsed by Nicholas.

Oxford,
Jan. 18.

1815. *The King to Ormond.* *Original.*

In cypher, not decyphered.

Endorsed, "Duplicate of a letter from his Matie, ye original 15 Dec., this of the 18 of Jan. Rec. 6 of March, 1644. By Coll. John Barry."

Jan. 18.

1816. *Last Will and Testament of Archbishop Laud* (dated Jan. 13, 1643-4). It consists of ten closely-written pages, and contains numerous legacies, notably to St. Paul's Church (800*l.*), the King (1000*l.*), and a debt of 2000*l.* forgiven). St. John's College, Oxford (500*l.* and plate). Duchess of Buckingham (10*l.*), many children of half-brothers and sisters, his chaplains, and the poor of several parishes of Oxford, Northampton, and elsewhere. It concludes thus: "For the money to bear the charge of those Legacies expressed in my Will, and other Intendments, I have, for fear of the present storm, committed it to honest and, I trust in God, safe hands, and I doubt not but they will deliver the money in their several custodies to my Executors for the uses expressed. But I forbear to name them, lest the same storm should fall on them which hath driven me out of all I have considerable in my own possession." *Copy.*

Printed in his Works, Lib. Ang. Cath. Theol.

Oxford,
Jan. 28.

1817. *The King to Ormond.* Commends the bearer, Brian O'Neill, to him. *Original.*

Endorsed, "Recd. July 2, 1645, found with S^r Br. O'Nril after his committall to ye Castle."

1818. *Powers* of the Commissioners from the Parliament to treat with those from the King in the matter of religion.   1644-5. Jan. 28.
Copy.

<small>The names of the Commissioners herein are the same as those printed in Hist. Rebell. bk. viii. p. 510. Printed in King Charles's Works, part II. p. 431.</small>

1819. *Additional charges against the Earl of Sussex* (Lord Savile), founded principally on the friendships and conversation of his daughter, Lady Temple.   No date*.
Copy.
<small>Endorsed by Nicholas with the name of Mr. Bridges.</small>

1820. *Reply of the Earl of Sussex* to the charges brought against him by the King, of reflecting upon him for breach of privilege of Parliament by demanding the six members, of vilifying the jurisdiction of the Lords at Oxford, of a design to seize the Queen on her return from Holland, and of correspondence with Sir Peter Temple and other rebels.   Jan. 28.

1821. *His Majesty to Secretary Nicholas.* Approves of what the Commissioners have done concerning religion, and desires him to ascertain whether the rebels will allow the treaty to be laid open, that the disagreeing to one or more articles on either side hinder not the treating on the rest, that all points of difference and the certain price of peace may be clearly known.   Oxford, Feb. 5.
<small>Written entirely in the King's hand, and endorsed by Nicholas. Cl. S. P. vol. ii. p. 186.</small>

1822. *Warrant of His Majesty* for a pension of 500l. per annum to Clara Harner, Countess of Forth, in consideration of the services of the late Lord Forth, her husband.   Oxford, Feb. 6.
Copy.

1823. *Contract* between Lord Cottington, as Lord High Treasurer, and Mr. Justus Collimar, of Antwerp, to deliver 1000 barrels of powder, 30 tons of brimstone, and 200 or 300 tons of saltpetre, at some of the King's magazines.   Feb. 6.

Account of moneys paid by Collimar on the King's account.   [Feb.]
Copy.

1824. *Paper* of resolutions with regard to concessions on the subject of episcopacy, apparently prepared for the Uxbridge Conference.   Feb. 10.
<small>Endorsed by Hyde. The substance of these is the same as those printed in Rapin, vol. ii. p. 512.</small>

1825. *The King to Ormond.* Recommends the bearer, Sir Tim. Fetherston †, to him. Refers him to (Ld.) Digby for   Oxford, Feb. 16.

<small>* This must have been in the year 1644-5. Lord Savile was created Earl of Sussex May 25, 1644, and died in 1646. The execution of the Hothams is mentioned in Lord Sussex's reply.   † Featherstonhaugh.</small>

1644-5.
particulars of his business. Prays him to hasten the Irish peace, and at all events not to fall into a new rupture with them. Encloses a copy of the postscript sent in the letter by Barry. *Original.*

Endorsed, "Recd. April 4, 1645."

Feb. 17.
1826. *Further Agreement* between Capt. Smith and Sir N. Crisp for division of prize-money. See July 9, 1644.

Oxford, Feb. 20.
1827. *Warrant of His Majesty to the Uxbridge Commissioners,* empowering them to name to the Parliament Commissioners certain persons into whose hands the militia shall be put. The list consists of thirty names the most considerable on both sides. *Two Copies.*

Both signed by the King and sealed, but one with a blank left for the list of names.

Oxford, Feb. 14.
1828. *The King to Ormond.* Answers two points in Ormond's letter to Digby. Directs him to imprison Sir Wm. Parsons, Sir Adam Loftus, and Sir Rt. Meredith, now at large on bail. As to the treason lately discovered, the King recommends severity (though contrary to his nature) against Sir Patrick Weemes. [Wemyss.]

Inserted.—A list of the Irish Council present May 14, 1645.

Signed by the King. Endorsed, "Read at the board 14 May, 1645; and by advice of the Council his Matie command the same day obeyed," &c.

Feb. 17.
1829. *The same to the same.* The English rebels having given the command of Ireland to the Scots shows their aim to be a subversion of religion and regal power; this and the necessity of preserving the King's Irish subjects in Ireland, move him to enlarge Ormond's powers to conclude a peace, which is to be done at whatever cost. Empowers him even to suspend Poyning's Act and the penal laws against Papists, if only the Irish will engage themselves in the King's assistance against his English and Scotch rebels. *Original.*

In cypher, decyphered by Ormond. Also a duplicate in cypher, sent April 4. Endorsed, "Recd. 5 April by the Ld. Taafe."

No date.
1830. *Mr. Richard Kemp to His Majesty,* explaining his reasons for not executing the King's commands, having acted with the advice of the Council and the consent of the King's Commissioner, Mr. Leonard Calvert. Cl. S. P. vol. ii. p. 175.

Feb. 17.
1831. *The same to Sir William and Sir John Berkeley.* A full exposition of the causes which have rendered him unable

to carry out the King's commands touching the seizure of the ships, and an account of recent engagements with the natives, and erection of several forts, with special commendation of the gallantry of Capt. Raph. Wormeley. Enclosing— 1644-5.

> October, 1644. *The humble answer of the Grand Assembly to His Majesty's propositions for a Custom House to be erected in the colony, with tonnage and poundage, and the reasons thereupon*, pleading in excuse the poverty of the colony, the want of coin to pay in money, and their inability to pay in kind at the rate of 1 lb. of tobacco for every penny.
>
> Same date. *Address of the Grand Assembly to His Majesty*, alleging the same reasons for suspending his orders concerning the ships as Governor Kemp had done in his letter.
>
> Both signed "John Meade Cl. Dom. Commun."

1832. *The Prince of Wales to Lord Goring*, announcing his intended arrival at Bristol on Monday, and desiring immediate information on military matters. Bath, March 8.

> Without date or signature, but endorsed by Nicholas, "Letter from the Prince to Lord Goring, from Bath, March the 8th, 1644."

1833. *Lord Digby to Sir John Berkeley*, rebuking him, in kind terms, for being in garrison, and for so occasionless a tartness towards General Goring, shewing the necessity of friendly unity. Oxford, March 11.

Copy.

1834. *Lord Goring to the Prince of Wales*, giving an account of his forces, and plans to meet Waller, and desiring instructions. Has about 1500 foot and 3000 horse, and will be joined this day by Sir John Berkeley with 1000 foot and 500 horse. March 12.

1835. *Lord Culpeper to Lord Goring*, promising him from the Prince every assistance against Skippon, and leaving the conduct of the business to his own judgement. Sir John Berkeley is ordered to join him. Bristol, March 12.

> No signature, but endorsed with Lord Culpeper's and Lord Goring's names.

1836. *Order from the Prince of Wales* to draw together under Sir Francis Doddington all soldiers of the county of Somerset who have heretofore lived in any of His Majesty's armies or garrisons and have withdrawn themselves from their colours. Bristol, March 13.

Original.

> Signed, "Charles P.," and endorsed, "For Lord Goring." With a Copy certified by Ric. Fanshawe, endorsed, "For General Goring."

1644-5. March 17.	1837. *Warrant* of Lord-Keeper Littleton to enforce the King's warrant issued at York, Aug 13, 1642 (which is quoted at length), that in consequence of the King's distance from the Privy Seal, clerks of the Signet and Privy Seal shall receive their fees, though the grants are passed under the Great Seal. *Copy.*
Oxford, March 17.	1838. *Proclamation* by the King, requiring all such as have any office or command in Ireland, to make their speedy repair thither to attend their employments. *Printed.*
Bristol, March 21.	1839. *Despatch* from the Prince to Lord Goring, advising him to follow Waller on his retreat as far as Wiltshire. *Rough Draught.* Written by Sir E. Hyde, and interlined in places by Lord Culpeper, who directs a juncture with Sir Richard Grenville's forces. See Hist. Rebell. bk. ix. p. 544.
No date.	1840. *Lord Goring to Lord Culpeper.* He was misinformed about Waller's retreat. Complains bitterly of the absence of officers without leave, especially Col. Hutchinson and Col. Mulesworth.
From the rendezvous at West House, March 22.	1841. *The same to the same.* Will follow Waller's retreat, as ordered, but has no hope to overtake him. Desires provision be made for the forces he leaves behind him, and either definite instructions or absolute powers to act as he thinks fit.
Exeter, March 23.	1842. *Sir John Berkeley to Lord Digby*, answering with great spirit the charge of inactivity brought against him, by shewing that he acted against his own wishes, under command from Lord Hopton, and that he has not been idle in the matter of the recusant clergy, though that business was entrusted to Sir George Parry and not to him. Justifies his angry mention of Lord Goring, but declares that he has faithfully served and obeyed him, and quotes his forgiveness of an outrage of Sir William Courtenay as a proof of his desire for unity.
March 23.	1843. *Orders* of Lord Goring, to regulate the levying of contributions in the Western counties. Every horseman to be allowed 6d. a day and free quarters by the parishes where they are quartered. Plunder and extortion punishable by death. *Copy.* On these Orders, see Hist. Rebell. bk. ix. p. 555.
1645. Bristol, March 26.	1844. *Account* of several sums paid Mr. Justus Collimar out of the excise of this city; extending from Feb. 20 to March 26 (1645), and amounting to 1324l. 1s. 6½d. *Endorsed by Nicholas.*

1845. *Lord Goring to Lord Culpeper.* Waller is reported to be much stronger than he had anticipated, and the siege of Taunton will be more difficult than had been expected. Advises that the siege be pressed, instead of following Waller's retreat.
  1845.
  Shafton,
  March 26.

1846. *Lord Culpeper to Lord Goring*, desiring him, from the Prince, to receive back Col. Molesworth and his soldiers, and to forgive their offence.
  Bristol,
  March 26.

1847. *The same to the same*, expressing the Prince's consent to his design upon Taunton, and giving him leave to act as he thinks fit.
  Bristol,
  March 27.

1848. *Lord Goring to Lord Culpeper.* Complains of illness which entirely incapacitates him, and if continued one day longer will force him to ask for two of the Council to relieve him of the command.
  Shafton,
  March 27.

1849. *Sir Lewis Dyve to Lord Goring.* Sir Richard Grenville will be hard pressed by the forces from Taunton, which have marched out to join Cromwell's horse, and 1500 foot expected from Portsmouth, unless immediate aid arrive from Goring or Sir John Berkeley.
  Sherborne,
  March 27.

1850. *Sir Richard Grenville to the same.* Has defeated the Taunton forces in three several encounters. They are said now to be about Exminster, with forces from Lyme, and Cromwell's horse, aiming at Devon. He is about at once to march for Honiton.
  Chard,
  March 27.

1851. *Lord Goring to Lord Culpeper*, for match to be sent to Ilchester, and that Sir John Browne and Col. Hutchinson be sent at once from Bristol to their command.
  Shafton,
  March 28.

1852. *Lord Culpeper to Lord Goring.* Directs him to march immediately to try and get Cromwell between himself and Sir Richard Grenville. Taunton must be left alone, until the decision of a battle shall give it them without siege; or if the Taunton forces be drawn off to join Cromwell, Grenville may surprise and burn the town. *Rough Draught.*
In his own hand.
  Bristol,
  March 28.

1853. *Lord Goring to Lord Culpeper.* Waller's strength is so great that they must prepare for fighting rather than a siege. Grenville's force should follow the Taunton forces, and if they join Waller, should join Goring; taking Wellington and burning Taunton on the way, if they can.
  Shafton,
  March 28.

1645.

Bristol,
March 28.
1854. *Lord Culpeper to Lord Goring.* Is greatly concerned to hear of his illness. Sir William Ogle has intercepted letters which give apprehension of a design on Bristol, and necessitate immediate action. *Copy.*
In his own hand.

March 30.
1855. *Sir Fr. Mackworth to the same,* by Mr. Cooper, acquainting him of the receipt of 5000 lbs. of bread and 4000 lbs. of cheese, and congratulating him on his success yesterday near Dorchester. *Copy.*
No signature, but endorsed with the names.

Rendezvous at Lye Common, March 30.
1856. *Lord Goring to Lord Culpeper.* An account of his surprise of Cromwell's forces near Dorchester. Grenville should now burn Taunton, which has only 400 foot and three troops of horse to defend it.

Newtown by Evill, March 31.
1857. *The same to the same.* New rebel forces have landed at Poole and Weymouth. Is waiting till Sir Richard Grenville has burnt Taunton, for which purpose he gives him all the help he can. Speculates on Waller's probable line of march in Somersetshire, and desires that Sir John Berkeley and others be ordered to march at once to the aid of Grenville.

Bristol, March 31.
1858. *Lord Culpeper to Lord Goring,* congratulating him on his defeat of Cromwell's horse, and approving, in the Prince's name, all his plans for the future. Two Commissioners shall be sent to assist in provisioning the army. *Copy.*

Bristol, April 1.
1859. *The same to the same.* Having received intelligence that Waller, Cromwell, and the Taunton forces are all united, suggests that an attack may be contemplated on Bath or Bristol, and advises that Grenville join Goring, putting himself under his command, and that the Taunton scheme be for the present laid aside. *Rough Draught.*
In his own hand.

Bruton, April 1.
1860. *Lord Goring to Lord Culpeper.* Relates a successful surprise by Sir John Digby, with 1000 horse, of Waller's quarters at Cucklington, near Wincanton. Several officers are taken. Urges that orders be sent to Grenville to press on Taunton. *Original.*
In duplicate.

Bristol, April 2.
1861. *Lord Culpeper to Lord Goring.* Congratulates him heartily on his success, and suggests the deferring of his former designs until he has chased Waller out of those parts, "except his courage would adventure upon the second part of Roundway Downs."

1862. *Lord Goring to Lord Culpeper.* Is strong enough to keep Waller in check, though not to force his quarters. Grenville should be pressed to finish the Taunton business at once, and then join him in dislodging Waller, or else leave Apsley's men and Sir John Berkeley in Wellington, and so join him. — Bruton, April 3.

1863. *The same to the same.* Waller has retreated by way of Shaftesbury, but whither he does not at present know. — April 3.

1864. *Lord Culpeper to Lord Goring.* The Prince has written to hasten Grenville on in the Taunton business. Not being able to conjecture anything of Waller's plans, leaves all to Goring's judgment. *Rough Draught.* In his own hand. — Bristol, April 4.

1865. *Lord Wentworth to the same.* The enemy have returned to their old quarters at Shaftesbury. Desires directions as to his own movements. *Imperfect.* — Glastonbury, April 9.

1866. *Lord Goring to Lord Culpeper.* Has received the Prince's orders, and marched his men accordingly for Taunton. Proposes going to Bath for four or five days for his lameness. Hopes that the Taunton business will either be finished in that time, or not persisted in. Has little hope of any good coming of it, and is afraid it will only disclose the weakness of their foot. Had it not been for this they might have dislodged Waller and forced him to fight. Begs that the Prince send his orders to Sir R. Grenville and Sir Joseph Wagstaffo, to avoid disputes about command. — Wells, April 11.

Reference is made to this letter in Hist. Rebell. bk ix. p. 544, but the words and tone are entirely different from those quoted there.

A *Note* stating how odious Lord Culpeper, Sir Edw. Hyde, and Lord Hopton are to the commissioners, gentry, and county [of Devon] generally. Request will be made to the King and Council that Lord Hopton may be removed and Lord Culpeper and Sir Edw. Hyde come back to Oxford. We want the Marquis of Hertford more than is to be imagined.*

1867. *Lord Goring to Lord Culpeper.* Has received the King's commands to march in search of Fairfax, of whom he hopes to give a good account. — No date.

1868. *Sir Edward Hyde to Lord Goring,* upbraiding him for his behaviour in withdrawing himself from the forces, and strongly deprecating ill humours. *Copy.* — Bristol, April 12.

* Signed and addressed in cypher and dated only April. It cannot refer to the commissioners of the Uxbridge Treaty, who had separated before April in this year. It probably refers, therefore, to the transactions in the West. See Hist. Rebell. bk. ix. pp. 545-548.

1645. Oxford, April 18.	1869. *Lord Digby to Lord Goring,* ordering him, in the King's name, to march at once to Farringdon with 3000 horse at least, to convey the King within reach of Prince Rupert's army, the rebels having captured 300 of George Lyle's men at Hampton-in-the-Bush, and apprehensions being entertained that Oxford will be besieged. A postscript is added, signed by the King, to countermand his orders of the night before, which required only 2000 horse to come with Goring. *Copy.* Certified by Lord Goring thus, "A true Copy of a letter sent me in cypher."
Wells, April 30.	1870. *Lord Goring to the Earl of Berkshire.* Encloses a letter from Ld. Digby. Informs him of the King having sent for him. Intends to march to-morrow with near 3000 horse and dragoons to Marlborough, and next day between Farringdon and Oxford. Earnestly recommends that in his absence all the horse stationed in the country be drawn together under Sir Francis Dorrington, [Doddington] on the borders of Wilts and Somerset, to prevent the rebels relieving Taunton, and to favour his own retreat if he finds the enemy at Farringdon too strong for him. The levies should also be urged on. *Original.*
No date.	1871. *[The Earl of Berkshire and others of the Prince's Council] to [Lord Digby],* assuring him of the speedy execution of his orders by Lord Hopton, and that due communication of his despatches has been made to Lords Capel and Culpeper, and Sir E. Hyde, now at Exeter. *Copy.* Without signature or address.
Oxford, May 5.	1872. *Warrant of His Majesty* to Sir Nicholas Crisp to receive and audit the accounts of the sequestered estates of delinquents in Cornwall. *Copy.*
Oxford, May 6.	1873. *Warrant of His Majesty* to Sir Edward Walker, Garter King of Arms, to grant to such loyal subjects as distinguish themselves against the rebels such augmentations of their coats of arms as may fitly express their merits. *Two Copies.*
No date.	1874. *Sir Thomas Fairfax to Mr. Hugh Peters,* desiring him, as he is going to Bristol, to communicate with Col. Pinder and Col. Layton about money for the army.
Droitwich, May 13.	1875. *The King to Ormond.* Refers to his public letter of Jan. 22, in which he forbad Ormond to consent to a repeal of the penal laws against recusants. Now that apparently nothing can preserve his Protestant subjects from ruin but a peace with the Irish, he revokes the former restriction, and commands him to yield to his Roman Catholic subjects. Desires him to hasten the settlement of the peace. *Original.* Endorsed, "Recd. May 19, by Cornet Pilkington."

1876. *The King to Ormond.* Finds by Ormond's letter to Digby that he is cautious not to conclude the peace without the concurrence of the Council. Sends therefore a letter to be communicated to them, taking off the former restrictions. Commands him to execute the directions sent Feb. 27, with or without the approbation of the Council; promising on the word of a King that he shall receive no prejudice. *Original.* 1645. Droitwich, May 13.

In cypher, decyphered by Ormond. Also a duplicate and triplicate signed by the King. Endorsed, "Recd. 29th May, 1645. By Fra Penley."

1877. *Petition* of Sir John Buckhouse, Knt. of the Bath, to the Committee of Sequestrations, complaining that his property in Berkshire has been seized, though no proof of his delinquency or any definite accusation has been made against him. *Copy.* May 13.

1878. [*Col.*] *Jo. Bamfylde* to ——, defending himself against the charge of allowing the enemy to raise the siege of Taunton without fighting, which has occasioned a dispute between him and Lord Hopton, and desiring his correspondent to set him right with the King. No date.

Endorsed, "Jo. Bampfield, 1645, 14 May. Taunton relieved soon after that."

1879. *Lord Goring to Lord Culpeper.* Sends a list of the forces set free by the raising of the siege of Taunton, which will be sufficient to face Fairfax, if Cromwell be not joined with him. Desires ammunition, and instructions. Advises that the enemy be kept out of Devonshire and the east of Somerset. Has between 7000 and 8000 horse and foot with him. Somerton, May 15.

1880. *Lord Culpeper to Lord Goring.* The Prince refers the place of quartering and the arrangement of the troops entirely to his judgment. *Rough Draught.* Bristol, May 16.

In Lord Culpeper's hand.

1881. *The same to the same.* If Sir Richard Grenville be recovered, he is to bring up the forces to join Goring, otherwise Sir John Berkeley. The rebels are in great force about Newbury and Thatcham, but their designs are not known. Bath, May 20.

1882. *The King to Ormond.* His last letter (of which he sends a duplicate) is so full an answer to Ormond's despatch, that he has only to thank him for what he has done, and desires him to secure the peace, making the best bargain he can; assuring him that secrecy shall be observed. *Original.* Drayton, May 21.

In cypher, decyphered by Ormond. Endorsed, "Recd. 29 May."

1883. *The Lords of the Prince's Council to His Majesty.* If Goring's army march from the West, all that part will be lost to the King, and the Prince must accompany him. They have therefore respited the march till further orders. *Copy.* Bath, May 24.

266   CALENDAR OF

1645.
Bodmin,
May 14.

1884. *Order of removal* of General van Hacsdonck's prisoners from Falmouth to Truro.   *Copy.*

Bath,
May 14.

1885. *The Prince of Wales and Council to Lord Goring,* ordering him to suspend his march till further orders.   *Copy.*

Bath,
May 15.

1886. *The same to Lord Digby,* representing that it will be dangerous to withdraw all the forces from the West, and requesting that Goring should be accompanied only by the forces which he brought with him. Also that commissions should be issued in the Prince's name, instead of the Commander-in-Chief under him, and that the Prince be under no restraint as to marching or not marching with the army.   *Copy.*

See on this letter, Hist. Rebell. bk. ix. p. 545.

Bath,
May 2d.

1887. *The Prince of Wales to Lord Hopton,* desiring him to give every assistance to Sir Francis Mackworth in strengthening the garrison at Lamport. Annexed is the Prince's warrant to Lord Hopton as Master General of the Ordnance, to supply Mackworth with 100 muskets.   *Copy.*

In Lord Culpeper's hand.

Tutbury,
May 16.

1888. *Lord Digby to Lord Culpeper.* Sends him a copy of his letter to Lord Goring that he may enter into and assist their schemes. Desires him to hasten ammunition to Bristol, and prevent the delay complained of in the adjudication of prizes.

No date.

1889. *The same to Lord Goring,* enclosed in the last. His former orders are altered so far as that instead of marching to Harborough in Leicestershire, he is to march to Newbury and watch opportunity to relieve Oxford, or harass the besiegers. If Oxford can hold out six weeks, it will give the King's forces time to arrange all they wish in the North, and then they will at once march southward. In three days they hope to join Charles Gerrard at Leicester, where they will wait for Goring's answer. Enjoins haste and frequent communication.   *Copy.*

In his own hand.

No date.

1890. *The Prince's Council to His Majesty,* in reference to the orders sent from time to time to the Western forces, and the chief command there. They represent that such orders tend to diminish the powers granted to the Prince in his commission, and to place the command in Lord Goring, which would, in their opinion, be very injurious.   *Rough Draught.*

In Hyde's hand. See Hist. Rebell. bk. ix. p. 551.

1891. *Extracts from letters of His Majesty and Lord Digby to the Prince and his Council,* concerning the powers to be granted to Lord Goring, and dating from March 4 to May 19.   1645. No date.

 In Hyde's hand, and evidently prepared with reference to the preceding paper.

1892. *Sir Richard Grenville to Lord Culpeper,* complaining of the uncertainty of his position in the associated army, and the infringement of his authority by the commissioners of Cornwall and Devon.   Exeter, May 28.

1893. *[Prince Rupert] to [Lord Goring].* A short note in these words, "What ye desier in your lettre from the 22 of May (?) shall be observed, and assure yourself that P. Rupert shall lose his life rather than G. Goring shall sufer for P. Rupert, but shall mantayn G. G. honor and power."   No date.

 Apparently an extract. No signature or address, but endorsed by Hyde, "Pr. Rup. to Goring." See Hist. Rebell. bk. ix. p. 572.

1894. *His Highness' Answer to a Petition* presented to him at Wells, the 2nd of June, 1645, from divers of the inhabitants of the county of Somerset, assembled in a field near Castle Cary in the same county, reminding them that the evils of which they complain are necessitated by their county being the seat of war, but promising to do his best to mitigate them, and to obtain pardon for any who have assisted the rebels, on their return to their allegiance.   *Copy.*   June 2.

 Certified by Sec. Fanshawe.

1895. *His Majesty to the Prince of Wales,* explaining that his letter of May 20 was not intended to diminish the Prince's power, and giving him leave to reside, by advice of his Council, wherever he may judge most expedient.   Wolverhampton, June 17.

 Signed by the King.

1896. *The King to Ormond.* The late misfortune makes the Irish assistance more necessary. Recommends to him its speedy performance; else he may be put to great straits. Fitzwilliams came recommended by the Queen; recommends him to Ormond. Desires him to send speedy intelligence to what port to direct the ship for transporting Ormond's men.   *Original.*   Bewdley, June 18.

 Endorsed, "Recd. 19 June, by Col. Fitzwilliams."

1897. *Lord Goring to Lord Culpeper,* relating the progress of the works at Taunton, which town he hopes soon to take. Massy, who is on his march, is not likely to have force sufficient to compel him to raise the siege. Desires that Sir Richard Grenville be directed to join him.   Hilbishops, June 18.

1645.
Barnstaple,
June 10.

1898. *Lord Culpeper to Lord Goring.* The forces to act under Goring shall be sent in command of Sir Richard Grenville, who seems willing to comply with the Prince's pleasure. Desires frequent intelligence, as they know nothing of what goes on eastward. *Copy.*

In his own hand.

Barnstaple,
June 11.

1899. *The Prince of Wales to the same,* complaining of the insolence of the club-men of Somersetshire to the garrison at Lamport, and ordering him to take steps for reducing them to reason. *Copy.*

See Hist. Rebell. bk. iv. p. 556.

Hereford,
June 23.

1900. *The King to the Prince of Wales.* Should the King be taken by the rebels, the Prince is never to submit to any dishonourable condition, even to save the King's life. Urges him to constancy, as he values his father's blessing. Directs him not to communicate this letter to the Council until occasion arise. *Copy.*

By Hyde, from the King's cypher. With another dated March 22, 1644.

Another copy, by a different hand.

See Hist. Rebell. p. 486.

June 24.

1901. *A Particular of the Pieces, &c., of Tin blown at the Blowing House of St. Nyott,* from Midsummer 1644 to Midsummer 1645, the mark of the House being a flower de luce; John Cole and Walter Hodge, owners; Walter Hodge and John Cole blowers. The total is 6320 lbs.

Fonderford,
June 24.

1902. *Lord Goring to Lord Culpeper.* Complains greatly of the want of powder, and also of provisions, which will cause him, if not relieved, to raise the siege of Taunton within two days. Had hopes that the club-men of the county would have declared for the King, till the news came of the late blow *.

No date.

1903. *The same to the same,* desiring supplies of match, and that the Cornish runaways be sent back to the army. Hears that the enemy are detained before Bridgewater, which is well provided. Will quarter at Torrington and Bideford to-night.

Barnstaple,
June 25.

1904. *Sir Edward Hyde to Secretary Nicholas,* lamenting the defeat of Naseby, where they thought themselves strongest, as has always been the case. Complains grievously of the efforts made at Court to dishonour the Prince and frustrate all their endeavours. Goring does as he likes. Will not give

* The battle of Naseby was fought June 14th.

Goring their cyphor, as Nicholas knows his old way of opening letters. Wishes the King would come West to prevent any mischief by Goring. If Goring had been the soldier they expected, Plymouth would have been taken long ago, but he does nothing but drink and play. Desires Nicholas to comfort his [Hyde's] wife, and lend her 100*l*.   *Copy.*

1645.

Endorsed by himself.

1905. *The Lords of the Prince's Council to Lord Goring*, in answer to a letter of the previous day, complaining of lack of provisions. They express their surprise at this, and desire instructions from him; for which purpose they will send Commissioners to confer with him, if he thinks it necessary. *Copy.*

June 25.

In Hyde's hand.

1906. *The King to Ormond.* Recommends O'Neil to him. Trusts the peace will be concluded before this reaches him. O'Neil will speak of the Master of the Ward's place and the V. Treasurer's.   *Original.*

Hereford. June 26.

Endorsed, "Recd. 8 Aug. by D. O'Neil."

1907. *Lord Goring to Lord Culpeper*, renewing his complaints of scarcity of provisions, and desiring that Commissioners be sent to him at once. If the club-men of that county would declare for the King, they would be strong enough to face the enemy, but of this there is little hope, some violence having passed between them and the garrison at Lamport. Otherwise they must strengthen the garrisons and defend the passes into Devon.

Pondsford. June 27.

For the quarrel at Lamport, see Hist. Rebell. bk. ix. p. 556.

1908. *Warrant of His Majesty to Sir Edward Hyde*, as Chancellor of the Exchequer, to pay 500*l*. to Lady Catherine Aubigney.   Signed by the King.

Hereford, June 27.

1909. *Lord Goring to Lord Culpeper.* Informs him of his intention to withdraw all his forces to Chard in consequence of Massey's advance. Desires that Sir Richard Grenville be not allowed to come to the army in capacity of marshal of the field, as he will thereby supersede Lord Wentworth.

Pondsford, June 29.

1910. *Sir Richard Grenville to Secretary Fanshawe*, enclosing a petition to the Prince for a trial by court-martial, or else for leave to retire out of England.

[June (?) 29.]

No date, but endorsed "29 June (?) 1645." See Hist. Rebell. bk. ix. p. 562.

1645.
Ottery St. Mary, July 3.

1911. *Sir Richard Grenville to the Lords of the Prince's Council*, resigning his commission, with a long account of his grievances, especially his being superseded by Sir John Berkeley before Plymouth; and offering to serve as a volunteer.

See Hist. Rebell. bk. ix. p. 559.

Penrhyn, July 6.

1912. *General van Haesdonck to Sir Edward Hyde*, pressing for money to enable him to revictual his ships.

No date.

1913. *List* of ships now at sea under Haesdonck's command, ten in number.

Truro, July 7.

1914. *Warrant* of the Commissioners of Cornwall to the Custom Officers, to permit the shipping of 90*l*. worth of wool at 14*d*. a lb., for the procuring of ammunition for the county.

July 15.

1915. *Warrant* to stay goods at a custom house in Cornwall till the duties be paid.

July 16.

1916. *A Note*, signed "John Penhallows," relating to the same business as the last.

July 17.

1917. *Notes* concerning some persons employed by van Haesdonck.

No date.

1918. *Notes* similar to those contained in the last paper.

Bideford, July 18.

1919. *Lord Goring to Lord Culpeper*, with complaints of want of pay for the men and officers, and the frequent desertions from the army. The differences between Sir R. Grenville and Sir John Berkeley increase daily, and if not reconciled, all will go to wreck.

Stevenston, July 20.

1920. *The same to the same.* Desires assistance to be given to Col. Arundell in recovering the Cornish runaways. Makes great complaint of want of provisions and pay. The rebels are said to be still before Bridgewater, and to have suffered considerable loss.

Liskeard, July 21.

1921. *[Lord Culpeper] to Lord Goring*. The Prince desires him to attend him at Launceston, whither he goes to-morrow, to confer with him on the state of the army. *Copy.*

Without signature.

Launceston, July 24.

1922. *Orders in Council* of the Prince concerning the reformation of the forces under Lord Goring into a life-guard for the Prince: that the forces be at present quartered at Kirton, and that provision be made for quartering at Exeter.

The Prince, the Earl of Berks, and the Earl of Brentford are mentioned as present.

CLARENDON PAPERS.   271

1923. *Mr. Thomas Mounce to Capt. Robert Moulton*, his kinsman, thanking him for kindness done him.   1645. Ridreth, (Redruth) July 14.

1924. *Sir Richard Grenville to Lord Hopton*, recommending the bearer, Capt. William Hamlyn, for a majority. Has just heard that the enemy's van is advanced to Collumpton.   Exe. July 17.

1925. *Lord Goring to Lord Culpeper*. Has not above 1300 foot left. Want of pay is drawing both officers and men away from the army. Advises a quarter about Tiverton, when a force can be got together.   Stevenston, July 17.

This letter is quoted in Hist. Rebell. bk. ix. p. 559.

1926. *The same to the Lords of the Council*, by Sir Joseph Wagstaffe, who desires to represent to the Prince the condition of his forces. Now that Bridgewater is taken, the rebels will not be likely to remain where they are.   July 17.

1927. *Lord Culpeper to Lord Goring*, promising to send back what runaways he can, and leaving other matters to his own judgment.   *Rough Draught*.   Launceston, July 18.

In his own hand

1928. *Lord Goring to Lord Culpeper*, renewing his complaints of the Cornish runaways and Sir R. Grenville's backwardness.   Stevenston, July 18.

1929. *Lord Culpeper to Lord Goring*. Lord Hopton and Mr. Chancellor are gone to Bodmin to meet the Cornish gentry, and on their return plans may be formed. Is just setting out to endeavour to get passage to the King.   *Copy*.   Launceston, July 19.

1930. *Robert Harris to Sir Nicholas Crisp*, enclosing the next, and recommending that the exchange be made.   Plympton, July 20.

Plymouth, July 22. *Capt. James Kerr to the captain of the garrison at Mount Edgcumbe*, requesting an exchange of prisoners; offering Richard Rundell for Robert Ribell, and another seafaring man for John Pomeroy.

1931. *Lord Goring to Lord Digby*, giving an account of his defeat by Fairfax, and his forced retreat to Bridgewater.   [July.]

Copy.

Part of this letter is printed in Hist. Rebell. bk. v. p. 559.

1932. *Address* "to the valiant and loyal Cornish men of all ranks and degrees whatsoever." Recites the Parliamentary protestation (1641) in favour of the Protestant religion of the Church of England, allegiance to the King, privileges of Parliament, and the liberty of the subject. Notices the attacks   July (?).

1645. of Anabaptists and other heretics, Archer, Crisp, Eton, Goodwin &c., on the established religion. Enters into ecclesiastical controversies, and the sacrilegious spoiling of churches. Rehearses the attacks made on the King. Discusses the power and privilege of Parliament, and the lawful rights and liberties of the subject. The Protestation to be observed, and its upholders protected. Peace and union to be preserved between the three kingdoms. Duties of those who have made the Protestation. Laments the triumph of their adversaries. Objections and answers. Further objections, with seven answers. General exhortation to arouse and exert themselves in so noble a cause.

Draught.

(Thirty-seven pages.) Endorsed, "In Mr. Gatford's hand, who was Chaplain to them in the West, and at Jersey."

Stevraston, Aug. 1.
1933. *Lord Goring to Sir Edward Hyde,* laying before the Prince and Council propositions for re-forming an army from the troops under his command joined with those of Sir Richard Grenville, Sir Henry Cary, Col. Fortescue, and Col. Walker, with the old Cornish forces and a new Devonshire levy. That 5000*l.* of the Cornish contribution be assigned to the army, and supplies of ammunition, otherwise the army will speedily break. If this be done, engages shortly to have an army of 10,000 or 12,000 in good order, to march wherever the King desires. If the Commissioners are backward in consenting to these propositions, he must be his own carer. Sees some light now of having a brave army on foot. Is sending a copy of this to the King, pledging his life and honour to its performance, if his demands be granted.

Part of this letter is printed in Hist. Rebell. bk. ix. p. 364.

Launceston, Aug. 2.
1934. *The Prince of Wales in Council to Lord Goring,* expressing their willingness to comply with all his propositions.

Rough Draught.

Annexed is a *Warrant* for the recovery of all the Cornish officers and soldiers who have left the army. *Copy.*

In Hyde's hand. See Hist. Rebell. bk. ix. p. 364.

Cardiff, Aug. 4.
1935. *His Majesty to Secretary Nicholas,* explaining a passage in one of his letters to the Queen, seized at Naseby, and published by the Parliament, wherein he writes impatiently of Lord Sussex's faction.

Copy of an extract, in Nicholas's hand. The whole letter is printed in King Charles's Works, part I. p. 345.

Brecknock, Aug. 5.
1936. *The same to the Prince of Wales,* ordering him in case of danger to fly to his mother in France.

This is the letter printed in Hist. Rebell. bk. ix. p. 364.

1937. *Warrant of His Majesty* to Francis Godolphin, Governor of the Island of Scilly, for the committal of the Duke of Hamilton to that island. — 1645. Brecknock, Aug. 6.

1938. *Instructions* of the Prince of Wales to Sir E. Hyde, to raise what money he could in advance from the Cornish Customs, and to visit Pendennis and the Mount, to provision them for a year. — Padstow, Aug. 13.

1939. *Petition* of Martin Schomacher, master of the ship 'Gideon,' of Lubeck, to the Prince of Wales, touching a dispute between him and Sir John Mucknell, who had made prize of his ship. Endorsed with a reference of the case by the Prince to Sir Edw. Hyde. — Aug. 17.

   i. Aug. 13. *Depositions* of Philip Lawson and Thomas Williams in the case.

   ii. Aug. 14. *Sir F. Mackworth and Sir F. Bassett to Sir E. Hyde*, about the same business.

   iii. Same date. *The same to Lord Hopton*, about the same business.

   iv. Aug. 20. *Affidavit* of Martin Schomacher in the case.

   v. Penrhyn, Aug. 21. *Report* of Sir E. Hyde to the Prince of Wales in favour of the petitioner, Martin Schomacher, and deciding that the 'Gideon,' with its freight of flax, be restored to him.   *Rough Draught.*
In his own hand.

1940. *Lord Jermyn to Sir Edward Hyde*. Did not know that a grant had been made to the Prince of the tin, which had previously been granted to the Queen, who would have made a much greater benefit of it than the Prince. She is in great disquiet for the safety of the Prince; to whom she has sent 300 barrels of powder. — St. Germains, Aug. 19.

1941. *Warrant* of Sir E. Hyde to Cadwallader Jones, Collector-General of Customs, to deliver 500*l.* worth of wool to George Potter for the use of Sir Allan Apsley, Governor of Barnstaple. — Bodmin, Aug. 21.

1942. *The Commanding Officers at Exeter to the Lords of the Prince's Council*, representing that the quarters of their forces are so contracted by the enemy's advance to Bristol, that they will not be able to maintain themselves longer without supplies of provision. Desire that some of the Council visit Exeter for a conference. — Exeter, Aug. 21.

Signed, "George Goring. John Berkeley. Peter Balle. Geo. Parry. Peter Spinthill. Gilbert Yarde. Hum. Prowzy."

CALENDAR OF

1645.
Launceston,
Aug. 15.

1943. *Order* of the Lords of the Prince's Council that the expenses of victualling Pendennis Castle be paid out of the Cornish contributions.

Aug. 15.

1944. *The Lords of the Prince's Council to Lord Goring*, desiring him to draw together speedily all the available forces, according to the plan agreed on at Okehampton, to be ready for the relief of Bristol if necessary. The Prince will soon repair to Exeter. Also, on the same sheet—

    i. *The same to the Commissioners for Devonshire*, requesting supplies of clothing and provisions for the army.
    Rough Draught.
    In Lord Culpeper's hand.

    ii. *Orders of Council* concerning Pendennis Castle (the same as the preceding) and a prize laded with cloth, taken into Ilfracombe by the 'Tenth Whelp.'
    Rough Draughts.
    In Hyde's hand.

Aug. 16.

1945. *Deposition* of Capt. Richard Jones, of the 'Rose,' touching the capture of the 'Francis.'
Endorsed by Hyde, "Concerning Mr. Allen's ship."

Annexed to this are—

    i. *A Paper* concerning the same business, which shows that the 'Francis' was taken in August, 1643, and was therefore lawful prize; the cessation of hostilities not commencing till the 15th of September.

    ii. Sept. 18, 1643. *Appraisement* of the cargo of the 'Francis' at 480*l.*

    iii. *Demand* of Patrick Allen, the owner, amounting to 5985*l.*

    iv. *A Schedule* of the cargo of the 'Francis.'

    v. May 15, 1645. *Additional valuation* of the 'Francis,' and other prizes, with a schedule of such prizes as have been brought into Cornish ports without paying the tenths and fifteenths to Sir Charles Trevanian, Vice-Admiral of those parts.
Signed, "P. Edgcumbe and W. Scawen."

Rome,
Aug. 28.

1946. *Sir H. Bennett to Lord ———*, praising Sir Kenelm Digby for his adroitness and success in his negotiations, and desiring his own recall to England.
A great part of this is in cypher, which is still undeciphered.

Aug. 31.

1047. *Lord Jermyn to Sir Edward Hyde.* Complains greatly of the diversion of the grant of tin from the Queen to the Prince. She would not only have made the 15*s.* a hundred profit, which the Prince will get, but intended to be her own merchant, and in the faith of that had obtained 12000 pistoles, being four months' advance of her pension from that Court, and the loan of a ship from the Prince of Orange, whereby, with the help of the French duties, she would have made more than double her money at every return, and have paid the advance of her pension in three weeks. The tin was granted her to pay the interest of the money borrowed on her jewels in Holland, pawned for a quarter their value. Has great hopes of the King's success, which he founds upon assurances of succour from France in the North and West, the French Queen-Regent's affection for the King and Queen, and an offer of the Duke of Bouillon to raise and land in England an army entirely at his own expense. The Queen is about to send to meet him at Cologne to settle the matter. She recommends Sir Nicholas Crisp to Hyde's favour.

1645.

Principally in cypher.

1948. *His Majesty to Prince Rupert,* desiring him not to hearken to treaties for peace. *Two Copies.*

Cardiff, Aug.

Printed in Hist. Rebell. bk. ix. p. 561, verbatim, except that "this cause" is printed "his cause" in the 9th line from the top of the page.

1949. *Sir Richard Prideaux to Sir Edward Hyde,* informing him of the rout of a small body of insurgents, who had attempted to surprise the troops on their march to Launceston. Their discontent is about accounts; and their prayer, contained in a paper picked up near Bodmin, he desires may be carried into execution.

Tregarden, Sept. 1.

1950. *Mr. Francis Hyde to the same.* Complains of the sharpness of his Grace's edge towards him, and of some other person too. The French have entered Milan, that province being to be shared among the confederates, and the city being allotted to the Duke of Savoy, the French King's generalissimo in Italy. Venice moves slowly, pleasing thereby the Spaniard more than the French, but will declare for the stronger.

Venice, Sept. 7.

The date endorsed by Hyde seems to be "1645," but it is addressed to "Mr. Edward Hyde, of Purton."

1951. *Sir Edward Hyde to the Governors of Penzance, St. Ives, and Pendennis,* requiring, in the Prince's name, lists of their garrisons, and that soldiers taking refuge there be sent to the Prince. *Copies.*

No date.

In his own hand.

1646.
From before Bristol, Sept. 8.

1952. *Address* of the Parliamentary Generals to the people of Cornwall, warning them that they are now the only considerable party left to the King, desiring them to withdraw from his cause, and menacing them, in case of persistence, with the greatest severities of war. *Original.*

<blockquote>Addressed to the High Sheriff of the county of Cornwall and the well-affected gentry and inhabitants of that county. Signed by Tho. Fairfax and Oliver Cromwell.</blockquote>

Exeter, Sept. 8.

1953. *Warrant* to deliver to Sir Richard Vyvyan one ton of flax for making match to supply the fleet of Pendennis.
Copy.

No date.

1954. *Note of a Warrant* to deliver to Sir N. Crisp, wool in part payment for 100 barrels of powder.

Sept. 8.

1955. *Affidavit* of Howell Price, Custom-house Officer, concerning some smuggled goods.

Sept. 8.

1956. *Affidavit* of the same, concerning rolls of tobacco and other goods seized at Brixham.

    i. *Appraisement* of the goods last mentioned.

    ii–v. *Four Warrants* of Sir Edw. Hyde, the two last dated Sept. 8, to seize the above-named and other goods.   *Two Originals and two Copies.*

Ragland, Sept. 9.

1957. *His Majesty to Secretary Nicholas.* Desires him to proclaim positively that the truth is exactly contrary to the rebels' assertion concerning the discovery of his commission in a letter to the two Queens about the Irish Papists. Far from expressing approbation of Hartegan's foolish proposition, he finally denied it in a letter to the Queen, the Queen's answer to which the rebels refuse to publish, because it would prove the truth. *Copy.*

<blockquote>Certified and endorsed by Nicholas. Cl. S. P. vol. B. p. 187 (where is a note touching the commission mentioned).</blockquote>

St. Germains, Sept. 13.

1958. *Lord Jermyn to Lord* ———, giving at length the Queen's opinion on the proposition to refer Church questions to the judgment of Parliament, which if made with a view to a general settlement, would be yielding all they had struggled for; if with a view to gain the Scots, the Queen approves of it with some limitations. Probably some news of Montrose's success, or of the Irish peace, has altered affairs since he heard last. Entertains hope of assistance from the King of Denmark, whose troops are now set free by a peace with Sweden. The Duke of Bouillon has offered the Queen to raise and transport

to the West at his own charge, 1500 horse and 500 dragoons, 1645.
which might be profitably changed for foot-soldiers, who would
both fight and remain with them. Has great hopes of a good
fleet being shortly at their disposal.

Almost entirely in cypher, but decyphered.

1959. *His Majesty to Prince Rupert*, after the surrender of Hereford,
Bristol, desiring him to retire beyond seas.   *Copy.* Sept. 14.

In the King's own hand, and endorsed by him. "Copy of my letter to my nephew Rupert." Printed in Hist. Rebell. bk. ix. p. 569.

1960. *Revocation* by His Majesty of all Prince Rupert's Ragland,
commissions.   *Copy.* Sept. 14.

1961. *Sir Richard Grenville to the Prince of Wales.* Has Truro,
a suspicion that St. Ives had invited the rebels to come by sea, Sept. 16.
against which he has taken precautions by placing a garrison
there, disarming the townsmen, and causing three ringleaders
to be executed at St. Ives, Helston, and Truro respectively, as
the three most rotten towns in the West. Encloses depositions
touching the treason of Major Hannibal Bonithon, Governor of
the Castle of St. Mawes.

    i. Bodmin, Nov. 22, 1643. *Informations* of several soldiers
        of the garrison of St. Mawes, touching the same
        charges against the Governor.   *Copies.*

    ii. Truro, Jan. 11, 1643. *Articles* exhibited at the Gene-
        ral Sessions of the Peace, charging Major Bonithon
        with smuggling tobacco, embezzling the soldiers' pay,
        and disaffection to the King's cause.   *Copy.*

    iii. [No date.] *Articles* of the above and other charges
        against Bonithon.

    iv. Sept. 15, 1645. *Depositions* of witnesses to prove the
        preceding Articles.   *Copies.*

See Hist. Rebell. bk. ix. p. 565.

1962. *Lord Culpeper to Lord Digby.* Laments the great Barnstaple,
misfortune of the loss of Bristol, which is not counterbalanced Sept. 18.
even by Montrose's great successes. Submits a plan, as the
only thing left, of the King breaking through to the Scotch
with all the horse he can get together, and so marching
at once on London, which one battle would give them;
succours from Ireland and France meanwhile to attack
Wales and the West. The Scotch army under Leslie and
Callendor to be courted, and all the lazy licentiousness which
has hitherto enerved the forces, to be checked. The care of
the King's person to be the centre of all action. Digby should

1645. meet Goring at Newark or Oxford. If Goring stay in the West till Fairfax come up, all the horse will be lost; he should therefore break away at once, for if his horse miscarry, the King's chance of joining Montrose would be greatly weakened.
Rough Draught.
Corrected by himself. Cl. S. P. vol. ii. p. 188.

Sept. 18. 1063. *Instructions* for the Lord Hopton and the Chancellor of the Exchequer, employed by the Prince in the West of Cornwall upon important affairs having reference to the fortifying and victualling the Western forts, especially Pendennis.
Hist. Rebell. bk. ix. p. 573.

[Sept. 18.] 1064. *Lord Digby to the Earls of Leven and Callender, &c.* Desires them to consider Montrose's victories in Scotland, and their own desperate condition here, and invites them to a conjunction with the King. None of them can disbelieve that the King is a sincere Protestant. He will engage not to disturb the Scotch Government now or hereafter, to assent to all propositions for the civil liberty of Scotland, and to pass a general act of oblivion. *Copy.*
Cl. S. P. vol. ii. p. 189.

Launceston, Sept. 19. 1065. *The Earl of Berkshire to Lord Goring.* The Prince expects that Goring will go to the assistance of the King, and that force enough will be left to protect the West against Massy.

Bath, Sept. 19. 1066. *Sir Thomas Fairfax to the Prince of Wales.* Will willingly acquaint the Houses of his request for passes to the Lords mentioned in his letter, and assures him of his desire for peace.
Cl. S. P. vol. ii. p. 192.

Pendennis, Sept. 21. 1067. *Petition* of Nicholas Fishbourne, chief mate to Sir E. Hyde, for a share in a prize taken into Dartmouth.
Endorsed by Sir E. Hyde, with a reference to Capt. King for an answer.

The Mount, Sept. 26. 1068. *Mr. Roger Polkinhorne to Sir E. Hyde*, with professions of devotion. Enclosing the next—

1643. *Certificate* of Irish cloths and lead sent to Mr. Abraham Biggs, by appointment of Mr. Hghe, Sheriff, and Sir Charles Trevanion, Vice-Admiral of the South of Cornwall. Signed by Polkinhorne.

Truro, Sept. 27. 1069. *Examinations* of Scotch mariners, taken prisoners by Hacsdonck, touching the value of prizes taken by him.
Endorsed by Hyde.

1970. *Richard Slingsby to Sir E. Hyde*, excusing himself for not having delivered his accounts as paymaster at Bristol, having been plundered by the club-men on his way to the King after the loss of that town. Doubts not that Hyde has the particulars of that siege and this of Chester, from better hands.

1645. Denbigh, Sept. 27.

Endorsed, "Cap. Slingsby;" apparently the Col. Slingsby who is mentioned in Hist. Rebell. bk. vii. p. 408, and who supplied Hyde with the accounts of several battles, among others the siege of Bristol.

1971. *List* of five prizes taken by Hacsdonck, and the estimated value of the ships and cargoes, amounting to 5300*l*. altogether.

Sept. 27.

Endorsed by Hyde, "Scotch prizes taken by Hacsdonck."

1972. *Account* given in by Hacsdonck of his prizes.

Sept. 27.

Endorsed by Hyde.

1973. *A Note* of the ammunition taken out of the 'Eagle' by Sir Baldwyn Wake.

Sept. 27.

1974. *Lord Goring to Lord Culpeper*, recapitulating the trivial reasons which Hyde had alleged against the granting of his commission, and desiring to know positively what he is to trust to. Would not press it, if he had not been promised it several times by the King.

Thorverton, (Tiverton or Thorverton). Sept. 28.

This letter is quoted in Hist. Rebell. bk. ix. p. 567.

1975. *Lord Culpeper to the Lords of the Prince's Council*. Sir John Berkeley and himself have had an interview with Lord Goring, who complains greatly of the disobedience of Sir James Smith, and of words used by Sir R. Grenville, whom he desires to be sent speedily to the army with the Cornish forces, to take command of the whole infantry (inasmuch as the Cornish troops are not willing to serve under any other commander), receiving orders only from Goring. Grenville to have entire command in case of Goring's being obliged to march eastward to the King's assistance, and to be at once informed of such intention.

Exeter, Sept. 28.

1976. *His Majesty to Lord Culpeper*. Goring must break through to Oxford, and thence join him, probably about Newark. The Prince must be transported to France at once, to be under his mother in all except his religion, which must still be under the care of the Bishop of Salisbury.

Chirk Castle, Sept. 29.

Printed in Hist. Rebell. bk. ix. p. 570.

1645.
Sept. 29.

1977. *Demands* of Lord Goring, as printed in Hist. Rebell. bk. ix. p. 566, with the additions that all movements in the field be presented immediately and singly by him to the Prince, and all orders to the army issued to him singly. That he be empowered to take such arms and ammunition from all garrisons as he thinks necessary. That the powers of the Prince's commission be inserted in his as Lieutenant-General, to be signed at Oxford, with instructions added to it from the Prince, that Goring is not to remove any commissioned governor of a garrison. That an establishment of pay for his general officers be assigned out of the Devon and Cornish contributions.

> No date, but a note is annexed by Lord Culpeper, dated as in the margin, stating that the paper was delivered to him by Lord Wentworth at Launceston, without any present desire to communicate it, but that now Lord Goring desires it to be presented to the Prince.

Sept.

1978. *Minutes of Resolutions* at the Prince's Council, touching Goring's complaint against Sir J. Smith and Sir R. Grenville's charge of broken promise, which the Prince indignantly repudiates.

In Hyde's hand.

No date.

1979. *Lord Goring and Sir James Smith.* Eleven resolutions of the Prince's Council relating to Lord Goring's complaint of Sir J. Smith, and the conduct of Sir Richard Grenville, who is severely reproved for charging the Prince with a breach of his promise. *Rough Draught.*

In the handwriting of Sir Edw. Hyde.

Launceston, Oct. 1.

1980. *The Prince of Wales to the Commissioners of Devon and Cornwall,* urging the necessity of a new loan.

Rough Draught.
In Hyde's hand, and endorsed by him.

Paris, Oct. 3.

1981. *Mr. Justus Collimar to Sir Edward Hyde,* defending himself against charges of neglecting to carry out his contract of supplying provisions and ammunition.

Oct. 4.

1982. *Articles of Agreement* between Lord Goring and the Commissioners of Devon, concerning the raising and distribution of a new rate for six weeks, half thereof to be assigned to the army. *Copy.*

See Hist. Rebell. bk. ix. p. 570.

Exeter, Oct. 4.

1983. *Lord Goring to Lord Culpeper.* News of the enemy's advance. Is confident that Fairfax will neither hurt Exeter nor the army. Sir R. Grenville distracts him extremely, but he hopes, when the Prince enables him, to bring Grenville into order, or keep him from doing hurt.

1984. *Sir John Berkeley to Sir Edward Hyde.* Lord Goring proposes, in order to remedy the disorder of the troops, that Sir Richard Grenville, or in his default Lord Hopton, be ordered to march up with the Cornish forces, and put himself under Goring's command. If there is any difficulty in this, he will lend his forces to Lord Hopton for the present, to be restored to him when the objection is removed. He wishes this proposal to be communicated only to Lord Culpeper.

Poltimore, Oct. 5.

No signature, but endorsed by Hyde with Sir John Berkeley's name.

1985. *Warrant* of Sir E. Hyde to Cadwallader Jones to allow certain goods to be re-shipped for exportation without payment of customs. *Copy.*

Oct. 8.

1986. *Lord Goring to the Prince of Wales.* Inasmuch as he begged the honour of the commission chiefly to enable him to do better service, and since it is most for the service at this time to have it respited, he thinks the substance of his petition granted; having no other ambition than to sacrifice his life in the Prince's service.

Poltimore, Oct. 8.

1987. *Lord Norwich to Sir E. Hyde.* Will be with him in a few days if he can pass through the Parliament forces. With great professions of affection renews his propositions, sent by his servant, for the government of Pendennis Castle: if they are not entertained, he has discharged his duty and will write on the gate as he passes that you can have no more of a cat than her skin. Urges most strongly that the Prince be not sent to France. Has read seven romances of ten volumes to make him valiant enough to relieve Exeter. If he can only get Orandates and Arsace over with him, he is made, and England saved. If he is not to have Pendennis, will steer his course some other way, where he may hope to do the King service, and not follow after him with his thumbs in his girdle.

Havre, Oct. 9.

1988. *Lord Goring to the Lords of the Prince's Council,* requesting them to consent to the arrangements he has made with the Commissioners concerning the new rate to be levied.

Exeter, Oct. 10.

1989. *The Commissioners of Devon to Sir E. Hyde,* representing Mr. Brown's claims for payment for the arms and ammunition he has brought from France, and assigning him 500*l.* of the Privy Seal. He promises to make powder at 6*l.* 10*s.* a barrel.

Exeter, Oct. 13.

1990. *Lord Goring to Lord Culpeper.* Urges the hastening of the Cornish forces, lest on Fairfax, Cromwell, and Massy

Exeter, Oct. 13.

1645. advancing to the Exe, he be forced to retreat. All the troops possible should be got together, and a battle fought, as soon as possible, to check the animosities now prevailing, and to anticipate the Cornish returning home. If his advice be followed is confident of success.

Oct. 14. 1991. *The Prince of Wales to Lord Goring.* All that he desires shall be done, except that no troops can be drawn from before Plymouth. *Rough Draught.*
In Lord Culpeper's hand.

Shipton, Oct. 17. 1992. *Lord Digby to His Majesty*, detailing the affair of Sherborne, which he represents as only failing of being a complete victory by the unfortunate mistake which some of Sir Marmaduke Langdale's men made in mistaking their own troops in chase for victorious rebels, and thereupon flying in panic, leaving the prisoners which his mistaken mercy had spared. *Copy.*
Endorsed by himself and Hyde.

Exeter, Oct. 17. 1993. *Lord Goring to Lord Culpeper.* Has held a Council of War upon Fairfax's advance, and resolved to send General Webbe with all the horse but 1000 westward to meet the Cornish troops, if they will come up. Desires instructions from the Prince what to do.
See Hist. Rebell. bk. ix. p. 570.

Fowey, Oct. 20. 1994. *Mr. Cadw. Jones to Sir E. Hyde,* certifying to Mr. Brown's account for wools delivered at Dartmouth, and enclosing the next.

Account of wools delivered from the 'Fame' of London, and sold to various persons, the whole amount realized being 4020*l* 13*s*. 8*d*.

Exeter, Oct. 20. 1995. [*Mr. Triplett*] *to the same.* If the rebels take a year's fortification in one hour, by proportion we are gone in two hours. It is a ridiculous business that the rebels should have been better at letting down a bridge at Tiverton, than we at keeping it up, which two hooks or a bedcord would have done. It is a terrible thing to turn soldiers out of command and put in ambassadors. Had he a command he would take Montrose's course with the factious Cornish, who reduced the quarrelsome to loyalty by hanging and firing.
Signed "T," and endorsed with Triplett's name.

CLARENDON PAPERS.

1996. *Lord Goring to Lord Culpeper*, desiring that any command given over his horse to others than their own officers may be temporary, and wishing to know whether he may send orders to Sir R. Grenville.

1645.
Exeter,
Oct. 20.

1997. *The Prince of Wales to Lord Goring*, appointing Sir Richard Grenville to advance with the Cornish and take command of the horse sent under General Webbe to Newton Bushell. *Rough Draught.*
    In Hyde's hand.   See Clar. Hist. Rebell. bk. ix. p. 570.

Launceston,
Oct. 21.

1998. *Lord Goring to Lord Culpeper.* Has withdrawn from Exeter to join the rest of his horse, and desires to know whether Sir R. Grenville, if he come up with the Cornish, is to receive orders from him. Offers to resign his command to any one whom the Prince appoints.

 No date, but endorsed as received Oct. 23, and the event evidences that it was written Oct 22. The greater part is printed in Hist. Rebell. bk. ix. p. 570.

[Oct. 22.]

1999. *The Prince of Wales to Lord Goring*, informing him that he has directed Sir R. Grenville to put himself under Goring's command. The Prince retires to-morrow to Liskeard. *Rough Draught.*
    In Hyde's hand.

Launceston,
Oct. 23.

2000. *Lord Goring to Lord Culpeper.* Has received the Prince's answer to his last, and is willing to comply with Sir R. Grenville all that lies in his power, but is prevented by illness from riding on horse or in coach at present.

Totness,
Oct. 24.

2001. *The Prince of Wales to Lord Goring*, desiring that, in consequence of the distressed state of the garrison at Barnstaple, the twelve weeks' contribution for that hundred may be suspended for the present. *Rough Draught.*
    Without address, but endorsed, "To the Lord Goring."

Launceston,
Oct. 25.

2002. *Lord Goring to Lord Culpeper.* Is quartered in sight of the enemy on the other side of the river Fedder, but cannot attack from the nature of the position and the want of match. Proposes that Sir John Berkeley attack them in concert with himself. Cannot attend to the Somersetshire levies at present.

 Dated merely "This present Sunday, 1645." Probably either Sunday Oct. 26, or Sunday Nov. 2.

Ashe,
[Oct. 26.]

2003. *Lord Digby and Sir Marmaduke Langdale to His Majesty.* An account of their endeavour after the affair at

Douglas,
Oct. 27.

1645.	Sherborne to pass into Scotland and force a passage to Montrose, their failure and dispersion at Cartmell and Furness, and their embarkation at Ravenglass with forty or fifty of their officers for the Isle of Man. *Copy.* Endorsed by himself and Hyde.
Oct. 27.	2004. *Prince Rupert to Major-General Poyntz,* desiring passes through the Parliamentary forces to Worcester for himself, Prince Maurice, Lord Gerard, Lord Hawley, Sir Richard Willis, and others, as having retired from service; also a convoy for Lieut.-Col. Osborne to the Parliament, to ask for passes to go beyond seas. *Copy.*
No date.	2005. *Sir Richard Grenville to the Prince of Wales,* justifying the conduct of his troops quartered in North Petherwyn, in a dispute with Lord Wentworth's horse also quartered there, and pointing out that he has no other quarters left him, Goring having occupied and plundered all Devonshire and some of Cornwall, and he, as Sheriff of Devon, being compelled by his oath to keep to his county.
Oct. 27.	2006. *Instructions* for obtaining the redemption of a ship which had been captured. Endorsed, "Instructions to Mr. Hamer."
Oct. 28.	2007. *Application of the Parliament to the Governor of Flanders,* to close the ports to the King's ships of war, to prevent the sale of prizes and transport of arms, and to cause restitution to be made of the prizes already sold. The answers of the Governor to each of the four requests are given severally, expressing his intentions to be guided by the treaties in force and the law of nations.—French. *Copy.*
Havre, Oct. 14.	2008. *Lord Norwich to Sir E. Hyde,* pressing his propositions for the command of Pendennis, with extravagant professions of attachment to his sweet dear young master, with the King and Queen, on whom his soul dotes. Hopes much from the discontent of the Scots with the Parliament.
Oct. 14.	2009. *The same to the same,* recommending to his good offices Capt. Henry Bushell, who desires to revictual his ship, and to be re-imbursed his outlay in the King's service.
Oct. 29.	2010. *The Prince of Wales to Lord Hopton and Sir E. Hyde,* at Pendennis. Directs them to order the regiment of Pendennis to Sir Richard Gronville, and to put the castle in order for His Highness's reception and abode there the ensuing winter. *Original.* Countersigned by Sir Rich. Fanshawe.

2011. *Prince Rupert to the Parliament.* Has determined, with Prince Maurice, Lord Hawley, Lord Gerard, Sir Rich. Willis, and others, to leave England. Engages their honour that they have no hostile design. Sends Lieut.-Col. Osborne to assure them of this. Requests a safe-conduct. *Copy.*
1645. Wyverton, Oct. 19.

2012. *Sir Richard Fanshawe to Lord Hopton and Sir E. Hyde,* at Pendennis. Directions as to the march of the trained bands from the several Cornish garrisons. Orders to be given respecting them as they shall see convenient. *Original.*
Bodmin, Oct. 30.

2013. ——— *to* ———. An officer of the Parliamentary army informs his correspondent of the safe-conduct asked by Prince Rupert; and its conditions.
Anonymous, without address.
Melton-Mowbray, Oct. 30.

2014. *Warrant* to Mr. Cadwallader Jones, Receiver-General, to pay Mr. Abraham Biggs the fees for the office of Customs of Plymouth and Cornwall. *Copy.*
Truro, Oct. 31.

2015. *Warrant of the Prince of Wales to the Governor of Pendennis.* Orders the establishment of twenty gentlemen to be added to the companies of the garrison. *Original.*
Countersigned by Sir R. Fanshawe.
Liskeard, Nov. 2.

2016. *Sir Richard Grenville to Sir Thomas Fairfax,* desiring to know what answer he has received from the Parliament to the Prince's message forwarded through him that he would be glad to send Lord Hopton and Lord Culpeper with overtures of peace to them. *Rough Draught.*
Partly in Hyde's hand, addressed to "Sir R. Grenville," with a note signed "R. F.," desiring him to transcribe it and forward it to Fairfax.
Liskeard, Nov. 3.

2017. *Deposition* of Capt. Browne concerning the ship 'Newcastle,' pressed at Newcastle for the King's service by the Marquis of Newcastle.
Nov. 3.

2018. D. P——— *to* ———. An account of Lord Digby's defeat at Sherborne after his attempted passage into Scotland, and of the victory of Denbigh. Digby's letters taken at Sherborne and read in the Houses, have disclosed most important secrets, the negotiations with Holland and other foreign states, a treaty for a match between the Prince of Orange's daughter and the Prince of Wales, the Irish business, and Scotch intrigues.
Endorsed by Fairfax, "Copy of a letter from a member of Parliament at London to several members of Parliament residing in the army, and confirmed by other hands to the General."
Partly printed in Cl. S. P. vol. ii. p. 193.
London, Nov. 4.

1645.
Nov. 5.

2019. *Warrant addressed to Capt. Walrond.* Recites the Prince's order of Oct. 4th. Orders him to receive certain contributions from places in Cornwall. *Draught.*
By Hyde.

Boscawark, Nov. 6.

2020. *Warrant* of the Prince of Wales for the payment of such sums as shall be required by Lord Hopton and Sir E. Hyde during their performances of special service near Pendennis. Signed by the Prince.

Nov. 7.

2021. *Instructions of the Houses of Parliament to their Agent in Denmark*, to remonstrate on the employment of Sir John Henderson on the King of Denmark's mission to them, as having been guilty of treason, and to decline the King's offer of mediation, as being themselves about to proffer propositions for peace. *Copy.*
Cl. S. P. vol. II. p. 193.

To which are annexed—

i. *Letter from the Houses to the King of Denmark*, to the same purport as the above instructions.—Latin. *Copy.*

ii. *Two Letters from the Houses to the States-General*, requesting justice against Nicholas de Witte for plundering two merchant vessels of Hull.—Latin. *Copy.*

Endorsed by Hyde, "Copies of a letter to the King of Denmark sent by Jenks, and his instructions from the rebels. Copies of letters from the rebels to the States, that the united Parliament sent by Strickland their Agent there."

Oxford,
Nov. 7.

2022. *The King to the Prince of Wales.* Directs him, if in danger of falling into the hands of the rebels, to fly to Denmark. His going beyond sea is necessary. Forbids him to go to Scotland or Ireland. *Original.*
In cypher, and a copy decyphered. Endorsed by Hyde. Cf. Hist. Rebell. bk. ix. p. 469, ed. 1732.

Antry (?),
Nov. 7.

2023. *Mr. John Mylles, [Milles] Advocate-General to Fairfax's army, to Dr. George Morley* at Exeter. Informs him that the General has granted a pass in order to a conference between them at Silverton. *Copy.*

Nov. 8.

2024. *Sir Thomas Fairfax to Sir Richard Grenville*, forwarding a letter to the Prince in answer to the last.

Nov. 8.

2025. *The same to the Prince of Wales.* Has not yet received an answer to his request from the Parliament, who

perhaps think the design fruitless, if not hurtful. Advises the 1645.
Prince to disband his forces, and go in person to the Parliament, and so gain for his followers the benefit of the propositions tendered to all who come in before Dec. 1, and good
conditions for his soldiers. Cl. S. P. vol. II. p. 194.

2026. *Sir Richard Grenville to Sir Thomas Fairfax*, expressing the Prince's indignation at the attempt made in his No date.
letter to seduce him from his loyalty. *Rough Draught.*
In Hyde's hand. Cl. S. P. vol. II. p. 195.

2027. *Dr. He[nry] J'anson to Sir E. Hyde.* Gives an Jersey,
account of his imprisonment, and bad treatment by the rebels Nov. 15.
last year. Advises the King to secure Guernsey. Six frigates
and the three islands would be protection enough were all else
lost. *Original.*
Endorsed by Hyde, "Dr. Janson."

2028. *Lord Culpeper to Lord Hopton* at Truro. News of Nov. 17.
the King's victory near Worcester. There has been a long
discourse with Lords Goring and Wentworth, and Sir John
Berkeley. The treaty is at an end. Lord Goring proposes
to go into France. Lord Wentworth is to go to the Prince.
Dr. Staynes came to visit Lord Goring with a pass from Fairfax, to ask questions about Lord Saville's report that Lord
Goring would come in to them; which Lord Goring denied;
and about what Lady Poulett said. *Original.*
Endorsed by Hyde.

2029. *Lord [Henry] Jermyn to Sir E. Hyde.* Has not Paris,
heard from him since Sir John Winter came. Begs a particular Nov. 17.
answer to his by Charles Murray. Begs to be believed as to
the business of the tin. Recommends Sir Nicholas Crisp to
him. Thanks him for his kindness to Sir Peter Bull.
Original.
Endorsed by Hyde.

2030. *Sir John Wintour to the same.* A note of compliment. St. Germains,
Original. Nov. ⁂.

2031. *The Marquis Antrim to the same.* Has more Paris (?),
trouble in setting out his frigates than in procuring them. Is Nov. 19.
forced to offer his powder for sale to pay the seamen. Begs
permission to sell the ammunition, and the Prince's safe-conduct for both his frigates. *Original.*
Endorsed by Hyde.

288   CALENDAR OF

1645.
Truro,
Nov. 22.

2032. *Sir E. Hyde to the Lord Marquis Antrim.* Has received his of the 19th. The Prince does not understand how there can be expectation of support from him; nor can he give licence to sell the powder, nor can Sir E. Hyde buy it. Suggests that he should bring Sir Nicholas Crisp to them.
Copy.
Endorsed by Hyde.

Exeter,
Nov. 22.

2033. *Lord [George] Goring to the Prince.* Both forces being settled in winter quarters, begs leave for his health's sake to go into France. Professes great devotion to the Prince's service. *Original.*

Exeter,
Nov. 22.

2034. *Mr. Henry Croone to Mr. William Edgeman* (Secretary to Sir E. Hyde), begging him to solicit Hyde in his favour, to get some money which he claims with interest, and detailing his great losses at sea.

Nov. 24.

2035. *Receipt* for 21l. received from Captain Cottle for tools and nails for Pendennis Castle, ordered by Secretary Fanshawe.

No date.

2036. *Letter to Captain Cottle,* to order him to pay the sum due for match to Sir N. Crisp on behalf of Mr. Abraham Biggs.
Copy.
Without signature.

Exeter,
Nov. 26.

2037. *Mr. T. Triplett to Mr. W. Edgeman.* Is much moved at "my Lord of Armagh's tragedy." Mentions movements in Wiltshire and Dorsetshire, Sadler's condemnation, and Fulford House. *Original.*

St. Germains,
Nov. 27.

2038. *Lord [Henry] Jermyn to Sir E. Hyde.* By the Queen's commands he informs him that Lord Goring has been asking leave of absence for two months, to go to France, and that she approves his request. The Queen has written to the Prince to give him notice of this. *Original.*
Endorsed by Hyde.

Morlaix,
Nov. 30.

2039. *Sir F. Mackworth to the same.* Landed at Conquest, Nov. 23. Has had an interview with Master Hitchcock, a merchant, who was employed by the Queen. He promised a supply of deal boards. The French are enraged against the Parliament for taking their ship; thinks a breach may be made between them. *Original.*
Partly in cypher, decyphered.   Endorsed by Hyde.

2040. *The King to Ormond.* Ormond's long silence prevents the King from coming to a resolution with respect to assistance from Ireland, which will be of no service unless it comes before the beginning of April next. Peace must not be concluded without an assurance of assistance, and if that be refused the King is to be at once advertised of it. Urges, in a postscript, the connection of the Irish peace with that of England. *Original.*

1645.
Oxford,
Dec. 1.

In cypher, decyphered by Ormond. Endorsed, "Recd. 13 Jan. 1645, by Mr. Garet Moore."

2041. *Warrant* to authorize payment of Ecclesiastical Tenths and Firstfruits to Mr. Robert Long for His Majesty's use.

Truro,
Dec. 4.

Also *Warrant* to Mr. Henry Grenville to get in the arrears of the contributions for the county of Cornwall. *Copies.*

2042. *The King to Prince Charles.* Has resolved to propose a personal treaty to the rebels in London. The Prince's being in another country will be the King's real security. Commands him to go out of the country on receipt of this letter. *Original.*

Oxford,
Dec. 7.

In cypher, and a copy decyphered. Endorsed by Hyde. Hist. Rebel. bk. ix. p. 469. ed. 1731.

2043. *Prince Rupert to His Majesty,* tendering his humble submission, and asking pardon for his conduct. *Copy.*

Woodstock,
Dec. 8.

Cl. S. P. vol. II, p. 195.

2044. *Sir E. Hyde to Mr. Pooley,* stating his reasons for not allowing the free exportation of wool from Cornwall to Jersey, Cornwall and part of Devon being the only ports now left to the King, and the manufactories therefore requiring to be carefully kept up; the people also having publicly petitioned against the transport of wool. *Copy.*

Penryn,
Dec. 9.

2045. *Mr. Hitchcock to Sir E. Hyde.* Encloses a letter entrusted to him by Sir Francis Mackworth. Promises the deal boards, and anything else he can do for the King. His partner, John Samborne, accompanies Sir F. M. *Original.*

Morlaix,
Dec. 8?

2046. *Mr. John Ashburnham to [Lord Culpeper?].* Repeats news given in former despatches which have miscarried, of Digby's defeat in Scotland, and flight to the Isle of Man, the loss of Skipton and Bolton, the only garrisons for the King on this side Trent, the storm of Shelford (with slaughter of the

Oxford,
Dec. 13.

1648. whole garrison), and surrender of Worton, which last, however, by occupying the rebels, enabled the King to escape from Newark to Oxford. The garrisons of Worcester, Exeter, Newark, Chester, and Oxford, have orders to slight their works, and march to a rendezvous near Worcester by Feb. 20, when the King will either march west to Grenville, or to Norfolk and Suffolk, or to Kent. Lord Astley is coming to Worcester, where he hopes to raise 2000 foot by April. If foreign succour comes not before that time, it will be no use. The Duke of York is to be conveyed by Lord Astley to Beaumaris for Ireland, if peace be made, or if not, for France. However, they hope the peace with Ireland is not made, being now fully aware of the base intentions of the Irish. The King's determination to offer a personal treaty in London, or else at Oxford, Newark, or Worcester, with his reasons for this course. The King gives him full liberty to act as he will with a view to gain the Scotch, only provided he destroy not the Church of England to set up Presbytery. The Queen is treating with Scotland through Sir Robert Murray, not having sent Will. Murray, as the Scotch Commissioners requested, knowing the offence it would give to Montrose. The King earnestly wishes (Culpeper) and Lord Hopton not to go with the Prince, but leaves it to their judgment. A despatch has just come from Lord Sinclair and David Leslie, inviting the King to come to their army. *Decyphered Copy.*

With no address, headed " Be sure to decypher this yourself."
Partly printed in Cl. S. P. vol. II. p. 196.

Ashburton, Dec. 15. 2047. *Lord [Thomas] Wentworth to Lord Culpeper.* Has received his and the Prince's letters. Cannot leave the army to wait on him at Tavistock. The enemy's motions are uncertain. Would be glad to speak with him and Sir Richard Grenville. Will not send for Sir Joseph Wagstaffe until they can march nearer to Exeter. They are not strong enough to attempt to force the enemy from Kirton. Has just informed Sir E. Hyde that the enemy have taken Fulford House. Wants a supply of biscuit for horse and foot. Will inform Sir J. Berkeley of the Prince's resolution. *Original.*

Signed by Wentworth. Endorsed by Hyde.

Dec. 16. 2048. *Mr. Godolphin to Sir E. Hyde,* requiring the use of a vessel lying at Penzance in order to convey provisions to Scilly.

Dartmouth, Dec. 16. 2049. *Sir Hugh Pollard to [Sir E. Hyde].* Sends enclosed papers from Sir W. Davenant, from Havre, where he and the

general * landed Dec. 20, and went thence to Paris. There met 1645.
"an expresse from the Queen attending a passage for Dartmouth." Trusts relief will soon come to Exeter. Sir J. Berkeley is sick, J. Hervye in danger, and Lady Dalkeith very ill. Relates current news. Is despondent. Dartmouth garrison is in a bad state. Has heard from Apsley. Sends this by Lord Wentworth. *Original.*
Endorsed by Hyde.

2050. *Sir Arthur Bassett to Sir E. Hyde*, desiring that a   The prize with its cargo lately brought in thither may be assigned   Mount, to him for the use of the garrison, and to cover his expenses,   Dec. 18. with the arrears of rates due from widows and others who are unable to pay.

 i. Dec. 17. *Appraisement* of the 'Richard and William,' the prize mentioned above, with its cargo of paper, oakum, and dowlas, amounting in all to 252*l.* 7*s.*

 ii. *Letter from Richard Simpson*, the master, putting his   No date. expenses at 30*l.*, which he desires may be allowed him.

2051. *James Apsley to Sir E. Hyde.* Asks for a commission   Dec. 20. to set out his ship as a man-of-war; and a warrant to press some frigate as an attendant. The rogues at Swansea have stopped all their coal barques; wishes to be revenged on such rascals. *Original.*
Endorsed by Hyde.

2052. *Sir Allan Apsley to the same.* Refers to his   Barnstaple, brother. Has got some bells, having been obliged to pull   Dec. 20. down the steeple. Expected to have heard of the coming of French and Irish forces. Hopes he will grant his brother's petition for a warrant to seize and a license to rob at sea. Sir Samuel Rolle's woods partly made up for their want of coal. *Original.*
Endorsed by Hyde.

2053. *Reasons why His Majesty thought good to send his*   Dec. 20. *Propositions of the 26th of Dec. to London*, being a summary of the King's miserable position in England, the failure of peace in Ireland, and the little hope of help from Montrose, France, or Holland. *Copy.*

 Endorsed by Nicholas. The date in the MS. is 1646, as also in the endorsement, but it is evidently a mistake.   Cl. S. P. vol. ii. p. 198.

* Lord Goring.

1645.
Truro,
Dec. 12.

2054. *Warrant* to the Deputy Comptrollers of the Cornish ports, to send their accounts to Mr. Anthony Harrison of Penryn, during the vacancy of the office of Comptroller, void by the decease of Mr. Deane. *Copy.*

Pendennis,
Dec. 13.

2055. *Col. Slingsby to Sir E. Hyde*, desiring a mortarpiece for the defence of the castle, and some cases for grenades.

Bodmin,
Dec. 13.

2056. *Lord Capell to the same.* The sheriff's warrants are vigorously enforced. Three regiments have marched from Launceston to Okehampton.

Liskeard,
Dec. 14.

2057. *The same to the same.* Advises a great saving by making the corn into bread instead of biscuit, and that arrangements be made for the postage of provisions to and fro, and the prevention of plundering. Considers the Prince's removal to be absolutely necessary. Addressed to Sir E. Hyde, at Truro.

Pendennis
Castle,
Dec. 14.

2058. *John Arundell of Trevise, Governor of Pendennis, to the same.* Details of matchmakers' wages, and supplies for the castle. *Original.*
Endorsed by Hyde.

Liskeard,
Dec. 14.

2059. *Lord [Arthur] Capell to the same.* Thinks the sooner the Prince advances the faster the Cornish will move. Has provided shoes, but cannot get stockings. *Original.*
Endorsed by Hyde.

Cambridge,
Dec. 17.

2060. *Thomas Shepard to Hugh Peters.* Compliments him on the service he is to God's cause. Speaks against toleration and liberty of conscience. Asks him to furnish the college with books, e. g. a Bishop's library. *Original.*

Dec. 30.

2061. *An Order to the Keeper of the University Library* for D'Aubigne's "Histoire Universelle," for the King's use.

No date.

2062. *An Account* of the defence of Donnington Castle by Sir Jo. Boys, and its surrender to the Parliamentary forces under Dalben *.

No date.

2063. *An Account* of the siege of Winchester and its surrender by Lord Ogle to Cromwell *.
This and the preceding endorsed by Hyde as "Capt. Knight's Relations."

* These surrenders took place after the defeat of Lord Hopton by Fairfax, and before the close of this year. (See Hist. Rebell. bk. ix. p. 588.)

2064. An *Account* of the military proceedings in the North 1645. from 1641 to 1645 inclusive, chiefly those in which the Marquis of Newcastle was concerned, and which relate to the town of Newcastle: drawn up, as it seems, by the Mayor, acting as Governor of that town, after the flight of the Marquis abroad.

2065. *Petition* of Sir John Mucknell to the Prince of Wales No date. for another ship, having lost his former one off Scilly in an engagement with the rebels.

2066. *A List of the Prince's Servants*, with the wages which No date. they have received, varying from 1*l.* to 2*l.*
     Endorsed as described, with the date of this year.

2067. *A List of Parishes within the Hundred of Penwith*, No date. with the names of their clergy, and the amount of the weekly payment of each parish to the contribution, amounting in all to 75*l.* 18*s.* 2*d.*   Signed "Hugh Thomas and Simon Priest."

2068. *Sir N. Crisp*, on seeking help from Holland. Seven- No date. teen paragraphs suggesting a marriage between the Prince of Wales and the daughter of the Prince of Orange, and several inducements in matters of trade to an alliance with the Low Countries, with the advantages proposed to be granted to them in a treaty for that purpose.
 Endorsed by Hyde, "Considerations of Sir N. Crispe concerning Holland, for their men of War."

2069. *Petition of Dr. Robert Creighton, Dean of Buryan, to* No date. *Prince Charles.* Complains of a conspiracy amongst his people to resist payment of tithes. He is disabled from paying the rates for the King's service.   *Original.*
    See Walker's Sufferings of the Clergy, pt. ii. p. 72.

2070. *Complaint* of Capt. Smith against Sir Nicholas Crisp, No date. for abuse of his privileges in shipping business.

 i. *A Note* taken about All Saints' Day last touching Sir N. Crisp's fleet.

 ii. *Sir N. Crisp's Answer* to your Lordships concerning the shipping.

 iii. *Answer* of the same to the petition of Sir Charles Trevanian and Lieut.-Col. Scawen, Judge of the Vice Admiralty; their charge against him being for intercepting the tenths of prizes, and other abuses of his commission.

1645.
    iv. *Notes* on the case, in Hyde's hand.

    v. Oxford, May 3, 1645. *Warrant* of His Majesty to Sir N. Crisp, granting the tenths of such prizes as he shall make.   *Copy.*

    vi. *List* of ships with commissions for reprisals renewed by Sir N. Crisp.

    vii. *List* of ships at sea under Sir N. Crisp's commission.

No date.   2071. *The King to certain Merchants in the city of Exeter.* In answer to their remonstrance respecting an imposition of 15 per cent. on goods carried into the enemy's quarters. The imposition to be 10 per cent. besides customs and excise.
    No signature or endorsement.

No date.   2072. *Sir E. Hyde to Lord Jermyn.* Has received a letter by Sir D. Wyatt. Will with Lord Culpeper enter into the particulars of the despatch, and first concerning the Princess at Exeter and the governess, Lady Dalkeith. Quotes Sir F. Wenman's saying on friends. The governess has faithfully obeyed the Queen's directions, and had received her letter at the end of September, when the Prince was at Exeter; and until that city was in danger to be besieged she was not to remove. Upon rumours that the Prince was being carried into France, protests were raised in Exeter and Cornwall against it; a petition suppressed by H. Killigrew. The Prince's arrival was expected in France. If the Princess had been then removed, the Prince's security would have been destroyed. In all these difficulties there are not six persons on whom Lord Culpeper and himself can rely. Letters taken at Dartwell exposed designs for removing the Princess. Prays him to intercede with the Queen for Lady Dalkeith. They can no more take the Prince to France than beat Fairfax with one regiment. Prays for help from Lord Goring in the defence of Pendennis. Lord Hopton will willingly lay down the government of the army. Does not wish to meddle with the army, but to fulfil the King's trust. Is weary of his part. Has seen Lord Jermyn's letter to Lord Culpeper. Tells him to be careful of their reputations, and impute this plainness to the kindness and affection of faithful friends. Sir D. Wyatt will inform him of the supplies spared to the castle by the Prince; who has undertaken for 500*l.* to be paid. Hopes that the Queen will speedily send further supplies. *Original.*
    Endorsed, "My letter to Ld. Jermyn."   Cl. S. P. vol. ii. p. 203.

    2073. *Disbursements* of the ship 'St. George,' during the years 1640-5, consisting of several sheets of accounts.

2074. *Relation* by Sir Joseph Fane of the state of parties in Cornwall from the commencement of the rebellion, and the campaigns there till Sir Richard Grenville's arrival. 1645. No date.

No signature, but endorsed by Hyde, "Sir Joseph Fane's [report] of the state of Cornwall."

2075. [*The Lords of the Prince's Council*] *to Lady P[awlet]*, desiring her to obtain information whether there be any reality in the professions of peace made by the Parliamentary commanders; in what persons the civil power of the Parliament lies, what party is likely to prevail among them, and what government they aim at in Church and State. No date.

No signature or address, but endorsed by Hyde, "Instructions to L. P."

2076. *Dr. William Harvey to [Sir E. Hyde]*, desiring his favour with the King to be restored to his place as Physician of the Household, which he hears he has lost by absenting himself. No date.

2077. *List* of five delinquents in Cornwall, Thomas Mayow, Antony Nicholls, Humphrey Lower, Hannibal Randall, and Francis Buller, who have never compounded, and who have great store of corn. No date.

2078. *Instructions* to demand abstract of accounts of the profits from the Dean Forest Ironworks, the total given in by the merchants being 3865*l*. 6*s*. 4*d*. profit, made of the fifth year's wood received by the farmers of the ironworks. To make which sum they account 2397*l*. 9*s*. 6*d*. in debts due from several men, and 1463*l*. in iron remaining unsold. No date.

2079. *Transcendent and multiplyed Rebellion and Treason discovered by the Laws of the Land*. A long treatise, without signature, against the proceedings of the Parliament. No date.

2080. *Account* of Mr. Abraham Biggs with Capt. Cottle for malt received from Sept. 13th to the end of the year.
Endorsed by Hyde.

2081. *Sir Richard Grenville to the Prince*. Sends an account of the miseries of the soldiers. Captain Bligh of Launceston has promised shoes and stockings. Col. R. Arundell and Sir C. Trevanian's subalterns promised that their regiments should be in Tavistock on Monday. Will attend his Highness' commands then and there. Has ordered his own regiment to be at Bridgestowe to observe Major Molesworth's commands at Okehampton. Begs him to send orders to Capt. Blyth. *Original.* 1645-6. Warrington, Jan. 2.

1645-6.
Jan. 4.

2082. *Extract of a letter from the Lord Lieutenant and Council of Ireland to Mr. Secretary Nicholas.* Recites proceedings in Council from Dec. 26th last as to the Earl of Glamorgan and his dealings with the confederate Catholics; impugning his authority from the King, and giving a warrant for his committal, on the ground of the scandal given by him. With

    Copy of the "pretended" warrant given by the King to the Earl of Glamorgan.
Addressed "For your Highness." See Carte's Life of Ormond, vol. III. p. 437.

Dublin.
Jan. 7.

2083. *Lord Digby to Sir E. Hyde.* Encloses papers of information. Having lost so many of the King's horse, his enemies will accuse him of disservice. Thinks that the King should have gone from Welbeck into Scotland if Montrose were on this side Forth, but not otherwise. Gives details of the movements of the Southern horse under Gerard, Montrose, Sir Marmaduke Langdale, and himself. His employment in this desperate service brought about by the King's agreement with him in thinking a temporary separation between them advisable. What has befallen at Newark, with Prince Rupert and Gerard, whose violent designs are known, will explain his remove. He could not concur in the policy of submission that many had urged on the King against his own resolution: and finding that he was supposed to be the cause of the King's constancy, thought it time to free His Majesty from that injury. Prays the Chancellor to convey these reasons to the Prince of Wales. Has been windbound for a month in the Isle of Man, where he was received by the Earl and Countess of Derby: from thence to Dublin, where, at a conference between Lord Glamorgan, the Lord Lieutenant, and himself, concerning the disposal of the aids prepared for the King's service, the business contained in the enclosed papers obliged him to vindicate the King as he alone could do. He was hated both by Puritans and Papists. Enjoys the friendship of that generous and virtuous person the Marquis of Ormond. *Original.*
Partly in cypher. Endorsed by Hyde. Cl. S. P. vol. II. p. 199.

June 11,
1650.

2084.* *The Marquis of Worcester* (late Earl of Glamorgan) *to the same.* His passionate affection to the late King's service is the chief key to the secret passages between his late Majesty and himself. Gives details of the King's designs (in 1645) concerning the forces in North and South Wales under Sir H. Gage, Liègois under Sir F. Edmonds, Lorriners under Col. Browne, and others out of Flanders and Holland, with other aids by the Prince of Orange and the Governor of Lyne. This army to have been maintained by the Pope and certain Catholic

* Placed here as being necessarily connected with No. 2083.

princes, with whom he had power to treat. The seal was put to this commission by Mr. End. Porter and himself. Though he had power to employ any of the King's moneys he used it not, when the design was broken by his commitment in Ireland: nor had any self-interest or benefit. Commits all this to the King's consideration and the Chancellor's judgment. Prays the continuance of that care of him which was recommended to the Chancellor by the late King *. *Original.* 1645-6.
Endorsed by Hyde. Cl. S. P. vol. ii. p. 201.

2085. *Sir E. Hyde to Mr. Long.* Repeats his order to provide money in readiness for the Prince; that brought by Mr. Johnson being insufficient. Hose and shoes and a magazine of bread at Totnes have swallowed up all receipts. The Receiver and Mr. Potter are to assist him in obtaining money. Much depends on the success of the Prince's present undertaking. He goes to Totnes on Monday. *Copy.* Tavistock, Jan. 7.
By Edgeman.

2086. *Sir Richard Grenville to the Prince.* Has heard from Okehampton that the enemy's forces have appeared there. Has advised Major-Gen. Molesworth to maintain his post if possible, and if not, to retreat to Bridgestowe, or by way of the Moor. Will attend the Prince to-morrow. *Original.* Worington, Jan. 8.

2087. *Sir John Berkeley to Sir E. Hyde.* Has sent out a party of horse towards Crediton, who brought intelligence of the enemy's forces there, and the departure of some of them for Moreton. Has taken a copy of a despatch sent from Oxford to Lord Culpeper. Begs for information. *Original.* Exeter, Jan. 10.
Endorsed by Hyde.

2088. *The King to M. Montreuil.* The Queen Regent has proposed by M. Montreuil that the King would establish Presbyterianism in England as the means of agreement with the Scots. Not only the King's conscience, but the opposition of Independents forbids it. But for the sake of the Scotch treaty the King will engage to keep the Presbyterian government in Scotland. Is content that all ecclesiastical differences be determined by a national synod; the Scots to be represented thereat (as the English were at Dort) and to have free exercise of their religion in England. Will also pay their arrears. By the business of Ireland and other ways is confident to give them satisfaction. Will adhere to the Queen's answer given to Sir R. Murray. Is resolved that the Marquis of Montrose and his party be received without reserve. Graciously embraces the affection of the Scots. Oxford, Jan. 10.

Note by Sec. Nicholas.—" The Queen must be spoken to for the answer given to Sir R. Murray." *Copy*
By Edgeman. Cl. S. P. vol. ii. pp. 209, 110.

* See No. 2103.

1645-6.
Jan. 15.

2089. *M. Montreuil to the King.* There is much surprise shown at the King's rejection of the care taken by the deputies of Scotland. They are now more like to take up with the Independents. Yesterday the Scotch and English Presbyterians took the covenant afresh, and to-day a petition is sent to Parliament to establish Presbyterianism. Thinks the King should submit. Represents all this without disguise. The messenger goes to France to-day. The Parliament calls on the Prince to lay down his arms. Fairfax will soon be here. Prays the King to act speedily and willingly, that the English and Scotch may come to terms with him. *Copy.*

Cl. S. P. vol. II. p. 211.

Worington,
Jan. 16.

2090. *Sir R. Grenville to the Lords of the Prince's Council at Launceston.* Has a bad cold and cannot attend them. Prays them to appoint a commander-in-chief of the King's forces in the West. Suggests Lord Brentford or Lord Hopton. Declines it for himself. Is hated by Lord Goring's forces and others for his strictness of discipline. *Original.*

Launceston,
Jan. 16.

2091. *The Prince to Sir R. Grenville.* Has received his of the same day. Will follow his counsel. Encloses an order to the officers of the army.

"Order to the Colonels of Brigades." The Prince has taken on himself the charge of the whole army. The officers to be informed of this.

Major-General Webb has the confidence of the Prince. Orders to Goring, Lord Capell, and Major Carter. Postscript to Lord Major-General Webb. *Rough Draught.*

By Hyde.

Worington,
Jan. 17.

2092. *Sir R. Grenville to Mr. Fanshawe, Secretary of War.* Has received his of yesterday, requesting him to pacify a quarrel between Lord Wentworth's and his own men about quarters. Enters into details of the dispute. Complains of Lord Goring's troopers. Is rather hurt at the treatment he has received. *Original.*

Oxford,
Jan. 17.

2093. *Secretary Nicholas to M. Montreuil.* Sends a copy of the King's message of the 15th inst. about the treaty, by his command. Desires him to learn what assurance the Scots will give for the King's safety if he comes to London; and for their junction with Montrose. Though the King relies on France as his best security, it will be convenient to have the engagement of the Scots, and details of what is to be done. (By the King's command and dictation.)

Cl. S. P. vol. II. p. 211.

2094. *Lord Jermyn to Lord Culpeper.* Gives reasons for not having written. Leave is given to raise troops in Brittany and Guienne for the reinforcement of the Western army. Ships will be ready for transportation. Writes at large and in general terms on current affairs; more particularly of Lord Goring. *Principally in cypher, decyphered. Endorsed by Hyde.* 1645-6. Paris, Jan. 17.

2095. *The King to Ormond.* Is sorry to find by Colonel Harry the sad condition of his fortune. Commands him to despatch the peace of Ireland out of hand. "As for Poynings act I referre yo to my other later, and for maters of Religion, though I have not found it fit to take publique notice of the prayer wch Browne gave you, yet I must command you to give him, the Lord Muskry and Plunket particular thankes for it." Promises repeal of the penal laws against Roman Catholics, when he receives help from the Irish, but the laws against appeals to Rome, and præmunire, must stand. Commands great secrecy and speedy despatch of the peace.
In a postscript added to a duplicate—Gives further powers in order to obtain a peace, but trusts his affairs will be so bettered that the Irish will accept less. *Decyphered by Ormond.* Oxford. Jan. 18.

2096. *Sir R. Grenville to the Prince.* Has received his commands about the regulation of the army. Begs the Prince not to expect any more service in the field from himself. Hopes soon to wait on him. *Original.* Worlington, Jan. 18.

2097. *M. Montreuil to the King.* The King's message has pleased neither party. They had just read the commission for liberty of conscience in Ireland. Fairfax is successful at Plymouth, and is about to besiege Dartmouth. Part of his horse will come between Oxford and Newark. The King has no time to lose. *Copy.*
By Edgeman. Cl. S. P. vol. II. p. 212. Jan. 18.

2098. *Prince Charles to Sir Arthur Bassett, Governor of the Mount.* Orders him to take charge of Sir Richard Grenville. *Original. With corrections.* Jan. 21.

2099. *The King to M. Montreuil.* Adds to Secretary Nicholas' answer to Montreuil's of the 15th, his thanks for representing things without disguise. Can comply with no further demands, having refused the two Queens. His shop can afford no more. Montreuil must make the best bargain he can. Begs him to hasten Will. Murray, who is sent by the Queen. *Copy.*
By Edgeman. Cl. S. P. vol. II. p. 213. Jan. 21.

1645-6.
Launceston,
Jan. 31.
2100. *The Prince to Lord Goring.* Encloses the order for uniting all the King's forces in the West under one command. Explains this order. No commissions to be issued but by himself. The command shall be restored to Goring on his return.
Draught.
Not signed.

Jan. 31.
2101. *Act* of the Council of War held at Holdsworthy by the principal officers of Lord Goring's army. They obey the Prince's order; and receive Lord Hopton on condition that Lord Goring be not superseded by him in case he return.
Copy.
Endorsed by Hyde.

Jan. 25.
2102. The *Account* between Capt. Cottell and Mr. Abraham Biggs for match supplied since Sept. 13th, with a copy of the Prince's order of July 19, 1645, for delivery of the same to the magazine at Launceston.
Copy.
Endorsed by Hyde.

Oxford,
Jan. 30.
2103.* *The King to Ormond.* Never intended Glamorgan to supersede Ormond. Blames him heavily. Directs Ormond to prosecute him, but to suspend the execution of the sentence. Adds in a postscript, in cypher, "I would not have you sentence Glamorgan except you find that the omitting it will much prejudice my service."
Original.
Endorsed, "Recd. 25 Apr. '48."

Launceston,
Jan. 30.
2104. *Warrant* of the Prince of Wales enabling the master and mariners of the 'Young Tobias' of Hamburg (brought into Fowey by a man-of-war) to return home, and allowing them their expenses in Fowey.
Copy.

Annexed is a reference of the case by Sir E. Hyde to Mr. Cadwallader Jones, dated Pendennis, Feb. 8.

i. Fowey, Feb. 19. *Statement* of the expenses of the master and mariners.

ii. Feb. 23. *Decision* of Mr. Cadwallader Jones, allowing 176*l.* 19*s.* 5*d.* for their expenses.

Tavistock,
Jan.
2105. *Petition* to the Prince. Recites the distractions of the kingdom. Prays that a national synod be assembled to settle religion, that the militia be entrusted to "the ancient nobility," that Irish rebels be chastised by the law, and Irish "papists" converted by "instruction," rather than that they should be destroyed and extirpated. That in order to these ends the King should endeavour at another treaty with the Parliament.
Draught.
Endorsed by Hyde, "Overtures at T. by Sir H. B."

* See No. 2084.

2106. *Copy of Verses* addressed to the Prince. Imitation of Buchanan's "Genothliacon" (addressed to King James) applied to the Prince. (100 lines.) — 1645-6. Jan.—Feb.

" Grow up brave youth borne for thy country's good

. . . .

As first to rule himselfe, and then a land." *Copy.*

2107. —— *to Sir E. Hyde.* Complaints against Lord Goring for misapplying and embezzling contributions. By a collector of the contributions, extending from Jan. 1644 at Salisbury, Bridgewater, Christchurch, and other places. — Jan.—Feb.

(Five pages.) Endorsed by Hyde, "Cornelius concerning Goring."

2108. *Sir E. Hyde to Mr. Secretary Nicholas.* Complains of the declining state of affairs. Pendennis is victualled for a year. They will soon retreat there. Complains of his not writing. Is left in ignorance of the resolutions taken at Oxford. *Draught.* — Jan.—Feb.

Endorsed by himself.

2109. *An Order* to Sir Arthur Bassett, Governor of the Mount, to send Sir R. Grenville to Scilly. *Copy.* — Feb. 1.

Not signed.

2110. *The King to the Lords Capell, Hopton, Culpeper, and Sir E. Hyde.* Is satisfied that the Prince should not go beyond sea unless there be hazard of his falling into the rebels' hands. Likes that he should be at the head of the army. Will have 1500 horse and 1000 dragoons by the end of the month. Purposes to march into Kent and Sussex to Rochester. Has directed the Queen to cause the 5000 men out of France to land at Hastings. If these succours fail will join the Prince of Wales. As to the London journey, thinks that the personal treaty will fail. Is resolved never to part with the Church, the crown, or his friends. *Copy.* — Feb. 1.

By Hyde from cypher. Endorsed by the same. Cl. S. P. vol. ii. p. 203.

2111. *Secretary Nicholas to Lord Culpeper.* Refers Lord Culpeper to his letter to Mr. Chancellor of the Exchequer. Has sent the Prince news of the Earl of Glamorgan and the Scots army. The King will come to Lord Culpeper's aid in two months. The Earl of Newport reports that Lord Capell's Lieutenant has undertaken to betray the Prince. — Oxon, Feb. 4.

Mostly in cypher. Cl. S. P. vol. ii. p. 206.

2112. *M. de Montreuil to the King.* Has omitted no occa- — Feb. 5.

1645-6. sion to persuade the Scots to be content with what has been granted them: and has played off the Independents against them. Urges the King to grant their demand and disregard the Independents. Favours shown to the latter content neither them nor the Presbyterians. These two would be united by bringing in foreigners; so that the best policy is to adhere to the Scotch and English Presbyterians alone. Parliament is not satisfied with the King's letter concerning Ireland and the Independents. Vane says it is a trick to win the latter. Again urges him to join with the Scots. Will. Murray is imprisoned at Canterbury, but his letters are safe. Another messenger has been stopped, but the letters are recovered. The King ought quickly to resolve on joining the Scotch army. Reports a vessel and 4000 stand of arms taken at Dartmouth; with letters concerning the marriage of the Prince and Mademoiselle.
Copy.

By Edgeman. Cl. S. P. vol. ii. p. 213.

Jan. 30. 2113. *Order* of Prince Charles by Richard Fanshawe for allowance to be made to Joachim Hardwick, skipper of the 'Young Tobias' of Hamburg, lately captured by a man-of-war. With

Pendennis, Feb. 8. Copy of Mr. Chancellor's [Sir E. Hyde] reference upon the above.

Pendennis, Feb. 8. 2114. *Order* to Mr. Jones for an allowance to the Hamburg skipper. *Copy.*
By Edgeman.

Pendennis, Feb. 9. 2115. *Warrant* to the officers of His Majesty's customs giving leave to Mr. John Collison to unload and sell in Cornwall part of his cargo of wine and aqua vitæ bought for the use of the garrison of Exeter, and transport the rest, without payment of custom, to a foreign port, where he may with greater security convoy it to Exeter. *Copy.*

Feb. 9. 2116. *Sir T. Fanshawe's receipt* to Mr. Andrew King for two bills of exchange payable by T. Park in St. Malo for 200l. received from Sir E. Hyde.

Feb. 9. 2117. *Receipt* of Sir T. Fanshawe to Mr. King for two bills of exchange for 200l. (2600 francs) payable at St. Malo.

Paris, Feb. 9. 2118. *Lord Jermyn to Sir E. Hyde.* Has received volumes from him by Sir Francis Doddington, to all which he will find

answers in a despatch of Sir Dudley Wyatt, of which he begs him to inform Sir J. Berkeley and Sir H. Pollard. Urges him to attend to the instructions concerning the bringing away of the young Prince from Exeter. Represents the Queen's resentment against Lady Dalkeith for not having brought her charge, the young Prince, from Exeter. *Original.*
Endorsed by Hyde.

1645-6.

2110. *M. de Montreuil to the King.* Has received an answer to one only of his letters. Repeats the information about Murray. Supposes the Parliament will refuse him a pardon; and that he will be tried by martial law. The indignation of the Scotch at his messenger's seizure may incline France to break with the Parliament. Refers to his former letters for an account of what he has done. *Copy.*
By Edgeman. Cl. S. P. vol. ii. p. 216.

Feb. 12.

2120. *Lord Jermyn to Lord Culpeper and Sir E. Hyde.* The bearer will give particulars of a design, disclosed by the Earl of Newport, to deliver the Prince to Fairfax. Begs him to defeat the mischief. Encloses a duplicate of Sir Dudley Wyatt's despatch. *Original.*
Endorsed by Hyde, "Received 16th March by Mr. Seymour."

Paris.
Feb. 15.
(N.S.)

2121. *Sir E. Hyde to the Queen.* Mr. Grant and Sir Dudley Wyatt go with information. The Prince is between this and Truro. Lord Hopton and Lord Capell are at Torrington with 6800 horse and foot. Exeter is resisting Fairfax. Barnstaple is well prepared. If help comes soon the West may be kept. Assures the Queen of her servant's devotion. Prays for her compassion if they be liable to censure. *Original.*
Cl. S. P. vol. ii. p. 208.

Pendennis
Castle.
Feb. 17.

2122. *Joachim Hardwick's Account* of expenses in the matter of ship and crew of the 'Young Tobias.' (Two leaves.)

Fowey,
Feb. 19.

2123. *The Prince to the Governor of Pendennis Castle.* Order to place the military stores brought by Lord Antrim in the castle. *Rough Draught.*
By Hyde.

Pendennis,
Feb. 19.

2124. *The same to Lord Hopton.* Orders him, after his defeat by Fairfax at Torrington, to make a stand about Stratton, and so defend Cornwall. The Prince will await intelligence from him at Truro. *Rough Draught.*
By Hyde.

Pendennis,
Feb. 19.

1645-6.
Paris,
Feb. 18.

2125. *Lord Jermyn's Despatch to Sir Dudley Wyatt.* The Queen has heard of the danger Dartmouth is in. Is commanded to give orders, in consequence of some received from the King, for the Prince's removal from the West, if it be thought that he is in danger. The Queen desires the Prince to come to France, that he may be sent thence to Denmark.

Duplicate. Partly in cypher, decyphered. See Hist. Rebell. bk. x. p. 405.

Pendennis,
Feb. 12.

2126. *Sir E. Hyde to Mr. Edgeman.* Mr. Biggs' presence is necessary at Truro. Muskets are wanted there, and pigs. Mr. Jones is ordered to find candles at Foy. Has received his letter. *Original.*

Feb. 13.

2127. *Certificate* by Cadwallader Jones for allowance to be made to Joachim Hardwick, skipper of the 'Young Tobias,' of Hamburg, under an order from Prince Charles of Jan. 30, 164$\frac{5}{6}$. 171*l.* 19*s.* 6*d.*

Torrington,
Feb. 15.

2128. *Lord Fairfax to Hugh Peters and Lieut.-Col. Burgh.* Desires them to acquaint the Governor of Plymouth with his intention to advance with the army into Cornwall; and with his wish that aid should be given in settling that county in obedience to the Parliament. *Original.*

Pendennis,
Feb. 15.

2129. *Prince Charles to the Chancellor of the Exchequer.* Order to grant licences for the transportation of wool.

Original.

Countersigned by Sir R. Fanshawe.

London,
Feb. 16.

2130. *M. de Montreuil to Sec. Nicholas.* Has received the King's letters. Things in London are well disposed for the King's service. Repeats information about W. Murray. The Scotch deputies desire to know the authors of two letters which pretend to disclose the King's dealings with France and the Scotch. The thanks of the Scotch Parliament to the City for money furnished for the war has pleased the Council but dissatisfied the Parliament; there are other presages of a rupture between the nations. Has demanded a passport for Scotland by way of Oxford, but sends this before lest he should be waylaid. Adds in a postscript that he has his passport, and that the discovery of certain letters is pretended. *Copy.*

By Edgeman. Cl. S. P. vol. ii. p. 117.

Waterford,
Feb. 18.

2131. *Earl of Glamorgan to Lord Calpeper.* Prays him to move the Prince to transport 6000 men who are ready to the relief of Chester; the other 4000 in May. Capt. Allen has moved for 300 men for the Prince's lifeguard, and proposes a Post-bark to ply between this and the King. *Original.*

Endorsed by Hyde.

2132. *Mr. Robert Boyle to Mr. Arthur Annesley.* Begs that his interest in the Abbey of Rossacke and other places belonging to him in the north of Ireland, that have been taken by Annesley's forces, may be preserved for himself and returned to his sister, Lady Ranelagh. Authorizes him to receive rents and arrears. *Original.*
1645-6. London, Feb. 16.

Endorsed. "Received April 12, by Jeremy Tomlins."

2133. *The Prince's proposal to erect a Chapel in Pendennis Castle.* Rehearses his motives for dedicating a place of worship within the garrison. Invites contributions. This resolution and request to be published in all churches and chapels in the Duchy. Contributors' coats of arms to be fixed up in the chapel. Lionel Gatford, B.D., chaplain to the garrison, to receive and pay moneys. *Draught.*
Pendennis. Feb.

2134. *Sir E. Hyde to [the Earl of]* ——. They say they will go beyond Exeter. His servant Parsons is dead. Has received his of Jan. 18. Mentions the siege of Corfe Castle and taking of Wareham. Has received his of Jan. 18 and 19. Mentions the last message of the King, Jan. 29. Speaks of the King's resolution. As soon as Fairfax is master of the West the Scots will be cudgelled out of the kingdom. *Copy.*
Feb.

(A fragment.) By Edg mss.

2135. *Lord Culpeper to [John] Ashburnham.* The Scotch treaty is the only way to save the realm. The King will soon have no towns in the West. "Ireland will be a broken reed." Foreign forces are a dream. If Fairfax advance, the horse is lost. The Scotch treaty must be an avowed one, with Lesley and Calander. The King is safer in Scotland than in Newcastle. Commends the bearer, whose lord must be a party to the treaty. *Rough Draught.*
Feb.

Endorsed by Hyde.   (L. S. P. vol. II. p. 207.

2136. *Journal of Sir W. Vavasour's military motions.* Proceedings in the neighbourhood of Gloucester, Tewkesbury, Ledbury, Taynton, Upleadon, Maismore, Minsterworth, Micheldean, Worcester, Ross, Hereford, in concert with Sir W. St. Leger, Col. Crofts, and Sir J. Wintour. *Original.*
Feb.

(Seven pages.)   Endorsed by Hyde.

2137. *The King to Sir H. Vane the younger.* Urges him and his friends to prevail that the King may come to London. Makes large promises concerning Presbytery.
March 2.

"A true Cople. C. R."

1645-6.
No date.

2138. *The King to Sir H. Vane the younger.* Repeats his requests and promises. Looks for an answer in four days.

"A true Copia. C.R."

Endorsed by Sec. Nicholas, "Coppye of a lre sent to the Independents party by His Matie command." Cl. S. P. vol. ii. pp. 216, 217.

March 1.

2139. *A Narrative* of the affairs of the West, since the defeat of the Earl of Essex at Lostwithiel in Cornwall, anno 1644. Printed anno 1647. This defeat being given the 2nd of September, 1644.

"Affairs of the West from Sept. 2, 1644, to March 2, 1644/5; a defence of Sir Rd. Grenville's conduct in that period." (Eight pages.)

Printed, with some immaterial variations, in Carte's Collection, vol. I. p. 96.

Jersey.
March 16.

2140. *Sir E. Hyde to Lord Hopton,* on the death of his wife. A second letter to him. Mr. Bogan has sent him all the news. Encloses letters received from Lord Capell and "my Lord" of Norwich. Has received his of March 12. Longs for his coming. Will. Hinton assures him the French cook is admirable. Of all comforters mere divines are the most unpleasant. Quotes Pliny. Approves the silence of Job's friends. Mentions the preparations for strengthening the defences of the Island. *Copy.*

By Edgeman.

Caen.
March 17.
(U. S.)

2141. *Lord Culpeper to Sir E. Hyde.* Mr. Scrope is at Havre. Sir Thomas Fanshawe is at Jersey. Sir Richard Grenville has taken a boat to carry him to the West of Brittany. Jones is in danger of arrest for goood. about the sale of the Hamburg ship. Begs him to send the Dunkirk frigate to Brest to meet him on his return. *Original.*

Endorsed by Hyde.

March 18.

2142. *Thomas Fairfax to the Governor of Pendennis Castle.* Summons him to deliver the castle, with fitting conditions. Expects an answer in two hours. *Copy.*

Endorsed by Hyde. Cl. S. P. vol. ii. p. 227.

March 18.

2143. *John Arundell to Thomas Fairfax.* The castle is the King's. Wonders that Fairfax has demanded it without the King's authority. Will not brand himself as a traitor. Has taken two minutes' resolution. No threat more formidable than loss of loyalty and conscience. *Copy.*

Endorsed by Hyde. Cl. S. P. vol. ii. p. 228.

London,
March 19.

2144. *M. Montreuil to Sec. Nicholas.* His passport is at length granted. Hopes to see the King this week. The Prince's departure is held for certain. Fairfax has written

disobligingly about the Earl of Essex. The King of Spain 1645-6. has ordered his plenipotentiaries to give up his interests into the Queen Regent's hands. Prays that a room may be prepared for him near the Court.—French. *Copy.*
By Edgeman. Cl. S. P. vol. ii. p. 218.

2145. *Dutchman's bill* for sailing tackle to Captain Warren, March 20. amounting to 1049 gulden.

2146. *Account* of some sails and ropes, with a note annexed March 20. by Sir Baldwin Wake, stating that they are put on board the Prince's frigate the 'Spread Eagle.'

2147. *Receipt* by James Warren for the sails and ropes on March 20. board the 'Spread Eagle' frigate.
Countersigned by Sir Baldwin Wake.

2148. *The King to the Prince.* Is glad to think that the Oxford, Prince is with his mother. Urges constancy to religion, March 22. obedience to his father and to the rules of honour. Warns him against Roman and Presbyterian doctrine; in all else to be directed by his mother. *Copy.*
By Hyde from the King's cypher, with another dated June 23, 1645.
Two other copies in different hands.

2149. *The same to the Commissioners of Scotland in London.* March 23. Upon M. Montreuil's representation will satisfy them as to Church government in all points not against his conscience. There will be little difference on other matters. Should the King's message be rejected by Parliament, he hopes he and his family shall be secure in the Scotch army, into which he will in any hazard put himself.
Copied from cypher by Montreuil. Cl. S. P. vol. ii. p. 218.

2150. *Supplement* to the King's message by M. Montreuil March 23. to the Commissioners of Scotland in London. (Not sent.) Expects the Marquis of Montrose's forces to join theirs with all possible speed. Has designed for that employment a person who is to be sent ambassador extraordinary into France.

2151. *Postscript* to the above.—Has sent orders that Newark March 24. be delivered into the hands of the Scotch. Empowers them to make a promise to the city of London of a grant of the militia and other demands made at Uxbridge. *Copies.*
By Edgeman. Cl. S. P. vol. ii. p. 219.

1645-6.
St. Malo,
March 14.

2152. *Order* from the Prince for provisions and military stores to be sent to Sir E. Hyde at Scilly: with engagement to pay Mr. Potter and Mr. Alford. A vessel of forty-seven tons to transport the goods, or two vessels of lesser burden.
Not signed.

St. Malo,
March 14.

2153. *Lord Culpeper to Sir E. Hyde.* Has just arrived in France. Gives an account of what he has done in procuring provisions, and raising money to pay for them. Encloses letters. [Sir] Bernard Gascoyne is returned to Paris, whither he himself is about to go. Col. Munke has arrived from Havre. Has heard of Montrose's victories. *Original.*
Endorsed by Hyde, " Recd. in Jersey."

March 15.

2154. *Guerret Reynardson's bill*, amounting to 17l. 9s., acknowledged by the receiver of the goods.

March 15.

2155. *Charge* of 122l. 7s. by bill of exchange upon Mr. Gregory Alford. *Memorandum.*

March 15.

2156. *Two Bills of Expenses* (Dutch), with a receipt attached to one of them.

March.

2157. *Treaty* between the Marquis of Ormond on behalf of the King, and Richard Lord Viscount Mountgarret and others on behalf of His Majesty's Roman Catholic subjects.
Imperfect Copy.
(Twenty-five clauses on sixteen pages.)
See Carte's Life of Ormond, vol. I. bk. iv. pp. 545–566.

No date.

2158. *Customs.* The names of the several officers belonging to the custom-house in Bristol, with their fees, amounting to 553l.

1646.
March 17.

2159. *The King to the Scotch Commissioners in London.* Desires them to send, with all speed, power to M. Montreuil to assure the King that he will be safe in the Scotch army. Promises on coming to the army to send the note concerning the Duke of Hamilton.
Copied from cypher by Montreuil. Transcribed by Edgeman.
Cl. S. P. vol. ii. p. 119.

[March 28.]

2160. *Articles of Peace* between Lord Ormond and the Irish rebels. *Copy.*
This is the treaty which was finally concluded on March 28, 1646, the substance of which is given in Carte's Life of Ormond, vol. I. bk. iv. pp. 545, 546.

2161. *Lord Ormond to Sir E. Hyde.* Is sorry that letters have miscarried. Begs him to accept Lord Digby's assurances of his good will. Invites the Prince to Dublin. *Original.*   1646. Dublin Castle, March 30.
Endorsed by Hyde.

2162. *The Speakers of the Houses of Lords and Commons to the Prince.* Hearing he is in Scilly, they invite him to reside where and with what attendants the Houses of Parliament shall think fit to appoint. *Copy.*   Westminster, March 30.

2163. *Sir J. Berkeley to Sir E. Hyde.* Refers to his own letters of Feb. 4th, 7th, and 9th. Gives intelligence of public affairs. Will. Murray is in the Tower. The Scotch and London parties. Siege of Banbury and Sir W. Compton. Abingdon nearly surprised. Has heard of Fairfax and Lord Hopton at Torrington. Lord Byron is gone to secure Anglesey. The Duke of Buckingham and his brother are come to London. The Duke is to marry the Earl of Northumberland's daughter. Has been summoned (to surrender) a second time. The Independents have invited the Prince, with a design to put him at their head. *Copy.*   March 31.
By Edgeman.

2164. *The King to the Scotch Commissioners in London.* Promises that none shall come with him to the Scots army but his two nephews and Ashburnham. Stipulates that all who adhere to his person be saved from ruin and dishonour; a condition insisted on by the Queen and Cardinal Mazarin. Is very willing to be instructed concerning the Presbyterian Church government.   April 1.
Copied from cypher by Montreuil. Transcribed by Edgeman. Cl. S. P. vol. ii. p. 220.

2165. *M. Montreuil.—A Stipulation and Promise.* Promises for the King and Queen that if the King puts himself into the Scots army he shall be received as their Sovereign, and his servants protected; and that the army be employed in procuring a favourable peace. *Copy.*   April 1.
By Edgeman. Endorsed by E. Nicholas. Cl. S. P. vol. ii. p. 220.

2166. *The King to Ormond.* Refers him to what he has written to Digby. The King's commands to Digby are directions to Ormond. Laments false friends, and avers he will never change his side. *Original.*   Oxford, April 4.
Endorsed, "Recd. 20 May, by Walsingham."

1646.
Paris,
April 5.
(N. S.)

2167. *Lord Culpeper to Sir E. Hyde.* Lord Jermyn has showed him the Queen's letter to Sir E. Hyde. Is detained by the victualling and manning of two frigates. The great expense this hiring of vessels is to the Queen. Hopes soon to return with money. The King's cause is desperate unless he join the Scots. *Original.*
Endorsed by Hyde.

Paris,
April 6.

2168. *The Queen to the same.* Lord Culpeper has informed her of the condition of Scilly, and its fitness for the Prince's abode. Presses very earnestly for his removal to Jersey. Should he touch at France, a safe-conduct is assured him. *Original.*
Partly in cypher. Endorsed by Hyde.

Paris,
April 6.

2169. *Lord Culpeper to the same.* Has excellent news from London. The Scots join with the King, and have broken with the English. Desires him to leave Scilly with the Prince at once for Jersey, or any port of France; and to invite the Duke of Hamilton from the Mount to join him. *Original.*
Endorsed by Hyde.

Paris,
April 6.

2170. *Lord Jermyn to the same.* Urges them to leave Scilly, as the Queen and Lord Culpeper have already written. The bearer has instructions. *Original.*
Endorsed by Hyde.

Pendennis,
April 11.

2171. *The Council of War at Pendennis to the Prince.* The enemy's quarters are at Arwenack House, with a line from sea to sea. The garrison is in a bad state; great want of clothes. Prays that supplies may be speedily sent from France and Ireland. *Original.*
Endorsed by Hyde. Signed by John Arundell, John Digby, Ab. Shipman, and nineteen others, and a duplicate signed by John Arundell and nine others.

Oxford,
April 11.

2172. *The King to the Queen.* Does not follow her example in omitting occasions of writing. Her last melancholy letter troubles him. Fears she is displeased. Prays her to write, "for nothing but wilful silence can look like unkindness between us." *Original.*

Kilkenny,
April 11.

2173. *The Supreme Council of the Confederate Catholics of Ireland to General Preston, Lord General of Leinster.* Twelve instructions for the expedition into Connaught, under the command of the Marquis of Clanricarde. *Original.*
Signed by Hen. McDonnell, R Bellings, Patr. Darby, and four others. Some of the signatures mutilated.

CLARENDON PAPERS. 311

2174. *Lord Taafe to Sir E. Hyde.* Commends Ireland to him in the hope he may come thither. Trusts he will further Lord Digby's intentions. *Original.* Endorsed by Hyde. — 1646. Waterford, April 12.

2175. *The King to M. Montreuil.* Has been waiting for a letter. Is quite ready to join the Scots army. Desires him to consult with the Commanders what commands he should make to his garrisons. Offers to order the Marquis of Montrose to join them. Exeter is to be given up to-morrow, so he must join the Scots army at all hazards. Has written particulars to the Queen. *Copy.* — April 12.

By Edgeman. "Sent by Sir Tho. Gand's sister y⁰ 13th of ye 1ˢᵗ Month. A duplicate sent ye 14th by Col. Gifford. A triplicate sent . . ." Cl. S. P. vol. ii. p. 221.

2176. *King Charles the First's Vow* to restore all lay impropriations held by the Crown, if he recover his right. — Oxford, April 13.

"This is a true coppy of the King's Vow, which was preserved thirteen years under ground by me Aug. 31, 1660." Gilb. Sheldon.

2177. *Lord Jermyn's Bill of Credit.* Promises to accept bills of the Prince of Wales to the value of 2000 pistoles. *Original.* Endorsed by Hyde. — Paris, April 13.

2178. *The King to the Queen.* Has not heard from Montreuil, but is resolved to run all risks for his deliverance. Charges her to command their son's presence. Will certainly not stay where he is. Recommends the hastening of the ambassador he proposed in his letter of March 30th. *Copy.* Cl. S. P. vol. ii. p. 250. — April 15.

2179. *The Prince to the Parliament.* Has received their message of March 30 and April 11. Echoes their desires for peace. Is compelled to remove to Jersey, whence he will be able to correspond with them. Begs them to send him a safe-conduct for Lord Capel. *Copy.* Endorsed by Hyde. — April 15.

2180. *M. Montreuil to Mr. Secretary Nicholas.* One of his messengers has been intercepted at Oxford. Had hoped that the interview with the Chancellor of Scotland and the Earl of Dunfermline and ... at Royston would have brought about the performance of all he had promised to the King. They are now determined to meet the King at Burton-on-Trent, and send horse to Bosworth. The King must declare his in- — Southwell, April 15 or 16.

1646. tention of going into Scotland, and must join the army unattended, except by the two Princes and Mr. Ashburnham, until they are demanded by the Parliament. The Marquis of Montrose must not go ambassador to France. The King is to grant the Presbyterian government as soon as possible. Has stated these conditions of the Parliament, and thinks the King must accept them if he cannot make better. Has burnt the order for the Governor of Newark, lest it should be used against the King. The Earl of Seaford is said to have declared for peace. Hears that the King's party is very strong in Scotland.

2181. April 16.—M. Montreuil had spoken with the Scotch deputies before they had the particulars of the design concluded at Royston. The Scotch will meet the King at the place appointed, at the time he shall choose, when he shall be received into the army. His conscience shall not be forced. *Copia.*
By Edgeman. Cl. S. P. vol. ii. pp. 221–223.

April 16. 2182. *M. de Montreuil to Mr. Secretary Nicholas and the King.* Since the arrival of the messenger has urged them to advance beyond Burton; but they will only send horse to Bosworth. Thinks that the King will be secure, if not satisfied. Will send two of his own horses. *Copy.*
By Edgeman. Cl. S. P. vol. ii. p. 223.

April 17. 2183. *Col. Robert Hammond to J. Arundell, Governor of Pendennis.* Summons him to surrender the castle. A second demand. *Copy.*
Endorsed by Hyde.

Pendennis, April 17. 2184. *J. Arundell to Robert Hammond.* Has already answered Sir Thomas Fairfax's demand. Refuses to surrender. Thanks him for his civility. *Copy.*
Endorsed by Hyde.

Waterford, April 17. 2185. *Lord Antrim to Sir E. Hyde.* Explains his inability to lend Lord Digby the frigates he asked for. Believes that the Marquis of Ormond and himself will shortly be reconciled. Refers him to Lord Digby for the state of Ireland. Expresses his readiness to serve the Prince. *Original.*
Endorsed by Hyde.

April 18. 2186. *Secretary Nicholas to M. Montreuil.* The King's letter to the Marquis of Montrose to be decyphered and sent to him. It contains the King's last conditions. The King has received no despatch; and is close begirt. Fairfax and Cromwell are coming, now that Exeter and Barnstaple are given up. *Copy.*
By Edgeman. Cl. S. P. vol. ii. p. 223.

2187. *The King to the Marquis of Montrose.* Having upon the engagement of the French King and Queen Regent made an agreement to join the Scotch army, desires him to unite his forces to theirs, upon certain information that the Scotch have declared for the King, and that they are friendly to Montrose.
Copy.
By Edgeman.   Cl. S. P. vol. II. p. 224.

1646.
April 18.

2188. *John Arundell to Mr. Edgeman.* About his grey gelding. Mr. Harrison and other neighbours have invited the enemy. Prays him to obtain a place for himself from Sir E. Hyde. 800 of the Plymouth forces are coming to besiege them. Col.* Hamon is near Exeter. Both Pendennis and the Mount must soon surrender.   *Original.*

April 19.

2189. *Mr. A. Cowley to Lord Culpeper.* The King is resolved to put himself into the hands of the Scotch; has promised to obtain the release of Duke Hamilton, and to command the Marquis of Montrose to retire into France: as Sir R. Murray writes to the Cardinal, while pressing him to remember his promises of assistance.   *Original.*
Endorsed by Hyde.

Paris,
April 20.

2190. *M. Montreuil to the King and me.* The Scotch make great promises, to which the King is not wholly to trust. The enterprise is full of danger. Has received a note from Lord Bellasis, urging him to press the King to come hither, for if taken in Oxford he would be lost. The Scotch troops are near Burton. The King's arrival in their army will no longer serve for the reconciliation of the Independents and the Scotch. Has shewn Lord Bellasis' letter to the Scotch. General Lever and the Earls of Lothian and Dunfermlin favour the King. The Chancellor of Scotland will arrive as soon as the King.   *Copy.*
By Edgeman.   Cl. S. P. vol. II. p. 224.

April 20.

2191. *Mr. Sec. Nicholas to M. Montreuil.* Conveys the King's thanks to him for his noble dealing. The King, in spite of well-grounded mistrust, wishes him to try to further prevail with them. The King trusts he will do him right in his despatches to France as to his respect for the treaty which has cost him the "hazard of [being taken at] Oxford." Thinks this and other monarchies will fall, if other monarchs "shall not instantly appear for an imbargue of trade, and some declaration or ambassage."   *Copy.*
By Edgeman.   Cl. S. P. vol. II. p. 225.

April 22.

* Sir Hamon L'Estrange.

1646.
April 24.

2192. *Mr. Sec. Nicholas to Mr. Montreuil.* The King, hearing that the English Presbyterians desire him to join the Scotch army, wishes him to acquaint them with the King's readiness to comply, which the Scots have themselves hindered: nevertheless the King desires him to continue his negotiations, hearing a more favourable report from London, which he trusts will influence the Scots. The King cannot venture so far as Burton or Bosworth without more forces. Oxford is blocked up with 5000 troops, and Fairfax and Cromwell are marching with the rest.
Copy.

By Edgeman. Cl. S. P. vol. II. p. 215.

April 25.

2193. *The King's Instructions* for the Earls of Lindsey and Southampton; Sir W. Fleetewood and John Ashbournham to treat with Col. Raynsborrow for the King's safe-conduct to London.
Copy.

By Sec. Nicholas's clerk.

April 29.

2194. *Bill of Items* amounting to 3057 livres, due from Mr. Osborne.—French.

Receipted. Endorsed, "For Sir Thomas Fanshawe."

No date.

2195. *A Paper,* endorsed by Hyde, "Provisions designed" for the garrison of Pendennis for 1500 men for six months, to be sent from Ireland. Enclosed in the letter of the Council of war. Ending with twenty gross of tobacco pipes.

(Single sheet.)

No date.

2196. *Oath taken on Composition.* Form of oath not to assist the King against the Parliament, and to submit to the Parliament without prejudice to the proceedings of the two Houses.

See Ant. à Wood's "Hist. et Antiq. Univ. Oxon." L L p. 373.

Havre,
May 1.
(N. S.)

2197. *Lord Culpeper to Sir E. Hyde.* Has received his welcome letter from Jersey. Hears there is a fleet in the Downs designed for Scilly. Encloses London news. Has sent Mr. Progers with letters. Has talked with Lord Jermyn about the intended reduction of Guernsey. The bearer will give him particulars of the moneys received. The Prince's letters are of great importance.
Original.

Endorsed by Hyde.

Paris,
May 4.

2198. *Lord Jermyn to the same.* Urges them to come to France. Excuses himself for not attending the Prince at Jersey. The Queen adds her letters to the Prince to hasten his coming, and with a small train.
Original.

Endorsed by Hyde.

2199. *Mr. Robert Long to Sir E. Hyde.* Wrote both by Mr. Progers and Lord Culpeper, but fears that the letters have not reached him. Congratulates him on leaving Scilly, and the Queen's pleasure at the Prince's arrival in Jersey. He will be welcome in France; if he comes, the Prince's train should be lessened. Hopes the King has left Oxford. Exeter is surrendered. Mentions current reports from England. The Queen is now in Paris, but returns shortly to St. Germains. *Original.* — Paris, May 4. (N. S.) 1646.

2200. *Two Orders of Parliament.* All harbourers of the King's person to be treated as traitors; and the order to be published by the Militia. *Copy.* — May 4.

2201. *Lord Culpeper to Sir E. Hyde.* Proposes that Duke Hamilton shall be taken to Jersey or Scilly; prefers the latter. Begs him to persuade the Prince to do it in the most obliging way he can. Prays to be commended to Lord Brentford, Lord Capell, and Lord Hopton. *Original.* — Havre, May 5.

2202. *Sir W. Davenant to the same.* News from London about the City and the Parliament. Fairfax is advancing to Middlesex; he and the greater part of Westminster are against the whole City and the Scots. This news comes from one of the leading Members. *Original.* *Endorsed by Hyde.* — Paris, May 5.

2203. *Richard Smith to Mr. Fanshawe.* A receipt for 15*l.* — May 5.

2204. *Sir Baldwin Wake's Note of Expenses* amounting to 5*l.* 8*s.* 6*d.*, with memorandum by R. Fanshawe, and receipt from Owen Swinson. — May 6.

2205. *G. Carteret to Mr. Fanshawe.* Order to pay the bearer 500 livres, with receipt for the same. (For the expenses of the Prince's household, as are the two notes above.) *Original.* — May 6.

2206. *Lord Culpeper to Sir E. Hyde.* Thinks it best that the Prince should not leave the castle. Let all persons instantly take the protestation. It were better if the Irish were in the two castles. *Original.* *Endorsed by Hyde.* — Containville, May 11.

2207. *Mr. G. Potter to Mr. Edgeman.* The barque is gone to Scilly; wishes for a frigate to be sent to St. Malo for the goods, or to conduct the barque to Jersey. *Original.* — St. Malo, May 12.

1646.
St. Germains,
May 13.

2208. *Mr. Mason to Mr. Edgeman.* Thanks him for his letters. The French are in the field, and go towards Flanders. The King is gone into Picardy. Fairfax and Cromwell are at Oxford. "They of London affirm they will have Episcopacy rather than Presbitery." *Original.*

Jersey,
May 15.

2209. *Sir E. Hyde to Lord Digby.* Has received his of the 11th, when Digby's brother was with him, who brought 300 men to Scilly six days after the Prince left it. Sir T. Bassett refused to receive them, so that 200 had to be sent back, and 100 have come to Jersey. Has written to "Dick Arundell." Is satisfied of the security of the island. Does not think the Prince will be moved to go to France, unless he is driven from Jersey. There is a report that the King is gone to Ireland. *Copy.*
By Edgeman. Endorsed by Hyde.

Jersey,
May 15.

2210. *The same to Mr. Gatford.* Thanks him for his letter by Sir T. Hooper. Is much pleased with the island. Has ordered provisions to be sent to them from France. Begs him to have an eye to a certain officer. *Copy.*
By Edgeman.

May 15.

2211. [*Sir E. Hyde*] *to Col. Arundell.* Sir T. Hooper arrived on the 2nd from Pendennis. Despatched an express to him of the reasons of the Prince's resolve to come to Jersey. Lords Hopton and Capell came to Scilly April 11th, with a summons from Fairfax. Next day a fleet encompassed the island; and after its dispersion by a storm the Prince sailed for Jersey; having answered the Parliament that he would concur with their advice as far as he might. Sent his message by Sir J. Seymour. The Parliament and the Scots are at mortal defiance. It was his Highness' first care to send Lord Culpeper into France. The news brought by Sir T. Hooper put an end to their resolution. The next day the Prince sent an express to the Queen. Both the Prince's person and the place shall be preserved. Expects an account from H. Killigrew, of Coryton, Edgecombe, and Trelawny.
In the hand of Edgeman.
Cl. S. P. vol. II. p. 219.

Rouen,
May 14.

2212. *Lord Culpeper to Sir E. Hyde.* Is well pleased that the King is with the Scots. Capt. Pindar brings word that Lesley accepted the promise of the Garter. News of Fairfax's movements. Fears that Newark will be delivered to the Parliament and not to the Scots, but has hopes, on the whole, of a peace. With

> *A postscript* on a separate paper, containing further reports of the King's movements. J. Ashburnham is voted to the gallows. *Original.*

2213. [*Sir F.*] *Godolphin to Sir E. Hyde.* Had a short letter from Sir T. Bassett on the 5th. Complains that as a Parliament man he cannot compound under a third part of his land. Has great difficulties in raising money to defray the charges of the vessel and seamen. Prays to be relieved of this burthen, and to be repaid for goods disbursed by Capt. Amy. *Original.*
With schedule of disbursements.

1646.
Caen,
May 16.

2214. *The Queen to the Prince.* "Deare Charles, hauing resceaued a lettre from the King I haue dispatch this bercar Dudly Wiatt to you with the copie of the letter by which you may see the King's commands to you and to me. I make no douts but you will obey it and sudenley: for sertainly your coming hother is the securitie of the King your father, thorfore make all the hast you can to shew your selfe a dutifull sonne and a carefull one to doe all that is in your power to serue him: otherwise you may ruine the King and your selfe: now that the King is gone from Oxford, wether to the Scotch or to Irlande, the Parlement will with all ther power force you to come to them: there is no time to be lost, therefore loose none, but come speedeley: I haue writt more at large to milord Culpeper to shew it to your counsell. He say no more to you, hoping to see you shortley. I would haue send you Henry Jermin, but he is goinge to the court with some commands from the King to the Queene Regente. He adde no more to this but that I am your most affectionat mother,
"For me deareat sonne." HENRIETTE MARIE R."
Original.
Endorsed by Hyde. Cl. S. P. vol. II. p. 230.

St. Germains,
May 17.

2215. *The same to Lord Culpeper.* Sends the bearer with copy of the King's letter. Urges him to bring the Prince at once into France. The King's commands must be obeyed.—French. *Original.*
Endorsed by Hyde. Cl. S. P. vol. II. p. 231.

May 17.

2216. *Capt. Thomas Amy to Sir E. Hyde.* Has come from Scilly and knocked a hole in the ship's bottom. Has no money for wages or repairs. On the 26th of April met with thirty-four sail of the English fleet; and heard of seventeen sail of Parliament ships bound for Scilly to take the Prince to London.
Note.—Capt. Amy was employed by the Prince from Scilly to France. He had on board Mr. Godolphin and a cargo of tin. *Original.*

Brest,
May 18.

2217. *Lord Jermyn to Lord Culpeper.* Enforces the King's and Queen's orders for the Prince to go to France. The King

St. Germains,
May 18.

1646. left Oxford at 2 a.m. last Monday with Ashburnham and his servant, and a servant of Lord Digby. Begs him to take no further steps at present concerning the composition with Sir Peter Osborne. *Original.*

Endorsed by Hyde.

St. Germains, May 18.
2218. *Lord Jermyn to Sir E. Hyde.* Letters to Lord Culpeper will explain the bearer's mission. No resolution is to be taken at present touching the composition with Sir Peter Osborne in the matter of Guernsey Castle. Begs him to make his excuses to the Prince for not attending him. Has to go to Compiegne. *Original.*

Endorsed by Hyde.

Newcastle, May 18.
2219. *The King to the Houses of Parliament.* Having understood that it was not safe for him to come to London, he enters into the questions of Religion, Militia, and Ireland, of which he trusts they will come speedily to a settlement. *Copy.*

St. Germains, May 18.
2220. *Lord Jermyn to the Prince.* Pleads the affliction he has that he cannot yet wait upon the Prince; moves him to beg the Prince to believe that it is with grief he is withheld from attending him. *Original.*

Endorsed by Hyde.

Newcastle, May 19.
2221. *The King to the City of London*, about the proposals for peace sent to the two Houses of Parliament. *Copy.*

King Charles's Works, p. 113; Rapin, vol. II. p. 524.

Jersey, May 20.
2222. *Sir E. Hyde to Lord Jermyn.* Would gladly go to Paris, but as he is to live in retiredness will explain his motives. The transport of the Prince into France will prove either the preservation or ruin of himself, the King, the Queen, and the crown of England. Sees not much force in the arguments urged for the Prince's going to France. Points out several inconveniences that will attend his leaving the King's dominions; but upon the least probability of his being surprised by the rebels, will advise his going thither at once. *Draught.*

Cl. S. P. vol. II. p. 231.

London, May 21.
2223. *Letter of Intelligence.* There has been a general muster in Hyde Park, where many kissed the Duke of Gloucester's hand. Debates in Parliament on the disposal of the King. *Original.*

Anonymous.

CLARENDON PAPERS.   319

2224. *Lord Jermyn to Lord Culpeper.* Has received the letters about the relief of Pendennis Castle; gives directions for the same; and guarantees to repay Hitchcock. *Original.*
Endorsed by Hyde.

1646.
St. Germains,
May 31.

2225. *The King to Alexander Henderson.* Does not pretend to equal ability in divinity. Has been well settled in religion by his father. Proceeds to state his belief. His mother, the Church of England, taught him to reverence the Reformation. Bishops are necessary for a Church. Is supported by his Coronation Oath. Episcopacy has always subsisted in England. *Copy.*

Newcastle,
May 29.

2226. "*Brief Memorials* of the unfortunate successe of his Maties army and affaires in the yeare 1645, being only such as the lapse of tyme, want of papers, and the sadnesse of the subject haue suffered mee to reteyne in memory." Forty-one pages, chiefly military affairs, ending thus:—"To conclude this sadd discourse, which is an accumulation of misfortunes, it is observable, that if from May 1645 unto that time 1646, his Matie had beene successfull in any one of his undertakings, or had donne the contrary to what hee did, hee had beene eyther M^r of all, or at least had kept himself on foote a much longer time."
Endorsed by Hyde, "Passages in the King's affairs in the year 1645, before the battle of Naseby to the King's leaving Oxford."
Probably one of the two papers sent by the King from Oxford to Hyde (see Life, p. 103), and used as materials for the History of the Rebellion.

May.

2227. *Sir E. Hyde to Sec. Nicholas.* Has received his letter of the 22nd by Col. Bovil. Has not been fully trusted. Lord Culpeper has changed his opinion on the Prince's going to France. He and Lord Capell are with the Queen. Will shut himself up with Sir G. Cartwright rather than be hurried in the matter of the Prince's leaving Jersey. Is glad to hear of the King's honourable reception by the Scots. Would not buy a dear peace. England seems ready to take any religion. Hopes yet to wait on Lord Southampton at Litchfield. Begs him to tell Lady Hyde that Lady Wenman owes him 100*l.*
Copy.
By himself.   Cl. S. P. vol. II. p. 236.

June 1.

2228. *The same to Mr. Brett.* Thanks him for his loyalty. Will be glad to do him a service in return. Begs him to send information of anything that may happen of importance.
Copy.
By himself.

June 2.

1646.
St. Germains,
June 1.

2229. *Sir William Davenant to Sir E. Hyde.* Montrose is upon the borders. Reports the King's movements, and orders; and the strength of the Presbyterian party in London. Lord Digby is about to set out for Ireland. Suggests a motive for the Prince's leaving Jersey. *Original.*
Endorsed by Hyde.

Gresbois,
June 1.

2230. *Henry de Bourbon (brother of the King of France) to the Queen of England.* Hopes to see her soon. Sends extracts from a letter he has received from Cardinal Mazarin. Is entirely devoted to her service.
Extract.—Is glad to inform him that the interests of the King of England are in a better condition. M. de Bellievre is about to go as ambassador extraordinary. Has received information of the Parliament's design on the Prince of Wales. *Original.*

Newcastle,
June 3.

2231. *Mr. A. Henderson to the King.* Does not wish to dispute with divines. Quotes Picus Mirandula for the supremacy of reason as against the will and the schoolmen on the other side, St. Ambrose and Symmachus on education. Instances Jacob and the Kings of Judah as reformers. Henry VIIIth's Reformation imperfect. More schism and separation in England than anywhere else. Now is the time to reform perfectly. Argues against bishops. To quote the primitive church and the fathers is to argue as the Papists do. Overrules the argument for the Coronation Oath. King James swore and subscribed to the doctrine, worship, and discipline of the Church of Scotland. *Copy.*
Corrected by the King.

Newcastle,
June 6.

2232. *The King to Mr. A. Henderson.* A disputation of well-chosen divines would be best. Traverses his arguments. Edward VI. and Queen Elizabeth began and perfected the English Reformation. Presbyterianism not primitive. The King and clergy without Parliament made the Reformation. Knows his father better than Mr. Henderson knew him. *Copy.*
Corrected by the King.

St. Germains,
June 9.

2233. *Lord Culpepper to Sir E. Hyde.* Has received his packet of May 23rd, but is still in doubt concerning Scilly or Jersey. Trusts he will get 400 pistoles from Sir G. Carteret. The Queen relies on the speedy coming of the Prince. A letter has lately been received from Cockram, agent in Denmark. The Queen does not mislike Mr. Pooly's journey. They are waiting news from London. Wintour Grant is ready to go to the King. *Original.*
Endorsed by Hyde.

2234. *Mr. Godolphin to Sir E. Hyde.* Complains much of Capt. Amy, who refuses to deliver the tin, and threatened to open his trunks to seek for money. Begs him to obtain a release either for his tin or his money, but not to let Bullen have anything to do with it. *Original.*
1646. Caen, June 11.

* Printed in Dr. Hoskins' "Charles II. in the Channel Islands," vol. ii. p. 400.

2235. *Thomas Coke to Mr. Edgeman*, at Jersey. Thanks him for his letter. Hopes to return soon with satisfaction to himself and Mr. Auditor Johnson. Hears that another war is like to break out near London, and that the Parliament and Scotch forces in Yorkshire disagree. Oxford has made some fierce sallies. *Original.*
Rouen, June 11.

2236. *Lord Culpeper to Sir E. Hyde.* Thanks him for his letter. There is bad news from Newcastle. J. Ashburnham is sent away from the King. There is a proclamation against Royalists. Is in fear and perplexity. Goes to the Cardinal about the instructions for M. Dellievre. *Original.*
Endorsed by Hyde. Dr. Hoskins, vol. i. p. 425.
June 14.

2237. *Mr. A. Henderson to the King.* Is adverse to a disputation of divines. Repeats his arguments against those of the King. The right to reform is not confined to rulers. No difference between a Bishop and a Presbyter. Private interpretation of Scripture. Presbyters may ordain. Reform may be made without the consent of the clergy. Kings should not force the Church to prayers and tears. How conscience may be forced. *Copy.*
Newcastle, June 17.

2238. *The King to the Marquis of Antrim.* Sends Sir James Lesley with commands to lay down arms. Has sent the same to Montrose. None shall be ruined for their obedience to the King. *Copy.*
Cl. S. P. vol. ii. p. 237.
Newcastle, June 19.

2239. *The Queen to the Prince of Wales.* Requires him to obey the King's commands sent by Sir Dudley Wyatt, and reiterated in a letter from the King sent by M. Montrenil. France has given full assurance for honourable treatment. Sends an extract from the King's letter of March 22.
St. Germains, June 10.

Encloses:—1. Copy of the King's letter signed by the Queen. 2. Extract of the King's letter to the Queen of May 28th, 1646. 3. Extract from the King's letter to the Queen of June 3rd, *Copies.*
By Edgeman. Endorsed by Hyde. Cl. S. P. vol. ii. pp. 238, 239.

* Nos. 2216, 2217, 2224, 2229, and 2233 are also printed in the same work.

1646.
May 30—
June 30.

2240. *Narrative* of affairs at Oxford from Monday, April 27, 1646, to May 30 of the same year, with copies of the treaty between Sir Thomas Fairfax's Commissioners and the Commissioners for Oxford; and Sir Thomas Fairfax's letter to Sir Thomas Glemham.

(Five pages folio.) Endorsed by Hyde.
See Hist. Rebell. bk. x. p. 496. Wood, Hist. et Antiq. I. i. p. 364.

Jersey.
June 22.

2241. *Prince Charles to Capt. Amy.* Warrant ordering Captain Amy, commander of the 'Little George,' to deliver the ship, with all her stores and armament. *Original.*
Endorsed by Hyde.

Newcastle,
June 11.

2242. *The King to Mr. A. Henderson.* Argues the points of the Reforming Power, the English Reformation, the equality of Bishops and Presbyters, private interpretation of Scripture, ordination without Bishops, the Coronation Oath, King James's opinion, unlawfulness of war made by subjects, forcing of conscience. *Copy.*

Hereford,
June 23.

2243. *The same to the Prince.* Commands him, should his father be taken prisoner, not to yield to any conditions dishonourable or unsafe to his person or authority; not even to save the life of the King, who will die cheerfully if only his son be constant. Charges him to keep this letter by him, and not shew it to the Council until occasion require. *Copy.*
Hist. Rebell. p. 488, ed. 1732.

Caen,
June 23.

2244. *Mr. Godolphin to Sir E. Hyde.* Is in great distress on his own and his wife's account. Prays him to consider of a settlement for Scilly. *Original.*
Endorsed by Hyde. Hopkins, vol. II. p. 40.

Cockloft in
Newgate,
June 23.

2245. *Lieut.-Col. John Lilburne to Mr. Wollaston, Keeper of Newgate.* Refuses to acknowledge the competency of the Lords to judge him. Will not appear before them unless by violence.
(A printed broadsheet.) Endorsed by Hyde. With a copy of the Order of the Lords.

June 23.

2246. *The Prince of Wales to the Marquis of Ormond.* Lord Digby will inform him of the Prince's good will. Prays him to employ Mr. Fanshawe, whom he recommends to his service. *Copy.*
By Hyde. Hopkins, vol. II. p. 34.

Caen,
June 24.

2247. *Mr. Godolphin to Sir E. Hyde.* Capt. Amy has sold all his tin. Prays for redress and assistance in his great strait. Trethcney and Spernon have come. *Original.*

2248. *Lords Capell and Hopton, with Sir E. Hyde, to the Queen.* Have presented to the Prince their advice for suspending his journey to France, and their reasons for not attending him thither. Prays the Queen to make a gracious interpretation of their absence. *Rough Draught.*
By Hyde. Cl. S. P. vol. II. p. 239.
1646. June 15.

2249. *Sir Edw. Hyde's Memorandum* concerning the Prince's remove from Jersey. Debate in the Prince's Council on June 20. Lords Capell, Culpeper, Jermyn, Digby, Wentworth, and Withrington, Sir Marmaduke Langdale, Sir Wm. Davenant and others. Notes of Hyde's conversation with Lords Digby and Jermyn. Another Council on Sunday; the Queen's letter again read. A third Council on Monday; when the Prince's accounts, the garrisons of Pendennis and Scilly, and the Prince's immediate departure for France were discussed. On Tuesday morning the Prince made an attempt to leave for France, but was detained by baffling winds. The Prince remained with great impatience until the evening, when he was able to reach France. Notes of conversations held by Lords Capell, Hopton, Digby, and the Chancellor of the Exchequer.
Holograph.
(Six pages.) Endorsed by Hyde.
June 15.

2250. *Ant. Lightfoote to W. Edgeman.* Thanks him for the sack out of the Chancellor's cellar, and other entertainments.
Original.
A merry and familiar letter.
Caen, June 17.

2251. *Letter from John Digby, H. Killigrew, A. Shipman, Richard Arundell, Will. Slaughter, Chas. Jennings, Math. Wyse, Jo. Hurley, John Arundell, Walter Slingsby, Joseph Jane, Rob. Harris, Henry Shelley, Lewis Tremayne, to the Prince.* Informs him that they are reduced to the last extremity, and must, if not relieved, surrender in three weeks.
Copy.
Endorsed by Hyde, "Received July 13, at Jersey, and sent at once to the Prince."
Pendennis, June 27.

2252. *Mr. A. Henderson to the King.* Omits subordinate points. Questions of the Primitive Church, and interpretation of Scripture. King James preferred Calvin to Augustine.
Copy.
Corrected by the King.
Newcastle, July 1.

2253. *The King to Mr. A. Henderson.* Refuses to admit his interpretation of Scripture; and retains his own opinion on that point.
Copy.
The above controversy is printed in King Charles's Works.
Newcastle, July 3.

1648.
Sept. 3,
1612 —
July 4,
1646.

2254. *Prince Rupert's Journal in England.*

Each day occupies a line. The journal is little more than a list of names of places and persons. Twelve leaves: eighteen pages. Endorsed by Hyde, to whom it was sent by the Prince. See Hyde's letter of thanks, April 18, 1648.

Jersey,
July 5.

2255. *Lords Capell and Hopton, and Sir E. Hyde, to the King.* They cannot attend the Prince into France. Will always find any opportunity of serving the King. *Copy.*

By Edgeman. C. S. P. vol. II. p. 140.

Caen,
July 8.

2256. *Mr. Godolphin to Sir E. Hyde.* Sir John Berkeley, Col. Ashburnham, and Mr. Denham, arrived from Hampton the day after the Lords went towards Jersey. Amy is returned to Brest. Prays for redress. Letters to be forwarded by Richard Alford at St. Malo. *Original.*

Endorsed by Hyde.

Jersey,
July 10.

2257. *Sir E. Hyde to ———.* Has received his letter of June 25. Will forward the Princess's letter to his Highness. Lords Capell and Hopton stay with him. The Earl of Berkshire is before his time at the Hague. Lord Goring has good reason not to censure him. Is glad to hear the Prince of Orange is able to take the field. His hopes for England depend on the Prince. *Copy.*

By Edgeman.

Jersey,
July 12.

2258. *The same to Sir John Berkeley.* Has received his of the 13th (N.S.) on the 9th (O.S.). Has heard from Dr. Fraser he had been at Caen. Had a justifiable reason for remaining in Jersey. Is well treated by Sir G. Carteret, and is willing to rest and wait a time to serve the King or Prince. Is afflicted at Berkeley's bad condition. [Is well satisfied that the Prince and Princess have trespassed on him. Recapitulates circumstances connected with trade in the West; the imposition laid upon it, and certain communication between themselves. Berkeley's losses are no fault of his. Lady Dalkeith's sufferings trouble him exceedingly; wrote to her and Lord and Lady Wilmot last week*.] Repels the charge of speaking ill of him. Prays him in their banishment from the world to preserve their old friendship. Desires to hear of Dr. Morley, Pollard, and Nat. Apsley. *Copy.*

By Edgeman. Endorsed by Hyde. C. S. P. vol. II. p. 140. * [Not in C. S. P.]

Jersey,
July 12.

2259. *The same to Mr. Long.* Received his of the 13th (N.S.) Returns his certificate. Was solicitous for Mr. Alford. Recommends the bearer, Mr. Butterworth. *Original.*

2260. *Richard Mason to Mr. Edgeman.* The Articles of Oxford are sent to the Chancellor by Mr. Alesford. Hopes he will prevent Capt. Amy making a prize of a ship of Mr. Potter's that he has taken at Brest. *Original.*
1646. Paris, July 14.

2261. *Cadwallader Jones to the same.* Has sent the Chancellor a hogshead of beer. Hopes to be at Jersey shortly. Mr. Hinton's business is ready. *Original.*
St. Malo, July 19.

2262. *The same to Sir E. Hyde.* In answer to his letter of June 27th. Is ready to pay the Prince the money due to him. Mentions current topics of intelligence from Oxford, Scotland, Ireland, and London. *Original.*
St. Malo, July 19.

2263. *The King to the Lords Jermyn and Culpeper, and J. Ashburnham.* Received six letters from them last Saturday, but only answers that of July 19. Complains of the impudence with which he has been assaulted to yield to the London Propositions. Conjures them and the Queen to remain constant. Cannot concur in their advice as to the Church, for the change of Church government is but a "pretext to take away the dependency of the Church from the Crowne; which, let me tell you, I hold to be of equal consequence to that of the Militia, for people are governed by pulpits more than the sword, in times of peace; nor will the Scots be content with alteration of government, except the Covenant be likewise established." As to the theological part, "the change would be no less, and worse than if Popery were brought in, for we should have neither lawful priests, nor sacraments duly administered." He will never yield to this; yet the Scots are "to be sought with all possible industry usque ad Aras." Permits a treaty with the Independents. *Original.*
Newcastle, July 22.

Cl. S. P. vol. II. p. 142.

2264. *The same to the Marquis of Antrim.* Sir James Lesley bears his repeated commands for laying down arms. Can promise him no assistance.
Newcastle, July 29.

Cl. S. P. vol. II. p. 242.

2265. *The King's Answer to the Propositions tendered by the Parliament Commissioners.* Cannot give a particular and positive answer before a full debate; to which end the King proposes to come to London to discuss the power of the Crown, the liberty of the subject, and the privileges of Parliament. Upon assurance of an agreement the King will send for the Prince and answer for his obedience. *Copy.*
Newcastle, Aug. 1.

By Edgeman. Endorsed by Hyde. King Charles's Works. p. 114.

1646.
Newcastle,
Aug. 1.

2206. *The King to the Houses of Parliament.* Proposals for a personal interview in London, in order to a settlement of affairs. *Copy.*

With postscript, offering to send for the Prince.

Dublin,
Aug. 1.

2267. *John Poingdexter [to Sir E. Hyde].* The peace is completed notwithstanding their alarm at the King's letter ordering the Lord Lieutenant to break it off. The Scots entirely defeated in Connaught. Enters into details of the risk that was run of destroying the peace. Trusts the peace will find favour with all parties, including the Pope's Nuncio; and that Ireland, with some help from France, may free itself from the Scots and Parliament. *Original.*

Endorsed by Hyde. See Birch, on Lord Glamorgan's Transactions.

Dublin,
Aug. 2.

2268. *Lord Digby to Sir E. Hyde.* Rejoices over the proclamation of the peace. They have 22,000 foot and horse; the enemy not above 7000. Joins with the Lord Lieutenant in urging Hyde to come with R. Fanshawe to Ireland. His despatch is carried by a French frigate. *Original.*

Endorsed by Hyde.

Athlone,
Aug. 2.

2269. *Lawrence Rouen to Nicholas French, the Bishop of Ferns.* Attacks the Supreme Council. Went to Capt. Brabazon, in Connaught, where he stayed fourteen months. Hearing that the Nuncio, prelates, and clergy have disclaimed the peace, begs a commission to raise horse and a patent to command them, to be called the Nuncio's guard. *Original.*

Jersey,
Aug. 5.

2270. *Sir E. Hyde to the Lord Withrington.* Has "prevailed with himself to endeavour the compiling a plain, faithful narrative of the proceedings of these last ill years." Prays him to obtain such information as he can concerning the recovery of the North of England to the King. Cl. S. P. vol. ii. p. 146.

St. Germains,
July 27—
Aug. 6.

2271. *Lords Jermyn and Culpeper, and Mr. J. Ashburnham, to the King.* Their despatch from Fontainbleau three days since went by a dispatch from Cardinal Mazarin. Point out to him the probable results of yielding to the Presbyterians, who hate and fear the Independents. They rely on his courage and constancy. Touching his letter of July 8, they represent to him the danger of the attempt, and the provocation given to the Parliament if successful. *Original.*

In cypher, decyphered by the King, and endorsed by him, "Rec⁴. 7/17 Aug." Cl. S. P. vol. ii. p. 244.

2272. *The Corporation of Cashell to the Nuncio and Congregation.* A Latin letter in answer to an application not to proclaim the peace. They excuse their not complying on account of the oath they had taken on entering into the confederacy to obey the command of the Supreme Council, whose commands to publish the peace they had already received; but promise to delay it as long as possible. *Original.*

1646.
Cashell,
Aug. 7.

2273. *F. Bartholomew Hamlyn to the Bishop of Ferns.* The Mayor and Council of Wexford have readily obeyed the decree of the Nuncio. They are ready to spend their blood in this cause and the defence of the ancient Roman religion. *Original.*

Wexford,
Aug. 7.

2274. *The Marquis of Ormond to Sir E. Hyde.* Is sorry Hyde did not come with Lord Digby. Trusts the Irish peace may help to settle the other kingdoms. Promises him all contentment. *Original.*
Endorsed by Hyde. Printed in Carte's Life of Ormond, vol. iii. p. 492.

Dublin
Castle,
Aug. 7.

2275. *To the Prince from the Lords.* Inform him of their destitute state, and difficulty in holding the castle. Sir Baldwin Wake and Sir Geo. Carteret help to support them. Pray for relief. *Rough Draught.*
By Hyde.

Castle
Cornet,
Aug. 9.

2276. *To the Mayor and Clergy of Kilkenny.* A circular letter, in Latin, enclosing a copy of their letter to the Supreme Council, about suspending the proclamation of the peace. *Draught.*

Waterford,
Aug. 10.

2277. *The King to the Lords Jermyn and Culpeper and Mr. (John) Ashburnham.* Has received letters from them all since the first of the month. Thanks Lord Jermyn for news of his daughter's arrival in France. Does not think that Presbyterian government, and abolition of Episcopacy, without the Covenant, will please the Scotch. Thinks Presbyterian doctrine anti-monarchical and more erroneous than Roman: nevertheless the Scots must be gained over if possible. Cannot get a libel in defence of Lilburne answered. The appearance of a strong force for him, which must begin abroad, is the only thing to bring the Scots to declare for him. The Queen will be careful of his preservation. Must soon be a prisoner in his own dominions, or at liberty elsewhere. Begs them not to press him against his conscience. Notes some mistakes in the cypher. *Draught.*
Endorsed by himself, "Not to be burned."
Cl. S. P. vol. ii. p. 246.

Newcastle,
Aug. 12.

1646. 2278. *Decretum Perjurii.* Per congregationem ecclesiasti-
Waterford, cam utriusque cleri Hibernici, in Spiritu Sancto congregatam
Aug. 12. Waterfordiæ, coram illustrissimo Domino Archiepiscopo Fir-
manensi, Nuntio in Hiberniam Apostolico. [Et
Waterford, Epistola tertia ad supremum concilium*.] *Draught.*
Aug. 11.   Cl. S. P. vol. ii. p. 249. *[Not in Cl. S. P.]

Aug. 13. 2279. *The first Oath taken at Duncannon*, with note dispensing
with its observance in the case of General Preston's demand
for surrender; due regard being had to the General's agreement with the Nuncio and clergy.
Cl. S. P. vol. ii. p. 250.

Jersey, 2280. *Sir E. Hyde to Sir J. Berkeley.* Has received his of
Aug. 14. the 9th. Defends himself from "negligent discourse" of him
with Sir Hugh Pollard; and from any unexact performance
of his duty to the King and the Prince. Gives his opinion of
the Propositions sent to the King at Newcastle. Tells him he
is writing the History of the Rebellion, and begs to be furnished
with materials. *Copy.*
By Edgeman. Endorsed by Hyde.

Paris, 2281. *Cadwallader Jones to Sir E. Hyde.* Pendennis is in
Aug. 14. great distress. Wallingford and Worcester is taken. Fairfax
is gone to Bath. The King is at Newcastle and refuses
to subscribe the Propositions. Montrose resolves not to quit
his army. *Original.*
Endorsed by Hyde.

St. Ger- 2282. *Lord Culpeper to the same.* Prays him to hasten
mains, their business. Mentions certain difficulties on which he wishes
Aug. 14. to hear from him and Sir G. Carteret. The Prince goes to
Fontainbleau. *Original.*

Newcastle, 2283. *The King to Ormond.* Has received his despatches
Aug. 15. by Rob. Leslie, but cannot read a word, not having
the cypher. Rates him for his fault. Is glad the Irish peace
is made, but can at present give no further directions, being
himself a sort of prisoner. Refers him to the Queens of England and France, to whom he looks for relief. *Original.*
Endorsed, "Recd. 16 Sept. by Ro. Lesley."

Waterford, 2284. *From the Congregation at Waterford to Piers Fitz-*
Aug. 15. *Gerald.* Acquaints him with the resolutions they have taken
against the peace. Refers him for particulars to the bearer.
Copy.

2285. *The King to the Lords Jermyn and Culpeper, and Mr. Ashburnham.* Received theirs of the 17th last Monday. Answers what they have said respecting Religion, and the Militia. Mentions the report that the London rebels will seek to satisfy the Scots; and desire to make the Duke of York King. No eloquence but that of a good army will touch the rebels. The business of Ireland stops the way. Thinks that France should be urged to move. *Original Draught.*
　1640.
Newcastle, Aug. 19.

Endorsed "By London." Cl. S. P. vol. II. p. 148.

2286. *Dr. Walter Lynch, Titular Warden of the College of Galway, to the Lords Bishops of Waterford, of Ferns, or any of them; or in their absence, to the Very Rev. Robert Barry.* Hastened to Limerick to divert the sudden resolution of the Council in proclaiming the peace: and distributed the papers of excommunication to Mr. Dominic Fanning and others. Disputed on the excommunication with Dr. White and Dr. Arthur, urging the danger of losing nearly all the churches. Heard that the Commons were ready to oppose the proclamation, which they did yesterday with much rioting, the Sergeant-at-Arms and others being wounded. *Original.*
Limerick, Aug. 11.

Cl. S. P. vol. II. p. 150.

2287. *Mr. John Jane to Mr. Edgeman.* Has been to St. Germains in behalf of Capt. Nicolas of Pendennis Castle. Gives many details. Final success of his application to the Prince. *Original.*
St. Malo, Aug. 12.

Hoskins, vol. II. p. 19.

2288. *Lord Culpeper to Sir E. Hyde.* Has received his two letters of the 2nd and 4th. Private and money matters. *Original.*
Paris, Aug. 14.

Endorsed by Hyde.

2289. *[Lords] Mountgarret, [Dillon, Bellasis] to [the Bishop of Ferns].* Have received his letter written at the command of the Nuncio. Will be ready to do all in their power to advance the Catholic cause. *Original.*
Kilkenny, Aug. 16.

Partly defaced.

2290. *The King to the Prince of Wales.* Sends Dr. Steward to him to be admitted Dean of the Prince's chapel. Enlarges on his infallible maxim, that as the Church can never flourish without the Crown, so the dependency of the Church on the Crown is the chief support of regal authority; next to which is the sword. Counsels him never to abandon his friends. *Original.*
Newcastle, Aug. 26.

Endorsed, "To my sone Charles." Cl. S. P. vol. II. p. 253.

u u

1646.
Aug. 28.

2291. *Preston to [the Bishop of Ferns]*. After F. Darcie's departure the peace was proclaimed by the Marquis of Clanricarde. Did not then know of its being disapproved by the Congregation, to whom he professes his devotion. Hopes his army will be paid their arrears. *Original.*

Waterford,
Aug. 28.

2292. *The Nuncio and Ecclesiastical Congregation in Ireland to the Marquis of Antrim.* Have censured all that adhere to the peace of late concluded at Dublin. Have sent their declaration, with five Propositions to the late Supreme Council. Cannot concur with those, who without their consent have contracted for Religion, the Church, and Sacraments; but rely on the Marquis as a protector of the Roman Catholic faith. Have sent all acts and papers of the Congregation concerning the peace; and ordered the Lord of Ferns to procure eighty barrels of powder and two field pieces. *Copy.*

Signed by "Nicolaus Fernensis Episcopus." Endorsed by him. Cl. S. P. vol. ii. p. 253.

St. Germains,
Aug. 28.

2293. *Charles Murray to Sir E. Hyde.* The King has refused to sign the Propositions, and Lords Loudon and Argyle have returned with the Lords that carried them. Duke Hamilton has gone for Scotland. The Prince has been received with as much respect as could be, and has gotten the love of all that have seen him. Trusts that a peace will be made without the Propositions. The Prince remembers the three at Jersey with much kindness. *Original.*

Endorsed by Hyde. Cl. S. P. vol. ii. p. 254.

Newcastle,
Aug. 31.

2294. *The King to the Lords Jermyn and Culpeper, and Mr. John Ashburnham.* Has received the despatches of two weeks. Is deeply grieved that they condemn his wilfulness. Is certain that nothing short of the destruction of the monarchy will content the Scots. And with this Episcopacy would be totally abolished, "the dependency of the Church torn from the Crowne, and the Covenant firmly established." Is firmly convinced of this, and begs them, if his arguments prevail not, to shew him particularly why. *Original Draught.*

Endorsed by himself. Cl. S. P. vol. ii. p. 255.

2295. *Two Anecdotes* of a weaver, and a woman who preached and created disturbances in London and Weymouth. *Copy.*

Endorsed by Hyde, "Shippen."

Aug.

2296. *Extracts of letters of intelligence.* The affairs of King, a vintner in Smithfield, and of Sir John Eveland. The barbarous punishment of a woman at Henley-on-Thames.

Endorsed by Hyde, "Shippon's relation of some particular extravagancies of the Parliament." In part Cl. S. P. vol. ii. App.

2297. *Memorandum by the Prince of Wales* of the King of France, his augmentation of the Queen of England's appointment of 30,000 to 40,000 livres a month. — 1646. Aug.

2298. *The same* for the Prince, during his stay, until the end of 1648. With note of payments by Sir E. Hyde. — Aug.

2299. "*Six Reasons* offered by the Congregation of both secular and regular clergy by which they justifie the displacing of Colonel Richard Butler from the conduct of that regiment." (Three pages.) *Rough Draught.* — Aug.

2300. "*A memento for Fa. Diffinitor.*" Nine articles relating to the Castle of Athlone; its defence and garrison. — Aug.

2301. *Memorandum.* Eleven particulars agreed on by the Nuncio and Congregation as to what they were to do after disclaiming the peace.—Latin. *Rough Draught.* — Aug.

2302. *Nine Instructions* of the Congregation, after the peace, about calling a General Assembly, and taking measures for carrying on the war. *Copy.* — Aug.

2303. "*The Bishop of Ferns'* engagement to be answerable for the ammunition delivered, and moneys lent for the use of the confederate Catholics." Fourteen items amounting to 3711*l*. 8*s*. 11*d*. *Original.*
Endorsed by Hyde. Hoskins, vol. ii. p. 10. — Aug.

2304. *Lord Culpeper to Sir E. Hyde.* Begs a remittance. Hopes he will visit his friends. *Original.* — St. Germains, Sept. 1.

2305. *The same to the same.* Has received his of August 14th. Capt. Amy's business to be despatched at once. Personal matters. *Original.*
Endorsed by Hyde. — Paris, Sept. 4.

2306. *Walter Lynch to Patrick, Lord Bishop of Waterford, and Nicholas, Lord Bishop of Ferns.* Asks the question, "How shall temporal justice be administered, now that the authority of the Supreme Council has ceased?" All at Tuam are well affected to the measures of the Congregation. Lieut.-General John Bourke and Capt. Moyles Bourke are amongst others ready to embrace the motion of the Church. Prays for full directions and information. *Original.*
With a Latin version. (Two Papers.) — Tuam, Sept. 4.

1646.
Newcastle,
Sept. 7.

2307. *The King to Lords Jermyn and Culpeper, and Mr. John Ashburnham.* Denies the possibility of the union of Presbyterian and regal government. If the former be established the dependency of the Church on the Crown will be taken away. Is assured that there can be no satisfaction unless the Covenant be established. Recommends Dr. Steward to them as his accredited adviser in matters of religion. Has received no letters from France by the last packet. *Draught.*

Endorsed, " By London."

St. Malo,
Sept. 10.

2308. *Cadw. Jones to Sir E. Hyde.* Has received two of his letters. Gives details of current news. Forwarded his letter to Mr. Hitchcock. Has heard of the surrender of Pendennis. Fairfax is before Ragland Castle. *Original.*

Endorsed by Hyde.

Waterford,
Sept. 10.

2309. *Protestation of the Clergy of Ireland.* In behalf of the confederate Catholics, a solemn protestation of the clergy's faith to God and fidelity to their Sovereign. Detail the assistance in money and arms they have given to the King. Lord Glamorgan, after he had concluded peace with them, was imprisoned. Refusing to accept an unjust peace, the Ecclesiastical Congregation vow to maintain the Catholic faith, planted by St. Patrick, professed by St. Edward the Confessor, confirmed by Henry II. and his successors; and the privileges of the Catholic Church granted by Magna Charta; and will endeavour the repeal of all penal laws against Catholics. They will bear true allegiance to King Charles, their lawful Sovereign, and will defend his government and possessions; they will also endeavour, by the aid of Catholic allies, to reinstate the King in his dominions. They repudiate any distinction between the ancient Irish and the new English in the confederate Catholics. This protestation to be printed, and published in all parish churches. *Copy.*

By Edgeman. Endorsed by Hyde. Signed by " Nicolaus Fernensis Episcopus."
Cl. S. P. vol. ii. p. 257.

Sept. 11.

2310. *Articles of Scilly.* Fifteen Articles, agreed upon at the surrender of Scilly to the Parliament fleet, between Francis Godolphin, Christopher Grosse, and John Whiting, on behalf of Sir Tho. Bassett, Knight, Commander of the fort of St. Mary, and John Seyntabin, George Ayscue, and Tho. Jennings on behalf of Capt. William Batten, Commander of the fleet.

(Three papers.) *Copy.*

Kilkenny,
Sept. 15.

2311. *The Bishop of Clogher to the Bishop of Ferns.* Encourages him to proceed with all prudence and diligence in carrying out the plans of the confederacy against the peace.—Latin. *Original.*

2312. *The King to Ormond.* Wishes to find a safe way of intelligence between them; begs an answer to a proposition.
In cypher.
A duplicate original; not decyphered. Endorsed, "15 Aug. from Newcastle."

1646.
Newcastle,
Sept. 16.

2313. *Lords Jermyn and Culpeper to the King.* Perceive that neither their letters nor the King's make any impression on the other. They would be silent were not so much at stake. Urge at length his union with the Scotch and Presbyterians against the Independent and anti-monarchical party. Differ wholly from the King's assertion, that Episcopacy is *jure divino* exclusive: there are not "six persons of the Protestant religion" of that opinion. The Crown must not be identified with Episcopacy. The question is, Whether he will choose to be a King of Presbitery, or no King? A sound Irish peace will encourage the Scots to join him. Episcopacy to be parted with only on a full engagement of the Scots for his defence. If satisfaction be given in this, he will not be much pressed in the matter of the Militia. Beg him to employ the French ambassador in transacting the whole, that so the French crown may be engaged. *Copy.*
By the King, from cypher. Endorsed, "Recd. 1/12 Oct. To be kept."
Cl. S. P. vol. ii. p. 261.

St. Germains,
Sept. 15.

2314. *The King to Lords Jermyn and Culpeper, and Mr. J. Ashburnham.* Finds their draught of his answer to the London Propositions against his conscience, and the maintenance of monarchy. So much care is taken for the establishing Presbyterian government, that not even the universities are spared. As to Ireland, their answer is poor and juggling. What if his concessions fail of their purpose! Will rather leave the kingdom than yield in the point of religion. Some day they will persuade him to submit to the Pope. Indeed, "it is less ill to submit to one, than many Popes." Recommends Dr. Steward to them. *Draught.*
By himself. Endorsed, "Sensure upon their draught of an answer to the Propositions."
Cl. S. P. vol. ii. p. 264.

Newcastle,
Sept. 21.

2315. "*Instructions* agreed on by the Lord Lieutenant and Council of Ireland, to be observed by our Right Trustie and well-beloved Sir Gerrard Lowther, knight, Lord Chief Justice of his Majesty's Court of Common Pleas, and Sir Francis Willoughby, knight, Serjeant-Major-General of the Army, and our trustie and well-beloved Sir Paul Davys, knight, Clerk of the Council."

Sept. 26.

Eighteen Instructions sent to those who were to treat with the English Parliament for succours after the peace

1646.

with the rebels was rejected by a great part of them. (Signed) *Ormonde.* Ri. Bolton. Canc. Roscommon. Geo. Cloyne. Cha. Lambert. Fr. Chichester. He. Titchborne. Tho. Lucas. Rob. Forth. J. Ware.

(Three papers.) *Copy.*

See "Dismall effects of the Irish Insurrection," p. 167.

Sept. 16. 2316. "*Instructions* agreed on by the Council of Ireland, to bee observed by Sir Gerrard Lowther," &c. (as above.) Respecting the suppression of the Irish rebellion, with certain reservations. *Copy.*

Signed as above, with the exception of Ormonde.

Sept. 16. 2317. "*Propositions* of the Lord Lieutenant of Ireland, to be presented to the most honb^{le} the Lower House of Parliament of the kingdom of England."

Four Propositions respecting the prosecution of the war against the Irish rebels. Signed by Ormonde.

Propositions of the Lord Lieutenant and Council of Ireland, to be presented, &c. (as above).

Five Propositions respecting recruits, Protestants, and prisoners. *Copies.*

On one paper. Signed by Ormonde and ten others.
Whitelock, p. 224.

Sept. 16. 2318. *Letter of the Lord Lieutenant and Council of Ireland to the Speaker of the House of Lords.* Recite the Articles of the peace; the acts of the Nuncio and the Catholics; and set forth the general state of Ireland. Have sent deputies with full instructions. Trust they shall be enabled to take vengeance on their foreign enemies and domestic rebels. *Copy.*

Sept. 16. 2319. *The Lord Lieutenant and Council of Ireland to the Lord Mayor of the City of London.* Appeal to the City for succours and relief. Give an account of the destitute condition of the army, and what has been done to raise money. Beg a contribution. *Copy.*

Signed by Ormond and nine others.

Jersey, Sept. 16. 2320. *Sir E. Hyde to Lord Digby.* Has received his of Aug. 2nd. Has received no advice from Paris how to dispose himself. Complains of ill-treatment at the hands of the Queen and others in France. [A portion of the letter interspersed with cypher, which is not decyphered.] Believes his brother, (Col. John Arundell), will shortly be with him, for Pendennis is

lost for want of bread. Scilly will probably go the same way. Wrote last week by Mr. Butterwell to Lord Ormond and himself. Desires him to direct letters by Mr. Alford, or Mr. Hitchcock, and no more by Paris. Dick Fanshawe is at Caen. If the King's hand be at the disposal of the rebels, how right soever his heart be, his servants may be easily oppressed. Assures him that he has good friends in Jersey. Wrote to the King a week since. Major Cooke takes this letter. Begs for supplies of wool, hides, cloth, and victual. *Original.*
With a Copy by Edgeman. Cl. S. P. vol. ii. p. 259.

1646.

2321. *Sir E. Hyde to the Marquis of Ormond.* Has received his letters of August 1st. Receives with joy his leave to come to Ireland, and hopes to hear from Lord Digby from what port he shall find a passage. Urges his suit on behalf of Jersey for a supply of wool. Sir G. Carteret thinks the island may be made of great use to England, especially if Guernsey be reduced. *Original.*
With a Copy by Mr. Edgeman. Cl. S. P. vol. ii. p. 259.

Jersey, Sept. 25.

2322. *Lord Culpeper to Sir E. Hyde.* Writes a fourth time for money; suggests means of sending it. *Original.*
Hoskins, vol. ii. p. 11.

St. Germains, Sept. 27.

2323. *The King to the Bishop of London.* Puts a case of conscience to him; "How far he may give way to the proposed temporary compliance, with a resolution to recover and maintain the Episcopal doctrine and discipline." Gives him leave to take the assistance of the Bishop of Salisbury and Dr. Sheldon. *Copy.*
By W. Murray. Endorsed by the King. Cl. S. P. vol. ii. p. 265.

Newcastle, Sept. 30.

With, *A proposition for settling religion.* Proposing a debate by a well-chosen number of divines of each opinion. *Copy.*
By W. Murray. Cl. S. P. vol. ii. p. 266.

2324. *A letter from Scotland.* The King went to Stirling, July 24. Movements of the forces on either side. The King at Dunfermlin; and subsequent events. Lord Jermyn is on his way to the Princess Royal. Has received a letter for Prince Rupert. Begs him to send money.
Without signature or address. Endorsed by Hyde.

Sept.

2325. *The King to the Lords Jermyn and Culpeper, and Mr. J. Ashburnham.* Is well assured of their loyalty. Laments that his stedfastness in the matter of Episcopacy is not understood. Is much moved at Davenant's threat that [the Queen] will retire into a monastery. Has received from them and the Queen, two despatches. *Rough Draught.*
Endorsed by himself, "To be kept." Cl. S. P. vol. ii. p. 270.

St. Germains, Oct. 5.

1646.

2326. *The Lords Jermyn and Culpeper to the King**. The Earl of Crawford has arrived by way of Ireland to propose in Montrose's name to raise 30,000 men to reduce Scotland, and set the King free. Ireland will supply 6000 men upon conditions. Lord Branford is satisfied with the list of names. M. Bellievre has another design which may be combined with this. The Queen sends an express to the Highlands in her own name; and Winter Grant goes to Ireland with large powers. [Then follows a list of 19 names with the number of men for which each makes himself responsible.] *Copy.*

By the King. Endorsed by him. Cl. S. P. vol. II. p. 171.

Oct. 1⁄8.

2327. *The Queen to the same.* Discusses the position of affairs. Lord Crawford has arrived. Has received assurances of friendship from Sweden. Encourages him to hope for a return to his throne. *Copy.*

By the King. Endorsed by him. "Received Oct. 31." Cl. S. P. vol. II. p. 171.

Newcastle, Oct. 10.

2328. *The King to Lords Jermyn and Culpeper, and J. Ashburnham.* Is grieved to find by their letter of the 28th Sept., that his argument concerning Religion does not weigh with them. Will never forsake his conscience, his crown, or his friends. Is experiencing the truth that Presbyterian government is incompatible with Monarchy. The government of the Church is as necessary a flower of the crown as the Militia. Hopes much from the rebels' distractions. Will do all he can to obtain union with the Scots. *Rough Draught.*

Endorsed by the King. Cl. S. P. vol. II. p. 173.

Paris, Oct. 12.

2329. *The Lords Jermyn and Culpeper to the King.* Have received the King's of Sept. 21st. Cannot but still advise him to yield in the matter of the Presbytery. Recommends delay on other points. Montreuil has conferred at London with the Presbyterians; they give the heads of the Propositions. Beseeches him to encourage M. Bellievre's treaty. Winter Grant goes to Ireland. The Queen is at St. Germains; they have received the King's letters of Sept. 7th and 14th. *Copy.*

By the King. Endorsed by him. "Recd. Oct. 17." Cl. S. P. vol. II. p. 168.

Oct. 13.

2330. *Will. Long to Mr. Edgeman.* Reminds him of the letter he was to write to the Prince about the reward for the linen cloth. Lord Branford and Lord Fane are gone to Scotland, present their service to Sir Geo. and Lady Cartaret. *Original.*

---

* At the head of this paper is a copy by the King of a short letter from the same to the same, dated Paris, Oct. 1⁄8, promising a letter at large by the next dispatch.

2331. *The Bishops of London and Salisbury to the King.* Resolve the King's doubt arising on the proposition. The King's determination to return to Episcopacy relieves him from any violation of his oath in complying with the present demand of the Presbyterians. They suggest that the temporary toleration should be made only an accessory, and necessary concession, not as the principle of the proposition. *Original.*

1646. Pelham, Oct. 14.

Endorsed by the King. Cl. S. P. vol. ii. p. 267.

2332. *The King to Will. Murray.* Sends his Answer to the Propositions, with the additions. Instructs him as to the acts of the Great Seal, Ireland, and the Universities. Directs him to bargain for the establishment of a regulated Episcopacy at the end of five years. Offers terms in the matter of the Militia. *Draught.*

Newcastle, Oct. 15.

Endorsed by the King. Cl. S. P. vol. ii. p. 275.

2333. *The King's Answers to the Propositions,* tendered to him by the Commissioners from the Lords and Commons in the Parliament of England at Westminster, and the Commissioners of the Parliament of Scotland.

Oct. 12 and 15.

Three Draughts:

i. *A Holograph* by the King.

ii. *A Copy,* signed by him and endorsed " Sent, but not made use of."

iii. *Additional Answers.* A holograph, addressed "To the Speaker of the House of Peers *pro tempore,* to be communicated to the House of Commons and the Commissioners for the Kingdom of Scotland."

See Burnet's Memoirs of the Dukes of Hamilton, p. 299.

2334. *To Mr. Annesley from his wife.* Complains of his not writing. *Original.*

Oct. 16.

2335. *The King to the Queen.* Trusts she will be satisfied with the account that Davenant, and the enclosed copies [of answers to the Resolutions], will give her. The absolute establishment of Presbyterian government would make him but a titulary King. Supremacy in Church affairs is a chief flower of the crown. Under the pretence of a reformation they will place Ecclesiastical government in Parliament, and the supreme power in the people. *Draught.*

Newcastle, Oct. 16.

Endorsed by the King. Cl. S. P. vol. ii. p. 277.

1646.
Jersey,
Oct. 16.

2336. *Minutes* of a conversation between Sir E. Hyde and Dr. Johnson. Dr. Johnson came the night before out of France, with messages from Lord Jermyn. Their design in France was to make the King tributary to them, that the Scots moved as they directed. Lord Jermyn and the Queen desired it. The Prince's coming into France had not hindered the division between Presbyterians and Independents. The King did all he could to procure peace. The Prince was treated with much familiarity by the French. *Original.*

Cl. S. P. vol. II. p. 276.

Newcastle,
Oct. 11.

2337. *The King to the Lords Jermyn and Culpeper, and Mr. J. Ashburnham.* His remaining in the kingdom is the only way to secure the Scots, and settle a new government without a breach between the nations. Has discussed this opinion with M. de Bellievre. *Rough Draught.*

Endorsed by the King. Cl. S. P. vol. II. p. 278.

Paris,
Oct. 18.

2338. *Lord Culpeper to Sir E. Hyde.* Has received his of Sept. 25. Money and business matters. Ashburnham is at Rouen. The Scots threaten to give up the King if he does not give up all to them. *Original.*

Endorsed by Hyde. Hoskins, vol. B. p. 12.

Jersey,
Oct. 18.

2339. *Articles of Association* entered into between the Lords Capell and Hopton, and Sir E. Hyde, and Sir G. Carteret, for the defence of the island of Jersey, against a supposed design of Lord Jermyn to give it up to the French. Lord Jermyn was to have 200,000 pistoles, was to buy Aurigny for 50,000 pistoles. His secretary, Mr. Cooly, is implicated. Lord Jermyn's neglect of the islands, his intention of drawing the Prince into France; the loss of the sovereignty of the seas, which England, since Dunkirk is in French hands, would suffer by the cession of the islands, determines them to agree upon the following particulars:

(1) Lord Capell's mission to Paris and Holland to obtain information and give warning.

(2) That Sir G. Carteret communicate with the Earl of Northumberland in order to obtain assistance and guarantee.

(3) That Lord Capell solicit relief from Holland against the French.

(4) That the castle of Guernsey be put in a state of defence.

(5) That their signatures shall bind them to the maintenance of these Articles.

One of four draughts, autograph signatures. Cl. S. P. vol. II. p. 279.

2340. *William Loring to Mr. Edgeman.* Has received a letter from Mr. Colston, of Exeter, about the linen cloth. Looks for a reward. Lord Crauford is come from Ireland. Dublin was besieged. *Original.*

1646. St. Germains, Oct. 10.

2341. *Lieut.-Col. Traill to Arthur Annesley, Esq., at Belfast.* Mr. Allen, the bearer, will bring news. Last week's close sitting at Derby-house despatched the affair concerning the Marquis of Ormond and Dublin, who is to be superseded. Sir F. Willoughby went last Friday. Five Commissioners go for Dublin to-day. W. Murray is come from Newcastle. Lord Valentin is in London. *Original.*

London, Oct. 11.

Endorsed. " Recd. Nov. 28, at London, on being returned from Ireland, by Mr Cliffe."

2342. *The King to William Murray.* Has not revealed to any one besides himself the private instructions given him. Disclaims as his own any propositions made by Grignon. Never gave him hope of approving the Covenant. Cannot make any changes in his original purpose with regard to the Militia and officers. *Rough Draught.*

Newcastle, Oct. 12.

By himself. Endorsed, " To answer to his of the 18th."
Cl. S. P. vol. ii. p. 283.

2343. *Sir E. Hyde to Lady Dalkeith.* Many men of honour are running to compound. Cannot tell himself how anything can be honest to recover an estate that had not been so to preserve it. Their sufferings are no more than they had reason to expect, when they engaged themselves in the King's service. Reliance on God's Providence, and honest principles, is now reproached and laughed at. Men would give their Christianity and two years' purchase for the preservation of their estates. As it is, they have to add to the price of compounding so many oaths and lies. *Copy.*

Oct. 14.

Endorsed by himself. Cl. S. P. vol. ii. p. 284.

2344. *Engagement* of the Lords Capell and Hopton and Sir E. Hyde to repay Sir Geo. Carteret (failing public payment) his expenses in repairing the fortifications of Jersey, and provisioning it. *Copy.*

Oct. 14.

By Hyde. Cl. S. P. vol. ii. p. 282.

2345. *Certificate* of Sir Geo. Carteret. To repay Sir Geo. Carteret, as Governor of Jersey, a portion of expenses incurred by him in fortifying and provisioning it; in the case of his papers being lost, were the island delivered to the French. *Rough Draught.*

Oct. 14.

To be signed by Lords Capell and Hopton, and Sir E. Hyde.
Endorsed by Hyde, " The certificate was signed concerning the debt due to the garrison."

1646.
St. Germains,
Oct. 26.

2346. *The Prince of Wales to the Marquis of Antrim.* Has been assured of his zeal and merits in the King's service by the Earl of Crauford. Accepts the offer of his services and assistance. Desires him to keep his men in readiness. Captain Alex. Blackader carries this letter. *Copy.*
(S. P. vol. 8. p. 285.

The Hague,
Oct. 27.

2347. *The Earl of Berkshire to Sir E. Hyde, at Jersey.* Probability of a general peace, and invasion of England. A report that the people of Jersey are separating themselves from the English interest. Is surprised that the Dutch are inclined to a peace with Spain. *Original.*
Hoskins, vol. ii. p. 59.

Dublin,
Oct. 18.

2348. *Sir Maurice Eustace to [Arthur Annesley].* Thanks him for his letter of the 13th, by Colonel Chichester. Defends him against aspersions. Is wholly English, and in that interest. Has been nearly ruined by the rebels. Sir Francis Willoughby is despatched from London, and is now at Hoston shipping horse and foot for the rebels. Trading is now open. Owen O'Neil's movements. Desires him and his father to remember him. *Original.*
Endorsed by Annesley, "Recd. Nov. 29, at London."

Chester,
Oct. 29.

2349. *Sir John Clotworthy to Mr. Arthur Annesley (at Belfast.)* Acknowledges his obligations. Entreats him to remain where he is. Store of arms and ammunition is already sent. Enters into further details of his preparations. Begs him to let them hear from him at Dublin; they are only waiting for Sir Tho. Wharton and Mr. Sallewy. Speaks of what he has done with the rest of the Commissioners. 2000 foot and 300 horse are ready to be shipped for Dublin. *Original.*
Endorsed, "Recd. Nov. 28, at London."

Paris,
Nov. 1.

2350. *Lord Culpeper to Sir E. Hyde.* A draught for 300 pistoles, payable to Clement Chevalier; with his signature. *Original.*
Hoskins, vol. ii. p. 13.

The Camp,
Nov. 2.

2351. *General Preston and General O'Neil to the Marquis of Ormond.* By command of the confederate Catholics they enclose six Propositions, in order to the establishment of their religion and the security and happiness of the King and country.

Propositions:—i. Freedom of religion. ii. Constitution of the Council. iii. iv. Garrison towns. v. Engagement against Parliament. vi. Protestation. *Copy.*
Printed in the History of the execrable Irish Rebellion, p. 166. See Carte's Life of Ormond, vol. i. p. 588.

2352. *Order* of the House of Commons. Those comprised within the Articles of Oxford shall be admitted to compound without taking the oath. *Order* respecting the rents of such persons. (Signed) H. ELSYNG. *Copy.*
Endorsed by Hyde.

1646.
Nov. 3.

2353. *The Duke of Ormond to the Council of Confederate Catholics.* Has received the Propositions from Generals Preston and O'Neil*. Begs to be informed by whom the Propositions are offered, by what authority the Council of Confederate Catholics is established. *Original.*

Dublin Castle, Nov. 4.

Endorsed, "When the Duke writ this letter, the two generals were with their armies at Lucan bridge, with a design to besiege Dublin, and that within two months after they had perfidiously broke the peace which had been made with them."

2354. *Sir E. Hyde to Secretary Nicholas.* Is not surprised to hear he is at Caen. Will write to him weekly. Reminds him of their old meetings at Oriel College. Cypher need rarely be used. Asks him whether the King's approbation of his living at Caen implies disapprobation of Jersey. Begs him, if he corresponds with Newcastle, to keep up the reputation of his friends. The Lord Treasurer consents to the correspondence. My Lord of Borks thinks the Independents honester than the Presbyterians. Many think it safe to take a part, who would willingly have the heads of their own party hanged. There can be no peace in England "till there be some great examples of God's justice on the heads of this rebellion." Fears equal judgments on the Atheism of some enemies to the rebellion, who forswear themselves, and laugh at those who, relying on God's justice, refuse to compound. Concurs with him in the case of "aliening" church lands; questions him as to discipline and government. Pray him to send particulars of the treaty and business of Oxford. Prince Rupert has reported that the town might have held out till Christmas. Thinks the Marquis of Ormond chose the right in giving Ireland up to Parliament. Has been urged by Lord Digby to go with him into Ireland, but their opinions on public affairs being contrary, has sent a refusal by Butterworth. The French Protestants incline to a popular government, and the English clergy in France have neither language nor reputation to reform them. Has returned the letter for W. Smith. Since coming to this island his Highness has borrowed 1500 pistoles for his support. The command for his

Jersey, Nov. 15.

* Note by the editor of the printed Papers. "The letter to which this is an answer, is in this collection, but not published because it occurs in the History of the execrable Irish Rebellion, p. 106. Mr. Carte, in his History of Ormond, vol. i. p. 1646, says the duke sent no answer—'Tis true this is no answer to the Propositions, yet it is not an entire neglecting of them."

1646.

removal to France has been unwillingly obeyed. Has been obliged to raise money by the Prince's borrowing on Lord Culpeper and himself, and hopes to share with Lord Hopton. His chief expenses being meat, paper, and ink. Has received much kindness from the Governor of Jersey and his lady. Lord Essex's death has so disordered Lord Capell's estate, that the latter is obliged to go to Holland for a time. Only Lord Hopton, himself, Sir Edm. Stamel, W. Hinton, Auditor Kynesman, and others, are resolved to remain. Trusts they shall escape at least until Ireland and Scotland are subdued. Has one good meal a day; goes to church Wednesdays and Fridays, and has a good sermon on Sundays, from some good English clergymen. Has resolved to write the history of this rebellion; has written about 60 sheets, beginning from the death of King James. Gives further details of what he has written, which if it were now printed, "would exceed what Daniell hath written of 12 kings; to what a Book of Martyrs will the whole volume swell." Writes with all fidelity and freedom of all he knows. Has appointed it (if finished) to be delivered after his death to Nicholas; for the King, "who will not find himself flattered in it, nor irreverently handled: though the truth will better become a dead than a living man." Writes this history three hours a day. Begs for informations of all kinds. Hopes to obtain papers from London. Thanks him for kindness shewn to his wife. Is a loser by the death of Lord Essex. Will be able hereafter to write longer letters. Takes him to task for having parted with his secretaries. *Copy.*

Endorsed, "My letter to Secy. Nicholas." Cl. S. P. vol. ii. p. 285.

Jersey, Nov. 18.

2355. *Sir E. Hyde to the Lord Treasurer Cottington.* Received yesterday his letter of the 12th (N. S.) Is now confirmed of his stay at Rouen. Reminds him of their Oriel College meetings. Thinks he should have betaken himself to the King's rather than a foreign Prince's service. Jersey, like St. Ursula's field, rejects all but honest people. Has no intention of leaving the island. Rallies him on his preference for the neighbourhood of St. Germains. Is grieved that the hopes of the King depend on French counsels. Cannot imagine why those who refuse the Covenant remain in England, unless they are of "Jack Mince's mind," in the "Bowling Green." Thinks Lord Essex's death will discompose the Marquis. The Independents are not to be compounded with. Has not had Sir Toby Matthew's good fortune, in procuring materials for his volume. Is impatient to hear from Lord Capell. Lord Hopton is unsettled, and wants counsel. The ambassador's nephew disappoints him. *Copy.*

By Edgeman. Endorsed by Hyde. Cl. S. P. vol. ii. p. 290.

2356. *Sir E. Hyde to Lady Dalkeith.* There has been no correspondence with Normandy for ten days. Is glad to hear of his wife's courage and magnanimity; which are a barrier against temptation. Reflects severely on certain compounders. Prays her to write to him; and also to the Duke of Hamilton, that he may do her justice with Lord Morton and the family, in observance of the agreement between them. *Copy.*
  By Edgeman. Endorsed by Hyde. Cl. S. P. vol. ii. p. 292.

1646.
Jersey, Nov. 20.

2357. *The Queen to the King.* Davenant's account gives her more fears than hope. Thinks the Scots will hardly deliver him up at Westminster. Has taken measures for the coming of persons from herself to the King, as proposed by the Scots. Has received his letter of Nov. 1, and another to Jermyn, Culpeper, and Ashburnham, with a copy of his Answer to the Propositions sent to him from London. Prays him not to send this, as it would be a desertion of his principles. Ashburnham is to go to the Hague to see to the jewells, and settle a friendship between Prince Charles and the Prince of Orange. Has appointed Lords Jermyn and Culpeper to attend Card. Mazarin. Urges him not to leave the kingdom till the Scots declare they will not protect him. His doing this would destroy their hopes of peace. *Copy.*
  By the King. Endorsed, "From my Wyfe." Cl. S. P. vol. ii. p. 297.

St. Germains, Nov. 16.

2358. *Sir E. Hyde to Sir John Berkeley.* This is the third letter since he has received any answer. Has now received his of Nov. 22 (N. S.) Writes at large on composition, and the inexcusableness of some who now compound. One might as well commit adultery as take the Covenant. Innocence is the best wealth. Fears that the atheism of those who oppose the rebellion will increase the calamities and miseries caused by it. *Copy.*
  By Edgeman. Endorsed by Hyde.

Jersey, Nov. 21.

2359. *The same to the King, and to Lord ——.* Does not know whether the account presented by Lord Capell, Lord Hopton, and himself has reached the King. Sends these expressions of devotion by Col. Collins. Thinks he is doing the King the best service he can by remaining in Jersey and preparing the story of the King's sufferings. Prays the King to find means for supplying wool from the North of England, in order to compose fears in Jersey; and so lead to the reduction of Guernsey. Points out the danger of these islands falling to some foreign state.

Kisses his grace's hands. Can only pray for the success of those who strive to stanch the wounds of the nation. Prays him to present the enclosed to the King. *Copy.*
  By Edgeman. Endorsed by Hyde, "Never delivered."
    Cl. S. P. vol. ii. p. 293.

Jersey, Nov. 21.

1646.
Newcastle,
Nov. 11.

2360. *The King to the Queen.* No man can study more than he has to give her contentment. Has no small estimation of the Militia, which, except religion be preserved, will not be much useful to the Crowne; for it seems more to hold off ill than to do much good; and will do none if the pulpits teach not obedience, and that the Presbyterian will not do. The three years' concession of Presbyterian government would content the Scots, if it were not for their adhering to the Covenant. So far from this offer being looked upon as a disclaimer of the argument of his conscience, his constancy to religion is the more believed. If his conscience be injured, it is by his own want of courage. Acknowledges his weakness in this respect in the instances of the perpetual Parliament, the death of Strafford, and the taking away the Bishop's votes. But a new relapse, such as abandonment of Episcopacy, would argue despair. Is sure the Scots will not engage for him, except he establish the Covenant, and lay down regal authority. Has said so much to clear his conscience. The ambassador refused to go to the Scotch Parliament with the condition that the King should have nothing to do with any capitulation more than to give [the Prince of Wales] full power to execute his authority. Prays the Queen either to procure the ambassador a command to accept his offer; or else that she will join in his way. Is confident that he shall soon be recalled with much honour. Has received hers of the 16th, not yet deciphered.
Draught.

Endorsed, "To my Wyfe." Cl. S. P. vol. ii. p. 193.

Nov. 11.

2361. (*Sir E. Hyde*) *to Lady Isabella Thynne.* Has received hers of Oct. 29. Reflects on the coldness of some of his old friends towards him, which has been noticed by her. They are happy enough in the island. Touches on the compounders.
Copy.
By Edgeman.

St. Germains,
Nov. 11.

2362. *The Queen to the King.* Has received his letter containing the account of W. Murray's demands. Is rejoiced to hear that he has resisted them. Prays him to be firm. Questions his consistency in the matter of the three years' concession of Presbyterian government. Concessions should not be made without the certainty of some benefit in return. Begs him not to yield to Murray's demands as to the Great Seal. Firmness in the future will be the best remedy for the past; especially in the matters of the Militia, Ireland, and the Covenant; this last would involve the destruction of themselves and their cause.
Copy.

By the King. Endorsed, "From my Wyfe." Cl. S. P. vol. ii. p. 194.

2363. *Cadwallader Jones.* A private account with Sir E. Hyde, amounting to 32*l*. *Original.* Signed by Jones. 1646. Nov. 14—26.

2364. *Lady Clotworthy to Arthur Annesley*, (*Belfast.*) Lord Lisle is about to depart. Domestic matters. *Original.* Nov. 28.

2365. *Camillo Card. Panfilio.* Eleven conditions committed to Monsignor Rinuccini, the Pope's Nuncio in Ireland: Rome, Nov. 30.

   i. Free exercise of Roman Catholic religion, with restoration of the hierarchy. The free Parliament of Ireland to be consulted as to the released monasteries, and the three bishopricks.

   ii. All penal laws against Catholics to be revoked.

   iii. A free Parliament, independent of that of England, to be granted.

   iv. The chief offices to be in the hands of Catholics; all disabilities to be removed.

   v. Dublin and two other places to be put in the hands of Irish or approved English Catholics.

   vi. The King's and the Irish forces to join in driving the Scots and Parliamentarians out of Ireland.

   vii. The above conditions, subject to modifications approved by M. Rinuccini, being performed the Pope will pay to the Queen 100,000 crowns.

   viii. Oaths of supremacy and allegiance to be revoked; and the revocation confirmed on the establishment of affairs in England.

   ix. 12,000 Irish foot, and 3000 English horse, under Catholick officers, to be conducted in England.

   x. The Pope's subsidy to be paid monthly for three years, according to the success of the army.

   xi. The first six conditions to be completed in six months, the eighth and ninth in four more.

An Italian transcript, with a translation endorsed by Hyde, "The Pope's promises, by Sir Ke. Digby, Novemb. 1646." Cl. S. P. vol. ii. p. 298.

2366. *The King to the Queen.* Is pleased with her letter of the 23rd. Repeats arguments on the three years' concession of Presbyterian government. Cannot consent to an act of oblivion. Will not think of an escape until the Scots desert Newcastle, Dec. 5.

1646. him. Has written to M. Bellievre to interest European Princes in his cause, and to take measures to oblige Spain not to meddle with Ireland. Begs her to assure the Irish that he will not abandon them. *Rough Draught.*
Endorsed by himself. Cl. S. P. vol. II. p. 304.

Chester, Dec. 5. 2367. *Alderman John Johnson, of Chester, to Arthur Annesley.* Details of his wardrobe; making, mending, and dyeing, by Mr. Brock. *Original.*
Endorsed by Annesley.

Paris, Dec. 7/17. 2368. *The Lords Jermyn and Culpeper to the King.* The despatch, which M. Bellievre has orders from Card. Mazarin to present, will shew him how dangerous they think his project of going to London; and that France is desirous to give him real assistance. Suggest remedies for the unlimited concessions made by the King in the matter of the Militia; and his abandonment of the Irish. Wish him to insist on the Oath of Allegiance if not on the Oath of Supremacy. Think the Scots should be further satisfied in the Presbytery; but not as to the Covenant. Beg him not to repeat his "Sad proposition." M. de Bellievre has orders from Card. Mazarin to enter into a treaty with the Scots; and if they declare for the King, France will also declare for him. The grant of the Militia to the Parliament for ten years, should be made subject to the continuance of Parliament; and it should be resumed by the King alone, not by the King and Parliament. As their interpretations of the verses of Scripture he recommends to their reading are diverse, they can return no answer to them without his comment. Prince Rupert is chosen General of the English forces, the Queen and Prince Charles having answered for the King's consent. *Copy.*
By the King. Endorsed by him. Cl. S. P. vol. II. p. 301.

Paris, Dec. 7/17. 2369. *The Queen to the same.* Has received his letter of the 14th Nov. Is surprised at his giving over the Militia to the Parliament for ten years. Conjures him to make no more concessions, those already made are suicidal. So long as Parliament lasts he is not King. Her own life might be a necessary concession if she came to England. If his offers are not accepted at London, there will be the better ground for future resistance. Ireland must not be abandoned; the Irish are ready to transfer their allegiance. Refers him to Lords Jermyn and Culpeper and M. Bellievre, who brings orders from France. Wishes he were as firm in the matter of the Militia as he is that of the Bishops. Can in no way approve the Covenant. Nothing short of an act of oblivion will ensure security. *Copy.*
By the King. Cl. S. P. vol. II. p. 300.

2370. *Sir E. Hyde to Sir Baldwin Wake.* Has received his of Dec. 3rd. Has heard from St. Germains that order is to be taken in the supply of Castle Cornet. They are left in Jersey only as sojourners; and the uncivil treatment that some have received there is due to the imputations of treachery they have laid upon those from whom they expect courtesies. Thinks that the misapprehensions of others have begotten unreasonable opinions in him. He can expect a solid relief of the castle from none but the Prince. *Copy.*
By Edgeman. Endorsed by Hyde. Cl. S. P. vol. ii. p. 311.

1648.
Jersey,
Dec. 12.

2371. *The same to Lord Bristol.* Is encouraged by his approval of the task he has undertaken. Has heard from St. Malo that Lord Digby is still in Dublin with Lord Ormond, in whose difficulties Lord Bristol's son no doubt partakes. A union of all the Irish for the King's service seems desperate. Discusses the position of the Scotch, the Independents, and the King's party. Ashburnham goes no further than Holland. Censures the compounders. Approves Dr. Hinshaw's conduct. Hopes Sir Baldwin Wake will soon receive supplies. Animadverts on Sir Peter Osborne, and the Governor of Jersey. *Copy.*
By Edgeman. Endorsed by Hyde.

Jersey,
Dec. 12.

2372. *The same to Sec. Nicholas.* Has three letters of his to answer. Impatiently expects his opinion on his staying in Jersey. Has written to Lord Digby's father on the breach between Lord Ormond and certain persons. Wonders at those who venture themselves in the rebels' army to do the King service. Sees no reason for obeying the King's intentions when they oppose his written warrants. Hopes the peace between France and Spain will not be concluded. Dunkirk and Flanders cannot be restored. Fears a French army more than Presbyterians and Independents; but a julep from the North may be well applied to the fever of the South; for if the English are made a conquered people they will never vindicate their loyalty, religion, or their valour. Does not doubt that the Scotch and Parliament will agree. Fears the complications that may arise from the Scotch interference. Does not think they will change Monarchy to Aristocracy or Democracy, but rather change the Monarch for one who shall owe his crown to them. Cannot therefore yet choose his side, Presbyterian or Independent. Though Monarchy and Episcopacy are not so *jure divino* as that all other forms of government are anti-Christian, yet when they are changed he will not look to see good days in England. Butterworth was sent to Ireland for provisions about the time of the pacification. The imprisonment of Sir Richard Grenville was a necessary

Jersey,
Dec. 12.

1646. act. Wrote to Lord Culpeper to intreat J. Ashburnham to send an exact relation of the King's journey to the Scots. All his information of late events has come from Sir E. Walker, who is now in France. Is surprised at Lord Hatton's behaviour to Nicholas. The Marquis of Dorchester will surely not take the Covenant. Cannot submit to the three conditions required for compounding; though the negative oath may honestly be taken temporarily. Inquires whether Nicholas's brother is still Dean of Bristol. Is troubled at the danger apprehended in Sir Thomas Fanshaw. Cannot believe that the King purposed to break his engagement with the Scots, and go to London. Thinks it better to trust God rather than either Presbyterians or Independents. Col. Collins has not fulfilled his commission. Has been accused of a design to deliver up the Prince to the Parliament. Is thankful to hear of his wife's constancy and courage. Would be glad to see Mr. Attorney-General in Jersey. Will have nothing to do with the compounders. The Chaloner who made the foolish speech is son to Sir Tho. C., and was committed ten years before for sedition. Prays him to keep up his spirits: it is innocence that begets cheerfulness. *Copy.*

By Edgeman. Endorsed by Hyde. Cl. S. P. vol. ii. p. 306.

Dec. 14. 2373. *The Queen to the King.* Has received his letter of the 21st Nov., which she answers in English that it may the more easily be put into cypher. Cannot suffer him to rest in errors that will prove fatal. Refers him to the advice already sent, and prays him to recur to it. Will use no more arguments about the pulpits and Presbyterian government. Does not think his subtilty in the matter of the three years' concession will avail. Desires him not to recede from his demand of a general act of oblivion. Begs him to arrange that some persons may be admitted to come privately to him, and the Scots, in order to the satisfaction of both. The proposition to Bellievre is hateful and mischievous. Requests him to modify his message about the Militia and Ireland. Awaits intelligence from Sir S. Crow concerning the business of Constantinople. If Sir S. Crow is recalled, Sir W. Killigrew and Sir R. Brown are the next candidates. *Copy.*

By the King. Endorsed, "From my Wyfe." Cl. S. P. vol. ii. p. 303.

Cart, Dec. 14. 2374. *A Return of the Citizens and Burgesses to serve on the Supreme Council at Kilkenny.* The undersigned have appointed William Howe and John Gould to represent them at the Assembly to be held at Kilkenny on the 10th of Jan. next, in pursuance of a letter received from the Supreme Council dated Nov. 13. (Thirty signatures.)

"A true copy." Compared and examined April 28, 1664.

CLARENDON PAPERS. 349

2375. *Sir E. Hyde to Lady Dalkeith.* Has received hers of the 6th. Private business. So long as the King's person is safe he is not much troubled. Discusses the position of affairs. "When men have turned round a little longer, they will end where they begun, without removing foundations." *Copy.*
Endorsed by Hyde.
1646.
Dec. 15.
(O. S.)

2376. *The same to Mr. Richard Harding.* Has received his of the 4th. Pleasure of correspondence. Current topics, the Lovellers, John Lilburne. Defends one of his friends; recommending candour in judging of others in these times. *Copy.*
Endorsed by Hyde. (This and that to Lady Dalkeith on one paper.)
Dec. 15.

2377. *The Bishop of Clogher to Owen O'Neil, the Lord General of Ulster.* Encourages him. Wexford is the only sea-coast free from the enemy. The Bishop of Ferns and Dr. Peter Butler are especially forward in the cause. Dalton is harassing Wexford, threatening death to Butler and Captain James Nolan. Desires him to collect his scattered troops.—Latin. *Original.*
Kilkenny, Dec. 18.

2378. (*Sir E. Hyde*) *to the Bishop of Londonderry.* Jersey is still Episcopalian. Uses Sir George Carteret's name to recommend the bearer, Mr. Cooter, as a candidate for orders, to fill a vacant benefice in the island. *Copy.*
Endorsed by Hyde. Hoskins, vol. ii. p. 75.
Dec. 19.

2379. *Lords Jermyn and Culpeper to the King.* All the good the King can expect from the better party in London is on that message which, they grieve to hear from his letter to the Queen of Dec. 5, was not then sent to Westminster. This delay, and the quick advancement of the treaty concerning the receipt of the 200,000 have much allayed their hopes that the Scots will join with the Presbyterians and City of London in the King's interests. Think that if he find freedom and safety neither with the Scots nor in London, a voluntary imprisonment with the English would be better than liberty elsewhere, for they cannot assure him that France will declare for him. With all this the Queen agrees. She has been much troubled with the toothache. They are commanded by her, after advice with Cardinal Mazarin, to add that if the King be refused safe conduct by the Parliament and is forsaken by the Scots, he is to choose Ireland, the Highlands, or Jersey; but is not, save in extremity, to leave his dominions. *Copy.*
By the King. Endorsed by him, " From L. Jer. and J. Cul. ¾¾ De. received Jan. ¾."
Cl. S. P. vol. ii. p. 312.
Dec. 14.

1646.
Newcastle,
Dec. 19.

2380. *The King to the Lords Jermyn and Culpeper.* Makes only a few observations on theirs of Dec. 11. Presbyterian discipline would be forbidden by the oath of allegiance. Episcopacy less hateful to them than royal supremacy. Is much hurt at its being supposed he could yield to Presbyterian government. Prays them not to bring him to the hazard of as ill effects as any that his "melancholy offer" could bring about. *Rough Draught.*
By himself. Cl. S. P. vol. ii. p. 314.

Newcastle,
Dec. 11. 16.

2381. *The same to the Queen.* Has not heard from her for a week. His answer to London is disapproved in Scotland. If Hamilton and Lanerick do as they say (which he doubts) his cause is not desperate. 19th. Received her answers to his of Nov. 14 or Dec. 16. Now answers hers of Dec. 11 and 14. Sends a copy by F. Ambrose of his substituted answer to the London Propositions, being that of Aug. 1. No alterations can make the damned Covenant passable. Must uphold Monarchy no less than Episcopacy. *Rough Draught.*
By himself. Endorsed by Hyde, "To my Wyfe."
Cl. S. P. vol. ii. p. 313.

Dec. 20.

2382. *The same to the Speaker of the House of Peers.* His offer of a personal debate being refused, and his answer to the Propositions misconstrued. Proposes to come to London. Prays them to accept this offer as a means to a general settlement. To be communicated to the House of Commons and the Scotch Commissioners. *Copy.*
Endorsed by Hyde, "The King's last message to the Parliament."
King Charles's Works, p. 571.

Jersey,
Oct. and
Dec. 24.

2383. *Collections by Sir E. Hyde.* Fourteen paragraphs numbered 12 to 25 on "Imposition." Eleven paragraphs, "Remonstrance and argument against the King's power to impose in 7 Jaco. published by order of this Parliament." Five paragraphs, "The Lord Egerton's argument upon the Post-nati." 101 paragraphs, "Sir. Edw. Coke's jurisdiction of Courts."* 1–60. "Courts of Parliament." 61–66. "Of the Starr Chamber." 66 (bis) 67. "Court of Chivalry." 68, 69. "Ecclesiastical Courts." 70–78. "Of Ireland." 79–101. "Lord Coke's Pleas of the Crowne. High Treason." 97. "Bribery."

(13 leaves, 20 pages.) In Sir E. Hyde's handwriting, with the exception of a copy of "28 Hen. VI. Stat. de Resump. in Turri Lond. not printed."

* "When he writt this treatise the house of Peeres consisted of 24 Bpps., Dukes, Marquises, Earls, Viscounts and Barons, 106; and the H. of Commons of 493."

2384. *Sir E. Hyde to Sir J. Berkeley.* Would grow melancholy did he not have news from Paris, Rouen, and Caen. Thinks the public interest of the nation will prevail against that of any particular persons. Refers him to an uncompromising canon of the Council of Eliberis which meets the case of the compounders. Evasions and subtleties in taking the Oath are worse than the Covenant itself. Cannot imagine how Lord Ormond can trust those who have broken faith with him. Wishes Lord Northumberland were general in Sir T. Fairfax's place. Berkeley does well not to venture himself in England. Will not share in the guilt of those who would preserve England by a dishonourable composition. Instances the Earl of Castlehaven's answer to those who would persuade him to beg a commutation of his capital sentence. Has often heard the King say that if he could not live a King he would die a gentleman, and applauds him for not consenting to the Propositions. Is much refreshed by his little retirement. *Copy.*

1646. Dec. 26.

By Edgeman. Endorsed by himself. Cl. S. P. vol. ii. p. 315.

2385. *Sir John Cochran, Knt., Envoy from the King of England to the King of Denmark.* An acknowledgment of his having received 2600 rix dollars of Lord Hannibal Schestedt, Counsellor of State to his Danish Majesty; which he promised to repay with interest; and in the meanwhile leaves a quantity of arms and ammunition in his hands by way of pledge, with a schedule of moneys and arms.

Dec. 31.

Endorsed by Hyde, "The arms at Bergen."

2386. *The King's Answer to the Propositions tendered to him by the Commissioners from the Lords and Commons in the Parliament of England at Westminster, and the Commissioners of the Parliament of Scotland.* Assents to the first Proposition; will authorize Presbyterian government, and the Directory for three years. Agrees to the seventh, eighth, and with reserve to the ninth. Promises acts against Papists, Sabbath breaking, Innovations, and Pluralities. Will pass acts for raising money to pay debts, his own inclusive. Grants the Militia to Parliament for ten years. All the above to apply to Ireland also. Approves an act of oblivion upon conditions. Will grant the disposal of certain offices to Parliament for ten years. Consents to the confirmation of all privileges of the city of London. An act of oblivion, a settlement of revenue upon himself and his family, and his safe conduct to Westminster are the Propositions he makes on his side. *Copy.*

Newcastle, Dec.

Endorsed by the King. "A particular answer to the London Propositions which I intended but did not send because rejected by the Scots."
Printed in Burnett's Memoirs of the Dukes of Hamilton, p. 299, ed. 1674; p. 311, ed. 1852.

1648. No date.	2387. *Petition of Sir John Mucknall to Prince Charles.* Has had an engagement with the rebels off the Isle of Scilly, and has lost his ship. Asks for another ship, and for employment in some service. *Endorsed by Hyde.*
No date.	2388. *Sir E. Hyde to [Mr. Edgeman.]* Has received his of the 3rd and 10th. George Carteret promised to pay him 10 pistoles. Has not halfe so much for himself and therefore cannot accommodate General Digby. The enclosed to be sent to W. Hyde. *Original.*
No date.	2389. *An Account* of moneys towards the relief of Castle Cornet.
No date.	2390. *A Balance Sheet,* total 556 pistoles. *Signed by Sir T. Fanshawe.*
No date.	2391. *A Fragment,* without address or signature. Is sorry Tice is slow. The enclosed has been just received by Mr. Diggons. Lady Godolphin has been prodigal in her offers of Sir William's kindness.
No date.	2392. *Account* by Richard Fanshawe of moneys repaid to himself by the Prince's order of May 20; 2008 livres. *Original.* *Hoskins, vol. 2. p. 33.*
1646-7. Jersey, Jan. 1.	2393. *Sir E. Hyde to Sec. Nicholas.* Has received his of Jan. 3rd; but is uncertain whether his own of the 12th [Dec.] has reachod him. Is glad that Will. Hyde is his factor at London. Does not think the Independents will suffer the money to be paid to the Scots, or that the Scots, if they receive it, will go out of England. The purchasers of Church lands will never consent to a peace that will endanger their property. Urges several reasons in support of this opinion, and refers him to the book of the treaty of Uxbridge. Lord Sligo's carriage towards those of Charenton brought discredit on the Church of England. English churchmen ought to communicate with Lutherans, and other Protestants, as the best means to wipe away the aspersions on the King's party in point of religion. The business of Rochelle has set the French against the whole nation, and not any particular party in it. Adverts to Mr. Cardonell's overture for the press, but does not think that the proposed tract to awaken Christian Princes to sense of the injuries done to their neighbours would be of service. The absence of the chief elements of the Christian religion, and of the civil obligations of alliance and marriage from the policy of States, makes an appeal to them ridiculous. Thinks the present destruction of Principalities is the just

punishment for the absence of religion. Tells him of the progress of his own History of the Rebellion. Begs him to send materials for details of confederacies; and passages in the war remembered only by Sir E. Walker. Will send the original MS. when it has been copied by Edgeman, who will shortly go to France. Inquires, on the instance of Lord Portland opening Lord Holland's letters, what the commission of an ambassador is. Hears that Lord Jermyn has assumed the hearing of civil causes. Inquires after Lords Lindsey and Portland. Savile's imprisonment at Oxford has proved to be just. Hears that Lord Seymour is with the Lord Treasurer, and is resolved to die in prison. [Sir J. Berkeley] is unfit to be sent to London. Dr. Earles and Mr. Hobbs read with the Prince. May go to Caen, but not to Paris. Mislikes Irish affairs. Wishes him a good new year. *Copy.*
By Edgeman. Cl. S. P. vol. ii. p. 317.

2394. *Sir E. Hyde to the Lord Treasurer Cottington.* Has received his of Dec. 19th. Is concerned at an affront put upon him. Wonders that those who desire repose do not choose this convenient island. Inquires after Lord Hatton and the Lord Keeper. The troops, whom promised by France were not even levied, nor was there any purpose to levy them. The Hamburg ship was not sold under the writer's warrant, but under that of the Prince, who at Sir George Parrey's request reversed Dr. Martin's knavish sentence of disunision. Suggests that Mr. Jones's accounts be taken by the auditor. Is glad to have his encouragement to look further after the business of Bristol. Approves Lord Seymour's resolution. Thinks Lord Saye's motion will do more hurt than Lord Northumberland's; for the Independents would not do that which would endanger their best titles to their estates. There is little danger of the success of any French attempt on these islands. Would be glad to hear that Parliament was adjourned to Oxford, even if Cromwell were left Governor of London. Approves, on the whole, of the City Petition. Begs him to send his judgment on the writer's stay in the island. *Copy.*
By Edgeman. Cl. S. P. vol. ii. p. 319.

2395. *The same to the Earl of Bristol.* Thanks him for his of Jan. 4th. Begs him to send particulars that may serve as materials for the History he is writing. Thinks the Scots will not desert the King. Lord Digby will probably send him an account from Ireland. No more believes that Digby is Lieut.-General of the Horse than that the Nuncio has twice given him the lie. Will observe his commands with Sir Baldwin Wake. Upon hearing from the latter in September last,

1646-7.

Jersey,*
Jan. 1.

Jan. 1.

* See Chevalier's account, of which an abstract is given in the second report of the Historical Commission, 1871.

1646-7. the writer, with Lords Capell and Hopton, urged the Prince to relieve him. Has had no answer from Paris on the subject.
Copy.
By Edgeman.   Cl. S. P. vol. II. p. 321.

Jersey,
Jan. 1.

2396. *Sir E. Hyde to Dr. John Earles.* Takes him to task for laziness and bad writing. Nothing can be more diametrically opposite than the Covenant and the aims of the Independents. Wishes he was as sure that the King would not desert his principles as he is that the Scots will not desert the King. Is glad that the Doctor is so well at London; and of the recovery of the Dean of St. Paul's. Reflects on Mr. Cressy's taking Orders in the Roman Catholic Church; thinks that if a clergyman of the Church of England joins the former Church he should remain a layman. Sydney Godolphin has left Mr. Hobbs a legacy of 200l. Inquires after the Bp. of Salisbury.
Copy.
By Edgeman.   Cl. S. P. vol. II. p. 322.

Jersey,
Jan. 1.

2397. *The same to Lord Jermyn.* Thanks him for his favour in his last to the Governor, who makes much of the writer. They study without his Tully, and serve God without his velvet, though they would be the better for both. Has great faith in the Scots. Wishes they were all back in that ill-inhabited city, which is pleasanter than either Paris or Jersey.
Copy.
By Edgeman.   Cl. S. P. vol. II. p. 323.

Jersey,
Jan. 1..

2398. *The same to Lord Culpeper.* Complains of his neglect of him. Begs him to dispatch the warrant from the Prince concerning the ship. The merchants call for it weekly. *Copy.*
By Edgeman.

Jersey,
Jan. 1.

2399. *The same to Sir Tho. Dayrell, at Paris.* Has received his of Dec. 31st. Trusts they shall meet again in England; or if he gets tired of Paris before long, then in Jersey.
Copy.
By Edgeman.

Newcastle,
Jan. 1.

2400. *The King to the Queen.* Has been a strict prisoner these four days. Now that it is clear that the demands concerning religion are destructive both to Crown and conscience, the Queen and Prince must declare publicly that they will dissuade the King from granting more; for if it is supposed that the Prince will grant more than his father, the King's life is not safe. In this F. Ambrose and Montreuil concur. The former goes to France next Monday. Commends himself and the Prince to her care. *Rough Draught.*
By himself.   Endorsed, "To my Wife."   Cl. S. P. vol. II. p. 324.

2401. *The King to Ormond.* Has received with much contentment the large despatch from Ormond and Digby of the 2nd and 3rd Dec. *Original.* 1646-7. Newcastle, Jan. 5.
Cypher. In duplicate, not decyphered.

2402. *Sir E. Hyde to Capt. St. John.* Has received his of the 4th of Jan., and three others from St. Malo. Desires him to send letters by Mr. Nicholls, at Sir Richard Browne's, the King's resident. Begs him to send a book on the Ecclesiastical Orders of his Church. Is not at all satisfied by the Protestation of the Irish clergy. [Sept. 10, 1646.] *Copy.* Jersey, Jan. 6.
By Edgeman.

2403. *The same to Capt. Brett.* Has received his of Dec. 25 and Jan. 4th. Has sent his letter to Mr. Alex. James's house, but finds he has left the island. Returns the Irish Protestation. Thinks the protesters are ignorant of the true history of their own religion. The Catholics cannot do better than preserve the King's power over the laws. *Copy.* Jersey, Jan. 6.
By Edgeman. Cl. S. P. vol. ii. p. 324.

2404. *The same to Dr. Creighton, Dean of St. Buryan's, Cornwall.* Has received his of Dec. 15th; but has had no answer to his own letter of Dec. 12th. Begs him to send a Greek Test. and Grotius's Comment. Asks the explanation of a passage from the first book of Cicero's Offices, on the military oath. Wishes to understand the Ecclesiastical position of the people with whom Dr. Creighton is now living. Does not look forward to a speedy settlement of affairs; and cannot think the Scotch will desert their King. *Copy.* Jan. 8.
By Edgeman.

2405. *The same to Lord Jermyn.* Has received his of the 8th [N. S.]. Is not alarmed at the King's removal to Holmby. The message is a prudent one. Is willing to let Presbyterians and Independents fight it out. Discusses the relative position of parties, as in former letters. *Copy.* Jersey, Jan. 8.
By Edgeman.

2406. *The same to Lord Culpeper.* Has received his of Jan. 5th. Is much relieved to hear from him at last. Thanks him for the enclosure by Sir Edw. Walker, and other helps towards his History of the Rebellion; of the progress of which he gives details. Prays for further materials. Urges several arguments in the matter of the warrant for the ship (Jan. 1), which must be sent immediately. Does not think the Scots will leave the King, or the kingdom. Trusts that the King will listen to none who would have him leave his dominions; so will he "be glorious to posterity." Inquires about a duel in which Thomas Sandys was concerned. *Copy.* Jersey, Jan. 8.
By Edgeman. Cl. S. P. vol. ii. p. 325.

1646-7.
Jersey,
Jan. 7.

2407. *Sir E. Hyde to Sir John Berkeley.* Has received his of Jan. 9th. Answers complaints of negligence and reservedness in writing to him. Wrote to the King last month, and the Duke of Hamilton, by Colonel Collins, who is now at Paris. Begs him to require the packet of Colonel Collins, and send it on by Lady Dalkeith. *Copy.*
By Edgeman. Cl. S. P. vol. ii. p. 327.

Jersey,
Jan. 8.

2408. *The same to Dr. Stewart.* Is glad to hear of his recovery. Wishes he could send as good an account of the King's mind as of his body. Prays him to send materials for the History of the Rebellion; as to the treaty of Uxbridge, and the Archbishop of Canterbury; also to verify a quotation from Grotius, on the rights of banished Kings, bk. ii. ch. 18, De Juro Belli et Pacis. *Copy.*
By Edgeman. Cl. S. P. vol. ii. p. 329.

Jersey,
Jan. 8.

2409. *The same to Dr. Earles.* Upbraids him with not writing. Puts a query to him upon the extent of the *Charitas Patriæ.* Quotes examples of Alcibiades and Jocasta. *Copy.*
By Edgeman. Endorsed by Hyde. Cl. S. P. vol. ii. p. 329.

Jersey,
Jan. 8.

2410. *The same to Lady Dalkeith.* Has not heard from her for a month. Speaks of the London plots. Begs her not to be dispirited on account of the distractions of the time. Relief will come soon. *Copy.*
By Edgeman.

Newcastle,
Jan. 9.

2411. *The King to the Lords Jermyn and Culpeper.* Theirs of Dec. 20 has made him wonder not a little. Their corrections of his message would have done more harm than good. Thought that they had relied on Francis declaring for him if he were a prisoner. Neither the Highlands, Ireland, nor Jersey are open to him; the only question now is, whether he shall be a prisoner in England or Scotland. Recommends to them the opinion he sent the Queen concerning her and the Prince's declaration. *Rough Draught.*
By himself. Endorsed as above. Cl. S. P. vol. ii. p. 329.

Jersey,
Jan. 10.

2412. *Sir E. Hyde to Mr. Joseph Jane.* Has received his of the 10th [N. S.] Discusses current affairs. Begs his service to Lord Hatton. Has no confidence in the fair appearance of things in Ireland. Mentions Mr. Jones, Mr. Rashleigh, and his cousin John Jane. *Copy.*
By Edgeman. Partly printed in Hopkins, vol. ii. p. 80.

Paris,
Jan. 11.

2413. *News from Paris.* The Prince of Condé's corps has made a progress through the city, and is now at St. Vallery. The Prince has entered the Council. The Parliament of Paris

has been debating on duties on merchandise. There are still
disturbances at Montpellier. The Count of Harcourt is returned to Barcelona. Caro is taken to secure l'iombino.
Father Philip, the Queen's confessor, is dead.

1646-7.

2414. *Mr. John Croft to Mr. Edgeman.* Has been in the
country for eighteen months. Is now with Lady Butler. Has
spent a merry Christmas. *Original.*

London,
Jan. 11.

2415. *Certificate* of expenses paid for the Lords Lieutenants
of Ireland, June 30, 1641; July 30, 1642; June 27, 1646;
Jan. 14, 164⅞. (Signed) H. ALDRICH.

June 30,
1641—
Jan. 14,
164⅞.

2416. *Extracts of Letters of Intelligence.* Commissioners
appointed to receive the King. The French ambassador is
coming to London. Several Malignants and tub preachers are
apprehended. A letter of the King's has been intercepted.
Infamous books are printed. The West-country soldiers are
marching towards London. *Copy.*

Jan. 1⅟.

   Endorsed by Hyde.   Partly printed in Cl. S. P. vol. ii. App.

2417. *Extracts of Letters of Intelligence.* Reports about
Sir H. Vane, jun., and the Scots Commissioners. The Earls
of Pembroke and Northumberland will impeach Mr. Lloyd.
The former carries messages from the King's children to their
father. Particulars of the King's attendants. The Lords have
suspended the letter of the Commons to be sent to France.
Items of current news. Parliament is jealous of the City.
General David Lesley is resolved not to deliver the King.
Movements in Ireland. *Copy.*

Jan. 1⅟.

   Endorsed by Hyde.   Partly printed in Cl. S. P. vol. ii. App.

2418. *Sir E. Hyde to Lord Jermyn.* Begs him to assure
the Queen of his devotion. Position of Scotch and English
affairs. Sends this by Mr. Nicolls. *Copy.*

Jersey,
Jan. 16.

   Endorsed by Hyde.

2419. *The same to Lord Digby.* Has received his of Jan. 3.
Complains that he has sent no materials for the History of the
Rebellion. Points out to him the dishonour of serving another
Crown, while his master is in such distress. Suggests to him
a year's retirement and reflection, after which he may return
with the greater vigour. Prays for information about Ireland,
the Duke of Hamilton, and the Marquis of Montrose. *Copy.*

Jan. 16.

  Corrected and endorsed by himself.   Cl. S. P. vol. ii. p. 330.

1646-7.
Jan. 11.

2420. *Extracts of Letters of Intelligence.* Large sums are spent in public compensations. Disturbances about the Kentish Committee. The differences of the Houses are most apparent in the business of the Great Seal. Sir T. Bendish is to succeed Sir S. Crow at Constantinople. Difficulty in getting men to Ireland. Hudson is in the Tower. The King will have it declared whether he is a prisoner or no. London and Ipswich desire the King. A commotion made by Massey's "Reformadoes" in Westminster Hall. The Scots show an intention to quit England. The Independents incline to a moderate Episcopacy. *Copy.*
Endorsed by Hyde.

Jan. 18.

2421. *Sir E. Hyde to Mr. Edgeman.* Has received a letter from him. Has sent him some money. Personal matters. Complains of the want of conveyance between London and St. Malo. Asks him to inquire of Mr. Dickinson what is become of R. Fanshawe. *Original.*

Jersey,
Jan. 10.

2422. *The same to Mr. Brett.* Has received his of Jan. 13 [N. S.]. Begs to be commended to Capt. Wright. Wishes to send a letter to Lord Antrim. Looks for good news from Ireland, but questions the advantage to Catholics of their present policy, and fears that the English Catholics will pay dearly for immunities obtained by the Irish. Is sorry that the Marquis of Worcester is so much misunderstood. *Copy.*
By Edgeman.

Peter Port,
Jan. 16.

2423.* *Robert Russell to Sir Baldwin Wake.* Has received intelligence that the King is at Holmby. This and the proposed surrender of Jersey move him to urge a surrender of Castle Cornet.
Hoskins, vol. ii. p. 90.

Castle
Cornet,
Jan. 17.

Sir Baldwin Wake to Robert Russell. Nothing shall make him fail in his resolution to hold the castle for the King. Does not understand the intelligence about Sir G. Carteret's surrender of Jersey. Hopes he will honour his resolution. *Copies.*
(One paper.) Endorsed by Hyde.

Newcastle,
Jan. 17.

2424. *The King to Ormond.* *Original.*
In cypher, not decyphered. A duplicate and triplicate. Decyphered on following paper.

Newcastle,
Jan. 27.

2425. *The same to the same.* Confirms his approval of the London treaty, and that with General Preston. He must "repeece" the Irish peace, yet without raining conscience. He is to follow the Queen's and Prince's direction, and not to

* See Tupper's Chronicles of Castle Cornet, 2nd ed., 1851.

stick at anything for want of legal power from the King. Commands him to declare publicly that he will obey none of the King's commands but such as he shall receive by trustworthy hands.
Decyphered by Ormond. Endorsed, " Recd. 6 March 1646."

1646-7.

2426. *Mr. Hyde to Mr. W. Edgeman.* A short friendly letter.
Original.

Jersey, Jan. 13.

2427. *Sir E. Hyde to Lord Treasurer Cottington.* Has received his of the 26th. Wrote to him on the 15th. Is sorry for Lord Hatton's misfortune through trusting Willoughby, who is a notorious libeller, and could injure Lords Dorset and Chichester more than he has Lord Hatton. Is not alarmed at the report of a treaty for delivering up the island, unless the King and the Parliament concur in it. Is glad that Oriel College was so just in the case of the Hamburger. Mr. Jones is to arrive in fourteen days. If the Queen's choice lie between Ireland and a monastery, the last would be the better. *Copy.*
By Edgeman. Endorsed by himself. Cl. S. P. vol. ii. p. 332.

Jersey, Jan. 15.

2428. *The same to Sir J. Berkeley.* Has received his of the 25th. Thinks his last packet containing letters to Lady Dalkeith and Harding must have miscarried. Cannot think the Scots will leave England. Until the King recedes from his resolutions of honour and conscience his case is not desperate. Is not sorry for the admission of the three Lords. Peace can only be made on the old foundations of government in Church and State. Ireland, if relied upon, will prove a reed. "They well understand your condition in France, you do not theirs," so that proposals must come from thence, not from England.
Copy.
By Edgeman. Cl. S. P. vol. ii. p. 337.

Jersey, Jan. 28.

2429. *The same to Secretary Nicholas.* Received his last four letters together last Tuesday. Has heard from the Lord Treasurer. Lady Hyde cannot come to him. The island is secure. Is concerned to hear of his sending some prisoners to London, and others from London to Barbadoes. Touches on Irish matters. Fears some precipitate resolution at Paris. The King's vacillations are his undoing. Gives the character of one of his friends*. Is sorry to hear of the proposition from Charenton. Mentions Lord Hatton and Philip Willoughby; Portland and Willmot.
Copy.
By Edgeman. Hopkins, vol. ii. p. 93.

Jersey, Jan. 28.

* Name in cypher.

1646-7.
Jan. 30.

2430. *Anthony Lightfoot to Mr. Edgeman.* A letter of humour and pleasantry on current affairs. *Original.*
Endorsed by Edgeman.

Feb. 1.

2431. *Mr. William Loring to Mr. William Edgeman.* Thanks him for his of Dec. 26th. Has no news. *Original.*

It nees,
Feb. 1.

2432. *Mr. Clutterbuck to the same.* Has received his of Jan. 3rd and 4th. Complains of the miscarriage of letters. Mentions John Crofts. *Original.*

Jersey,
Feb. 2.

2433. *Sir E. Hyde to the Earl of Bristol.* Has received his of Jan. 23rd and 28th, with Dr. Henshaw's. Explains the method and probable extent of the History of the Rebellion. Mentions the discourse on Kingly government *. *Copy.*
By Edgeman.   Cl. S. P. vol. ii. p. 313.

Feb. 4.

2434. *Extracts of Letters of Intelligence.* Particulars of the King's progress to Holmby. The French ambassador is in London. Twelve Lords have been added to the Committee for Compositions. Details of the course for Compositions. The Lords refuse to pass the Pardons ordered by Parliament. Things in Ireland are in no good condition for the Parliament. The Marquis of Ormond is closing with the Irish, and they are very strong. *Copy.*
Endorsed by Hyde, on the same paper with those of Feb. 18.
Partly printed in Cl. S. P. vol. II. App.

Feb. 11.

2435. *Letter of News from England.* Discusses current affairs. The King is an absolute prisoner. *Copy.*
Endorsed by Hyde.

Jersey,
Feb. 8.

2436. *Sir E. Hyde to Dr. Robert Creighton, Dean of St. Buryan's, Cornwall.* Has received his of Jan. 17th and 26th. His own of the 8th is still unanswered. No apology was necessary for the writer's letter to Dr. Frayser. Though he has no good opinion of Dr. Creighton's countrymen, he is not out of hope of them. Discusses the question of the division of the books of the Bible into Canonical and Apocryphal. Begs his service to his "pretty pupil," and through him to his mother. *Copy.*
By Edgeman.   Cl. S. P. vol. II. p. 336.

Paris,
Feb. 8.

2437. *Tho. Johnson to [W. Edgeman.]* Has received his of Dec. 9th. Money matters between Mr. Long and Cadw. Jones. Mentions a duel lately fought between Capt. Straughan and another. *Original.*

* A paper answering to this description is among the Clarendon MSS.

2438. *Extracts of Letters of Intelligence.* The Court is well satisfied with M. Servient's endeavours at the Hague. News of marriages at Court and at Rome. Movements in Burgundy, Brittany, and Languedoc. The Queen-Regent is going to Dunkirk. The Prince of Condé and the Duke of Orleans agree. Affairs in relation to Sweden. *Copy.*

1646-7.
Paris,
Feb. 8.

Partly in French.

2439. *Extract of Letter of Intelligence from London.* The King has come from Leicester to Holmby. The Excise produces much discontent. Cromwell is dangerously ill. Account of the King and the Commissioners. Sir P. Killigrew is returned from Scotland. Lord Lisle is at Bristol, on his way to Ireland. Captain Marrow is committed for abating the tumult in Smithfield. *Copy.*

Feb. 11.

Endorsed by Hyde.

2440. *Sir E. Hyde to Secretary Nicholas.* Has received his of the 4th Jan. Is troubled that his own of the 18th has not reached him. Looks on the entertaining of Panzani, Con, and Rosetti as a scandal to religion no less than ship money was to liberty and property. Defends the King from the imputation of slowness in declaring against the Irish rebels. A King may be gracious to his Catholic subjects, yet not incline to their opinions. The King's instruction to Glamorgan in Ireland inexcusable to justice, piety, and prudence. Sees nothing to object to the Prince's going to Charenton, but cannot look favourably on the letter to the Pope. In the reigns of Elizabeth and James it was thought well to use clemency towards Papists lest other Princes should deal hardly with Protestants. The condition of Catholics in England and that of Protestants elsewhere. Lord Hopton leaves Jersey within twenty days.
Copy.

Jersey,
Feb. 12.

By Edgeman. Cl. & P. vol. ii. p. 336.

2441. *Extracts of Letters of Intelligence.* The Venetian ambassador declares that the Republic will make an independent peace with the Turks.—French. *Copy.*

Feb. 15.

Endorsed by Hyde. On the same paper with those of 11 Feb.

2442. *Sir E. Hyde to Dr. John Earles.* Has received his of the 14th. Would rather the King should have defended Oxford to the last and been taken prisoner, than have thrown himself into the arms of the Scots. Tells him the motives of his question concerning *Charitas Patriæ.* Is opposed to the employment of any foreign force, and is not sorry to hear that there is no danger of such interference with the experience and

Jersey,
Feb. 12.

1646-7. interest of the nation. Prays him to send relations of military affairs, and of the transactions with Sir John Hotham. Mr. Hobbes's legacy is well assured if Frank Godolphin do not inform against him. *Copy.*
By Edgeman. Endorsed by himself. Cl. S. P. vol. II. p. 338.

Bodmin, Feb. 11.
2443. *Extract of Letter of Intelligence.* A prophetess in Cornwall, who upholds the "old form of Prayer," and predicts the restoration of the King. *Copy.*

Jersey, Feb. 12.
2444. *Sir E. Hyde to Lord Cottington, the Lord Treasurer.* Has his of Jan 30. No religious indifference will enable Presbyterians and Independents to live quietly together. Quotes a judgment of Lord Jermyn on a demand of Mr. Porter.
Copy.
By Edgeman. Endorsed by Hyde.

Jersey, Feb. 16.
2445. *The same to Mr. Joseph Jane.* Has received his of the 16th (N. S.). Asks for an account of affairs in Cornwall during the Rebellion. Touches on Scotch and Irish matters. Lord Hopton goes to Rouen; he himself to the castle. *Copy.*
By Edgeman.

Dublin Castle, Feb. 19.
2446. *Lords of the Council to the King, Queen, and Prince.* Representation of the state of that part of Ireland still subject to the King. They are reduced to great extremity; have no pay. Dublin can no longer support troops. State of Drogheda, Trim, Dundalk, Carlingford, Newry, Greencastle, &c. State of the twenty-seven troops of horse. Stores at Dublin. No means but the Excise. No magazine of victuals. Garrisons are not fortified. Numbers leave them. *Copy.*
Signed by Ormond. Roscommon. Ri. Bolton. Geo. Cloyne. Edw. Bolton. Cha. Lambart. Art. Chichester. Ja. Ware. Rob. Forde.

Jersey, Feb. 24.
2447. *Sir E. Hyde to Secretary Nicholas.* Has received his of the 22nd. Sir H. de Vic is shortly to be in Jersey, being recalled from Brussels, and Mr. Sandys put in his place. * Mr. Nicholls, heretofore secretary to Lord Dorchester, sends constant intelligence from Paris. It was an unkingly act to ask or take good usage from the Scots. The example of the King's virtue will do more than the strength of his armies. France is in no way to be trusted. Lord Percy is hated by the Queen and Lord Jermyn. * Butterworth is in Ireland. Lord Digby's ill fortune there. White is an honest fellow : inquires after his Lordship's pranks at Oxford. The King's confirmation of the new Great Seal is necessary to the advancing

* i. e. John Nicolle, a native of Jersey. Hoskins, vol. ii. p. 123.

upon a summons. "Of my favourite, or his Bill, I know 1646-7.
nothing more than that he hath received vast sums of money
for the King, the whole revenue of the Customs, and these
seizures at Dartmouth, and never made any account.... I
expect him every day.... My Lord Treasurer having appointed honest Auditor Kingsman, who is here to examine and
state his accounts." Relates proceedings in which Col. Smyth
(Sir Alex. Denton's son-in-law), under protection of a letter
from J. Ashburnham, a warrant under the King's signature,
and a letter from the Prince to the Governor, was engaged in
Jersey. Lord Hopton alone is to hear of this. *Copy.*
By Edgeman.   Cl. S. P. vol. II. p. 341.

2448. *Sir E. Hyde to Secretary Nicholas.* Has received his Feb. 27.
of Feb. 26 (N. S.), and two letters from Dr. Hyde since he
came to Rouen. The island is prepared for an attack. Discourses current affairs. [Several lines in cypher]; apparently
the position and motions of members of the two parties. *Copy.*
By Edgeman.

2449. *The same to Dean Creighton.* Has received his of the Jersey,
18th and 25th. Thanks him for the books he has sent. Visited Feb. 28.
Mr. Pointdexter a few weeks ago, but found no books in his
study. Again discusses the military oath. Inquires about
books. Lord Hopton is with his uncle in Rouen. *Copy.*
By Edgeman.

2450. *Credentials* of Mr. Walter Strickland, sent to the Westminster.
States-General.—Latin. March 2.

2451. "*To the Illustrious Assembly of the Confederate Catho-* From
likes of Ireland." A series of expostulations and arguments to England,
induce them to throw themselves "at the feet of the royal Jan.—
mercy," and either share their King's victory or perish with March.
him. *Draught.*
(Sixteen leaves.)   The signature is erased.

2452. *Letter of Intelligence.* The King is isolated from his Feb. 25.
friends. A new committee is to be appointed. The King's
chaplains are refused access to him. If the King refuse the
Covenant and Propositions a declaration will be set forth to
inform the people. The Common Council have received a
Petition. Payment of the Excise is ordered to be continued.
The Marquis of Argyle and Lord Lauderdale are coming to
treat of the union of the kingdoms. Lord Maltravers is confined in his house. The ordinance banishing the King's party
from London is renewed. Mr. Strickland's instructions for
his going into Holland are renewed. *Copy.*

1646-7.
Paris,
Feb. 25.

2453. *Lord Fitzwilliam to the Supreme Council at Kilkenny.* Has followed their instructions towards the Queen, Cardinal, &c. Complains of scandalous reports of himself. Will always persist in working for the establishment of the true Catholic faith and the King's rights in Ireland. Dr. Tyrrel will vouch for the writer's fidelity. Mr. Grant, who had instructions from the Queen to the Lord Lieutenant to grant all churches of which he was possessed, is delayed. Lord Lisle is commanded to be ready to go for Ireland: he is appointed Lord Lieutenant. The Marquis of Antrim must be presently supplied. Lord Wilmot is expected in Paris from the Parliament. *Original.*
Cl. S. P. vol. ii. p. 342.

Jersey,
Feb. 26.

2454. *Sir E. Hyde to Lady Dalkeith.* Has received hers of the 22nd. His stay in the island has given him leisure to call himself to a stricter account than late years have given him leave to do. Although his affection for the Scots has not increased since their last infamous act, he thinks that Lady Dalkeith should forbear to hate that nation. Her pension, though not great, is as much as the times can afford. Piety is the only true guide in religious difficulties. Cressy and Grant, now Catholics, are still his friends. Is glad that she is in no danger of change. The Church in which she was bred, and not herself, should be the judge of controversy. Prays her to keep his letters to the King. Were the writer in Paris, the Prince would not follow his counsels. *Copy.*
By Edgeman. Partly printed in Cl. S. P. vol. ii. p. 344.

London,
Feb. 28,
March 2.

2455. *Letter of Intelligence.* Reports of what the Scots will do. There is discontent among the soldiers against Cromwell and Langhorne. Information about Judge Jenkins. The Earl of Roscommon is fallen mad. There is sickness among the soldiers at Whitehall. Mr. Haselrig has written information of the King's order to remove reports of Star Chamber examinations about the poisoning of King James. The General, Lieut.-General, Mr. Pridenux, and Mr. Allen have consulted on Propositions to be sent from the army to the King. A mutiny among the General's life-guard. Discusses matters between the Scots and the Parliament. Sir M. Langdale and Sir L. Dives are in Scotland. The design of carrying the Prince into Holland. Mr. Maule and Mr. Murray are sent away from the King. *Copy.*
Endorsed by Hyde.

Feb.

2456. *Vote of the Lords* in Parliament that the King should reside at Newmarket with such attendants as Parliament shall appoint, with respect to the safety of his person, and the preservation of the Protestant religion, and the liberties of the kingdom. *Copy.*
By Mr. Murray.

2457. *Mr. Secretary Nicholas to Sir E. Hyde.* The Queen has made a marriage between two of her French servants that cost her 2000 pistoles. She has received her money, but does not pay her servants. *Original.*
　　　In cypher, decyphered by Edgeman.　　　Cl. S. P. vol. ii. p. 344.

1646-7.
March 1.

2458. *The Confederate Catholics of Ireland to the Lord Lieutenant, with replies.* Overtures for an accommodation delivered by Dr. E. Fennel and Geoffry Baron, esq. Eight propositions. Eight questions demanded thereupon by the Lord Lieutenant. Eight answers made to the aforesaid questions. An offensive alliance against the King's enemies is the principal point. Enjoyment of religion. Tenants on the Lord Lieutenant's estates and garrisons are the subjects of the questions and replies. *Copy.*
　　　Endorsed by Hyde, "State of Ireland."
　　　See Carte's Life of Ormond, vol. i. p. 601.

March 3, 4.

2459. *Mr. Secretary Nicholas to Sir E. Hyde.* "I pray keepe it to yourself that I have the sig[n]et." A report that Sir W. Waller hath twenty ships and 3000 men to take Jersey. "What advice you conceive fit to be given if Prince Charles, being sent for by the Parliament, demand it of his father's councell[or]s in this kingdom." *Copy.*
　　　By Hyde.　　Principally in cypher.　　Decyphered.

March 4.

2460. *Extracts of Letters of Intelligence.* Reports of a charge against the King for his father's death. Sir Walter Earle's representations on the King's behalf disapproved by Parliament. Account of the French ambassador's audience. The Presbyterians' Petition received and committed. The City have received no answer to their Petition. The Earl of Arundel is permitted to go abroad, and Lord Capell to return to England. *Copy.*

March 4.

2461. *The King to the Speaker of the House of Commons.* Has received no answer to his letter of seventeen days since. Repeats his request to have some of his chaplains with him in order to help him in resolving the points of conscience. Will not strive for victory in argument, but will seek to submit to truth, and give contentment to the two Houses of Parliament. *Copy.*
　　　Endorsed by Hyde.　　Parl. Hist. vol. xv. p. 333.

Holdenby.
March 6.

2462. *Sir E. Hyde to Mr. Secretary Nicholas.* Has received his of the 4th and 11th. Warneford's expectations. They are prepared for a defence of the island and castle. The Prince borrowed here 1650 pistoles, of which none are paid.

Castle Elizabeth,
March 7.

1646-7. The Governor has written to Lord Jermyn. About thirty of the Irish company are returned. Had already warned Lord Digby against O'Neal. "I will write to my Lord Hatton, but if Mr. Dugdale be in England, I have no great hope of getting much from him to my purpose: I cannot enough wonder at the recommendation still, though now you have told me the instrument, I warrant you the suggestion was to keep the Prince right in the business of the Church." Will read his French book and study that language, leaving his Law and Greek. Has no certainty of the report of the Prince's going into the field, nor of Lord Wilmot being in France. [Lord] Leicester having excused himself from going to Paris, it is likely that Lord Denbigh will go to invite the Prince. Is confident that France will side with the disturbers of England, and deal with the Prince in order to that. Has received the new book of ordinances, in which is published Lord Digby's cabinet with intercepted letters from the King to the Queen, "of which my Lord of Southampton said that all the business was in words and the love in figures." Wishes the King would suffer resolutely; Denbigh would serve him faithfully. Is confident that Lord Digby knew not of Lord Glamorgan's commission in Ireland. Wants more particulars of foreign affairs. The Independents will not give over their designs upon any disadvantage in the House. Parliament will not implicitly govern the people. Is not sure that the intelligence of the Prince's marriage is false. Has heard of the great wedding at Paris; and that Lord Jermyn has received hard messages from the English who want money. *Copy.*

By himself. Partly printed in Cl. S. P. vol. ii. p. 345.

Paris, March 8.

2463. *Letter of Intelligence.* Mentions the carnival, opera, and balls. The Prince of Condé is about to go. The treaty between Spain and Holland is in suspense; and the peace between France and Spain advances slowly; but the peace of the Empire is nearly settled. Cardinal Mazarin holds Corbie. The Duke of Nemours is out of danger of death. *Copy.*

Paris, March 9.

2464. *Letter of Intelligence.* Reports of the King. Riots in Smithfield about the Excise. General discontent at the taxations. Reports of military movements in the North. The peace with Spain and Holland is broken. Lord Goring will take employment under the Spaniard. The Prince of Condé does not go for a fortnight. *Copy.*

Endorsed by Hyde.

Paris, March 15.

2465. *Letter of Intelligence.* Movements of the Prince of Condé and his troops; and of Cardinal Grimaldi. The Count

of Harcourt is ordered to retire to Poigny. The Paris trades- 1646-7.
men still refuse to pay taxes. The Duke of Nemours and
Mdlle. de Guebriant are dead. *Copy.*

Endorsed by Hyde.

2466. *Sir E. Hyde to Dr. J. Earles.* Has received his of March 16.
the 10th. He must not complain of a long letter. The City
petition was signed but by a party of 400. "I think I told
you formerly my author (an incorrupt one) of the testimony
Marshall should give the King. I had it from my Lord
Capell. . . ." The King has given no provocation but that of
refusing an absolute submission; his replies to Lord Pembroke
and Holland struck the party deeper. Is well pleased with
the King's carriage, and not troubled at his restraint from his
servants and chaplains. Cannot believe that more residence
in Earles parsonage at Bishopstone (in this horrid alteration)
is a restoration of the comfort he formerly enjoyed. "How
could you and I live in any tolerable degree of happiness in a
place where all conversation must be snares and all commerce
reproaches?" Either things will mend, or if not, they may be
thankful that they are at a distance. Would not have him
importune Lord Newcastle any further. Must suspend his
confidence in Godolphin's integrity. Is glad to hear Lady
Dalkeith is out of danger. Inquires for Dr. Holden, Tom
Triplett, and the prophetess of Bodmin. *Copy.*

By Edgeman. Cl. S. P. vol. ii. p. 348.

2467. *The same to Mr. Secretary Nicholas.* Has received Jersey.
his of the 16th. Is not satisfied with Sir Richard Browne's March 16.
letter to Nicholas. Sir H. de Vic, and his successor, Sandys.
Can England spare 3000 men for Hispaniola, or are they for
Jersey? That island is now well supplied with intercepted
Irish stores. Lord Culpeper told Mr. Nicholls that a French
garrison would be the best defence for Jersey; but no such
stratagems shall hurt them. Wishes the Prince were out of
France; but thinks Holland better than Denmark. Quotes a
letter brought by Sir J. Henderson to the Prince from his
uncle. Why were so many Lords made at Oxford,—Brunkard
[Bruncker], Bard, Ogle? Heard yesterday from the Lord
Treasurer, who tells him of the King's resolution to live and
die by his principles. It would be hard were the Lord Treasurer sent to Paris. Advises him what to do if required to
attend the Prince, who, he thinks, should do nothing but by
his father's command. Innis is not to be trusted. *Copy.*

By Edgeman. Partly printed in Cl. S. P. vol. ii. p. 347.

2468. *The same to the Earl of Norwich.* Has received his Jersey.
of March 9th. Lord Hopton is at Rouen. Has heard that March 16.

1616-7. the Prince is to go into Flanders with his uncle. The French think that the treaty between the States and Spain will come to nothing. Hopes they will be allowed to keep Mr. Gatford, who is well fitted for a castle. Has received great kindness from the people. Is most willing to serve him. Quotes Ecclus. xxxviii. 24. *Copy.*

By Edgeman.

March 17. 2469. *The Marquis of Ormond to the King.* Refers to his letter of Feb. 20. Has been forced to a second application to the Parliament. Gives particulars of the origin and purpose of the treaty of which he wrote last December. Complains of General Preston's falling off, and the consequences that resulted from it to his own forces. Expected in vain some redress from the Kilkenny meetings. Can hold out no longer. Has received no commands from the Queen or Prince since August last. Hopes the King will approve what necessity has forced upon him. Will soon kiss his hands. With

"An extract out of the Marquis of Ormond's instructions to Sir George Hamilton, intended to be sent to His Mat¹⁰ about the time he was delivered by the Scots.*
Copy.

Carte's Life of Ormond, vol. iii. p. 549, without the extract.

Jersey, March 18. 2470. *Sir E. Hyde to the Lady Dalkeith.* Has received hers of the 8th and 11th. His letter to the King is not now to be sent. They are well prepared to defend the castle. Thinks Lord Digby will hardly escape out of England. Does not censure, though he cannot consent, to certain counsels that seem easy to other men. Has no less desire than herself for their meeting. *Copy.*

By Edgeman. Endorsed by himself. Cl. S. P. vol. ii. p. 351.

Jersey, (the best island in Christendom ever under a monarch,) March 18. 2471. *The same to Lord Hatton.* Hears he is fixed at Paris. Wishes to obtain some of Mr. Dugdale's memorials of the late years. Quotes "He that hath little business shall become wise." Ecclus. xxxviii. 24. Hopes to hear from him "if you write largely and kindly, and like the man I used to feast with at Oxford." *Copy.*

By Edgeman.

March 21. 2472. *Extracts of Letters of Intelligence.* Compositions of the Marquis of Dorchester and the Marquis of Hertford. Details of the City Petition to both Houses. The King has worsted Sir James Harrington in an argument. Particulars of the King's condition. Reports from Ireland. *Copy.*

Endorsed by Hyde. Partly printed in Cl. S. P. vol. ii. App.

* Consisting of plans to obtain time till he can receive the King's commands.

2473. *Extracts from Letters of Intelligence.* Report of the ratification of the articles of peace between the King of Spain and Holland. The Prince of Orange died last Thursday morning*.
  1646-7. The Hague, March 19.

  The Prince of Condé has spoken in behalf of the Count of Harcourt. The young Prince of Orange is more inclined to France than his father. The French think of giving the Swedes a greater subsidy. The Governor of Dunkirk is arrived. The Prince of Conti is to be made a Cardinal.
  Paris, March 19.

  Marshall de Grammont is gone to Lyons. The young Duke of Richelieu is General of the Galleys. The Duke of Orleans is going to the waters of Bourbon. Particulars of the Dukes of Bavaria and Longueville. *Copy.*
  Paris, April 5.

2474. *Extracts of Letters of Intelligence.* News of the movements of the Prince of Condé. The Duke of Lorraine has made fresh overtures. An ambassador extraordinary goes to Rome. Commissioners are appointed to value the lands about Sedan, and those the King gives in exchange. *Copy.*
  Paris, March 17.

2475. *Extracts of Letters of Intelligence.* The convoy of the money sent from London for the Scots. The Independents are troubled by the City's Petition. Mr. E. Kirton is committed for letters received from France. Part of Wilton House burnt down. Lord Digby is in Dublin. Proceeding of the Goldsmiths' Hall Committee. Cavaliers imprisoned for living in London. 12,000*l.* paid to the Scots in London. The Presbyterian party had a majority of twenty in the House of Commons. Hudson is apprehended. Ormond has made a truce with the Catholics. *Copy.*
  Dec. 11—Dec. 25 Jan. 1.

  Endorsed by Hyde.

2476. *The Scots Apostacy* (a satire). Sixty-six verses. The first and last lines are—
  No date.

  "Is't come to this? what? shall the cheekes of Fame
  . . . .
  To afford one act of mercy to a Scot." *Copy.*

  Endorsed by Hyde.

2477. † "Diuers remarkable orders at ye Spring Garden by the Ladyes in Parliament assembled. Together with certain votes of ye unlawful assembly at Kate's in Covent Garden. Both sent abroad to prevent misinformacion. Vespere Veneris, Marty 26, 1647." "Ordered by the Ladies in Parliament
  1647. March 16.

* March 14.
† By Hen. Neville. See Aubrey's letters, vol. ii, pt. i. p. 243, and Wood's Athenæ. Printed in Somers' Tracts.

3 B

1647. assembled that their orders and votes be forthwith printed and published, to prevent all such misreports and scandalls as either malice or want of witt, heightened with snuffs of ale or stummed claret, may rayse to ye dishonour of their said votes and proceedings. J. KYNASMAN, Clerica. Parliam."

(Four pages.) Printed in the year 1647.
A satirical piece reflecting on some of the Ladies of the time.
In Edgeman's hand. Endorsed by Hyde.

London,
April 1.
2478. *Letter of Intelligence.* Items of information. The Independents' Petition. Marquis of Dorchester's fine. Marquis of Hertford's composition. Lord Lauderdale's arrival from Edinburgh. Declaration prepared by Mr. Greene, the chairman for the navy. The Duke of York's health and appearance. Mr. Sedgewick's revelations, and the prophecies of a maid in Cornwall. Proceedings in Parliament and the Council of War.

London,
April 5.
Judge Reeves' charge to the jury, and death. Mr. Hollis, Major Ireton, and Sir W. Waller. Independents and Presbyterians. *Copy.*
Endorsed by Hyde.

Castle
Cornet,
April 2.
2479. *Sir Baldwin Wake to Mr. Edgeman.* Thanks him for his services. Is sorry he is going to leave Jersey. Inquires after his own nephew, Mr. Fanshawe, and Mr. Harrison.
Original.

Paris,
April 12.
2480. *Letter of Intelligence.* Movements of the Prince of Condé, the Count of Harcourt, and the Duke and Duchess of Orleans. News from Holland and Brissac. Letters from Munster on events after the accord at Ulm. Reports of insurrection in Andalusia. The Duke of Guise is returning from Rome. Mdlle. de Pont has entered a convent. *Copy.*
Endorsed by Hyde.

Jersey,
April 4.
2481.* *Sir E. Hyde to the King.* Vindicates his course of action in retiring to Jersey with the Prince; of which the Lords Capell and Hopton, and Sir G. Carteret will give a fuller account. Prays the King to show compassion to his wife and children. *Original.*
Cl. S. P. vol. ii. p. 352.

Jersey,
April 4.
2482. *The same to the Prince of Wales.* Is confident of his Highness' favourable opinion. Prays him to extend his bounty and protection to the writer's wife and children.
Original.
Cl. S. P. vol. ii. p. 354.

* The seven letters and papers immediately following were written when he thought his life in danger from an expected attempt of the Parliament upon Jersey. They were not to be delivered until after his death.

2483. *Sir E. Hyde to the Duke of Richmond.* Confidence in his Grace's good-will prompts him to beg his favour in behalf of his wife and children. *Original.*
Cl. S. P. vol. ii. p. 354.

Jersey, April 4.

2484. *The same to the Earl of Southampton.* Being in danger of death and loss of fortune, he prays him to continue his care to the writer's wife and children. *Original.*
Cl. S. P. vol. ii. p. 355.

Jersey, April 3.

2485. *The same to Lady Hyde.* Comforts her in view of his death and loss of fortune. The above letters to be delivered by her. Commends her also to her own family; and Lord Seymour; the Lord Keeper, and Sir T. Gardiner. *Original.*
Cl. S. P. vol. ii. p. 356.

Jersey, April 3.

2486. *Sir E. Hyde.* "My desires concerning my papers." Names Mr. Secretary Nicholas, the Lord Keeper, Sir T. Gardiner, Mr. Geoffry Palmer, Dr. Sheldon, Dr. Earles, and Dr. Morley to peruse his papers and receive the King's direction concerning them; after which they are to be delivered to his eldest son. *Original.*
Cl. S. P. vol. ii. p. 357.

Jersey, April 4.

2487. *Sir E. Hyde.* "My last will and profession." The condition of his country, and his own banishment from it, makes a formal will impossible. Professes himself a true Protestant according to the doctrine of the Church of England established in the Thirty-nine Articles. Bequeaths his whole property to his wife, whom he desires to rear his children in the true Protestant religion; and charges them never to be so corrupted as to receive in any way lands or other dues of the Church; either as lords, tenants, or owners. Desires also that they be brought up dutiful and loyal subjects of the King. Has no means of giving an exact account of his debts. Arranges for his sisters' portions, and the payment of certain unsecured debts. States the account of Archdeacon Marler's money. Desires his cousin, Serjeant Hyde, and Mr. Geoffry Palmer to advise his wife and children; and commends them to the care of certain noble friends, and his servant, Edgeman, for whom he has obtained the reversion of a Clerk's place of the Privy Seal. Arranges for the repayment of 300*l.* lent by Secretary Nicholas. With the following protestation:—

Castle Elizabeth, April 3.

1. During his service in the House of Commons he always endeavoured to observe the bounds between the King's power and the subject's right.

Jersey, April 6.

2. Did never aim at the King's favour.

1647.
3. Did declare himself before the King unworthy of the place of Solicitor-General.

4. Performed no service but out of the sense of duty.

5. Endeavoured to decline any thought of preferment.

6. Having received from the King the offer of the Secretary's place, declined it as unfit.

7. Submitted to the appointment of Chancellor of the Exchequer out of an opinion he should be better able to serve the King.

8. Has never gotten a penny by that office more than the small fee due to it.

9. Has been constantly impartial in his service and attendance. *Original.*

Cl. S. P. vol. ii. pp. 358–363.

Jersey, April 7.

2488. *Sir E. Hyde to Secretary Nicholas.* Has received his of the 8th and 10th (N. S.). Complains of the loss of several letters. This goes by Edgeman. Discusses the King's present position, and the policy of France. Finds great benefit by reading ill books, such as Lilburne's, Prynne's, and Mr. Milton on Wedlock. Is having Nicholas's book translated into French. Has just heard of Sir T. Fanshawe's going to England. Will never compound unless he fall into the hands of the Parliament. So long as the King is kept from his crown, no man can expect to enjoy his private fortune. Urges many other arguments against compounding. Discusses the business of Ireland. Is vexed at the levity of the managers in France, who conceal nothing from the meanest people. The Jersey boat is not yet returned. The Governor is 1500 pistoles out of purse for the relief of the castle. The order touching receiving the King has been printed. "I am glad to hear that our feminine clergy get any assignments out of their husbands' estates; it is a sign no new incumbents are presented in their places." Would rather take a gaol than skulk up and down the country; a gaol is worth a hundred of compounding. Answers a question on private business with Jones. Sends some of his papers by Edgeman, and begs him to criticise them. The sealed bundle contains his will and other things, only to be opened in case of his death. Expects Will. Hyde from London. *Copy.*

By Edgeman. Endorsed by himself.
Partly printed in Cl. S. P. vol. ii. p. 363.

Paris, April 8.

2489. *Extract of a Letter from Paris to a French General in Caen.* Information about Bellievro's negotiation; and what must be done if the Parliament demand the Prince. *Copy.*

2490. *Prince Rupert to* ———— (in England). The King of France has given him command of all the English in France, with power to make levies. Invites those whom he addresses to enter this service. Col. Dorell will bring particulars. Enclosing:— 1647. Paris, April.

An *Order* from the King to Captain Stradling, of the 'Bonadventure,' to transport the Queen and Princess to the Low Countries, dated 1641. [Erased.] *Copies.*

The first in Cl. S. P. vol. ii. p. 351.

2491. *Sir E. Hyde to Lord Hopton,* at Rouen. Has received his of April 6 (N. S.) by Cornelius [Jasper]. Three of his letters have miscarried. No pies or presents have come. Has a touch of the gout; as has also the Lord Treasurer. Is glad to hear Sir George Ratcliffe is at Rouen. Speaks of the treaty of Uxbridge. The Governor has received orders to take care of Guernsey. Mentions Sir W. Chichele. Animadverts on the compounders. *Copy.* April 6.

Endorsed by Hyde.

2492. *Mr. Justice Jenkins's Answer to the Committee of Examinations.* Denies that his adherence to the King is treason. Argues that the King is the fountain of justice, and life of the law, so that without power from the King the Parliament has no jurisdiction. *Draught.* April 10.

Endorsed by Hyde. Cl. S. P. vol. ii. p. 365.

2493. *Thomas Joyce to William Edgeman.* A friendly letter, with many Latin quotations. *Original.* April 10.

2494. *Sir E. Hyde to Lord Culpeper.* When Sir Peter Osborn last sent a boat of Guernsey, Lord Hopton was informed that Sir Baldwin Wake had become distracted. Wishes to take measures to prevent any misadventure arising from the Governor's distemper. *Copy.* Jersey, April 14.

Hoskins, vol. ii. p. 71.

2495. *Extract of Letters of Intelligence.* News from Ireland. Sir. P. Killigrew brings a report of the King's condition. An epitaph on the present Earl of Pembroke, who is still very weak. Rumour of a duel between Hollis and Ireton. Surmises of what will be done about the Propositions. Report of a libel on the King, and a pretended plot against the Parliament. Items of general news. *Copy.* April 14.

Endorsed by Hyde. Partly printed in Cl. S. P. vol. ii. App.

2496. *The King's Answer to a question about the keeping of Easter.* Easter celebrated by the same authority that changed Holmby, April 18.

1047. the Sabbath to the Lord's Day. Therefore, those who will not keep this feast should return to the observance of Saturday.
Copy.

King Charles's Works, p. 91.

April 12. 2407. *Extract of Letters of Intelligence.* News of the Earl of Pembroke; and of scenes at a church in Eastcheap on Easter Day; sermons by Dr. Soames and Dr. Sherwood. Particulars from the City, and the Parliament Committee sent to the army. The foreign ministers are offended with the Dutch ambassador. An agent has arrived in Ireland from France. Sir J. Munson's fine is abated. Col. Harvey accepts Fulham and London House if the King confirm the alienation of them. A meeting of Apprentices is called. Details of the King's conduct and conversation. *Copy.*

Partly printed in Cl. S. P. vol. ii. App.

Paris, April 19. 2498. *Memorandum* on the war between France and Spain. The Prince of Condé is taking all the troops he can get together into Catalonia. "At Pont St. Esprit he met the Count of Harcourt." The fleet is at Hyeres. Mons. de Tracy has come with the ratification of the treaty with the Duke of Bavaria. The French are unwilling to believe what they fear of the Hollander's treaty with Spain. A tavern-keeper's wife whipped to death for a political offence. *Copy.*

Endorsed by Hyde, "For y'e noble Lieut.-Governor."

April 21. 2499. *Petition* from the Army, with the King's Answer. Prays him "to give himself to be guarded by them unto the head of their army; who would restore to him his honour, crown, and dignity." Answered—

That the King will not engage in another war, but will auspiciously look on their loyal intentions. *Draught.*

Endorsed by Hyde. Cl. S. P. vol. ii. p. 365.

Jersey, April 24. 2500. *Sir E. Hyde to Lord Hopton.* Has received his of the 3rd and 7th by Mr. Nicolls. Thanks an unknown donor for "six faire pyes" of lamprey. They have been visited by a severe tempest. Mentions Lady Kingsmill, Colonel Slingsby, Captain Cade, and Ned Stowell. Criticises the King's proceedings. The Governor of the island is disturbed at the Prince's revocation of all commissions at sea. *Copy.*

Hoskins, vol. ii. p. 147.

Jersey, April 25. 2501. *The same to Lord Jermyn.* Thanks him for his letter by Mr. Nicolls. Has had some speech with the Governor, of whose fidelity and zeal he has a high opinion; and who deserves all kindness from Lord Jermyn. *Copy.*

Hoskins, vol. ii. p. 125.

2502. *Extract of Letters of Intelligence.* Exceptions taken to Lord Lauderdale's credentials. The army is indisposed to go to Ireland. Martin's remarks on touching for the King's evil, and sending the Propositions to the King. Details of general news. *Copy.*

1617.
April 16.

Partly printed in Cl. S. P. vol. II. App.

2503. *Letter of Intelligence.* The Prince of Condé is at Barcelona. The Count of Harcourt has been well received here. The army is to be moved towards Flanders. The King has received a grant of 5,600,000 livres from Brittany and Languedoc. The articles of the general treaty are all concluded except that concerning Portugal. Disturbances at Nantes between Dutch and French residents. *Copy.*

Paris,
April 16.

Endorsed by Hyde.

2504. *Letter of Intelligence.* Lord Digby has been rescued by the Marquis of Ormond, and conveyed to France. Further news of the army and the Parliament. The provincial Presbytery of London sits at St. Paul's. No Independents elected Militia officers. Offers are made underhand to the Marquis of Newcastle and Earl of Derby. The King will do nothing but in public. *Copy.*

April 19.

Endorsed by Hyde.

2505. *Sir E. Hyde to Secretary Nicholas.* Has received his of the 28th [N. S.]. (*Nearly all in cypher, not decyphered.*) Some expressions point to a secret commission under the Great Seal; possibly that of Glamorgan.) Received a letter about Michaelmas last on some private matter, on which he asks the Secretary's advice (*cypher*). Does not understand the movements of the Presbyterians. Approves his declaration on the army's petition. Thought Sir W. Earle an Independent. Warns him against one who promises fairly (*cypher*). *Copy.*

Jersey,
April 19.

Endorsed by Hyde.

2506. *The same to Mr. Richard Harding.* Believes the news he heard from London was true, yet does not think all things ready for his reception. The impetuosity of the Scotch clergy will do more to convert the nobility and gentry than anything else except an army: therefore the clergy must be governed; and that can be only by bi-hops. Wishes more places would declare against the Parliament or army (*two lines in cypher*). Presumes he has received letters with enclosure for the Prince. Thanks him for his advice to write to Lord Ormond, whom he takes to be the most excellent subject of the King. Mentions the behaviour of several persons whose names he gives only in cypher. *Copy.*

May 1.

Endorsed by himself.   Cl. S. P. vol. II. p. 345.

1647.
May 5.

2507. *Sir E. Hyde to Lady Dalkeith.* A letter of friendly banter. "If *Ned be but a poor Platonick he may find some examples to justify him; but you will hardly make him set it under his hand that he is of that sect." Touches on public affairs. Begs her to chide Jack Berkeley for not writing.
Copy.

Endorsed by himself.   Cl. S. P. vol. ii. p. 366.

May 3.

2508. *Letters of Intelligence.* News of the Spaniards approach. The Duke of Orleans is sent for. The Prince of Condé is in the field. The Duke of Richelieu is put to sea. Disturbances at Nantes.

Paris, May 10.

The King and Queen-Regent are gone to Chantilly. The French fleet expected at Tortosa. The Danish ambassador is gone. The Duchess of Longueville is arrived.
Copies.

Endorsed by Hyde.

Castle Elizabeth, May 6.

2509. *The Governor of Jersey [Carteret] to the Earl of Warwick.* Has just received his of Feb. 5. Refuses to betray his trust.

The same to [*Russell*]. Has received his letters of the 5th, concerning the captain taken by an Irishman. Jersey has no correspondence with Ireland. Begs him to convey the above letter to the Earl of Warwick. Denies the truth of the report about the surrender of the island.
Copies.

Endorsed by Hyde, "Answer to the Summons from the E. of Warwick."
Hoskins, vol. ii. pp. 128, 129.

Jersey, May 10.

2510. *Sir E. Stowell* (signed Stawell) *to Mr. Edgeman.* Thanks him for performing some commissions. Mentions Sir F. Dodington and Mr. Trethwey.
Original.

Endorsed by Edgeman.

May 10.

2511. *Extracts from the Register of the Council of State* (France). Ordains that all decrees and adjudications made at St. Malo or elsewhere, contrary to the French King's ordinance of July 10, 1643, be annulled. The said edict forbidding the King of England's ships to bring prizes taken from the Parliament into any French port, or to dispose of them as prizes. Directs that all complaints of the Parliament be decided by a Commissioner, the Sieur Bouchart.

Signed by Phillipeaux.   Endorsed by Hyde.   In French, with a translation by the same hand.
(These ordinances and decrees were obtained by Augier, Resident for the Parliament.)

* Probably Sir Edm. Stawell.

2512. *The King's Message or Letter to the two Houses of Parliament, by way of answer to the Propositions.* Complains that his servants are denied access to him. Disclaims all purpose of withdrawing from his promises. Answers the Propositions touching religion. Consents to the seventh and eighth Propositions. Desires further information as to the ninth. Is ready to pass an Act of Parliament against Papists. Will consent to other acts concerning religion. Reserves some points relating to the Militia. Will give satisfaction touching Ireland. Remarks on the Declarations, the new Great Seals, and the officers mentioned in the seventeenth article. Consents to the act for the confirmation of the privileges of the City of London. *Copy.*

1647.
Holmby.
May 12.

King Charles's Works, p. 116.

2513. *Sir E. Hyde to the Marquis of Ormond.* Writes at Mr. Harding's desire to congratulate him on his arrival in France. *Copy.*

Jersey,
May 13.

Endorsed by Hyde.

2514. *The same to Lady Dalkeith.* Is glad that the Queen received his letter. Hopes to be able to serve her Majesty again. Thinks the Scots will not have power to destroy the Church of England. *Copy.*

Jersey.
May 13.

Endorsed by Hyde.

2515. *Letter of Intelligence.* Colonel Rainsborough is making preparation to reduce Jersey. A fight near the Isle of Wight between Parliament and Swedish ships. A committee from the Parliament go to meet the army at Saffron Walden. Opposition of Independents and Presbyterians. The King remains firm. The peace between Spain and Holland will be concluded notwithstanding the opposition of France. *Copy.*

May 12.

Endorsed by Hyde.

2516. *Anonymous letter*, lamenting the refractoriness of the army. A suspicion has arisen that they are in treaty with the King, who is now strictly guarded. *Copy.*

London.
May 18.

By Mr. Trethewy.

2517. *Letter to Lord (Jermyn or Culpeper).* The differences between Independents and Presbyterians are growing. To take advantage of this the King should be urged not to give way to the Presbyterians. Begs him to use his influence in the French Council. *Copy.*

London,
May 19.

By Mr. Trethewy.

1647.
Amiens,
May 10.

2518. *An Edict of the King of France.* Ordains that captains of English ships, having held commissions (since revoked) under the King of England or the Prince of Wales, presuming to make prizes of any ships of the English Parliament, and bringing them into French ports, shall be treated as pirates, and the ships be restored to their owners. *Copy.*

Endorsed by Hyde. Signed by the King and De Lomenie.
Another copy not endorsed, and an English translation.

Hoskins, vol. II. p. 143.

London,
May 22.

2519. *Bowman to ———.* The Duke of Hamilton, Lord Callandor, and Sir Marmaduke Langdale are taking the field. Cromwell is still detained by the resistance of the Welsh. Mentions Sir Harbottle Grimston's speech. John Ashburnham and Colonel Legge are taken to Windsor. *Original.*

Endorsed by Hyde.

May 24.

2520. *Letter of Intelligence.* How the King's Message was received in Parliament. The City has another Petition in hand. The Marquis of Ormond wishes to justify himself to the King. The Irish rebels are getting the upper hand. None can leave England for the French or Spanish service. Cromwell's report from the army. *Copy.*

Endorsed by Hyde.

May 27.

2521. *Copy of the printed Declaration of Judge David Jenkins.* Asserts the right of every man to be tried by his peers, confirmed by Magna Charta, &c.

Endorsed by Secretary Nicholas and by Hyde.

London,
May 27 &
31—
June 4.

2522. *Letter of Intelligence.* Difficulties about the disbanding of the army, which is adverse to the business of Ireland. Large sums demanded from the City. Opposition to the King's coming to Oatlands. Complaints from Colonel Greaves. Disturbances about the Excise. Independents and Presbyterians squabble. Colonel Rainsborough and the Parliament. The army and the Parliament. News from Holmby. The Prince's colours worn by many on his birthday. Some of the army are gone to Oxford to secure the magazine there. Proposals to raise more men for the security of the Parliament. *Copy.*

Endorsed by Hyde.

Paris,
May 31.

2523. *Letter of Intelligence.* Cardinal Mazarin is with the Court at Amiens. Movements of the army and the Duke of Orleans. Lerida is invested. The Archbishop of Aix goes from Toulon to Rome. New orders are sent to Marshal Turenne. *Copy.*

Endorsed by Hyde.

2524. *The Army's Resolution:* seven articles, subscribed "These are our desires, and the contrary our grievances." 1647. May.
Copy.
Endorsed by Hyde.

2525. *The Army's Resolution and positive Answer to the Propositions.* *Seven articles. The soldiers' queries, signed by many, upon the Parliament declaration that the Petition was of dangerous consequence, and the petitioners should be declared enemies to the State. Twenty questions. May.
Copy.
By Mr. Trethewy. Endorsed by Hyde.

2526. *Sir E. Hyde to Lady Dalkeith.* Has received hers of May 28 (N. S.). Hopes Lord Digby will retire out of Ireland. Gives an account of a difference between two Royalists [names in cypher]. "If men thought as much of Heaven as they do of Whitehall, I am persuaded we should come the sooner to the last as well as to the first." Thinks the Queen should write to Lord Moreton in Lady Dalkeith's behalf. Jersey, June 1.
Copy.
By Edgeman. Endorsed by Hyde.

2527. *Letter of Intelligence.* A post is come for the Commissioners at Holdenby. Many in the Parliament army use the Common Prayer-book. London, June 3.

Council of the army at Bury, where the King has been carried. Further reports from Oxford and London. Rouen, June 6.
Copy.
Endorsed by Hyde.

2528. *Letter of Intelligence.* Presbyterians and the army. Colonel Massey in the City. The army's declaration. The army is coming to Brentwood. The King is in good health. Proposed meeting of the Apprentices. Some members of Parliament insulted by men of the City. The message delivered from the King by the Earl of Dunfermline is not authentic. Answer of the Scots Commissioners to the Parliament. June 7.
Copy.
Endorsed by Hyde.

2529. *Sir E. Hyde to Lord Hopton.* Compares the Church of England with other reformed churches, in regard of Orders and Communion. Instances Burges and Caroll. Discusses Ecclesiastical jurisdiction. Purposes "to write a discourse of the weakness of the consideration of the Church of England of the conformity to other reformed churches." Gives his opinion on the movements of the Prince. Warns him against consenting to any treaty that should lessen the power of the Crown. June 9.

* See No. 2540.

1647.

Defends the King from his accusers [partly in cypher]. Argues on the effect of recent petitions. Begs him to confer with Dr. Steward on the Gallican liberties. Puts him in mind of Major Cooke. *Copy.*

Endorsed by himself. Partly printed in Cl. S. P. vol. ii. p. 367.

London, June 10.

2530. *Extract of Letters of Intelligence.* Proceedings of Presbyterians and Independents. The Earl of Dumfermline is gone to Paris to fetch Prince Charles. Commissioners are despatched to the army. Reports of the King's movements. Fairfax, Cromwell, the Earl of Pembroke, and the Presbyterians. Affairs at Oxford, the Eastern Counties, and in the North. *Copy.*

Endorsed by Hyde. Partly printed in Cl. S. P. vol. ii. App.

June 14.

2531. *Letter of Intelligence.* The army is at St. Alban's, the King at Newmarket. The army's declaration about the Parliament. Presbyterian offers to the King are of no value. Train bands disturbance in the City. Permission given to the King to come to Richmond or Greenwich. *Copy.*

June 19.

2532. *Eight "Heads presented to his Majesty by the army June 19th, drawn into a declaration and printing at Cambridge."* *Copy.*

Endorsed by Hyde.

Paris, June 21.

2533. *Letter of Intelligence.* Movements of French and Spanish armies. A sortie from Lerida. Gallant act of the Prince of Condé. The ambassador from the Duke of Bavaria has orders to propose a marriage between the Emperor and Mademoiselle. *Copy.*

Endorsed by Hyde.

June 21.

2534. *Extract of Letter of Intelligence.* Major Scott sends good news from the army. Proceedings in Parliament. Details of what happened between the King and Colonel Whaley. It is reported that the King will engage himself to the best bidder, Presbyterian or Independent. Particulars of matters relating to the City; the Navy; the Bishops about the person of the King; the Prince's going to Scotland; the adjournment of Parliament; the King's movements; the Presbyterians; and the new declaration from the army. *Copy.*

Partly printed in Cl. S. P. vol. ii. App.

June 21.

2535. *Letter of Intelligence.* Commines is taken. Movements of Marshal de Turenne. News from Lerida. Cardinal Mazarin's nieces are come into France. *Copy.*

Endorsed by Hyde.

2536. *Letter of Intelligence.* The King is to come to Richmond. Relations of the City, the army, and the Parliament. The army holds all places of access about London. 1647. June 11.

The army offers that the Queen may return, with liberty of conscience, and other concessions. Proposals relating to the King from the army and the Parliament. The business of the Militia is the chief difference between the Parliament and the army. Sir Edward Forde is come to the King from the Queen. *Copy.* June 14.

Endorsed by Hyde.

2537. *Humble advice* concerning the business of Ireland, in relation to an accommodation between the Lord Lieutenant and the Confederate Catholics. June 15.

1. The Marquis of Ormond was so far engaged with the Parliament when Mr. Grant came to him, that he could conclude no accommodation with the Irish.

2. That had he not been so engaged, he would have put himself into the power of the Irish, unless they had made their submission to the peace.

3. Three reasons against the pretended accommodation between the Lord Lieutenant and the Confederate Catholics offered by Dr. Fennell and Geoffry Baron.

4. In the face of so great opposition to the accommodation it cannot be carried through.

The Lord Lieutenant should refuse to deliver those places to a faction of Parliament that he has to deliver to the whole Parliament. *Draught.*

By Mr. Poingdexter.   Cl. S. P. vol. ii. p. 370.

2538. *Extract of Letters of Intelligence.* Independents and Presbyterians. Fairfax's demands. It is reported that Scotland is in disorder; and that the King's declaration is being printed at Cambridge. The King is at Hatfield and has his chaplains about him. Mentions the state of feeling in the army and amongst the people. Lord Capell is still under restraint. Fairfax is said to "intend really to the King." The eleven excepted, and impeached by the army, after a speech by Mr. Hollis, left the House. The Commissioners have gone to Uxbridge to treat with the army. *Copy.* June 18.

With notes.   Partly printed in Cl. S. P. vol. ii. App.

2539. *Sir E. Hyde to Secretary Nicholas.* Discusses the position of affairs upon the King's seizure at Holmby. "If the Parliament were wise they would now renew the treaty of Jersey, June 19.

1647.

Uxbridge." Answers in detail his letters, one of June 23rd (chiefly in cypher), and criticises some appointments. Gives an account of the progress of his History; with particulars of events (mostly in cypher). The Marquis of Ormond is the only man who can carry on the war in Ireland. The army has impeached several members of both Houses of Parliament.

Copy.
By Edgeman.

June 30. 2540. *Letter to the Earl of Bristol.* Brings arguments against the article of excepted persons. Mentions the cases of Lord Castlehaven and Sir Giles Mompesson. The power of pardon is, with certain restrictions, in the Crown.

Copy.
Endorsed by Hyde.

June. 2541. *The Account* given by the Commissioners who kept the King at Holmby, of what passed concerning their taking him thence. To the Houses of Parliament:—Cornet Joyce and the Commissioners dispute with the King: Major Tomlins also addresses him. *Copy.*

Parl. Hist. vol. xv. p. 416.

London, July 1. 2542. *Letter of Intelligence.* The army and the Parliament in relation to the King. Dr. Sheldon and Dr. Hammond are with the King. The army and the Parliament. Eleven Presbyterian members have suspended themselves. Lord Lindsay is with the King. *Copy.*

Endorsed by Hyde.

Caen, July 3. 2543. *Sir G. Strode to Secretary Nicholas.* Acquaints him with particulars of the Lent Assizes at Maidstone in 1641-2. Mr. Richards, Sir Roger Twisden, Sir Edward Dering, and himself framed the Petition and presented it to the Bench. A copy was sent to Justice Mallett, who communicated it to the Earl of Bristol, upon which they were both imprisoned, and the authors of the Petition apprehended, and he himself impeached for having said he found nothing of treason in the impeachment of the Earl of Strafford. *Original.*

See Hist. Rebell. bk. v. p. 160.

Lord Craven's House, near Reading, July 4. 2544. *Letter of Intelligence.* Dr. Hammond, Dr. Sheldon, Mr. Crofts, and Mr. Peters are with the King. The treaty between the army and the Parliament Commissioners is begun. The officers' civility towards the King is great. The King's answer to Dugdale about Lord Halton. Cromwell, Hamon, and Lambert have been with the King. *Copy.*

Endorsed by Hyde.

2545. *John Thruppe to W. Edgeman.* Thanks him for his letters. Details of family news. *Original.*   1647. Bristol, July 5.

2546. *Letter of Intelligence.* The siege of Lerida has been raised by the Prince of Condé. The Count of Harcourt's last year's actions are now justified. News of the Spanish army in Flanders, whither the French army is gone. The Swedes under Marshal Turenne are returned with him beyond the Rhine, as they will not serve against Spain without express order from the Crown of Sweden. *Copy.*   Paris, July 5.
Endorsed by Hyde.

2547. *Letter of Intelligence.* The King's movements; aims of the Independents. The King at Caversham. A Petition of London lately delivered to the Houses. Men are enlisted in the City. Alderman Gibbs's explanation at a committee in the army. "Saint John's did lately send to Cromwell that they should not do the King's business so fast; his answer was it could not be helped, because the army was so inclined to the King." *Copy.*   London, July 5.
Endorsed by Hyde.

2548. *Extract of Letters of Intelligence.* The Dutch ambassador has taken his leave of the King. The Prince Elector has been used very friendly by the King. Details relating to the Militia, the treaty, and the agitators. The General's letter to the Parliament on the King's behalf. The Duke of Richmond is at Cobham, but will probably return to the King. *Copy.*   July 7.
Endorsed by Hyde.   Partly printed in Cl. S. P. vol. ii. App.

2549. *Letter of Intelligence (from Mr. Trethewy).* Arrival of the King. News of the eleven excepted members' flight. The Duke of Richmond, Dr. Sheldon, and Dr. Hammond are here. Liberal proposals made to the King. The army and Parliament are treating. *Copy.*   Hatfield, July 8.
Endorsed by Hyde.

2550. * *Heads from the Army to the Parliament;* ten in number; and   July.

The Army's Resolution and positive Answer to the Propositions; seven clauses; and

The Soldiers' Queries, signed by many, upon the Parliament's declaration that the Petition was of dangerous consequence, and the petitioners shall be declared enemies to the State. Twenty queries. *Copy.*
Endorsed by Hyde.

* See No. 2525.

1647.
Hatfield.
July 8.

2551. *Letter of Intelligence.* Mr. Ashburnham must hasten to the King. The votes of the Houses are now independent. The King not restrained from personal interviews or private correspondence. "The Earls of Manchester and Warwick tack about." *Copy.*
Endorsed by Hyde.

London,
July 12.

2552. *Letter of Intelligence.* The Duke (of Richmond) returned home. Favourable prospects. "The Parliament is packing theire listed Reformadoes out of London." *Copy.*
Endorsed by Hyde.

Paris,
July 12.

2553. *Letter of Intelligence.* The Court is at Amiens. There is little hope of saving Landrecy. The agreement between Marshal de Turenne and his army. The Chevalier de l'Escale is sent to the Bastile. "Sarrazin is faine to fly for having made a song upon the Prince of Condé." There is great disorder at Naples. 2000 men are sent into Sicily. *Copy.*
Endorsed by Hyde.

July 15.

2554. *Sir E. Hyde to Dr. Earles.* Discusses current affairs. Is satisfied that they who had an impious design on the King's conscience would not have suffered Dr. Sheldon and Dr. Hammond to have ministered to him. It is probable from the behaviour of the army that things will soon take a favourable turn. There are good hopes from the Independents. *Copy.*
By Edgeman.

July 16.

2555. *Four Resolutions* passed at a General Council of War to be tendered to the Parliament, and an Answer to be given by July 21st. *Copy.*
Endorsed by Hyde.

July 18.

2556. *Letter of Intelligence.* Proposed movements of the army. The King's children were with him at Caversham; he sent a letter to the Earl of Northumberland by the Princess Elizabeth. Col. Birch and his brother are seized in Wales.
Copy.
Endorsed by Hyde.

Paris,
July 19.

2557. *Letter of Intelligence.* News of the two parts of the French army. The revolt of Sicily is appeased. The Venetian fleet has defeated fifty Turkish galleys. *Copy.*
Endorsed by Hyde.

July 21.

2558. ——— *to (Lord Hopton).* Has received his of the 14th. Proposed movements of the King and the army. Difficulties about the dissolution of the Bishops' lands. The Parliament and the Militia. Sir T. Fairfax is voted Generalissimo of all the forces. The government of the Church to be left to the King.
Not signed nor addressed.

CLARENDON PAPERS.   385

2550. *Letter of News to Lord Hopton.* Vote about the   1647.
Militia; nine heads of proposals to be sent from the army. July 22.
The business stands between the grandees of the Parliament,
of the Army, and the Agitators. The King's children have
returned to St. James's. The King has turned away Dr.
Crofts for bowing to the altar. Petitions are being addressed
to Parliament to bring home the King.   *Original.*
                    By Sir E. Forde. Not signed.
            One sentence is printed in Cl. S. P. vol. ii. App.

2560. *Letter of Intelligence.* Military successes and move- Paris,
ments in France.   *Copy.*   July 26.

2561. *Sir E. Hyde to the King.* Is uncertain whether the Castle
joint letter of Lords Capell and Hopton and himself has reached Elizabeth,
the King. Mr. Fanshawe is the bearer of this. Tells the July 27.
King he is writing the story of his sufferings. In the event
of his death his papers will be placed at the King's disposal.
Fanshawe will give the King an account of the islands: Sir G.
Carteret still holding the castle at Guernsey. Jersey has been
much infested by the Parliament ships.   *Copy.*
                              Cl. S. P. vol. ii. p. 371.

2562. *The same to Dr. Gilbert Sheldon.* Has received great July 27.
content by his of the 12th. Congratulates him on the prospect of a redemption of the kingdom.   *Copy.*
            Endorsed by himself.   Cl. S. P. vol. ii. p. 373.

2563. *Hertfordshire Petition to Parliament* against raising a July.
second army or re-engaging the Scots.   *Copy.*
                              Endorsed by Hyde.

2564. *Proposals sent from the Army to the King.* Eleven Aug. 1.
heads relating to the Parliament, *Four* to the Militia, *Seven* to
its disposal in England or Ireland. *Eleven* relating to various
acts to be passed. *Eleven* relating to composition. *One* to an
act of oblivion. *Eleven* to various privileges, duties, courts of
law, tithes, imprisonment for debt, &c.   *Draught.*
    Signed by " Ja. Rushworth," by the appointment of his Excellency Sir Tho.
        Fairfax and the Council of War.   Rapin, vol. ii. pp. 347, 537.

2565. *Letter of Intelligence.* The City prepares for war. Aug. 4.
Tilbury and Gravesend held by the army. The City horse
under Sir R. Pye and Col. Greaves defeated at Deptford. Sir
John Berkeley, Mr. Ashburnham, and two chaplains have
carried the King's final resolution to the army. The King's
prospects are favourable. Movements of the Peers in and out
of Parliament. Tumults in the City. The suburbs are revolted from the City. Hopes soon to meet his correspondent
in London.

1647.
Paris,
Aug. 3.

2566. *Letter of Intelligence.* The Court is at Abbeville. The Duke of Orleans is in Paris. No news since the taking of La Baséo. The Prince of Condé is intrenched seventy miles from Tarragona and six from Lerida, waiting reinforcements. The Bavarian ambassador returns to take command in the Bavarian army. *Copy.*

Endorsed by Hyde.

Stoke,
Aug. 3.

2567. *The King to Sir T. Fairfax.* Writes to dispel the false report that he has consented to the engagement of any persons in the City of London in opposition to the army about his person. Is glad to find that Episcopacy is not abolished nor the Covenant urged against the conscience of himself or others. These and other considerations afford good grounds for hope that the Proposals to the Commissioners of the Army may be the means of obtaining peace in the kingdom. Exhorts him therefore to make good his professions. *Rough Draught.*

Cl. S. P. vol. ii. p. 373. See Parl. Hist. vol. xv. p. 305.

Aug. 5.

2568. *Letter of Intelligence.* The army's five proposals to the City agreed to at Southwark. Further punishment to be inflicted on the City. The Earl of Lauderdale is refused access to the King. *Copy.*

Endorsed by Hyde.

London,
Aug. 5.

2569. *Letter of Intelligence.* Affairs in the City and Southwark. Enthusiastic forecast of events. *Copy.*

Endorsed by Hyde.

Aug. 8.

2570. *Jo. Wilcocks (Secretary Nicholas) to Mr. Edgeman.* Sickness having broken out in Reading, the King and army are gone to Woburn. Expects to receive no more intelligence until Bartholomewtide. *Original.*

Endorsed, " Mr. Secretary."

London,
Aug. 9.

2571. *Letter of Intelligence (from Sir Edw. Forde).* The Speaker's return to the House with military and civil processions. Proceedings in Parliament. A Thanksgiving day and preachers appointed, viz. Marshall and Nye. The Bishops of Salisbury, Exeter, and London, and other divines are with the King. Four counties are armed for the King. The Mayor and Common Council have been to Whitehall, and met the Speaker at Charing Cross. Only eight Peers in the House of Lords this day. Holles and Stapleton have sent for all their friends to be in the House. *Original.*

Endorsed by Hyde.

2572. *Letter of Intelligence to Mr. John Gardiner.* Sir T. Fairfax is voted Constable of the Tower. The King is at Stoke. "Jack Berkeley and Jack Denham" are in Town; "Jack Ashburnham is not far off." *Original.*
Endorsed by Hyde. Not signed.

1647.
London,
Aug. 9.

2573. *Letter of Intelligence from J. I. to J. T.*, at Rouen. Has received his of the 14th. Affairs in the City. The antipathy of the two factions will help the royal cause. The King is very merry, and has his friends about him; his security is the Prince's absence. *Original.*

London,
Aug. 11.

2574. *Letter of Intelligence from Sir E. Forde.* Proceedings in Parliament on Monday and Tuesday. Mr. Ashworth's bill brought in on Wednesday. Col. Titchborne made Lieutenant of the Tower. A bason and ewer of gold has been offered by the City to Sir T. Fairfax. *Original.*
Endorsed by Hyde.

London,
Aug. 11.

2575. *Letter of Intelligence from Oatlands.* The King approves of what has been done in the West, and is glad to hear that the opposition to the Prince's leaving Jersey was not of design. Sends thanks to Sir E. Hyde; well knows the importance of Jersey, and has given orders to Lord Jermyn about it. Highly values the services of Sir G. Cartoret. The army professes much for the King. *Original.*
Endorsed by Hyde. Decyphered by Mr. Trethewy.

Oatlands,
Aug. 13.

2576. *Letter of Intelligence from Sir E. Forde.* Proceedings in Parliament. Sir T. Fairfax and the City. The King hunts at Oatlands. He is very firm for Bishops: he will let those who have not compounded go free. *Original.*

Aug. 16.

2577. *Sir E. Hyde to Dr. Gilbert Sheldon.* Has received his of the 10th. Expresses his satisfaction in the present prospect of a settlement of affairs. Instances Cato's reply to Cæsar's offer of pardon, and vindicates himself from any guilt in the affair of the Prince's going to France. Has read Livy, Tacitus, and Cicero, and written 300 sheets of paper since he came to Jersey. *Copy.*
Endorsed by himself. Cl. S. P. vol. ii. p. 374.

Aug. 19.

2578. (*Sir E. Hyde*) *to the Lord Treasurer*, at St. Germains. Will send the auditor to meet him at Rouen. Prays him to present his duty to the Queen and Prince, and to vindicate to the former his conduct to her and the Prince. *Copy.*
Endorsed by Hyde.

Jersey,
Aug. 19.

1647.
Aug. 29.

2579. *Sir E. Hyde to John Ashburnham.* A friendly and hearty letter. *Copy.*
By Edgeman. Endorsed by Hyde.

Aug. 31.

2580. *Jo. Wilcocks (Secretary Nicholas) to Mr. Edgeman.* Is about to start for Rouen, thence to St. Germains. Will be back in three weeks. Hopes to go to England before winter. *Original.*

Jersey,
Aug. 30.

2581. *Sir E. Hyde to William Ashburnham.* Thanks him for a friendly letter received after some estrangement between them. Disdains all ill-will, and hopes their correspondence will be kept up. *Copy.*
Endorsed by Hyde.

Sept. 4.

2582. *Letter of Intelligence.* Copy of six private resolutions of Parliament. Col. Hammond is to succeed the Earl of Pembroke in the Isle of Wight. A son of Lord Say is to be Governor of Gloucester. Malmesbury is fortifying. Disturbances in Wales and in the West. *Copy.*

London,
Sept. 6.

2583. *Letter of Intelligence.* Has been with the King at Hampton Court. The Propositions will be sent to-morrow, so that the army may be able to interpose, if their divisions do not hinder the business. There is a general animosity amongst them against the Scots. *Original.*
Endorsed by Hyde. Signed in cypher (13).

Sept. 9.

2584. *The King's Answer to the Propositions* presented to him at Hampton Court the 7th of September by the Earls of Pembroke and Lauderdale, Sir Charles Erskine, Sir John Holland, Sir John Coke, Sir James Harrington, Mr. Richard Browne, Mr. Hugh Kennedy, and Mr. Robert Berkeley, in the name of the Parliament of England, and in behalf of the kingdom of Scotland. Can return no other answer than he did to the like Propositions offered him at Newcastle. Urges Parliament to consider the proposals of the army to the Commissioners; upon which there may be a personal treaty with himself. *Copy.*
Corrected by the King.
Another copy with the Earl of Pembroke's speech when he presented the Propositions. King Charles's Works, p. 387.

Sept. 9.

2585. *Sir E. Forde to Lord Hopton.* Gives details of the Recorder's trial. The Earls of Lincoln, Suffolk, and Middlesex, and Lords Rochford, Berkeley, Willoughby of Parham, and Maynard are impeached. The Earl of Pembroke's impeachment is deferred. The Militia is settled. Proceedings in

Parliament. Cromwell has visited the prisoners at the Tower. 1647.
Fairfax is enlisting all the men he can get. Tells a story of
rats crossing the Tweed. *Original.*
   Endorsed by Hyde. Partly printed in Cl. S. P. vol. ii. App.

2586. *W. Dickinson to* ———. The head-quarters of the Hampton
army is still at Putney. Maynard and Glyn are impeached Court,
of high treason. Other items of news about the Militia, Scots, Sept. 9.
and adjournment of Parliament.

 Postscript.—Probable answer of the King to the Propositions. Some of the City Aldermen have laid down their
gowns. *Original.*

2587. *Letter of Intelligence from* "13." Has received a London,
message through Mr. Trethewy. The Scots Commissioners Sept. 13.
are not satisfied with Sir T. Fairfax's passes. The King has
again sent to the Earl of Lauerick. *Original.*
   Endorsed by Hyde. Signed in cypher (13).

2588. *Letter of Intelligence from (Sir E. Forde) to Lord* London,
H(opton). The King's Answer returned by the Earl of Pembroke will not be opened by the Houses until to-morrow. Sept. 13.
Reports and surmises on it. Affairs in the City. Col. Copley
condemned to the Tower. Maguire not yet hanged. Mr.
Giles Strangways presents his service. Mr. Palmer, the Presbyterian, is dead. The City have given their reasons for not
paying Sir T. Fairfax's demands, but will have to do so.
            Original.
          Endorsed by Hyde.
  The signature of this and others of Sir E. Forde is a pseudonym.

2589. *Letter of Intelligence.* Assembly of Parliament. Paris,
Tumult of citizens. A majority of votes against the King. Sept. 14.
News from the army. Endorsed by Hyde, "For Sir Geo. Carteret."

2590. *Sir E. Hyde to the King.* Has received the King's Sept. 15.
of Aug. 19th. Trusts that any misapprehension as to his exact
obedience to the King will be removed. Thanks the King for
himself and the Governor of the island for his favour to them.
Mr. Hinton can give information of the state of the island.
            Draught.
   By himself. Cl. S. P. vol. ii. p. 375.

2591. *W. Dickinson to (Sir E. Hyde).* Begs him to send London,
an enclosed letter from Dr. Hinton. Probable result of the Sept. 15.
King's answer to the Propositions. *Original.*

1647.
London,
Sept. 15.

2592. *E. Upton to Mr. Edwards, at Rouen, for Lord Hopton.* Report of an agreement between the King and the army. State of the latter. Impeachment of seven Peers and commitment of Maynard and Glyn. *Original.*
Endorsed by Hyde.

Jersey,
Sept. 16.

2593. *Sir E. Hyde to Mr. Edgeman.* Is impatient for his box. Has received a letter from the King, which may take him away. Tells him to write to Will. Hyde to comfort him on the loss of a paper; and to — Stowell* on money matters. Recommends him to read Dr. Ossalt's letters, and those of Cardinal Perron, as models of style and despatch of business.
Original.

The Hague,
Sept. 16.

2594. *Sir F. Mackworth to Lord Hopton.* Mr. Mason, a kinsman of Sir Humphrey Bennet, has received an answer from Sir T. Fairfax, assuring him he might come with safety into England. Sir Christopher Lewkenor is bound for England. Discusses English Ecclesiastical affairs. There is a report that Lord Hopton is married, and that the Princess Royal is with child. Lord Stafford is lately come over. *Original.*
Endorsed by Hyde.

London,
Sept. 16.

2595. *Letter of Intelligence from Sir E. Forde.* Proceedings in Parliament. Petition from the Independents of London. Other Petitions from four counties against tithes. "Divers forces are gone northward." *Original.*
Endorsed by Hyde.

London,
Sept. 20.

2596. *Letter of Intelligence from* "13." Relations of the King and the Parliament. Death of the old Marchioness of Hamilton. Rallies his correspondent on a lady at St. Germains. The press sends forth storms of pamphlets, most are against the army. *Original.*
Endorsed by Hyde.

London,
Sept. 20.

2597. *Sir E. Forde to Lord (Hopton).* Hopes he will soon return. Details of the standing army for Ireland voted by the Houses. Relations of the army and the Parliament. High language at a Council of War between Cromwell and Rainsborough. Another part of the army is for the King. Behaviour of Col. Lilburne in the Tower. The Earls of Lincoln and Suffolk, and Lord Maynard are at the Black Rod. Lord Willoughby is not to be found. "Pembroke hath got off, but Harry Martyn . . . ." *Original.*
Endorsed by Hyde.

* Probably Sir Edw. Stawell.

2598. *Sir E. Hyde to Dr. Gilbert Sheldon.* Wishes to know whether the King is satisfied with what he has written to him. Does not understand what is meant by an invitation from the Queen to go into France: thinks he has served the King better in Jersey than he could have done elsewhere. Fears arrest in France. Is not surprised that he is the object of envy; but is not conscious of being unjust to any. *Draught.*
By himself.   Cl. S. P. vol. II. p. 376.

1647. Sept. 14.

2599. *From the Committee of Estates of Scotland to the King.* Nominate the Lord Chancellor and the Earl of Lanerick to act jointly with their Commissioners. *Original.*
Endorsed, "D^d to his Mat^{ie} 22 Oct. 1647."
Signed by Hamilton, Argyll, and eight others.

Sept. 24.

2600. *Sir E. Hyde to the King.* Answers the queries sent by Dr. Sheldon:—1. Did not conceive the King's judgment was declared in that particular; 2. Believed his choice was grounded on reasons that the King would approve. Prays him to speak for him to the Queen. Protests that he has discharged his duty faithfully. *Draught.*
By himself.   Cl. S. P. vol. II. p. 378.

Sept. 24.

2601. *The same to Lord Ashburnham.* Has lately heard from the Clerk of the Closet. Trusts that he received a letter of Aug. 29th. Would write more if he had a cypher. Wishes to be thought honest by honest men. *Draught.*
By himself.

Sept. 24.

2602. *Extracts of Letters of Intelligence.* An account of the debate in the House on the King's Answer to the former Propositions; and of those now resolved on. The army is sending Commissioners to the counties for sequestration. The Presbytery has possession of the Churches. *Copy.*
Endorsed by Hyde.   Partly printed in Cl. S. P. vol. ii. App.

London, Sept. 27.

2603. *Sir E. Forde to Mr. ———.* A short friendly letter, excusing himself for being unable to send no good news. *Original.*

Putney, Sept. 27.

2604. *Sir E. Forde to Lord (Hopton).* Gives an account of proceedings in Parliament; and of the impeachment of the Lord Mayor, Langham, Adams, and Bunch, three aldermen, three common councilmen, and three officers, Colonels Bromfield and Hooker, and Captain Jones. *Original.*
Partly printed in Cl. S. P. vol. II. App.

Sept. 28.

1647. London, Sept. 30.	2605. *Sir E. Hyde to Lord (Hopton).* Has received his of Oct. 2. Wrote on Sept. 16th, 20th, 23rd, and 27th. The Commons have made Rainsborough Vice-Admiral; the Earl of Northumberland opposes it. No issue comes of communications between the head-quarters at Putney and the King at Hampton Court. The City refuse to pay. "Sir Sackville Crow will not present the new ambassador." *Original.* Endorsed by Hyde.
France, Sept.	2606. *Letter of Intelligence.* Report of the treaty between the King and the army. News from London about the Militia, and impeachment of the seven lords. General Gassion has defeated 1200 horse and taken 600 prisoners; but was afterwards killed. *Copy.* Endorsed by Hyde.
Sept.	2607. "*The Proceedings of the Parliament Army after it was newly modelled in April 1645 to the King's escape from Hampton Court Sept. 6, 1647.*" With the names of the Colonels of horse and foot. Drawn up by E. Wogan, till then an officer in that army. (Twenty pages folio.) The first thirteen pages are printed in Carte's collection of Original Letters, vol. I. p. 136, with some omissions. See Hist. Rebell. p. 477, bk. a. p. 498, ed. 1732.
Sept.	2608. *Thomas Bassett, Vicar of Llantrissant, his Protestation,* addressed to Mr. Eltonhead and Mr. Parker, by way of answer to Sir T. Lewis, denying the jurisdiction of Mr. Eltonhead and Mr. Parker, they not holding the King's commission, which Sir Marmaduke Lloyd and Walter Rumsey held as judges sitting in assizes at Cardiff. *Copy.* Endorsed by Hyde.
Sept.	2609. *The Scotch Commissioners to the King.* Cannot concur in the new Propositions, which are prejudicial to religion, the Crown, and the union and interests of the kingdoms. *Copy.* Signed by Loudon, Lauderdale, and three others.
Oct. ?	2610. *Jo. Wilcocks (Secretary Nicholas) to Mr. Edgeman.* Encloses a letter from Lord Hopton. Mentions the duel between Lords Digby and Wilmot. "The Queen hath reconciled Prince Rupert and Lord Digby.". *Original.*
London, Oct. 4 and 5.	2611. *Extracts of Letters of Intelligence.* The King's agents negotiate with the army. The Oxford Commissioners are ordered to press the Covenant and Negative Oath on the University. The Scots are excluded from what concerns England. The Lord Dyall [de Lisle], Sir W. Fleming, and Robert Lesley are

removed from the King. The army proposes to reduce the | 1647.
estates of the nobility. The Scots army is to be disbanded by
the 20th. The King's answer to some Agitators' question about
the Prince. Divisions in the army grow high. *Copy.*
Endorsed by Hyde. Partly printed in Cl. S. P. vol. ii. App.

2612. *Letter of Intelligence.* The Queen has come to visit | Paris,
her son, the Duke d'Anjou, who is sick. Marshal Gas- | Oct. 5.
sion mortally wounded. M. de la Feuillade also wounded.
Marshall de Turenne is in Lorraine. The Prince of Condé is
expected at Dijon on the 20th. The Archbishop of Aix goes
to be viceroy in Catalonia. The French fleet is again at sea.
Cardinal d'Este is sent for. The Duke of Vendôme's process
is now in hand. Prince Robert is come to Court. *Original.*
Endorsed, "For Sir Geo. Carteret."

2613. *Sir E. Hyde to Sir J. Berkeley.* Has greater hopes | Oct. 6.
from the army than from the conclusions of the two Houses.
Begs him to make no unreasonable concessions. If God has
determined the ruin of the kingdom, he has not determined it
by dishonest means. *Rough Draught.*
By himself. Cl. S. P. vol. ii. p. 379.

2614. *Sir E. Forde to Lord (Hopton).* "Sir Edward Bayn- | Paris,
ton's son was suspended the House for his activity among the | Oct. 6.
'Prentices;" others were accused. Glyn and Maynard will
have to appear to-morrow. "Two votes were sent the City
from the Houses," one to dismantle the line of communication,
the other to pay 5000*l.* Indictment and sentence of Col. Poins
and others. Col. Hammond is made Governor of the Isle of
Wight. Military movements in Wales and in the West.
Original.
Endorsed by Hyde, "6. 8ber."

2615. *Jo. Wilcocks (Secretary Nicholas) to Mr. Edgeman.* | Oct. 7.
Has received his of Oct. 7/17, and two letters from the Chancellor of the 24th and 25th Sept. (O. S.). Has seen the
apology, "though the Ea. of Bristol keeps it secret." Some
items of news from England. *Original.*

2616. *Letter of Intelligence.* The Propositions are being | London,
considered in Parliament. The King has sent for the Marquis | Oct. 7.
of Hertford, the Marquis of Ormond, the Earl of Southampton,
and the Duke of Richmond, and they are admitted. Parliament has voted 8000*l.* (or 6000) to be paid monthly to the
army. Opposition in Gloucestershire and at Marlborough.
Ministers in the City have petitioned the House to be per-

1647. mitted to exercise their office without ordination. Lilburne's faction intend to impeach Sir Tho. Cromwell. "Yesterday came a message to the House by Fleetwood, Waller, and another." Cromwell and Ireton have spoken for the King. Fairfax is in London. Danger of rebellion in the North. *Copy.*
Endorsed by Hyde.

Caen, Oct. 8. 2617. *Jo. Wilcocks (Secretary Nicholas) to Mr. Edgeman.* Sends some letters and pamphlets of Lord Hopton for Sir E. Hyde. Asks for "stirrup stockinges," and "worsted slides." Mentions current reports. *Original.*

Oct. 10. 2618. *The same to the same.* Thanks him for his letter of the 5th. Gives further directions about the underclothes he had ordered. Has not heard from Sir E. Hyde since Mr. Hinton came. Inquires where Mr. Hill is. *Original.*

Oct. 11. 2619. *The same to the same.* Has received his of Oct. 7th and 12th, and one from the Chancellor. "The Earl of Downe hath been here these ten days." *Original.*

Oct. 11. 2620. *Sir E. Hyde to the same.* Has received his of 14th (N. S.). Approves his correspondence with Thrupp. Details of private money matters. *Original.*

Paris, Oct. 11. 2621. *Military News.* The Duke of Anjou is better. There is talk of the Prince of Wales going to Fontainbleau. "Sens being rendered upon composition, 'tis here deliberated to raze that place, and to goe presently to the siege of Douay or Armentiers, leaving Dixmudio to defend itself with the forces that are in it." Marshal de Gassion's death is not much felt at Court; gives particulars of the transfer of his government and the amount of his estate. Marshal de Turenne hastens back to the Empire with troops. The Prince of Condé will stay to see the Archbishop of Aix settled in the government. The King of France will propose the marriage of the Landgrave of Hesse with the sister of Brandenbourg, and the Landgrave's sister with the Prince of Talmont. *Copy.*

London, Oct. 11. 2622. *Letter of Intelligence.* The army will get the Customs; and demands payment of their arrears by the sale of Church lands. Neither the people, nor the Agitators, nor the army, nor the Parliament, can be ruled by the power that called them.* Prospects of the King's party. Proceedings in Parliament. Differences between Cromwell and Ireton. Names of six of the seven delinquents. Has spoken with the Earl of Lanerick, who brings information of the Scots intentions.
Copy.
Endorsed by Hyde.

* This is in a letter from Secretary Nicholas to Mr. Edgeman, dated 28 Oct. 1647.

2623. *The Marquis of Worcester to the Roman Catholic Bishop of Ferns.* Has found a way to bring the Queen to befriend this nation. Beseeches him with the Bishop of Clogher and Dr. Rochfort to be sure that General O'Neile, to whom the copy of the letter and the Nuncio's recommendation are addressed, dissent not from the letter approved by the Bishop of Ferns: the contents thereof have been recommended to the King. *Original.*
Galway, Oct. 12. 1647.
Cl. S. P. vol. ii. p. 380.

2624. *Extracts of Letters of Intelligence.* Proceedings in Parliament. The Agitators are grown powerful. A Council of War on the disposal of the King's person is to be held at Putney. Visitors sent by Parliament have reached Oxford. Presbyterians and Independents are disturbed by Rationalists. Quakers have come to Southwark;* and other sects are coming forth. Judge Jenkins is sent to Newgate. The army is purging the Militia of "Malignants." *Copy.*
London, Oct. 14.
Endorsed by Hyde. Partly printed in Cl. S. P. vol. II. App.

2625. *Jo. Wilcocks (Secretary Nicholas) to Mr. Edgeman.* Has received his of the 22nd. Is unable to send to Guernsey. Thinks the Scots will enter the kingdom. *Original.*
Oct. 14.

2626. *Dr. Jo. Henshawe to the same.* Has received his of the 15th. Will attend to the money matters. Lord Digby has fought a duel with Lord Wilmot, who was wounded. One of Sir K. Digby's sons parted the duelists and the seconds. *Original.*
Caen, Oct. 17.

2627. *Extracts of Letters of Intelligence;* one of them from Lord Capell. It is intended to settle the government of the kingdom by a Council, without the King or any of his issue. Cromwell and Ireton are to be accused. The Propositions are almost perfected. Balance of probabilities, of which the issue is unfavourable to the King. The number of excepted persons is not to exceed seven. The Scots Commissioners have arrived. Lord Capell thinks the King's business very hopeful. *Copy.*
London, Oct. 18 and 20.
Endorsed by Hyde.

2628. *Jo. Wilcocks (Sec. Nicholas) to Mr. Edgeman.* Encloses a letter from himself to Sir E. Hyde. The King raised a Parliament he could not rule, and the Parliament raised an army it cannot rule, and the army has raised Agitators they cannot rule, and the Agitators are setting up the people whom they will be unable to rule. Things are in great confusion. *Original.*
Oct. 12.
Cl. S. P. vol. ii. p. 381.

* Copied in a letter from Sec. Nicholas to Edgeman, Nov. 4, 1647.

1647.
Oct. 18.

2629. *Sir E. Hyde to Mr. Edgeman.* Mr. Abraham Durell is to see him. Letters have not reached him for almost a month. *Original.*

Oct. 21.

2630. *The same to the same.* Has received his of the 17th, 21st, and 25th of October. Had heard of Mr. Hollis's being by Sherbrook [Cherbourg], but not of his great wealth. Is sorry Dickinson is gone from London. *Original.*

Oct. 12.

2631. *The Scots Commissioners' paper* delivered at Hampton Court. Address to the King on his removal from Holdenby by Sir T. Fairfax. The Scotch Parliament has commanded them to know from the King his present true condition. They desire to live in such obedience as their predecessors have done under 107 of the King's progenitors. (Signed), Loudoun, Lauderdaill, Lanerick, Charles Erskine, Hen. Kennedy, Ro. Barclay. *Original.*
Cl. S. P. vol. ii. p. 380.

London,
Oct. 27, 28.

2632. *Extracts of Letters of Intelligence.* Sir J. Berkeley and Col. Ashburnham are gone to Hampton Court for protection. The officers of the army are resolved to cashier their Agitators. Ireton has spoken in behalf of the King, and pretends he must leave the House. The Scots demand reparation of honour for the King's delivery, and produce a contract between the Parliament and themselves. The King has received the Propositions, and also the message of the Scots Commissioners. The army aims at dispossessing the Church. Cromwell and Ireton are accused of receiving a bribe from the City. *Copy.*
Endorsed by Hyde. Partly printed in Cl. S. P. vol. ii. App.

Oct. 28.

2633. "*Extract* of a letter of the 28th Oct. 1647. St. Vet. from my Servt." The Scots Commissioners have delivered a letter to the King. The answer is expected this night.
(Apparently addressed to Secretary Nicholas.)
This and that of Nov. 4/14 are endorsed, "Extracts for Sir E. H."

Oct. 31.

2634. *Jo. Wilcocks (Secretary Nicholas) to Mr. Edgeman.* Desires him to convey the enclosed to the Chancellor, from whom he has received a letter. Commends the King's magnanimity. *Original.*

Oct.

2635. *Appeal* of the University of Oxford against the Visitation. State their privileges in point of Visitation. Refer to the Protest of May 5, 1641. With

Postscript.—Addressed to the Right Worshipful Nathaniel Brent and the rest of the Commissioners sitting at Merton College. *Copy.*
(Seven pages.) By Mr. Trethewy.
See Wood, Hist. et Antiq. Univ. Oxon, L i. p. 389.

2636. *Anonymous Letter*, giving an account of the reception of the ordinance of the two Houses and a Commission under the Great Seal on Sept. 28. The Vice-Chancellor (Dr. Fell) and Proctors resisted all that was done.
           Endorsed by Hyde.
  See Wood, Hist. et Antiq. Univ. Oxon, l. i. pp 389, 390.

1647.
Oxford,
Oct.

2637. *Extracts from Letters of Intelligence*. Sir T. Fairfax is ill. The army is about to remove to Windsor. The King will accept the Propositions if they come to him unaltered. There is news from St Germains, by Sir F. Cornwallis, of the Prince's illness and recovery.   *Copy.*

Oct.

2638. *Extracts of Letters of Intelligence*. The army governs all, and the Agitators it. A Council of War has been held at Putney. The violent party keep a fast this day. On Saturday last the two Houses had a conference about the Propositions to be sent to the King. The five regiments, with Lilburne's and others, have petitioned the Council, and aim at levelling all in the kingdom, which the army declares is theirs by conquest. They say there must be a new Parliament. Cromwell's, Ireton's, and Whaley's wives have been to Court, and have met Ashburnham. He and Sir J. Berkeley are removed from the King.   *Copy.*
 Endorsed by Hyde.   Partly printed in Cl. S. P. vol. ii. App.

Nov. 1.

2639. *Jo. Willcocks (Secretary Nicholas) to Mr. Edgeman.* Has received his of the 29th Oct. Mr. Hinton is safely arrived, and has been with the King, who still remains firm. The Scots Commissioners are expected daily. The Commons have again voted the settlement of Presbytery, with liberty for tender consciences. Socinians appear under the title of Rationalists. Foreign women called Quakers are arrived in Southwark.   *Original.*
         Cl. S. P. vol. ii. p. 383.

Nov. 4.

2640. *Extract of a Letter of Intelligence from London.* The ascendancy of the army. The Commons have voted a prosecution against the King. The Presbyterians will probably submit to the army. All the King's servants but two are warned from him. The Scots may interfere on behalf of the King. Probable future proceedings in Parliament. Has been sent by Sir T. Fairfax to Hampton Court. The King has withdrawn his parole. The Propositions are not yet finished. The Scots Commissioners wait on the King twice a week. There is great division in Scotland.   *Copy.*
 Endorsed by Hyde.   Partly printed in Cl. S. P. vol. ii. App.

Nov. 4.

1647.
Nov. 4.

2641. "*Extract of a part of my l{re} to my Ser{vt}.*" Sir E. Hyde asks for Sir E. Walker's journal of the Western business. Desires him to procure Mr. Dugdale's notes and collections for Sir E. Hyde, who also desires materials for his History from the loyal lawyers and clerks of the Council.

Apparently from Sec. Nicholas. Chiefly in cypher, decyphered by Hyde. See his letter of Jan. 1, '48. Cl. S. P. vol. ii. p. 382.

London, Nov. 4.

2642. *Sir E. Forde to Lord (Hopton).* The King's servants are all recalled, except the Scots. Disturbance amongst the soldiers at Dunstable. The army has voted down the negative voice of the King and of the House of Lords; and have voted that the Parliament shall end in July. The King is resolved not to stir, except by force. When the Scots have got Berwick and Carlisle they will declare themselves. *Original.*

Endorsed by Hyde.

Constantinople, Nov. 4.

2643. *Letter of Intelligence.* Mr. Hyde apprehended and detained at Lord Bendish's house four days: then sent on a false pretence to Sir Sackville Crow, who was then forced away to Lord Bendish's, whence he was sent to Smyrna. His lady and Mr. Hyde are to follow him. *Copy.*

Endorsed by Hyde, "Coppy of a relacōn of ye mad exit of Sir Sa. Crow, being barbarously used by Sir Tho. Bendish."

London, Nov. 4.

2644. *Extract of a Letter of Intelligence.* Colonels Rainsborough and Proud, and H. Martin have won Cromwell through fear to side against the King. Cromwell and others are like to be impeached. Contents of the army declaration not yet published. The Scots have had their answer. Parliament has voted that seven persons still excepted shall not yet be named. *Copy.*

Endorsed by Hyde. Partly printed in Cl. S. P. vol. ii. App.

London, Nov. 4.

2645. *Letter of Intelligence.* The King's removal from Hampton Court is discussed. The five discontented regiments demand justice on the chief delinquent. Cromwell and Ireton not to be trusted. Proceedings in Parliament. "A little time" will shew "them ugly rogues or honest men."

Signed in cypher "3." Endorsed by Hyde.

Nov. 5.

2646. *The Scots Commissioners to the House of Lords.* Recount the steps they have taken since the King's removal from Holdenby. Desire to know the certainty of the King's condition; and the Propositions to be tendered to the King be communicated to them: also that there may be a personal treaty with the King, either in London, or, without restraint of his person, or interference with themselves, at Hampton Court. *Copy.*

2647. *Extract of a Letter of Intelligence from London.* The Scots Commissioners press for a personal treaty. The army opposes the making any more addresses to the King; Ireton left the Council of War in consequence. The Lords are scared by the Levellers. Ashburnham and Berkeley are protected by the army from Speaker Lenthall's warrant. The Oxford delegates are summoned to attend the Visitation Commissioners. 1647. Nov. 6.
Copy.

Endorsed by Hyde. Partly printed in Cl. S. P. vol. ii. App.

2648. *Sir E. Hyde to Mr. Edgeman.* Has received his of the 4th and 14th, and one from Mr. Secretary of the later date. Gives directions about his boxes. Is sorry his correspondence with Dickenson is broken off. Sends enclosure to W. Hyde. Nov. 8.
Original.

2649. *Jo. Wilcocks (Secretary Nicholas) to the same.* Has received his of the 11th. Thanks him for conveying letters from Lord Hopton and himself to Jersey. Relates items of current news from London and Oxford. The seamen at Cherbourg have called Mr. Hollis traitor. Sends and receives letters by Mr. Pullon. Nov. 11.
Original.

2650. *Extract of Letters from London.* Dares not write some particulars. The Agitators are discharged. If they had been in fear of the Levellers one day longer, the King would have been at St. James's on good terms. The King's servants are removed except Maule. W. Legg comes away to-night. Major Huntington is taken from the King's guard. The Scots Commissioners are still clear for the King. Difficulties about taking away the King's veto. The message from the Scots Commissioners to the two Houses has startled the army. The General is taking precautions against the Agitators. London, Nov. 11.
Copy.

Endorsed by Hyde.

2651. *Extract of Letters from London.* The King's escape on Thursday saved him from being murdered on the following day. He is in the Isle of Wight. Cromwell is at the rendezvous of the army. Encloses copies of letters found on the King's table at Hampton Court. Fairfax was at Richmond on Thursday. The head-quarters is at Ware. Col. Lilburne is ordered to the North. Col. Rainsborough has tried to prevent a division in the army. There have been disturbances about the soldiers' pay at St. Albans, Dunstable, Luton, &c. Nye's prayer. Rainsborough and H. Martin laboured to impeach Cromwell of treason. Movements of Sir T. Fairfax and Major White's regiment. Speech of a member of the House of Commons for the King. London, Nov. 15.
Copy.

Endorsed by Hyde.

1647.
Rouen,
Nov. 16.

2652. *Mr. Trethewy to Mr. Edgeman.* Hopes Watson will soon come to him. The Prince has been sick and is not fully recovered. "Mr. Clutterbuck, your nephew W., and my brother L. present their service." *Original.*

Nov. 17.

2653. *The Scots Commissioners to the House of Lords.* Have received no answer to their paper of Nov. 5. Complain of the alteration of the Propositions. Regret the King's hard usage. Repeat their suggestion that a personal treaty be held. *Copy.*

Rome,
Nov. 18.

2654. *Letter of Intelligence.* Detailed account of affairs at Naples after "poor Massianello's fate." Death of Prince Toralta and his son. Escape of the Marquis of Brancavio. The Duke of Guise invited to be King. Details of his expedition, the design of which is due to Sir Kenelm Digby. Some "say that the whole kingdom is come in again to the Spaniards," others that a great part of the nobility is declared for the Duke. Sir K. Digby has taken leave of the Pope; he has done more honour to the English nation here than ever any man did. *Copy.*
Endorsed by Hyde.

London,
Nov. 18.

2655. *Extracts of Letters of Intelligence.* Proceedings in Parliament. All well and quiet at the rendezvous at Ware. Another rendezvous appointed at Watford. The King will sign no Propositions, but is ready to treat in person; in this the Scots agree. The King is in the Isle of Wight. "The knott of all will rest in the Bishopps." *Copy.*
Endorsed by Hyde.

London,
Nov. 14.

2656. *Letter of Intelligence.* Col. Rainsborough and Major Scott are suspended the House. Cromwell reduced the mutiny of Lilburne's regiment at Ware. The next rendezvous is at Hounslow Heath. The Levellers are disappointed. Dr. Oldsworth's sermon on Nov. 5. *Copy.*
Endorsed by Hyde.

Rouen,
Nov. 20.

2657. *Mr. Trethewy to Edgeman.* Has received his of the 15th. Mentions Mr. Hurman and Mr. Watson. Mr. A. Durell returns to-morrow. Will give an account of the boxes consigned to Mr. Lamborne. Enters into some details about the Governor's sister, and familiar matters. *Original.*

Jersey,
Nov. 21.

2658. *Sir E. Hyde to Lord Digby.* Has received his letter of Nov. 15th. Prays him to send materials for his History. They who continue firm will see fine days after this dismal storm. Desires him, if it be in his power, to restore the writer to the Queen's favour. *Copy.*
Endorsed by himself. Cl. S. P. vol. II. p. 383.

2659. *Extract of a Letter of Intelligence.* Fears the King was overreached by the army in the matter of his removal from Hampton Court. Hammond, upon the Parliament's demand of Ashburnham, Berkeley, and Legg, returned a dilatory answer in excuse of his honour. Lilburne and others, upon going to the Parliament to demand justice for the death of the Agitator, were imprisoned. *Copy.* 1647. Nov. 23.
Dated by Hyde.

2660. *The King's Answer to the Paper of the Scots Commissioners.* Wonders that the paper received Oct. 22 was not sent many months ago. Was kept at Holdenby with all rigour, and was carried thence against his will by Sir T. Fairfax, since which time he has been treated with greater civility and freedom. Refers them for an account of his present condition to the Houses of Parliament and the army. *Draught.* Nov.
Corrected by the King. Cl. S. P. vol. ii, p. 381.

2661. "Mr. Hen. Martyn, being grievously troubled with an evil spirit, desires the prayers of the congregation." "Sir, you are required and commanded by an hundred thousand honest Christians that desire the prayers of this congregation for the conversion or final destruction of the bloody taskmasters that sit at Westminster," &c. Nov.
Endorsed by Hyde.

2662. *Extract of Letters of Intelligence.* Sir John Berkeley is come from the King. The army and the Parliament are agreed. The City and people are disheartened. The Scots go away discontented. "The Parliament, City, and army clave one another as they find it serves their turns." All who enter the Isle of Wight are examined. The Houses have agreed to a personal treaty. There has been a difference between Lord Sinclair and David Lesley; the former is committed to Edinburgh Castle. *Copy.* Dec. 3. Dec. 2. Nov. 29.
Endorsed by Hyde.

2663. *Two Orders* of the King of Portugal in censure of Cornelius (or Constantine) Mahun's book.* *Copy.* Lisbon. April 6. Dec. 3.

2664. "*Propositiones* [sex] quædam scandalosæ et seditiosæ. Desumptæ ex libro quodam dicto, Disputatio apologetica de jure Regni Hiberniæ pro Catholicis Hibernis adversus hæreticos Anglos. Authore C. M. Hiberno (alias P. Cornelio de Seto. Patritio, o Soc. Jesu). Artium et sacræ theologiæ magistro, impress. Francofurti (alias Ulyssipone) 1645." Followed by "In exhortatione ad Catholicos Hibernos eodem authore Cornelio Mahun, e Soc. Jesu." [Nino propositiones.] *Copy.* April 6. Dec. 6.

* Constantine Mahony; Oliver, p. 257.

1647.
Paris,
Dec. 6.

2665. *Letter of Intelligence.* The French King is better, but the Queen-Mother has a fever. The French fleet is looked for at Naples. The Pope has refused to interfere. Expedition of the Duke of Guise. Movement for half-yearly Parliaments in France. The Princes of Italy will remain firm in their union against Spain.   *Endorsed by Hyde.*

Carisbrook,
Dec. 6.

2666. *The King's Message to the two Houses of Parliament, and the Parliament of Scotland.* A personal treaty is superior to all other means of peace. The decay of trade, and increase of prices and taxes, further moves the King to use all his endeavours for peace. The blame of retarding it does not fall on him. He will meet them if they will wait on him.   *Copy.*
Endorsed by Hyde.
King Charles's Works, p. 122; Bapin, vol. ii. p. 541.

London,
Dec. 6.

2667. *Extract of a Letter of Intelligence.* Reported movement of the army and the Agitators. Sir J. Berkeley is returned to the Isle of Wight. Parliament is drawing up the bill for the four Propositions to be sent to the King. The Earl of Norwich is in London. The King is closely guarded: he has intended to escape to Jersey. "His Majesty's negotiators" now exclaim against Cromwell for his "good parts." The Speaker is sick. The army is divided from the Parliament and the City. A report of Mr. Windham being killed. The Cavaliers' hope is in the Scots. The King will sign the four bills "the first half-hour of the personal treaty." *Copy.*
Endorsed by Hyde.

London,
Dec. 6.

2668. *Extract of a Letter of Intelligence.* The General approves of the King's being in the Isle of Wight. A personal treaty may be brought about. The army and the Agitators' disturbances. Lord Inchiquin's victory over Lord Taaffe, and the seizure of the latter's cabinet, has prejudiced many against the King. The Scots influence used for the King does not find much favour in England.   *Copy.*
Endorsed by Hyde.

Dec. 9.

2669. *A Letter of Intelligence.* Describes the dispositions of the superior officers, of Cromwell, and of Ireton, and of their opposition to the Agitators; which is not from any friendship to the King. It was arranged that the King should fall into Hammond's hands.   *Copy.*
Endorsed by Hyde.   On the same paper with that of Dec. 16.

Dec. 12.

2670. "*Sir E. Hyde to the King and Lord B. or Lord Ash.*" Trusts, by means of a vessel and messenger to be despatched to the Isle of Wight, to hear of the King's safety. Fears that the King's remove from Hampton Court will hinder his obtaining materials for his History, in compiling which he has now to depend on his memory and a few papers. 1647.

* Cl. S. P. vol. ii. p. 384.

The news of the King's being in the Isle of Wight was long in reaching them. The messenger is directed to either of his correspondents, whom he prays to send intelligence as soon as possible. *Rough Draughts.*

On one page. By himself.

2671. *Extracts of Letters of Intelligence.* The Propositions are pressed upon the King by those who wish him most harm. The Scots are of no more account than a last year's almanack. The army receives 30,000l. from the City. Gloomy prospects. Relations between the Parliament, the army, and the City. There is 100,000l. preparing to stop the Scots' months. The King and Lanerick frequently correspond. Petitions from several counties against the army. Trading decays. Proceedings in the House about Col. Rainsborough. Failure of Presbyterian attempt to dissolve Parliament. Above sixty condemned for murder and robbery. The Recorder is freed from the Tower. Hammond has the King's parole on condition that no more forces be admitted to the island. *Copy.*
London, Dec. 13.

Endorsed by Hyde.

2672. *Extract of a Letter of Intelligence.* The Commons have made an alteration in the bills for the Militia, and adjournment of Parliament. The strength of the Presbyterian party in the House moved the Independents to hasten on the impeachment of the seven lords. Dr. Sheldon, Dr. Oldisworth, and Dr. Haywood are with the King. The warrants against Ashburnham, Berkeley, and Legg are called in. The King's allowance will be lessened 20l. a day if the Commissioners do not go to the Isle of Wight. *Copy.*
Dec. 13.

Endorsed by Hyde.

2673. *Sir E. Hyde to Dr. J. Earles.* Refers to the events of the battle of Newbury, his mention of Lord Falkland and Hampden; and generally to the style and progress of the History he is writing. *Copy.*
Jersey, Dec. 14.

Endorsed by the writer. Cl. S. P. vol. ii. p. 386.

2674. *The same to Sir F. Cornwallis.* Has received his letter of the 14th* (N. S.). Defends himself from imputations of neglect and haughtiness. Trusts that he will remain firm, and that they will meet happily again. *Copy.*
Jersey, Dec. 15.

Endorsed by himself. Cl. S. P. vol. ii. p. 385.

* This may be a mistake for Nov. 14.

1647.
Dec. 16.

2675. *Part of a Letter of Intelligence.* Incloses a [Mercurius] "Pragmaticus." The army will probably settle a military government in the City. The Scots will declare themselves for the King in the spring, when matters will be more ripe; meanwhile the counties are to appear with their Petitions at Westminster. *Copy.*

Endorsed by Hyde. On the same paper with that of Dec. 9.

Dec. 16.

2676. *Sir E. Hyde to Lord Hopton.* Has received his 57th and 58th letters. Refers to the King's message from the Isle of Wight* of Nov. 17. The Scots message to Parliament gives no ground of reasonable expectation of great service to the King. [*A portion in cypher.*] The concession of Presbyterial government alters no legal possession or tithe. Comments on a letter he received from the King Nov. 23 [*in cypher*]. Gives two reasons upon which the King might be persuaded to send (the concession), yet could on no account be the adviser of it. The King's constancy is so great, as that if it do not fail all will be well. The proffer that (*a name in cypher*) has made is ridiculous. Prays him to recommend Sir J. Clotworthy to the Lord Treasurer. (*A passage in cypher.*) Criticises Sir R. Grenville's declaration, and proposes that an answer to it be drawn up, of which he gives an outline. *Copy.*

Endorsed by the writer. Partly printed in Cl. S. P. vol. II. p. 386.

London.
Dec. 16.

2677. *Letter of Intelligence.* The Earl of Southampton forbidden to go to the King. Saltmarsh's rebuke to Sir T. Fairfax, and subsequent death. All Cavaliers to leave London for three months. It is supposed the Scots are waiting to be bribed. *Copy.*

Endorsed by Hyde.

Dec. 16.

2678. *Letter of Intelligence.* The King is in good health. Both army and Scotland court him. The Earl of Traquhair left him for Scotland on receipt of a packet from the Duke of Hamilton. *Copy.*

Endorsed by Hyde.

Dec. 16.

2679. *Jo. Wilcocks (Secretary Nicholas) to (Mr. Edgeman).* Mentions Sir W. Lewis and Mr. Hollis. A few items of current news. *Original.*

Dec. 17.

2680. *Answer of the Scots Commissioners concerning the four Bills.* Five short paragraphs on religion, the Militia; consent of both kingdoms to a peace, and restoration of the King's rights (being heads of their long Answer of Dec. 18).

In Hyde's hand.

Parl. Hist. vol. xvi. p. 437. Rapin, vol. ii. pp. 542, 543, who refers to Rushworth and to Whitelock.

* See King Charles's Works, p. 110.

2681. *A just and solemn Protestation* of the free-born people of England and free citizens of London against a clause in the late Ordinance, to deprive them of their free elections and to enslave them. For Parliament to make or declare new treasons is a matter to which they cannot submit; all elections ought to be free; but the late Ordinance of Dec. 17 is a violation of the liberties of the citizens of London. They denounce it as a plot of the confederate Independent party. They defend themselves against the charge of treason, and demand a full hearing and judicial decision.   Endorsed by Hyde.   Cl. H. P. vol. II. p. 388.

1647. Dec. 10.

2682. *Letter of Intelligence.* Proceedings in Parliament. The Scots Commissioners follow the English to the Isle of Wight. Hopes that gold will not have the power to unite them. The army demands payment of arrears. An order from both Houses for all the King's party and all Catholics to leave the City in three days. A son is born to the Countess of Lanerick.   *Copy.*
                 Endorsed by Hyde.

London, Dec. 10.

2683. *Letters of Intelligence.* The King has written to the Parliament in higher language than usual; but the letter is suppressed. The Commissioners in the Isle of Wight. The King is advised by a private message from the Peers to offer half what is desired; which will be accepted.   *Copy.*
                 Endorsed by Hyde.

Dec. 10— 13.

2684. *Part of a Letter of Intelligence.* The Commissioners from both Houses are expected to-day; and also the Scots Commissioners. No English lord of the King's party has been with him since he has been in the island. He is under strict surveillance, which is increased by the nearness of the Dutch fleet. Rainsborough is to watch the island with four ships.   *Copy.*
                 Endorsed by Hyde.
   On the same paper with that of Dec. 30.

Carisbrook Castle, Dec. 12.

2685. *Agreement at Carisbrook, signed by the King.* The King will confirm the League and Covenant in both kingdoms, and Presbyterian government, the Directory, and Assembly of Divines for three years. Will suppress Antitrinitarians, Arians, Socinians, Antiscripturists, Anabaptists, Antinomians, Arminians, Familists, Brownists, Separatists, Independents, Libertines and Seekers. Nothing shall be done without the consent of the Kingdom of Scotland. An act of oblivion shall follow the settling of a peace. Scotland shall be aided in every way, the charges of their army paid, and a complete union of the two kingdoms effected.   *Two Copies.*
   One by Hyde; another in cypher decyphered.
  Countersigned and confirmed by Loudon, Lauderdale, and Lanerick.

Dec. 26.

1647.
St. Germains,
Dec. 17.

2686. *The Rev. Richard Watson to W. Edgeman.* Mr. Cruso is at Bristol. Has been summoned by Dr. Earles, as he supposed, to act as chaplain. Mr. Lewellyn is gone to England. Mentions Dr. Clare and Dr. Wolley. *Original.*

Dec. 17.

2687. *Jo. Wilcocks (Secretary Nicholas) to Edgeman.* Has received his of the 24th and 28th. Discourses about affairs in England and Scotland. *Original.*

London,
Dec. 30.

2688. *Letter of Intelligence.* Position of the Presbyterian and Independent parties. The army has appointed a general rendezvous. A declaration is being framed by Parliament against the Scots. *Copy.*

Endorsed by Hyde.

London,
Dec. 30.

2689. *Part of a Letter of Intelligence.* The Militia is being settled; and all who are suspected of loyalty turned out. Rainsborough is to be hastened to his command at sea. There is a report that the Scots will be assisted by the Swedes and Danes. Proceedings at a public Fast. "Sir John Evelyn, j^r, becomes a *purus putus* Indep." Merchants are withdrawing their stock. Little or no bullion is brought into the Mint. Christmas observed as usual, except that no sermons were permitted. Dr. Griffith and Mr. Hall imprisoned for intending to preach. Some Presbyterian ministers have been threatened. *Copy.*

Endorsed by Hyde. On the same paper with that of Dec. 22.

Dec.

2690. *Draught of a Message to be sent by the King to the Parliament;* drawn up by Sir E. Hyde. The King's conscience cannot suffer him to acknowledge that the proceedings taken against him are just. He desires a personal free treaty in which all particulars may be clearly laid before him. He will consent to no preliminary determinations that may defeat a peaceful settlement; but will die a King if he be not suffered to live one. *Original.*

(See the King's message of Dec. 28.) Cl. S. P. vol. II. p. 388.

No date.

2691. *The Earl of Bristol to (Sir E. Hyde).* "I have according to your desire reduced into writing that discourse which I held to you concerning that vote of the Houses whereby divers persons are excepted from all pardon and mercie." Argues against the censure and sentence as severe, illegal, and unjust; and therefore null.

(Fourteen pages.) Endorsed by Hyde.

2692. *A Paper*, commencing with a reference to the treaty of confederation between the Crowns of England and France, in answer to the charge of the King's having assisted his Christian Majesty against Rochelle. *Copy.* — 1647-8. Jan. 1.

2693. *Votes of the Commons on Jan.* 1st, 3rd, 5th, 1644. Col. Hammond to secure the King in Carisbrook Castle. No more addresses be made to the King under penalty of high treason. Will receive no more messages from the King. Sir W. Constable and Col. Hammond may remove from the King any suspected person. The Scots are excluded from all business of design and policy. *Copy.* — Jan. 1—5.

2694. *Letter of Intelligence.* The disorders in Anjou are in a fair way of being composed. Details of the Duke of Guise's movements in Italy. The French fleet has again put to sea from Piombino. Continued illness of the Pope. Mentions the Marshal de Turenne and the Duke of Longueville. *Copy.* — Paris, Jan. 3.

2695. *Jo. Wilcocks (Secretary Nicholas) to Mr. Edgeman.* Incloses a letter from Lord Hopton to Sir E. Hyde. Gives some news from England. Has received his of the 11th. Sir W. Lewis was with Mr. Hollis and Mr. Clotworthy. Is very severe against the Covenant. *Original.* — Jan. 4.

2696. *Sir E. Hyde to the same.* Has written three letters without an answer. Gives directions about private matters. *Original.* — Jan. 5.

2697. *Jo. Wilcocks (Secretary Nicholas) to the same.* A kinsman of Sir G. Carteret carried his last letters to Sir E. Hyde. Discusses English affairs. Mr. Saltmarsh is dead. *Original.* — Jan. 6.

2698. *Letter of Intelligence.* Col. Hammond has discharged from about the King Mr. John Ashburnham, Sir John Berkeley, Col. Legg, the chaplains, and all other friends and servants. Every man is officially questioned whether he be for King or Parliament. Discontent in the country; insurrections for Christmas customs against the officers opposing them. Another levy about to be made. *Copy.*
Endorsed by Hyde. — London, Jan. 6.

2699. *Letter of Intelligence.* Since his refusal of the four bills, the King is treated with greater severity, and is now a close prisoner. The Independents carried the vote of no addresses by fifty-two voices. The Presbyterians are retired in discontent. Report of a conversation between the King and Hammond. *Copy.*
Endorsed by Hyde. — London, Jan. 6.

1647-8.
Jan. 7.

2700. *Jo. Wilcocks (Secretary Nicholas) to Mr. Edgeman.* Incloses a letter to Sir E. Hyde. Mr. Hollis is sending his son from Cherbourg into England. *Original.*

Jan. 9.

2701. *The same to the same.* Repays him for stockings purchased. Has just received his of the 7th. *Original.*

Paris,
Jan. 10.

2702. *Letter of Intelligence.* Proceedings in the Paris Parliament; that of Aix interdicted. Probable continuance of the war. Communications held with the Duke of Lorraine. A Council of War has resolved to have two armies in Flanders. The Pope has held a Consistory. *Copy.*

London,
Jan. 13.

2703. *Letter of Intelligence.* The prevailing party are carrying things with a high hand. Divers unnecessary offices are suppressed. The six Colonels who brought in the declaration from the General Council of the army have received the thanks of the Commons. 'Tis said that Saltmarshe's ghost appears to the General. Measures are taken against the Scots. The King is to be impeached. Behaviour of the Duke of York on hearing of his father's imprisonment. Scott, the Leveller, is dead. The tax-collectors are roughly treated. Votes in the two Houses. The King hunted last Tuesday. Particulars of the doings of a Yorkshire fanatic, furnished by Col. Slingsby. *Copy.*

Endorsed by Hyde.

Jan. 14.

2704. *Jo. Wilcocks (Secretary Nicholas) to Mr. Edgeman.* Sir J. Berkeley and Mr. Ashburnham are seeking a passage into France. Reports other items of news from England. Mr. Overbury is a Presbyterian. *Original.*

Carisbrook,
Jan. 18.

2705. *"The King's Declaration* to all my people of whatsoever nation, quality, or condition." Refers to the vote of no more addresses. Vindicates his character as a husband and as a King. Enters into the particulars of the propositions tendered him; and his proposals for a personal treaty.

King Charles's Works, p. 516.

Jan. 18.

2706. *Earl of Brentford to the Marquis of Montrose.* His Highness does not wish him to go to Scotland yet, but desires him to encourage the Highland gentlemen in their good will towards himself, of which he will make use at a more fitting opportunity, when the resolutions of the Parliament of Scotland shall be known. *Rough Draught.*

By Hyde. Cl. S. P. vol. 8. p. 466.

CLARENDON PAPERS. 409

2707. *Letter of Intelligence.* Parliament treats with the King. Probable war with the Scots. The army is very strong, though divided, as is the Parliament. *Copy.*
Endorsed by Hyde.

1647-8. London, Jan. 10.

2708. *Letter of Intelligence.* A reward offered for Lord Byron and Sir Marmaduke Langdale. Votes of the Lords prohibiting any communication with the King. Lieut.-Col. Lilburne to be tried at the King's Bench. Sir L. Diues is escaped from prison. Capt. Burley is being tried at Winchester. Visitors sent to Oxford are made Heads of Houses. The King desires to send a new message to the Parliament. *Copy.*
Endorsed by Hyde.

London, Jan. 12.

2709. *Sir E. Hyde to the Marquis of Montrose.* Has received orders from the Prince to wait on the Marquis. There is great jealousy of a treaty between the Prince and his Lordship. It will not be well for him to be seen at Antwerp or Brussels; suggests Breda, Bergen, or Gythrenberg, as a place of meeting. *Copy.*
By Edgeman. Endorsed by Hyde. Cl. S. P. vol. II. p. 463.

The Hague, Jan. 20.

2710. *The same to Mr. R. Fanshawe.* Is sure he is now in Ireland. Has received a packet of private letters in cypher, to which he has not the key. Does not like the country. The preservation of the fleet must be ascribed to Prince Rupert, Batten and Jordan having played the rogue. Charges him to preserve a right understanding between the Prince and the Lord Lieutenant. Is willing enough to go to Ireland. Has kept the despatch from the King for Spain. There is no probability of the Prince's going to Scotland.
Rough Draught.
By Hyde. Partly printed in Cl. S. P. vol. II. p. 467.

Jan. 21.

2711. *Letter of Intelligence.* Reports of a personal proceeding against the King: and that the Earl of Denbigh be sent to invite the Prince. Sir Lewis Diues has got away; but Sir J. Stowell and Judge Jenkins will be brought to trial. The Duke of Hamilton's and Argyle's faction are agreed. Northumberland is gone to Petworth. Lord Rocheford alone of the impeached lords is not received into the House. A fort is being built by the Tower. *Copy.*
Endorsed by Hyde.

London, Jan. 24.

2712. *Letters of Intelligence.* Northumberland is out of favour by reason of his speech against the last votes of the Commons. The Scots are bribed. Their policy. Some

London, Jan. 24—28.

3 D

1647-8. Western garrisons refuse to disband without their arrears are paid. Arthur Trevor, Col. Langhorne, and Col. Milton have been plotting together. Affairs at Newcastle. A letter from the Assize in Hampshire to the Parliament. Capt. Burley is condemned for mutiny. More Commissioners to be sent to the King. Westminster Hall and Scotland Yard fortified. Sir W. Constable is returned from the Isle of Wight. *Copy.*

Endorsed by Hyde.

Jan. 16. 2713. *John May to Sir Thomas Aylesbury.* Desires him to restore the white mare to this bearer that she may be sent to grass. *Original.*

London, Jan. 27. 2714. *Letter of Intelligence.* The King is patient and cheerful. A fort is to be built in Lambeth. Mr. Fiennes's answer to the Scots declaration is ready for press. A mad soldier. Regiments appointed for Ireland refuse to disband. Disorders in Gloucester, Pembroke, and Plymouth. Some of the Commons repent of their votes against the King. Precautions taken against suspected persons. *Copy.*

Endorsed by Hyde.

The Hague, Jan. 27. 2715. *Sir E. Hyde to Prince Rupert.* Has received his of the 24th by Capt. Ulbert, whom he has sent to Amsterdam to get men. The order for wearing the standard has been sent. Informs him, at the Prince's request, of the debate concerning it. Warns him against those who would bring about a misunderstanding between his Highness and the Marquis of Ormond. Thinks that Dr. Hart should accompany him. Sends warrants for payment of moneys advanced, and salaries. Hopes the prize he has taken is not a Hamburgher. Gives him notice of reported movements of the enemy. *Copy.*

By Edgeman, with additions and endorsement by Hyde.
Partly printed in Cl. S. P. vol. ii. p. 468.

Jan. 27, 30, 31, and Feb. 3. 2716. *Letter of Intelligence.* Capt. Burley condemned on a breach of the statute that condemns his judges. Affairs in the City. Private instructions are given to the Commissioners that go to Scotland to cajole the Estates there. The Swedes, and perhaps Holland, will join with Denmark to assist the Scots on the King's behalf. The King's refractoriness forces the Parliament to extremes. If Cromwell do not ruin Lilburne, he will be ruined by him. The General is in Queen Street. Soldiers to be quartered in St. Paul's. All parties in Ireland will side with the King. Langham, the late Mayor, Ald. Bunce, and others will be proceeded against. Playhouses are being voted down. Many Cavaliers sent to prison. Probabilities of a Scotch

invasion. Newcastle reinforced. Proposed new treaty between 1647-8.
the Scots and the Parliament. The greater part of the army
disavows the declaration of the Council of War. The King
impeached by the Commons.   *Copy.*
                                                        Endorsed by Hyde.

2717. *Jo. Wilcocks (Secretary Nicholas) to Mr. Edgeman.*   Feb. 5.
Sir T. Fairfax has seen Saltmarsh's ghost. Mentions the vote
of no more addresses. Draws a parallel between the behaviour
of the Independents and the Scots towards the King.
                                                         Original.

2718. *An Account* of the last illness and death of King   Feb.
James, with the proceedings against the Duke of Buckingham.
— French.   *Endorsed by Hyde.*

2719. "*Sir E. H[yde] to Lord H.*" [*Holland?*] The Scots,   Feb. 6.
unless they are strictly treated with, are not to be trusted. [Erroneously
Ill use made of the first Protestation, which many thought so marked
innocent. Moderate Episcopacy is a new word "to cozen men by the
into a consent for extirpation." The ill success of the King's editor
affairs to be imputed to no one thing more (drinke excepted) Feb. 4.]
than the supine temper of many honest men in endeavouring
expedients to satisfy those who were in the wrong. Concessions
increase demands. He would not, to preserve himself, wife,
and children from want and famine, consent to the lessening
any part of the function of a Bishop or the taking away the
smallest prebendary.
      Cl. S. P. vol. III. p. 1, where it is suggested that it may have been written
      to Lord Hatton.

2720. *Sir E. Forde to Lord Hopton.* Has been ill. Pro-   Feb. 9.
ceedings in Parliament. Lord Willoughby of Parham is gone.
Sir John Maynard is before the House. Charges against the
King. All the Scots of any quality except two are gone into
their own country. Informers employed by the Parliament.
Fatal affray between some Welshmen and soldiers. The Earl
of Stamford resists the billeting of soldiers on him. *Original.*
                                                   Endorsed by Hyde.

2721. *Jo. Wilcocks (Secretary Nicholas) to Mr. Edgeman.*   Feb. 10.
Has received his of the 4th. Retails news from England.
Overbury says that he is Sir Gil. Overbury's son, who is
brother to Sir T. Overbury. Mentions Martin and Lilburne.
                                                   Original.

1647-8.
Feb. 10.

2722. *Letter of Intelligence.* A new oath and other securities to be imposed by Parliament. Proceedings in Parliament; charges against the King. Henry Martin's scandalous book. The Scots press for a personal treaty. Riots in Shrewsbury against the Excise officers. Lord Willoughby is gone; perhaps to Barbadoes. English merchants seized by the Emperor of Russia. The Mayor's feast for the General. The King allowed only thirty servants. H. Martin's disreputable behaviour. Griffith commits violence and murder. *Copy.*
Endorsed, and with marginal notes, by Hyde.

London,
Feb. 11.

2723. *Letter of Intelligence.* Great hopes excited by the Prince's proposed going into Scotland. Sir H. Vane, jun., has left the prevailing party. Cromwell fears for his personal safety. Sir T. Fairfax has been polled. Proceedings in Parliament. Activity of Sir H. Mildmay and H. Martin. Reports of the Scotch Convention. Many of the King's party in London are imprisoned. *Copy.*
Endorsed by Hyde.

Feb. 14.
Feb. 17.

2724. *Letters of Intelligence.* Lords Ormond and Willoughby are reported to have gone to Scotland. The King has been visited by a Cavalier; he is secured by five well-locked doors. Relates proceedings in Parliament in which Mr. Selden, the Lieut.-General, and Sir Simon D'Ewes, took part. Two of Lord Holland's servants have been imprisoned for drinking the King's health. Post letters have been opened. Money is to come to 5 per cent.; that lent to the State to 8 per cent. Sir Tho. Barwis has written to the Committee of Indemnity. Gives an account of Judge Jenkins's appearance at the bar of the House. *Copies.*
On the same paper. Endorsed by Hyde.

London,
Feb. 17.

2725. *Letter of Intelligence.* Particulars of the debate on the Parliament's declaration against the King: Mr. Selden, Sir Simon D'Ewes. Judge Jenkins's business.
Endorsed by Hyde.

Paris,
Feb. 22.

2726. *Letter of Intelligence.* The Prince of Condé is to go into Catalonia. Details of Army Corps. Marshal de la Moillonay will command the naval forces. Mons. de Fountenay Marcüill goes ambassador extraordinary to Rome. Declaration of the Venetian ambassador. *Copy.*
Endorsed by Hyde.

Feb. 23.

2727. *Papers* sent to Mr. Secretary Nicholas by Sir Richard Browne, the ambassador at Paris; viz. his general instructions when sent first to that Court, dated July 23, 1641. A letter from the King to him, Sept. 12, 1642, commanding him to

remonstrate against the reception there of Augier in a public 1647-8.
character from the Parliament, and in case he should be received to protest against it. A letter from Sir Richard Browne
to Mr. Secretary Nicholas, Feb. 23, 1644, acquainting him
that he is at a loss how to get a sight of Augier's instructions,
but will endeavour to procure his credentials, if the Secretary
of State [find] them.

2728. *Instructions from the King to Richard Browne, Esq.* Feb. 23.
Appoints him in the place of the Earl of Leicester, who will
present him to the French King, with whom he is to continue
the friendly relations that have hitherto subsisted. He is to
watch all motions of the State, and to communicate from time
to time with the authorities at home. (Signed) H. VANE.
Copy.

2729. *The King to Sir Richard Browne.* Walter Strickland Feb. 23.
has been sent by the Parliament to treat with the States-
General of the United Netherlands; and Augier into France.
Instructs him to use his utmost means "to hinder and oppose
any audience, countenance or treaty in any kind to be afforded
the said Augier or other whatsoever," and to protest against it.
Copy.
Endorsed by Secretary Nicholas.

2730. *Sir Richard Browne to Secretary Nicholas.* Has re- Feb. 23.
ceived his of the $\frac{1}{11}$ and $\frac{2}{11}$. Sends copies of his own instructions, orders, and credentials. Gives what information he can
of M. Augier, who came to Paris Dec. 1, 1644; and still
"appears in all business in the name of the Parliament."
Copy.
Endorsed by Secretary Nicholas.

2731. *Letter of Intelligence.* Sir T. Gell has heard that the Feb. 24.
Scots are resolved to break with the Parliament. Col. Ponsonby's regiment has gone to the Scots. Mentions reports
from Ireland. Aberconway and Pembroke Castles, and Langhorne's regiment refuse to disband. Gives an account of an
attempted delivery of a letter from the Duke of York to the
King, and the examination and confession of the former. Col.
Jephson's wife brings good reports from Ireland. Reports
proceedings from Scotland. Langhorne's regiment has seized
Swansea. Further particulars of Judge Jenkins. Debates in
the House on sending the fleet to sea, and on the Oxford
articles. *Copy.*

1647-8.
Feb. 25
—29.

2732. *Warrant* of the States-General of the United Provinces, translated out of Dutch. For the conveyance, duty free, by Mr. "Alesbury," of sixteen chests of pictures belonging to the Lord Duke of Buckingham, from London to Amsterdam, and thence to England. *Copy.*

With apparently original signature of Beddel.
Subscribed Johan Van Hende, and countersigned by Banel. Beddel.

Feb. 26.

2733. *Francis Dodsworth to Sir Thomas Aylesbury, Bart., at Cranborne Lodge, near Windsor.* Encloses a letter received from Mr. John Mayo, three weeks ago, about a white mare. *Original.*

Feb. 28.

2734. *Letter of Intelligence.* Mr. Marshall has returned from Scotland with no good news. The Lords and Commons met on Sunday. Edinburgh is full of English Cavaliers. Monro is recalled from Ireland into Scotland. "If the Prince were here nine parts of ten of the kingdom would join with him." Report of an "underhand treaty" between the King and Cromwell. The Duke of York has confessed that he was ordered by his father to escape out of the kingdom. There is much buying and selling of gold; viz. "worth ten pound in the hundred exchange." The Earl of Northumberland's goods "are stayed going into Holland." *Copy.*

Endorsed by Hyde.

March.

2735. *The proceedings against the University of Oxford.* Account of the proceedings of the Committee of Lords and Commons for the reformation of the University. Dec. 28, 1647. Mr. Rouse, chairman, Lord North, Mr. Selden, Mr. Poole, Mr. Whitelock, and other speakers. *Draught.*

Cl. S. P. vol. ii. p. 397.

March 6 and 9.

2736. *Letter of Intelligence.* All comers out of England are countenanced and entertained in Scotland. Sir L. Dives, Sir M. Langdale, and Lord Willoughby of Parham are expected. Negotiations of the Commissioners. Marshall is much vilified, and is ordered to return. Men are to be forced to compound. It is suspected that Massey, Waller, Hollis, and Long are in Scotland. Relations of Scotch and English. Pembroke Castle holds out. Proceedings in Parliament. Volunteers are being raised for Ireland. The Scotch and English Commissioners. Mr. Herle's sermon at Edinburgh. Affairs at Plymouth and Gloucester; Col. Welden, Col. Morgan, and Sir W. Constable. A mad Petition that the King should be recrowned by Parliament. *Copy.*

Endorsed by Hyde.

CLARENDON PAPERS. 415

2737. [*Sir E. Hyde*] *to Sir John Berkeley.* Has received his of the 8th. Discusses the King's situation. The King "hath quitted so much authority to other men, and made them so much above him, that it may be questionable whether the exercise of any power over him be an act of oppression .. we have yet no example of a King of England who hath been destroyed without his own consent, or who hath been preserved after his consent to what might reasonably destroy him." *Copy.*
Endorsed by Hyde.

1647-8.
Jersey,
March 8.

2738. *Letter of Intelligence.* Proceedings in the Parliament at Edinburgh. The English flock fast to the North. London "Mercuries" and other pamphlets to be treated with severity. The Independents will not oppose the Scotch.
Copy.
Endorsed by Hyde.

London,
March 13.

2739. *Major-General Lambert to the two Cols. Partington, Col. Wheatley, Lieut.-Col. Ashton, Sir John Digby, and Sir Hugh Cartwright.* Invites them to surrender Pomfret Castle within fourteen days. Adds three conditions. *Original.*

Norwich.
March 17.

2740. *Sir E. Hyde to the Lord Treasurer.* Has received his of Feb. 27. Is well satisfied with the King's constancy. Wishes to procure Lord Dankes's discourse through Mr. Clutterbuck. Is busy about his garden. Mentions Lord Hopton. Mr. Jones is now come, and the auditor has his books. They are prepared for any attempt by the Parliament on the island. *Copy.*
Endorsed by Hyde.

Jersey,
March 16.

2741. *Letter of Intelligence.* The Edinburgh Parliament began March 2. Opposition between Argyle and Hamilton, and nearly a duel between Argyle and Lindsay (Lord Crawford). Disturbances at Berwick. Large sums of money offered to the Scots and refused. A treaty with the King opposed. The City laugh at the impeachment of the Aldermen. Distractions in the army. Cromwell is gone to Bury to quiet them. Fairfax moves northward. "Many members begin to be civill." *Copy.*
Endorsed by Hyde.

London,
March 20.

2742. *Extract of a Letter of Intelligence to the Earl of Brainford.* Precautions taken about Berwick. Proceedings of the Committee: and the Parliament. Opposition of the clergy. *Copy.*
Endorsed by Hyde.

Edinburgh,
March 21.

1647-8.
March 11
—13.

2743. *Letters of Intelligence.* Forecasts the result of present affairs. Cromwell is blamed for inveigling the King from Hampton Court. Likelihood of his faction being quelled. "Things begin to work to some purpose in Scotland." South Wales will appear for the King. Describes a scene in St. Martin's Church after sermon on Sunday. It is reported that Lord Say has been in the Isle of Wight, and that Hammond in searching for private papers had a tussle with the King.

Copies.
On the same paper. Endorsed by Hyde.

No date.
2744. *A Summary* of military operations from June 1642, when the King, being forced from Westminster, sent away the Queen for her safety, to March 1644, when Pontefract Castle was taken. (Twenty-seven pages.)

No date.
2745. *A Ballad.* "A newe Letanie for our new Lent." Fifty-two stanzas of three lines. Endorsed by Hyde.

No date.
2746. "*Plain English to the people of England.*" "An address to the people of England, particularly the Citizens, to rouse and defend themselves from the tyranny of the then Powers." Violent language, classical allusions, abuse of Mildmay, Evelyn, Martyn, Selden, Luke Robinson, John Blackstone, and Sir Simon D'Ewes.
(Three pages.) Endorsed by Hyde.

No date.
2747. *Rev. Mr. Gatford* on the "places of Holy Scripture applied by the Rebels to their purpose."* Accounts of discourses at Bury St. Edmunds, and other places in Norfolk and Suffolk; London and Sussex. The texts quoted are from Proverbs xxv.; Judges v. 23; Exod. xxxii. 29; Deut. vii. 1, 2; Jeremiah xlviii. 20; Numbers xxii. 25; St. Luke ix. 54, 55; Jeremiah v. 30, 31; 2 Sam. xxiii. 12; Daniel xi. 32; Jeremiah xxxii. 31; 2 Sam. xxiv. 45. Endorsed by Hyde.

No date.
2748. "*An Answer* to the poysonous sedicious paper of Mr. David Jenkins, by H. P.†, Barrester of Lincolnes Inn, 1647. London, printed for Robert Bostock, dwelling at the signe of the Kinges Head in Paul's Churchyard, 1647." *Copy.*
Endorsed by Hyde.

No date.
2749. "*Some heads of an Answer to some particulars in the Declaration in the House of Commons against the King.*" Recapitulation of the King's offers. Denial of the right of the House of Commons to meddle with the King's marriage, and

* Mr. Gatford was minister of the church in Jersey which the Chancellor attended. † Parker.

CLARENDON PAPERS. 417

the treaty thereupon. Answer to the charge of keeping up a 1647-8.
correspondence with Rome. Replies in detail to "proceedings
and passages in Parliament concerning the death of" King
James; the business of Rochelle; the supposed plot of bringing in an army of German horse; a pretended proclamation
against Parliaments; and "the searching of cabinets, closets,
&c." Explanations concerning the Rebellion in Ireland, and
the Queen's tampering with Papists. *Draught.*

<sub>Corrected and endorsed by Secretary Nicholas. In answer to the declaration
of the vote of no more addresses. Hist. Rebell. bk. x. p. 519, ed. 1752.
Cl. S. P. vol. ii. p. 391.</sub>

2750. *Letter of Intelligence.* The Masters of Requests or- 1648.
dered to register all documents in their hands. The Chevalier Paris,
Garnier ordered to take seven or eight vessels to Naples before March 17.
the return of the Spanish armada. M. d'Avaux will return from
Munster. The King and Queen have paid a visit to Chartres.
 Copy.
 Endorsed by Hyde.

2751. *Letter of Intelligence.* The Northern parts are ready March 15.
to join with the Scots in the King's quarrel. Montrose is to
attend the Prince, who is to be in Holland, where he will procure the foundation for an army. Report of the fall of Berwick and Carlisle; a disturbance in Worcestershire; the
Speaker going to the Spa; seizure of some moneys of Lord
Gray of Warke. Conduct of the Sheriffs of Lancashire and
Bucks. Proceedings at Chelmsford Assizes. Bonfires in
London. Summons to surrender sent to Pembroke Castle,
which holds out still. Proceedings in Parliament. Details of
the army voted by the Scots. *Copy.*
 Endorsed by Hyde.

2752. *Sir E. Hyde to John Berkeley.* Has received his of March 29.
the 26th. Thanks him for the hopes he has received of being
restored to the Queen's favour; and is glad of the good
opinion Lord Jermyn has of him. Gives reasons why he
should not be invited to the councils of the Queen and Prince.
Discusses the imposition upon wines. Cannot imagine what
Sir Baldwin Wake can complain of the Governor. Adds a
postscript, *chiefly in cypher.* *Copy.*

2753. *Letter of Intelligence.* Scotland and the Parliament. London,
Berwick is to be occupied. Sir John Strangways has com- March 29.
pounded. Fairfax goes to Bury. The King has given seven
commissions to Scotchmen.

The Marquis of Montrose is off from the employment of Paris,
 April 8.

3 H

1648.

St. Germains,
April 10.

the French. French affairs in Naples go ill. Peace negotiations at Munster fail.

The Prince of Condé has lately come to St. Germains to visit the Prince. There is a report that Tenby Castle joins Pembroke against the Parliament.
Copy.
Endorsed by Hyde.

London,
March 30.

2754. *Letter of Intelligence.* Military movements in Wales. Lord Inchiquin and his soldiers are to be satisfied. Rejoicings in the City on the King's coronation day (March 27). Fewer soldiers in Westminster Hall. Lord Say is out of town. Sir W. Russell is ill-used and threatened. *Copy.*
Endorsed by Hyde.

London,
April 3—8.

2755. *Letter of Intelligence.* Proposals for a personal treaty with the King. "Wales will suddainly be in actual warre." Commissioners are going to hinder Lord Inchiquin's purpose. Balance of parties. Lord Say's behaviour. Scotch affairs. Proceedings in the House. Details of the siege of Pembroke Castle. Bonfires on the coronation day. Lord Denbigh hurt. Disturbances at St. Martin's Church. Sam. Crispe and wife killed by the fall of their house. *Copy.*
Endorsed by Hyde.

Paris,
April 8.

2756. *Letter of Intelligence.* The resolutions for the campaign settled at a Council of War. Expedient proposed for arranging the business of the Masters of Requests. The chief points accorded at Munster. Affairs at Naples.

Constantinople,
Dec. 26.

The Janissaries drew the Sultan out of his seraglio, but were appeased with large sums of money.

The Hague,
March 23.

The French ambassador's propositions. France and Spain; the States and the Prince of Orange. Recriminations, but probable pacification. *Copy.*
Endorsed by Hyde. (On one paper.)

April 10.

2757. *Colonel Poyer's Declaration.* "The declaration of Colonel Poyer, and Colonel Powell, and the officers and soldiers under their command, which they desired to be published to the whole kingdom, wherein they declare their intentions for restoring his Majesty to his just prerogative and the laws to their due course for the maintenance of the Protestant religion and the liberty of the subject: which was the ground of their first taking up arms, and for which they are resolved to live and die." *Copy.*

2758. *Letter of Intelligence.* Proceedings in the Parliament. An army to be raised for the King's interest. Argyle's opposition will fail; Lord Balmerino voted against him. *Copy.*   1648. Edinburgh, April 11.
Endorsed by Hyde.

2759. *Letter of Intelligence.* Prospects of peace. Movements of Generals Königsmark and Wrangel, and M. de Turenne. Duke Ernest of Saxony mediates between Hesse Cassel and Darmstadt.—French. *Copy.*   Frankfort, April 12.
Endorsed by Hyde.

2760. *Letter of Intelligence.* Apprentice riots in London. "Playing at Catt." Violence of the troops; blood shed on both sides. Letters from Scotland to the Committee of Derby House. [Mercurius] "Elenticus is come out this week upon a merry pin with the Parl^t." Lords Southampton, Bath, and Arundel have been solicited to go to the King to make way for a treaty. "Coll. Poyer and Powell of Tenby Castle are still resolute," and expect reinforcements from Ireland. Bp. Williams holds several places in North Wales for the King. *Copy.*   April 13.
Endorsed by Hyde.

2761. *Sir E. Hyde to the Prince of Wales.* Thanks him for Harding's memorials of Prince Rupert's marches. Gives some particulars of the progress of his History. *Copy.*   Castle Elizabeth, April 16.
Endorsed by himself.   Cl. S. P. vol. II. p. 400.

2762. *The same to the Queen.* Has suffered much from fear of her displeasure. Will never otherwise appeal than from her justice to her mercy. *Copy.*   Jersey, April 16.
Endorsed by himself.   Cl. S. P. vol. II. p. 401.

2763. (*Sir E. Ford*) *to* (*Lord Hopton*). Interchange of civilities between the City and the Parliament. Affairs in Pembrokeshire. Inchiquin and Lord Taafe have declared for the King. The former's son of nine years of age sent to the Tower. The Earl of Southampton's reply in the House. Sir Sackville Crow sent to the Tower. Affairs in Wales, Devonshire, and Cornwall. Sir H. Waller imprisoned in Plymouth. *Original.*   April 16 and 17.
Endorsed by Hyde.

2764. *Letter of Intelligence.* Affairs in Scotland, Ireland, and Wales. "I am clearly of opinion that Hamilton is not now acting your King's interest, but his owne, and pursuing the old designe of his family." Compliments between the City and the Parliament. Essex's Petition prosecuted at   April 17—20.

420   CALENDAR OF

1648.   Quarter Sessions; disorderly proceedings. Sir H. Waller
                repulsed by Fortescue of Pendennis. The Oxford scholars
                made cat's-paws of by the Visitors. Military movements in
                Wales. Reports from Ireland. Burglary at Lady Wynne's
                house at Wimbledon.   *Copy.*
                                                       Endorsed by Hyde.

Edinburgh,   2765. *Letter of Intelligence.* The general Declaration pre-
April 18.   sented in Parliament. Preparation for war. "The Kirke
                are very unsatisfied." Argyle left this day.   *Original.*
                              Endorsed by Hyde.   Not signed or addressed.

The Hague,   2766. *Letter of Intelligence.* Sir W. Boswell's care in order-
April 22.   ing Webster of Amsterdam to send provisions to Jersey.
                                                                 Copy.
                                                       Endorsed by Hyde.

London,   2767. *Letter of Intelligence.* The Duke of York has escaped
April 24.   and gone to Flushing. Proceedings in Parliament. The City
                will be fined. (Signed) BOWMAN.   Endorsed by Hyde.

Paris,   2768. *Letter of Intelligence.* The purposes of the Scots
April 25.   gathered from the Propositions printed by them. The Mar-
                quis of Montrose is to be Lieut.-General to the Duke of Lor-
                raine. Two of the Earl of Northumberland's men employed
                at Paris from the Independents are sent away unsatisfied.
                French reverses at Naples.   *Copy.*
                                                       Endorsed by Hyde.

April 25.   2769. *Mr. Roberts to Mr. Aylesbury.* Tells him how to
                address his letters. Wishes to have some talk with him.
                                                              Original.

April 30,   2770. *Sir E. Hyde to Lord Hopton.* Has received his of
May 1.   the 16th with enclosures. [*A passage in cypher.*] Thinks it
                possible he may exercise too much charity towards the mis-
                reformed Churches. Indulgence is due to them because their
                reformation being without the concurrence of the Crown, their
                combination is imperfect. Are the Huguenots really so much
                opposed to bishops? Despite their defect in orders, the Church
                of England has admitted them to Communion for their conformity
                in opinion. Yet they are presumptuous in desiring the dises-
                tablishment of the English Church, because the King of France
                will not establish them. Would as soon receive the Sacrament
                from Cromwell as from one ordained by Burges and Caroll.
                Does not know how to have ministers without bishops, except
                in case of necessity, which must be carefully determined. Can
                hardly refrain from writing against Mons. Amyrant's apology.

Prophesies that the want of bishops will bring reformed Churches, and the Kirk of Scotland, to ruin. Episcopacy is the bulwark of Protestantism in England, as the Papists well know. Is contented with the present complexion of affairs. [*A passage in cypher.*] Prays him to send particulars of the actions in Hampshire; and other matters for his History. Has heard from Sir Hugh Cholmley. Is suffering from gout. Asks for the reversion of Sutton's Hospital. Encloses a letter to Lady Dalkeith. *Copy.*

Endorsed twice by Hyde.   Cl. S. P. vol. ii. p. 401.

1648.

2771. *Letter of Intelligence.* The City fears the advance of troops. Cromwell is gone to Bow. Proceedings in Parliament. Details of military affairs in Wales. Appointment of officers to the Scotch army; preparations to enter England. The army approaches London. Presbyterian discontent. Duke of York at Flushing. *Copy.*

Endorsed by Hyde.

London, May 1.

2772. *Anonymous letter.* Has received his of 14/24 of April. The Princess Royal sent him to Dort to wait upon the Duke of York, who has come over with Col. Bamfield. Gives a particular account of his escape. He was attended at Dort by Mr. Mayart, Capt. Armorer, Mr. Johnson, and Mr. Fitz-James. From Dort they came, in Capt. Hart's vessel, with Lord Willoughby, Col. Massey, and Mr. Alexander, and were met by the Prince of Orange, Herr Zulenstein, and others. The Duke has since visited the Queen of Bohemia. The States, French, and Portuguese deputies have welcomed the Prince. (*Some erasures.*)

Honselaersdyck,† May 4/14.

2773. *Letter of Intelligence.* Negotiations between Scotland and England. Affairs in Wales, Bristol, and Liverpool. The City and the Parliament. The Duke of York and Rainsborough. The Petition from Essex. Details of the Norwich business. "Nullum bonum ex Aquilone." The Scots Declaration. *Copy.*

Endorsed by Hyde.

London, May 4.

2774. *Letter of Intelligence (from Lord Hopton).* Military affairs in Wales and the West. Alarms at London. The Scots demand the Covenant. Major Hopton sent into Wales with 800 horse. *Copy.*

Endorsed by Hyde.

St. Germains, May 5.

* Signature erased.
† A house of the Prince of Orange, five miles from the Hague.

1648.
St. Germains,
May 8.

2775. *Letter of Intelligence.* Escape of the Duke of York. Langhorne is also escaped and gone to Wales. The Swedes have received a great blow in Germany. Trouble in France.
Copy.
Endorsed by Hyde.

Paris,
May 8.

2776. *Letter of Intelligence.* Rendezvous of the army at Peronne. Details of the affairs of Naples. The Duke of Schomberg, Viceroy of Catalonia. The verification of the Edicts is hindered. Mademoiselle's offer of marriage from the Archduke Leopold.
Copy.
Endorsed by Hyde.

London,
May 8.

2777. *Letter of Intelligence from Jo. Wilcocks* (i. e. *Secretary Nicholas*). Cromwell superseded in his command by Sir Hard. Waller. Proposals of Dr. Hammond's chaplain.
Endorsed.

London,
May 8 and 11.

2778. *Letter of Intelligence.* The King and the Independents. Cromwell's movements. Relations of the Independents, Presbyterians, and the City. The King's forces in the West and North. Troops to be raised by the Parliament. Mr. Squibb taken with Parliament letters. Behaviour of the townsmen of Newcastle. Affairs on the borders of Wales. Answer of Parliament to the Scots messenger; and to the Essex Petition. Sir M. Langdale, Lord Biron, and Sir T. Glenham in the North. The Scots are disunited. The policy of the Parliament. The King is in good health. *Copy.*
Endorsed by Hyde.

Edinburgh,
May 9.

2779. *Letter of Intelligence.* Appointment of officers for the field; strength of the regiments. Opposition of the clergy. Munitions sent to Berwick.
Copy.
On the same paper with that of Paris, May 30.

London,
May 11.

2780. *Letter of Intelligence.* The City have the Militia and the Tower in their own hands. False report of a defeat of the Welsh. Military movements in the North.
(Signed) BOWMAN.
Endorsed by Hyde.

London,
May 15.

2781. *Letter of Intelligence.* Details of the fight near Cardiff on the 18th; and a subsequent engagement. Result of the trial at Canterbury for Church riots. Disturbances at Bury about a Maypole.
Copy.

St. Germains,
May 15.

2782. *Letter of Intelligence.* The Duke of York is in Holland. The Marquis of Ormond and the Marquis of Clanricarde are appointed to treat with the Irish Commissioners.

News of military movements in Wales. They have voted in London for a government by the King and two Houses of Parliament. *Copy.* 1648.
Endorsed by Hyde.

2783. *Letter of Intelligence.* The Scots and the Parliament. Loyal forces in the North. The defeat in Wales. Petitions from Surrey and from Kent will shortly be presented. Thanksgiving for the victory over the Welsh. Military movements in the West and North. Details of the late trial at Canterbury. Disturbances at Bury and Ipswich. *Copy.* May 15.
Endorsed by Hyde.

2784. *Letter of Intelligence.* Movements of the Prince of Condé and Marshal de la Meilleray. News from Naples. Unsettled state of affairs in the French Government. "Mademoiselle's business is reconciled." *Original.* Paris, May 15.
Endorsed, "For my noble friend Sir Geo. Carteret," &c.

2785. *Letter of Intelligence.* Affairs in Wales. The Scotch messengers at St. Germains. Several counties are making associations in pursuance of certain Petitions. Relations of the City and Parliament. "The Presbyterians and Independents are minded rather to submit themselves to the inconveniences of each other's friendship, than by variance to lay themselves open to the Prelatical and Popish party." *Original.* London, May 18.
Endorsed by Hyde.

2786. *Letters of Intelligence.* News from Wales. Murder of the miller of Wandsworth, one of the Surrey Petitioners. Emptiness of the churches. Affairs in the City. News from the North and from Suffolk. Scotch and Irish forces raised for the King. Details of the reception of the Surrey Petition. Probable effect of the discontent in the City and Counties. London, May 18.
Endorsed by Hyde.

2787. *Letters of Intelligence.* Bad policy of the City. News from Wales. The Kentish Petition. Divers Cavaliers imprisoned. The City and the Parliament. It is ordered that on Wednesday next there shall be a debate on an address to the King. The Mayor of Sandwich reports that the Prince is landed there, and in concealment. London, May 21.
Endorsed by Hyde.

2788. *Letter of Intelligence from "Thomas Smyth."* News from England of the Parliament; military movements in the North. Disorders and mutinies in the army. News sent from Langhorne to the Marquis of Worcester. All is quiet in Italy. Arrival of troops in Flanders. A French convoy taken by the Spaniards. Paris, May 23.
Endorsed.

1648.
Edinburgh,
May 13.

2789. *Letter of Intelligence.* An army of 30,000 foot and 9000 horse will be ready in a short time. Sir M. Langdale is in Lancashire. Col. Gray commands in Berwick. The Duke of Hamilton's brother-in-law will command the Scotch army.
Two Copies.
(On the same paper with that of St. Germains, June 12.)

London,
May 15.

2790. *Letters of Intelligence.* The disturbances in Kent delay the advance of the army to the North, and caused the Commons to vote a personal treaty with the King. Petition of the City to the Parliament. New ordinance against Papists and Cavaliers in London. Details of affairs in Kent. The Parliament apologizes to the County of Surrey. Reverses in the North. Proceedings in Parliament. Endorsed by Hyde.

London,
May 19.
(Edinburgh,
May 13.
St. Germains,
June 12.)

2791. *Letters of Intelligence.* Reports from Wales and Scotland. Relations of the City and the Parliament. Deptford Bridge held by the Kentish men. The navy is joined with them. Rainsborough's narrow escape from being hanged. Warwick appointed Admiral. Fairfax ordered to do what he pleases with the Kentish men. Rising of 20,000 Essex men; a bridge of boats making between the two counties. The Tower delivered to West. *Two Copies.*
(On one paper.) In Mr. Trethewy's hand.

London,
May 29.

2792. *Letters of Intelligence.* Effects of the Kentish insurrection: a rendezvous appointed at Blackheath. News from the North and West. Affairs in the City. The revolt of the ships. Endorsed by Hyde.

Paris,
May 30.

2793. *Letter of Intelligence.* The Queen and Prince have been with the King of France and the Queen-Regent; the Cardinal has visited them. Speedy departure of the Prince.
Copy.
(On the same paper with that of Edinburgh, May 9.)

May 30.

2794. *Relation of the business of Kent, in a letter to Lord Culpeper.* The face of the country is wholly changed. It has been always well affected to the King. Particulars of the disturbance at Canterbury last December; entry of Sir M. Levizey and 1000 men. Commission of Oyer and Terminer, May 10, 11, Serjeants Wild and Tresswell being of the Quorum. Sir W. Man, Mr. Lovelace, and Ald. Savin committed. Meeting of Deputy-Lieutenants at Maidstone; the Petition declared seditious. The Deputy-Lieutenants' forces defeated: castles and ships gained. A body of 20,000 men marching to Blackheath. Sir R. Hardress and Sir A. Archer marched towards Sandwich, and after taking Cornelius Evans (a counterfeit

Prince of Wales), they proceeded by Deal towards Dover, and 1648. thence to Rochester. The Admiral returning to London in a Weymouth coaster. They pray Lord Culpeper to come to Calais and send them advice and assistance. *Draught.*
Endorsed by Hyde. Cl. S. P. vol. II. p. 404.

2795. *A Paper* in explanation of the Scots Declaration, Edinburgh, particularly of that part which relates to the solemn League May. and Covenant, and the refusal to put such power into the King's hands as shall be dangerous to religion. *Copy.*
Endorsed by Hyde.

2796. *Letter of Intelligence.* Tenby is blockaded by Horton; London, Pembroke is free. Langherne's forces are untouched. Pe- June 1. tition of the City to Parliament. Lord Fairfax has baffled the Kentish men under Hales. Dover Castle is relieved. The Common Council of the City has voted to adhere to the associate counties. Failure of the King's attempt to escape from Carisbrook. The King's restitution very likely if the matters of the Church hinder it not. Account of a debate on the proposal to increase the Committee of Safety at Derby House. Reports from the fleet and from Kent. *Copy.*

2797. *Letter of Intelligence.* Account of the business of June 1. Kent and the associated counties. News from Wales and the North, and from the fleet. Particulars of movements in Kent, and the refusal of the set to admit the Earl of Warwick as Admiral. Sermon preached on the fast day in the House of Commons. Reception of the Petition of the Common Council. Major-General Brown's speech in the House. Reports from the North. A Frenchman taken at Sandwich supposed to be the Prince. Eleven of the Surrey Petitioners killed. Further account of the resources of the associated counties. Relations between Independents and Presbyterians. The Irish are marching towards Dublin. *Copy.*
Endorsed.

2798. *Names of the Lords* who were summoned to wait on June 1. the Queen and Prince at the Louvre on June 1. Twenty-two names. *Copy.*

2799. *Letter of Intelligence.* The Duke of Vendome's son Paris, has escaped from Vincennes. Two more of the Parliament June 1. have been arrested. The Prince has come from St. Germains.
Addressed to Mr. Clutterbuck, secretary to Lord Cottington.

1648.
Calais,
June 3.

2800. *Letter of Intelligence.* Reception of the Petition of the Kentish men. News from the fleet, which has left the Downs. Strength of the Kentish forces. Dover Castle holds out. Reports from the Isle of Wight, and from Wales.
Copy.

London,
June 5.

2801. *Letters of Intelligence.* Details of affairs in Kent and Essex. Lady Mildmay intercepted. The Earl of Warwick is sent to Portsmouth. The Earl of Norwich crossed with troops from Greenwich into Essex. Unsettled state of the City. News from Wales, the North, and Ireland. The revolt of the navy.
Copy.

London,
June 5.

2802. *James B[onnithon] to* ———. In accordance with instructions received from Mr. Morley, he awaits his correspondent's return, and places himself at his disposal.
Original.
(Mutilated.)

June 7.

2803. *(Secretary Nicholas) to the King.* Has received his of the 9th. Obeys the King's command to give advice on the Prince's remove into Holland, of which he fully approves. Will always be ready, in spite of his necessities, to serve the King in person.
Copy.
Endorsed by Secretary Nicholas.

June 8.

2804. *Mr. R. H[ollins] to Mr. Denman.* His departure has occasioned much surprise and inconvenience. Kentish fire is "now vanished into smoak."
Original.

Paris,
June 8.

2805. *Francis Chapman [Marquis of Antrim] to Mr. William.* Believes he is a friend of "my sister Crombie." Has received his messages through Mr. Robert. Desires him to assist in maintaining "my sister in France," as Mr. Trayle and Mr. Robert advise him. Cannot keep correspondence with Mr. Crombie and his brother-in-law.
Original.
Endorsed, "Marq. of Antrim."
(Seal, an arm holding a cross patée with palm branches on either side, surmounted by an Earl's coronet.)

St. Germain en Laye,
June 10.

2806. *The Prince (Charles) of Wales to Sir E. Hyde.* Tells him of his own purpose to go into Holland. Desires his advice therein.
Signed by the Prince.

St. Germains,
June 12.

2807. *Letter of Intelligence.* The Queen has good news from Sir Marm. Langdale; who will be speedily supplied with arms and ammunition from Holland.
Two Copies.

2808. *Letter of Intelligence.* Movements of the Queen and the Prince; Lord and Lady Hatton and friends. *Copy.* Partly in cypher. St. Germains, June 14. 1648.

2809. *Sir E. Hyde to the Queen.* Has received her letter of the 9th, and another from the Prince. Approves of the Queen's resolution for his Highness' remove into Holland. *Copy.* June 14.
Endorsed by himself. Cl. S. P. vol. ii. p. 407.

2810. *The same to the Prince.* Has received his letter of the 10th. Does not so well understand the state of affairs in the three kingdoms as to be able to offer particular advice as to the Prince's resolution to remove into Holland, but believes that it is seasonable, and may prove of singular advantage to his service. *Copy.* Jersey, June 14.
Endorsed by himself.

2811. *The same to Lord Jermyn.* Has received his of the 16th (N. S.), and will despatch an answer the same day. Prays him to thank the Queen and Prince for the great favour of their commands. Will come to St. Germains as soon as he has boots to put on. Thanks him for sending supplies. Will now put off sending for a physician for himself and Sir Philip Carteret. Makes arrangements for receiving money for his journey. *Copy.* Jersey, June 16.
Endorsed by himself. Cl. S. P. vol. ii. p. 407.

2812. *The same to Lord Culpeper.* Thinks that the commands he has received from Lord Jermyn to attend the Prince to Holland are partly due to Lord Culpeper. Thanks him for his favour and assures him of his constancy. Has received a letter from Mr. Nicholls with orders to send a trunk of Lord Culpeper's to St. Malo. Gives reasons for keeping it in the island. *Copy.* Jersey, June 16.
Endorsed by himself.

2813. *Mr. Roberts to Mr. William Aylesbury*, by M. le Chevalier du Vic. Has received a letter from Mrs. Susan Wagh. Is glad to hear he is in Holland. Hears that Mr. John Trayle has delivered him 130*l.* for himself. Sends this letter by Fr. D'Arcy of Bruxelles, Sir H. du Vic, Mr. Porter, or Mr. Webster. Mr. Whitman is gone. He is to assist Mr. J. Trayle and Roberts in Mrs. Crombie's affairs. Wants money badly. Inquires after jewels, and other private matters. Mr. Rich. Masson is daily expected. Sir K. Digby is come from Rome. *Original.* Paris, June 18.

1648.
Mynde,
June 19.

2814. *Sir W. Pye to ———.* The uncertainty of his correspondent's return out of Holland and other difficulties have forced him to make use of the interest he has in the Bailiff of Leominster's Oare, and take 100*l.* of the Duke's money. Desires him to procure a discharge for the same. *Original.*

June 20.

2815. *Dr. Isaac Dorislaus' Credentials from the Parliament.* Letters credential addressed to the States, and sent by Dorislaus, in which complaint is made of an act of violence committed by some of their ships in the port of Bristol. Signed by E. Manchester and Gul. Lenthall (in Latin), with a letter of Dorislaus to the States, dated Aug. 12, 1648, in Dutch, on the occasion. *Copy.*

With an (apparently) original signature to the letter.

Bramford,
June 20.

2816. *C. Alleyn* [endorsed "Sir Chas. Cotterell"] *to Mr. W. Denman, at Amsterdam.* All is subdued in Kent but Deal, Sandowne, and Sandwich. Fairfax lies near Colchester. "My Lord of Norwich, Lord Capell, Sir Ch. Lucas, keepe the town." Gives various reports. *Original.*

St. Germaine,
June 21.

2817. *Letter of Intelligence.* Particulars of the Duke of York's order to the seven ships that had signed the Kentish Petition, and their subsequent movements. Lord Willoughby of Parham sent to advise with them. The Prince is to take the command. Loyalty of the town of Yarmouth. Sir J. Berkeley besieged in Peronne by the Archduke's forces that are now very strong about Aix-la-Chapelle. *Copy.*

Paris,
June 23.

2818. *Lord Digby to Sir E. Hyde.* Urges him to hasten his departure in order to wait upon the Prince, who is on his way to Calais, where will be the rendezvous of most of the King's Council in France, who are to make a settlement in the business of the ships that are declared for the King.
Original.
Endorsed by Hyde.   Cl. S. P. vol. ii. p. 408.

The Hague,
June 25.

2819. *Dr. Stephen Goffe to Mr. Aylesbury.* He will find a better sale for his "commodities" in Antwerp than in Amsterdam. The royal fleet is come into Gorèe, "9 brave ships." Gives news reports from England. *Original.*

Paris,
June 26.

2820. *Lord Jermyn to the same.* Thanks him for two letters. Hears from Dr. Goffe that he can do in Holland that which in England he failed of. Will do the Duke [of Buckingham] all the service he can. *Original.*

CLARENDON PAPERS. 429

2821. *Mr. Roberts to Mr. Aylesbury, at Amsterdam.* Has received his of May 15. Has sent a letter to him by Fr. Charles Daray. Hopes to go to Holland. Mentions Mrs. Crongby's [Crombie's] affairs. Wants the 130*l.* Gives details of several private matters. Prince Charles has taken leave of the King of France. Mr. Masson is come safe. Reports news from Scotland. *Original.*
<small>1648. Paris, June 26.</small>

2822. *Joseph Ashe to the same, at Amsterdam.* Has received his of May 19th for June 19th. Gives information about the letting of a house. *Original.*
<small>Antwerp, June 27.</small>

2823. *Mr. R. Sydney to the same.* A complimentary letter. *Original.*
<small>The Hague, June 19.</small>

2824. *Anonymous Letter to Sir E. Hyde.* Answers the Chancellor's request to give him an account of the Prince's journey, and who stay behind. Dr. Goffe has 1000*l.* a year for being supervisor to Sir W. Boswell. "The Ki. was very earnest with me to goe with Ld. Ch. and is very angry. QE. will not let Ld. Dig. goe. . . . He urged my meeting Sir E. H." Mr. Dugdale is with him. The Prince's first station is Calais, whence he will either go with Lord Willoughby of Parham and his ships, or by land to Holland. *Original.*
<small>June 19.</small>
<small>In cypher, decyphered by Hyde.</small>

2825. *Sir E. Hyde to Sir J. Berkeley.* Hopes the former letter, inclosed in one to Sir H. Boswell, has reached him. Gives a short account of the misfortunes he met with when he first left Jersey to meet the Prince at Calais. Mentions the affair of Ostend. *Copy.*
<small>Middleburgh, July 1.</small>
<small>Endorsed by Hyde. See Life, pp. 104-7.</small>

2826. *Mr. Roberts to Mr. Aylesbury.* Has received his of May 15 and 19 for June 15 and 19. Will venture imprisonment at Cambray rather than wait for money or passes. The Prince is about to go to Calais, where he will be met by most of the English nobility, some of whom will proceed to Holland. Prays him to send 20 pistoles to pay interest for the jewels. Has got money at 6½ per cent.
<small>Paris, July 3.</small>

Another letter of the same purport of the above date from the same to the same, sent by a different hand. *Original.*

2827. *Stephen Gough to William Aylesbury, at Amsterdam;* endorsed "Dr. Goffe." Good news from Essex. The Prince is to be at Calais this night, and the ships are to meet him
<small>[St. Germains.] July 4.</small>

1648. there; whither they will sail is not determined. "My lord Duke [of Buckingham] hath many hearty wishers in France; pray God bless him in this engagement in Essex." Sir E. Hyde is summoned to attend the Prince.

July 8. 2828. *Mr. A. Woodhead to Mr. Denman.* Sir Charles Cotterell is at Cranborne. Mentions Mr. Hides and Mr. Dayrell. Reports news from England, of a "fight about Kingston." Lady Cotterell has executed his commissions. *Original.*

Paris,
July 9. 2829. *Mr. Roberts to Mr. Aylesbury.* A third letter of the same purport as those of July 3. Mentions Trayle and Whitman. *Original.*

July 5 and 11. 2830. *Order of the House of Commons.* To appoint a Committee to treat with the Common Council of the City and other officers concerning their engagement for the safety of the King and the Parliament during the intended personal treaty. Articles agreed upon between them in case the proposed treaty should be held in the City.—Printed.

July 13. 2831. *Lady Aylesbury to Mr. William Aylesbury.* They have concluded with Mr. Goodwin; and are in full possession. Is glad he is away from them, and the sad accidents that have happened. His sisters desire to be remembered to him. *Original.*

Cranborne,
July 13. 2832. *Sir Chas. Cotterell to Mr. Wm. Denman.* The Duke of Buckingham, with his brother and my Lord of Holland and Peterborough and others, met together at Kingston on Wednesday was se'nnight with 600 horse. The Lord Francis was slain. Details of private and money matters.

July 14. 2833. *Mr. Woodhead to the same.* Since Lord Francis was killed the forces have been routed at St. Neots. "The Lord Holland taken, the Duke of Buckingham escaped with some few horse. . . . The procuring of an act of indemnity for him . . . is much laboured. . . . Mr. Dayrell is suing for his goods." A Petition delivered by the London Independents against any personal treaty was received with thanks. *Original.*

July 18. 2834. *Mr. T. Remington to Mr. Alesbury.* Has received his of the 14th. Has enclosed letters to Mr. Arthur Dee. *Original.*

2835. *A Pass* from the Prince of Wales to Mr. Edgeman, to go to Rouen, Dieppe, and other places.
Signed by the Prince. Countersigned by Robert Long.
1648. Calais, July 19.

2836. *Mons. Vallois to* ———. Has suffered loss in the death of his patron and is in great distress. After God, has no helper but the person he addresses. Has some debts. Prays him not to refuse help. *Original.*
July 11.

2837. *John Hopkins [W. Hyde] to [Sir E. Hyde].* Has received his of June 21, and another with an inclosure to Mr. Johnson. Prepares him for a visit from himself.* *Original.*
London, July 11.

2838. *Mr. A. Woodhead to Mr. W. Denman.* Reports news from England. Mr. Dayrell hopes to have his goods. Colchester holds out. The City has drawn up articles against Skippon. It is reported that Portsmouth is surprised. *Original.*
July 11.

2839. *Edmund Grisvald (or Grissel) to* ———. Begs him to remind Mr. Aylesbury of the writer's business with him. Mr. Edwards and another complain much of Aylesbury's dealings. *Original.*
July 15.

2840. *The Prince of Wales to the Duke of Hamilton, the Earl of Lindsay, Lords Lauderdale, Lanerick, and Callender.* Earnestly desires to be with them. Expects their Commissioners upon the subject of Sir W. Fleming's instructions. Begs them to give credit to the bearer, W. Murray.
Rough Draught.
From the Fleet, July 16.

2841. *Order* by the Prince for the setting forth a declaration, with the reason and grounds of his present appearing upon the fleet in action.
(Eight reasons, as in the printed paper.) Signed by the Prince. Endorsed by Hyde.
The Downs, July 17.

2842. *The Lord Treasurer, Lord Cottington, and Sir E. Hyde to the Prince.* Gives an account of their movements after their leaving Dieppe, and being taken to Ostend. Beg the Prince to complain to the Archduke of the inhuman treatment they received.
In Hyde's hand. Signed by Lord Cottington and himself.
See Life, p. 104.
July 18.

2843. *Mr. A. Woodhead to Mr. Denman.* Mr. Dayroll has his goods. The claims of others have caused a demur in the Committee for disposing of them. *Original.*
July 18.

* Apparently so; speaking of himself in the third person.

432   CALENDAR OF

1648.
July 18.
2844. *Mons. Vallois to* ———. Another appeal of the same purport as that of July 21.   *Rough Draught.*

From the Fleet,
July 19.
2845. *The Prince to the Lord Mayor, Aldermen, and Common Council of the City of London.* Desires them to supply him with 20,000*l.* for the subsistence of the navy, which shall be repaid out of the Customs. If they make this grant he will restore the merchant ships now detained by him.

See Hist. Rebell. and Parl. Hist.

The Downs,
July 29.
2846. "*The Prince's Declaration* to all his Majesty's loving subjects concerning the grounds and ends of his present engagement upon the fleet in the Downs." The peace of the kingdom and the relief of his father's distress is his principal aim. Embodies the eight reasons given in the order of July 27. Promises pay and indemnity to Fairfax's soldiers and Warwick's seamen if they leave their service.   Endorsed by Hyde.

(This is very different from the printed paper dated July 31.) See Parl. Hist. vol. xvii. p. 342.

Amsterdam,
July 30.
2847. *Mr. John Webster to Mr. John Aylesbury, at Antwerp.* Has received his of July 26. The cabinet is still unsold. Cannot send 300*l.* Gives a statement of the account between them.   *Original.*

The Hague,
July 30.
2848. *Sir E. Brett to Mr. W. Aylesbury.* Would have sent off the arms and pistols, but a report of the rout of the forces brought by Mr. Smith makes him wait for further instructions.   *Original.*

From the Navy,
July 31.
2849. "*Prince Charles, his declaration, for satisfaction of all his Majesties loyall subjects in England, Scotland, and Ireland.*" (Signed) Willoughby, Hopton, Culpeper.

(Eight pages, uncut.)   Printed in the year 1648, with a declaration of eight reasons of his appearing upon the fleet in action.

July or Aug.
2850. "*Relation* of the last secret business." The engagement of Duke Hamilton. "I hold myself obliged to render to the world the account, &c. ... This I protest to do with that undoubted impartiality, that not a person living, whether he be of the Hamilton faction, or of that of Argyle's, &c. ... When not only the lawfulness, but the unavoidable necessity of engaging in a War against the Breakers of the Covenant, of ever cursed memory, with England, &c. ... If the Duke's designe was to ruin the well affected to the King and the Royal

party, &c. . . . Sir Marmaduke Langdale is treated with; . . . he is permitted to take Berwick and Carlisle, &c. . . ." 1648.

(Two pages.) An imperfect paper.

2851. "Mr. W. Murrey's explanation of a passage in the Scotch Parliament's declaration." ["In D. Hamilton's Engagement."] Undertakes to clear some things at which he might scruple in their declaration, made by Earl Lanerick so that there is an evasion for every passage. Instances some of these. *Copy.* July or Aug.

Endorsed as above.

2852. *The Earl of Peterborough to Sir E. Hyde.* Has heard of his movements from Dr. Fraser. Has been hindered from following him. Begs him to deliver an enclosed letter to the Prince. Was boarded in crossing by a Parliament vessel. *Original.* Rotterdam, Aug. 7.

Endorsed by Hyde.

2853. *The Lord Treasurer to Sir Henry de Vic, afterwards Chancellor of the Garter.* Desires him to apply to the Archduke for the restoration of the goods of which they were plundered when they were carried to Ostend. *Copy.* Treasure, Aug. 8.

By Edgeman. Corrected by Hyde.

2854, 2855. *The Lord Treasurer (Lord Cottington) and Sir E. Hyde to the Prince.* Mr. Carteret will inform him of their movements. Sent a letter by Col. Washington. Have been eleven or twelve days at Middleborough; are about to go to Rotterdam, whence they may wait on the Princess Royal and the Duke of York. Have frequently written to the Prince. *Rough Draught.* Middleborough, Aug. 9.

By Hyde. See letter of July 28, 1648.

2856. *The same to the same.* Inform the Prince, by Mr. Carteret, of their movements. Beg him to send them his commands. *Original.* Treasure, Aug. 15.

See Life, p. 109.

2857. *Earl of Lauderdale* [on behalf of the *Committee of Estates of the Parliament of Scotland*] *to the Prince of Wales.* The Scottish army having marched into England for the rescue of the King, the Prince is invited to come into Scotland or join the army, with full assurance of honour, freedom, and safety. He is requested to use the way of divine worship established by law in Scotland, and since that kingdom cannot admit the The Downs, Aug. 16.

3 K

1648.	Book of Common Prayer, to bring no chaplains who have not taken the Covenant. *Copy.* Endorsed by Hyde.
Aug. 17.	2858. *Draught* of the Prince's reply to Lauderdale. He will, as soon as the fleet is settled, begin a voyage towards the Scots army; and consents while in Scotland or with the army to use their way of divine worship, and not to bring with him any chaplains.
Brussels, Aug. 19.	2859. *Mr. Endymion Porter to Mr. W. Aylesbury, at Antwerp.* Has received his of the 18th. Hears he wishes to see his brother Hyde. Mentions F. Clayton and F. D'Arcy. Sends a complimentary message to "Mr. Chancellor." *Original.*
Flushing, Aug. 19.	2860. *Sir E. Hyde to Lord Culpeper.* Relates the difficulties they encountered in their passage; being forced to put back to Flushing, whence they had sailed a week before, and where they are still weather-bound. The Lord Treasurer suffers from the ill-accommodation of the ship. This letter will probably not precede them. There is much discourse of the Scotch Commissioners being sent to invite the Prince into the North to their army. Discusses the purpose and possible consequence of their entry into England under the Duke of Hamilton, and thinks that the Prince should not join them until a full and particular agreement be made. The Prince continuing in the fleet is like, in the present conjuncture, to be more formidable to the rebels than landing and joining the Scots army. Suggests points for consideration as to the management of the navy. Proposes that Guernsey be reduced and made the rendezvous of the ships, and a centre for purposes of administration. Shows how money may be raised for the Prince's expenses and the supply of the fleet. Another unsuccessful attempt to leave this port has just been made. Points out that the King's assent to all laws is that necessary condition for which they are contending; and that if the King give way to Parliament there will be no end to their demands. Does not wholly approve of the Prince's declaration. *Copy.* By Edgeman. Endorsed by himself. Partly printed in Cl. S. P. vol. ii. p. 409.
The Downs, Aug. 22.	2861. *The Prince to the Scots Committee of Estates of the Parliament of Scotland.* Has received their letter by Lord Lauderdale, to whom answer has been given that the Prince will repair immediately to their army in England. Encourages them to promote the interests of the King. *Rough Draught.* By Mr. Long. See Burnet's Memoirs of the Duke of Hamilton, p. 366.

2862. *Sir Marmaduke Langdale's relation of the defeat of the Scots*, addressed to the Prince. Gives details of the movements of the armies in Lancashire. The Scots, on crossing the river, neglected to secure a lane near the bridge, whereby Sir M. Langdale's flank was turned; after which the Scots forces were beaten from the bridge. Six Scotch lords, of whom Lord Traquhaire was one, left them. Three of the officers are in Nottingham Castle. *Three Copies.*

1648.
Aug. 16.

Two written in the first person. One by Edgeman, in the third person. See Hist. Rebell. bk. ii. pp. 537, 538, ed. 1732. Printed in Carte's Original Letters.

2863. *The Earl of Lauderdale to the Prince [of Wales]*. Was ready the previous day to have waited on the Prince when he resolved to fight. The writer's ship cannot go within the sands. Desires to know the Prince's condition now that his resolution of going straight to Holland is abandoned. *Original.*

Margate Roads.
Aug. 17.

Cl. S. P. vol. ii. p. 412.

2864. *The Prince [of Wales] to Lord Lauderdale*. Is well satisfied with the loyalty of the kingdom of Scotland. Is now engaged in an expedition against the Earl of Warwick. Will soon follow Lord Lauderdale into Holland, and there fulfil the engagement to which he adheres. *Copy.*

Aug. 19.

Cl. S. P. vol. ii. p. 413.

2865. *The Prince of Wales to the Prince of Orange*. Recommends Lord Lauderdale to him, and begs him to further his negotiation. *Three Rough Draughts.*

Aug. 19.

On the same page, by Mr. Long.

2866. *The Prince of Wales' Proposals* to the company of merchants at Rotterdam for a supply for the service of his fleet. The Prince engages himself to procure an act of indemnity, and to protect their ships, and to repay their subsidy. *Copy.*

Aug.

By Hyde. Endorsed by him, " Paper delivered by Dr. Goffe to the company at Rotterdam." See Hist. Rebell. bk. ii. p. 556.

2867. *Sir Philip Musgrave's relation of the Scots engagement*. The Scotch Commissioners, "Lord Lowdon, Lord Lancrick, and Lord Lotherdaile," imparted to the writer, amongst others, their purpose to raise an army to restore the King. Mentions Sir M. Langdale, Mr. A. Barclay, Sir T. Glenham, the Duke of Hamilton, Col. Denton, John Eglionby, Major Charnley, Mr. Barwis, Sir H. Bellingham, Sir Patrick Curmen, Sir E. Musgrave, Sir W. Huddleston, Sir H. Fether-

No date.

1648. ston, Col. Chater, Col. Carleton, Col. Lockhart, Sir T. Tildesley, Sir W. Leveston, Major-Gen. Ashton, and others. Gives a detailed account of events from April 27 to August 1648.
Original.
(Six pages.) Endorsed by Hyde.

Sept. 1. 2868. *The Lord Treasurer (Lord Cottington) to Lord Hopton.* Complains of his not having written, "for which I could be very cholerick, but that Mr. Chancellor's meekness restroyned me." Hears with surprise of the Prince's movements. Begs him to read Hyde's letter to Lord Culpeper, to himself, and then, if he think fit, to the Prince. Mr. Wansford will inform him of the condition they are reduced to. *Rough Draught.*
By Hyde. Endorsed by him.

Bruges, Sept. 1. 2869. *Lord Goring (Earl of Newport) to the Lord Treasurer Cottington.* Prays him to procure subsistence for some men on their coming to the fleet, and consider of a place for their landing; also some money for the Prince. Begs him to inquire what Dr. Goffe has done in the matter of meeting an offer of troops; and to show this letter to the Chancellor.*
Original.
Endorsed by Hyde. (Three pages.) Apparently the second sheet of a letter.

Flushing, Sept. 1. 2870. *The Lord Treasurer and Sir E. Hyde to the Prince.* Sends this by Mr. Wansford, who has come with them from Rouen. Have been hindered from obeying his commands to come to him. Understand that the Prince is on his return from the Downs to the Hague. Send the bearer to receive his commands there. *Original.*
With a draught by Hyde. Endorsed by him.

Middleborough, Sept. 2. 2871. *Sir E. Hyde to Lord Goring.* Has received his letter to himself and another to the Lord Treasurer, who is in too much pain to write. Henry de Vic and Mr. Taylor arrived last Monday. They hear that the Prince was resolved to leave the Downs for Scarborough. Col. Slaughter reported yesterday was on his way.'. . . They therefore suspend their voyage, and have sent an express to the Hague for information. Has heard of some assistance from the Duke of Lorraine, in which Lord Goring was to be employed. Whenever the writer and the Lord Treasurer meet the Prince they will advance Lord Goring's desires with all their interest; and if they see Dr. Goffe, will inquire the state of the business with Vanderpat. Lord Goring's training in the Spanish army raises great expectations of his generalship. *Copy.*
By Edgeman. Endorsed by Hyde. Cl. S. P. vol. ii. p. 413.

* This probably relates to some scheme for assisting the Kentish men.

2872. Sir E. Hyde to "My Lords in the Downs." The report of the Prince's being on his return from the Downs to the Hague is the reason of their staying at Middleborough. Mentions Sir W. Vavasour, Mr. Wansford, Sir W. Batten, and Major Charles Dawson. *Copy.*
By Hyde. Endorsed by him. (See letter of Sept. 8.)

1648. Middleborough, Sept. 2.

2873. A *Journal* of the movements of the Royal Fleet. Heard of the approach of the Earl of Warwick, whose fleet they found in the river. After some manœuvring, being short of provision, they sailed from Holland and came to Helvoetsluys. *Copy.*
By Edgeman. Endorsed by Hyde.

The Downs and Helvoetsluys, Aug. 26— Sept. 2.

2874. Sir E. Hyde to "*their Lordships in the Downes*, by the captain of the frigate." The wind is still contrary. Repeats a rumour of the arrival of the Duke of York. Mentions Captain Burley and Captain Stanton. "I do not think any one of you is left in the Downs that can read my own hand." The Lord Treasurer has been ill of the gout. *Copy.*
By Edgeman. Endorsed by Hyde. (See letter of Sept. 2.)

Middleborough, Sept. 8.

2875. "*Mr. J. May to my Lord* * [addressed to Mr. Johnson]. If he give himself up to the General, he will probably be received into protection without conditions, except that of thanking the General, "who in his owne nature is affable and courteous." Has written on other topics to Mr. Denman.

London, Sept. 10.

2876. Sir T. A. to Mr. Denman. Informs him of the taking of Colchester, and the death of Sir Charles Lucas and Sir George Lisle. The Earl of Norwich, Lord Capell, and Lord Loughborough are prisoners in Windsor Castle. Has difficulties in paying his composition. Mentions H. Cogan.
Original.
(Two pages.)

Sept. 14.

2877. The Prince of Wales to Lord Cottington and Sir E. Hyde. Has received their letter by Mr. Wansford. Approves what they have done. Directs them to attend him at the Hague.
Signed by the Prince.

Sept. 15.

2878. "Dr. Stewart's relation of the management of the fleet under Prince Charles," (commencing "My Lord"). They cared chiefly for help from the Scots. Lord Cottington and Chancellor Hyde are come to the Hague this day. Took 120,000*l.* worth of prizes. A mutiny detained the Prince.

The Hague, Sept. 17.

* The Duke of Buckingham.

1648. Captain Jordan nearly came up with the Vice-Admiral of Warwick's fleet. They passed by the Portsmouth fleet in the night. The Prince has behaved very gallantly.

(Two pages.)   Endorsed by Hyde.

The Hague, Sept. 18.

2870. "A relation of the Prince's motions, councils, and actions in the fleet." Mentions Button, Lord Brainford, Lord Withorington. "Sir W. Bellenden is gone for Scotland with 10,000 arms and ammunition." Probable rupture between the Knights of Malta and the States.

(Four pages.) By the same hand as that of Sept. 17th, but more circumstantial.   Endorsed by Hyde.

Sept. 19.   2880. *The Prince's Answer to the summons of the Earl of Warwick.* None but the King can make a Lord High Admiral of England. Offers pardon, pay, and protection to any officers and men who shall leave Lord Warwick's command; and will receive Lord Warwick himself with sincerity and affection.   *Rough Draught.*

In Hyde's hand.

The Hague, Sept. 21.

2881. [*Endorsement.*] "Relation concerning the management of the fleet under the Prince, for Sir E. H., written I suppose by Mr. L." They are at length on dry land. Relates the divisions of the Council and mutinies of the men. Met Lord Warwick's fleet at Lee Road; followed it to Queenborough; anchored within cannon shot; but without fighting; weighed for Holland, followed by Warwick, who cast anchor at night; they themselves going on, "and here we are, I thank God; and if they ever get me into their sea voyages again I am much mistaken." The Prince behaved gallantly. Culpeper is hated by all. They have released several rich ships on easy compositions. The States allow the Prince 1000 guilders a day. The Scots here look very blank. They have no thoughts of going northward. W. L. came to them in the Downs with commands from the King to bring the fleet to the Isle of Wight. Lord Cottington and the Chancellor are come to them as counsellors.

Endorsed as above.   Cl. S. P. vol. ii. p. 414.

Sept. 22.   2882. *Sir E. Hyde to the Queen.* Last Thursday he and the Lord Treasurer presented themselves to the Prince. Regrets that he did not see the Queen in France and learn her wishes. Is so devoted to the government of the Church of England that he cannot consent to anything that may destroy or alter it, for if that were done the rights of the Crown could not be preserved; and he will resist all attempts, even those of the King or Queen themselves, to deprive them of the power of the Crown. Begs her therefore to consider how unfit he is for the transaction entrusted to him. The Prince's putting himself into the hands of the Scots cause the writer great perplexity, which the defeat of the Duke of Hamilton does not remove. Trusts he shall not lose the Queen's favour if he do not accompany the Prince into Scotland, in case he go there on the present conditions, but prays he may be appointed to some other service. Will obey the Queen's commands received by Lord Culpeper. *Original.*

1648.

<small>And a draught by Edgeman, on which latter is endorsed by Hyde. "Draught of a letter to the Queen which I after waved and writ it to my Ld. Jermyn by Mr. Freeman." Cl. S. P. vol. ii. p. 416.</small>

2883. *Mr. Woodhead to* ———. "Col. A." desires him to inclose a letter this week. Cromwell's men have taken Scarborough. Pontefract stands out. Scilly is taken by some French, it is supposed under the Prince's command. Other items of news. *Original.*

Sept. 23.

2884. [*Mr. Peter Roberts*] *to Mr. Aylesbury.* Encloses a warrant he has obtained; and some letters from England relating to private affairs. *Original.*

The Hague. Sept. 24.

2885. *Mr. Nicolls' Memorial* of the "results of the several conferences which passed in the month of September betwixt Sir George Carteret and Sir Baldwin Wake about the expedition then on foot for reduction of the Isle of Guernsey to his Maty" obedience." Chiefly an account of their disputes, and the failure of the expedition, through the obstinacy of Sir Baldwin Wake. Mentions Capt. Sherwood.

Sept.

<small>(Four pages.) Drawn up after the King's death. Endorsed by Hyde.</small>

2886. "*Earl of Warwick's first summons to the Fleete.*" As Lord High Admiral of England requires the Admiral of the King's fleet to take down his standard. *Copy.*

Sept.

<small>By Edgeman. Hist. Rebell. bk. ii. p. 549; Parl. Hist. vol. xvii. p 496.</small>

2887. *Lord Byron's Account* of his proceedings since his coming into Cheshire, and of what happened in those parts from Feb. 20, 1648 till the middle of Sept. following. Found the King's party so unwilling to undertake anything that he applied to Col. John Booth, who having received a commission undertook to raise two regiments and secure Warrington and Liverpool: but upon urging him to declare, having in view the relief of Pembroke Castle, he being influenced by Holland, Shuttleworth, and other Presbyterians, did not stir until Byron himself, having a warrant out against him, was obliged to

Sept.

1648. escape, after appointing a rendezvous in Dallamour Forest on May 18, for which 200 engaged themselves, but only a tenth part appeared, with Col. Roger Whiteley. They then being surrounded by Parliament troops dispersed, soon after which sixty of their party arrived at the place of meeting, and finding none there, separated. Booth, though warned of the approach of Cromwell's horse under Major Huntingdon, suffered himself to be taken in Warrington, with arms and ammunition, but was soon after set at liberty. Cromwell's horse then marched on to Lambert, leaving Rigby in Lancashire. About the same time Berwick and Carlisle were surprised by Sir M. Langdale and Sir P. Musgrave with 5000 foot and 200 horse, who had already reduced Cumberland and Westmoreland. The Lancashire rebels being thus terrified, the Presbyterians in that county, with those of Yorkshire and Durham, sent to treat with Sir Marmaduke, who nevertheless, though urged also by Lord Byron, retreated to Carlisle, where he continued till the Scotch army came in, and gave Lambert time to recruit. Byron then endeavoured to raise men in Shropshire and North Wales, and would have succeeded had the money promised been sent out of France. Their designs in North Wales were hindered by the Archbishop of York. Denbigh Castle lost through a panic. Col. Robinson and Capt. Symkis caused the Isle of Anglesea to declare for the King. Sir J. Owen defeated Mytton in Carnarvonshire, and would have followed up his success with the help of Col. Whiteley, had not the Archbishop of York interfered. Henry Lingen gave assurances of Hereford; Col. Stopkins of Stafford, and others of Chester, but none of the attempts succeeded; Stopkins was betrayed and killed. Lingen on his way to North Wales was defeated and taken by Col. Horton. Meanwhile the Anglesea party having cleared that island and gone as far as Llanrwst, Col. Whiteley was sent to join them and wait for the Duke of Hamilton's advance with the Scotch army, of whose overthrow there soon came assurance, Hamilton having given himself up at Uttoxeter to Lord Grey; a disaster that more than outweighed Sir M. Langdale's success. Thereupon the party at Llanrwst fell back into Anglesea. "The Archbishop of York, whilst the Scotch cloud hung over him, made his countrymen believe he was for the King," but soon returned to his old practices, and nearly obtained the expulsion of Lord Byron from Anglesea, who, finding his command opposed, retired to Col. Robinson's house near Holyhead, having first written to the gentlemen of the island declaring the commission he had from the Prince of Wales. The Archbishop represents to the islanders the hopelessness of the King's cause; and Mytton with 1500 horse and foot invades the island and defeats Bulkeley and Col. Whiteley.

Sir Arthur Blayney is killed. Col. Robinson makes his escape 1648. to the Isle of Man. *Original.*

Endorsed by Hyde. "Lord Byron's relation of his actions, summer 1648, received from him at the Hague 27th of March."
Partly printed in Cl. S. P. vol. ii. p. 418.

2888. *Edw. du Jardin to Mr. Aylesbury.* Has been in the Oct. 1. service of "my Lord Duke and my Lord his brother." Is nearly destitute. Prays for relief. Adds an account amounting to 93*l*. of which 12*l*. is "with my lord Frances."
Original.

2889. "*An Account* of the forty-five barrels of indigo re- Oct. 3. ceived out of the 'Danyell' of London, in the Downs the 19th of August, 1648, twelve thereof delivered to Sir Baldwin Wake by order, the other thirty-three returned the owner upon composition of one guilder per pound for Helvoetsluys the 3rd of October following." Paid 8000 guilders to Mr. Hammond, treasurer of the fleet, by appointment of my Lord Treasurer Willoughby. (Signed) Tho. Fisher. *Original.*
Endorsed by Hyde.

2890. *Mr. (T.) Dayrell to Mr. W. Aylesbury.* Has sent his Oct. 3. letter to "Dover." It is not yet safe for him to come to England. The Isle of Wight treaty will probably come to nothing. "Sir Ch. Cott[erell] writ to me for your great horizontal Dyal for Mr. Chichley." *Original.*

2891. *Algernon Sydney to the same.* Heard from him a London, month ago. Thinks he may come to London with safety, and Oct. 4. with a fair prospect of transacting the business he has in hand with good success. *Original.*
Cl. S. P. vol. ii. p. 431.

2892. *An Attestation* by a notary, Gabriel Gabrielli, to his Oct. 5. having made a true copy in Italian of a document in English signed by "Prince Charles," appointing Joseph Kent to be the English Consul at Venice and Zante. Signed by Prince Charles in consequence of the King's being then "a prisoner and in a deplorable condition."—Italian. (Four pages.)
The Italian copy of the document is on the second and third pages; the attestation is on the first and part of the third and fourth pages.

2893. *Mr. R. Wiseman to Mr. Edgeman.* Sends him a letter Rouen, of Oct. 2, that he had received, commencing "My deare unkle," Oct. 6. giving an account of what the writer has done at St. Germains, where he spoke with the Prince. Saw Mr. Harding, Col. Hamer, Tho. Johnson, Mr. Lightfoot, and others. Mr. Heath and Nic. Bowden are gone to England. *Original.*

442   CALENDAR OF

1648.
Inchiro-
gahan,
Oct. 10.

2894. *Lord Inchiquin to the Marquis of Ormond.* Lord Taaffe, Sir R. Talbot, and J. Walsh met here this day to negotiate the reorganization of the army of Ballynakill, which needs brogues and stockings; and has no better food than rooks. No peace will be obtained till the churches are granted to their clergy. Will urge them to accept a settlement: but thinks they are prepared to seek better terms elsewhere. Some wish Owen O'Neill to be invited, and that Bishop Darcie should be one of the Commissioners. Will wait on Lord Ormond in a few days to learn his pleasure on this matter. *Original.*

Cl. S. P. vol. II. p. 422.

(This and several other papers were lent by Ormond to Clarendon while the latter was composing his History. In the Carte Papers, vol. 219, 4to. p. 141, is a letter from Lord Ormond to the Earl of Arran, dated 13 April, 1681, in which mention is made of the papers having been borrowed, and a request is preferred that they may be returned.)

Oct. 10.

2895. *Letter of News from Oxford to Mr. Deaman,* signed "A. W." and endorsed "Mr. Woodhead." Alludes to Monk's having beaten Monroe in Ireland; to the progress of Monroe [Montrose] in Scotland and his defeat of Argyle; to the treaty, "yet the proceedings here are fierce against the caval., many daily imprisoned." Major Gibbon was stabbed yesterday by two Cavaliers, and is dead. The writer has been voted here out of his fellowship; and desires his Grace's leave to find some employment for himself, if anything offer, "as any occasion of going behond sea with sombody, or pedanting in some gentleman's house, &c., for clergy-employment I will accept of none."

Isle of
Wight,
Oct. 14.

2896. *Letter of Intelligence.* The Bishop of Salisbury has supplied the King with a distinction, by which his concession in the matter of proclamations against traitors may not tie his hands. Particulars about the Militia, Ireland, and the Church lands. Thinks the King will not be able to make his escape, nor will he have his liberty whatever concessions he makes. Papers for the taking away of civil honours and ecclesiastical preferments are presented. Cromwell is expected in London. *Draught.*

Partly in cypher, decyphered.

Paris,
Oct. 16.

2897. *Lord Jermyn to Sir E. Hyde.* Is not convinced by his arguments against the Prince's going to Scotland, but that in no longer a question. Has received a letter from him. Has hopes from Ireland. Has written to Lord Culpeper. Presents his services to Lord Cottington. "The Queen makes you no answer by this occasion." *Original.*

Endorsed by Hyde.

2898. "*Sir John Berkeley's account* of all he received since his being in Holland for his Highness' use." Receipts 12,500 gulden; paid 11,777 gulden. *Signed by Sir J. Berkeley.* 1648. Oct. 16.

2899. *The Committee of Estates in Scotland to the Prince of Wales.* Having heard of the Prince's preparations in Holland, they think it right to acquaint him with the true state of affairs. They send papers by Lieut.-Col. Carmichael relating to their attempt to preserve the peace of the kingdom, which they pray him not to disturb by prosecuting a course of war, but to use his endeavours to remove the differences between the King and his subjects; specially those which concern religion. *Copy.*
By Edgeman. Endorsed by Hyde.
Signed by the Earl of Loudoun, Lord Chancellor of Scotland, in the name and by the warrant of the Committee of Estates.
Cl. S. P. vol. ii. p. 422. Edinburgh, Oct. 17.

2900. *The Commissioners of the General Assembly in Scotland to the same.* After a preface of assurances of loyalty they pray him to consider whose principles and interests he owns, to be diligent in reading the Scriptures, and frequent in prayer, that so he may join the League and Covenant, which is the best means for securing the King's throne. *Copy.*
By Edgeman. Endorsed by Hyde. Signed by Robert Douglas, Moderator, in the names of the Commissioners. Cl. S. P. vol. ii. p. 413. Edinburgh, Oct. 17.

2901. *Father Clayton to Mr. W. Aylesbury.* Thanks him for his services in the matter of the jewels. Informs him of certain money transactions. Mentions Mr. Ash, F. Parcy, and Mr. Hans. *Original.* Antwerp, Oct. 22.

2902. *John Pulford* "a Mons. Mons. Denman dans la maison de Hoboke a Anvers." The treaty goes on with great hope of good agreement: the King hath hitherto granted in effect all the Propositions. This day the Lords voted that he should not be further pressed to take the Covenant, and the Commons are at this present upon debate thereof. It is reported that a letter is intercepted from Ormond and Inchiquin to the Catholic Committee in Ireland. Oct. 27.

2903. *The King to the Prince of Wales.* Has sent this journal and memorials to be preserved by the Prince. (1) Of the things preparatory to the treaty in the Isle of Wight. (2) Those that were acted in the treaty. (3) What is to be observed from both. Newport, Nov. 6.
    1. Recapitulates events and attempts from the treaty of Uxbridge to September 18, when the treaty began.
    2. Progress of the treaty during ten days when the first

1648.

Proposition was granted. Then the Propositions relating to the Church and the Militia, with their limitations. Next, Delinquents. After which the King's Propositions for his liberty, revenue, and act of oblivion were sent up. Then the Propositions for nominating Crown officers, and concerning the City of London were granted, so that by Oct. 21 all the Propositions of the two Houses were granted. No return was received until Nov. 1, and none at any time to the King's Propositions. On Nov. 1 the Commissioners' paper concerning the Marquis of Ormond's proceedings in Ireland was received: and upon the close of all was given to them some additional satisfaction concerning the Church, as to making no new bishops for three years; the disuse of the Common Prayer-book, and restrictions on saying mass in Court: all further matters being reserved in point of conscience. The King's present determinations not absolutely unalterable. The Commissioners were dismissed with a request that they would plead as well before Parliament as they had before the King, who forbore to mention his own condition, and thanks the Commissioners for their personal civilities.

The Hague. Nov. 7.
2904. *The Prince's judgment on Sir Robt. Walsh (or Welch).* Recites his attempt on Lord Culpeper. Forbids him the Court. *Copy.*
By Edgeman. See Hist. Rebell. bk. ii. p. 548.

London, Nov. 9.
2905. *Letter of Intelligence.* Account of Rainsborough's death at Doncaster, by Capt. Palden's party of horse. Alarm of the Parliament at the proceedings in Ireland. *Copy.*

Helvoet-sluys, Nov. 10.
2906. *Lord Hopton and Sir E. Hyde to the Lords of the Council with the Prince at the Hague.* Have taken measures in concert with Sir Will. Batten, Capt. Jordan, some Kentish gentlemen, Mr. Rich and Mr. Welden, for making provision for the pay, victualling, and fitting of the fleet. Many difficulties stand in their way. *Draught.*
In Hyde's hand, and signed by himself and Lord Hopton. (Three pages.)

Nov. 11.
2907. *Account of Moneys owing by his Highness the Duke of York.*

	£	s.
Personal expenses amounting to	9936	14
And "more left behind by Col. Bampfield" and "other small bills"	6643	1
	£16,579	15

2908. "*A List of the Servants which are to attend his Highness at Sea.*" Sir John Berkeley, three servants; Mr. George Howard, two servants; Mr. Bennett, one servant; Mr. Charles May, two servants; Mr. Tho. Killigrew, two servants; Dr. Killigrew, Mr. Baptist May, Thomas Walpole (barber), Tho. Ramago (yeoman of the robes), Daniel Coghlan (page of the bedchamber), John Mackinney, Roger Vaughan, Patrick Coghlan, Redman Maguire (footmen), William Hall (sticher to the robes), John Clarke (cook).
1648. Nov. 11.
Signed and endorsed by Sir John Berkeley.

2909. *Mr. John Wandesforde to Sir E. Hyde.* Has inspected powder and made preparation for its purchase and conveyance. "There is here a Colonell from London named Willoughby, formerly a meane carpenter, his designe is said to be to corrupt Sir William Battin and other seamen ... here is likewise Sir Robert Welch."   *Original.*
Amsterdam, Nov. 12.
Endorsed by Hyde.

2910. *Memorandum* relating to the fleet. Powder, bullets, beef, petty warrants, &c.; with memorandum by Hyde to Sir W. Boswell concerning the States ships, the Provost Marshall, letter to the Admiralty at Rotterdam, &c., and further notes on provisions and pay. Mentions Mr. Forde, Mr. Low, and Sir W. Batten.
Nov. 13.

2911. "*A List of the Duke's Servants which are dismissed.*" Twenty-three names.   Signed by Sir John Berkeley.
Nov. 14.

2912. *The Prince of Wales to the Duke of York.* Sends information by Sir John Berkeley. Desires his immediate presence with the fleet.   *Draught.*
Nov. 15.
In Hyde's hand.

2913. *Sir E. Hyde to Lady St. Paull.* Has received hers of Oct. 11, on bonds to Mr. John Ayliffe and himself, whose name was used only in trust, which he is willing to assign. Incloses a letter to Mr. Jeffrey Palmer, of the Middle Temple, who will peruse Mr. St. John's will and advise him thereon.
Copy.
The Hague, Nov. 15.
By Edgeman. Endorsed by Hyde.

2914. *The same to Mr. Jeffrey Palmer.* Encloses a letter to himself from Lady St. Paull. Instructs him to peruse evidence and advise him on it.   *Copy.*
The Hague, Nov. 15.
By Edgeman. Endorsed by Hyde.

446   CALENDAR OF

1648. 2915. *Mr. John Wandesforde to Sir E. Hyde.* Has re-
Amster- ceived and answered his of the 9th. Has taken care to pro-
dam, vide powder. Directions to be sent to Mr. Forde of Rotterdam.
Nov. 16. Mr. Webster has supplied match and shot. Condoles with
him on a fit of the gout. *Original.*
Endorsed by Hyde.

Nov. 17. 2916. *The Prince of Wales to the Duke of York.* Has received his letter by Sir J. Berkeley. Resolves not to venture
his person at sea, but directs him to go to the Brill and advise
with Prince Rupert for the preservation of the fleet.
Rough Draught.
By Hyde.

Amster- 2917. *Mr. John Wansford or Wandesforde to [Sir E. Hyde].*
dam, Has received his by Secretary Long; with a money bill. Has
Nov. 18. made provision for conveyance of ammunition. Mentions Mr.
Dox, Mr. Neale, Mr. Webster. Begs for more money to discharge himself to Prince Rupert. Mr. Secretary has acquainted
him with his business of borrowing moneys. A vessel has
arrived from Hull with news of Sir H. Cholmeley, Ingram, and
Col. Rainsborough. *Original.*
Endorsed by Hyde.

The 'Ad- 2918. *Sir Francis Dodington to Sir E. Hyde.* The appear-
miral,' ance of Lord Warwick's fleet has alarmed them. They are in
(a ship). no condition to resist the expected attack. The Duke of York
Nov. 18. must hasten to the Brill. There is disorder on the 'Hind'
frigate. (With a rough sketch of the position of the ships.)
Names of ships—
"Satisfact. Char. Hind. Ro. Bu. Dl. Lady.
Tho. Ad^{ll}. Convert. Loue. R. Ad^{ll}. V. Ad^{ll}."
Original.
Endorsed by Hyde.

Brill, 2919. *Lord Hopton to the Lords of the Council of the Prince
Nov. 19. of Wales.* Arrival of the Prince. Account of the state of the
fleet on the approach of the Earl of Warwick. *Original.*

London, 2920. *Letter of Intelligence.* The declaration from the army
Nov. 20. has destroyed the good understanding between the King and
the Parliament. Particulars of their extravagant demands,
and probable intentions. The declaration penned by Ireton.
Copy.
Endorsed by Hyde.

2921. *Letter of Intelligence.* The Commissioners have given in an answer concerning Episcopacy. There is some "muttering" against the Primate's sermon yesterday, on the King's birthday. — Newport, Nov. 10, 1648.

Endorsed by Hyde. On the same paper with that of Nov. 25.

2922. *Lord Chr. Hatton to Sir E. Hyde, at the Hague.* Has had no letter before his going to Calais. Expresses his love and esteem for the Chancellor. — Paris, Nov. 21. *Original.*

Endorsed by Hyde.

2923. *Letter of Intelligence.* The treaty is to end on the 25th. Head-quarters are removed to Windsor. Sir H. Cholmeley is confined, and his regiment disbanded. Sir J. Maynard, Mr. Prynne, Mr. Tate, Col. Rich, and Col. Cecil opposed the remonstrance. "'Tis feared Inchiquin may play the Presbyter." The Commissioners profess satisfaction in his Majesty's grants. — London, Nov. 23. *Copy.*

Endorsed by Hyde. On the same paper with that of Nov. 10, from Newport.

2924. *The King to the Prince of Wales.* Continuation of the treaty to Nov. 21st. — Newport, Nov. 25.

    1st Proposition. Ten years granted for naming great officers extended to twenty.

    2nd Proposition. Approval of a short Catechism.

    3rd Proposition. The King's revenue of 100,000*l.* a year voted by Parliament agreed to.

    4th Proposition. Declaration against the Marquis of Ormond.

    5th Proposition. Absolute taking away the Bishops and entire alienating their lands.

Then what passed concerning the King's Propositions—

1. As to the King's revenue.
2. Compensation of profits of the Crown.
3. That the King be settled in a condition of honour, freedom and safety.
4. Consent to an act of oblivion.
5. Nothing in the King's Proposition shall impair any agreement in the treaty.

Concludes his letter with advice and warnings for the future.
Copy.

By Oudart. Cl. S. P. vol. II. p. 444.

1648.
Paris,
Nov. 18

2925. *Scout-Master Watson to a brother Independent.* "A true copie of a letter written by an independent agent for y° armie from Paris in France to an independent member of the House of Commons," &c. Has made acquaintance with some Catholics. Thinks their opposition to the King is not to be reconciled. [*Here are inserted in the margin three apostills.*] Lord Say has undertaken to procure a pass for Sir K. Digby to come to England; and begs him to promote the motion when it comes before the House. Wishes Mr. Westrow and the Doctor [Staines] would bring him over into France.

Endorsed by Nicholas.   Cl. S. P. vol. ii. p. 544.

The Hague,
Nov. 18.

2926. *Sir E. Hyde to Lord Jermyn.* His being aspersed for differing in opinion from Doctor Goffe in the matter of the Duke of Lorraine's levies, and his probable loss of the Queen's favour, moves him to give Lord Jermyn a full account of the matter. He gives details of the engagement of the Duke of Lorraine; in which Lord Goring, Sir M. Langdale, and others were concerned. On Dr. Goffe's return from France he brought the Queen's orders respecting the employment of the expedition against Guernsey, which was not thought practicable. He deprecates any prejudice that may have arisen against him, and begs Lord Jermyn to remove it.   *Copy.*

By Edgeman. Endorsed by himself.   Cl. S. P. vol. ii. p. 455.

Newport,
Nov. 29.

2927. *The King to the Prince of Wales.* Continuation of the treaty to Nov. 25: during which was discussed the votes of the House concerning Delinquents; the clergy; the Scotch Proposition; and, after a further extension of the treaty to Nov. 28, the business of the Church was again returned to, when the King, refusing to abolish Episcopacy out of the Church, agreed to its suspension.   *Copy.*

By Oudart.   Cl. S. P. vol. ii. p. 449.

The Hague,
Nov. 30.

2928. *Sir E. Hyde to the Lord Digby.* Has received his of the 23rd. Could not agree to the directions given to Dr. Goffe. [*A sentence in cypher.*] Has written of this to Lord Jermyn. Is ready to join the Lord Treasurer in going to Ireland. Dr. Goffe has used much civility. Does not repent his coming from Jersey. [*A sentence in cypher.*] Keeping to the foundation of established government will not contribute to any ill-advised alterations. Is fitter for a monastery than a Court. Wishes the Queen could be persuaded to appoint some place in France for the King's counsellors to attend the Prince. [*A sentence in cypher.*]   *Copy.*

By Edgeman. Endorsed by himself.   Cl. S. P. vol. ii. p. 458.

2929. *Minutes* relating to the employment of the Duke of Lorraine's men in taking Guernsey. Mentions Dr. Goffe and Sir G. Carteret. The strangers will do great damage in Jersey.
In Hyde's hand.

1648.
Nov. 23.*

2930. *Prince Rupert, by Sir E. Hyde, to Sir William Batten.* Desires him to go at once to the fleet and assist the Prince at Helvoetsluys with his advice and assistance in allaying the mutinous spirit. *Draught.*
In Hyde's hand.

The Hague, Nov.

2931. *Mr. Morton's Propositions.* Proposes that a detachment shall be sent by the Prince from the fleet to the Mediterranean to intercept the Parliament ships that are engaged in the Levant trade; or to negotiate for ships with the Duchess of Savoy. Mr. Morton was the King's agent with the Duchess of Savoy. *Copy.*
Endorsed by Hyde.

Nov.

2932. "*A Memorial* of things necessary to be considered before his Highness' going to Helvoetsluys, and before his going to sea, humbly tendered by me." [Sir John Berkeley.] The Duke of York's debts and current expenses to be provided for; and officers appointed to accompany the Prince in the expedition.
Signed by Sir John Berkeley.

Nov.

2933. *Heads of the Treaty in the Isle of Wight.*
1. The Proposition for—
   Recalling Declarations.
   Taking away all the Hierarchy but the Bishop.
   Confirming the Assembly of Divines.
   The several Acts about Papists.
   For the due observance of the Lord's Day.
   Suppressing Innovations.
   Advancing of Preaching.
   Against Plurality and Non-residency.
   Regulating the two Universities.
   Militia of England, Wales, Guernsey, Jersey, Berwick.
   Disabling now Peers.
   Voiding the cessation of Ireland; war to be prosecuted there; with all matters else belonging to that kingdom.
   Nomination of great officers in England and Ireland.
   Militia of London, and their charter, &c.

Treaty of the Isle of Wight.
—
No date.

* See Hyde to Jermyn of this date.

1648.
Treaty of
the Isle of
Wight.

The Great Seal made by both Houses, confirmed: and all grants made under it to be valid, as proposed. Court of Wards and Liveries.

2. What was not granted was—
Not taking away the Bishop, whom nevertheless we
    Suspended for three years,
    Lessened in Revenues,
    Limited jurisdiction, &c., and desired but a free debate about him too.
The not absolute alienating of Bishops' lands, which we charged with leases for ninety-nine years, &c.
The not consenting wholly to the proposition about Delinquents, whom we submitted all to composition.
    Some to Banishment,
    Some to distance from Court, &c.
    Others from serving in Parliament for three years.
The Covenant, which being an oath for our former reasons we declined, and yet satisfied them in the ends of it.
Lastly: The Lord of Ormond's engagement, which was not part of the treaty, and which we granted if this treaty concluded in a peace as is before mentioned.

3. Leaves the question of who showed most affection to the peace of the kingdoms to judgment, to decide as to the King's conscience against taking away a Bishop and selling Church lands.

It can ill be called a treaty, yet the King trusts his concessions will prove the King's good will. The treaty being now continued, and the issue doubtful, the King reserves the conclusion to this discourse. *Copy.*

    By Mr. Oudart. Cl. S. P. vol. ii. p. 425.

2984. *The Papers which passed in the Treaty of the Isle of Wight.* *

Sept. 6.
1. The first paper delivered in by the Commissioners, being a copy of their commission. Signed by H. Elsynge.

Newport,
Sept. 18.
2. The King's first paper delivered into the Commissioners, requesting copies of propositions and instructions.
    Copy.
    Parl. Hist. vol. xvii. p. 470.

---

* These papers are printed in Sir E. Walker's Historical Discourses, Lond. 1705. Sir E. W.'s own transcript from which the above is printed is among the Rawlinson MSS. in the Bodleian Library. The endorsements are Sir E. Walker's. The papers are also printed, with few exceptions, in the Parliamentary History.

3. Paper delivered by the Commissioners in answer to the above. Signed by   1648.
Treaty of the Isle of Wight.

    Northumberland   Pembroke and Montgomery
    Salisbury   Middlesex
    W. Say and Seale   Tho. Wenman
    Denzell Holles   W. Pierrepoint
    J. Potts   Har. Grimston
    H. Vane   Jo. Bulkley
    Jo. Crewe   Sam. Browne.

Newport, Sept. 18.

Original.
Parl. Hist. vol. xvii. p. 471.

4. For Mr. Hudson to go into Scotland for persons to be sent thence duly authorized to the King in order to treat of a peace together with the Commissioners from the English Parliament.   *Original.*   Sept. 18.

5. Proposition delivered by the Commissioners to revoke Declarations, Oaths, and Proclamations against Parliament. Signed by the same as 3.   *Original.*   Newport, Sept. 18.
Parl. Hist. vol. xvii. p. 470.

6. The second paper delivered to the King by the Commissioners for the treaty at Newport.   Newport, Sept. 18.

7. Draught of the King's second paper delivered to the Commissioners at Newport.   Sept. 18.

8. The Commissioners' answer to the King's second paper of the same day, that they will acquaint the Parliament with the King's declaration.   *Original.*   Newport, Sept. 18.
Parl. Hist. vol. xvii. p. 472.

9. The King in answer to the paper of September concerning the recalling of oaths, declarations, &c.   *Copy.*   Sept. 19.

10. The Commissioners' answer to the King's third paper, concerning the propositions and instructions. Signed by the Commissioners.   *Original.*   Sept. 19.

11. Commissioners' reply to the King's paper of the 19th, about recalling oaths, &c. Signed as 5.   *Original.*   Newport, Sept. 20.
Parl. Hist. vol. xvii. p. 474.

12. The Commissioners' answer to the King's paper of Sept. 20. Signed by the Commissioners.   *Original.*   Sept. 20.

13. i. Copy of 11, by Edgeman.
    ii. The King's consent to an Act to declare all oaths, &c., against Parliament null and void.   *Copy.*   Sept. 20.

1648.
Treaty of the Isle of Wight.

Newport, Oct. 2.

  iii. Copy of 5.
  iv. The King's consent to the Commissioners' proposition of the 18th. With memoranda of other papers.
  v. The King's paper concerning episcopal government.
                Copy.

Sept. 20.
 14. i. Copy of 11.
  ii. Copy of 13, ii.
  iii. Copy of 5.
  iv. Copy of 13, iv.

Sept. 20.
 15. Endorsed, "Reasons in debate if offered, whether power to consent."

Sept. 23.
 16. Draught of a bill to recall the King's proclamations and declarations. *Copy of the printed Draught.*

Newport, Sept. 21.
 17. The King's answer to the Commissioners' reply of the 20th.   *Rough Draught.*
        Parl. Hist. vol. xvii. p. 475.

Sept. 25.
 18. Commissioners' reply that they will transmit papers to London. Signed as above, with J. Glynn. *Original.*
        Parl. Hist. vol. xvii. p. 477.

Sept. 25.
 19. Commissioners' paper concerning the Church. Signed as above.   *Original.*
        Parl. Hist. vol. xviii. p. 3.

Sept. 28.
 20. The King's propositions.   *Draught.*
    (Seven leaves.) Parl. Hist. vol. xviii. p. 5.

Sept. 28.
 21. A Copy of the King's propositions delivered to the Commissioners.   Walker, p. 29.
  At the end is added a copy of the answer of the Commissioners, dated the same day, which is not printed by Walker. They refuse to alter their prescribed mode of procedure, which is, to consider their own Propositions severally in their order. The following note is added: "The originals of these two papers doe yet lye upon the table, but the cople of the King's was sent by his Matie the last weeke to the Parliament, in a letter to ye Speaker; there being cause to suppose that if this Treaty should breake of upon the following proposition concerning the Church, neither the Parliament nor the kingdom would be made to know how far his Matie was contented to condescend for a peace to his people."

Sept. 19.
 22. "The King's reasons why the Commissioners should transmit his proposition tendered but refused to be taken."   Parl. Hist. vol. xviii. p. 14.

Sept. 29.
 23. The King's paper.   *Rough Draught.*
        Parl. Hist. vol. xviii. p. 16.

CLARENDON PAPERS.   453

24. The King to the Speaker of the House of Peers, to be communicated to the Lord and Commons. *Draught.*
Parl. Hist. vol. xviii. p. 17.
1648.
Treaty of the Isle of Wight.

25. Commissioners desire an answer to their proposition concerning the Church. Signed as above. *Original.*
Parl. Hist. vol. xviii. p. 16.
Sept. 29. Sept. 29.

26. Copy of the King's answer to the proposition concerning the Church. Parl. Hist. vol. xviii. p. 36.
Sept. 30.

27. Copy of 11 v. King Charles's Works, p. 612.
Oct. 2.

28. The King's second paper concerning the Church. *Draught.*
Parl. Hist. vol. xviii. p. 42.
Oct. 9.

29. Another paper about religions allowed or forbidden. In substance, Parl. Hist. vol. xviii. p. 42.
No date.

30. The Commissioners will transmit the King's final answer concerning the Church. Signed as above. *Original.*
Parl. Hist. vol. xviii. p. 42.
Oct. 9.

31. The Commissioners will transmit the King's answer to the Militia. Signed as above. *Original.*
Parl. Hist. vol. xviii. p. 50.
Oct. 9.

32. The Commissioners will transmit the King's answer concerning Ireland. Signed as above. *Original.*
Parl. Hist. vol. xviii. p. 54.
Oct. 11.

33. The Commissioners request an answer to their proposition for the payment of public debts. Signed as above. *Original.*
Parl. Hist. vol. xviii. p. 57.
Oct. 11.

34. The answer to the proposition for the payment of public debts. *Rough Draught.*
Parl. Hist. vol. xviii. p. 58.
Oct. 12.

35. The Commissioners' acknowledgment of the answer concerning the public debts. Signed by the Commissioners. *Original.*
Newport, Oct. 12.

36. The Commissioners transmit resolutions of Parliament in answer to the King's proposition concerning the Church, dated Oct. 9. Signed by twelve Commissioners. *Original.*
Parl. Hist. vol. xviii. p. 79.
Oct. 16.

37. The King's final answer to the proposition concerning Delinquents. *Draught.*
Parl. Hist. vol. xviii. p. 80.
Oct. 17.

1648.
Treaty of the Isle of Wight.

Newport,
Oct. 17.
Oct. 11.
Oct. 21.

38. Letter from the Commissioners requiring a full answer to the proposition concerning the Church. Signed by the Commissioners. *Original.*

39. The King's propositions to his two Houses of Parliament. *Copy.*
   Parl. Hist. vol. xviii. p. 81.

40. The Commissioners request the King's consent to a proposition concerning the city of London. Signed by fourteen Commissioners. *Original.*
   Parl. Hist. vol. xviii. p. 96.

Nov. 1. 41. Letter from the Commissioners to the King, with the resolutions of the Lords and Commons of the 30th Oct. Signed by the Commissioners. *Original.*

Nov. 1. 42. Two Letters from the Commissioners respecting Ireland. Signed by the Commissioners. *Original.*

Nov. 1. 43. i. Letter from the King to the Commissioners respecting the Marquis of Ormond.

Nov. 1. ii. Rough Draught of the King's paper respecting Ireland.

Nov. 1. 44. The King's reply to the Commissioners' paper of the same day.

Nov. 1. 45. Two Letters from the Commissioners respecting the days allotted for the treaty, and the enlargement of the time allotted. Signed by the Commissioners. *Original.*

Nov. 3. 46. From the Commissioners respecting the King's exceptions to the proposition concerning the Church. Signed by the Commissioners. *Original.*

Nov. 4. 47. Rough Draughts of the King's two final answers to the proposition concerning the Church.

Nov. 4. 48. The three Letters from the Commissioners of the same date, respecting the proposition concerning the Church. Signed by the Commissioners. *Original.*

Newport, Nov. 6. 49. The King's first answer respecting the Wards and Liveries. Signed by himself. *Original.*

Nov. 6. 50. The Commissioners' reply concerning the nomination of officers. Signed by the Commissioners. *Original.*

Nov. 6. 51. The King's consent to the additional fourteen days for the treaty. *Copy.*

Nov. 6. 52. Paper from the Commissioners, with the votes of the Houses of Parliament on Nov. 2nd and 4th. Signed by the Commissioners. *Original.*

53.	The King's final answer concerning the nomination of officers.	1648. *Treaty of the Isle of Wight.*
54.	Reasons and grounds of the King's answer to the first proposition of Sept. 18. *Draught.* (Three leaves.)	Nov. 8. Nov. 8.
55.	The Commissioners desire the King's approbation of the Catechism. Signed by five Commissioners. *Original.*	Nov. 8.
56.	The King's final answer to the Catechism. *Draught.* Parl. Hist. vol. xviii. p. 150.	Nov. 10.
57.	Letter from the Commissioners on the King's answer respecting the Catechism. *Original.* Signed by Northumberland, Wenman, Denzell Holles, Pierrepont, Crewe.	Newport, Nov. 10.
58.	The King's final answer respecting the Wards and Liveries. *Copy.* On the same paper with that of Nov. 6.	Nov. 11.
59.	The Commissioners will transmit the King's consent to the votes of the Parliament about the 100,000*l.*, in lieu of the Court of Wards. Signed by five Commissioners. *Original.*	Nov. 11.
60.	Votes of the two Houses of Parliament. Parl. Hist. vol. xviii. pp. 145, 148, 151, 154.	Nov. 10, 11, 15.
61.	The King's final answer to the papers of Nov. 11, concerning the Marquis of Ormond. *Draught.* With copies of papers of the Commissioners of the 6th, 8th, 10th, and 11th of November. Parl. Hist. vol. xviii. p. 156.	Nov. 14.
62.	A fuller answer than 61. *Original.*	Nov. 16.
63.	Another answer on the same point. *Draught.* Parl. Hist. vol. xviii. p. 157.	Nov. 16.
64.	The Commissioners having debated on the King's answer, press for a fuller and more satisfactory one. Signed by six Commissioners. *Original.* Parl. Hist. vol. xviii. p. 157.	Nov. 16.
65.	The King's final answer concerning the Marquis of Ormond. *Rough Draught.* Parl. Hist. vol. xviii. p. 157.	Nov 17.
66.	The Commissioners will transmit the King's final answer about the Marquis Ormond. Signed by six Commissioners. *Original.*	Nov. 17.

1648. *Treaty of the Isle of Wight.*	67. The Commissioners deliver the satisfactory votes of the two Houses (Nov. 15) concerning the Church. Signed by six Commissioners. *Original.*
Nov. 17. Nov. 17.	68. The Commissioners report the two Houses' votes of dissatisfaction upon some parts of the King's answer concerning the Church. Signed by six Commissioners. *Original.*
Nov. 18.	69. The King's answer to the votes of the Houses respecting his answer concerning the Church.
Nov. 20.	70. The Commissioners' answer, with reasons for dissatisfaction with the King's paper concerning the Church. *Original.*
Nov. 21.	71. The Commissioners present to the King the votes of both Houses on the King's propositions respecting the treaty. Signed by six Commissioners. *Original.* Parl. Hist. vol. xviii. p. 160.
Nov. 21.	72. The King's acceptance of both Houses' votes concerning the propositions. *Two Rough Draughts.* Parl. Hist. vol. xviii. p. 252.
Nov. 21.	73. The Commissioners will communicate to both Houses the King's answer to their votes on the propositions. Signed by six Commissioners. *Original.*
Newport, Nov. 23.	74. Answer to the Commissioners, consenting to the continuation of the treaty to Nov. 25th. *Draught.*
Nov. 23.	75. The Commissioners report to the King both Houses' unsatisfactory votes (Nov. 1, 11, and 21), concerning Delinquents. Signed by six Commissioners. *Original.*
Nov. 24.	76. The King's answer to the Commissioners' paper of the 23rd, concerning Delinquents. *Rough Draught.* Parl. Hist. vol. xviii. p. 272.
Nov. 23.	77. The Commissioners present the votes of the two Houses for a continuation of the treaty until Saturday the 25th. Signed by six Commissioners. *Original.*
Nov. 23.	78. The King's acceptance of the continuation of the treaty. *Copy.*
Nov. 24.	79. The Commissioners' answer to the King's paper about Delinquents. Signed by five Commissioners. *Original.* Parl. Hist. vol. xviii. p. 273.

80. The Commissioners will communicate to both Houses the King's final answer about the Marquis Ormond. Signed by five Commissioners. *Original.* 1648. *Treaty of the Isle of Wight.*

80a. The King's final answer concerning new Delinquents. *Rough Draught.* Nov. 15.
Parl. Hist. vol. xviii. p. 275. Nov. 15.

81. The Commissioners will communicate the King's final answer concerning Delinquents to both Houses. Signed by five Commissioners. *Original.* Nov. 15.

82. The Commissioners present the votes of both Houses concerning the new Delinquents. Signed by six Commissioners. *Original.* Nov. 15.

83. The King's final answer touching Delinquents. A fair copy, signed by the King, with a page of rough draught additions. Parl. Hist. vol. xviii. p. 273. Nov. 15.

84. The Commissioners will communicate to both Houses the King's final answer concerning new Delinquents. Signed by five Commissioners. *Original.* Nov. 15.

85. The Commissioners report to the King the votes of both Houses concerning the King's answer of the 17th. Signed by six Commissioners. *Original.*
Parl. Hist. vol. xviii. p. 241. Nov. 15.

86. The King's final answer concerning the Marquis Ormond. Signed by the King. *Original.* With erasures. Parl. Hist. vol. xviii. p. 276. Nov. 15.

87. The King's letter to the Marquis of Ormond, informing him that he is superceded in the management of the Irish war. *Rough Draught.*
Parl. Hist. vol. xviii. p. 276. Nov. 15.

88. The Commissioners present to the King the unsatisfactory votes of both Houses on the King's paper of the 21st, concerning the Church. Signed by six Commissioners. *Original.*
Parl. Hist. vol. xviii. p. 253. Nov. 27.

89. The Commissioners present the vote for the continuance of the treaty until this night. Signed by six Commissioners. *Original.*
Parl. Hist. vol. xviii. p. 253. Nov. 27.

90. The Commissioners present the two Houses' new proposition concerning Scotland. Signed by six Commissioners. *Original.*
Parl. Hist. vol. xviii. p. 241. Nov. 27.

1648.
Treaty of the Isle of Wight.

Nov. 27.
Nov. 27.

Nov. 27.

Nov. 27.

Nov. 27.

91. The Commissioners will communicate to both Houses the King's final answer concerning the Church. Signed by six Commissioners. *Original.*

92. The Commissioners will communicate to both Houses the King's final answer touching Ireland. Signed by five Commissioners. *Original.*

93. The King's final answer to the proposition concerning the Church. Signed by the King. *Copy.*
With erasures. Parl. Hist. vol. xviii. p. 278.

94. The King's consent to the continuation of the treaty until this night. *Rough Draught.*

95. The King's final answer to the new proposition concerning Scotland. *Rough Draught.*
Parl. Hist. vol. xviii. p. 277.

96. *The King's account of the treaty, in a letter to the Prince, dated Newport, Nov. 29, 1648. *Copy.*
(Thirteen leaves.) By Edgeman, with corrections by Hyde.

Nov.

2961. *Memorandum of the Fleet.* List of eight names of Captains; with memoranda relating to Bardo the surgeon, Sir W. Boswell, Mr. Forde, and Lord Craven.
In Hyde's hand.

Nov.

2962. *Judgment of the Prince upon Sir R. Welch* for his attempt on the person of Lord Culpeper. Forbids him the Court. *Rough Draught.*

Dec. 4.

2963. *Resolutions and Orders of the Council of War in Scarborough Castle* upon the reception of Col. Bethell's summons to surrender. (Two pages.)

Dec. 4.

†2964. *John Lawrans to Secretary Nicholas.* Some private matter in which C. Jones is concerned. The King is in great danger. Every one is to subscribe to a new form of government. Fairfax and his army have come to London. Gives a list of their quarters. Reports that the King is carried to Corfe Castle. There is some hope of an agreement between the King and Parliament, as the former yields in the matter of Bishops. Nat. Fiennes has enraged the Independents by his exposure of Sir H. Vane's partial report to the King's prejudice. Gives an account of proceedings in the House. Forecasts probable events.
Two letters on the same paper, endorsed by Hyde.

* These papers are placed together in one volume.
† The writer, who is probably a son of Secretary Nicholas, seems to have received intelligence in writing from others, which he transcribes for the Secretary.

2965. *Sir E. Hyde's minutes relating to a conversation between himself, Mr. Mowbray, and Mr. Mungo Murray.* Mowbray's information from Scotland of the Earl of Lanerick's continued attachment to the Prince, his willingness to serve under Montrose, and bring 10,000 or 12,000 men to meet the Prince. Mowbray saw the King at the Isle of Wight, and carried his message to the Prince concerning his satisfaction at the intelligence received by Mason, with directions to the Prince to follow his instructions. Lord Lanerick thought that Lord Lauderdale's severity had done harm. The same day Lord Culpeper told them the contents of the King's letter. Murray's information from Scotland, that the governing party there would raise an army of 20,000 men to support the Prince, if he came to them. W. Murray advised the Prince to answer the letters from the Committee and Assembly with gentleness; to take the Covenant if pressed to do so, and to send Mr. Denham into Scotland. Did not wholly approve of Mowbray's advice and Lord Lanerick's propositions. — 1648. Dec. 5, 7. In Hyde's hand. Cl. S. P. vol. ii. pp. 460, 461.

2966. *Eight Articles* agreed upon between Col. Chr. Legard, Lieut.-Col. W. Spencer, Lieut.-Col. Barrington Bourchier, Capt. Nicholas Conyers, and Capt. John Lawson on behalf of Col. Hugh Bethell, Commander-in-Chief of the Parliament forces, and Col. T. Fairfax, Major E. Gower, Major T. Preston, Capt. Roger Nevinson, Capt. T. Wilkins, for Col. Matt. Boynton, Governor of Scarborough Castle. — Dec. 17. Signed by the first-named officers, and ratified by Bethell. Endorsed by Hyde.

2967. [*John Lawrans to Secretary Nicholas*]. Hamilton has refused to impeach the King. Probable course to be taken against the King. The imprisoned members expect a remove. — Dec. 19. Endorsed by Hyde. On the same paper with that of Dec. 21.

2968. *The same to the same.* Lords Pembroke, Salisbury, Denbigh, and North abased themselves before the General without effect. Mr. Prynne accompanied sixteen of the secluded members to Whitehall, and was attacked by Ireton, and after railing at the army was carried away. Twelve of the others received a promise of release. The Presbyterian party are strengthening their interest. In Ireland things proceed happily. Aston will soon be in open hostility with the Parliament. Thinks it probable that Cromwell will preserve the King. A letter has been sent to Col. Pride and the Council of War. — Dec. 21. Endorsed by Hyde. On the same paper with that of Dec. 18.

1648.
Dec. 13.

2969. *The Prince of Wales to the Lord Chancellor of Scotland.* Received his letter by Mr. Carmichael, dated Oct. 17, on Dec. 5. Thanks him for it, and hopes that he will find many to join with him in restoring the King to freedom.

Rough Draught.

By Hyde.   Cl. S. P. vol. ii, p. 461.

Dec 13.

2970. *The same to the Commissioners of the General Assembly of the Kirk of Scotland.* Received their letter with the Chancellor's. Thanks them for their affection. Prays them to use their endeavours to restore the King; an act worthy of the ministers of the Gospel of Christ.

Rough Draught.

By Hyde.   Endorsed by him.   Cl. S. P. vol. ii. p. 462.

Dec. 13.

2971. *Lord Balmerino to Lord Lauderdale.* This letter is sent under the Earl of Abercorn's cover. Ten days are allowed to those out of the country to declare their acceptance of the treaty of Stirling. "There will be a penitential speech expected of yourself before your reconciliation to the Kirk," for the share he had in the Duke of Hamilton's engagement. Mentions Mr. Gillespie.   *Original.*

Endorsed by Hyde.

Dec. 25.

2972. *(John Lawrans) to (Secretary Nicholas).* Eighteen members are still under restraint, Sir W. Lewis, Swinson, Birch, Greene; Pryn, Walker, Edw. Stephens, and Gower; Sir R. Harley and his son, Col. W. Strowd, Leigh, and Wheeler; Waller, Clotworthy, Massey, Browne, and Copley. Enters into details of the Independent, Leveller's, and Presbyterian interests. General Widdrington, Mr. Whitelocke, Mr. Nich. Low, and other moderate men are on the committee for considering the charge against the King. The King has been at Farnham on his way to Windsor.

Endorsed by Hyde.   On the same paper with those of Dec. 18 and 19.

Dec. 26.

2973. *John Lawrans to Mr. John Francis [Secretary Nicholas].* The Earl of Warwick has brought his excuses for leaving Goree. Imputes motives to the Marquis of Hamilton. The King is expected at Windsor, where it is thought Langhorne, Powell, and Poyer will be brought to die. Pembroke is constable of the Castle, and Oldsworth ranger. A Declaration is voted to reverse the votes of the 5th of December. All private letters are examined at the post house. Has received his of the 17th. All the imprisoned members but sixteen are released. The army has interfered in the election of Common

Councilmen for the City. The Earl of Norwich and Sir W. Brereton have exchanged blows. *Original.*
Endorsed by Hyde.

1648.

2974. *The Earl of Abercorn to the Earl of Lauderdale.* Has been hawking in the West country till within ten days. The committee of the Barenthrow [Renfrew?] have made him a Malignant. On the 14th the Lord Chancellor made his repentance in Mr. R. Douglas's Kirk, in the presence of the Marquis of Argyll, Lord Wariston, and others. The Earl of Lanerick and other noblemen have been cited by the Committee. Details of his examination, and the bond he is required to sign. Fears that no less will be required of Lauderdale. *Original.*
Endorsed by Hyde. Cl. S. P. vol. ii. p. 461.

Edinburgh, Dec. 27.

2975. [*John Lawrans to Secretary Nicholas*]. Accounts for the policy of the Independents, and their relation to the Scotch Presbyterians. They used Argyle as their instrument. The Council of War intend the Admiralship to Lord Denbigh. There is discontent in Scotland and the North of England.
Endorsed by Hyde.
On the same paper with those of Dec. 25 and 29.

Dec. 28.

2976. *John Lawrans to [Secretary Nicholas].* The King is at Windsor, and Sir H. Mildmay, C. Holland, Sir G. Norton, — Edwards and others are appointed by the Commons to draw up a charge against him. Has received his of the 17th. Mentions some private money matters. Endorsed by Hyde.
On the same paper with those of Dec. 25 and 28.

Dec. 29.

2977. *A Clause of the Covenant.* "Wee shall in like manner, without respect of persons, endeavour the extirpation of Popery, Prelacy (that is, Church government by Archbishops, Bishops, their Chancellors and Commissaries, Deans, Deans and Chapters, Archdeacons, and all other ecclesiastical officers depending on that Hierarchy"), &c. *Copy.*
Apparently by the King's secretary; with a translation.
Endorsed by Hyde, "Clause in the Coven' in Latine by the presbiter."

Dec.

2978. *A Relation of the business of Pontefract.* His brother has had some meetings with Col. Morris, a confidant of Overton, Governor of Pomfret Castle, which they had a scheme to surprise. Overton went to Hull, and was succeeded at Pomfret by Major Cotteroll. Gives details of the failure of the first attempt and success of the second. In August, Pomfret was held by 400 horse and 800 foot, of which 300 went to Doncaster, whence they went to Lincoln and quartered a troop there. Describes the engagement with

No date.

1648. Rossiter, and their varied fortune before York, with particulars of the defence of Pomfret in September, and its being taken from them by Cromwell after his return from Scotland.

<small>Drawn up after the death of the King, " by one of those concerned in the dispatch of Rainsborough. Lambert is not mentioned." See Hist. Rebell. bk. ii. p. 545, from which this account differs in several particulars, specially with those which relate to Col. Morris.</small>

No date. 2979. *Richard Osborn to the Prince of Wales.* Account of his employment about the King's person, and narrative of the attempted escape, with details of intrigues to take the King's life: his own letter to Lord Wharton, and appearance at the bar of the House of Lords, with the trial of Major Rolph.
Original.
(Eight leaves.)

No date. 2980. *Memorandum* of some reply in behalf of the powers and privileges of the House of Lords.

No date. 2981. A similar *memorandum* respecting the alleging of precedents in favour of the House of Lords, apparently at some conference with the House of Commons. Beginning, "Introduce the præsidents with telling them."

No date. 2982. *Account* of receipts and disbursements by his Highness the Duke of York's command and for his service. Receipts amount to 20,000*l.* Disbursements 19,559*l.*
Endorsed, "Colonel Bampfield's account."

No date. 2983. *Memorandum* of the parentage and descendants of the younger brother of Pope Innocent the Tenth.
In Hyde's hand, headed " Innocent 10th Pamphilio."

No date. 2984. *Mr. Reade's relation of the Scots engagement.* "Some passages in Scotland, and observations on the last expedition of the Scots army into England, 1648." This account is in substance the same with that which Lord Clarendon has given in his History. The writer was Secretary to the English Commissioners in Scotland, and in that post did all he could for the King. He pretends it was through his means that Berwick and Carlisle Castles were not secured by Cromwell, and says that the Lords of the opposite parties in Scotland had privately a good understanding with each other, and Lauderdale particularly frequently conferred with Loudon in his chamber.
Copy.
(Eighteen pages.)

2985. *A Bull of Dispensation.* Richard Wake is dispensed from the observance of the strict fast of Lent, except Holy Week.—Spanish. *Printed.* 1648. No date.

2986. *List* of sixty-four gentlemen of the county of Salop. No date.

2987. *List* of persons in Flint and Denbigh shires continuing in arms after the suppression of the rebellion against the Parliament. Ninety-nine names in Flintshire, thirty-eight names in Denbighshire. *Copy.* No date.
(Four pages.)

2988. *Capt. Brissenden's Account* of bread, beer, beef, pork, peas, fish, butter, cheese for the fleet. With an abstract of such victuals as Capt. Brissenden has received from Mr. Harfleet, for the victualling of his Highness' fleet, with the difference of their accounts. No date.

2989. "*An Account* of victuals received from Thomas Harfleet, Esq., towards victualling his Maties fleet (now at Helvoetsluys) for three months." Sept. 6 to Dec. 8. Mentions Edward Mullet, C. Derickson, W. Droghart, R. Edwards, H. Clussoe, J. Adams, — Saunders, M. Devogle, P. Peterson, Capt. Stanton, A. Rose, Capt. Eakins. *Original.* Sept. 6— Dec. 8.
Endorsed by Hyde, "Brissenden's receipt for the victuals."

With an account of general provisions of boatswains' and carpenters' stores, which came from Rotterdam to Helvoetsluys for his Maties fleet there in anno 1648. A memorandum of and a month's provision after the 10th of December, for 1500 men. *By Hyde.*

2990. *Letter* of the ambassadors addressed to the King of Spain, just before their departure, praying him to assist the King of England by sending relief to Guernsey and Jersey. No date.
Draught.
By Hyde.

2991. *Lord Digby to Sir E. Hyde.* Is very impatient for a meeting with him, wanting to impart some of his thoughts, which he can vent to no one but himself. *Original.* No date.
Endorsed by Hyde, "Recd. at Middleborough."

2992. *Mr. Clutterbuck to* [*Lord Cottington*]. Has received his of Dec. 22. Will execute his commands in domestic matters. Trusts the soldiers will be removed. Dr. Winston's accident, with whom is Sir Jo. Penruddock. Dean Browne is at Paris. Encloses letters from Mr. Squibb and Secretary Nicholas. *Original.* 1648-9. Dec. 31 and Jan. 1.

1648–9. Jan. 1.	2993. *E. M[assey] to the Prince [of Wales].* Urges him to cast himself and his interests wholly on the Scots, and to put aside the thoughts of employing foreign force. Signed "E. M.," and endorsed by Hyde, "Delivered to his Highness at the Queene of Bohemia."
Jan. 7.	2994. *The Pope's Nuncio to the Bishop of Ferns and Sir Nicholas Plunket.* Thanks them for speaking well of him at Rome. Has had nothing to do with O'Neil or his army, his sole aim having been to recover the people from heresy. Has always desired that bygones should be bygones, and laments that the Catholic confederacy should have issued in violence; and that his labours of three years should have had such little good result. *Original.* (Signed) Jo. b. Archbp. Firman. Cl. S. P. vol. ii. p. 464.
Jan. 8.	2995. [*John Lawrans to Secretary Nicholas*]. They intend forthwith to proceed against the King. The Independent sticklers in the City and the Levellers agree in aiming at rooting out the King, but not in the intended oligarchical form of government by way of States. Enters into details of the position and relation of parties. The King has received a copy of the ordinance of attainder. Endorsed by Hyde. On the same paper with that of Jan. 11.
Jan. 11.	2996. *The same to the same.* Account of proceedings in the two Houses of Parliament. The trial was ordered to be proclaimed, and a committee appointed to consult with the judges. Cromwell obtained an adjournment. The Duke of Richmond and others have conferred with the Independents on behalf of the King. Endorsed by Hyde. On the same paper with that of Jan. 8.
Jan. 13.	2997. *The same to the same.* Has received his of the 7th. Gives information about the proclamation for the trial of the King, the proceedings of the High Court, and of Parliament. The Synod have sent some of their members with a rough message to the army, threatening them for expelling members of Parliament, and deposing the King. The Duke of Richmond, Marquis of Hertford, Dorset, and others have engaged themselves and their estates to the council of the army, that the King will perform whatever he yields to. Describes the form of the writ and the particulars of the new great seal. Endorsed by Hyde.
Kilkenny, Jan. 17.	2998. *Thomas Cashel, John, Archbishop of Tuam, David Ossory, and other Bishops of the Assembly to [the Officers of the*

Army.] The peace concluded between the King's lieutenant and the Roman Catholics speaks them a most loyal nation, and removes past suspicion. They have received a good satisfaction for the being and safety of religion. Pray that [the army] will happily wear this green laurel of a happy peace.

(Eleven signatures.) *Original.*
Endorsed, "Irish Catholic bishops in approbation of the peace."
Cl. S. P. vol. ii. p. 463.

1648-9.

2999. *The Marquis of Ormond to Prince Charles.* Has fulfilled his instructions, as will be seen by the Articles of Peace now concluded. Has been assisted by the Lord President of Munster, and the Assembly. The English and Irish armies and all the cities will readily submit to the peace; and those under O'Neale and the Marquis of Antrim will adhere to the cause. Trusts the Prince will come in person, or send supplies.
Carte's Life of Ormond, vol. iii. p. 601.

Kilkenny,
Jan. 11.

3000. [*Mr. Nicholls*] *to Mr. Edgeman.* Sir G. Carteret has mislaid a letter from him. Sir J. Dingley can do nothing until his return into Holland. Begs him to send the small trunk from Rotterdam to Mr. Tredenham at St. Malo. Sir John Grenville has been here this fortnight. Has seen nothing of the Prince and his fleet. Mr. E. Carteret is said to be on his way hither. Signed "J. N." *Original.*
Endorsed, "Mr. Nicholls."

Jan. 13.

3001. *The Prince of Wales to Lord Fairfax and the Council of War.* Has heard of the treatment the King has received. Urges them to restore their King, to whom their allegiance is only due. *Copy.*
With a rough draught in Hyde's hand. Hist. Rebell. bk. ii. p. 367.

The Hague,
Jan. 23.

3002. *Draught,* in Sir E. Hyde's handwriting, of a circular letter prepared to be sent to various States. Rehearses the desperate state of affairs, and the extreme danger the King's life is in. Trusts "that all Princes and States will be firm and united to assist the Prince in taking the highest vengeance on this transcendant villany." *Endorsed by Hyde.*

Jan. 13.

Also a fair copy of a similar letter, addressed by the Prince to the States, with rough draught of the same in Sir E. Hyde's hand. Dated as above, at the Hague.

3003. *John Lawrans to Secretary Nicholas.* Massey has escaped. Gives details of the King's trial. Abuses Cooke and Ludlow. The delay caused by the rumoured intervention

Jan. 16.

3 D

1648-9. of the Scotch and Dutch, and the aversion of the General, revives their spirits. Peers, judges, lawyers, and divines are against the High Court. Abuses Peters. Bradshaw receives 3000*l.* Sir H. Mildmay hath undertaken for 2000*l.* and Wimbleton to keep the King's children. Mr. Seymour is come, "with divers from the Prince." Mentions some private money matters, a certain knave Sadler, and Mr. Edwards.

Endorsed by Hyde.

Jan. 16. 3004. *John Lawrans to Secretary Nicholas.* Details of proceedings at the High Court. The General would not appear. The Scotch Commissioners and Dutch ambassadors endeavoured to stay the trial; the latter said they would assist the Prince. Gives the Hollanders' reasons for their intervention. Ashton in Lancashire, the Militia in Yorkshire, and the Irish are moving.

Under the endorsement of the next preceding letter.

Jan. 18. 3005. *Lord Montrose to Sir E. Hyde.* In accordance with his and the Prince's orders is prepared to wait on him at some private place. *Original.*

Endorsed by Hyde. See Hist. Rebell. bk. xii. p. 578, ed. 1732.

Jan. 18. 3006. *The same to the Prince.* Has received his letter. Expresses his devotion to the Prince, and obedience to his directions. *Original.*

Endorsed by Hyde.

Castle Elizabeth, Jan. 31. 3007. [*Mr. Nicholls*] to [*Mr. Edgeman*]. Has received his of the 4th; but not that said to be sent by Mr. Cornelius, who came with Mr. Mors. Sir John Gronville and Mr. Godolphin are to go with him to Scilly. The business between himself and Sir John Dingley remains as it was when the former left the Hague. Mentions Mr. John Smith, Francois Martin, and S^r. de Tredolian. Signed "A. N."

Jan. 3008. *List* of the names of the Judges of the High Court of Justice for trial of the King; appointed by an act of the Commons, &c. 139 names in all, printed with MS. additions of "Mr. Broughton of Maidstone," as one of the "Councellors assistant to the Court."

The Hague, Feb. 19. 3009. *Account of the state of affairs.* The now King cannot at present come to England, but may perhaps go to Scotland, so that his possession of that kingdom may enable him to come with an army into England. Arguments for and against this course of action.

(Four pages.) In Hyde's hand. *Endorsed by him.*

3010. *Jo. Wilcocks (Secretary Nicholas) to Sir E. Hyde.* 1648-9. Has received his of Feb. 22. The Queen desires to speak March 8. with the King, and hopes he will give her a meeting. The Earl of Lancrick's servant has gone with letters to St. Germains. Intends to come to him in Holland. If the King goes to Scotland and not to Ireland his hopes will be frustrated. Does not expect good fruit from the treaty for an accommodation at St. Germains. There is great scarcity now in Paris.
Original.
Endorsed by Edgeman.

ADDENDA.

[The following papers, Nos. 1—306, form the contents of one volume of official transcripts of letters on foreign affairs during the early part of the reign of Queen Elizabeth.]

1. *Queen Elizabeth to Maximilian, King of Bohemia.* Announces her succession to the Crown. Tho. Chaloner will assure him of her desire to maintain friendly relations with him.—Latin. *Copy.* 1558. London, Nov. 16.

2. *Safe-conduct* for Tho. Chaloner, addressed to Kings, Princes ecclesiastical and secular, &c.—Latin. *Copy.* London, Nov. 16.

3. *Letters Patent* for Christopher Mundt. Addressed to Kings, Princes, Bishops, &c. Mundt is to be received as her agent.—Latin. *Copy.*

4. *The Queen to Sigismund Augustus, King of Poland.* Begs him to permit free passage and trade to English merchants.—Latin. *Copy.* London, Dec. 16.

5. *The same to the Viceroy of the King of Poland in Lithuania.* To the same effect as the next preceding, and specially in behalf of the bearer, Tho. Alcock.—Latin. *Copy.* London, Dec. 16.

6. *The same to Albert, Duke of Prussia.* Acknowledges his letter of Nov. 15, addressed to her sister Mary. Thanks him for eight falcons. Hopes to continue friendship and alliance with him.—Latin. *Copy.* London, Dec. 18.

1558-9. 7. *The Queen to Philip, King of Spain.* Letters of credence
London,   for Nicholas Wotton, Dean of Canterbury, as her agent.—
Jan. 1.   Latin.   *Copy.*

1559.   8. *The same to Sebastian, King of Portugal.* Has received
Westm.   his letters of January 26, by John Poreira; thanks him for
April 15. his congratulations.—Latin.   *Copy.*

Westm.   9. *The same to Catherine, Queen of Portugal.* Thanks her
April 15. for her letter of January 26, received by John Poreira.—
          Latin.   *Copy.*

Strasburg, 10. *Letters* of commendation of John Sturmius. Christopher
April 15. Threcius, with his pupil Stanislaus Comespolius, son of the mili-
           tary profect of Wiolun, have behaved themselves with fidelity
           and diligence in the school.—Latin.   *Copy.*

No date. 11. *The Queen to the Emperor Ferdinand I.* Has received
          his letter dated March 29, and ambassador, Count Helffenstein.
          Assures him that her good will towards him is not less than
          that of her father, brother, or sister.—Latin.   *Copy.*

No date. 12. *The same to the Duke S. Adolphus* (*Duci Holsatium*).
          Has read his letters written to her dearest sister Mary, who
          died before she could receive them. Opens the question of
          trade between their countries; and sends (Sir Will.) Wade
          as ambassador to treat with him on this matter.—Latin.
                                                                      Copy.

No date. 13. *The same to Philip II, King of Spain.* Has received
          his letter of May 8, informing her that the Bishop of Aquila
          is to succeed to the crown of Foris. Speaks highly of the
          latter.—Latin.   *Copy.*

Westm.   14. *The same to Mac Art' Mors.* Has heard a good account
June 4.   of him from the Earl of Sussex. Commends him for his ser-
          vices. Next to the service of God nothing is of more conse-
          quence than obedience to the Prince.—Latin.   *Copy.*

No date. 15. "*Eighteen letters* sent to the lords and gentlemen of
          Ireland of this tenor." Commends his fidelity, of which she
          has heard from the Earl of Sussex. Desires him to influence
          his family and dependants. Warns him not to neglect this
          duty; and trusts there will be no breaches of the peace.—
          Latin. [A circular letter.]   *Copy.*

16. *The Queen to Princess Anne of East Friesland, Oldenburgh, and Delmenhorst.* Asks permission for Thomas Tomson, of London, to purchase military stores.—Latin. *Copy.* — 1559. June 17.

17. *The same to John Frederic, second Duke of Saxony.* Has received his letter of May 25, by John Elmer. Readily follows his counsel in the cause of religion, which she embraced at an early age and now diligently propagates. Will carry out the true worship of God, and the *Confessio Augustana*; and will maintain friendship with those Princes "qui Augustanæ Confessioni sese jam addicunt."—Latin. *Copy.* — Greenwich, July 2.

18. *The same to Augustus, Duke of Saxony.* Is pleased to hear that he accepts her professions of good will sent by Christopher Mundt, LL.D. Assures him of her zeal for religion, which with the consent of all her subjects is established throughout her kingdom. Will take care that the tradition in her Church is brought into conformity with the confession of Augsburg. Repeats the assurance contained in the preceding letter.—Latin. *Copy.* — Greenwich, July 2.

19. *The same to Philip, Landgrave of Hesse.* Has received his letter of May 3. Thanks him for congratulating her on her zeal for religion; does not doubt that God will perfect what he has begun in her. In order to establish religion according to the express word of God, intends to adopt the Augsburg confession; and will maintain friendship with those Princes that adhere to it.—Latin. *Copy.* — Greenwich, July 2.

20. *The same to Prince Albert, Duke of Prussia.* Has received his letter of Jan. 31, by William Barlow. Thanks him for his congratulations *de nostro in religione recto sensu*, and congratulates him on the same. Heartily accepts his advice to adopt the Augsburg confession. Commends William Barlow, whom at Duke Albert's request, and for his own merit, she has designated Bishop of Chichester.—Latin. *Copy.* — Greenwich, July 2.

21. *The same to the King of Spain.* Credentials of Sir Thomas Chaloner sent to his Court.—Latin. *Copy.* — No date.

22. *The same to the same.* More extended credentials of Sir Thomas Chaloner, whose instructions are to foster the good will that has so long subsisted between the two countries.—Latin. *Copy.* — Greenwich, July 5.

1559.
Greenwich,
July 1.

23. *The Queen to the Civic Authorities at Lubeck, and the other Cities of the Hanseatic League.* Affairs of State, war, peace, and religion have hindered her from writing. Thanks them for their congratulations. Expostulates with them on their breaking of the conditions of trade, and especially that of exporting corn during a famine in the two preceding reigns. Promises freedom of trade on the terms of the charter granted by Queen Mary.—Latin.   *Copy.*

Westm.
June 2.

24. *The same to* ———. Has received his Majesty's letter of May 8, by baron Caspar Preymer [or Proyner]. Discusses the question of her marriage with one of his sons. Thanks him and excuses herself.—Latin.   *Copy.*

Westm.
Oct. 6.

25. *The same to the Count Palatine and two others.* Thanks them for their letter of Aug. 15; and for their advice and proffers of assistance in the matter of religion in her Church.—Latin.   *Copy.*

Westm.
Oct. 10.

26. *The same to Adolphus, Duke of Holstein.* Thanks him for his letter of July 31, sent by his chancellor, Adam Thraciger. Enters into negotiations for a treaty of commerce between them.—Latin.   *Copy.*

Westm.
Oct. 11.

27. *The same to the same.* A complimentary letter of thanks for his expressions of good will. Urges him to take steps to bring the negotiations to an issue.—Latin.   *Copy.*

Westm.
Nov. 8.

28. *The same to Gustavus, King of Sweden.* Thanks him for his letter of July 26, sent by John, Duke of Finland [son of the King of Sweden], with whom Steno Ericson is associated to carry on negotiations about her marriage with the King's son, of whom she speaks highly, but declines to marry, as God has filled her heart with the joys of celibacy.—Latin.   *Copy.*

Westm.
Nov. 9.

29. *The same to Eric, King elect of Sweden.* Has received his letters sent in July by his brother, the Duke of Finland. Thanks him for the munificent offers and good will made and shewn to her.—Latin.   *Copy.*

Westm.
Nov. 16.

30. *The same to Augustus, Duke of Saxony.* Has received his letter of Oct. 1. Will purge religion in her kingdom in spite of the devil himself. Thanks him for his good offices.—Latin.   *Copy.*

Westm.
Dec. 14.

31. *The same to Philip, King of Spain.* Difficulties of transit by land and sea hinder her envoy from going to him;

has therefore committed the business to the Bishop of Aquila; but trusts that negotiations will proceed without hindrances.—Latin. *Copy.* — 1569.

32. *The Queen to Frederic, Prince Palatine of the Rhine.* Thanks him for his letters of congratulation. Sends to him Dr. Christopher Montius (Mundt) as envoy, whom she hopes will be favourably received.—Latin. *Copy.* — Westm. Dec. 10.

33. *The same to Christopher, Duke of Wurtemburg.* Thanks him for his congratulations. Has committed the care of negotiations on her side to Dr. Montius.—Latin. *Copy.* — Westm. Dec. 10.

34. *The same to the Senators and Council of Lubeck, and other Hanse Towns.* On the trade conference to be held in London. Free trade to be continued on either side until the 1st of April next. Trusts that all disputes will be settled and firm friendship exist between them.—Latin. *Copy.* — Westm. Dec. 31.

35. *The same to Duke Albert of Prussia.* Thanks him for eight falcons sent to her sister Mary, and a second set of the same, with letters of Oct. 25th.—Latin. *Copy.* — Westm. Dec. 31.

36. *The same to the Duke of Holstein.* Thanks him for his letter of Dec. 15; and political alliance with herself. Hopes he will visit England, as he appears to wish to do so.—Latin. *Copy.* — 1559-60 Jan. 10.

37. *The same to the Archduke Charles.* Has received his letter by Count Helffenstein. Thanks him for his good will. Has no inclination to matrimony.—Latin. *Copy.* — Jan. 11.

38. *The same to the Emperor Ferdinand.* Has received his letter dated Vienna, Sept. 29, by George, Count of Helffenstein, whom she is happy to receive as the Emperor's envoy, in place of Caspar Preyner. To the solicitations of both that she should marry, she replies that she has no inclination for a married life; and this determination is of long standing, as might have been seen during the reign of her sister Mary, when an honourable marriage might have saved her from prison and other misfortunes. Goes further into the matter of the marriage negotiations. Highly commends Caspar Preyner. —Latin. *Copy.* — Jan. 11.

39. *The same to Frederic, King of Denmark.* Sends John Spithoneus on certain business, and furnishes him with credentials.—Latin. *Copy.* — Westm. Jan. 16.

1559-60
Westm.
Jan. 16.

39 a. *The Queen to Princess Dorothy of Denmark.* John Spithonous will convey her expressions of good will, and communicate certain matters of business.—Latin. Copy.

Westm.
Jan. 16.

40. *The same to Princess Margaret of Parma.* Edward Basshe, who has charge of naval supplies, is authorized to recover 21*l*. 1*s*. 4*d*. balance of moneys due for corn supplied to Adolphus of Burgundy for King Philip's fleet, for which sum John Vander Lueren and Giles Hostman are sureties.—Latin. Copy.

Westm.
Feb. 4.

41. *The same to Prince Otto of Brunswick and Luneburg.* Has received his letter by Andrew Sauras and Theobald Ornmerus. Considers his request for letters patent and a pension granted by her brother Edward VI, which on the strength of their agreement in religion and other matters she allows. With conditions and articles agreed and concluded between them.—Latin. Copy.

Westm.
Feb. 6.

42. *The same to Frederic II, King of Denmark.* Thanks him for his letter of Dec. 17, received by Frederic Pede, in which Herbrand à Langen is commended to her. Thanks him for his expressions of good will, and should occasion for war arise, will employ à Langen.—Latin. Copy.

Westm.
Feb. 10.

43. *The same to Duke Augustus of Saxony.* Letters of credence for John Brigantin, sent as envoy to the Duke.—Latin. Copy.

Westm.
Feb. 18.

44. *The same to John Frederic II, Duke of Saxony.* Letters of credence for the same as the next preceding.—Latin. Copy.

Westm.
Feb. 10.

45. *The same to Otto, Duke of Brunswick and Luneburg.* Letters of credence for the same John Brigantin.—Latin. Copy.

Westm.
Feb. 20.

46. *The same to John, Lord Bishop of Osnaburg and Paderborn.* Letters of credence for the same John Brigantin, with expressions of gratitude and good will.—Latin. Copy.

Feb. 20.

47. *The same to Albert, Count de Hoye, in Nuremburg.* Letters of credence for the same John Brigantin.—Latin. Copy.

Westm.
Feb. 20.

48. *The same to Princess Anne of East Friesland.* Rejoices at their good understanding and agreement in religion. Accredits John Brigantin to her.—Latin. Copy.

49. *The Queen to Count Antony of Oldenburg, Delmenhorst, &c.* Thanks him for his expressions of good will. Accredits John Brigantin to him.—Latin. *Copy.*
  1559-60
  Westm.
  Feb. 20.

50. *The same to Cosmo, Duke of Florence.* On some money due from him to her, for payment of which, now that Italy is at peace, she urges, and expects to receive by Bartholomew Compagni of Florence, a London merchant.—Latin. *Copy.*
  Westm.
  Feb. 19.

51. *The same to the same.* Understands that the disturbed state of Italy has hindered him from paying a sum of money due to her; but does not doubt that a settlement will now be made by his agent in the matter, Barth. Compagni.—Latin. *Copy.*
  Westm.
  July 9.

52. *The same to Gustavus, King of Sweden.* Highly commends his son, the Duke of Finland, whose stay in England will, he hopes, increase their friendship.—Latin. *Copy.*
  1560.
  Westm.
  April 10.

53. *The same to Prince Eric of Sweden.* The Duke of Finland, his brother, will convey to him her sentiments. Speaks highly of his conduct of the negotiations.—Latin. *Copy.*
  Westm.
  April 10.

54. *The same to the Emperor Ferdinand.* Commends the Count of Helffenstein on his return from the Court; for his zeal and prudence in the cause he advocated.—Latin. *Copy.*
  Greenwich,
  May 16.

55. *The same to Princess Anne of East Friesland.* Two ships, conveying military stores from Hamburg to London, have been wrecked on the coast of East Friesland. Begs her to permit and assist in the recovery of the cargoes.—Latin. *Copy.*
  Westm.
  Nov. 18.

56. *The same to the Council, &c. of Revel.* Thanks them for their action in the case of widow Anne Milford and Rich. Hodgson, merchants of Newcastle, her subjects, with two of their citizens, Benedict Corke and Thomas Lover. Prays them to see that their sentence is carried out.—Latin. *Copy.*
  Westm.
  Dec. 6.

57. *The same to the King of Spain.* Has been asked by his agent for leave for the Countess of Feria and the Lady Clarentia to leave the kingdom. Her agent has instructions to confer with him on this and other matters.—Latin. *Copy.*
  Westm.
  Dec. 11.

58. *The same to Prince Eric of Sweden.* Condoles with him on the death of his father (Gustavus), of which his letter of Oct. 12 has informed her. Congratulates him on his new position. Hopes he has received her letter given to his agent last October.—Latin. *Copy.*
  1560-1.
  Westm.
  Jan. 1.

1860-1. Westm. Jan. 1.	59. *The Queen to Cosmo, Duke of Florence.* Repeated request for payment of moneys due. Readily grants what he asks for his merchants in his letter of August 13 last.—Latin. Copy.
Westm. Jan. 10.	60. *The same to Frederic, Palatine of the Rhine.* Has committed instructions for negotiations to Christopher Mundt, for whom he begs a favourable reception.—Latin. Copy.
Westm. Jan. 18.	61. *The same to Wolfgang, Count Palatine of the Rhine.* Letters of credence for Christopher Mundt.—Latin. Copy.
Westm. Jan. 18.	62. *The same to Christopher, Duke of Wurtemburg.* Letters of credence for Christopher Mundt.—Latin. Copy.
No date.	63. *The same to Philip, Landgrave of Hesse.* Letters of credence for Christopher Mundt.—Latin. Copy.
Westm. Jan. 10.	64. *The same to John Frederic, Duke of Saxony.* Letters of credence for Christopher Mundt.—Latin. Copy.
Westm. Jan. 10.	65. *The same to Augustus, Duke of Saxony.* Letters of credence to Christopher Mundt.—Latin. Copy.
Westm. Jan. 10.	66. *The same to the Margrave of Baden.* Letters of credence for Christopher Mundt.
Westm. Jan. 10.	67. *The same to Duke Albert of Prussia.* Thanks him for his letter of Oct. 14, with ten falcons.—Latin. Copy.
Westm. Jan. 14.	68. *The same to Philip, Landgrave of Hesse.* Has received his letter written in favour of J. Godgaffe, merchant. A bad season makes import of corn necessary; nevertheless, permits the aforesaid to export a hundred casks or tuns of beer.—Latin. Copy.
Westm. Jan. 14.	69. *The same to Anne, Countess of East Friesland.* One Tiart Mannon has delivered, with the Countess's letter, a paper of the authenticity of which she has some doubt, as it is written in German, and not in Latin, and wants her signature.—Latin. Copy.
London, Jan. 17.	70. *Edmund Clynton to Prince Eric of Sweden.* Has received his letter dated Ellsburgh, October 12. As soon as he is informed of the season for sailing he will send him, with the Queen's permission, mariners whose skill and fidelity will be at his service, for the purpose he has in hand.—Latin. Copy.

71. *The Queen to Frederic II, King of Denmark.* Has received his letter of Dec. 25 last. Enters into the matter of customs and port dues in the preceding and present reign. His subjects have been treated on exactly the same footing as those of other European Princes. Trusts that friendly feeling will continue to exist between them.—Latin. *Copy.*

1560-1. Westm. Jan. 10.

72. *The same to Sigismund II, King of Poland.* Has heard that three Englishmen, citizens of Dantzic, William Dickenson, Humphrey Carr and Roger Watson, forfeited their recognizances by the non-appearance of Cuthbert Blunt, merchant of Newcastle. Has heard also that he has written to the King of Spain, desiring Blunt to be sent to Poland. Explains that Blunt, at the time he should have appeared, was engaged in business that could not be deferred, by the command of Queen Mary. Blunt is now dead, but they are in possession of evidence about the goods sold by Gerard Innighfield of Dantzic. Prays him to grant a new commission, by which the case may be referred to the Council of Dantzic.—Latin. *Copy.*

Westm. Feb. 8.

73. *The same to the City of Dantzic.* In the matter of the case detailed in the preceding letter.—Latin. *Copy.*

Westm. Feb. 8.

74. *The same to the same.* In the matter of a dispute between two Englishmen, Henry Saxey and William Hudson, the former of whom has produced an instrument, sealed, as he says, with their civic seal, but which is believed in England to be a forgery. Prays them therefore to say what ought to be done in this matter.—Latin. *Copy.*

Westm. Feb. 8.

75. *The same to the Council and Senators of Lubeck.* Has received their letter of Oct. 17, in favour of Henry Bullinger and other citizens in the matter of a ship and merchandize said to have been sunk by John Ashe in the preceding reign. Ashe is dead and his companions dispersed, but she will give every facility to the agent appointed by the city to proceed against whomsoever can be found. Gives them information as to the proper method of procedure.—Latin. *Copy.*

Westm. March 8.

76. *The same to Catherine, relict of the Duke of Saxony.* Thanks her for her letter in behalf of the persons named in the preceding letter. Will assist the course of justice in the prosecution of the representatives of John Ashe, but can do nothing more.—Latin. *Copy.*

Westm. March 8.

77. *The same to Henry, Duke of Brunswick and Luneburg.* Had ordered guns of long range, called Carryers, from

Westm. March 12.

1560-1.	Germany. Ten cases full of these were, on their way to Hamburg, detained in some town of his dominions. Begs him to permit their free passage.—Latin. *Copy.*
Westm. March 11.	78. *The Queen to the King of Spain.* Anthony Hickman and Edward Castellin, two London merchants, have agents in the Canary Islands, for whom he begs his favour and protection; promises that his subjects in her kingdom shall be treated as she would have him treat hers.—Latin. *Copy.*
Westm. March 18.	79. *The same to the Doge of Venice.* Has heard that Guido Janetti, a faithful servant of Henry VIII and Edward VI, is imprisoned at Venice at the order of the envoy of the Pope. Begs that his case may be enquired into. Trusts that their friendly relations will continue.—Latin. *Copy.*
Westm. March 18.	80. *A Letter to James Ragazzoni, a noble of Venice.* Prays him to assist in the liberation of Guido Janetti. Signed "Tui amici," &c.—Latin. *Copy.*
1561. Westm. March 30.	81. *The Queen to Frederic, King of Denmark.* Tho. Alan, merchant, has orders to provide the English fleet with stores for the East; for whom, as successor to William Watson, she begs free passage, and certain exemptions; both for him and other merchants trading to the East.—Latin. *Copy.*
Westm. March 25.	82. *The same to the Emperor of Russia.* Thanks him for past kindness. Recommends the bearer, Anthony Jenkinson, and begs the Emperor to permit him to trade freely in his own dominions, and to furnish him with credentials to the Emperor of Persia and other Princes.—Latin. *Copy.*
Westm.	83. *The same to the Emperor of Persia, &c.* Begs him to protect and assist Anthony Jenkinson.—Latin. *Copy.*
Greenwich, June 15.	84. *The same to Eric, King of Sweden.* Nich. Guldenstein, his chancellor and envoy, came to her on the 15th of this month, with his letter of April 11th. Enters into the matter of John Dymocke's agency "*in causa matrimoniali;*" his conduct will be explained by Donis Borrhous. Adds many particulars about Dymocke and Borrhous. Declines, with some vehemence, all proposals of marriage.—Latin. *Copy.*
No date.	85. *Letters patent* in behalf of John Spithovius, collated by her to the prebendary of Gillingham Major, granting him leave of absence to travel without loss of the proceeds, provided that

during his absence all things are done in the church of his prebend according to the laws of England and her injunctions.—Latin. *Copy.* 1601.

86. *The Queen to Adolphus, Duke of Holstein.* Thanks him for kindness done by his subjects in saving goods wrecked on Ditmarsh. Sends William Hearle, citizen of London, to convey her thanks, and bring the war materials from Hamburg.—Latin. *Copy.* June 29.

87. *The same to the Council and Senators of Hamburg.* Begs them to favour and assist William Hearle to transport the goods he has charge of.—Latin. *Copy.* Greenwich, June 29.

88. *The same to Otto, Duke of Brunswick and Luneburg.* Credentials for William Hearle.—Latin. *Copy.* Greenwich, June 29.

89. *The same to Henry, Duke of Brunswick and Luneburg.* Credentials for William Hearle.—Latin. *Copy.* Greenwich, June 29.

90. *The same to Francis, Duke of Saxony and Lauenburg.* Credentials for William Hearle.—Latin. *Copy.* Greenwich, June 29.

91. *Circular letter from the Queen to the European Princes.* Contradicts rumours current in Germany that the war material ordered for England was to be sent to the Emperor of Austria. Will reward any one who shall give information of the author of these false reports.—Latin. *Copy.* June 29.

92. *The Queen to the Emperor Ferdinand.* Has received his letter of May 31, in which he speaks of Livonia; and the increasing power of Muscovy. Promises to prevent the export of war material or supplies; but must allow her merchants to trade in skins. Has enforced this strict neutrality by a public edict.—Latin. *Copy.* Greenwich, July 7.

93. *The same to the King of Spain.* Complains of restrictions placed on traders between the two countries, which she begs may be removed. *Copy.* Greenwich, July 7.

94. *The same to the Magistrates of the Hanse Towns.* Has received their letter of May 15, containing their answer to the articles relating to their privileges that were exhibited to their commissaries in the preceding year, to which she replies, offering privileges and facilities for trade; and urging them not to be backward in accepting her terms, which might Greenwich, July 7.

1562. have been made more stringent. Meanwhile she will permit their merchants to trade on the terms of the aforesaid articles.—Latin. *Copy.*

July 12. 95. *The Queen to the King of Denmark.* Cuthbert Vachan complains of the treatment he has received from certain officials in Norway. Sends a statement of the case, and begs him to take order that justice may be done.—Latin. *Copy.*

London, July 14. 96. *The same to Cosmo, Duke of Florence.* Edward Lord Beauchamp and Earl of Hertford is travelling to enlarge his experience. Begs the Duke to give him a favourable reception at Florence.—Latin. *Copy.*

Greenwich, July 21. 97. *The same to the King of Spain.* Several of her subjects resident in Spain complain of the treatment received by them. Desires a conference on the matter, that the injustice may be remedied.—Latin. *Copy.*

St. James's, Oct. 5. 98. *The same to the same.* Recalls Thomas Chamberlain, her envoy, and sends Sir Thomas Chaloner in his place; whom she furnishes with letters of credence.—Latin. *Copy.*

St. James's, Oct. 6. 99. *The same to Frederic II, King of Denmark.* Has received his letter of Sept. 4. Enters into the case of Simon Sorberke, merchant of Weapond island, alleged to have received injuries at the hands of Englishmen. Has given orders that the matter shall be investigated. It appears that the complainant himself offered violence to James Spenser.—Latin. *Copy.*

St. James's, Oct. 8. 100. *The same to the same.* William Causton, William Smith, and others, English merchants, have been fishing at Weapond island, but on their entering the harbour certain Scotchmen, Tho. Nicholson, John Hogg and others, made an attack on them and destroyed their property. Understands that he has written to the Queen of Scots in behalf of the English merchants. Places her letters to them in his hands, and hopes that the case will have a favourable issue.—Latin. *Copy.*

St. James's, Nov. 11. 101. *The same to Sebastian, King of Portugal.* Has received his letter of Oct. 22, and has heard with attention the statement made on his behalf by the Bishop of Aquila. Informs him that she has fulfilled all the points explained to him last summer by Emmanuel Aravius, and has given orders to English merchants in accordance with his desires. Hopes that her compliance in thus restricting her subjects will be taken in good part by him.—Latin. *Copy.*

CLARENDON PAPERS.   479

102. *The Queen to Frederic, Palatine of the Rhine.* Letters of credence for Christopher Mundt.—Latin.   *Copy.*
    1562.
    Westm.
    March 16.

103. *The same to Philip, Landgrave of Hesse.* Is glad that she occupies no lower a place in his affection than did Henry VIII and Edward VI. Gives letters of credence for Christopher Mundt.—Latin.   *Copy.*
    Westm.
    March 16.

104. *The same to Christopher, Duke of Wurtemburg.* Letters of credence for Christopher Mundt.—Latin.   *Copy.*
    Westm.
    March 16.

105. *The same to Albert, Duke of Prussia.* Thanks him for his letter of Oct. 10, and ten hawks, by his falconer.—Latin. *Copy.*
    Westm.
    Dec. 13.

106. *The same to Eric, King of Sweden.* Touches of business she has discussed with his envoy. Refers to his letter of Sept. 17th, and the articles conditionally ratified under the treaty of marriage, and with sundry complaints begs him to cease from taking any further steps in these negotiations.—Latin.
    Copy.
    Westm.
    Dec. 14.

107. *The same to the same.* Has received his letter of April, by his chancellor, Nicholas Guldenstein, who now wishes to leave the kingdom, but is furnished with no letters from the King to that effect. Declines to say anything about the matrimonial project.—Latin.   *Copy.*
    Westm.
    March 27.

108. *The same to the King of Denmark.* Thomas Allen, merchant of London, has a commission to obtain supplies for the navy. Begs that he may be allowed to trade freely.—Latin.   *Copy.*
    Westm.
    March 27.

109. *The same to Sigismund II, King of Poland.* Thomas Martin, an Englishman, has sued Nicholas Backer and Bernard Tuke, of Dantzic, for a sum of money, but having gained the cause cannot get his money. The cause has been transferred to Poland "ad judices istic, qui nominantur terrestres." Thomas Martin is dead, his son William seeks to recover the debt. Prays him to further the cause.—Latin.   *Copy.*
    Westm.

110. *The same to the Council and Senators of Dantzic.* Lays before them the case of Thomas Martin, as stated in the preceding letter. Begs that justice may be done.—Latin. *Copy.*
    Westm.

111. *The same to Albert, Duke of Prussia.* Thomas Martin, having failed to recover goods due to him in Prussia during
    Greenwich.

1562. her father's reign, left his property to his son William, on whose behalf she prays that justice may be done without delay.—Latin. *Copy.*

Greenwich, April 5.
112. *The Queen to Frederic, King of Denmark.* An English ship, the 'Christophers,' of Lynn, has been detained at Fleckerye for the offence of one of the crew. Prays that the person of the sailor be attached and the ship restored to her owners Tho. Grove, Tho. Clayborne, and Geo. Walden.—Latin. *Copy.*

Greenwich.
113. *The same to Sebastian, King of Portugal.* Has received his letter by his envoy, John Pereira. Speaks highly of Pereira's conduct of negotiations, which she trusts will be satisfactorily arranged.—Latin. *Copy.*

Greenwich.
114. *The same to the Princes, States, orders, &c. of the Augsburg Confession.* Letters of credence for Henry Knolles and Christopher Mundt.—Latin. *Copy.*

Greenwich.
115. *The same to Philip, Landgrave of Hesse.* Letters of credence for Henry Knolles and Christopher Mundt.—Latin. *Copy.*

Greenwich.
116. *The same to Augustus, Elector of Saxony.* Letters of credence for Henry Knolles and Christopher Mundt.—Latin. *Copy.*

Greenwich
117. *The same to Frederic II, Duke of Saxony.* Letters of credence for Henry Knolles and Christopher Mundt.—Latin. *Copy.*

Greenwich.
118. *The same to Christopher, Duke of Wurtemburg.* Letters of credence for Henry Knolles and Christopher Mundt.—Latin. *Copy.*

Greenwich.
119. *The same to Frederic, Palatine of the Rhine.* Letters of credence for Henry Knolles and Christopher Mundt.—Latin. *Copy.*

Greenwich.
120. *The same to Wolfgang, Duke of Deux Ponts* (gemini Pontis). Letters of credence for Henry Knolles and Christopher Mundt.—Latin. *Copy.*

Greenwich.
121. *The same to the Margrave of Baden.* Letters of credence for Henry Knolles and Christopher Mundt.—Latin. *Copy.*

122. *The Queen to Philip, King of Spain.* His envoy, Bishop Alvares de Quadra, will have informed him of her sentiments on the state of affairs in France. Enters at large into this matter. Mentions the Duke of Guise; and recalls various grievances. Calais ought to be restored; and she will take measures to recover it; in which enterprise she expects his assistance.—Latin. *Copy.*   1562. Hampton Court, Sept. 12.

123. *The same "Romano Imperatori."* Letters of credence for Henry Knolles and Christopher Mundt.—Latin. *Copy.*   Hampton Court, Sept. 25.

124. *The same to Maximilian, King of Bohemia.* Letters of credence for Henry Knolles and Christopher Mundt.—Latin. *Copy.*   Hampton Court, Sept. 25.

125. *The President and Company of London Merchants to Princess Anne of East Friesland.* William Gnaphous, her agent, has informed them of her pleasure that they should freely trade in the port of Embden. Enters into details of terms and conditions.—Latin. *Copy.*   London, Nov. 13.

126. *The Queen to the King of Spain.* Informs him of several circumstances that may tend to lessen their friendship. Doubts whether Bishop de Quadra deals openly with her. Has instructed her envoy to explain matters, and trusts that a good understanding will be arrived at.—Latin. *Copy.*   1562-3. Westm. Jan. 9.

127. *The same to Duke Albert of Prussia.* Has received his letter of Oct. 9, with ten falcons. Thanks him for this annual gift.—Latin. *Copy.*   Westm. Jan. 16.

128. *The same to the same.* Another letter to the same effect as the next preceding.—Latin. *Copy.*   Westm. Jan. 16.

129. *The Queen's Representatives to Sir Maurice Ranczow and Paul Brocktorp.* Their letters of Nov. 27 have been received. Puts off the payment of their money until August next.—Latin. *Copy.*   Westm. Jan. 16.

130. *The Queen to Eric, King of Sweden.* Has received both his letters of October last. Will investigate the affair in which Francis Berti and his chancellor (lately his envoy in England) are concerned; and also that of opening the navigation to certain Russian ports. His third letter of Oct 31 has also engaged her attention. Will serve his interest in any way she can. A postscript, explaining why she cannot grant certain privileges of trade to his merchants.—Latin. *Copy.*   Westm. Feb. 10.

1562–3.
Westm.
March 14.

131. *The Queen to Count Anthony of Oldenburg and Delmenhorst.* Commends to him William Horle, the bearer of this letter.—Latin. *Copy.*

Westm.
March 14.

132. *The same to Count Isard of Oldenburg and Delmenhorst.* Commends to him the bearer, William Horle.—Latin. *Copy.*

Westm.
March 14.

133. *The same to the Council and Senators of Hamburg.* Commends to them William Horle, the bearer of this letter.—Latin. *Copy.*

1563.
Westm.
March 24.

134. *The same to Philip, Landgrave of Hesse.* Has received his expressions of good will by Henry Knolles. Speaks of the alliance of Protestant Princes, which must be firmly maintained and widely spread.—Latin. *Copy.*

Westm.
March 26.

135. *The same to the Duke of Wurtemburg.* Has received assurance of his friendship by Henry Knolles. Trusts that he will join with those who wish to further the Protestant cause in France; and that their alliance against Rome and Trent will be firm and powerful.—Latin. *Copy.*

March 16.

136. *The same to Frederic, Count Palatine of the Rhine.* Henry Knolles has informed her of his adherence to the Protestant cause, which his letter of December 10 confirms; and in answer to it writes at length of the alliance of Protestant Princes.—Latin. *Copy.*

Westm.
March 26.

137. *The same to the Hanseatic League.* Has received their letter of July 6 last. Rejoices at the continuance of their alliance, and trusts that the conditions contained in the articles may be observed to the benefit of merchants concerned.—Latin. *Copy.*

Windsor,
Nov. 3.

138. *The same to the Emperor Ferdinand.* Thanks him for his letter of Sept. 24. Pardons, at his request, those who have offended against the laws about religion; but cannot permit them freedom of worship, as she professes to follow the mind of the early Fathers. Both law and prudence forbid toleration of any other religion. Is much grieved at being obliged to refuse his request.—Latin. *Copy.*

Windsor,
Nov. 9.

139. *The same to Frederic, King of Denmark.* Has received both his letters of Sept. 18. Grieves at the audacious offence of an English youth, by which their Majesties of Denmark and Sweden have been insulted; but hopes that the affair will be settled to their satisfaction. Gives details of the case of Henry Bullinghausen and the Amsterdam merchants.—Latin. *Copy.*

140. *The Queen to Adolphus, Duke of Holstein.* Has received his letter about the affair of Henry Bullinghausen, and certain subjects of the King of Spain; which she trusts will be satisfactorily settled.—Latin. *Copy.* 1563. Windsor, Nov. 14.

141. *The same to Cosmo, Duke of Florence.* Urges him again to pay the money claimed in a former letter.—Latin. *Copy.* Windsor, Nov. 21.

142. *The same to Philip, King of Spain.* Her envoy at his Court is in ill health and wishes to return home; begs the King to permit him to do so. Will send another in his place either to Spain, or to the Regent in Belgium; to whom also a special messenger will be sent to explain what has been done in satisfaction of certain demands.—Latin. *Copy.* Windsor, Dec. 11.

143. *The same to Frederic II, King of Denmark.* William Peterson, Francis Chatfield, George Chatfield, Thomas Lovesham, London merchants, complain that their shipload of merchandize bought in Sweden has been seized on its way to Dantzic. Prays that it may be restored.—Latin. *Copy.* Windsor, Dec. 11.

144. *The Merchants of London to Anne, Countess of East Friesland.* Thank her for certain privileges granted in the interests of trade. Have appointed George Neda and George Roo to complete the negotiations. (Signed) Joan. Marshe.—Latin. *Copy.* 1563–4. Jan. 18.

145. *The Queen to Otto of Brunswick and Luneburg.* George Neda has a commission to buy war supplies in Germany. Begs that he may receive protection and assistance.—Latin. *Copy.* Jan. 18.

146. *The same to the Count of Mansfield.* Thanks him for commending to her one skilled in military affairs. Will certainly entertain his proposal if occasion arise.—Latin. *Copy.* Windsor, Jan. 14.

147. *John White, William Allen, Thomas Bannister, James Morley, Robert Dowe, John Rivers, John Barnes, merchants of the City of London, to the Queen.* Lately sent their agents with eight ships into Spain. About Nov. 20 last, as their vessels with return cargoes were in the port of Gibraltar, a French ship of Rouen entered the harbour and threatened and insulted the English crews, one of which retaliated. After some loss of life on both sides, the English ships were battered from the town and attacked with five vessels by Don Alvarez, and their crews imprisoned. Give details of further injuries, and pray the Queen to write to the King of Spain.—Latin. *Copy.* No date.

1563-4.
Windsor.

148. *The Queen to Philip, King of Spain.* Gives an account of the affair related in the next preceding letter, which she sends to him, and trusts that the matter will be justly and amicably settled.—Latin. *Copy.*

Windsor,
Feb. 20.

149. *The same to Frederic II, King of Denmark.* Bertram Anderson and other merchants of Newcastle have suffered from the war between Denmark and Sweden; one of their crews, with their agent, William Anderson, being imprisoned, and the ship seized at the siege of the castle of Elsbrough. Prays him to see to this, and to give all the assistance he can to English north-country merchants.—Latin. *Copy.*

Windsor,
Feb. 25.

150. *The same to Eric, King of Sweden.* Has heard of the brilliant talents of his sister Cecilia, whom she will be happy to receive at her Court. Has written to the King of Denmark to beg him to waive his right as a belligerent in her behalf and permit her to pass through his dominions.—Latin. *Copy.*

Windsor,
Feb. 25.

151. *The same to Frederic II, King of Denmark.* Begs him to permit the King of Sweden's sister to pass through his dominions.—Latin. *Copy.*

Windsor.
Feb. 15.

152. *The same to Cecilia, Princess of Sweden.* Has written to her brother of her purpose to visit England. Is grieved at her recent loss. Hopes to see her soon.—Latin. *Copy.*

Windsor,
Feb. 25.

153. *The same to John* ["*comiti in Thenes. capitaneo Rhohasinensi*"]. Has received his letter dated Copenhagen, Jan. 10, by Leo Curio and George North. Condoles with him on the death of the Palatine Belsko. Hopes he will meet the Princess Cecilia in England and prosecute his suit.—Latin. *Copy.*

Windsor,
March 2.

154. *The same to Sebastian, King of Portugal.* Anthony Courtney armed a ship against France last year, and having captured a vessel laden with a French cargo put eight sailors on board as prize crew, who from stress of weather took her into Lisbon, and were there imprisoned as pirates. Begs that they may be released.—Latin. *Copy.*

Windsor,
March 17.

155. *The same to Philip, King of Spain.* Has taken precautions in order to avoid complications with him, arising from her war with France; but finds that English merchants trading to Spain are ill treated, on the ground of reprisals. Prays that these practices may be restrained, and due punishment inflicted.—Latin. *Copy.*

156. *The Queen to Sigismund, King of Poland.* Thanks him for what he has done in the case of William Martin at Dantzic; begs him to take measures for the complete settlement of the same.—Latin. *Copy.*
　　1564. Windsor, April 25.

157. *The same to the Councillors and Magistrates of Dantzic.* Urges them to give satisfaction in the matter of William Martin.—Latin. *Copy.*
　　Windsor, April 25.

158. *The same to Frederic II, King of Denmark.* In behalf of English merchants, who run great risks and suffer loss, especially during the present war, from pirates. Prays him to protect them within his dominions.—Latin. *Copy.*
　　Windsor, April 25.

159. *The same to the Councillors and Senators of the City of Hamburg.* Thanks them for their letter of March 17. In the matter of a dispute between English merchants and others. Readily entertains their petition for free trade, subject to the arbitration of those most interested in it.—Latin. *Copy.*
　　April 25.

160. *The same to Cosmo, Duke of Florence.* Commends the bearer, Guido Cavalcanti, of Florence, who came when a boy with his father to England, and served Henry VIII, Edward VI, and herself; and now desires to return to Florence. Urges him again to pay the money due.—Latin. *Copy.*
　　Richmond, May 27.

161. *The same to the Emperor of Russia.* Thanks him for his kindness to English subjects visiting Russia. Commends to him Raphael Barborini, an Italian, for whom she begs a free passage and protection in his dominions.—Latin. *Copy.*
　　June 14.

162. *The same to Frederic II, King of Denmark.* Dennis Dorrheus and Nicholas Goldnister, lately agents to the King of Sweden, were obliged to borrow money from William Hemet, Lionel Duckett, Nicholas Springam, Geoffry Duckett, Edward Osborne, and other English merchants, which has not yet been repaid. Thomas Valentine, sent to the King of Sweden to demand payment, has been detained at Copenhagen; his letters and 150 thalers being taken from him. Begs him to let her messenger proceed to Sweden, and his property be restored to him.—Latin. *Copy.*
　　St. James's, Sept. 14.

163. *Certificate* for the importation of yew into England. Adrian Pavelsenius, of Hamburg, has bought yew for bows of Nicolas Angulus for the English market, but has been forbidden to bring it out of Saxony; there being a suspicion that
　　St. James's, Nov. 4.

1564.	it was for barbarians. Explains that it is for England, and begs all Princes through whose dominions it may have to pass will assist Pavelsenius.—Latin. *Copy.*
St. James's, Nov. 8.	164. *The Queen to Frederic II, King of Denmark.* Geoffry Preston, a young gentleman on his travels, who left England in company with John, Duke of Finland, has been detained and imprisoned by Danish magistrates. Begs that he may be released.—Latin. *Copy.*
St. James's, Sept. 24.	165. *The same to Eric, King of Sweden.* Fears that her letter of Aug. 16 in last year has been lost. Repeats her request on behalf of the London merchants, who cannot recover a sum of money from the King's agent, Nicholas Goldnister.—Latin. *Copy.*
St. James's, Nov. 25.	166. *The same to Sigismund Augustus, King of Poland.* John Copp, by his servant John Epte, has transacted business with the agents of Tho. Allen. Part of the money due for cloth sent to Dantzic is still due. Begs him to see to the payment.—Latin. *Copy.*
St. James's, Nov. 27.	167. *The same to the King of Hungary.* The Marchioness of Northampton, who suffers from a severe acute disorder, having heard of his physician, Dr. Michael ab Othen; and has been attended by him. Begs the King to permit her stay to be prolonged.—Latin. *Copy.*
Westm. Dec. 21.	168. *The same to the King of Spain.* On the recall of her agent, who was in ill health; and the disturbances between Spanish and English merchants. Has had communication with the Duchess of Parma.—Latin. *Copy.*
1564-5. Westm. Feb. 10.	169. *The same to Princess Anne and others, of East Friesland.* Is glad to hear of her kindness to English merchants in the former year, and is therefore the more sorry at the difficulties that have recently arisen. Trusts that the negotiation may yet be concluded.—Latin. *Copy.*
1565. Westm. April 3.	170. *The same to Frederic II, King of Denmark.* Repeats her request made in her letter of September last in the matter of Tho. Valentin and English merchants.—Latin. *Copy.*
Westm. April 17.	171. *The same to Jerome, Doge of Venice.* Guido de Casone desires to return from his exile. Begs that he may be permitted to spend the rest of his life in his native country.—Latin. *Copy.*

172. *(Secretary of State) to Dr. Albert Knopper, Secretary to the King of Denmark.* His friends William Rowle and Robert Boste, English merchants, are sending a ship to Russia. Certifies that there is no war material on board. Begs that the ship may be allowed to proceed to her destination without hindrance.—Latin.   *Copy.*

1565. April 21.

173. *The Queen to the King of Denmark.* Thomas Allan, agent for the English navy, is sending four ships, the 'Saviour,' of London; the 'Christ,' of Newcastle; the 'Mary George' and the barque 'Gray,' of London, for naval stores to Dantzic. The vessels are loaded with English cloth and rabbit-skins. Begs for a safe-conduct for them.—Latin.   *Copy.*

Westm. May 3.

174. *The same to the King of Sweden.* To the same effect as the next preceding letter.—Latin.   *Copy.*

Westm. May 3.

175. *The same to the King of Denmark.* Begs him to remove the grievances of which the English merchants complain. —Latin.   *Copy.*

Westm. May 7.

176. *The same to Cosmo, Duke of Florence.* Alexander and Julius Augustino, English subjects, have for five years been trying to get their paternal inheritance from Baptist Canalsanti and Vincent Geraldi. Augustino was a favourite physician of Henry VIII. Commends these men and their cause to him.— Latin.   *Copy.*

May 7.

177. *The same to Eric, King of Sweden.* Has just received his letter of June 1, 1564. Is grieved at his war with Denmark. Hopes to be of some use in making peace. Trusts that their intercourse may be maintained, and makes offers of friendly assistance.—Latin.   *Copy.*

Westm. May 19.

178. *Conditions and articles of a convention between Queen Elizabeth and John, Count of East Friesland.*—Latin.   *Copy.*

Westm. May 14.

179. *The Queen to Anne, Countess of East Friesland, and others.* Endeavours to enlist their sympathy and assistance in the controversy about the merchants. Arnold Walwick will explain particular details.—Latin.

Westm. May 17.

180. *The same to the King of Poland.* Thanks him for the orders he has given to the Council of Dantzic in behalf of William Martin. Prays that the same measure may be extended to John Martin, that he and other English agents may be treated with justice and consideration.—Latin.   *Copy.*

Greenwich, July 17.

1565.
Richmond,
Aug. 5.

161. *The Queen to the Emperor Maximilian II.* Adam Sweckovitz, Baron Mittenburg, his ambassador, has delivered his letter of March 15. Will return him a full answer by the ambassador. Assures him of her friendship and good will.—Latin. *Copy.*

Richmond,
Aug. 5.

162. *The same to Charles, Archduke of Austria.* To the same effect as the next preceding.—Latin. *Copy.*

Westm.
Sept. 25.

163. *The same to the King of Sweden.* Thomas Knapp has delivered two of his letters. Enters at length into their contents, and the relations of England and Denmark. Has spoken more fully with his sister (the Princess) Cecilia.—Latin. *Copy.*

Westm.
Oct. 6.

164. *The same to the same.* In the matter of his brother John, Duke of Finland, and the matrimonial scheme. Trusts that all offence will be passed over.—Latin. *Copy.*

Westm.
Oct. 14.

165. *The same to the King of Spain.* Recites the assurances she received from him as to the character of the proceedings at the conference of Bayonne. Prays him to give no heed to rumours or anything that may lessen their friendship and alliance. Hears that his ambassador has orders to go to Brussels to be present at the marriage of the Prince of Parma. Offers accommodation to the fleet in English ports. Mentions the death of Thomas Chaloner; will shortly send another agent.—Latin. *Copy.*

Westm.
Nov. 9.

166. *The Secretary of State to the Mayor, &c. of Dunkirk.* In the matter of Nicasius and James Notswerf.—Latin. *Copy.*

Nov. 22.

167. *The Queen to the King of Portugal.* In the matter of Thomas Pope and John Kyrrie, whose ship, the 'Margaret,' of Minehead, has been attacked by Louis of Almeda; they themselves, after trial before Manuel of Almeda, were set free, but their property was not restored. Prays for redress.—Latin. *Copy.*

Westm.
Nov. 22.

168. *Letters Patent* conceded to Prince Christopher, of Baden, husband of the Princess Cecilia of Sweden, granting him a portion of 1000 crowns.—Latin. *Copy.*

Westm.
Dec. 4.

169. *The Queen to Duke Albert of Prussia.* Thanks him for his letter and present of eight hawks.—Latin. *Copy.*

Westm.
Dec. 4.

170. *The same to Frederic, King of Denmark.* In the matter of safe-conducts for the English merchant ships in war time.—Latin. *Copy.*

191. *The Queen to the King of Sweden.* To the same effect as the next preceding. Promises that there shall be no breach of neutrality.—Latin.   *Copy.*
  Westm. Dec. 4. 1565.

192. *The same to the same.* In the matter of John Dymock, whose ruin has involved that of others, and on whose behalf she begs that justice may be done and restitution made.—Latin.   *Copy.*
  Westm. Dec. 9.

193. *The same to the King of Spain.* In the matter of Henry Fallowfield, merchant of London, whose ship has been seized on a charge of piracy.—Latin.   *Copy.*
  Westm. Dec. 11.

194. *The same to the King of Denmark.* Further explanations in the affair of H. Bullinghausen, Dr. Knopper, and Will. Peterson.—Latin. (Six pages.)   *Copy.*
  Westm. Dec. 16.

195. *The same to the King of Sweden.* At the request of the Princess Cecilia permits some woollen cloth to be exported for Sweden.
  Westm. Dec. 28.

196. *The same to the King of Denmark.* Requests a safe-conduct for merchants trading to Lubeck, Dantzic, and Poland. —Latin.   *Copy.*
  1565-6. Jan. 1.

197. *The same to the King of Spain.* In commendation of the Condé d'Arro, who has lately visited England.—Latin.   *Copy.*
  Westm. Jan. 7.

198. *The same to the same.* Sends John Man, Dean of Gloucester, in place of Tho. Chaloner.—Latin.   *Copy.*
  Jan. 16.

199. *The same to the King of Denmark.* Explains why permission cannot be granted to James Cullam to bring a naval contingent into her kingdom.—Latin.   *Copy.*
  Jan. 18.

200. *The same to the Princess Regent of Flanders.* In the matter of Edward Souchenorthe, merchant of London, and Arnold Vandale.—Latin.   *Copy.*
  Westm. Jan. 30.

201. *The same to the Count Palatine of the Rhine.* Thanks him for his letter of Dec. 27, in which he had expressed his gratitude to her for her reception of the Princess Cecilia and her husband.—Latin.   *Copy.*
  Westm. Feb. 1.

202. *The same to Anne, Countess Palatine.* Mentions the visit of her sister, the Princess Cecilia. A letter of compliment. —Latin.   *Copy.*
  Westm. Feb. 1.

1565–6.
London,
Feb. 10.

203. *Letters Patent* for William George, who desires to enter foreign service against the Turks. Commends him to the favour and protection of European powers.—Latin. *Copy.*

Greenwich,
Feb. 17.

204. *The Queen to the King of Spain.* Begs his intervention in behalf of the English subjects whose ships and property have been detained in Spain for two years, since the disturbance in the harbour of Gibraltar.—Latin. *Copy.*

Greenwich,
Feb. 22.

205. *The same to the Landgrave of Hesse.* In authorization of the mission of Christopher Mundt.—Latin. *Copy.*

Greenwich,
Feb. 22.

206. *The same to Frederic, Count Palatine.* To the same effect as the next preceding letter.—Latin. *Copy.*

Greenwich,
Feb. 22.

207. *The same to the Duke of Wurtemberg.* Accrediting Christopher Mundt.—Latin. *Copy.*

Greenwich,
Feb. 22.

208. *The same to John Frederic, Duke of Saxony.* To the same effect as the last.—Latin. *Copy.*

Greenwich,
Feb. 21.

209. *The same to Augustus, Duke of Saxony, Prince Elector.* Appoints Christopher Mundt to be her representative in the forthcoming conference.—Latin. *Copy.*

Greenwich,
Feb. 22.

210. *The same to the Emperor Maximilian II.* Accrediting Dr. Christopher Mundt.—Latin. *Copy.*

Greenwich,
Feb. 22.

211. *The same to Wolfgang, Count Palatine of the Rhine.* To the same effect as the next preceding.

Greenwich,
March 8.

212. *The same to the King of Poland.* In the matter of Thomas Allen, merchant of London, and John Cop.—Latin. *Copy.*

Greenwich,
Feb. 22.

213. *The same to Joachim, Marquis of Brandenburg.* Accrediting Dr. Christopher Mundt. *Copy.*

Greenwich,
March 14.

214. *The same to the King of Sweden.* Complaints have arisen about certain moneys placed by some London merchants in the hands of Nicolas Goldmister. Begs that a settlement may be made.—Latin. *Copy.*

Greenwich,
March 14.

215. *The same to the King of Denmark.* About the same business as the last. Begs for a safe-conduct for John Keill.—Latin. *Copy.*

216. *The Queen to the King of Denmark.* Repeats the request made in her letter of Dec. 4, in behalf of the London merchants; which she sends by Christopher Haddesdon (or Hoddesdon).—Latin. *Copy.* — 1565-6. Greenwich, March 16.

217. *The same to the King of Sweden.* To the same effect as the last.—Latin. *Copy.* — Greenwich, March 16.

218. *William Cecil (Lord Burleigh) to Gonsalo Perez (chief secretary to the King of Spain).* Thanks him for the messages conveyed to him in letters to the ambassador. Assures him of his friendship and gratitude.—Latin. *Copy.* — Greenwich, Feb. 20.

219. *The Queen to the Emperor of Russia.* Sends Anthony Jenkenson as her agent. Mentions Raphael Barberini, who went to him last year with letters from herself.—Latin. *Copy.* — 1566. Greenwich, April 20.

220. *The same to Gerard, Bishop of Liege.* Begs that Walter Diepenraex may be permitted to return to England.—Latin. *Copy.* — Greenwich, March 28.

221. *The same to the King of Denmark.* Has received his letter of Jan. 26, by Dr. Albert Knopper. Writes to him on behalf of certain merchants and others who have just cause of complaint.—Latin. *Copy.* — Greenwich, April 22.

222. *The same to the same.* Begs a free transit for timber and other naval stores to be procured from Dantzic and elsewhere by Tho. Alan. Has spoken on the matter to Dr. Knopper.—Latin. *Copy.* — Greenwich, May 3.

223. *The Secretary of State to Dr. Knopper.* Further expostulations, and a request that the business referred to in the letter of April 22 may be settled.—Latin. *Copy.* — Greenwich, May 12.

224. *The Queen to the Magistrates and Council of the Hanse Towns.* Approves the appointment of Peter Eiffler (afterwards written Giffler) as their agent in London.—Latin. *Copy.* — Greenwich, May 28.

225. *The same to the Emperor Maximilian.* Philip Salvage, Baron of Ruigraffe, has been delayed in returning from his visit to England, by going to Hungary to join the Christian forces against the Turks. Begs that the delay may be excused.—Latin. *Copy.* — Greenwich, May 25.

226. *The same to (the King of Denmark).* Ralph Clayton, with his ship, the 'Julinna' and the cargo, is detained at — Westm. Nov. 6.

1606. Copenhagen. He is accused of offences of which he is innocent: begs that he may take his trial and be released.—Latin. *Copy.*

London,
Nov. 13.
227. (*The Secretary of State*) *to Dr. Albert Knopper.* Congratulates him on his advancement. Begs him to undertake some business in regard of causes in the Admiralty Court; and specially the affair of Ralph Clayton.—Latin. *Copy.*

This and the next preceding letter has the superscription " For my Lord Admirall."

Westm.
Dec. 6.
228. *The Queen to the Magistrates of Dantzic.* In behalf of Giles Gray. Complains of the harsh treatment he has received. Begs that he may be released from prison, and his ship and goods be restored to him, and a compensation made.—Latin. *Copy.*

Westm.
Nov. 30.
229. *The same to the King of Denmark.* John Petre, George Periman, and John Pope, merchants of Exeter, sent a vessel to Dantzic. The ship and two of their agents, Nicholas Denys and Richard Jordan, have been captured and detained. Prays for their release.—Latin. *Copy.*

London,
Nov. 3.
230. *The Lords of the Council to the Doge and Council of Venice.* In the matter of Daniel Foscarini and the Earl of Arundel.—Latin. *Copy.*

(Four pages.)

Westm.
Dec. 6.
231. *To the Magistrates of Dantzic.* Complaints of the treatment received by Robert Nayler, merchant of Hull.—Latin. *Copy.*

Westm.
Dec. 7.
232. *The Queen to the King of Denmark.* About the Exeter merchants (No. 229). The owners of the vessel are John and William Haukey.—Latin. *Copy.*

Westm.
Dec. 13.
233. *A letter* with superscription about a temporary concession for the export of cloth.—Latin. *Copy.*

Westm.
Dec. 18.
234. *The Queen to the King of Denmark.* Writes in praise of Dr. Knopper. Enters into the case of John Robins and John Cualling, about whom he had written. Begs that none may suffer unjustly by reason of the war.—Latin. *Copy.*

1606-7.
Jan. 14.
235. *The same to the Emperor.* Olave, Count of Arro, who is returning from England, takes this letter. Replies to his letter received by Tho. Damett.—Latin. *Copy.*

235. *The Queen to the King of Sweden.* In the matter of John Porter, merchant of Lynn, and his ship, the 'St. John Evangelist,' of Malden, which has been seized. Prays for redress.—Latin.   *Copy.*   1566-7. Westm. Jan. 10.

236 a. *The same to the King of Denmark.* About the same business as the last.—Latin.   *Copy.*   Westm. Jan. 10.

237. *To the Count de Feren.* Mentions their friend, the Lady Charenoux, lately deceased. Begs his assistance in resisting some malicious efforts made by George Kempe.—Latin.   *Copy.*   No date.

238. *The Queen to the King of Denmark.* Refers to her letter of March 16 last. Mentions Christopher Hodson, who has been well treated by him. Sends a list of English merchant vessels.—Latin.   *Copy.*   Westm. Feb. 10.

239. *The same to the King of Sweden.* Begs protection for the ships of English merchants, of which a list is sent.—Latin.   *Copy.*   Westm. Feb. 20.

240. *The same to the Council of Hamburg.* In behalf of the society of London merchants. Refers to her letter of April 30, 1564.—Latin.   *Copy.*   Westm. March 2.

241. *To the same.* Thanks them for their letter of Oct. 13 last. Sends Fr. Robinson, Fr. Benson, and others, as negotiators. Endorsed "Gubernator et societas Anglorum mercatorum peraegre negotiantium."   March 9.

242. *The President of the Society of English Merchants to the same*, superscribed "Pro Jo. Marshe, Gubernatore." In behalf of the English merchants.—Latin.   *Copy.*   March 6.

243. *Circular letter of credence* for Fr. Robinson and Fr. Benson, London merchants, who are going to East Germany.—Latin.   *Copy.*   London, March 8.

244. *The Queen to the Magistrates of Dantzic.* In behalf of the English merchants.—Latin.   *Copy.*   Westm. March 10.

245. *The same to the King of Denmark.* In the matter of Tho. Alan and his business at Dantzic.—Latin.   *Copy.*   Westm. March 10.

246. *The same to the King of Sweden.* On the same subject as the last.—Latin.   *Copy.*   Westm. March 10.

1567.
Westm.
March 19.

247. *The Queen to the King of Spain.* Refers to her former letter about the Count of Arro, for whom she asks a place vacant by the death of Ferdinand Cascalti.—Latin. *Copy.*

Westm.
April 18.

248. *To the City of Dantzic.* Thomas Bowes, Anthony Sauvage, Tho. Walker, London merchants, have suffered injuries. Begs that satisfaction may be made.—Latin. *Copy.*

Westm.
May 1.

249. *To the City of Lubeck.* William Peterson, George and Francis Chatfield, Tho. Louisham, Ph. Abney, Gerard Gore, Arthur Dawbney, Giles Vawdye, Arthur Maude, John Bournell, London merchants, have suffered great injuries. Sends John Foxall to lay the case before them. Prays for redress.—Latin. *Copy.*

Westm.
May 4.

250. *The Queen to the King of Denmark.* Thanks him for his letter of February last. Enters into the matter of William Winter, and his ship, and other cases of a like nature, which had already been laid before him both by her letters and by Dr. Knopper. Refers to her letter of Dec. 18 last. Sends John Foxall to him as her agent in this business.—Latin. *Copy.*

May 1.

251. *To the City of Lubeck and the other Hanse Towns.* Among their agents sent to England four years ago, was one Peter Schimbell, of Lubeck, whose private affairs have suffered by his attention to public business. Begs them to replace his losses.—Latin. *Copy.*

Westm.
May 6.

252. *The Queen to the King of Portugal.* In the matter of William and George Winter, and others. Complains of the pirates. Sends Dr. Tho. Wilson to him as her agent. Prays for redress. Mentions also the cases of William Gerreard and William Chester, in 1564; and of Thomas Fleming and others, in 1566.—Latin. *Copy.*

April 10.

253. *The Petition of William and George Winter.*—Latin. *Copy.*

Westm.
May 12.

254. *To the Council of the City of Stralsund.* Martin Swart has ill-treated George Norwood, the agent of John Gilbert. Begs that the affair may be settled.—Latin. *Copy.*

Westm.
May 12.

255. *The Queen to the Duke of Pomerania, &c.* In the matter of John Gilbert and Martin Swart.—Latin. *Copy.*

Westm.
May 13.

256. *The same to the King of Denmark.* Begs for a safe-conduct for Thomas Allen.—Latin. *Copy.*

257. *The Queen to the Emperor of Russia.* In behalf of Anthony Jenkinson (president) and the society of English merchants.—Latin. *Copy.* 1567. Westm. May 18.

258. *The same to the King of Denmark.* Refers to her having sent John Foxall. Writes in behalf of Ralph Clayton.—Latin. *Copy.* Westm. June 10.

259. "*For my Lord Admiral.*" To G. Bilde, *the Danish Admiral.* In the matter of Ralph Clayton.—Latin. *Copy.* Westm. June 5.

260. "*For the Duke of Norfolk.*" *To the same.* In the matter of John Hawkins, whose ship has been detained at Fleckeroe.—Latin. *Copy.* No date.

261. *The Queen to Cosmo, Duke of Florence.* Refers to her letter of May 7, 1565, in behalf of Alexander and Julius Augustine, whose inherited property has been seized by Bernard Bonsi. Francis Alford, Julius' stepfather, has endeavoured to recover the property. Begs that justice may be done.—Latin. *Copy.* Richmond, July 10.

262. *Letters Patent* of safe-conduct for Anthony de Conti, of Italy, and Lucretia his wife.—Latin. *Copy.* Windsor, Sept. 29.

263. *The Queen to Sigismund, King of Poland.* Thanks him for his letter of July 13. Writes about the affair between Dantzic and the English merchants.—Latin. *Copy.* Windsor, Sept. 29.

264. *The same to the King of Sweden.* The 'Roberta' of Newcastle, loaded with salt, has been seized, and the captain, George Anderson, and crew detained. Prays that they may be released.—Latin. *Copy.* Windsor, Oct. 8.

265. *The same to the same.* Two ships, with their captains, Henry Sterrene and Horman Petock, have been detained. Begs that they may be restored.—Latin. *Copy.* Windsor, Oct. 13.

266. *The same to the Emperor of Russia.* The society of London merchants sends to him their agents, Laurence Manley and Nicolas Procter. Commends them to his favour and protection.—Latin. *Copy.* Windsor, Oct. 14.

267. *Letter* of safe-conduct for Laurence Manley, Matthew de Quester, and Giles Vaud.—Latin. *Copy.* Hampton Court, Oct. 28.

268. *The Queen to the King of Poland.* Duplicate of 263. No date.

1567.
Hampton Court,
Nov. 1.

269. *The Queen to the King of Poland.* A fuller answer to his letter of July 13, which she had answered briefly on Sept. 29.—Latin. *Copy.*
(Eight pages.)

Hampton Court,
Nov. 1.

270. *The same to the Magistrates of Dantzic.* Thanks them for their letter of July 30. Complains that they say one thing and do another.—Latin. *Copy.*

Hampton Court,
Nov. 2.

271. *The same to Sebastian, King of Portugal.* Some officers of his fleet have ill-treated certain English subjects, viz. Eustace Oliver and John Walron, merchants of Exeter, whose ship, the 'Mynion Gale,' of Topsham, with her captain, John Pocam, and cargo of cloth, &c. has been seized near Lisbon. Demands redress.—Latin. *Copy.*

Hampton Court,
Dec. 9.

272. *The same to Albert, Duke of Prussia.* Thanks him for his letter of Sept. 25, and present of twelve hawks.—Latin.
Copy.

1567-8.
Westm.
Feb. 7.

273. *The same to Eric, King of Sweden.* In the matter of John Porter, of Lynn, and his ship, about which she had written in the foregoing year.—Latin. *Copy.*

Feb. 6.

274. *F. Clynton to Peter Oxe,* one of his Danish Majesty's Privy Councillors. "For my Lord Admiral." In behalf of Ralph Clayton.—Latin. *Copy.*

London,
Feb. 10.

275. *The Queen to the Emperor of Russia.* Thanks him for his letter of September last, received by Ant. Jenkinson. Refers to her letter sent by the agents, Laurence Manley and Nicolas Procter. Sends another agent, George Middleton, on other business of importance, about some Englishmen who, having surreptitiously contracted marriage with Poles, are to be arrested before they escape into Poland.—Latin. *Copy.*

Westm.
Feb. 10.

276. *The same to the King of Denmark.* The society of London merchants have sent the ship 'Juliana' to trade in the Baltic. Begs that the vessel may have free passage.—Latin. *Copy.*

Westm.
Feb. 13.

277. *The same to the King of Sweden.* William Garton, and other merchants of Yarmouth, have suffered loss by the detention of the cargo of their ship, the 'Luke,' which has been wrecked. Begs that it may be restored.—Latin. *Copy.*

Westm.
Feb. 17.

278. *The same to the King of Denmark.* On the same business as the last.—Latin. *Copy.*

279. *The Queen to the King of Poland.* James Spencer or Spenser, wishes to trade in Poland. Begs his permission and protection.—Latin. *Copy.* 1567-8. Westm. March 4.

280. *The same to Duke Albert of Prussia.* On the same subject as the last.—Latin. *Copy.* Westm. March 4.

281. *The same to Frederic II, King of Denmark.* On the same subject as 279.—Latin. *Copy.* Westm. March 4.

282. *The same to the same.* In the matter of Tho. Alan.—Latin. *Copy.* Westm. March 8.

283. *To the City of Dantzic.* To the same effect as the last. —Latin. *Copy.* Westm. March 2.

284. *To Duke Albert of Prussia,* superscribed "Pro domina Suffolch." Sends this letter by James Spencer, to thank him for his kindness to her husband and herself when they were in Prussia. Recommends Spencer to his favour.—Latin. *Copy.* London, March 6.

285. *To the same,* superscribed "Pro D. Pellam." Thanks him for kindness received at his hands. Military service has hindered him from writing. The bearer of this letter (Spencer) has married his sister.—Latin. *Copy.* London, March 6.

286. *The Queen to the King of Spain.* Thanks him for his letter of Dec. 22, in behalf of Mr. Inglefield, to which she replies.—Latin. *Copy.* Westm. March 4.

287. *The same to William, Landgrave of Hesse.* Thanks him for his letter of Jan. 1, enclosing the petition of Adolphus Zenck against Edmund Roberts.—Latin. *Copy.* Westm. March 10.

288. *The same to the King of Denmark.* Mentions the death of Henry, Earl of Darnley. Begs that Bothwell may be given up.—Latin. *Copy.* 1568. Westm. March 19.

289. *The same to Frederic, Count Palatine of the Rhine.* Thanks him for his letter of Feb. 12, received by Emanuel Tremellius. Enters at some length into the motives of the war in France and the conduct of the French King.—Latin. *Copy.* Westm. April 23.

289 a. *The same to the Emperor of Russia.* Thanks him for his letter of April 10, received by Stephen Twerdic and Feod. Pogorvella, whose business she has taken care to forward.—Latin. *Copy.* Greenwich, May 9.

299. *To the Magistrates of Dantzic.* About the complaints of the English merchants.—Latin. *Copy.* 1568. Greenwich, July 3.

300. *The Queen to Edgar, Count of East Friesland.* Has received his letter of June 1, by his agents, Dr. Duirkin and John Knell. Is grieved to hear of the disturbances in Friesland. Discusses the causes that have led to the rupture between him and the King of Spain.—Latin. *Copy.* London, July 11.
(Four pages.)

301. *The same to William, Duke of Cleves.* Walter Baylie, M.D., professor at Oxford, the bearer of this letter, has married one of the Duke's subjects. Begs the Duke to assist him in obtaining the property that comes to him with his wife. —Latin. *Copy.* London, July 4.

302. *The same to the Emperor of Russia.* Sent Lawrence Manley to him Oct. 14, 1567, and George Middleton Feb. 10, 156⅞, to apprehend certain Englishmen. Complains of the way they have been treated. Lest further mischief should ensue to Thomas Randolph, she sends this letter to explain the business in behalf of the English merchants. Mentions Thomas Glover, Ralph Ruttor, James Watson, Thomas Hawtree, Richard Usconio, Thomas Southam, Robert Boroughe, Nicholas Chancellor, Richard Poyntington, Benjamin Clarke, John Chappell, Christopher Bennet, Smythe, Bourman, Birkett, Plasshington, Aslabye.—Latin. *Copy.* Sept. 16.
(Sixteen pages.)

303. *To the Governors of the Company of Russia Merchants.* Two agents, Lawrence Manley and George Middleton, have been sent to the Emperor of Russia. Begs a favourable reception for them, and whatever assistance they can give them.—Latin. *Copy.* Windsor, Sept. 16.

304. *The Queen to the King of Poland.* Thanks him for his two letters of March and April last: in the matter of Thomas Howes and William Martin. Enters at some length into the case of Martin.—Latin. *Copy.* Windsor, Oct. 3.
(Seven pages.)

305. *To the Magistrates of Dantzic.* Their letter of March last has been referred to councillors for your consideration, and has been apostilled by them. The edict granted to William Martin respecting their ships and merchandize has been revoked. Begs that they will give every facility to English merchants.—Latin. *Copy.* Windsor, Oct. 3.

500 CALENDAR OF

1585. 306. *To Don Ferdinand de Castro, Marquis of Saria.*
Windsor, Thanks him for his letter, scented gloves, and other presents
Oct. 8. received by Ossorius. Has given orders that the things he
wants from Ireland be sent to him.—Latin. *Copy.*

1586. 307. *R. H. to Sir Walter Raleigh.* News of the French
Paris, Court, and of an interview between the Queen-Mother and
Dec. 30. the King of Navarre, at Cogniac. Roucroix is surrendered
on fair conditions. Wishes to hear whether he accepts the
dedication of his History of the Eight Decads of Peter Martyr.
His map of Antonio de Espeio's voyage is in the hands of
Andrew Home, the prince of cosmographers. Gives advice
with reference to his Virginian enterprise, that the best settlement will be about the Bay of the Theatopians, acknowledged
by the Spaniards to have been discovered first by Cabot and
the English. Praises Mr. Charles Thynne's acquirements.

*Partly printed in Cl. S. P. vol. B. App. p. L.: the part there omitted is con-
cerning the doings of the various notabilities of the French Court.*

No date. 308. *A Paper* endorsed "Commission for Capt. Lane."
Draught.

1603. 309. *The Poor Man's Petition to the King,* consisting of
May 7. thirteen heads, against Papistry and Puritanism, simony, abuses
of law-courts, and licenses, monopolies and taxes; the last two
heads being, (12) Good King, make not the L. of good Lincoln duke of Shoreditch, for he is, &c.; (13) Good King, make
not Sir Walter Rawleigh Earl of Pankeridge, for he is a, &c.
Copy.

Apparently a satirical production.

Woodstock, 310. *Commission* read when the Garter was delivered to
Sept. 18. Frederic, Duke of Wurtemberg.—Latin. *Copy.*

*A note is added: "This commission was read immediately before the deli-
very of the Order to the Duke, Garter then making a speech unto him
touching the Order."*

1604. 311. *Capita Fœderis inter Regem Angliæ Jacobum primum,*
London, *et Regem Hisp. Phillip. 3. et Archiduces Albertum et Isabellam*
Aug. 18. *Claram Eugeniam.* A treaty of alliance against Holland.—
Latin. *Copy.*

*Less full in the beginning and end; but in substance the same as that
printed in Rymer's Fœdera, vol. xvi. p. 580, &c. See Rapin, vol. II.
p. 169.*

CLARENDON PAPERS. 501

312. *Letters Patent* granting to George Hume the title and dignity of Earl of Dunbar.—Latin. *Copy.*   1605. Windsor, July 3.

313. *James to the Committee of the Higher House of Parliament.* Craves "sevin skoire thousande poundis" a year in clear addition to his former expenses. *Original.* Signed "James R."   No date.

314. *Articles of agreement* between the King of Great Britain and the King of France, for the marriage of Henrietta Marie with the Prince of Wales. With the letters patent signed by James I. confirming the treaty.   1624. Cambridge, Dec. 12.

    The articles are on paper; the letters patent on vellum, to which is attached the Great Seal of England.

315. *A Paper* sent in a letter bearing date Feb. 2, 1624, from the Duke of Buckingham unto the Earl of Bristol, containing certain propositions, the which the Duke requireth that the said Earl should acknowledge; with the answer of the Earl of Bristol subjoined, defending, at full length, his conduct in the negotiations with Spain for the restitution of the Palatinate. *Copy.*   1624-5. Feb. 2.

    Consisting of four sheets, one or more others missing at the end.

316. *The Lord Keeper Coventry's Speech* to the Houses of Parliament.   1627-8. March 17.

    Printed in full in Rapin, vol. ii. p. 262, with the exception of a short preface and an immaterial paragraph at the end, dismissing the Commons to choose their Speaker.

    Also—*The Speech of Sir John Finch*, the New Speaker, on his admission, praying in usual form, that the rights and privileges of the Commons be allowed. *Copies.*   March 19.

317. *Mrs. Lisle to her cousin, Mr. Edward Hyde;* addressed to him at Christ Church, Oxford, jesting with him on his assumption of petticoats (probably in some play) and advising him to marry.   1628. London, Aug. 27.

    Hyde married his first wife in 1629, and his second in 1632 (who did not die till 1667), and was knighted in 1643.

318. *Case* of Dr. Lloyd, fellow of All Souls College, Oxford, as to fees due from him to the University on his promotion to the degrees of B.C.L. and D.C.L.   No date.

319. *Mr. Francis Hyde to Mr. Edward Hyde.* Of the cardinal's hat, which is not yet given away; the number of English   1635-6. Venice. Jan. 11.

1636. in Rome greater than at any time since Henry VIII; and the quarrel of the Pope with Venice, ambassadors on each side being withdrawn. *Cl. S. P. vol. II. App. p. xxvi.*

Ratisbon, Sept. 8. 320. *The Earl Marshal to Secretary Windebank.* His servant, Lamplugh, and William Smith, one of the King's trumpeters, have been made away with. Details progress of negotiations. "What France will doe in the treaty to the prejudice of Bavaria I doubte."..."If our treaty be lofte out, where are we?"..."Spain will doe little." *Original.*
Cl. S. P. vol. I. p. 629.

Dublin, Dec. 16. 321. *A Certificate by Arnold Boate,* of Lord Mount-Norris' ill health, and the climate of Ireland.

1637. April. 322. *The King of France (Louis XIII) to the King of England.* Congratulates him on the Queen's safe deliverance of a daughter (the Princess Anne, born March 17). *Original.*

1639-40. Jan. 2. 323. *Bond* of John Latche and others, to Mr. Edward Hyde for 206*l*. 13*s*. 4*d*.

No date. 324. "*A declaration* of the customes and usages of the church of Windsor, about the dividing of rents and tithes."
Signed by Da. Stokes. William Brough. Tho. Brown. Geo. Gillingham.
Endorsed by Hyde, "Bp. of Hereford's case with the chapter of Windsor."

1641. Whitehall, July 30. 325. *Promise by the King* to pay to Lord Ettrick 5000*l*. on the surrender of Edinburgh Castle, and till the sum is paid to assign him 200*l*. per annum. *Copy.*

Oct. 28. 326. "*Capitulacions of the English nation,* wherein all the old were reviewed, altered, and set in order, with the additions and privileges newly obtained by Sir Thomas Roo, knt., his Majesty's ambassador to the Grand Signior. Anno 1622." A long treaty of free commerce with the Turks, made by the Sultan Mustapha Han [*sic*], with confirmations thereof added by succeeding Sultans, the last bearing date as in the margin. *Copy.*

Edinburgh, Oct. 31. 327. *The King to Ormond* Is glad that he has such a faithful servant on this occasion of the rebellion in Ireland. Desires him to accept the charge over the army. Will send further instructions by Capt. Weemes. *Original.*
Endorsed, "Rec^d. 10 Nov."

328. *Extracts from Scotch Acts of Parliament* passed during the years 1640–41; chiefly concerning the powers granted to the Committee of Establishment and the ratification of the Covenant. In Hyde's hand. — 1641-2. No date.

329. *Order* of His Majesty to Capt. Stradling, of the ship 'Bonadventure,' to take his ship to Portsmouth and lie off St. Helen's Point. Copy. — Whitehall, Jan. 8.

330. *Sir R. Brown to the Right Hon.*—— [one of the Secretaries of State]. Two regiments have been cashiered; and passes have been given by the Prince of Condé to the Irish commanders to return to their country. Has complained to the Prince of this, but could obtain no order to restrain the departure of the Irishmen. Has taken measures to have them intercepted. *Duplicate.* Cl. S. P. vol. II. App. — 1642. Paris, June 7.

331. *A paper of Minutes*, in Hyde's handwriting. "Proceedings of the Committee. Order of the 9th of Sept.;" and Memoranda of events in chronological order, prepared for the History of the Rebellion, Books III to VIII. (Twelve pages.) — 1644. No date.

332. "*A discourse* of my journey into Ireland, and my imployment there." Containing:—(1) Instructions. (2) Private instructions. (3) The Prince's approbation of both sorts of instructions. (4) Overtures for an accommodation from the general assembly of the Confederate Catholics, March 3, 1646. (5) Answer to the overtures and the papers of May 10, 1647. (6) Propositions made to the Committee, May 18, 1647, with details of further proceedings, copies of letters from Lord Digby, General Preston, and others. Forty-one pages, ending "and about the latter end of March following, in the soonest passage from Gallowaie I could find, in companie of my lord of Worcester and his Ladie, we sett sayle, arryving at Havre de Grace in five daies."
Endorsed by Hyde, "Winter Brook's relation of his journey into Ireland." — No date.

333. *Sir E. Hyde to Mr. Secretary*, sent by Mr. Gatford. Informs him of the summons that the Island had just received from a Parliament ship. The people of Guernsey are ready to rise. Notices Lord Digby's movements. Trusts that the King will be restored by his own courage and virtue. Mentions Porter's tale of a quarrel between Lady Marlborough and Mrs. Fretyevill. Does not wish to be sent to Paris. Has written about Mr. Thorndicke, and to Sir T. Fanshaw. Is expecting Will. Hyde. Has written a discourse upon the affairs of England, which he intends getting translated into French, and having it printed and dispersed in England. — 1647. Jersey, May 10.

Printed in Lister's Life of Clarendon, vol. iii. p. 50, and in part in Hoskins, vol. ii. p. 130.

1647.
July 31.

334. *Draught* of the King's reply to the eighteen propositions from the army, touching Parliaments, Militia, Ireland, and Religion.
     Endorsed by Hyde, "Sent by Mr. Ashb. and Sir Jo. Berkeley."

No date.

335. *Copy* of a paper sent by the King in answer to the Propositions of the Scotch Commissioners directing them to demand safe conduct for messengers, and to desire a treaty to be had at London, if possible; with further instructions and propositions.

1648.
Middleborough,
July 30.
No date.

336. "*Considerations* upon the present state of his Highness affairs."   By Hyde.

337. "*State Colors and Complections* in which are Reasons against the proceeding to try the King."
 (Signed) "John Clayton. This I delivered to Ireton about a fortnight before the King's trial." (Nine pages.)

INDEX.

A.

A[rmstrong?], Sir T., letter to Mr. Denman, 437.
Abbeville, French Court at, 386.
Abbot, George, Abp. of Canterbury, books carried to his library, 40.
Abdallah, (Muley), gives permission to the English to trade to Tetuan, 23.
Abdy, Alderman, his death, 205.
Abell, Alderman, is fined, 218.
Aberconway Castle, 113.
Aberdeen presbytery, their address to the Bishop, 19.
Abingdon, 302.
—— names of debtors of the King in, 247.
—— the rebels in, 249.
Absey, Ph., merchant, 494.
Acton, Sir Rob. Poyntz of, q. v.
—— Alderman, a design to prevent him becoming Lord Mayor, 207, 208; is rejected, 208.
Adams, ——, his impeachment, 301.
—— J., 463.
'Admiral,' the (ship), letter dated from, 446.
Admiralship, the, 461.
Admiralty Court, the, 492.
Admiralty, Lords of the, Captain Smith's complaint to, 250.
—— Vice, Judge of the, see Scawen, Lieut.-Col.
Adolphus of Burgundy, q. v.
—— Duke of Holstein, q. v.
Adriatic, pirates in the, 233.
Æneas, a pseudonym, 26.
Aerssen, Sieur François d', commission to him, 29; acts as commissioner in the treaty, 30.
Affidavits, three, 131.
Agitators in the army, 304, 307, 399, 401, 402.
Aiton, or Ayton, Sir Robert, warrant to him to use the Privy Seal, 76.
Aix, Abp. of, see Mazarini, Michel.

Aix, parliament of, interdicted, 408.
Aix-la-Chapelle, forces about, 128.
Alan, Thomas, see Allen.
Alay, Count d', his success in Italy; App. L 6.
Albert, Archduke of Austria, q. v.
—— Duke of Prussia, q. v.
Alluquerque, Duke of, his death, 136, 141.
Akala, Duke of, 127, 130.
Alcala wine, 166.
Akehaça, monastery of, 137.
Alcibiades and Jocasta, their example quoted, 356.
Alcock, Tho., bearer of a letter to the Viceroy of Lithuania, 467.
Aldbury, Lord Arundel's cottage at, 104.
Aldersgate Street, see London.
Aldrich, H., his signature, 357.
Aldworth, Col. Rich., letters to Col. Fiennes, 242.
Alegre, John, a courier, 24.
Alesbury, Mr., see Aylesbury.
Alexford, Mr., 325.
Alexander, Mr., 421.
Alexis, Emperor of Russia, q. v.
Alford, Francis, 495.
—— Gregory, charge by bill of exchange upon, 308.
—— Rich., payment to, 308.
—— of St. Malo, 324, 335.
Allan, Thomas, see Allen.
Allegiance, Oath of, q. v.
Allen, Mr., 364.
—— bearer of Lieut.-Col. Traill's letter, 332.
—— Capt., desires 300 men for the Prince's lifeguard, 304.
—— Patrick, capture of his ship 'Francis,' 274; his demand for money, ibid.
—— Allan, or Alan, Thomas, a merchant of London, 479, 491.
—— is to provide the English fleet with stores, 176.

J T

INDEX.

Allen or Alan, Thos., agents of, 486.
—— agent for the English navy, sends ships to Dantzic, 487.
—— letters in behalf of, 490, 493, 497.
—— a safe conduct desired for, 491.
Allen, William, a merchant of London, 483.
Alleyn, C., i. e. Sir Chas. Cotterell, q. v.
Alliance between England and the United Provinces against Spain, 29, 30.
Allon, letter dated from, 326.
Allott, or Elliott, John, complaint against, 2.
All Souls College, see Oxford.
Almeda, Louis of, attacks the 'Margaret,' 488.
—— Manuel of, trial before him, 488.
Alresford, relation of the battle of, 246.
Alsatia, 220.
—— disasters in, 151.
Alva, Duke of, 195.
Alvarez, Don, 483.
—— de Quadra, Bishop, 181.
—— envoy of the King of Spain, 481.
Alvaston, 239.
Alured, Mr., M.P., conversation with, about the train-bands of Hull, 232.
Amadeus, Victor, Duke of Savoy, q. v.
Amalia Elizabeth, Landgravine of Hesse, q. v.
Ambassadors resident abroad, keys to cyphers used by them, 214.
Amhurst, F., 350, 351.
—— St., quoad, 320.
Amiens, Card. Mazarin and the French Court at, 378, 381.
—— letters dated from, 378; App. 1. 8.
Amsterdam, residents at, 410, 414, 420, 428, 429.
—— letters dated from, 432, 445, 446.
—— merchants, case of Ll. Duffinghausen and, 482, 483.
Amurath IV, Emperor of Turkey, q. v.
Amy, Capt., 322, 324, 325, 331.
—— complaint against, 321.
—— goods of Sir T. Bassett disbursed by, 317.
—— commander of the 'Little George,' letter to, 322.

Amy, Capt. Thomas, letter to Sir E. Hyde, 317.
Amyrant, Mons., his 'apology' mentioned, 420.
Anabaptists, 272.
Andalusia, reports of insurrection in, 370.
Anderson, Bertram, a merchant of Newcastle, 181.
—— George, captain of the 'Roberts,' 495.
—— William, agent for merchants of Newcastle, 444.
Andover, Viscount or Lord, see Howard, Thos.
Andrews, Mr., claims lands in Dromore, 6, 8.
Anecdotes of preaching, 330.
Angelo, ——, a musician, 26.
Angelus, Nicolas, 485.
Angier, (French agent), 109, 195.
Anglesea or Anglesey, 309.
—— Isle of, caused to declare for the King, 440.
—— —— questions to the Sheriff of, for its protection, 249.
Anjou, disorders in, 407.
—— Gaston John Baptist, Duke of, afterwards Duke of Orleans, q. v.
Anne, Princess, daughter of Charles I, her birth, (1637), 126, 502.
Anne of Austria, Queen of Louis XIII, 149.
—— Queen-mother, 207, 208, 376.
—— Queen-Regent of France, 297, 307, 317, 324, 361, 424.
—— visits her son, the Duke d'Anjou, 393.
Anne (Princess) of East Friesland, q. v.
Annesley, Arthur, letter from his wife to, 337.
—— letters to, 122, 223, 305, 339, 340, 345, 346.
—— Francis, Viscount Valentia, in London, 339.
—— Mr. Francis, afterwards Sir F., and Lord Mount Norris, 40, 38.
—— letters to, 6, 7, 8, 9, 10, 11, 12, 15.
—— patent of his appointments in Ireland, 29.
—— petition to, 36.
—— letter from to Charles I, 75.
—— certificate of his ill health, 502.
—— the Earl of Strafford's treatment of, 219.
—— letter from to the Earl of Strafford, 220.

INDEX.   507

Annesley, Francis, Lord Mount Norris, letters to, 136.
—— witnesses in his case, against the Earl of Strafford, 221.
—— petition to Parliament for his losses, 238.
—— Lady, letter from to the Earl of Strafford, 87.
—— —— petition to the King, 103.
Anstruther, Sir Robert, 112.
Antony, Count, of Oldenburg, q. v.
Antrim, Earl and Marquis of, see Macdonnell, Randal.
Antry, letter dated from, 286.
Antwerp, 257, 409, 428.
—— la maison de Hoboke à Anvers, 443.
—— letters dated from, 66, 70, 184, 429, 443.
—— residents at, 432, 434.
Apprentices, and their meetings, 374, 379, 393.
—— rescue of two from the sheriffs, 222.
Apsley, ——, 263, 291.
—— Sir Allen, letter to, 14.
—— —— letter from to Lords of the Council, 15.
—— —— schedule of his debts, 31.
—— —— account of monies received by, 35.
—— —— petition in behalf of his children, 43.
—— —— letter to Sir E. Hyde, 291.
—— —— Governor of Barnstaple, warrant for delivery of wool for, 273.
—— James, letter to Sir E. Hyde, 291.
—— Nat., 321.
Aquila, Bishop of, 471, 478.
—— to succeed to the Count of Feria, 458.
Aranjuez, 127, 128.
—— marble busts at, 161; moulds taken from, 179, 185, 189, 200.
Aravius, Emmanuel, 478.
Archbould, Capt. H., letter to Col. N. Fiennes, 241.
Archduke, the, see Leopold of Austria.
Archer, ——, attacks the established religion, 272.
—— Sir A., 424.
Archot (or Arscot), Duke of, letter from to Lord Aston, 113.
Argyle, Earl and Marquis of, see Campbell, Archibald.
Arica, in Peru, 126.

Aristides, a pseudonym, 26.
Armagh, ploughing fires in, 5.
—— Lord of, 288.
Armentiers, 391.
Armorer, Capt., 421.
Arms, account of negotiations in 1643, for a cessation of, 240.
—— coats of, warrant concerning, 264.
—— Garter King of, see Walker, Sir Edward.
—— orders concerning Kings and other officers of arms, l.
Army, the, 274, 290, 376, 378, 379, 381, 382, 384, 385, 391, 397, 399, 402-406, 409, 415, 417, 423, 461.
—— and the Parliament commissioners, treaty between, 382.
—— at St. Alban's, 380; their declaration about the Parliament, ibid.
—— Commissioners for, 262.
—— corps, details of, 412.
—— engagement to, 461.
—— English and Irish armies submit to the peace, 165.
—— expenses of, per month, 203.
—— General Council of, their declaration mentioned, 402.
—— letter on the refractoriness of, 377.
—— letter and order to the Officers of, 298, 461.
—— military news, 394.
—— mutinies in, 423.
—— petitions against, mentioned, 401.
—— notice of their propositions to the King, 364.
—— the King's reply to their eighteen propositions (1647), 503.
—— their petition, with the King's answer, 374.
—— their resolutions, being their desires and grievances, 379; answer to the propositions, ibid.
—— resolution and answer to the propositions of Parliament, 383; the soldiers' queries, ibid.
—— their proposals sent to the King, 385.
—— proposals to their commissioners mentioned, 386.
—— their proposals to the City agreed to, 381.
—— relations of military affairs communicated to Sir E. Hyde, 246.
—— Serj.-Major-General of, see Willoughby, Sir F.

Army, summary of military operations from June 1642 to March 1647-8, 416.
—— their declaration mentioned, 446.
—— unfortunate success of the King's army in 1645, 319.
Arragon, the revolt and war in, 226, 232.
Arras, see Atrebatum.
Array, commission of, 235.
d'Arro, Olave, Condé, letter in commendation of, 469.
—— returns from Queen Elizabeth to the Emperor, 492.
—— letter from Queen Elizabeth in his behalf, 494.
Aracot, Duke of, his indictment, 193, 196, 199.
—— imprisoned, 44, 47.
—— Duchess of, 143.
Arthur, Dr., 329.
Articles concerning Religion, App. I. L.
Artois, proposed Spanish invasion by way of, 188.
Arundel House, letters dated from, 208, 242.
Arundel and Surrey, Earls of, see Howard, Thomas and Henry Fred.
Arundell, Col. John, of Trerise, Governor of Pendennis, 334.
—— his signature, 310.
—— letter from to W. Edgeman, 313.
—— —— to Thomas Fairfax, 306.
—— —— to Col. Rob. Hammond, 312.
—— —— to Sir E. Hyde, 292.
—— —— to the Prince of Wales, 323.
—— letters to, as Governor of Pendennis Castle, 275, 285, 303, 306, 312.
—— Col. Rich., 205.
—— letter to, 316.
Arwenack House, the Parliamentary forces at, 310.
Ash, Mr., see Ashe.
Ash, Lord, letter from Sir E. Hyde to, 402.
Ashburnham, Col., 309, 312, 324, 386.
—— Lord, letter to, 391.
Ashburnham, or Ashbournham, John, 314, 318, 343, 347, 348, 378, 384, 385, 387, 397, 399, 401, 406.

Ashburnham, or Ashbournham, John, at Rouen, 338.
—— agreement with Van Heesdonck, 245.
—— is removed from the King, 321, 407.
—— is voted to the gallows, 316.
—— letter from to Lord Culpeper, 289.
—— letters from to the King, 326.
—— letters to, 305, 325, 327, 329, 330, 332, 333, 335, 336, 338, 348.
—— warrant for a discharge to him for monies received for the King's use, 243.
—— warrant against, called in, 403.
—— William, letter to, 388.
Ashburton, letter dated from, 290.
Ashe, letter dated from, 283.
Ashe, or Ash, Mr., 449.
—— John, his representatives to be prosecuted for his sinking a ship, 475.
—— —— letter to Col. N. Fiennes, 241, 242.
—— Joseph, letter to Mr. Aylsbury, 429.
Ashley, Sir Jacob, 158.
—— appointed Commissary General, 162.
—— Lady, note of a suit between her and the Countess of Clare, 154.
Ashton, Lieut.-Col., letter to, 415.
—— Major-Gen., 436.
—— —— his movements in Lancashire, 466.
Ashworth, Mr., his Bill, 387.
Aslabye, —, 499.
Anje, Don Martio de, 148, 149.
Assembly of Divines, 449.
Astley, Jacob, Lord, 290.
Aston, Sir Walter, afterwards Lord, Baron of Forfar, 65, 79, 103.
—— secret instructions for him, 68.
—— leaves Madrid, 151, 152.
—— letter from to Mr. Hopton, 93, 94.
—— letters from to Secretary Calvert, 24.
—— letter from to the Prince of Wales, 28.
—— —— to Mr. Tho. Windebank, 123.
—— letters from to Secretary Windebank, 69, 70, 71, 75, 77, 78, 83, 85, 86, 89, 90, 91, 93, 95-102, 104, 106, 107, 109-111, 113-115,

INDEX.   509

117-119, 121-130, 133, 134, 136-
141, 143-145, 147-152.
Aston, Walter, Lord, letters from to
the King of Spain, 77, 121, 124,
138.
—— letters from to the Condé Duke
d'Olivares, 84, 118, 123-125.
—— to Lord Cottington, 84,
139.
—— to Secretary Coke, 71, 76,
78, 85, 86, 90, 93, 95, 96, 100,
102, 104, 106, 108, 110, 112, 114-
116, 119, 122, 123, 125, 126, 128-
130, 136, 139, 141, 143, 144, 147,
148, 150.
—— to Charles 1, 102, 145.
—— letters to, 70, 84, 85, 87, 103,
108, 113, 115, 117, 125-128, 131,
133, 134, 138-142, 144, 150.
—— his death, 183.
—— Walter, second Lord, 459.
—— his cypher, 214.
Athenry, Bishop of, 191.
Athlone Castle, articles relating to,
and its defence and garrison,
331.
Atrebatum, letter dated from, 60.
Attorney-General, the, see Banks,
Sir John; Herbert, Sir E.
Attwood, Edmund, letter to, 198.
d'Avaux, Mons., letter to, 173.
—— to Munster, 417.
Aubigney, Lady Catherine, warrant
for payment to, 269.
Audley, Lord, see Touchet, Mervyn.
Averie, John, the King's resident at
Hamburg, letter to Lord Falkland,
232.
Avery, Mr., 108.
—— his cypher, 215.
Augier, Mr., is sent by the Parlia-
ment to Paris, 254, 376.
—— the King's instruction to oppose
him, 413.
Augsburg Confession, the, adopted
by Queen Elizabeth, 469.
—— letter to the Princes, States,
orders, &c. of, 480.
Augusta, letter dated from, 106.
Augustana Confessio, see Augsburg.
Augustine, Alexander and Julius,
487.
—— their property seized, 495.
Augustus, Duke of Saxony, q. v.
Aurigny, 338.
Aust, on the Severn, 242.
Austen Friars, letter dated from, 15.
Austria and England, probable result
of their friendship, 112.

Austria and France, their antagonism,
56.
—— mediation offered between them,
105.
Austria, Albert and Isabella Clara
Eugenia, Archduke and Archduchess of, treaty with James I
against Holland, 500.
Austria and Sweden, proposed agreement between them, 133.
Austrian and Venetian ambassadors,
disgusts between them, 51.
Austria, Charles, Archduke of, letters
from Queen Elizabeth to, 471, 488.
—— sent as ambassador to the Duke
of Saxe, 22.
—— Leopold, Archduke of, 110, 431,
433.
—— —— his forces at Peronne, 428.
—— —— his offer of marriage to
Mademoiselle of France, 422.
—— Philip II, Emperor of (1561),
477.
Avignon, 232.
Awdley, Lord, see Audley.
Aylesbury, or Alesbury, Mr., 414.
—— complaint against, 431.
—— in Oxford, 3.
—— letters to, 19, 20, 21.
—— John, at Antwerp, letter to, 432.
—— Sir Tho., Navy Surveyor, letters
to, 31, 33.
—— Master of Requests, letter
to, 87.
—— at Cranborne Lodge, near
Windsor, letters to, 410, 414.
—— Lady, letter from to Will Ayles-
bury, 430.
—— William, letters from to Sir E.
Hyde, 212, 213, 216-218, 227.
—— letters to, 427-430, 432,
434, 439, 441.
Ayliffe, Sir George, 36.
—— letter from to Sir E. Hyde, 209.
—— John, 145.
Aysone, George, 332.
Ayton, Sir Rob., see Aiton.
Aytona, Marquis of, 52, 53.

B.

B., J., i.e. James Bossaithon, q. v.
Babila, taken by the Turks, 167.
Babthorpe, Tho., a Jesuit, 154.
Backer, Nicholas, of Dantsic, 479.
Backhouse, Sir John, affidavit of
assessment of his property, 253.
—— petition to the committee of
sequestrations, 263.
—— letter to, 35.

510 INDEX.

Backhouse, Sir W., of Swallowfield, 202.
Bacon, Sir Francis, appointed Lord Keeper, 12.
—— the King's Solicitor, his arguments on the jurisdiction of the Council of the Marches over the Western counties, 214.
Baddel, Bernd., warrant signed by, 414.
Baden, Christopher, Margrave of, letters to, 474, 480.
—— Prince Christopher of, husband of Princess Cecilia of Sweden, letters patent to, granting him a portion, 488.
Bagshot, letter dated from, 103.
Balançon, Baron de, 70.
—— besieges Limburg, 71, 73.
Ballad, 'A newe Letanie for our new Lent,' 416.
Balle, Peter, an officer at Exeter, 273.
Ballymore, letter dated from, 211.
Ballynakill, reorganisation of the army of, 412.
Balmerino, Lord, see Elphinstone, John.
Baltic Sea, the, 228, 496.
Bamberg, Bishop of, letter to his forces, 20.
Bamfield, Col., see Bampfield.
Bampfield, Col. Jo., 421, 444.
—— account of receipts, &c., for the service of the Duke of York, 462.
—— letter on the siege of Taunton, 265.
Bampton-in-the-Bush, capture of 300 of G. Lyle's men at, 261.
Banbury, siege of, 309.
Bandino, Cardinal, 27.
Banier, Bannier, or Banner, John, movements of his troops, 83, 131, 133, 135–137, 156, 176, 178–180.
Bankes, Lord, his discourse desired, 415.
Banks, Sir John, 175.
—— Attorney-General versus John Hampden, case of, 146.
Banner, John, see Banier.
Banning, Viscount, see Rayning, Paul, Viscount.
Bannister, Thomas, a merchant of London, 483, 498.
Bannock, petition concerning the lands of, 136.
Barbadoes, 359, 412.
Barbary pirates, 233.
Barber, William, receipt to Hyde for 100l., 239.

Barberini, Raphael, 481.
—— commended to the Emperor of Russia, 485.
Barberino, Cardinal, 52.
—— letters to, 34, 55, 56.
—— Francisco, audience with, 227.
Barcelona, 129, 357.
—— Prince of Condé at, 378.
Barclay, A., 135.
—— Ro., his signature, 396.
Bard, Henry, created Viscount Bellamont, 367.
Bardo, —, surgeon, with the fleet, 458.
Barenthrow, committee of the, 461.
Barham, Mr., 11.
Barkly, Mr., 152.
Barlow, Father, letter from to Secretary Windebank, 61.
—— William, designated Bishop of Chichester, 469.
Barnard, Clara, Countess of Forth, warrant for a pension to, 257.
Barnes, John, a merchant of London, 483.
Barnevelt, —, 12.
Barnstaple, 303, 312.
—— distressed state of its garrison, 283.
—— Governor of, see Apsley, Sir A.
—— letters dated from, 268, 277, 291.
Baron, Geoffry, 363, 381.
Barra, Juan de la, 115.
Barry, Col. John, 258, 299.
—— letter to, 231.
—— papers endorsed by, 256.
—— Very Rev. Robert, letter to, 329.
Barwis, Mr., 135.
—— Sir Tho., writes to the Committee of Indemnity, 412.
Basbili, Friar (a Minime), 127, 128, 130.
Basnett, Philip, letter to, 213.
Bassett, Sir Arthur, letter to Sir E. Hyde, 291.
—— Governor of the Mount, letter from the Prince to, 299.
—— order to, 301.
—— Sir Francis, commissioner of taxes, his dishonesty, 246.
—— —— letters to Sir E. Hyde and Lord Hopton, 273.
—— Sir Tho., Knight, commander of the fort of St. Mary, Scilly, 316, 332.
—— —— letter of, mentioned, 317.
—— Thomas, vicar of Llantrissant, his protestation, 392.

INDEX.   511

Bambe, Edward, his charge of naval supplies, 172.
Bassompierre, François, Baron de, troops under him, 80.
Bastile, the, 384.
Bastwick, Dr., report of his answer before the Lords, 146.
Bath, 240, 262, 263, 328.
—— letters dated from, 240-242, 250, 259, 265, 266, 278.
—— Earls of, see Bourchier, William and Henry.
Batten, Capt. William, commander of the Parliament fleet, at Scilly, 332.
Batten, or Battin, Sir William, 409, 437, 438, 444, 445.
—— letter to, 449.
Bavaria, 502.
Bavaria and France, 162, 165, 180.
Bavaria and Spain, 166.
Bavaria and the Brussels Conference, (1638), 148, 157.
—— "baculus arundineus," 167.
—— Maximilian the Great, Duke of, 21, 22, 42, 51, 56, 65, 66, 77, 79, 80, 86-88, 90, 94, 96, 99, 101, 105-107, 110, 113, 114, 116, 119, 122, 134, 135, 152, 160, 171, 172, 174, 229, 369.
—— —— his ambassador, 380, 386.
—— —— letters from to the Emperor Ferdinand II, 20.
—— —— treaty with, 374.
—— —— treaty against him, 36.
—— —— is suspected of a league with France, 47.
—— —— his diet, 78.
—— —— entertains the King of Hungary at Munich, 100.
—— —— arrives at Ratisbon, 106.
—— —— Mary Ann, Duchess of, 91.
Baylie, Walter, M.D., professor at Oxford, his marriage, 499.
Bayning, or Banning, Paul, Viscount, 35.
—— abstract of his Will, 54.
Baynton, Sir Edward, his son 'suspended the House,' 333.
—— his son Rogers, 244.
—— letter to Sir E. Hyde, ibid.
Bayonne, Conference of, 488.
—— invented, 116.
Beauchamp, Lord, see Seymour, Edward.
Beaumaris, 290.
Beauvais, W., letter to Col. N. Fiennes, 239.
Beck, John, Baron de, 220.

Beck, John, Baron de, Imperialist forces under him on the Rhine, 232.
Bedford, Lord, see Russell, Francis.
Bedinfield, alias Safinden, 101.
Beilievre, M., see Bellievre, M. de.
Belfast, residents at, 339, 340, 345.
Belgium, the Regent in, 183.
Bellarmine, Robert, Cardinal, 22.
Belhasis, Henry, Lord, 313.
—— letter to the Bishop of Ferns, 329.
Bellenden, Sir W., goes to Scotland with ammunition, 438.
Bellievre, Bellivre, or Beilievre, Mons. de, 320, 321, 336, 338, 318, 372.
—— ambassador extraordinary from France, 1-12, 116.
—— has orders from Cardinal Mazarin, 346.
Bellingham, Sir H., 135.
Bellings, R., his signature, 310.
Belasko, the Palatine, his death, 481.
Benavides, Don Christoval de, 70.
—— Don Juan de, General of the Armada, beheaded, 44.
Bendish, Lord, his barbarous usage of Sir S. Crow, 398.
—— Sir Thomas, is to succeed Sir S. Crow at Constantinople, 358.
Benedictines in England, 62.
Benefices, presentations to, 227.
Bennet, or Bennett, Sir Humphrey, his kinsman, Mr. Mason, 390.
—— letter to Lord ——, 271.
—— Christopher, 499.
Bennett, Mr., is to attend the Duke of York, 445.
Benson, Fr., a merchant of London, 493.
—— letter of credence for, ibid.
Bentivoglio, Guido, Cardinal, 62.
—— letter to, 49.
Bergen, 351, 409.
Berkeley, George, Lord, his impeachment, 388.
—— Sir John, 259, 261-263, 265, 270, 273, 279, 283, 287, 290, 291, 303, 324, 351, 353, 376, 385, 387, 396, 397, 400-403, 408, 416.
—— —— and his three servants to attend the Duke of York at sea, 445.
—— —— besieged in Peronne, 428.
—— —— documents signed by, 445.
—— —— his account of receipts for the Duke of York's use, 443.
—— —— his interview with Lord Goring, 279.

INDEX.

Berkeley, Sir John, his memorial on the Duke of York's going to Helvoetsluys, 449.
— is removed from the King, 407.
— letter from to Lord Digby, 260.
— letters from to Sir E. Hyde, 212, 281, 297, 309.
— letters to, 258, 259, 324, 328, 343, 351, 356, 359, 393, 402, 415, 417, 429.
— supersedes Sir Richard Grenville, 270.
— Sir William, 206.
— — letter to, 258.
— Robert, 388.
— Sir Robert, Justice of the King's Bench, his trial, 226.
Berkshire, petition of Sir J. Backhouse concerning his property in, 263.
— petition of recusants in, 175.
— Earl of, see Howard, Thomas.
Bernard, Duke of Saxony, see Saxony and Weimar.
Bernardines, General of the order, 137.
Bertovaldi, letter dated from, 36.
Berti, Francis, 481.
Bertie, Montagu, Earl of Lindsey, 353, 382.
— instructions for him, 314.
Bertram, Godfrey, 34.
Berwick, 398, 424, 433.
— Castle, 462.
— disturbances at, 415; precautions taken about, *ibid.*
— the King's camp at, 178.
— letter dated from, 181.
— militia of, 449.
— munitions sent to, 422.
— paymaster of the garrison, see Taylor, —.
— report of its fall, 417.
— Sir M. Langdale and Sir P. Musgrave's march against, 440.
Beskwood Park, 217.
Best, Capt., letter to, 29.
Beste, Robert, an English merchant, 487.
Betancos, letter dated from, 71.
Bethell, Col. Hugh, Commander-in-Chief of the Parliament forces, 450.
— his summons to Scarborough Castle to surrender, 158.
Bever, letter dated from, 105.
— Castle, letter dated from, 40.
Beverley, 233.

Bevil, Col., bearer of a letter from Secretary Nicholas, 319.
Bewdley, letters dated from, 249, 267.
Bible, discussion on the division of the Books of, 360.
Bickerstaffe, Robert, a servant of Gen. Fawley, his examination, 249.
Bideford, 268.
— letter dated from, 270.
Biggin, Captain Cornelius, 23.
Biggs, Abraham, 288.
— certificate of Irish cloths and lead sent to, 278.
— disbursement for arms, &c. for the King's garrisons in Cornwall, 249; his collection of customs in the ports of Cornwall, to 1664, with his expenditure, *ibid.*
— his accounts with Capt. Cottle, for match, 295, 300.
Biggs, Mr., his presence required at Truro, 304.
Bigle, —, secretary to the Marshal d'Estré, 125.
Bilbos, 44.
Bilde, G., Danish admiral, letters to, 495.
Bindon, Viscount, see Howard, Thos., Visc. Bindon.
Birch, —, M.P., 460.
— Col. and his brother, seized in Wales, 384.
Birkett, —, 499.
Biron, Lord, see Byron.
Biscay, bad success of the Spaniards at, 155.
— province of, 114.
Bisbaven, Condé de, 144.
Bishop, ordination of a, 62.
Bishops, 319–322, 346, 380, 400, 411, 420, 447, 458.
— Catholic, in Ireland, by whom to be nominated, 183.
— Deans, &c., 238.
— petition against, 212.
Bishops' lands, 450.
— dissolution of, 384.
— votes, 344.
Bishopston, letters dated from, 212, 216.
Bishopstone, parsonage at, 367.
Bishop's Wearmouth, parson of, see Johnson, —.
'Bl. Lady,' the (ship), 446.
Blackader, Capt. Alex., 340.
Blackheath, rendezvous at, 421.
Black Rod, the, 390.
Blackstone, John, abuse of, 416.

INDEX.   513

Blake, —, case of his prohibition against Violett, 11.
Blaney, Sir Edw., letter from to Mr. F. Annesley, 8.
Blayney, Sir Arthur, his death, 441.
Bligh, Capt., of Launceston, 215.
Blount, Sir Charles, discourse in defence of his marriage after divorce, 2.
—— Mountjoy, Earl of Newport, 301, 303.
—— —— Master of the Ordnance, memorial for him, 158.
Blundell, Mr., 10.
—— Sir A., conspiracy against him, 160.
—— Sir Francis, 20.
Blunt, Cuthbert, a merchant of Newcastle, 475.
Blyth, Capt., 205.
Boate, Arnold, his certificate of Lord Mountnorris's ill health, 502.
Boconnock, letter dated from, 286.
Bodleian Library, see Oxford.
Bodley, Sir Josias, 9.
Bodmin, 271, 275, 277.
—— letters dated from, 266, 273, 281, 292, 362.
—— the proprietors of, 367.
Bogan, Mr., 310.
Bohemia, wars in, 19-21.
—— Electorate of, 77 and folls.
—— Elizabeth, Princess of, (1635), 96.
—— fête at her marriage, 7.
—— pension granted to, 37.
—— Elizabeth, Queen of, 38, 119, 165, 464.
—— King of, his acceptance of the negotiations of a treaty for his restoration to his Electoral dominions, 37.
—— Maximilian, King of, letters to, 467, 421.
Bois-le-Duc, Bishop of, 229.
Bologna, 230.
Bolton, Edw., his signature, 362.
—— Sir Rich., Lord Chancellor of Ireland, his impeachment, 220.
—— —— his signatures, 331, 362.
Bolton, its loss to the King, 289.
'Bonaventure,' or 'Bonadventure,' the (ship), 233, 503.
—— the Captain of, see Stradling, Capt.
Bonithon, Major Hannibal, Governor of the Castle of St. Mawes, depositions touching his treason, 277; articles of charges against him, ibid.

Bonnefont, —, 181.
Bonnithon, James, letter of, 421.
Bonvi, Bernard, property of A. and J. Augustine seized by, 495.
Books, 269, 292, 357, 363, 366, 372, 390, 469.
—— Ballad, 52 stanzas, 416.
—— Buchanen's Genethliacon, 311.
—— Charitas Patriæ, 356, 361.
—— Const. Mahony's book, 401.
—— Corona Regia, 195.
—— Grotius's Comment, and Cicero's Offices, 355.
—— Grotius: De jure belli et pacis, 356.
—— H., R., his Hist. of the right decads of Peter Martyr, 500.
—— Hen. Marten's book, 412.
—— D'Aubigne's Histoire Universelle, 292.
—— Narrative of the Affairs of the West, (1644-7), 306.
—— H. Parker's answer to the seditious paper of Dav. Jenkins, 416.
—— "In Consideium nostrum," &c., 255.
—— Lilborne's letter to the keeper of Newgate, a printed broadsheet, 322.
—— Lord Banke's discourse, 415.
—— Lord Jermyn's 'Tully,' 354.
—— Mercuries, London and other, 415.
—— Mercurius Pragmaticus, 404.
—— Milton's book 'On Wedlock,' 372.
—— Picus Mirandula, 320.
—— Treaty of Uxbridge, 352.
Booth, Capt. Gerrard, 232.
—— letter from to Geo. Carr, ibid.
—— —— to Ormond, ibid.
—— letters to, ibid.
—— Col. John, receives a commission, 439.
Bordeaux, Abp. of, 179, 181.
Borgia, Cardinal, 90, 91, 100, 129.
—— ordered to return to Spain, 62.
—— goes to Naples, 63.
—— dismissed by the Pope, 82.
—— renounces his archbishopric of Seville, 102.
—— is required to return to Seville, 101.
—— recovers health, 128.
—— president of the Council of Arragon, 131.
—— Don Melchor de, 130.
Borough, Sir John, 97.

3 U

Borough, Sir John, letters from to Secretary Windebank, 98, 103-105, 107-109.
Boroughe, Robert, 109.
Borrheus, Dennis or Denis, agent to the King of Sweden, 476, 485.
Bost, Capt., see Best.
Bostock, Robt., book printed by, 416.
Boswell, Mr., agent in Holland, afterwards Sir William Boswell, q. v.
—— Sir 11., 429.
—— J., agent, resident with the States-General, his cypher, 214.
—— Sir William, 38, 159, 163, 458.
—— —— and the East India Company, 177.
—— —— his care in ordering provisions for Jersey, 420.
—— —— memorandum by Sir E. Hyde to, 445.
—— —— supervisor to, 429.
Bosworth, the Scotch offer to send horse there for the King, 311, 312, 314.
Bothwell, Earl of, see Hepburn, James.
Bouchart, Sieur, commissioner, 376.
Bouillon, Duke of, 275-277.
Bonlogne, App. I. 7.
Bourbon, waters of, 369.
—— Henry de, brother of the King of France, letter from to the Queen of England, 320.
Bourchier, Lieut.-Col. Barrington, 459.
—— Henry, Earl of Bath, 419.
—— —— petition against the Canons and the Oath, mentioned, 205.
—— William, Earl of Bath, letters from to the Lord High Admiral, 3, 25.
Bourke, Lieut.-Gen. John, 331.
—— Capt. Moyles, 331.
Bourman, ——, 409.
Bournell, John, 494.
Bousy, defeat of the Spaniards at, 170.
Bow, London, Cromwell at, 421.
Bowden, Nic., 441.
Bowen, Capt., royalist, a commission desired for him, 230.
Bowes, Thomas, a London merchant, 494, 499.
Bowman, ——, letters from London bearing his signature, 378, 420, 422.
Box, Mr., 416.
Boyle, ——, Lady Ranelagh, sister to Robert Boyle, 305.
—— letter to Sir E. Hyde, 248.

Boyle, Rich., Lord Cork, 241.
—— Rob., letter to A. Annesley, 305.
Boynton, Col. Matt., Governor of Scarborough Castle, articles agreed upon with Col. H. Bethell, 159.
Boys, Sir Jo., account of his defence of Donnington Castle, 292.
Brabant, French and Hollanders retire from, 69.
Bracamonte, Don Jasper de, Spanish ambassador to England, 148.
Bracbiano, Ursino, Duke of, 50.
Bradlng, 340.
Bradshaw, ——, receives 3000l., 466.
Brady, Mr., 34.
Braganza, Duke of, his rebellion, 221.
Brainford, Lord, see Ruthyn, Patr., Earl of Brentford.
Brainford, letter dated from, 428.
Bramhall, John, Bishop of Londonderry, letter to, 340.
Brancavio, Marq. of, escape of, 400.
Brandeis, 179.
Brandenburg, ambassador of, 119.
—— the Duchy of Juliers to be given to, 133.
—— Frederick William, Elector of, 232.
—— —— proposed marriage of his sister, 304.
—— George William, Marquis or Margrave of, 137.
—— —— movements of his troops, 154, 155.
—— —— letter to Charles I, 172.
—— Joachim, Marquis of, letter to, 400.
Brandi, John, 408.
Branford, Lord, or Brentford, q. v.
Brazil, 90, 178, 193.
—— destruction of Spanish sugar works in, 191.
—— hopes of recovering, 188, 189.
—— transports to, 129, 130.
Breadcake, Captain, 129.
Brecknock, letters dated from, 272, 273.
Breda, 143, 402.
Bremen and Denmark, 155.
Bremen, Archbishop of, and the sister of the Duke of Brunswick, match between, 232.
Bremen, Bishopric of, 78, 96.
Brent, Mr., recommended to Lord Ormond, 249.
—— Sir Nathan, Warden of Merton College, 255, 396.
Brentford, Earl of, see Ruthyn, Patr.

INDEX.

Brentford, letter dated from, 234.
Brentwood, 379.
Brereton, Sir W., 461.
Brest, 306, 324.
——— a ship taken at, 321.
——— fleet at, 225.
——— letter dated from, 317.
Bretons, 228.
——— 1500 at St. Malo, 225.
Brett, Capt., letters to, 319, 355, 358.
——— Capt. afterwards Major Arthur, 71, 73, 80, 121.
——— Mr E., letter to W. Aylesbury, 432.
Breze, Marshal de, defeats the Spaniards in Perpignan, 224.
Bribery, 330.
Bridges, Mr., his charges against the Earl of Sussex, 257.
Bridgestowe, 203, 207.
Bridgewater, 241, 268, 270, 301.
——— is taken, 271.
Brigantin, John, his letters of credence from various German Princes to Queen Elizabeth, 472, 473.
Brighte, Mr., royal shipwright, 12.
Brill, the, 446.
——— letter dated from, ibid.
Brindisi, Bishop of, 189.
Brion, Count de, 125.
Brisach, siege and taking of, 162, 163, 166.
——— garrison and siege of, 154, 157-161.
——— sermon on the loss of, 164.
——— news from, 370.
Brissenden, Capt., his account of provisions for the fleet, 463.
Bristol, 239, 241, 242, 259, 261, 262, 266, 273, 274, 406, 421.
——— Cols. Pinder and Layton at, 261.
——— enquiries why it was not fired, 239.
——— excise of, 260.
——— letters dated from, 239, 251, 259-263, 265, 276, 383.
——— names of the custom-house officers in, 308.
——— on the defence of, 239.
——— paymaster at, see Slingsby, R.
——— port of, 429.
——— relations of the siege of, 246.
——— R. Slingsby, paymaster at, plundered by the clubmen, 279.
——— surrender of, 277.
——— Dean of, see Nicholas, Matth.
——— Earl of, see Digby, John.

Bristol, Governor of, see Fiennes, Col. N.
——— Castle, letter dated from, 242.
Brittany, 299, 306, 375.
——— movements in, 361.
Brixham, tobacco and other goods seized at, 276; appraisement of, and warrants to seize the same, ibid.
Brock, Mr., 310.
Brockett, Dr. Col., letter to Ormond, 253.
Brocktorp, Paul, letter to, 181.
Bromfield, Col., his impeachment, 391.
Brook, Mr., 252.
——— Winter, relation of his journey into Ireland, 503.
Brooke, Lord, see Greville, Robert.
——— Nath., letter from to Capt. Best, 29.
Brough, William, his signature, 502.
Broughton, Mr., of Maidstone, Counsellor assistant to the High Court for trial of the King, 466.
Brown, Mr., claims payment for ammunition sent from France into England, 281.
——— his account for wools, 282.
——— Major-Gen., his speech in the House, 425.
——— Rich., see Browne, R.
——— Tho., his signature, 502.
——— —, M. P., 299, 400.
Browne, Capt., his deposition concerning the ship 'Newcastle,' 285.
——— Col., the Lorraine forces under him, 290.
——— Dean, at Paris, 463.
——— Sir John, at Bristol, 261.
——— or Brown, Richard, 162.
——— or Brown, Sir Rich., the King's resident at Paris, 348, 355, 388.
——— ——— instructions from the King to, 413; letter from the same to, ibid.
——— ——— ambassador at Paris, papers sent to Secretary Nicholas, viz. his instructions, when sent to that Court, &c., 412.
——— ——— letters to Lord Falkland, 228, 232.
——— ——— letter to one of the Secretaries of State, 503.
——— ——— letter to Secretary Nicholas, 413.
——— ——— letter to Nicholas, mentioned, 317.

Browne, Richard, English minister at Paris, letters of, 222, 224, 225.
—— Sam., his signature, 451.
Brownrigg, Ralph, Bishop of Exeter, with the King, 386.
Bruges, attempt to besiege it, 198.
—— letter dated from, 130.
Bruncker, Lord, 367.
Brunkard, or Bruncker, Lord.
Brunswick, Frederic II, Duke of, his sister, 232.
Brunswick and Luneburg, Henry, Duke of, letter from Queen Elizabeth to, 475, 477.
—— Prince Otto, Duke of, letters from Queen Elizabeth to, 472 (bis), 483.
Brussels, 201, 210, 229, 362, 409, 427, 486.
—— conference at, 164-166, 178, 181-183.
—— meeting of ambassadors at, (1637), 133, 138, 145, 148, 151.
—— Governor of, see Melo, Don Franc. de.
—— letters dated from, 20, 44, 60, 83, 93, 94, 159, 164, 167-172, 177, 187, 188, 190, 193-197, 224, 226, 229, 231-233, 434.
Bruton, letters dated from, 212, 262, 263.
Bruxelles, see Brussels.
Buccabella, Cardinal, 62.
Buchan, Earl of, see Erskine, James.
Buchanan, Gen., his 'Genethliacon' imitated, 301.
Buck, Sir Peter, letter from to the Lord High Admiral, 5.
Buckhouse, Sir John, Knt. of the Bath, see Backhouse.
Buckhurst, Lord, see Sackville, Thos.
Buckingham, Duchess of, see Villiers, Mary.
—— Marquis and Dukes of, see Villiers, George.
Buckinghamshire, conduct of the Sheriff of, 117.
Bulkeley, ——, defeated in Anglesea, 410.
Bulkley, Jn., his signature, 451.
Bull of Dispensation, Spanish, 461.
Bull, Sir Peter, 287.
Bullen, ——, 321.
Buller, Francis, 295.
Bullinger, Henry, 473.
Bullinghausen, Henry, and the Amsterdam merchants, case of, 482, 483, 489.
Bunce, Alderman, 110.

Bunch, ——, his impeachment, 391.
Burges, ——, see Burgess.
Burgess, or Burges, ——, and Caroll, ——, 379, 420.
Burgess, Dr., leaves York to present a petition, 206.
Burgh, Captain, Governor of Frankendale, 21.
—— Mr., i. e. Thomas Burke, q. v.
Burgh, or Burke, Mr., his death, 224.
Burgh, Lieut.-Col., letter to, 304.
—— Richard, Visc. Tunbridge, 73.
—— Ulick de, Earl of St. Albans, afterwards Marquis of Clanricarde, 173, 222, 253.
—— —— grant of lands to, 168.
—— —— instructions for the expedition into Connaught under his command, 310.
—— —— the peace in Ireland proclaimed by, 330.
—— —— appointed to treat with the Irish commissioners, 422.
Burghley, Lord, see Cecil, William, Lord Burleigh.
Burgundy, Adolphus of, moneys due for corn supplied to, 472.
Burgundy, 163.
—— invaded by the King of France, 161.
—— movements in, in 1646-7, 361.
—— troops in, in June 1637, 131.
Burke, or Burgh, Thomas, commissioner of the King, 237.
—— William, 144.
Burleigh, Lord, see Cecil, Will.
Burley, Capt., 437.
—— his trial at Winchester, 409.
—— is condemned for mutiny, 410.
—— Jo., an officer at Pendennis during the siege, 323.
Burnett, John, letter recommending his petition, 216.
Burton, or Burton-on-Trent, 311, 312, 314.
—— Scotch troops near, 313.
Burton, Mr., report of his answer before the Lords, 145.
Bury, Council of the army at, 379.
—— Cromwell there, 413.
—— disturbances at, 422, 423.
—— Fairfax goes to, 417.
Bury-St.-Edmunds, account of discourses at, 416.
Bushell, Capt. Henry, recommended to Sir E. Hyde, 284.
Butler, General, advances to Nuremburg, 106.
Butler, Lady, 357.

INDEX. 517

Butler, James, Earl and Marquis of Ormond, Lord Lieut. of Ireland, 252, 296, 312, 326, 335, 351, 360, 361, 375, 378, 393, 409, 410, 412, 425, 443, 444.
—— and Dublin, despatch of the affair concerning, 359.
—— and the Irish rebels, articles of peace between, 308.
—— is directed by the King to prosecute the Earl of Glamorgan, 300.
—— and Visc. Mountgarret, treaty between, on behalf of the King and his Roman Catholic subjects, 308.
—— propositions of the Lord Lieutenant to the Lower House of Parliament of England, 334.
—— and the Confederate Catholics of Ireland, advice in relation to an accommodation between, 381.
—— breach between him and others, 347.
—— declaration against, 447.
—— his engagement, not part of the Isle of Wight treaty, 450.
—— his signature, 311, 362.
—— letter to the Council of Confederate Catholics, 341.
—— letters from to Sir E. Hyde, 223, 309, 327.
—— —— to Sir Rob. Poyntz, 230.
—— —— to Prince Charles, 465.
—— —— to the King, 224, 368.
—— —— to Lord Inchiquin, 245, 250.
—— —— to Secretary Nicholas, 244.
—— letters to, 234, 236-238, 249-254, 256-258, 264, 265, 267, 269, 289, 299, 300, 322, 328, 333, 336, 340, 354, 358, 365, 377, 442, 502.
—— makes a truce with the Catholics, 360.
—— papers from the King and the Commissioners respecting him, 454, 455, 457.
—— the Queen's opinion of him, 253.
—— warrant from the King to, concerning the Lord Lieutenancy, 247.
Butler, Dr. Peter, 349.
—— Col. Rich., reasons for displacing him, 331.
—— Richard, Lord Mountgarret, letter to the Bishop of Ferns, 329.
—— —— and the Marquis of Ormond, treaty between, 308.
Butterwell, Mr., 335.
Butterworth, Mr., bearer of Sir E. Hyde's letters, 321, 341.
—— is sent to Ireland, 347, 362.

Button, Capt., acquittance from to Capt. Wood, 3.
Byrne, Serg.-Major, at Madrid, 192.
Byrne, or Birne, John, Lord, 309, 422.
—— account of his proceedings since his coming into Cheshire, Feb. to Sept. 1648; 439.
—— his account of the first battle of Newbury, 246.
—— reward offered for him, 409.
—— Sir Nicholas, Governor of Carlisle, petition to the King for payment of 3l. per diem, 235.

C.

Cabot, Sebastian, discovers the Bay of the Theatepians, Virginia, 500.
Cade, Capt., 374.
Cadiz, letters dated from, 23.
—— Spanish commissary at, 144.
—— the port of, closed, 141.
Cadman, George, a purser, 13.
Caen, 351, 353.
—— letter to a French general in, 372.
—— letters dated from, 306, 317, 321-324, 382, 394, 395.
—— residents at, 324, 335, 341.
Cæsar, Julius, mould from a marble bust of, 164.
—— his offer of pardon instanced, 382.
Calabaça weeds, 168.
Calais, 425, 447.
—— letters dated from, 426, 431.
—— endeavour to restore it, 481.
—— rendezvous of the King's Council at, 428, 429.
Calander, or Callender, Lord, see Livingstone, James, Earl of Calendar.
Calvert, Sir Geo., Secretary, letters from to the Lord High Admiral, 21; to the Earl of Bristol, 25, 26.
—— letters to, 22, 24, 27, 28.
—— minutes of a conversation with the King, 18.
—— Leonard, a commissioner of the King, 258.
Calvo, el Puerto, 129.
Cambray, 429.
—— defeat of the Spaniards at, 170.
—— Spanish victory near, 234.
Cambridge, declaration of the King printed at, 380, 381.
—— letters dated from, 292, 501.
—— order of the Privy Council respecting a Common, 34.

Camp, the, letter dated from, 340.
Campbell, Archibald, Earl and Marquis of Argyle, 169, 174, 187, 249, 250, 330, 363, 409, 419, 461.
—— defeated, 412.
—— his signature, 391.
—— leaves Edinburgh, 420.
—— and Hamilton, opposition in Parliament between, 115.
—— and Lindsay, nearly a duel between, ibid.
—— James, Lord Kintyre, 226.
—— John, Earl of Loudoun, Lord Chancellor of Scotland, 311, 313, 330, 391.
—— —— one of the Scotch Commissioners, 250, 435, 462.
—— —— agreement at Carisbrook confirmed by, 403.
—— —— letter to, 460.
—— —— liberated, 200.
—— —— letter from to the Lords of the Privy Council, 229.
—— —— his signature, 392, 396, 413.
—— —— makes his repentance, 461.
Canalentti, Baptist, 487 [? Cavalcanti].
Canary Islands, agents from London in, 476.
Canons, the reverend, 212.
—— of 1640, the Oath in, 214.
—— petition against, mentioned, 205.
Canterbury, 322.
—— letters dated from, 16.
—— trial at, for Church riots, 422–424.
—— Archbp. of, see Laud, William.
—— Dean of, see Wotton, Nich.
Cantarone, Medlle., her marriage, 198.
Capel, or Capell, Arthur, first Lord, 261, 303, 306, 311, 315, 316, 323, 324, 343, 354, 365, 367, 370, 381, 385, 395, 428.
—— articles of association between him, Sir E. Hyde, and others, 338.
—— engagement with others to repair the fortifications of Jersey, 339.
—— his estate disordered by Lord Essex' death, 342.
—— a report concerning his Lieutenant, 301.
—— letter from to the Queen, 323.
—— —— to the King, 324.
—— letters from to Sir E. Hyde, 292.
—— letter to, 301.
—— order to, 298.
—— prisoner in Windsor Castle, 437.
Capell, Lord, with the Queen, 319.
Capuchins, the, 205.

Capuchins, French, 53.
Caracalla, mould of a bust of, 200.
Caraminus, see Casimirus.
Cardeñas, Don Alonso de, 138, 149, 150, 153, 162, 163, 165, 168, 176, 177, 179, 181, 182, 185, 188, 201, 207.
—— requests protection for Spanish ships in English harbours, 171.
—— his complaint on the letters of marque granted to Lord Warwick and others, 214.
—— letters to Windebank, 162, 163.
—— letter to Charles I, 177.
—— memoranda of an interview with Windebank, ibid.
—— memorial from, ibid.
—— his submission, 183.
Cardiff, a ship rescued from pirates, brought into, 10.
—— details of the fight near, 422.
—— Judges of Assize at, 392.
—— letters dated from, 272, 275.
Cardinal, reasons for creating an English, 57.
Cardinals, 206.
Cardona, Duke of, 137, 140.
Cardonell, Mr., his overture for the press, 352.
Carey, Henry, Viscount Rochford, 272.
—— is impeached, 388.
—— is not received into the House, 409.
—— —— Earl of Dover, minutes by him of occurrences in Parliament, Aug. 1641—May, 1642, 230.
Carey, Lucius, Lord Falkland, 216, 218, 235, 243.
—— speech on ship-money, 212.
—— letters to, 223, 224, 233.
Carien, men of, to be tried for witchcraft, 65.
Carignan, or Carifian, Mary, Princess of, wife of Prince Thomas, 119, 210.
—— goes to Flanders, 124.
Carisbrook, agreement at, signed by the King, 403.
—— the King attempts to escape from, 426.
—— letters dated from, 402, 403.
—— Castle, letters dated from, 5, 405.
—— —— the King to be secured in, 407.
Carleton, Col., 436.
—— Mr., of Norwich, 61.
—— Anne, Viscountess Dorchester, allowance made to her three daughters, 35.
—— Sir Dudley, 18, 25.
—— —— letter from to Secretary Naunton, 18, 31.

INDEX.   519

Carlingford, 362.
Carlisle, 398, 433.
—— march against, 440.
—— report of its fall, 417.
—— Governor of, see Byron, Sir Nich.
—— Earl of, see Hay, James.
—— Castle, 462.
Carlos, the Infant Don, of Spain, q. v.
Carmichael, Lieut.-Col., bearer of papers to the Prince of Wales, 443, 460.
Carnarvon, Earl of, see Dormer, Rob.
Carnero, or Carnejo, Secretary to Olivares, 47, 97.
—— minutes of a conversation with him, 143.
Caroll, ——, 379.
Caron, Noel de, a commissioner for the Dutch alliance, (1624), 29.
Carr, Col., is exchanged prisoner for Col. Lansford, 243.
—— Geo., letter to, 252.
—— —— letter from to G. Booth, signed G. C., ibid.
—— —— letter from to Capt. G. Booth, ibid.
—— Humphrey, 175.
—— Robert, Viscount Rochester, 10.
—— Robert, Earl of Somerset, letter to, 7.
—— —— Lord Chamberlain, (1614), 9.
Carryers (guns of long range), ordered from Germany, 475.
Carter, Major, order to, 298.
Carteret, E., 465.
—— Sir George, Governor of Jersey, 320, 321, 328, 335, 336, 338, 342, 347, 349, 354, 363, 365, 370, 372-374, 385, 387, 389, 393, 435, 449, 465.
—— —— a kinsman of, 407.
—— —— and Sir Baldwin Wake, account of conferences between them for reducing Guernsey, 439.
—— —— promises payment to Sir E. Hyde, 352.
—— —— engagement to repay his expenses in repairing the fortifications of Jersey, 329; his certificate for repayment, ibid.
—— —— order for Mr. Fanshawe to pay expenses of the Prince's household, 315.
—— —— his surrender of Jersey reported, 358.
—— —— letter to the Earl of Warwick, 376.
—— —— letter to —— Russell, ibid.
—— Lady, 336.

Carteret, Sir Philip, 127.
Carthagena, sculptures from the King's house at, 34.
Cartmell, 284.
Cartwright, Sir George, 319, 327.
—— Sir Hugh, letter to, 415.
Cary, Sir Henry, see Carey.
Cary, Lucius, see Carey.
—— Thomas, the bearer of a present and letters to Princess (afterwards Queen) Henrietta Maria, App. I. 4, 5, 6.
Casaubon, Isaac, "Corona Regia" attributed to him, 195.
Cascahi, Ferdinand, his death, 404.
Cashel, Bishop of, see Walsh, Tho.
Cashell, letter dated from, 327.
—— Corporation of, letter from to the Nuncio and Congregation, ibid.
Casimirus, Prince of Polonia, 131, 135.
Casion, 117.
Casone, Guido de, 186.
Cassell, Landgrave of, 142.
Castaneda, Marquis of, 162, 183.
Castella, or Castilia, Almiranta de, appointed Captain-General on the coasts of the Bay of Biscay, 100.
—— superseded, 123.
Castelleone, the Pope's title to, 231.
Castellin, Edward, a merchant of London, 476.
Castil Rodrigo, Marquis de, ibid.
Castle Cary, Somerset, 267.
—— Cornet, in Guernsey, q. v.
—— Elizabeth, see Jersey.
—— Park, letter dated from His Majesty's fort at, 253.
Castlehaven, Earl of, see Touchet, Mervyn.
Castro, Condé de, 195.
—— Don Ferdinand de, Marquis of Saria, letter to, 500.
Catalans, the, 203, 204.
Catalonia, 210, 225, 374, 393, 412.
—— a Cortes held in, 193, 194.
—— disaffection in, 189, 198, 202.
—— French success in, 228.
—— the French in, 181.
—— Viceroy of, see Schomberg, Duke of.
Catechism, the short, papers of the King and the Commissioners respecting, 417, 453.
Catharine de Medicis, Queen-Mother of France, and the King of Navarre, interview between, at Cognac, 500.
Catherine, Princess, her birth and death, 165.

INDEX.

Catherine, relict of the Duke of Savoy, q. v.
—— Queen of Portugal, q. v.
Catholic Bishops for England, conditions to be observed in choosing them, 54.
Catholics, 355, 358, 361, 369, 448.
—— ammunition and moneys for the use of the Confederate, 311.
—— Confederate, of Ireland, propositions concerning their religion, 340.
—— —— letter to the Council of, 341.
—— clergy in England, reasons against the design of the Pope to send a Propositus, 163.
—— exhorted to pray for the King's success against the Scots, (1638), 162.
—— discipline in England, details considered, 57, 58.
—— James I and the penal laws against them, 21.
—— ordered to leave London, 405.
—— ordered by the Pope not to assist in the Northern expedition, 1639, 191.
—— penal laws against them, 345.
—— well treated in England, 58.
—— oaths required of those who serve in the fleet, 22.
Cato's reply to Cæsar's offer of pardon, instanced, 387.
Caulfield, Sir Toby, 10.
Causton, William, an English merchant, 478.
Cavalcanti, Guido, of Florence, commended to the Duke of Florence, 465.
Cavaliers, ordered to leave London, 404.
—— imprisoned for living in London, 360.
—— many imprisoned, 410.
—— their hope in the Scots, 402.
Cavarell, Abbot, letter to, 69.
—— letter from, 60.
Care, Lady Mary, monies due to, on the decease of her husband, Sir Thomas, 201.
Cavendish, William, Earl and Marquis of Newcastle, 285, 293, 341, 375.
—— as Lord Ogle, 367.
—— intrigue of Sir J. Hotham and his son with, 253.
—— letters from the King to, 240, 241.
—— letter to, on his appointment as Gentleman of the Bedchamber to the Prince of Wales, 150.

Cavendish, William, Earl and Marquis of Newcastle, letter from to Secretary Windebank, 150.
—— Lord Savile's answer to the charges sent by, 240.
—— account of his movements, to the surrender of York, 251.
—— his surrender of Winchester to Cromwell, 212.
Caversham, the King and his children at, 383, 384.
—— letter dated from, 241.
Cayrry, Sr, i.e. Thomas Cary, q. v.
Cecil, Col., 447.
—— Edward, Viscount Wimbleton, 70.
—— Robert, Earl of Salisbury, Lord Treasurer, letter from to the Stewards of the King's manors, 5.
—— William, Lord Burleigh, Lord Treasurer, letter to, 2.
—— letter from to Gonsalo Perez, 491.
—— William, Earl of Salisbury, 459.
—— his signature to the Isle of Wight treaty, 451.
Cecilia, Princess of Sweden, q. v.
Ceralvo, Marquis de, 181.
Cerbellon, Condé de, 137.
Ceylon, expedition prepared for, 193.
Challoner, Chaloner, or Chalanor, Sir Thos., envoy to the King of Spain (1562), 467, 478.
—— his credentials to the King of Spain, 469; extended credentials, ibid.
—— his death, (1565), 488.
—— J. Man succeeds him in Spain, 489.
—— safe-conduct for, addressed to Kings, &c., 467.
——, —, son to Sir Thomas, his speech, mentioned, 348.
Chamberlain, the Lord, 207.
Chamberlain, Thomas, envoy to the King of Spain, is recalled, 478.
"Champaign," letter to, 130.
Champney, Anthony, Dean of the Secular Catholic Clergy in England, his address, 162.
Chancellor, Nicholas, 499.
Chancery, case between the estate of Sir C. Egerton and his sister, 255.
—— notes of suits in, 154, 211.
Chantilly, the French King and Queen-Regent there, 376.
Chapman, Francis, i.e. Marquis of Antrim, q. v.

Chappell, John, 499.
'Char.', the (ship), 440.
Charl, Lord Goring's forces near, 209.
—— letters dated from, 253, 261.
Charneux, Lady, her death, 493.
Charenton, 361.
—— Lord Sligo's behaviour to those of, 352.
—— proposition from, 359.
Charing Cross, *see* London.
Charitas Patriæ, 356.
CHARLES I., 34, 36, 40, *et passim*.
—— as Prince of Wales, articles agreed on in his match with the Infanta Mary of Spain, App. I. 1.
—— articles of agreement for his marriage with Princess Henrietta Maria, 501.
—— letters on his marriage with Princess Henrietta Maria, App. L. 2.
—— letter to Lord Carlisle, *ibid.*
—— letter to Lord Kensington, *ibid.*
—— his betrothal deferred, 27, 28.
—— letters from, 28.
—— letters on his proposed reception in France, 1625, App. I. 4.
—— his escape from danger in a fall from his horse, App. L 4.
—— letters to, 20, 22, 23, 27, 28.
—— instructions to Sir F. Cottington, 27.
—— letters to him, App. L 2-6.
—— as King, letters to him, App. I. 6-8.
—— ill pleased with the King of Spain, 140.
—— is to be with troops at York, April 1, 1639, 170.
—— is to enter into a league with Spain, 190.
—— Ald. Acton, a friend to, 207.
—— lieutenants recommended to, 224.
—— his message from Newmarket, mentioned, 225.
—— Lord Paget's resolution to join the King, 232.
—— protestation made at the head of his army, 234.
—— the ship 'St. George' bought for his service, 245.
—— propositions for applying revenues from counties, &c., within the King's quarters at Oxford, for his use, 245.
Charles I., legacy of Abp. Laud to, 256.
—— account of monies paid for, 257.
—— reply to his charges against the Earl of Sussex, *ibid.*
—— answer to his propositions for a Custom House, 259.
—— the care of his person to be the centre of all action, 277.
—— his revocation of all Prince Rupert's commissions, *ibid.*
—— a sincere Protestant, 278.
—— promised a commission to Lord Goring, 279.
—— ships of war, 284.
—— reasons for sending his Propositions of Dec. 20, 1646, to London, 291.
—— his vow to restore all lay impropriations held by the Crown, 311.
—— movements with the Scots, 316.
—— leaves Oxford, 318.
—— memorials of the unfortunate success of his army and affairs in 1645, 319.
—— his reception by the Scots, *ibid.*
—— note of a relation of his journey to the Scots, 348.
—— remonstrance against his power to impose, 350.
—— particulars of his attendants, 357.
—— account of him, 361.
—— reports of a charge against him for his father's death, 365.
—— restoration predicted, 362.
—— report of a libel on, 373.
—— receives money from Brittany and Languedoc, 375.
—— movements of, 380.
—— on his seizure at Holmby, 381; account by the Commissioners on the same subject, 382.
—— the officers' civility towards him, *ibid.*
—— hunts at Oatlands, 387; and in the Isle of Wight, 402.
—— on the disposal of his person, 395.
—— servants removed from him, 397-399.
—— his veto, 399.
—— news of his being in the Isle of Wight, 402, 403.
—— allowance to be lessened, 403.
—— message from the Isle of Wight mentioned, 404.

3 x

Charles I, agreement at Carisbrook signed by him, 105.
—— to be secured in Carisbrook Castle, 407; no addresses to be made to him, ibid.; the Commons will receive no more messages from him, ibid.
—— proceedings against him, 409.
—— impeachment by the Commons, 411.
—— allowed only thirty servants, (1647-8), 412.
—— and Cromwell, reported treaty between, 414.
—— situation discussed, (1647-8), 415.
—— proposals of a personal treaty with, 418.
—— rejoicings on his coronation day, (1648), ibid.
—— refuses to abolish Episcopacy, 448.
—— account of the Isle of Wight treaty, in a letter to the Prince, 458.
—— account of Rich. Osborn's employment about the King's person, and of his attempted escape, 462.
—— his promise to pay Lord Ettrick 5000l. on the surrender of Edinburgh Castle, 502.
—— his reply to the eighteen propositions from the army, (1647), 503.
—— physician of the household, see Harvey, Dr. Wm.
—— his solicitor, see Bacon, Sir F.
—— trumpeter to, see Smith, Will.
—— powers and instructions to ambassadors and agents, 37, 48, 68, 73, 75, 80, 120, 152.
—— answer to Spanish ambassador, (1637), 132.
—— answer to the propositions of the Princess of Phalsburgh, 159, 160.
—— answer to Duke of Lorraine's proposition, 160.
—— answers to the London propositions, 337, 350.
—— answer to a question about the keeping of Easter, 373.
—— answer to some agitators' question about the Prince, 393.
—— answer to the charge of his having assisted the King of France against Rochelle, 407.
—— and the army, report of the treaty between, 392.
—— articles of agreement with Van Haesdonck, 215.

Charles I, assignations upon his ordinary revenue for 1643, 211.
—— at Holmby, 258.
—— at Newmarket, 380.
—— at Stirling and Dunfermline, 335.
—— at Windsor, 461.
—— calculation of his yearly revenue, 221.
—— certificate of receipts for the expenses of his household, 233.
—— chaplains refused access to, 363.
—— charges against him, 411, 412.
—— children, 384, 385, 461.
—— circular letter sent to various States in his behalf, Jan. 23, 1648-9, 465.
—— commission to Lord Falkland, 227.
—— commissioner of, 258.
—— corresponds with Lanerick, 403.
—— Covenanters intend no harm to, 252.
—— Council, letter to the Lords of, 273.
—— —— their orders concerning Pendennis Castle, 274.
—— order of the Lords of, ibid.
—— debate on the Parliament's declaration against, 412.
—— debates in Parliament on the disposal of him, 312.
—— declaration of Parliament presented to, 224.
—— declaration of his reasons for taking up arms (1642), 234.
—— declaration for committing Lords Sussex, Andover, and Percy to prison, 256.
—— declaration by the army presented to, 380.
—— his declaration on the vote of no more addresses, &c., 408.
—— declaration of Col. Poyer and officers for restoring him to his just prerogative, 418.
—— dissuaded from going to Scotland, 180.
—— sundry documents from, 38, 39, 52, 69, 79, 81, 97, 122, 134.
—— documents signed by, 258.
—— entreated not to confide in the Earl of Bristol and others, 244.
—— escape from Hampton Court, 329; letters found on his table there, mentioned, ibid.
—— fails to escape from Carisbrook, 425.
—— fleet, see Fleet and Ships.

INDEX. 523

Charles I, friends and servants about him discharged by Col. Hammond, 407; report of a conversation between the latter and the King, *ibid*.
—— grant of a pension, 32.
—— grant to Geo. Kirke, 184.
—— grant proposed for payment of his debts, 247; schedule of debts, with debtors' names, *ibid*.
—— harbourers of his person to be treated as traitors, 313.
—— design to exasperate him against Holland, 189, 191, 192.
—— agrees to break with Holland, 198.
—— instructions for the Earl of Antrim, 248.
—— instructions for the Earl of Lindsey, for his safe-conduct to London, 314.
—— instructions for the Duke of Richmond and Earl of Southampton, 251.
—— instructions to his Commissioners to treat with the Parliament, *ibid*.
—— instructions to Sir Rich. Browne, 413; letter to the same, *ibid*.
—— message to the Peers, offering to raise volunteers to suppress the Irish rebellion, 222.
—— proclamation declaring the Irish to be rebels, *ibid*.
—— petition from the Catholics of Ireland to, 234.
—— account of Irish affairs in 1642, sent to him, 235.
—— propositions of the Catholics of Ireland to, 242; answers of the Protestants of Ireland to the same, *ibid*.; summary of the propositions, *ibid*.
—— peace concluded between his Lieutenant (Ormond) and the Irish Roman Catholics, 465.
—— letters from to the Earl and Marquis of Antrim, 253, 255, 321, 323.
—— —— to Lords Capell, Hopton, &c., 301.
—— —— to the Infant Cardinal, 157.
—— —— to the Commissioners of Scotland in London, 307–309.
—— —— to the Commissioners at Oxford, 251.
—— —— to Lord Culpeper, 279.
—— —— to Sir T. Fairfax, 381.
—— —— to the Emperor Ferdinand, 80.

Charles I, letters from to the Earl of Forth, 237, 218.
—— letters from to Alex. Henderson, 319, 320, 322, 323.
—— —— to Princess (afterwards Queen) Henrietta Maria, App. II. 9.
—— —— to Sir Ed. Hyde, 231, 234, 248.
—— —— to Lords Jermyn and Culpeper, 329, 338, 350, 354.
—— —— to Lords Jermyn and Culpeper, and J. Ashburnham, 325, 327, 329, 330, 332, 333, 335, 336.
—— —— to the City of London, 318.
—— —— to the Bishop of London, 335.
—— —— to the Duke of Lorraine, 200.
—— —— to Lord Keeper Lyttleton, 221.
—— —— to the Masters of Requests, 82.
—— —— to merchants of Exeter, 291.
—— —— to M. Montreuil, 297, 299, 311.
—— —— to the Marq. of Montrose, 313.
—— —— to Will. Murray, 337, 339.
—— —— to the Earl of Newcastle, 240, 241.
—— —— to Secretary Nicholas, 257, 272, 276, 412.
—— —— to the Marq. of Ormond, 236–238, 249, 250, 254, 256–258, 264, 265, 267, 268, 288, 289, 300, 328, 333, 354, 358, 502.
—— —— to Parliament, 236, 318.
—— —— to the Parliament, suppressed, 405.
—— —— to the Earl of Pembroke, 69.
—— —— to the Prince of Wales, 267, 268, 272, 280, 289, 307, 322, 329, 443, 447, 448.
—— —— to the Prince of Wales and Council, 267.
—— —— to Prince Rupert, 275, 277.
—— —— to the Queen, 310, 311, 337, 344, 345, 350, 354.
—— extracts from his letters to the Queen, 321.
—— letters from to the Speaker of the House of Peers, 350, 453.

INDEX

Charles I, letter from to the Speaker of the House of Commons, 365.
— letter from to King of Sweden, 37.
— letters from to Sir H. Vane, 305, 306.
— — to Secretary Windebank, 39, 67, 68, 175, 176, 181, 202, 203, 205, 206.
— letters to, 28, 34, 38, 39, 52, 59–61, 80, 82, 87, 92–94, 97, 99, 102, 105, 107, 112, 117, 120, 126, 134, 141, 142, 145, 148, 149, 152–154, 156–158, 170, 172, 173, 175–182, 185, 190, 194–196, 199, 202–209, 213, 219, 224, 225, 229, 244, 258, 265, 266, 282, 283, 289, 299, 301, 309, 311, 320, 321, 324, 326, 333, 339, 370, 385, 389, 391, 392, 402, 426, 502.
— letter of, intercepted, 357.
— his infallible maxim on Church and State, 322.
— signature to the oath of allegiance, 128.
— order to Master and Council of the Court of Wards, 35.
— orders the appointment of a Commission on the petition of the Bishop of Killaloe, 36.
— order against his disposing of the jewels of the Crown, 232.
— order to Sir J. Stradling, 233.
— order to Capt. Stradling, to transport the Queen and Princess to the Low Countries, 373.
— order concerning warrants, 244.
— order for D'Aubigne's *Histoire Universelle*, for the King's use, 252.
— papers respecting the Marquis of Ormond, 454, 455, 457.
— papers respecting the Catechism, 455; Commissioners' answers to the same, *ibid.*
— orders of Parliament against him, 230.
— answer to the Parliament's declaration of May, 1642, 231.
— reply of Parliament to his demands (1642), 231.
— the Lords' contemplated answer to the King's message of April 12, 1643, 240.
— history of the dispute between the King and Parliament, to 1643, 247; corrected by him, *ibid.*
— letter to the Members of Parliament in London, 253.

Charles I, order to style the two Houses at Westminster a Parliament, 253.
— answer to the propositions of Parliament, 254.
— reply of Parliament to the King's letter, *ibid.*
— powers of Parliamentary Commissioners to treat with him, on religion, 257.
— answer to the propositions of the Commissioners of Parliament, 325.
— letter to the Houses of Parliament, 326.
— answer to the propositions of the Parliaments of England and Scotland, 351.
— message to the two Houses of Parliament, or an answer to the propositions, 377; how it was received in Parliament, 378.
— answer to the propositions of Parliament presented to him at Hampton Court, 388; probable answer, 389; reports on it, *ibid.*
— majority of votes in Parliament against, 392.
— the Commons vote a prosecution against him, 397.
— message to the Parliaments of England and Scotland, 402.
— order of Parliament for his party to leave London, 405.
— message to Parliament, 406.
— answer to the declaration in the House of Commons against him, 416.
— propositions to the Commissioners of the Isle of Wight treaty, 452; resolutions of Parliament in answer to the same, *ibid.*
— propositions to the Parliament, 454.
— answer to a petition concerning religion, 30.
— answer to a petition of Low Country merchants, 31.
— petitions addressed to, 25, 147, 220, 230, 235.
— petition to, for summoning a Parliament, with the King's answer, 204.
— petition from the Scotch to, with the King's answer, signed "Lanerick," 205.
— petition to, 206.
— a petition that he should be recrowned by Parliament, 414.

INDEX.   523

Charles I, proclamation against sending gold out of England, 217.
—— proclamation for adjournment of part of Hilary Term to Oxford, 235; answer against the same, *ibid.*
—— proclamation to those holding office in Ireland to repair thither, 260.
—— opinion of the Scots Privy Council against his visiting Ireland, 229.
—— the Scots Commissioners' address to him at Hampton Court, 396.
—— answer to the paper of the Scots Commissioners, 101.
—— answer to the propositions of the Scotch Commissioners, 503.
—— speech at the Scots' meeting, 207.
—— in Parliament (1628,) 32.
—— at the opening of Parliament (1640), 197, 209.
—— on the dissolution of Parliament, 198.
—— effect of his speech at York, 208.
—— his trial ordered to be proclaimed, 464; information about the same, *ibid.*
—— receives a copy of the ordinance of attainder, 464.
—— details of his trial, 465.
—— the Scotch and Dutch Commissioners try to stay his trial, 466.
—— High Court of Justice for his trial, Peers and others against, 466.
—— —— details of proceedings at, *ibid.*
—— —— list of names of the Judges, *ibid.*
—— reasons against the proceeding to try the King, 504.
—— warrant from Secretary Nicholas to print the Proclamation of Dec. 28, 1641; 222.
—— warrant to appoint Sir J. Colepepper, Chancellor of the Exchequer, *ibid.*
—— warrants to Sir Edw. Hyde, 235, 269.
—— warrant of the Committee concerning his revenue, 243.
—— warrant to Ormond, 247.
—— —— to John van Haesdonck, 249.
—— —— to Sir E. Herbert, 243.
—— warrants of, mentioned, 254, 363.
—— warrant for pension to the Countess of Forth, 257.

Charles I, warrant to the Uxbridge Commissioners, 258.
—— warrant to enforce his warrant issued at York, 261.
—— warrants to Sir N. Crisp, 264, 294.
—— —— to Sir Edw. Walker, 264.
—— —— to Francis Godolphin, Governor of Scilly, 273.
—— warrant for payment of Ecclesiastical Tenths and Firstfruits for his use, 282.
—— pretended warrant to the Earl of Glamorgan, 296.
CHARLES, Prince of Wales (afterwards Charles II), 259, 261–263, 265, 268, 270, 271, 275, 278–280, 285, 290, 292, 296, 297, 300, 309, 317, 318, 320, 330, 338, 341–344, 346, 348, 354, 356, 358, 361, 364–366, 368, 370, 372, 375, 379, 380, 387, 393, 394, 409, 414, 417, 418, 424, 429, 503.
—— Dean of his chapel, *see* Steward, Dr.
—— Master of the Harriers and Beagles to, *see* Pott, Thos.
—— his horoscope, 33.
—— a match proposed between him and the Emperor's daughter, 142.
—— order to draw Somersetshire soldiers together under Sir F. Doddington, 259.
—— despatch to Lord Goring, 260.
—— answer to a petition to him at Wells, 267.
—— his Council, 267, 268, 272.
—— orders of his Council concerning Lord Goring's forces, 270.
—— grant of tin made to, 273, 274.
—— instructions to Sir E. Hyde, on the Cornish customs, 273.
—— to be sent to France under the care of the Queen, 279; in his religion, to be under the care of the Bp. of Salisbury, *ibid.*
—— resolutions of his Council on the charge against him of breach of promise, 280; other resolutions against the charge, *ibid.*
—— warrant to the Governor of Pendennis, 285.
—— warrant for payments to Lord Hopton and Sir E. Hyde, 286.
—— order of, recited, *ibid.*
—— and the daughter of the Prince of Orange, on a marriage proposed between, 293.

INDEX

Charles, Prince of Wales, a list of his servants, with their wages, 292.
—— Lords of his Council, letter to Lady Pawlet, 295.
—— warrant for the master, &c., of the 'Young Tobias' of Hamburg, to return home, 300.
—— verses addressed to him, 301.
—— order for allowance to Joachim Hardwick, 302.
—— his proposal to erect a chapel in Pendennis Castle, 303.
—— his frigate, the 'Spread Eagle,' 307.
—— order for provisions to be sent to Sir E. Hyde, at Scilly, 308.
—— his arrival in Jersey, 315.
—— Lord Jermyn promises to accept bills of, 311.
—— order and receipts for expenses of his household, 315.
—— resolves to go to Jersey, 316.
—— the Parliament's design on, 320.
—— warrant to Capt. Amy, 322.
—— advice to him for suspending his journey to France, 323.
—— memorandum concerning the Prince's remove from Jersey, 323.
—— money due to, 325.
—— the King of France's allowance to, 311.
—— memorandum by him of the King of France's allowance to the Queen and Prince of Wales, ibid.
—— is treated with familiarity by the French, 332.
—— order for repayment to R. Fanshawe, 332.
—— Dr. Earle reads with, 351.
—— borrows money at Jersey, 365.
—— his revocation of all commissions at sea, 374.
—— his colours worn by many, 378.
—— his illness, 397, 400.
—— and the Marquis of Montrose, treaty between, 409.
—— proposes to go into Scotland, 412.
—— advice on his remove into Holland, 426.
—— Hyde goes to meet him at Calais, 429.
—— order by, with his reason for appearing upon the fleet in action, 431.
—— a pass from to Mr. Edgeman, to go to Rouen, &c., ibid.

Charles, Prince of Wales, his declaration from the navy, July 31, 1648, for satisfaction of His Majesty's subjects, 432.
—— his declaration concerning his engagement upon the fleet in the Downs, ibid.
—— reply to the Earl of Lauderdale's letter, agrees to join the Scottish army and to use their way of divine worship, 434.
—— relation of the defeat of the Scots addressed to, 435.
—— his proposals to the merchants of Rotterdam, for supplying his fleet, 435.
—— relations of the management of the fleet under his command, 437, 438; of his motions, councils, and actions in the fleet, 438.
—— his answer to the summons of the Earl of Warwick, ibid.
—— his gallant behaviour in the fleet, ibid.; his allowance from the States, ibid.
—— commission to Lord Byron, mentioned, 440.
—— on his going to Scotland, 412.
—— his judgment on Sir Rob. Walsh (or Welch), 444, 458.
—— a revenue of 100,000l. a year voted for him by Parliament, 447.
—— his movements, 422.
—— as King, arguments for and against his going to Scotland, Feb. 1648-9, 466.
—— letters to, 259, 267, 268, 277, 278, 281, 284, 286, 288, 289, 295, 297, 299, 307, 309, 310, 313, 317, 318, 321, 323, 327, 330, 337, 343, 344, 346, 348, 349, 362, 368, 370, 419, 427, 428, 431, 433, 435, 436, 443, 447, 448, 458, 462, 464-466.
—— letter from to Sir R. Grenville, 298.
—— —— to Sir A. Bassett, 299.
—— letters from to Lord Hopton and Sir E. Hyde, 284.
—— —— to Lord Hopton, 265, 303.
—— —— to Sir E. Hyde, 426.
—— —— to the Governor of Pendennis Castle, 303.
—— —— to Ormond, 322.
—— —— to the Parliament, 311.
—— —— to the Commissioners of Devon and Cornwall, 280.
—— —— to the Commissioners of the General Assembly of the Kirk of Scotland, 460.

INDEX. 527

Charles, Prince of Wales, letters from to the Committee of Estates of the Parliament of Scotland, 434.
—— letter from to the Lord Chancellor of Scotland, 460.
—— letters from to Lord Collington and Sir E. Hyde, 137.
—— to Lord Goring, 259, 266, 268, 282, 283, 300.
—— letter from his Council to Lord Digby, 244.
—— letter from to Lord Digby, 215.
—— letters from to the Duke of York, 445, 446.
—— —— to the Lord Mayor and Aldermen, 432.
—— to the Duke of Hamilton, Earl of Lindsay, Lords Lauderdale, Lanerick, and Callender, 431.
—— to the Prince of Orange, 435.
—— —— to the States on behalf of the King, Jan. 24, 1648-9, 465.
—— —— to the Marquis of Antrim, 340.
—— to the Governor of Jersey, mentioned, 363.
—— letter from the Lords of his Council to the King, 265, 266.
—— to Lord Goring, 209, 272, 274.
—— to the Commissioners for Devonshire, 274.
—— letter from to Lord Fairfax and the Council of War, 465.
—— letters to the Lords of his Council, 207, 270, 279, 281, 298, 444, 446.
—— letters alluded to, 314.
—— petitions to, 273, 293, 300, 352.
—— petition to, mentioned, 269.
Charles, Archduke of *Austria*, q. v.
Charles, Iofant of *Spain*, q. v.
Charles III, Duke of *Lorraine*, q. v.
Charles IX, King of France, L.
—— his conduct, 497.
Charles Emmanuel, Duke of *Savoy*, q. v.
Charles Louis, Prince Palatine, see Palatine.
Charleton, Lord Howard of, q. v.
Charnley, Major, 435.
Chartres, 417.
Chater, Col., 436.
Chatfield, Francis and George, merchants of London, 483, 494.
Chatillon, or Chastillon, —, taken prisoner, 151.
—— disaster in his French army, 198.
Chaworth, Lord, 181.

Chedzoy, letter dated from, 221.
Chelmsford Assizes, proceedings at, 417.
Chelsea, keepers of ale-houses in, 3.
—— letters dated from, 125, 138.
Chemnitz, capture of the fortress, 190.
Cherbourg, or Sherbrook, Mr. Hollis and seamen at, 396, 399, 408.
Cheshire, Lord Byron's proceedings since his coming into, 139.
Chester, 346, 440.
—— letters dated from, 14, 15, 340, 346.
—— on the siege of, 238, 279, 290, 304.
—— provisions from, 214.
Chester, Mr., warrant to seize his goods, 239.
—— William, 401.
Chevalier, Clement, payment to, 340.
Chevery, Christian de, Armador of the St. Sebastian squadron, 52.
Chevreuse, Chevreux, or Chevreaus, Claudius, Duke of, App. L 8.
Chevreuse, Mary, Duchess of, 143, 144, 147, 148, 196, 198, 199.
Chichels, Sir W., 373.
Chichester, Sir Arthur, afterwards Baron Chichester of Belfast, Lord Deputy of Ireland, 7, 8, 10, 169.
Chichester, Lord, 359.
—— letters to, 5, 6, 9, 11.
—— letters from to Sir H. May, 6.
—— —— to the Earl of Suffolk, 7.
—— —— to Capt. Trevor and Edw. Whitchurch, 11.
—— answer to a charge, 5.
—— his signature, 362.
—— Col., 340.
—— Fr., his signature, 334.
Chichester, letter dated from, 4.
—— Mayor of, letter from to the Lord High Admiral, 4.
—— Bishop of, see Barlow, W.
Chichley, Mr., desires W. Aylesbury's horizontal dial, 441.
Chillingworth, Mr., unable to join the Church of Rome, 80.
Chiroga, Father, the Queen of Hungary's confessor, 102.
Chivalry, Court of, 352.
Cholmeley, Sir Hugh, 421, 446.
—— account of his surrender of Scarborough to the Queen, 238.
—— memorials touching the battle of Marston Moor, 230.

Cholmeley, Sir Hugh, memorials touching the Hotham family, 255.
—— his regiment disbanded, 447.
Cholwick, Thomas, petition to Sir E. Hyde concerning the ship 'St. George,' 245.
'Christ,' the (ship), of Newcastle, 487.
Christchurch, 301.
Christian, Capt., bill of charges, 19.
Christian IV, King of Denmark, q. v.
Christmas, no sermons permitted at, 406.
—— customs, insurrections against officers opposing them, 407.
Christopher, Duke of Wurtemburg, q. v.
—— Prince of Baden, q. v.
'Christophers,' the (ship), of Lynn, detained at Fleckerye, 480.
Chudley, Capt., 219.
Church, 301, 307, 319, 321, 323, 325, 330, 336, 337, 352, 361, 371, 377, 381, 396, 425, 438, 444, 448, 452, 461, 462, [see also Ecclesiastical affairs.]
—— government of, by an assembly of divines, 240.
—— Lands, 442, 450.
—— —— sale of, 352, 391.
—— —— the King and the Commissioners' papers concerning, 453, 454, 456–458.
—— of England, admits the Huguenots to Communion, 420.
—— —— compared with other reformed Churches, 379.
—— —— how thought of at Ratisbon, 106.
—— —— its dependency on the Crown, 325, 329, 330, 332, 336.
—— —— why Catholics refuse communion with it, 198.
—— questions, the Queen's opinion on, 276.
—— University of Oxford's loyal attachment to, 210.
—— orders in the Roman Catholic, 354.
Churches, sacrilegious spoiling of, 271.
Cicero, M. T., 387.
Cicero's Offices, 353.
Ciudad Real, Duke of, reduces Bilboa to order, 44, 137.
—— his duel with the Duke of Marqueda, 202.
Clanricarde, Marquis of, see Burgh, Ulick de.

Clare, Dr., 406.
Clare, Dowager Countess of, see Holles, ——.
—— Father Francis, publication of his book hindered, 52–54.
Clarendon Park, 247.
Clarentia, Lady, 473.
Clarke, Benjamin, 499.
—— John, cook to the Duke of York, 445.
Clayborne, Tho., owner of a ship, 480.
Clayton, Dr., Master of Pembroke, 255.
—— F., 414.
—— John, 604.
—— Ralph, 402.
—— —— letters in behalf of, 495, 496.
—— —— and his ship the 'Juliana' detained at Copenhagen, 491.
Clemham, Sir Tho., executor to Lord Bayninge, 54.
Clergy, 217.
—— recusant, 260.
—— violent feeling in Parliament against, 211.
—— of Ireland, q. v.
Cleves, William, Duke of, letter to, 499.
Cleves, the land of to be seized, 167.
Cliffe, Mr., 339.
Clifford, Lord, at York, 162.
—— George, Earl of Cumberland, 2.
Clinton, Henry, Lord of Lincoln, 500.
—— Theophilus, Earl of Lincoln, is impeached, 388.
Clogher, Bishop of, 395.
—— letter to the Bp. of Ferns, 332.
—— letter to the Lord General of Ulster, 349.
Closet, Clerk of the, 391.
Cloth, a letter on the exportation of, (1606), 492.
Clotworthy, Lady, letter to Arthur Annesley, 345.
—— Sir John, 404, 460.
—— —— letter to A. Annesley, 340.
Cloyne, Geo., his signatures, 334, 362.
Clumnitz, see Chemnitz.
Clusnor, H., 463.
Clutterbuck, Mr., 400, 415.
—— letter to Lord Cottington, 463.
—— letter to W. Edgeman, 360.
Clynton, Edmund, letter to Prince Eric of Sweden, 474.

INDEX.   529

Clynton, F., letter to Peter Oxe, 196.
Cobb, Mr., of Sandringham, 61.
Cobham, the Duke of Richmond at, 383.
Cochran, or Cockram, Sir John, Knt., envoy to the King of Denmark, his acknowledgment of a debt to Lord H. Sebastedt, 351.
Cockpit, the, see London.
Cockram, Sir J., see Cochran.
Cocle, Sir Thomas, to be created a Baron, 7.
Codrington, John, royalist, letters signed by, 230.
Cogan, H., 437.
Coghlan, Daniel, page of the bed-chamber to the Duke of York, 445.
—— Patrick, footman to the Duke of York, ibid.
Cogniac, 500.
Coins of Ferdinand and Isabella, Charles V, and Philip II, 93.
Coke, Mr., letter from to the Lord High Admiral, 10.
—— Sir Edward, 25.
—— —— his daughter, Lady Purbeck, q. v.
—— —— his jurisdiction of Courts, 350.
—— Edward, Lord, his Pleas of the Crown, ibid.
Coke, or Cooke, George, Bishop of Hereford, his case with the Chapter of Windsor, 502.
—— Sir John, secretary, 82, 85, 101, 388.
—— —— letters and warrants from to Sir H. Vane, 37; to Secretary Windebank, 105.
—— —— warrant to John Veruge, 121.
—— —— letters to, 44, 47, 61, 76, 83, 85, 86, 90, 93, 95, 96, 100, 102, 104, 106, 108, 110, 112, 114-116, 119, 122-125, 128, 130, 143, 144, 147, 148, 174.
—— —— retires, 194.
—— Thomas, letter to W. Edgeman, 321.
Colarte (Flemish general), 136.
Colchester, siege of, 428, 431.
—— is taken, 437.
Cole, —, Mayor of Newcastle, 98.
—— John, owner of the tin blowing house of St. Neots, 258.
Colepeper, Sir John, afterwards Lord, see Culpeper.

Coliurure, siege of, 228; its walls 36 feet thick, ibid.
Collemer, Henry, 3.
Collimar, Justus, of Antwerp, account of monies paid by him for the King, 257.
—— contracts with Lord Cottington for powder, &c., ibid.
—— letter to Sir E. Hyde, 280.
—— sums paid to him out of the excise of Bristol, 260.
Collins, Col., bearer of a letter to the King, 313, 318.
—— at Paris, 356.
Collison, John, warrant for him to sell his wine, &c., in Cornwall, 302.
Collumpton, 271.
Cologne, 275.
—— ambassadors assemble at, 108.
—— conference at, 173, 175, 186, 188, 193.
—— Elector of, party to a league, 56.
—— letters dated from, 74, 96, 173.
Colon, Col., his regiment, 223.
Colonia, or Colonna, Don Carlos de, of Majorca, 83, 121.
—— his death, 143.
Coloredo, —, troops under him, 86.
Colston, Mr., of Exeter, 339.
Colt, Sir Henry, negotiation for his liberty, 66.
Colvil, —, 200.
Comerford, Patrick, R. C., Bishop of Waterford, letters to, 329, 331.
Comespolius, Stanislaus, pupil of C. Threcius, 468.
Commines, is taken, 380.
Commission of Oyer and Terminer, 424.
Common Pleas, Lord Chief Justice of H.M.'s Court of, see Lowther, Sir G.
Common Prayer-book, used by the Parliament army, 379.
Commons, House of, see Parliament.
Communion, the, as a test, 221.
Compagni, Bartholomew, of Florence, a merchant in London, 423 (bis).
Compiegne, 313.
—— letters dated from, App. L 3.
Composition, proposals from the army relating to, 385.
—— Committee for, 360.
Compounding, arguments against, 372.
Compton, Spencer, Earl of Northampton, business of, 238.
—— killed at the battle of Hopton-heath (March, 1643-4), 249.
—— Sir W., 309.

3 Y

INDEX.

Con, or Conn (Gregorio), 120, 115, 147, 158, 361.
— succeeds Panzani as Nuncio in England, 121.
— letter to, 97.
Condé, Henry II. Prince of, passes given by him to the Irish commanders, 503.
— Louis II, Duke or Prince of, 311, 366, 369, 374–376, 383, 384, 386, 393, 394.
— his corps at St. Vallery, 356.
— a gallant act of, 380.
— movements of his troops, 366, 369, 370, 423.
— goes into Catalonia, 412.
— at St. Germains, 418.
'Confessio Augustana' alluded to, 469.
Congregation of the clergy of Ireland, q. v.
Conn, G., see Con.
Connaught, 219.
— instructions for the expedition into, 310.
— the Scots defeated in, 326.
Conquest, Sir F. Mackworth at, 283.
Constable, Sir W., 407, 414.
— returns from the Isle of Wight, 410.
Constantinople, 348.
— the King's ambassador at, 253, 358.
— letters dated from, 398, 418.
Conti, Anthony de, and his wife Lucretia, letters patent of safe-conduct for, 405.
— Prince of (brother of the Prince of Condé), is to be made a Cardinal, 369.
Contreras, Col. Andres de, Spanish Governor of Frankendale, 99, 122, 139.
'Convert,' the (ship), 446.
Conway Castle, see Aberconway.
Conway, Sir Edw., afterwards Lord, Secretary of State, Commissioner for the Dutch alliance, and the treaty against Spain, 29, 30.
— Edward, second Viscount, narrative of his conduct in the action at Newburn, 213.
Conyers, Sir John, his appointment as Lieutenant of the Tower, 227.
— Capt. Nicholas, 459.
Cooke, —, 128, 165.
— Major, 335, 380.
— Edw., letter to Col. Fiennes, 212.
Conly, Mr., secretary to Lord Jermyn, 338.

Cooper, Mr., 262.
— Sir A. A., letter to Sir Edw. Hyde, 245.
— or Cowper, Sir Rich., letter from to the Lord High Admiral, 5.
— Coote, Sir Charles, petition of, 46.
Cooter, Mr., recommended as a candidate for Orders, 349.
Cop, John, letter concerning him, 490.
Copenhagen, letter dated from, 484.
— person detained at, 485.
— a ship detained at, 492.
— see Haffnia.
Copley, —, M. P., 460.
— Col., is condemned to the Tower, 389.
Copp, John, and his servant John Epte, 481.
Corbie, held by Card. Mazarin, 366.
Cordova, Don Gonzalo Fernandez de, Lieutenant-General, 22.
— letter from to the Landgrave of Darmstadt, 21.
— his death, 60.
Corfe Castle, M. P. for, 209.
— siege of, 305.
— reports of the King being taken to, 458.
Cork, letters dated from, 251, 252, 348.
— Parliament ship at, 252, 253.
Cork, Lord, see Boyle, Rich.
— his charge against Lord Inchiquin denied, 251.
Corke, Benedict, of Newcastle, 473.
'Cornelius,' letter to Sir E. Hyde, concerning Lord Goring, 301.
Cornelius, —, bearer of a letter of Sir E. Hyde's, 373.
— Mr., with Mr. More at Jersey, 466.
Cornwall, 268, 271, 274, 285, 286, 289, 292, 304, 312, 419.
— account for arms for the King's garrisons in, 249; account for the customs in the ports of, to 1664, ibid.
— address of Parliamentary generals to the people of, 276.
— address to the loyal men of, 271.
— Cornish contributions, 280.
— customs of, 285.
— Duchy of, 243.
— forces and forts of, 272, 278, 279, 281–283.
— instructions of the Prince of Wales concerning the customs of, 223.

INDEX.   531

Cornwall, letter to the Commissioners of, 280.
—— list of five delinquents in, 295.
—— the Mount, 310.
—— —— letter dated from, 291.
—— —— Governor of, see Bassett, Sir A.
—— petition of the County to the King, 230.
—— prizes brought into ports of, 271.
—— warrant to the deputy Comptrollers of the Cornish ports, 292.
—— prophecies of a maid in, 362, 370.
—— relation of the state of parties in, 295.
—— resolutions of persons in, concerning Sir F. Bassett, with their letter to the High Sheriff, 246.
—— High Sheriff of, 278.
—— Vice-Admiral of the South of, see Trevanian, Sir C.
—— warrant for recovery of deserters from the army in, 272.
—— warrant of the Commissioners of, to the Custom Officers, 270; warrant to stay goods at a Customhouse in, ibid.; note relating to the same, ibid.
—— warrant to Sir N. Crisp, concerning the sequestered estates in, 264.
—— warrant to get in the contributions for the county, 289.
—— warrant to the officers of H. M.'s customs in, 302.
Cornwallis, Sir F., 397.
—— letter to, 403.
—— Sir Thos., L
'Corona Regia,' title of a book falsely attributed to Casaubon, 193.
Coronation Oath, 322.
Corso, Cape, loss of the Armada from Italy on, 65.
Corunna, letter dated from, 184.
Coryton, ——, 316.
Coothill, letter dated from, 238.
Cosmo, Duke of Florence, q. v.
Cottell, Capt., see Cottle.
Cotterell, Major, Governor of Pomfret Castle, 461.
—— Sir Chas., letter to W. Denman, signed 'C. Alleyn,' 428.
—— —— at Cranborne, 130.
—— Lady Cotterell, ibid.
—— Sir Chas., letter to Wm. Denman, ibid.
—— —— letter of, mentioned, 441.

Cottington, Sir Francis, 24, 25.
—— afterwards Lord, 35, 43, 98, 117, 131, 159, 161, 164, 194.
—— Lord Treasurer, 201, 341, 353, 359, 367, 373, 414, 418, 442, 445.
—— as Constable of the Tower, 204.
—— strengthens the Tower, 205.
—— sends money to Windebank, 203, 206.
—— his plan for prolonging the loans, 206.
—— contract with J. Collimar, for powder, &c., 257.
—— appoints Kinesman auditor, 363.
—— is ill of the gout, 137.
—— letters from to Secretary Calvert, 27.
—— —— to Charles I, 31.
—— —— to Sir H. de Vic., 433.
—— —— to Lord Hopton, 436.
—— and Sir E. Hyde, letters from to the Prince, 431, 433, 436.
—— letters to, 43, 49, 51-53, 55, 59, 60, 62-69, 72-76, 79, 80, 83, 84, 86, 88-90, 92, 94, 103, 115, 119, 122, 124, 133, 139, 161, 166, 168, 171-175, 179, 186, 189, 193, 195, 196, 200, 202, 342, 354, 356, 362, 387, 413, 436, 437, 443.
—— and J. Boswell, cypher with, 214.
—— and Lord Fielding, cypher between, 215.
Cottle, Capt., receipt from, 268.
—— letter to, ibid.
—— or Cottell, Capt., accounts with, for match, 295, 300.
Cotton, Sir D., relation of his embassy into Persia, 32.
Covenant, the, 252, 325, 327, 330, 332, 339, 342-344, 346, 348, 350, 351, 354, 363, 386, 502, 443, 450, 459, 502.
—— a clause of, Latin and English, 461.
—— demanded by the Scots, 421.
Covenanters, 209.
—— repulsed at Edinburgh Castle, 200.
—— intend no harm to the King, 252.
Covent Garden, see London
Coventry, Sir Tho., Lord Keeper, 31, 34.
—— his speech in Parliament, 501.
—— his death, 194.
Council, see Privy Council.
Council of War, q. v.

Counsell, Capt. Thomas, letter to, signed "Jo. Seymour, Edw. Stephens, and J. Codrington," 239.
—— warrant to, to seize the goods of Sir R. Poyntz, &c., 239.
—— letters from Royalists to, 239.
Count *Palatine*, q. v.
Couriers, expenses of, 141.
Courland, Duke of, letter from the Ablegate of, 213.
Court, the English, 210, 268, 361, 444.
—— restrictions on saying Mass in, 444.
Courtenay, Edw. see Courtney.
—— Sir William, 260.
—— —— letter from, 13.
Courtney, Anthony, armed a ship against France, 484.
Courtney or Courtenay, Mr. Edw., 52, 63, 64, 74, 95.
—— remarks on his book, 67.
—— letter to, 45.
—— letter from to Sec. Windebank, 62.
—— extracts from his book, *ibid.*
—— his remonstrance, 63.
—— Howard, 45.
Coutainoville, letter dated from, 315.
Cowley, A., letter to Lord Culpeper, 313.
Cowper, Sir Rich., see Cooper.
Cracovia, 131.
Cranborne, letter dated from, 430.
—— Sir C. Cotterell at, 430.
Cranborne Lodge, near Windsor, 414.
Cranfield, James, Earl of Middlesex, is impeached, 388.
—— his signature, 151.
Craven, William, Lord, 458.
—— pays his ransom, 104.
—— letter dated from his house near Reading, 362.
Crauford, or Crawford, Earle of, see Lindsay, Ludovick and John.
Crediton, 297.
Creighton, Dr. Robert, Dean of St. Buryan's, Cornwall, 355.
—— letters to, 360, 363.
—— petition to Prince Charles, 293.
Creil, 125.
Crequi, Charles, Marquis de, forces under him, 112.
Cressy, Mr., takes Orders in the Roman Catholic Church, 354, 361.
Creutznach, letter dated from, 21.
—— taken, 71.
Crewe, Jo., 151.

Crisp, Sir Nicholas, 89, 272, 275, 288.
—— complaint against him concerning the 'St. George,' 250; his answer to the same, *ibid.*
—— account of sums expended, as between Capt. Smith and, *ibid.*
—— receipt from Capt. Smith to, 250; agreement with Capt. Smith for the use of the 'St. George,' *ibid.*
—— agreement with Capt. Smith for prize-money, 258.
—— warrant from the King to, 264.
—— letter to, 271.
—— warrant to deliver to him wool in payment for powder, 276.
—— recommended to Sir E. Hyde, 287.
—— complaint against him on the shipping business, 293; note touching his fleet, *ibid.*; his answer concerning the shipping, *ibid.*; his answer to the petition of Sir C. Trevanian, *ibid.*; notes on the case, 294; warrant to, granting him the tenths of prizes, *ibid.*; commissions for reprisals renewed by, *ibid.*; list of ships under his commission, *ibid.*
—— his considerations concerning Holland, 293.
Crispe, Sam., and his wife killed, 418.
Crofts, Col., 303.
—— John, 300.
—— —— letter to W. Edgeman, 357.
—— Mr., with the King, 382.
—— Dr., turned away by the King, 385.
Crombie, Mr., 426; Mrs. Crombie, 427, 429.
Crompton, Sir T., letter to, 3.
Cromwell, Oliver, 261, 265, 267, 270, 281, 280, 181, 361, 378, 380-383, 389, 390, 394-396, 398-400, 402, 410, 413, 415, 420, 442, 459, 462, 464.
—— surprise of his forces near Dorchester, 262; defeat of his horse, *ibid.*
—— address signed by, 276.
—— surrender of Winchester to, 292.
—— at Oxford, 316.
—— and Ireton, differences between, 391.
—— dispositions of his superior officers, 402; and of their opposition to the Agitators, *ibid.*
—— his fear for his personal safety, 412.

Cromwell, Oliver, blamed for inveigling the King from Hampton Court, 416.
— goes to Bow, 421.
— superseded in his command by Sir H. Waller, 422.
— marches of his horse under Major Huntingdon, 440.
— his aversion to the capital sentence against the King, 466.
— his report from the army, 378.
— his wife at Court, 397.
— his illness, 361.
— Scarborough taken by his men, 432.
Cromwell, Sir Tho., 394.
Crongby, Mrs., i. e. Mrs. Crombie, q. v.
Croobe, Henry, letter from to W. Edgeman, 284.
Cross, custom of heading letters with a, 130.
Cross, Sir R., commission to, L
Crow, Sir Sackville, the King's resident at Constantinople, 348, 358, 392.
— barbarously used by Sir T. Bendish, 398.
Crown, the, 333, 418.
— jewels, order against the King's disposing of, 232.
— officers, propositions for nominating, 444.
— Pleas of, 350.
— the power of, 325, 379, 382, 392.
— disputes the title to presentation of a living, 216.
— profits of, 447.
— Queen Elizabeth announces her succession to, 467.
Croydon, letters dated from, 3, 105, 106.
Cruso, Mr., at Bristol, 406.
Cualling, John, 492.
Cucklington, Digby's engagement with Waller's forces at, 262.
Cuirassiers, troop of, formed, 202, 206.
— the Captain to have 2hs. a day more than any other Captain of horse, 206.
Cullam, James, 489.
Culpeper, or Culpeper, Sir John, afterwards Lord, Master of the Rolls, 264, 281, 285, 290, 294, 315, 318, 319, 321, 342, 343, 348, 367, 425, 432, 4-9, 442, 444, 459.
— letter from to the Lords of the Prince's Council, 279.
— his speech, 209.

Culpeper, Sir John, afterwards Lord, warrant to appoint him Chancellor of the Exchequer, 222.
— agreement with Van Haesdonck, 245.
— odious to the gentry of Devon, 263.
— note by, concerning Lord Goring, 280.
— is sent into France, 316.
— hatred against, 438.
— attempt of Sir R. Welch upon his person, 458.
— letters from to J. Ashburnham, 305.
— — to Lord Digby, 272.
— — to Lord Goring, 259, 261–263, 265, 268, 270, 271.
— — to Lord Hopton, 287.
— — to Sir E. Hyde, 306, 308, 310, 314–316, 320, 321, 328, 329, 331, 335, 338, 340, 350, 354–356.
— — to the King, 326, 333, 336, 346, 349.
— letters to, 238, 260–263, 265–271, 277–283, 289, 290, 299, 301, 304, 313, 317, 319, 323, 327, 329, 330, 332, 333, 335, 336, 338, 350, 373, 377, 424, 427, 434.
Cumberland, 236, 410.
— Earl of, see Clifford, George.
Cunningham, —, in prison for refusing the oath, 209.
Curio, Leo, 484.
Curtius, William, 173.
— instructions to, 37.
— his cypher, 215.
— Mr. or Count, 91, 93, 94, 133, 140, 142, 156, 157, 159.
— — instructions to him, 120.
— — appointed Vice-Chancellor of the Empire, 142.
— — goes to Hamburg with powers to treat with Sweden, 149.
Curwen, Sir Patrick, 435.
Custom House, 259.
— officers, 276, see Price, Howell.
— officers in London, order to, 30.
Customs, the, 363, 394, 432.
— leased, 34.
— names of officers of the customhouse in Bristol, 308.
— warrant to the officers of His Majesty's, 302.
— and impositions, 221.
— revenue of Ireland, 75, 76.
Cyphers, five anonymous, 215.
— keys to various, used abroad, 214.

D.

Dade, Henry, letter from to Mr. Aylesbury, 17.
Daler, Mr., 61.
Dalkeith, Lady, see Scot, Mary.
Dalton, —, harasses Wexford, 349.
Daly, an Irish friar, 146.
Darrell, Tho., bearer of the Emperor's letter to Queen Elizabeth, 492.
Damport, i. e. Davenport, Father Francis, on Temporal and Spiritual supremacies, 86.
—— his book, 93.
Danby, Lord of, 255.
Daniel, the Prophet, 342.
Daniells, or Danylls, Mr., names of those present at his murder, 7.
Danish ambassador, see Denmark.
Dantzic, 479, 483, 485, 486, 489, 491, 495.
—— City of, letter from to Charles I., 141.
—— Council of, 475.
—— English citizens of, ibid.
—— letter to the Council and Senators of, 479.
—— letters to the City and magistrates of, 475, 485, 492-494, 496-499.
—— letters dated from, 141, 226.
—— orders to the Council at, 487.
—— ships sent to, for naval stores, ibid.
Danvers, Henry, Lord, letter from to the Lord High Admiral, 13.
'Danyell,' the (ship), of London, account of barrels of indigo received out of, 411.
Danylls, Mr., see Daniells.
Daray, Fr. Charles, 429.
Darcie, or Darcy, Fr., of Bruxelles, 330, 427, 431.
—— Bishop, 442.
Darcy, Mr., proposals to the King about the customs of Ireland, 75, 76.
Darmstadt, 419.
—— Lewis V, Landgrave of, letter to, 21.
Darnley, Earl of, see Stuart, Henry.
Darcy, Patrick, agent for the freeholders of Galway, propositions tendered by him to the King, 80.
—— his signature, 310.
Dartmouth, 282, 291, 299, 304.
—— a ship of, 245.
—— letter dated from, 290.

Dartmouth, petition concerning a prize taken into, 278.
—— seizures at, 363.
—— the King's fleet at, 249.
—— a vessel and arms taken at, 302.
Dartwell, 294.
D'Aubigné, Theod. Agrippa, order for his 'Histoire Universelle,' for the King's use, 202.
Daubney, or Dawbney, Arthur, 494, 498.
Davenant, Sir W., 290, 323, 337, 343.
—— letters from to Sir Edw. Hyde, 315, 320.
—— his threat that the Queen will retire into a monastery, 335.
Davenport, Francis, see Damport.
—— Humphrey, 129.
Davis, or Davys, Sir Paul, Knight, Clerk of the Council of Ireland, 333.
—— a witness against the Earl of Strafford, 221.
Dawbney, Arthur, see Daubney.
Dawson, Mr., cypher to correspond with, 215.
—— Major Charles, 437.
Dayrell, Mr., 430, 431.
—— sues for the goods of Lord Holland, 430, 431.
—— Sir Tho., at Paris, letter from to W. Aylesbury, 441.
—— letter to, 351.
Deal, 425, 428.
Dean Forest Ironworks, instructions to demand abstract of the accounts, 295.
Deane, Mr., Comptroller of the port of Penryn, his decease, 292.
Debts, papers relating to the payment of public, 453.
Decretum Perjurii, 328.
Dee, Arthur, letters to, mentioned, 430.
Delinquents, 444.
—— Commissioners' report of votes of Parliament concerning, 456, 457; the King's answer to, 453, 457.
—— votes of the House on, 448.
Dellamour Forest, rendezvous in, 410.
Delmenhorst, Princess of, see Friesland, East.
—— Count of, see Oldenburg.
De Lomenie, —, his signature, 378.
Delvyn, Baron of, and Baron of Killeene, dispute between, 6.

INDEX.   535

Denbigh, letter dated from, 279.
—— the victory of, 285.
—— Castle, is taken, 440.
Denbigh, Earl of, see Fielding, Basil.
Denbighshire, list of persons continuing in arms in, 463.
Denham, Mr., 459.
—— arrives at Caen, 324.
—— John, 387.
Denman, W., of Amsterdam, letters to, 426, 428, 431, 437, 442, 443.
—— —— letters to, 430, 431.
Denmark, 367, 410.
—— agent in, see Cochran, Sir J.
—— Danish admiral, see Bikie, G.
—— ambassadors of, 210, 376.
—— instructions of Parliament to their agent in, 286.
—— and Sweden, war between, 161.
Denmark, Christian IV, King of, 44, 153, 155, 157, 163, 232.
—— —— leagues with the Emperor against the Swedes, 92, 94.
—— —— envoy from the King of England to, see Cochran, Sir John.
—— —— hope of assistance from, 276; peace with Sweden, *ibid.*
—— —— letter from to Charles I, 40.
—— —— letter to, 286.
—— Frederic II, King of, letters from Queen Elizabeth to, 471, 472, 475, 476, 478-480, 482-498.
—— —— his secretary, see Knopper, Dr. A.
—— Princess Dorothy of, letter from Queen Elizabeth to, 472.
Denso, Paula, the Duke of Nothern's lieutenant, 124.
Denton, Col., 435.
—— Sir Alex., his son-in-law, Col. Smyth, 361.
Denys, Nicholas, 492.
Deptford, defeat of the City horse at, 385.
—— fire at, 14.
—— letters dated from, 2, 18.
—— Bridge, held by the Kentish men, 424.
Derby, Earl of, see Stanley, James.
Derby House, Committee of Safety at, 425.
—— letters from Scotland to the Committee of, 412.
—— Council at, on the affair concerning the Marq. of Ormond and Dublin, 339.
Derickson, C., 463.

Dering, Sir Edward, 382.
—— his speech, 203.
Desmond, Earl of, see Fielding, George.
Devenish, Henry, 17.
Devereux, Robert, Earl of Essex, 203, 205, 252, 307.
—— disputes a bequest to the College of Douay, 81.
—— letter from to the Deputy Lieutenants of Gloucestershire, 241.
—— letters attributed to him, 241.
—— his success at Plymouth, &c., 251.
—— his answer concerning a pass for the Duke of Richmond, quoted, 253.
—— his defeat at Lostwithiel, in Cornwall, 306.
—— his death, 312.
Devogle, M., 461.
Devon, or Devonshire, 261, 265, 267, 269, 272, 284, 289, 419.
—— petition from the gentry of, mentioned, 205.
—— observations on the general pardon for, 230.
—— odiousness of Lord Culpeper to the gentry of, 261.
—— letter from the Lords of the Prince's Council to the Commissioners of, 271.
—— Commissioners of, and Lord Goring, articles of agreement between, 280.
—— Devonshire contributions, *ibid.*
—— Devon and Cornwall, letter to the Commissioners of, *ibid.*
—— letter from the Commissioners of, to Sir E. Hyde, 281.
D'Ewes, Sir Simon, 412.
—— abuse of, 416.
Dickenson, or Dickinson, Mr., 358, 396, 399.
Dickenson, William, 475.
—— letter from, 389.
—— —— to Sir E. Hyde, *ibid.*
Dirgo de la Torse, Don, 226.
Diepeurnex, Walter, letter concerning him, 491.
Dieppe, pass to, 431.
—— Cottington and Hyde leave, *ibid.*
Diest, 229.
—— letter dated from, 71.
Diet, the Imperial, see Germany.
Digby, Mr. S., 26.
—— George, Lord, afterwards second Earl of Bristol, 230, 257, 309,

311, 312, 320, 322, 323, 327, 335, 341, 353, 355, 365, 368, 369, 379.
Digby, George, Lord, his speech upon grievances, 209.
—— duel with Lord Wilmot, 392, 395.
—— his brother, 316.
—— rescued by the Marquis of Ormond, 375.
—— letter from to Sir John Berkeley, 259.
—— —— to Lord Goring, 261, 266.
—— —— to Lord Culpeper, 266.
—— —— to Sir E. Hyde, 296, 301, 326, 428, 463.
—— —— to the King, 282, 283.
—— —— to the Earls of Leven and Callender, 278.
—— —— to Secretary Nicholas, 252.
—— —— to the Prince of Wales and his Council, 267.
—— copies of his letters, 603.
—— his defeat in Scotland, and flight to the Isle of Man, 289.
—— his defeat at Sherborne, 285; his letters taken from him, and read in Parliament, ibid.
—— his signature, 310.
—— servant of, 318.
—— in Dublin, 347.
—— his ill fortune in Ireland, 362.
—— letters to, 260, 264, 271, 277, 316, 334, 357, 400, 448.
—— letters from and to, mentioned, 258, 264, 265.
Digby, John, Earl of Bristol, 201, 241, 353, 361, 382, 393, App. L L.
—— propositions addressed to the Emperor, 21.
—— will not meddle with the Lords' petition, 205.
—— his son, 347.
—— discourse with Hyde concerning the vote of Parliament excepting divers persons from pardon, 408.
—— letters from to the Marquis of Buckingham, 20, 22.
—— —— to the Prince of Wales, 20, 22, 23, 27.
—— —— to the Commissioners for Germany, 21, 23.
—— —— to Secretary Calvert, 24, 28.
—— —— to Sir F. Cottington, 27.
—— —— to James I, 28.
—— letters to, 24, 25, 28, 317, 353, 360, 382.
—— letter to, on the negotiations with Spain for the restitution of the Palatinate, 501.

Digby, Sir John, is taken prisoner, 234.
—— letter from to the Prince of Wales, 323.
—— letter to, 115.
—— surprises Waller's forces at Cucklington, 262.
—— General John, 352.
—— Sir Kenelm, 118, 313, 400, 418.
—— success in his negotiations at Rome, 271.
—— his son, 393.
—— arrives at Paris from Rome, 427.
Diggens, Mr., 352.
Dijon, 393.
Dillon, Thomas, Lord, letter from to the Bishop of Ferns, 329.
—— letter to, 219.
—— Wentworth, Earl of Roscommon, his signature, 262.
—— is fallen mad, 364.
—— F. Edward, 191.
Dingley, Sir John, 465, 466.
Directory, the, 351.
Dishington, Sir Thomas, 78, 150.
Dispensation, Bull of, 463.
Dissenters, protestant, called Quakers; petition to the King, 147.
Ditmarsh, goods wrecked on, 477.
Dives, or Dives, Sir Lewis, see Dyve, Sir L.
Dixmudie, 394.
Docquetts, see Grants.
Doctors Commons, letters dated from, 14.
Doddington, Dodington, or Dorrington, Sir Francis, 259, 264, 302, 376.
—— letter from to Sir E. Hyde, 446.
Dodsworth, Francis, letter from to Sir Thos. Aylesbury, Bart., 111.
Dolben, ——, surrender of Donnington Castle to the Parliamentary forces under him, 292.
Donawert, held by the Duke of Bavaria, 21.
—— letter dated from, 101.
Doncaster, 444, 461.
—— letter dated from, 38.
Doncaster, Lord, see Hay, James.
Donne, Dr., letter from to Sir E. Hyde, 216.
—— his Sermons desired as a present for Lady Leicester, 218.
Donnington Castle, account of its defence by Sir Jo. Boys, 292; and of its surrender, ibid.

INDEX.   537

Dorchester, letter dated from, 239.
—— Lord Goring's success near, 262.
Dorchester, Marquis of, see Pierrepoint, Henry.
—— Viscountess (1631), see Carleton, Anne.
Dorell (Dayrell, or Durell), Col., 373.
Doria, Duke, sent prisoner to Narbonne, 224.
Dorislaus, Dr. Isaac, his credentials from the Parliament to the States, 428.
Dormer, ——, Lady Carnarvon, letter from Hyde to, 208.
—— Robert, Earl of Carnarvon, 60.
Dorothy, Princess, of Denmark, q. v.
Dorrington, Mr., 61.
—— Sir F., see Doddington.
Dorset, Earl of, see Sackville, Edw.
Dorsetshire, 288.
Dort, 297, 421.
Doway, College of, 19.
—— bequest to, 81.
—— letters dated from, 61.
—— siege of, 391.
Dover, 425, 141; App. L 4.
—— Castle, relieved, 425, 426.
—— Committee, 227.
—— letter dated from, 199.
Dover, Earl of, see Carey, Henry.
Douglas, letter dated from, 283.
Douglas, Mr., Scottish ambassador, 2.
—— Robert, moderator, a Commissioner of the General Assembly, 443.
—— Sir Arch., success of Lieut. Smith over him, 202.
—— R., his Kirk, 461.
—— William, Earl of Morton, 343, 370.
—— —— settlement on his daughter, 105.
Dowe, Robert, a merchant of London, 483.
Downe, Earl of, see Pope, Thomas.
Downs, the, fleet in, 314, 432, 436.
—— letters to Lords in, 437.
—— letters dated from, 45, 431-434, 437.
—— the ship 'Danyell' in, 441.
Dowridge, Lieut.-General, 170.
Dowry to be paid by the King of Spain in consideration of clemency shown to Roman Catholics in England, 28.
Drayton, letters dated from, 34, 205.
Drew, ——, one of Prince Charles' musicians, 26.

Droghart, W., 463.
Drogheda, 362.
—— a diary of the siege (Dec. 1641 to March, 1642), 227.
Droitwich, letters dated from, 264, 265.
Dromore, claim to lands in, 6, 8.
Droe, John le, narrative of his wrongs, 81.
Drury Lane, see London.
Dublin, 221, 226, 290, 309, 330, 340, 341, 345, 362, 369, 425.
—— an account of military operations about, 228.
—— is besieged, 339.
—— letters dated from, 4, 7, 11, 20, 44, 75, 89, 168, 221, 223-225, 229, 230, 234, 244, 245, 250, 252, 290, 326, 340, 502.
—— Lord Digby in, 347.
—— the affair concerning the Marquis of Ormond and, 339.
—— five commissioners for, ibid.
—— Castle, letters dated from, 40, 136, 252, 309, 327, 341, 362.
Duckett, Geoffry, 198.
—— Lionell, 485.
Dudley, Robert, Earl of Leicester (1584), circular letter of, 1.
Dugdale, William, 366, 368, 429.
—— his notes and collections, desired, 397.
—— the King's answer to, 382.
Duirkin, Dr., 499.
Don, Sir Daniel, letter from to the Lord High Admiral, 4.
—— warrant addressed to, 8.
Dunbar, Earl of, see Hume, Geo.
Duncanon, oath taken at, 328.
Dundalk, 362.
Dunfermline, the King at, 335.
—— or Dumferline, Earl of, 311, 313, 379, 380.
Dungan, Sir John, 224.
Dunkirk, 231, 347, 361.
—— behaviour of English ships there, 65.
—— preparation of arms at, 246.
—— defeat of the Spanish fleet at, 168, 170.
—— a fleet ready for, 202.
—— fleet, in the Groyne, 124.
—— frigate, 306.
—— Governor of, 502.
—— in French hands, 338.
—— letters dated from, 185, 186.
—— letter to the Mayor, &c. of, 488.
Dunsmore, Lord, 224.
Dunstable, 398, 399.

3 E

538   INDEX.

Duppa, John, letter from to Lord —, 23.
—— Brian, Bishop of Salisbury, 335, 354, 386, 412.
—— —— the Prince of Wales to be under his care in his religion, 279.
—— —— letter from to the King, 337.
Durell, Abraham, 396, 400.
—— see Dorell.
Durham, Bishop of, (1636), see Moreton, Thomas.
—— letter dated from, 212.
Dutch, the, 310.
—— ambassador, 374, 383.
—— fleet, 405.
—— frigates, Dunkirkers seized by, 120.
Dyall, Lord, 392.
Dymocke, John, agent from the King of Sweden to Queen Elizabeth, 176.
—— letter in behalf of, 489.
Dyve, or Dives, Sir Lewis, 364, 414.
—— escapes from prison, 409.
—— letter from to Lord Goring, 261.

E.

'Eagle,' the (ship), note of ammunition taken from, 279.
Eakins, Capt. R. N., 463.
Earl Marshal, the, see Howard, Thos., Earl of Arundel.
Earle, Sir Walter, 365, 375.
Earles, Dr. John, fellow of Merton Coll., Oxford, 371, 400.
—— reads with the Prince, 353.
—— letters from to Sir E. Hyde, 212, 216.
—— letters to, 354, 356, 361, 384, 403.
East, stores for the, 476.
Eastcheap, see London.
Easter, the King's answer about the keeping of, 373.
East Friesland, Prince and Princess of, see Friesland.
East India, see India.
Eberadorfe, letter dated from, 141.
Ecclesiastical affairs, English, 390.
—— Courts, 350.
—— Orders, 353.
—— Tenths and First fruits, warrant for payment of, 282.
Ecclesiasticus xxxviii. 4, quoted, 368.
Echemburg, Baron, President of the Council, 22.
Ecija in Granada, revolt of, 143.
Eckenburg, Prince of, 142.

Eden, Dr., 109.
—— to treat about the merchants' complaints in Spain, 201.
Edgar, Count, of East *Friesland*, q. v.
Edgebury, Mr., letter from to the Lord High Admiral, 18.
Fdgcombe, —, 316.
Edgecumbe, P., document signed by him, 274.
Edgeman, William, 371, 372.
—— his nephew W., 400.
—— a pass for him to Rouen, &c., 431.
—— Secretary to Sir E. Hyde, 135.
—— letters to, 288, 304, 313, 315, 316, 321, 323, 325, 328, 330, 339, 352, 357-360, 370, 373, 376, 383, 386, 388, 390, 392-397, 399, 400, 404, 406-408, 411, 441, 465, 466.
Edinburgh, letters dated from, 229, 250, 415, 419, 420, 422, 424, 443, 461, 502.
—— sermon at, 414.
—— full of English Cavaliers, *ibid*.
—— proceedings in the Parliament at, 115.
—— proceedings of the Committee, *ibid*.
—— Castle, attempt to surprise it, 170.
—— —— is given up, 181.
—— —— is defended by Lord Etrick, 207.
—— —— is yielded to the rebels, *ibid*.
—— —— Lord Sinclair committed to, 401.
—— —— a promise by the King to pay 5000*l*. for its surrender, 502.
Edmonds, Sir F., Liégois forces under him, 296.
Edward VI, 479, 485.
—— began the Reformation, 320.
—— King, pension granted to Prince Otto of Brunswick, 472.
—— a servant of, 470.
Edward the Confessor, St., 332.
Edwardes, Arthur, 498.
Edwards, Mr., 131, 466.
—— at Rouen, letter to him for Lord Hopton, 391.
—— appointed to draw up a charge against the King, 461.
—— R., 463.
Egerton, Lord, arguments upon the Post-nati, 350.
—— Sir Charles, case in Chancery between the estate of Sir C. Egerton and his sister Lucy, 255.

INDEX.   539

Egerton, Sir Rowland, business of, 239.
Eglionby, John, 135.
Egmont, Count, letters from to Charles I, 142, 153.
Kiffler, Peter, or Kiffler, q. v.
Elbe, inundation of, 37.
Elections, free, 247, 405.
Elector, Prince, letter to John Pym, 241.
Eliberis, Council of, canon of, 351.
Elizabeth, Queen, 1, 361.
—— official transcripts of letters on foreign affairs during the early part of her reign, 467-500.
—— her zeal for religion, 469.
—— negotiations about her marriage with the King of Sweden's son, 470, 471; declines to marry, 470, 471.
—— scented gloves presented to, 500.
—— letter of, 470.
—— letter from to the Princes, &c. of the Augsburg Confession, 480.
—— letters from to the Margrave of Baden, 474, 480.
—— to Maximilian, King of Bohemia, 467, 481.
—— to Joachim, Marquis of Brandenburg, 490.
—— to Henry, Duke of Brunswick, 475, 477.
—— to Prince Otto of Brunswick, 472, 483 (bis).
—— to the Archduke Charles, 471.
—— to William, Duke of Cleves, 499.
—— to the City and Magistrates of Dantzic, 475, 485, 492-494, 496-499.
—— to Frederic II, King of Denmark, 471, 472, 475, 476, 478-480, 482-498.
—— to Princess Dorothy of Denmark, 472.
—— to Cosmo, Duke of Florence, 473 (bis), 474, 478, 483, 485, 487, 495.
—— to the Princess Regent of Flanders, 489.
—— to Princess Anne of East Friesland, 469, 472-474, 486, 487.
—— to Edgar, Count of East Friesland, 499.
—— and John, Count of East Friesland, articles of a convention between, 487.

Elizabeth, Queen, letters from to the Emperor Ferdinand I, 468, 471, 473, 477, 482.
—— letters from to the Emperor Maximilian II, 468, 490-492.
—— to the Council of Ghent, 479.
—— to the Council and Senators of Hamburg, 477, 482, 493.
—— to the Magistrates of the Hanse Towns, 470, 471, 477, 482, 491, 494.
—— to Philip, Landgrave of Hesse, 469, 471 (bis), 479, 480, 482, 490.
—— to William, Landgrave of Hesse, 492.
—— to Adolphus, Duke of Holstein, 468, 470, 471, 477, 483.
—— to Albert, Count de Hoye, 472.
—— to the King of Hungary, 480.
—— to the lords and gentlemen of Ireland, 468.
—— to Gerard, Bishop of Liége, 491.
—— letter from the merchants of London to, 483.
—— letters from to the civic authorities at Lubeck, 470, 471, 494.
—— to the Council and Senators of Lubeck, 475.
—— to the Count of Mansfield, 483.
—— to Mac Art' More, 468.
—— to Count Anthony of Oldenburg, 473, 482.
—— to John, Bishop of Osnaburg, 472.
—— to the Count Palatine, 470.
—— to Frederic, Count Palatine of the Rhine, 471, 474, 479, 480, 489, 490, 497.
—— to Wolfgang, Count Palatine of the Rhine, 474, 490.
—— to Anne, Countess Palatine, 489.
—— to Princess Margaret of Parma, 472.
—— to the Emperor of Persia, &c., 476.
—— to the King of Poland, 467, 473, 479, 485-487, 490, 493-499.
—— to the Viceroy of the King of Poland in Lithuania, 467.

INDEX.

Elizabeth, Queen, letter from to the Duke of Pomerania, 494.
— letters from to the King of Portugal, 468, 478, 480, 484, 488, 494, 496.
— to the Queen of Portugal, 468.
— to Albert, Duke of Prussia, 467, 469, 471, 474, 479 (bis), 481, 488, 496, 497.
— to the Council of Revel, 473.
— "Romano Imperatori," 481.
— to the Emperor of Russia, 476, 488, 491, 495–499.
— to the governors of the company of Russia merchants, 499.
— to the Marquis of Saria, 500.
— to John Frederic II, Duke of Saxony, 469, 472, 474, 480, 490.
— to Augustus, Duke of Saxony, 469, 470, 472, 474, 480, 490, 498.
— to Francis, Duke of Saxony, 477.
— to Catherine, relict of the Duke of Saxony, 475.
— to Philip II, King of Spain, 468–470, 473, 476–478, 481, 483, 484, 486, 488–490, 494, 497, 498.
— to Gustavus, King of Sweden, 470, 473.
— to Eric, Prince, afterwards King of Sweden, 470, 473 (bis), 476, 479, 481, 484, 486–491, 493, 495, 496.
— to Cecilia, Princess of Sweden, 484.
— to the Doge and Council of Venice, 476, 486, 492.
— to Christopher, Duke of Wurtemberg, 471, 474, 479, 480, 482, 490.
— circular letter to the European Princes, 477.
— letters patent of safe conduct for A. de Conti, 495.
— letter from her representatives to Sir M. Ranezow and P. Broektorp, 481.
— letters patent to Prince Christopher of Baden, 488.
— to W. George, 490.
— commissions to her agents in Persia and Russia, 498.

Elizabeth, Queen, letter to, 481.
Elizabeth, Princess, 384.
Elizabeth, Princess, and Queen of Bohemia, q. v.
Elmer, John, 469.
Elphinston, John, Lord Balmerino, his appointment as a Scotch commissioner, 250.
— voted against Argyle, 419.
— letter from to Lord Lauderdale, 460.
Elsbrough, or Elisburgh, 474.
— siege of the castle of, 484.
Elson, Mr., cypher with, 215.
Elsyng, or Elsynge, H., papers signed by him, 341, 450.
Eltonhead, Mr., protestation denying his jurisdiction as judge of assizes, 372.
Emden, or Embden, 154, 481.
Empire, the, Aulic council of, 147, 148.
— jealousies between it, Spain, and Bavaria, 166.
— review of the power of (1638), 153.
Empson and Dudley, case of referred to, 25.
England, list of English agents abroad, 163.
— Father Semple's mission to, 201–203.
— petition of English Lords to the King, for summoning a Parliament, 204; the King's answer thereto, ibid.
— payment of English forces, 207.
— appointment of Scotch commissioners to make a treaty in, 250.
— reports from, 315.
— schism in, 320.
— letter dated from, 363.
— English merchants seized by the Emperor of Russia, 412.
— an address to the people to defend themselves from the tyranny of the then Powers (1647-8), 416.
— account of the state of affairs in, Feb. 19, 1648-9; 466.
— letters in behalf of English merchants, 467, 485.
— certificates for the importation of yew into, 485.
— on safe-conducts for English merchant ships, 488.
— list of English merchant vessels, 493.
— letter from the Society of Eng-

INDEX.

lish merchants to the Council of Hamburg, 193.
England, letters in behalf of the Society of English merchants, 493, 498, 499.
—— capitulations of the English nation (1622-41), a treaty of free commerce with the Turks, 502.
—— the English Protestant Church described, 57.
—— the English Reformation, 322.
—— account of the affairs in the West of, 240.
—— movements of forces in the Western counties, 260, 265, 266, 269, 277.
—— West of, 251.
—— —— order for uniting the King's forces in, 301.
—— —— a narrative of the affairs of, Sept. 1644, to March 2, 1645-6; 306.
—— —— Western garrisons, 110.
—— North of, 266.
—— account of the military proceedings in, from 1641-45; 291.
—— wool from, 313.
—— —— military movements in, 366.
—— Church of, *see* Church.
—— agent for English navy, *see* Allen, Thos.
—— English Presbyterians, *see* Presbyterians.
—— and France, rumoured league between, 115.
—— —— treaty between the crowns of, 407.
—— and Spain, league between, 198.
—— letter of the English ambassadors to the King of Spain, 463.
Englefield, Anthony, 175.
Enyon, James, grant of a baronetcy to, 227.
Episcopacy, 316, 319, 327, 330, 333, 335, 344, 358, 386, 387, 421.
—— petition in favour of, 227.
—— resolutions on the subject of, 257.
—— the King's determination to return to, 335, 337, 448.
—— Moderate, 411.
—— answer of the commissioners concerning, 447.
Episcopal government, 452.
Epte, John, a servant to John Copp, 480.
Eric, Prince of *Sweden*, q. v.

Ericson, Steno, negotiates about the proposed marriage of Queen Elizabeth, 470.
Ernest of Saxony, Duke, *see* Saxony.
Erule, Sir John, letter from to Lord Chief Justice Hyde, 34.
Erskine, Captain Alexander, 151, 153.
—— Sir Charles, 388.
—— —— his signature, 390.
—— James, Earl of Buchan, 165, 166, 172, 176, 179.
—— —— accused of forging credentials, 170.
—— —— conferences with the Spanish ambassador (1637), 122.
—— —— letters from to Secretary Windebank, 150, 151, 153, 154.
Escaglia, Abbot d', 131.
l'Escale, le Chevalier de, is sent to the Bastile, 384.
Escurial, Prior of the Convent made a Grandee of Spain, 148.
Espejo, Antonio de, map of his voyage, 500.
Esperoon, Duke of, 114.
Essex, 216, 426, 429, 430.
—— letter dated from, 110.
—— petition prosecuted at the Quarter Sessions, 419, 421.
—— petition, 422.
—— men, rising of, 424.
—— Earl of, *see* Devereux, Robert.
d'Este, Cardinal, 301.
d'Estre, Marshal, 125.
Eton, ——, attacks the established religion, 272.
Ettrick, Lord, 200.
—— his gallant defence of Edinburgh Castle, 207.
—— the King's promise to pay him 5000l. on the surrender of Edinburgh Castle, 502.
"Evangelici," the style first used, 148.
Evans, Cornelius, a counterfeit Prince of Wales, 421.
Eveland, Sir John, 330.
Evelyn, Sir John, jun., 406.
—— abused, 416.
Europe, summary of news (1619-20), 16; (1632), 37.
—— war preparations (1639), 173.
European Princes, circular letter to, 477.
Eustace, Sir Maurice, letter to Arth. Annesley, 340.
Examinations, answer to the Committee of, 373.

Exchequer, the, certificate of the Barons of, 129.
—— oath taken in, 208.
—— receipts and expenditure of the King's, at Oxford, 241.
—— account of moneys paid into, from the diocese of Oxford, 218.
—— processes of the Court of, to be sealed with the usual seal at Oxford, 248.
—— Chancellor of, *see* Culpeper, Sir J., and Hyde, Sir E.
—— on Sir E. Hyde's appointment as, 372.
Excise, 361–363, 366, 372.
Exe, the (river), 282.
Exeter, 270, 274, 280, 281, 283, 286, 290, 291, 294, 302, 304, 311, 312.
—— letters dated from, 2, 244, 260, 267, 273, 276, 279–283, 289, 297.
—— residents at, 261, 286, 339.
—— letter from the officers there, to the Lords of the Prince's Council, 273.
—— letter to certain merchants of, 294.
—— its surrender, 315.
—— merchants of, send a vessel to Dantsic, 452.
—— merchants of, 496.
—— Bishop of, *see* Brownrigg, Ralph.
Exminster, 261.

F.

F., R., note by, 285.
Fabroni, Cogneus, President, declaration of a plot of his, 159.
Fabian, Mr., his political opinions, 242.
Fabroni, Abbot, 181.
Fachados, Don Lewis, leaves Lisbon, 3.
Fairfax, Ferdinando, Lord, letter from to H. Peters and Lieut.-Col. Burgh, (1645–6), 364.
Fairfax, Sir Thomas, afterwards Lord, Lord General, 255, 278, 280–282, 287, 298, 299, 303, 305, 309, 312, 315, 316, 351, 380, 384, 385, 389, 391, 394, 397, 399, 401, 415, 417, 424, 428, 432, 458, 459.
—— interview with Capt. E. Scotten, at Reading, 259.
—— commands of the King to search for him, 263.
—— document signed by, 276.
—— news of his movements, 316.
—— at Oxford, *ibid.*

Fairfax, Sir Thomas, afterwards Lord, treaty between his commissioners and those for Oxford, 322.
—— at Bath, 328.
—— before Ragland Castle, 332.
—— his demands, 381.
—— is voted Generalissimo of the Forces (July, 1647), 381.
—— is voted Constable of the Tower (Aug. 1647), 387.
—— passes of, 389.
—— pelted at, 412.
—— rebuke to, 404.
—— Saltmarsh's ghost seen by, 411.
—— letter from to Hugh Peters, 204.
—— —— to the Prince of Wales, 278.
—— —— to Sir Thomas Glemham, 322.
—— —— to Sir Richard Grenville, 286.
—— —— to the Governor of Pendennis Castle, 306.
—— letters to, 245, 306, 386, 465.
—— Lord Goring's defeat by, 271.
—— Advocate-General to his army, *see* Mills, John.
Falconberg, Lord, 226.
Falcons presented to Queen Mary, 467, 471.
—— presented to Queen Elizabeth, 471.
Falkland, the Lady of, 79.
—— Lord, 109, 401.
—— —— letters to, 225–232.
—— —— letter from to Sir E. Hyde, 226.
—— —— commission from the King to, 227.
—— *see* Carey, Lucius.
Fallowfield, Henry, merchant of London, a letter concerning him and his ship, 482.
Falmouth, a ship arrested at, 98.
—— prisoners at, 216.
'Fame,' the (ship), of London, account of wools delivered from, 232.
Fane, Francis, his petition, 81.
Fane, Sir Joseph, his relation of the state of parties in Cornwall, 293.
—— Lord, goes to Scotland, 336.
Fanning, Dominic, excommunicated, 329.
Fanquan, ——, papers of 117.
Fanshawe, Mr., 104, 121, 322.
—— Richard, 259, 325, 335, 358.
—— —— receipt to, 315.
—— —— memorandum by, *ibid.*

INDEX.

Fanshawe, Sir Richard, account of moneys repaid to himself, 352.
— letter countersigned by, 281.
— letter to, 409.
— letter from to Lord Hopton and Sir E. Hyde, 285.
— bearer of a letter of Hyde's, 385.
—, nephew of Sir Baldwin Wake, 370.
— Secretary of War, 267, 288.
— letters to, 269, 238.
— Sir Thomas, 348, 372, 387.
— his receipts to Andrew King, 302.
— at Jersey, 306.
— balance sheet signed by, 352.
Faries, —, plots against Archbishop Laud, 175.
Farmers' hill of oblivion, mentioned, 220.
Farnham, the King at, 460.
Farrier's bill, a, 3.
Farringdon, 264.
Fast, proceedings at a public, 106.
Fawconer, William, sen., letter from to Sir E. Hyde, 210.
Fawley, George, his examination for corresponding with the rebels in Abingdon, 249.
Featherstonhaugh, or Fetherston, Sir Tim., 435.
— recommended by the King, 257.
Feilding, George, see Fielding.
Fell, Dr., Vice-Chancellor of Oxford, 233, 234, 397.
Fennel, Dr. E., 365, 381.
Fennyn, Don, secret discovery of gold mines, &c. made by him to the Duke of Buckingham, 29.
Feoffees, a case concerning the, 212.
Ferdinand I, Emperor of Germany, letters from Queen Elizabeth to, 468, 471, 473, 477, 482.
Ferdinand II, Emperor, 21, 22, 38, 41, 42, 47, 55, 56, 59, 64, 67–72, 74, 75, 77–80, 82–91, 94–97, 99–108, 110, 112, 113, 116, 118, 131.
— attempt to assassinate him, 134.
— his widow the Empress Dowager, 150.
— letters from to Lord Digby, 21, 23.
— — to Charles I, 62.
— — to Mr. Taylor, 86, 88.
— — to the Commissioners, 101.
— — to the Earl Marshal, 102.

Ferdinand II, Emperor, letters to, 20, 82, 89, 102.
Ferdinand III, Emperor, 133, 134, 135, 140, 170, 171, 177, 184–186, 207, 229, 231.
— birth of his son, 131.
— answer to Venetian ambassadors, 136.
— details of Mr. Taylor's audiences with, March, 1638; 149, 151.
— and Mademoiselle, proposed marriage between, 380.
— letters to, 145, 149.
Ferdinand (brother of Philip IV), Cardinal Infant, 43, 44, 47, 50, 52, 53, 66, 71–73, 82, 91, 95, 96, 102, 104, 107, 112, 114, 123, 131, 137, 140, 142, 148, 153, 163, 165–167, 169, 170, 172, 174, 176, 177, 181, 182, 184, 186, 190.
— letter from to the Emperor, 72.
— — to the Princess Phalsburg, 172.
— — to Charles I, 180, 185, 195, 199.
— letter to, 157.
— in Flanders, 210.
Ferdinand II, Duke of Florence, q. v.
Ferdinand III, King of Hungary, q. v.
Ferdinand, Duke of Tuscany, q. v.
Feria, Countess of, 473.
— the Count of, 468.
— or Feres, Count of, letter to, 493.
— Duke of, object of his army in Germany, 41.
Fernandino, Duke, 119, 128–130, 140.
Ferns, Bishop of, see French, Nich.
Fetherston, Sir Tim., see Featherstonhaugh.
Feuillade, M. de la, is wounded, 393.
Fouveradeel, R. de B. a F. G. de, United Provinces Commissioner for the treaty against Spain, 30.
Fez, King of, 24.
Ffolliott, Lord, recommended in place of Sir J. Nettersfield, 223.
Fielding, Basil, Earl of Denbigh, 366, 400, 459.
— bearer of a paper to the King, 254.
— is hurt, 418.
— the Admiralship intended for him, 461.
— George, Earl of Desmond, nephew to the Duke of Buckingham, 169.
— William, Lord, 77, 191.

Fielding, William, Lord, his cypher, 215.
—— letters from to Mr. Edw. Hyde, 70, 121.
Fiennes, Mr., his answer to the Scots declaration, mentioned, 410.
—— Col. John, letter to the Earl of Newcastle, 240.
—— John, letter to his brother Col. N. Fiennes, 242.
—— Col. N., Governor of Bristol, letters to, 239-242.
—— —— is joined to the Committee of Gloucestershire and Somersetshire, 242.
—— Nath., document signed by, 241.
—— —— the Independents enraged with, 458.
—— William, Viscount Say and Sele, 175, 176, 203, 214, 416, 418, 448.
—— —— documents signed by, 244, 451.
—— —— a son of his to be Governor of Gloucester, 388.
Finance, suggestions for providing Committees of, 245.
Finch, Sir John, succeeds Lord Keeper Coventry, 104.
—— speeches at the opening of Parliament, 107.
—— the new Speaker, speech on his admission to office, 501.
Finland, John, Duke of, son of the King of Sweden, 470, 486, 488.
—— commended by Queen Elizabeth, 471.
Fis, Mr. (or Fish), 122.
Fishbourne, Nicholas, petition for a share in a prize ship, 278.
Fisher, Mr., 41.
—— Tho., his signature, 441.
Fisheries, 166, 183.
—— question, the, 157, 159.
Fison, Capt., restoration of his ship, 63.
Fits-Gerald, Piers, letter to, 328.
Fitz-James, Mr., waits upon the Duke of York, 421.
Fitzwilliam, Lord, letter from to the Supreme Council at Kilkenny, 364.
—— Col., recommended by the King and Queen, 267.
Flanders, 153, 290, 347, 368, 375, 383.
—— troops sent to, 165, 166; their arrival in, 423.
—— proposition to place the coast under English protection, 171.

Flanders, defence of the coast, 201.
—— the Infant Cardinal in, 210.
—— application of the Parliament to, 284.
—— march of the French towards, 316.
—— armies in, 408.
—— Princess Regent of, letter to, 489.
—— Flemish money, English equivalent, 38.
Fleckeroe, or Fleckerye, a ship detained at, 460, 495.
Fleet, the, 317, 400, 446, 449, 465, 476.
—— the King's fleet at Dartmouth, 249.
—— surrender of Scilly to the Parliament fleet, 332.
—— the Prince's order and declaration concerning his engagement upon the fleet, 431, 432.
—— relations of its management under the Prince of Wales, 437, 438.
—— relation of the Prince's motions, councils, and actions in, 438.
—— the Earl of Warwick's first summons to the King's fleet, 430.
—— account of provisions for, 401.
—— debates on sending it to sea, 412.
—— news from the, 425, 426, 428.
—— letters dated from, 431, 432.
—— journal of the movements of the royal, 437.
—— measures taken for making provision for, 444.
—— memorandum relating to, 445; another, with list of captains' names, 458.
Fleetwood, Sir W., to treat with Col. Rainsborough, 314.
Fleetwood, ——, message to Parliament delivered by, 394.
Fleming, Sir Oliver, his cypher, 215.
—— Thomas, 494.
—— Sir W., 392.
—— —— on his instructions for Scotland, 431.
Fletcher, Anthony, letter from to Alderman Venn, 45.
Flint and Denbigh shires, list of persons continuing in arms in, 463.
Florence, letters dated from, 3.
—— Cosmo, Duke of, letters from Queen Elizabeth to him, 473 (bis), 474, 476, 483, 485, 487, 495.

INDEX.   545

Florence, Ferd. II., duke of, 119.
—— reported marriage of his sister, 167.
—— Grand duke of, summoned by the Pope to Rome, 231.
Fludd, Capt., letter from to the Lord High Admiral, 4.
Flügel, John, letter to the King, 213.
Flushing, 434.
—— the Duke of York at, 420, 421.
—— letters dated from, 431, 436.
Folliott, John, imprisoned on suspicion of being a priest, 61.
Fontainebleau, 326, 328, 394.
Fontaine-Françoise, in Burgundy, taken by the Duke of Lorraine, 125.
Fontarabia, see Fuentarabia.
Forbes, Alex., Bishop of Aberdeen, address of the presbytery to him, 19.
—— Alexander, Lord, his fleet ordered to be seized, 23d.
—— A., letter from to Col. N. Fiennes, 241.
Force, Marshal de la, his death, 66.
Forde, Mr., of Rotterdam, 415, 446, 458.
—— Sir Edward, is sent to the King, 381.
—— —— letters of intelligence from, 386, 387, 390, 391.
—— —— letters from to Lord Hopton, 388-393, 398, 411, 419.
Forde, or Forth, Robert, his signature, 362.
Forests, proposed sale of, for payment of the King's debts, 247.
Forster, Richard, his composition for recusancy reduced, 81.
Fortescue, George de, 104.
—— Col., troops under him, 272.
—— of Fendennis, repulses Sir H. Waller, 420.
Forth, Countess of, see Barnard, Clara.
Forth, Earl of, see Ruthven, Patrick.
Forth, or Forde, Rob., his signature, 321.
Foscarini, Daniel, letter on his behalf, 492.
Fountenay Mareüill, Mons. de, French ambassador extraordinary to Rome, 412.
Fowey, or Foy, 301.
—— the ship 'Young Tobias' brought into, 300; expenses of the master and mariners, and decision

of Cad. Jones allowing the same, 300.
Fowey, letters dated from, 249, 282, 301.
Foxall, John, sent to Lubeck in behalf of the London merchants, 494, 495.
Frackpitt, Richard, 81.
France, 225, 228, 242, 250, 272, 277, 279, 281, 287, 288, 290, 298, 301, 305, 306, 308, 310, 313, 314, 316, 317, 321, 326, 329, 340, 349, 353, 354, 357, 359, 362, 369, 372, 377, 379, 391, 429, 440, 448, 482, 491, 502. App. I. 4, 8.
—— misery in (1638), caused by the war, 152.
—— proposition that it should restore Lorraine, 160.
—— Irish regiments embark from, 224.
—— provisions ordered from, 310.
—— on the Prince's going into, 318, 319.
—— English clergy in, 341.
—— agent from, 374.
—— extracts from the register of the Council of State, 375.
—— is opposed to the peace between Spain and Holland, 377.
—— military movements in, 381.
—— movement for half-yearly parliaments in, 402.
—— Queen Elizabeth's opinion on the state of affairs in, 481.
—— motives of the war in, 497.
—— letter dated from, 392.
—— Mademoiselle of, offer of marriage from Archduke Leopold to, 422, 423.
—— Kings of, see Louis XIII and Louis XIV.
—— Queen Regent of, or 'the Queen-Mother,' see Anne of Austria.
—— Queen-Mother of (1586), see Catharine de Medicis.
France and Austria, their antagonism, 56; mediation offered between them, 105.
France and Bavaria, 189.
France and England, treaty with, 407.
France and Spain, rupture between, 81.
—— suspension of arms between (1638), 147.
—— strength of the former, 160.
—— peace between, 317.
—— treaty between, 380.

4 A

546   INDEX.

France and Spain, memorandum on the war between, 374.
—— and Sweden, league between, 142.
French, the, 338, 352.
—— French affairs in Naples, 418.
—— —— ambassadors, 357, 360.
—— —— ambassadors, letters to the magistrates of the Low Countries, 12, 13; at Venice, 120.
—— —— ambassador's speech at Frankfort [Ratisbon], 48.
—— —— ambassador, account of an audience with, 365.
—— —— ambassador, his propositions, April, 1618; 418.
—— —— Armada (1639), 179.
—— —— army, movements of, 380, 381.
—— —— capture of galleons by, 201.
—— —— Council, 377.
—— —— Court, 380, 393, 500. App. I. 4; at Amiens, 378.
—— —— defeated near St. Omer, 154.
—— —— defeat the Spaniards at Roseiglione, 229.
—— —— duties, 272.
—— —— enter Milan, ibid.
—— —— fleet, 376, 393, 402, 407.
—— —— in the Mediterranean, 106, 108, 110, 112, 119, 125.
—— —— frigate, 326.
—— —— General in Caen, 372.
—— —— Government, 423.
—— —— in Catalonia, 183.
—— —— march towards Flanders, 316.
—— —— linen, imported into Spain, 122.
—— —— merchants in London, 223.
—— —— ministers, App. I. 4.
—— —— not suffered to come to England, 178.
—— —— ports, edict on the rights of belligerents in, 243.
—— —— pretend a disinclination in King Charles I, 217.
—— —— Protestants, 341.
—— —— trade to Spain in English ships, 182.
Francis, John, *i.e.* Secretary Nicholas, q. v.
Francis de Lorraine, Duke of Guise, q. v.
Francis, Duke of Saxony, q. v.

'Francis,' the (ship), deposition touching its capture, 274; appraisement and schedule of the cargo, *ibid.*; additional valuation of, and other prizes, *ibid.*
Franciscans, the, in Peru, 133.
—— or Minims, 127.
Frankendale beleagured, 26, 74; Spanish commanders in, 26; Spanish governor of, 99, 123, 139.
—— governor of, *see* Burgh, Capt.
Frankfort on Maine, 138.
—— book printed at, 401.
—— letters dated from, 16, 74, 115, 119.
Franklin, Capt., 241.
Fraser, or Frayser, Dr., 324, 360, 431.
Frederic, Duke, resigns in favour of his nephew, James, 214.
Frederic II, Duke of *Brunswick*, q. v.
Frederic II, King of *Denmark*, q. v.
Frederic, Count or Prince *Palatine* of the Rhine, q. v.
Frederick William, Elector of *Brandenburgh*, q. v.
Freeman, Mr., 439.
—— Sir Ralph, Master of Requests, letter to, 87.
French, the, *see* France.
French, Nich., Bishop of Ferns, 330, 349.
—— his engagement on behalf of the Confederate Catholics, 331.
—— his signature, 332.
—— letters to him, 326, 327, 329, 330-332, 395, 464.
Freshford, letter dated from, 241.
Friesland, neutrality of broken, 153.
Friesland, East, ships wrecked on the coast of, 173.
—— Edgar, Count of, letter to, 499.
—— Oldenburgh, and Delmenhorst, Princess Anne of, letters to, 469, 472-474, 481, 483, 486, 487.
—— John, Count of, and Queen Elizabeth, articles of convention between, 487.
Fuentarabia, 156, 157, 160, 171.
Fuentes, Marquis de, commands naval forces in Flanders, 108.
Fulford House, 288, 290.
Fulham, 374.
—— letter dated from, 337.
Furness, 284.

INDEX.

G.

Gabier, Sir B., see Gerbier.
Gabor, Bethlem, takes up arms against the Emperor, 25, 111.
Gabrielli, Gabriel, a notary, attestation to his having made a copy of a document signed by Prince Charles, 411.
Gage, Mr., opposes English religious orders, 62.
—— George, English agent at Rome, 26, 163, 166, 182; letter from to James I., 27.
—— negotiates for an exchange of troops, 170.
—— letter from to Secretary Windebank, 168–170.
—— letters to, 25, 167, 177, 190.
—— Col. Henry, instructions for him, 167.
—— —— letters to, 181, 184, 190.
—— —— letter from to Mr. George Gage, 167, 177, 190, 198.
—— —— letter from to Sir Balthazar Gerbier, 197.
—— —— letters from to Secretary Windebank, 164, 167, 169, 171, 186–188, 190, 197; quarrel between him and Sir W. Tresham, 165.
—— Sir H., the forces in Wales under him, 236.
Galicia, King of, 221.
Gallas, Matthias, 139; movements of his troops, 65, 66, 104, 105, 118, 131, 133, 135, 137, 140, 143, 145, 153, 154, 156, 176.
—— superseded by Piccolomini, 184.
Gallawey, Sir James, 75.
Gallican liberties, 380.
Galway, agents for freeholders of, propositions tendered by them to the King, 80, 81.
—— letters dated from, 143, 395.
—— Warden of the College of, see Lynch, Dr. W.
Gant, see Ghent.
Gardiner, Col., 237.
—— John, letter of intelligence to, 387.
—— Sir T., 371.
Gardis, Dr. Ambrose de, 198.
Garnier, Chevalier, ordered to take vessels to Naples, 417.
Garter, constitutions of Hen. VIII., and orders concerning Garter King of Arms, 1.

Garter, Knight of the, 226.
—— Lesley accepts the promise of the, 316.
—— Order of the, delivered to the Duke of Wurtemberg, 500.
Gaston, William, and other merchants of Yarmouth, their ship the 'Luke,' 490.
Gartrie, warrant for calling out militia of the hundred of, 233.
Gascoyne, Sir Bernard, 308.
Gassion, Marshal de, or General, his victory and death, 392; mortally wounded, 393.
—— his death not much felt at Court, 394; amount of his estate, ibid.
Gaston, John Baptist, Duke of Anjou, afterwards Duke of Orleans, q. v.
Gateside, 204.
Gatford, Rev. —, chaplain at Jersey, 272, 368.
—— his discourses at Bury St. Edmunds, &c., on the places of Holy Scripture applied by the Rebels to their purpose, 416.
—— letter to, 316.
—— Lionel, B. D., chaplain to the garrison of Pendennis, 303.
Gatu, Father, 164.
Gazette Extraordinary (French), 125.
Gazetteer, the, 226.
Gebherd, Dr., commissioner appointed to treat with the Emperor on the restoration of the Prince Palatine, 100, 110.
Gerzeky, Capt., is desired to return to the royalists, 242.
Gekeine, —, movements of his troops, 133.
Gell, Sir T., 413.
General of the Galleys, see Richelieu, Duke of.
General, the, see Fairfax, Sir Thos.
Genep, 70, 71.
—— letters dated from, 71–73.
—— camp at, letter dated from, 71.
Genetti, Cardinal, letter to M. d'Avaux, 173.
Genoa, 106, 112.
Genoese, the, disavow the peace, 43.
George, William, letters patent for him, 490.
Geraldi, Vincent, 487.
Gerard, Father, 192.
—— Charles, Lord, 284, 285, 296.

Gerard, Gilbert, document signed by, 244.
Gerbier, Balthazar, afterwards Sir B., 134, 137, 149, 157, 160, 191, 193, 195, 196, 199-201.
—— declaration of a plot, 159.
—— misunderstanding between him and Count Leslie, 190, 192.
—— his cypher, 213.
—— letter from him to Secretary Windebank, 158, 159.
—— letters to, 160, 197.
Germains, St., see St. Germains.
German horse, supposed plot of bringing in an army of, 417.
—— Princes, list of thirteen, 10.
—— States, account of their contributions to the war, 152.
Germany, 422, 476, 477.
—— a review of the miserable state of (1635), 78.
—— review of the state of (1638), 151.
—— East, 493.
—— Emperors of, see Matthias, Maximilian II (1654), and Ferdinand I & II.
—— Lords Commissioners for the affairs of, letters to, 20, 23.
—— the Imperial Diet (1640), 200.
—— united, and desires peace, 157.
—— war supplies for, 483.
Gerrard, Aaron, 190.
—— Charles, 266.
Gerreard, William, and William Chester, their cases, 494.
Geta, news of the armies of, 140.
Ghent, letters dated from, 178, 192.
Ghost-houses, their establishment in every garrison, 245.
Gibbon, Major, his death, 442.
Gibbs, Alderman, 383.
—— W., letters from to Mr. Taylor, 176, 178, 180.
Gibraltar, 400.
—— English crews insulted at the port of, 483, 484.
Gibson, Col., 223.
'Gideon' of Lubeck, the (ship), M. Schomacher master of, 237; is taken by Sir J. Mucknell, ibid.; papers relating to the same, ibid.
Giffier, or Kiffier, Peter, appointed agent from the Hanse towns to Queen Elizabeth, 491.
Gifford, Col., 311.
—— Sir John, 126.
—— Richard, letter from to Mr. Lambey, 3.

Gilbert, John, and M. Swart, letter in the matter of, 494.
Gild, Mr., 10.
Gillespie, Mr., 460.
Gillingham Major, prebend of, see Spithurius, John.
Gillingham, Geo., his signature, 502.
Giustiniani, Georgio, letter from to the Lord High Admiral, 3.
Glamorgan, Earl of, see Somerset, Edward.
Glanville, Mr. Serjeant, speech on being presented to the King as Speaker, 197.
Glastonbury, letters dated from, 241, 263.
Glemham, or Glenham, Sir Thomas, 422, 435.
—— his movements till the surrender of York, 255.
—— letter to, 322.
Gloucester, 241, 303, 410, 414.
—— Bishop of, see Goodman, G.
—— Dean of, see Mas, John.
—— Duke of, see Henry.
—— a son of Lord Say to be Governor of, 388.
—— Governor of, for the Parliament, see Massie, Col. Edw.
—— letter dated from, 239.
Gloucester Hall, Oxford, see Oxford.
Gloucestershire, 214.
—— letter to the Deputy-Lieutenants of, 241.
—— opposition in, 333.
Glover, Samuel, in Holland, 244.
—— Thomas, 492.
Glyn, or Glynn, J., M.P., his impeachment, 389, 391.
—— his signature to the Commissioners' reply to the King, 452.
Gnapheus, William, agent of Princess Anne of East Friesland, 481.
Godgaffe, J., merchant, permitted to export beer, 474.
Godolphin, Sir Francis, 372, 362, 367, 466.
—— Governor of the Island of Scilly, warrant to, 273.
—— on board Captain Amy's ship, 317.
—— letters from to Sir E. Hyde, 290, 317, 321, 322, 324.
—— Lady, 352.
—— Sydney, bequest to Mr. Hobbs, 354.
Goffe, Dr., i.e. Stephen Gough, q. v.
Gold and silver thread smuggled, 36.

INDEX.

Goldnister, Nich., or *Goldenstein*, q.v.
Goldsmiths' Hall committee, proceeding of, 369.
Gonzaga, Marquis de, 106.
Good, Sir Thos., his sister, 311.
Goodeare, William, ale-house keeper, 3.
Goodman, Godfrey, Bishop of Gloucester, 158.
Goodwin, Mr., 430.
—— attacks the established religion, 271.
Gordon, Francis, letter from to Lord Falkland, 224.
—— Sir Robert, App. II. 14, 15.
—— messenger from the King to Queen Henrietta (when Princess), *ibid.*
—— his claim to a clerkship in the Common Pleas, 71.
Gore, Gerard, 494.
Gorée, royal fleet in, 428.
—— the Earl of Warwick's excuses for leaving, 460.
Gorge, Ferdinand, letter from to the Lords of the Privy Council, 2.
Goring, George, Lord, afterwards Earl of Norwich (created Nov. 8, 1644), 122, 248, 259, 250, 268, 270, 273, 276, 281, 284, 287, 288, 291, 298, 299, 306, 324, 396, 402, 428, 448, 461.
—— army of, 263.
—— charge made against him, 39.
—— orders on levying contributions in the West, 260.
—— letter from to the Earl of Berkshire, 264.
—— powers granted to, 267.
—— interview with Sir J. Berkeley, 279.
—— resolutions touching his complaint against Sir J. Smith and Sir R. Grenville, 280.
—— and the Commissioners of Devon, articles of agreement between, 280.
—— his demands concerning his movements in the field, *ibid.*
—— his commission as Lieutenant-General, *ibid.*
—— order to, 298.
—— officers of his army at Holdsworthy, 300.
—— complaints against him for misapplying contributions, 301.
—— crosses with troops from Greenwich into Essex, 426.

Goring, George, Lord, his training in the Spanish army, 436.
—— prisoner in Windsor Castle, 437.
—— sent by the King to Queen Henrietta (when Princess), App. II. 10, 11, 13, 14.
—— letter from to Lord Cottington, 136.
—— letters from to Lord Culpeper, 260-263, 265, 267-271, 279-283.
—— —— to Sir E. Hyde, 272, 281, 284.
—— —— to the Prince of Wales, 259, 281, 283.
—— —— to the Lords of the Prince's Council, 271, 281.
—— —— to the Queen, 247.
—— —— to Lord Digby, 271.
—— —— to Sir James Smith, 280.
—— letters to, 259, 264-369, 271, 272, 274, 281, 283, 300, 367, 436.
Goringe, William, ale-house keeper, warrant for him to appear before the Lord High Admiral, 3.
Gormanstown, Lord, letter from to the Earl of Ormond, 234.
Gottenburg, in Sweden, Scotch officers to leave there for Scotland, 207.
Gough, or Goffe, Dr. Stephen, 436, 449.
—— differs in opinion with Hyde in the matter of the Duke of Lorraine's levies, 448.
—— letters from to Mr. Aylesbury, 428, 429.
—— paper delivered by him to the company at Rotterdam, 435.
—— supervisor to Sir W. Boswell, 429.
Gould, John, appointed to serve on the Council at Kilkenny, 348.
—— W., letter from to Col. N. Fiennes, 241.
Gourdon, Sir, *see* Gordon, Sir R.
Gower, Major E., an officer in Scarborough Castle, 459.
——, M.P., under restraint, 460.
Græme, Sir John, his suit, 8, 9.
Graham, James, Marquis of Montrose, 204, 248, 278, 282, 284, 290, 296, 297, 311, 312, 320, 321, 328, 336, 357, 417, 459.
—— defeats Argyle, 442.
—— his successes and victories, 276-278, 308.
—— to attend the Prince in Holland, 417.

Graham, James, Marquis of Montrose, to be Lieut.-Gen. to the Duke of Lorraine, 120.
—— letter from to Sir E. Hyde, 406.
—— —— to the Prince of Wales, ibid.
—— letters to, 313, 408, 409.
—— letter to, mentioned, 312.
Grammont, Mons., 114.
—— Marshal de, at Lyons, 369.
Grand Assembly, answer to the King's propositions for a Custom House, 259.
—— address to the King concerning the ships, ibid.
Grandees, six made by the King of Spain, 192.
Grandison, Lord Deputy, letter from to Mr. Aylesbury, 20.
—— letter to Edw. Hyde, 228.
Grain, Marquis de, 167.
Grant, Mr., 303, 391.
—— Wintour or Winter, 320.
—— goes to Ireland, 336.
—— Mr., has instructions from the Queen to the Lord Lieutenant, 361.
Grants, eleven papers of, entitled Docquetts, 227.
Gravesend, 385.
Gray, Col., 222.
—— commands in Berwick, 424.
—— Mr., an officer of the High Commission Court, 200.
—— or Greye, Giles, letters in behalf of, 492, 498.
Gray of Warke, Lord, see Grey of Warke, Will., Lord.
—— the (barque), of London, 487.
Greaves, Col., complaints from, 378.
—— defeated at Deptford, 385.
Grave, Richard, 106.
Greene, —, chairman for the navy, 370.
—— M.P., under restraint, 460.
Greenecastle, 362.
Greenwich, permission for the King to come to, 380.
—— troops under the Earl of Norwich leave, 426.
—— letters dated from, 34, 35, 44, 469, 470, 473, 476-480, 487, 490, 491, 497-499.
Gregorio, Signor, see Con.
Grenoble, Bishop of, 56.
Grenville, Henry, warrant to, 289.
—— Sir John, 465, 466.

Grenville, Sir Richard, 223, 261-263, 265, 267-271, 279, 280, 281, 284, 290, 295, 300.
—— Lord Goring's complaint against, 280; his conduct is severely reproved, ibid.
—— is appointed to advance with the Cornish forces, 283.
—— an order to take charge of him, 299; another order to send him to Sicilly, 301.
—— troops under him, 272.
—— a defence of his conduct (1644-47), 306.
—— his imprisonment, 347.
—— his declaration criticised by Sir E. Hyde, 404.
—— letter from to Lord Culpeper, 267.
—— —— to Lord Hopton, 271.
—— letters from to Sir Thomas Fairfax, 285, 287.
—— —— to Secr. Fanshawe, 269, 298.
—— —— to Lord Goring, 261.
—— —— to the Prince of Wales, 277, 284, 286, 295, 297, 299.
—— —— to the Lords of the Prince's Council, 270, 298.
—— letters to, 286, 287, 298.
Greville, Sir Fulke, letter from to the Lord High Admiral, 15.
—— Francis, Lord Brook, 175, 176, 203, 214.
—— Robert, Baron Brooke, commissioner of the league against the King of Spain, 30.
Grey, —, evidence of his complicity in the plunder of a house, 218.
Grey of Warke, or Werke, William, Lord, some moneys of his seized, 417.
—— document signed by, 254.
Grey, Lord, takes the Duke of Hamilton at Uttoxeter, 110.
Grey of Ruthyn, Lord Henry, Parliamentary commissioner, warrant from (July 18, 1642), 233.
Grey, Henry, Earl of Stamford, letter from to the King, 241.
—— soldiers billeted on him, 411.
Greye, Giles, complains of injuries received at Dantzic, 498.
Grievances, speeches in the debate upon, 202.
Griffin, Capt., 121.
Griffith, Dr., imprisonment of, 406.

INDEX.   551

Griffith, —, murder committed by, 412.
Grignon, —, 339.
Grimaldi, Cardinal, movements of, 366.
Grimesditch, Mr., 186.
Grimston, Sir Harbottle, a speech of, mentioned, 378.
—— his signature, 451.
Grison ambassadors, 143.
Grisons and Spaniards, proposed treaty between, 144, 147, 150.
Grissel, or Grisvald, Edmund, letter of, 131.
Grievald, or Grissel, q. v.
Grilton, —, messenger of the Court of Wards, 97.
Grosbois, letter dated from, 320.
Grosse, Christopher, 332.
Grotius, Hugo, his Comment, 355.
—— quotation from his book 'De Jure Belli et Pacis,' 356.
Grove, Thomas, owner of a ship, 480.
Groyne, ships and fleet in the, 27, 71, 99, 102, 124, 136, 147, 179, 183, 202.
Guebriant, Count, 232.
—— Mdlle. de, her death, 367.
Guernsey, see Peter Port.
—— Isle of, 287, 335, 343, 373, 395, 448, 463.
—— intended reduction of, 314.
—— Castle, 318, 358, 385.
—— Castle Cornet, 327, 358.
—— —— account of moneys towards the relief of, 352; balance sheet, ibid.
—— letters dated from, 327, 358, 370.
—— proposed as the rendezvous of the ships, 434.
—— conferences between Carteret and Wake for the reduction of, 430.
—— militia of, 449.
—— minutes on the employment of the Duke of Lorraine's men in taking, 449.
Guets, —, movements of his forces, 153, 154, 156.
Guienne, 291.
Guipuscoa, 173.
Guise, Henry II, Duke of, returns from Rome (1647), 370.
—— his expedition, 402.
—— his movements in Italy, 407.

Guise, Henry II, Duke of, invited to be King of Naples (?), 400.
—— Francis de Lorraine, Duke of, (1562), 481.
Guldenstein, or Goldnister, Nich., chancellor and envoy of the King of Sweden, (1561), 470, 479.
—— letters on his holding moneys of London merchants, 490.
—— agent of the King of Sweden, 485, 486.
Gustavus Adolphus, King of Sweden, treaties with the Duke of Buckingham, 29; with Louis XIII, 36; with Charles I, 37.
Guzman, Don Gaspar de, Condé Duke of San Lucar, see Olivares.
Gythrenberg, 109.

H.

H., Col., 439.
H., Lord, i. e. Lord Holland (?), q. v.
H., R., i. e. R. Hollins, q. v.
H., R., i. e. Rd. Hakluyt, q. v.
Hackney, letter dated from, 20.
Haddenden, or Hoddesdon, Christopher, 491.
Haerdonck, John van, articles of agreement with the King, 245; with the Lords, ibid.
—— bond for 14,000l. to, ibid.
—— warrant from Charles I to, 249.
—— removal of his prisoners to Truro, 266.
—— notes concerning persons employed by, 270.
—— letter from to Sir E. Hyde, ibid.
—— list of ships under his command, ibid.
—— Scotch mariners taken prisoners by, 278.
—— list of prizes taken by, 279.
—— his account of the prizes, ibid.
Haffnia, letter dated from, 40.
Hague, the, 324, 343, 361, 438, 465, 466.
—— residents at, 244, 437, 447.
—— the Prince of Wales and his Council at, 444.
—— letters dated from, 12, 13, 18, 31, 94, 119, 142, 241, 340, 369, 390, 409, 410, 412, 418, 420, 428, 429, 432, 437–139, 444, 445, 448, 449, 465, 466.

INDEX.

Haines Hill, letters dated from, 107, 109, 112, 137, 138.
Hakeney (?), great statesman of, 217.
Hakluyt, Rd., letter from to Sir Walter Raleigh, 500.
—— dedicates his "History of the Eight Decads of Peter Martyr" to Sir Walter Raleigh, *ibid*.
Hales, ——, Kentish men under, 425.
Hall, Richard, letter from to the Lord High Admiral, 4.
—— William, sticker to the robes of the Duke of York, 115.
—— Mr., imprisoned for intending to preach, 406.
Hallinge, two letters dated from, 3.
Hamherall, Lord, his bill, 3.
Hambleton, Sir George, order to remove him from his command, 221.
Hamburg, 232, 476, 477.
—— magistrates of, letter from, 10.
—— company, paper on the affairs of a, 140.
—— ship, sold by warrant of the Prince, 353.
—— ships of, 300, 302, 304, 306, 359, 410, 473.
—— letters to the Council and Senators of, 477, 482, 493.
—— the King's resident at, *see* Averis, J.
—— residents at, 485.
—— letter dated from, 232.
Hamer, Mr., instructions to, for the redemption of a ship, 284.
—— Col., 441.
Hamilton, Duke of, *see* Hamilton, James.
—— Anne. Marchioness of, her death, 390.
—— Elizabeth, Countess of Lanerick, (afterwards Duchess of Hamilton), bears a son, 405.
—— Sir Geo., Ormond's instructions to, 368.
—— James, second Earl of Abercorn, 160.
—— —— letter from to the Earl of Lauderdale, 461.
—— James, Marquis of, 171.
—— —— his gallant service at sea, 178.
—— —— to treat with the Spanish ambassadors, 196.
—— —— his troops to be disbanded, 202.
—— —— commissioner for the treaty with the United Provinces, 29.

Hamilton, James, third Marquis and first Duke of, 273, 308, 310, 330, 343, 350, 356, 357, 378, 391, 404, 419, 434, 435, 439, 440.
—— proposal to take him to Jersey or Scilly, 315.
—— his release, 313.
—— his brother-in-law to command the Scotch army, 424.
—— letter to, 431.
—— relation of his engagement, 432.
—— and Argyle's faction, 409, 432.
—— refused to impeach the King, 450.
Hamilton, Sir William, 121, 158.
—— his mission to Rome, 97, 112.
—— letter from to Secretary Windebank, 117.
—— his cypher, 215.
Hamilton, William, Earl of Lanerick, or Lanark, (afterwards second Duke of Hamilton), 350, 391, 394, 403, 433, 435, 461.
—— the King's answer to the Scots' petition, signed, 205.
—— letters to, 207, 431.
—— the King sends to, 389.
—— his signature, 396.
—— agreement at Carisbrook confirmed by, 405.
—— his attachment to the Prince, 459.
—— servant of, 467.
Hamlyn, F. Bartholomew, letter from to the Bishop of Ferns, 327.
—— Capt. William, recommended for a majority, 271.
Hammond, Col. Robert, 384, 401, 403, 416.
—— letter from to J. Arundell, Governor of Pendennis, 312.
—— letter to, *ibid*.
—— to succeed the Earl of Pembroke in the Isle of Wight, 388.
—— is made Governor of the Isle of Wight, 392.
—— an arrangement for the King to fall into his hands, 402.
—— is to secure the King in Carisbrook Castle, 402.
—— removes from the King his friends and servants about him, *ibid*.
Hammond, Mr., treasurer of the Parliamentary fleet, payment to, 441.
—— Dr., with the King, 382, 383.

INDEX.

Hammond, Dr., proposals of his chaplain, 422.
Hamon, Col., see L'Estrange, Sir Hamon.
Hampden, John, 203, 403.
—— *versus* Attorney-General, case of, 146.
Hampshire, 421.
—— letter from the Assize of, to Parliament, 410.
Hampton, residents at, 324.
Hampton Court, 392, 397.
—— propositions of the Parliament presented to the King at, 388.
—— address to the King at, 396.
—— the King at, 388.
—— on the King's removal from, 398, 401, 403.
—— letters dated from, 1, 13, 14, 17, 24, 30, 52, 73, 116, 121, 158, 389, 481, 495, 496.
Hanaper, charges of, 243.
Henau, 138, 139.
Hankey, John and William, owners of a vessel detained at Dantzic, 402.
Hankinn, J., letter from to the Lord High Admiral, 2.
Hannibal, mould of a marble head of, 164, 200, 201.
Hans, Mr., 413.
Hanseatic League, or Hanse Towns, letter to the cities and magistrates of the, 470, 471, 477, 482, 491, 494.
Hanse Towns, letter from the Senate of, 40.
Harborough, Leicestershire, 266.
Harcourt, Count d', 247, 369, 375, 383.
—— returns to Barcelona, 357.
—— his movements, 370, 374.
—— is ordered to retire to Paigny, 367.
—— Mons. d', the business delivered to him at Oxford, concerning the dispute between the King and Parliament, 247.
—— Sir Simon, letter from to Sir E. Hyde, 217.
—— the King's wish to confer upon Sir S. Harcourt's widow and children lands in Ireland, 228.
Harding, Mr., 411.
—— Rich., 359, 372.
—— letters to, 349, 375.
Harding's memorials of Prince Rupert's marches, mentioned, 419.

Hardinge, Mr., letter from to Edw. Hyde, 226.
Hardress, Sir R., 424.
Hardwick, Joachim, his account of expenses for the ship 'Young Tobias,' 303; allowance to him, as skipper of the same, 304.
—— skipper of the 'Young Tobias' of Hamburg, order for allowance to be made to, 302; certificate for the allowance, 304.
Harfleet, Thomas, abstract of victuals received from him for the Prince's fleet, 463; an account of the same, *ibid.*
Harley, Sir R., and his son, M. P's., 460.
Harrington, Sir James, 398.
—— worsted by the King in an argument, 368.
Harriott, Mr., letter to, 3.
Harris, Robert, 323.
—— letter from to Sir N. Crisp, 271.
Harrison, Mr., 313, 370.
—— Anthony, of Penryn, 292.
Hart, Capt., the Duke of York on board his vessel, 421.
—— Dr., 410.
Hartegan, F., proposition of, 278.
Hartleton Lodge in Richmond Park, grant of the keepership to H. Rogers, 227.
Hartsfield, ——, 164.
—— refuses to deliver Prince Rupert to the Bavarians, 160.
Harvey, Col., 374.
—— Sir Francis, letters to, 33.
—— Dr. William, 114, 116.
—— —— letter from to Sir E. Hyde, 295.
Haselrig, Mr., 364.
—— Sir Arthur, Parliamentary Commissioner, warrant from, 233.
Haselworth Castle, 29.
Hastings, the French troops directed to land there, 301.
—— Henry, Lord Loughborough, a prisoner in Windsor Castle, 137.
—— Sir Edward, 1.
Hatfield, the King at, 381.
—— letters dated from, 383, 384.
Hatton, Christopher, Lord, 353, 358, 359, 366, 382.
—— cypher of, 215.
—— his behaviour to Secretary Nicholas, 348.
—— and Lady Hatton, 427.
—— letter from to Sir E. Hyde, 447.

554 INDEX.

Hatton, Christopher, Lord, letter to, 368.
Havre, 290, 306, 308.
Havre de Grace, 503.
—— letters dated from, 281, 284, 314, 315.
Hawes, James, 498.
Hawkins, John, his ship detained at Fleckeroe, 495.
—— Sir R., letter from to Sir T. Crompton, 3.
Hawley, Lord, 284, 285.
Hawtree, Thomas, 499.
Hay, James, Lord Doncaster, letter from, 16.
—— James, Lord Carlisle, letters from to Charles I. as Prince of Wales and as King, App. I. 3–8.
—— letters from the Prince to, App. I. 3.
—— letter from to the Duke of Buckingham, App. I. 6.
—— a commissioner for the treaty against Spain, 30.
—— bill of sale by him, 32.
—— App. II. 16.
Haynes, Charles, letter from to Col. Fiennes, 242.
Haywood, Dr., with the King, 103.
—— William, letter to, 67.
Hearle, William, see Herle.
Heath, Mr., 441.
—— Thomas, storekeeper at Newcastle, instructions for, 158.
Heede, Johan Van, warrant of the States-General subscribed with his name, 414.
Heidelberg, capture of, 21, 26, 96.
Heigen, Caspar, secretary of the Hanseatic Society in Bergen, 40.
Heilbronn, confederation of, 75.
Helffenstein, George, Count of, 473.
—— ambassador from the Emperor to Queen Elizabeth, 468, 471.
Helford, letter dated from, 4.
Helston, execution at, 277.
Helvoetsluys, 441, 449.
—— the fleet at, 437.
—— account of provisions for the fleet at, 463.
—— letters dated from, 437, 444.
Hemaw, letter dated from, 116.
Hemet, William, 485.
Henderson, A., letters from to the King, 320, 321.
—— letters to, 319, 320, 322, 323.
—— Sir John, 357.
—— —— his employment on the King of Denmark's mission to the Parliament, 286.
Henley-on-Thames, barbarous punishment of a woman at, 330.
Henrietta, Princess of Lorraine, q. v.
Henrietta Maria, Queen, 205, 207, 208, 267, 272, 275, 279, 284, 288, 290, 291, 294, 299, 301, 304, 309–311, 316, 318, 320, 325, 327, 328, 334–336, 338, 346, 349, 356–359, 362, 364, 368, 377, 379, 381, 387, 391, 395, 400, 416, 417, 424, 426, 433, 442, 448, 466, 467, App. I. 3.
—— as Princess of France, her picture, App. I. 3.
—— her beauties, ibid.
—— the Infant Don Carlos proposed for her, ibid.
—— Lord Kensington's interview with, App. I. 4.
—— of her exquisite singing, ibid.
—— a present recommended to be sent to, ibid.
—— preparations recommended for her reception in England, App. I. 5.
—— sends her colours to the Prince of Wales (Charles I), App. I. 6.
—— letters on her marriage with Charles I, App. I. 7; leaves Paris for England, App. I. 7, 8.
—— letters from to the King before their marriage (in French), App. II. 10–16.
—— letters from the King to, App. II. 9–15.
—— Queen of Charles I, extract from her Charter of Liberties, 35; with child, 47.
—— her accouchement (1637), 126
—— petition to, 175.
—— design to seize her on her return from Holland, 257.
—— account of the surrender of Scarborough to, 238.
—— expenses in conveying her to France in the ship 'St. George,' 250.
—— goes to Ireland, 253; her opinion of Ormond, Inchiquin, and Clanricarde, 253.
—— grant of tin made to, 273–275: her pension, 275.
—— her jewels pawned in Holland, ibid.
—— hastens the Prince's coming to Paris, 314.
—— answer to Nicholas' letter, mentioned, 276.

INDEX. 555

Henrietta Maria, Queen, her opinion on referring Church questions to Parliament, 276.
—— Hyde and Capell with, 312.
—— the King of France's allowance to, 331.
—— at St. Germains, 336.
—— makes a marriage between two of her French servants, 365.
—— order to transport them to the Low Countries, 373.
—— reconciles Prince Rupert and Lord Digby, 392.
—— on her tampering with Papists, 417.
—— and Prince at Paris, names of the Lords summoned to wait on, 425.
—— her movements, 427.
—— (as Princess), articles of agreement for her marriage with the Prince of Wales, 501.
—— birth of her daughter, Princess Anne, 502.
—— her confessor, *see* Philip, Father.
—— letters from to the Prince of Wales, 317, 321.
—— —— to Lord Culpeper, 317.
—— —— to Sir E. Hyde, 310.
—— —— to the King, 336, 343, 344, 346, 348.
—— letters to, 247, 303, 310, 320, 323, 337, 341, 345, 350, 351, 362, 419, 427, 438.
—— letter to, mentioned, 203.
'Henrietta Maria,' the (ship), letter dated from, 70.
Henriette, Princess, of Lorraine, q. v.
Henry II, King, 332.
Henry VIII, 479, 485.
—— his Reformation imperfect, 320.
—— a servant of, 478.
—— physician to, *see* Augustine, J.
Henry, Duke of Gloucester, homage to, 318.
Henry, Duke of Brunswick, q. v.
Henry II, Prince of Condé, q. v.
Henry II, Duke of Guise, q. v.
Henry, Frederick, Prince of Orange, q. v.
Henshaw, or Hinshaw, Dr. Jo., 347.
—— letter of, mentioned, 360.
—— letter from to W. Edgeman, 395.
Hepburn, James, Earl of Bothwell, Queen Elizabeth begs of the King of Denmark that Bothwell be given up, 197.
Herbert, Sir Edw., Attorney-General,

warrant from the King to, 243, 318.
Herbert, Edward, Lord, propositions touching Lord Beyninge's estate, 51.
—— a wife recommended for him, 99.
—— wishes to join his father at York, 206.
—— letters from to Hyde, 233–235.
—— recommended by the King, 254.
Herbert, Philip, Earl of Montgomery, bearer of a letter from Princess (afterwards Queen) Henrietta to the King, App. II. 16.
—— twenty-third Earl of Pembroke, letter to, 99.
—— Lord Chamberlain, 182, 224, 357, 367, 374, 380, 388, 459.
—— letter from to Hyde, 231.
—— his professions of good-will to the King, 234, 235.
—— epitaph on, 373.
—— declaration presented to the King by, 224.
—— speech of, 388.
—— his impeachment deferred, *ibid.*
—— his signature, 451.
—— constable of Windsor Castle, 460.
Herbert, William, Earl of Pembroke, commissioner for the alliance with the United Provinces, 29, 30.
Hereford, 305, 440.
—— letters dated from, 268, 269, 277, 322.
—— Bishop of, *see* Coke, George.
—— Dean of, *see* Richardson, John.
Herefordshire, 214.
Herle, Mr., his sermon at Edinburgh, 414.
—— William, his credentials to some German Princes, 477.
—— letters commending him to the Counts of Oldenburg and Council of Hamburgh, 482.
Herring fisheries, 156, 187.
Hertford, Earl of (1562), *see* Seymour, Edward.
—— Marquis of, *see* Seymour, William.
Hertfordshire petition to Parliament, 389.
Hervey, J., 291.
Hesdin, defeat of the Spanish garrison, 125.
Hesse Cassel and Darmstadt, mediation between, 419.
Hesse, Amalia Elizabeth, Landgravine of, 120.
—— letter from to Charles I, 219.

Hesse, Philip, Landgrave of, letters from Queen Elizabeth to, 469, 474 (bis), 479, 480, 482, 490.
—— William, Landgrave of, letter to, 479.
—— his proposed marriage with the sister of Brandenbourg, 394; and the Landgrave's sister with the Prince of Talmont, ibid.
—— William V, Landgrave of, his proscription delayed, 108.
Heston, Sir F. Willoughby at, 340.
Hewes, Capt., 14.
Hezekiah, King. 218.
Hibernus, C. M., alias P. Cornelius de Scto. Patritio. v. Mahony, C.
Hickman, Anthony, a merchant of London, 476.
Hides, Mr., 430.
High Commission, power of, 211.
—— Commission Court, sentence against Lady Purbeck in, 218.
—— Court of Justice for trial of the King, see Charles I.
High Treason, 350.
Highlands, 312.
Hilarion, Père, 125.
Hillbishops, letter dated from, 267.
Hill, Mr., 394.
Hilton, John, husband and father of recusants, 61.
'Iliad,' the (frigate), 446.
Hinshaw, Dr., see Henshaw.
Hinton, William, 306, 325, 342, 394, 397.
—— bearer of a letter to the King, 389.
Hispaniola, 367.
Hitchcock, Mr., 332, 335.
—— letter from to Sir E. Hyde, 280.
—— Master, a merchant, employed by the Queen, 288.
—— Lord Jermyn to repay him, 319.
Hobbs, or Hobbes, Mr., reads with the Prince, 353.
—— legacy to, 354, 362.
Hoboke, la maison de, à Anvers, 443.
Hoddesdon, Christopher, see Haddesdon.
Hodge, Walter, of St. Neots, 268.
Hodges, ——, 242.
Hodgson, Rich., a merchant of Newcastle, 173.
Hodson, Dr., Prebendary of York, letters from to Sir E. Hyde, 215, 217.

Hodson, Christopher, 493, see also Haddesdon.
Hogg, John, a Scotchman at Westpond island, 178.
Hokroft, Mr., 12.
Holden, Dr., 163, 367.
Holdenby, or Holmby, in Northamptonshire, 401.
—— commissioners at, 379, 398.
—— letters dated from, 305, 373, 377.
—— news from, 378.
—— the King at, 355, 358, 360, 361.
—— on the King's seizure at, 381; account by the commissioners of what passed concerning their taking him thence, 382.
Holdsworthy, or Holsworthy, act of the Council of War held at, 300.
Holland, 210, 224, 257, 273, 285, 290, 296, 338, 342, 347, 363, 367, 370, 410, 414, 429, 465, 467.
—— fishermen, licences granted to, 134, 141, 146.
—— H. Peters sent there to borrow money, 244.
—— considerations concerning, 293.
—— Dutchman's bill for sailing tackle, 307.
—— Dutch bills of expenses, 308.
—— letters on the Prince's resolution to go into, 426, 427.
—— ambassadors of try to stop the trial of the King, 466.
—— treaty of alliance against, 500.
Holland and England, rumoured rupture between, 176.
Holland and Spain, the treaty between, in suspense, 366, 364, 374.
Holland, the Hollanders, 127, 129.
—— defeated near Antwerp, 154.
—— their herring fishery, 156.
—— proposed seizure of their settlements, 188.
Holland, Frederick Henry, King of, 362.
Holland Fen, Lincolnshire, 184.
Holland, Earl of, see Rich, Henry.
——, a Presbyterian, 439.
—— C., 401.
—— Sir John, 388.
Holles, Denzell, see Hollis.
——, Dowager Countess of Clare, 154.
Hollins, R., letter from to Mr. Denman, 426.
Hollis, Denzell, 226, 370, 391, 396, 396, 399, 404.

Hollis, Denzell, a disputed settlement with a view to his marriage, 154.
—— his son at Cherbourg, 408.
—— a commissioner in the Isle of Wight treaty, his signature, 451.
—— and —— Ireton, report of a duel between, 373.
Holmby, see Holdenby.
Holstein, 232.
—— and Denmark, 153, 155.
—— Adolphus, Duke of, letters to him, 468, 470, 471, 477, 483.
Holy Islands, the, 159.
Holybead, Col. Robinson's house near, Lord Byron retires to it, 440.
Holyrood, letters dated from, 4, 32.
Home, Andrew, called the prince of cosmographers. 500.
—— George, see Hume.
Homicide, case of, in St. James' Park, 247.
Honiton, march to, 261.
Hood, Dr., Rector of Lincoln Coll., 255.
Hooker, Col., his impeachment, 391.
Hooper, Sir T., 316.
—— arrives at Jersey from Pendennis, *ibid.*
Hopkins, John, i. e. W. Hyde, q. v.
Hopper, Richard, bill of sale to, 32.
Hopton, Sir Arthur, 148, 149, 151, 163.
—— paper on the East India business delivered to the King of Spain, 67.
—— instructions to on his embassy to Spain, 152.
—— report of his conversations with F. Semple and the Condé Duke, 168.
—— instructions to him, 171.
—— paper delivered by him to the King of Spain, 189.
—— memorial to the King of Spain, in behalf of Prince Rupert, 202.
—— his cypher, 215.
—— letters from to Secretary Coke, 44, 47, 64, 171.
—— —— to Lord Cottington, 51, 55, 59, 61, 63–69, 72, 74–76, 79, 83, 84, 90, 97, 161, 166, 168, 171–175, 179, 186, 189, 196.
—— —— to the Condé Duke d'Olivares, 43.
—— —— to Lord Falkland, 225.
—— —— to Secretary Windebank, 42, 46–48, 50–56, 58–61, 63–70, 72, 74, 76, 79, 81, 83, 87, 90, 91, 92, 94, 153–157, 161, 165, 166,
168, 170–172, 174–176, 178, 179, 181–183, 187–190, 192–196, 198, 199, 201.
Hopton, Sir Arthur, letters to, 41, 42, 45, 51, 59, 60, 69, 78, 91, 94, 130, 159, 162, 163, 165, 170, 174, 176, 178, 180–182, 185–187, 190, 194–196, 198–201.
Hopton, Sir Ralph, afterwards Lord, 260, 263–265, 271, 281, 285, 290, 294, 298, 300, 303, 309, 315, 316, 324, 335, 342, 343, 354, 361–363, 370, 373, 385, 392, 399, 415, 432.
—— his army. 245.
—— account of affairs in the West, 246; continued, to the taking of Bristol, *ibid.*
—— relation of the battle of Alresford, 246.
—— as Master of Ordnance, 248.
—— Prince of Wales' warrant to, as Master General of the Ordnance, 266.
—— instructions for him concerning the Western forts, 278.
—— warrant for payment to, 280.
—— the death of his wife, 306.
—— articles of association between him and others, for the defence of Jersey, 338.
—— with his uncle in Rouen, 363, 367.
—— is sent into Wales, 421.
—— letters endorsed with his name, treating of the exchange of prisoners, 247.
—— letter from to Lord Cottington, 202.
—— letters from to Secretary Windebank, 202–204, 209.
—— —— to the Queen, 323.
—— —— to the King, 324.
—— —— to the Lords of the Prince's Council, 444, 446.
—— letter of intelligence from, 421.
—— letters and pamphlets of, mentioned, 394.
—— letter of news to, 385.
—— letters to, 204, 207, 208, 266, 271, 281, 287, 301, 303, 306, 373, 374, 379, 384, 388–393, 398, 404, 411, 419, 420, 436.
Hopton-heath, near Stafford, account of the battle of, 249.
Horoscope of Charles II. 33.
Hornserdyck, letter dated from, 421.

Horton, Col., Tenby blockaded by, 425.
—— defeats Ll. Lingen, 440.
Hostman, Giles, 472.
Hotham, Sir John, 218.
—— affidavits of two persons concerning him and the train-bands at Hull, 232.
—— memorials touching him and his son, and their execution, 255.
—— account of transactions with, wanted by Sir E. Hyde, 362.
Hounslow Heath, 400.
Howard, Mr., letters from to Sec. Windebank, 95, 100, 102, 103, 106, 107, 111, 112, 114, 116, 118.
Howard of Effingham, Charles, Lord, letter from to Lord Burghley, 2.
—— Charles, tenth Earl of Nottingham, letters to, 2, 4, 10, 19.
—— —— warrant of, 3; license from to Mr. Spruce, 8.
—— —— letters from to the Lords of the Council, 13, 14; to the Lord High Admiral, 17; to Mr. Aylesbury, 19.
—— —— George, and two servants, to attend the Duke of York, 445.
—— Henry Frederick, Earl of Arundel, 365, 419.
—— James, Earl of Suffolk, is impeached, 388, 390.
—— Thomas, Lord Maltravers (afterwards Earl of Norfolk), 97, 363.
—— —— letter to, 115.
—— Thomas, Earl of Arundel and Surrey, Earl Marshal, 92, 98, 105, 112, 118, 119, 121, 123, 172, 270.
—— —— a letter on his behalf, 402.
—— —— letters from to Secretary Windebank, 94-97, 99-102, 104, 106-111, 113-117.
—— —— letter from to Sec. Windebank, 502.
—— —— letters to, 185.
—— Thomas, Lord Andover (afterwards Earl of Berkshire), 209, 255, 256, 270, 341.
—— —— at the Hague, 324.
—— —— letter to, 254.
—— —— letter from to Lord Digby, ibid.
—— —— to Lord Goring, 278.
—— —— to Hyde, 340.
—— Thomas, Viscount Bindon, letter from to the Lord High Admiral, 5.
—— of Charleton, Thomas, Lord, Viscount Andover, allowance to him on his embassy to Venice, 227.
Howard, Thomas, fourth Duke of Norfolk, letter for him, 495.
—— Thomas, Earl of Suffolk, letters from to Mr. Annesley, 61; to the Lord Deputy Chichester, 7, 9.
—— Sir W., letters to, 167, 197.
—— William, Viscount Stafford, abroad, 390.
Howe, William, appointed to serve on the Council at Kilkenny, 348.
Howley, Lord Savile's property at, 240.
Hoyde (?), Sir Roland de la, petition against him, 40.
Hoye, Albert, Count de, in Nuremburgh, letter to, 172.
Huddleston, Sir W., 135.
Hudson, —, in the Tower, 358.
—— his apprehension, 369.
—— Mr., to go into Scotland, 451.
—— Rev. Michael, 216.
—— William, and Henry Saxey, dispute between, 475.
Hughes, Thomas, letter from to Sir E. Hyde, 238.
Huguenots, 56.
—— opposed to bishops, 420.
Hull, or Kingston-upon-Hull, 207, 461.
—— a fight near, 130.
—— preparations for war at, 155.
—— ordnance, &c. sent to, 158.
—— petition of two soldiers of the train-bands at, 232.
—— merchant vessels of, 286.
—— vessel from, 446.
—— a merchant of, 402.
—— letter dated from, 159, 161.
Hull, George, 40.
Huly, Mr., draper, letter to, 226.
—— his examination before Lord Falconberg, 226.
Humanes, Condé de, Spanish ambassador to England, 50, 60, 63-68, 81; his death, 70.
Hume, George, Earl of Dunbar, letter from to the Lord High Admiral, 4.
—— letters patent granting him the title, 501.
Hungary, 491.
—— ambassador of the King of, 170.
—— a diet to be held in, 135.
—— coronation of the Empress as Queen of, 148.
—— proposed descent into, 184.
—— threatened invasion of by the Turks, 193.

INDEX.   559

Hungary, Maximilian, King of, letter from Queen Elizabeth to, 186.
—— Ferdinand III, King of, 47, 50, 65, 66, 72, 74, 75, 8*, 91, 94, 96, 98-100, 107, 113-116, 119, 151, 153, 154.
—— —— proposed marriage of his daughter, 109.
—— —— letter from to Charles 1, 87.
Hungerford, Sir Edward, 240, 241.
—— letter from to Col. Fiennes, 240.
—— petition of, 44.
—— notice to tenants of his warrant to receive the rents of Papists, &c., 238.
Hunks, Sir Fulke, 223.
Hunt, R., letter to, 66.
Huntingdon, 225.
Huntingdon, or Huntington, Major, Cromwell's troop of horse under, 440.
—— is taken from the King's guard at Hampton Court, 329.
Hurman, Mr., 400.
Hutchinson, Col., 260, 261.
Hyde, Dr., at Rouen, 363.
—— Mr., apprehended at Lord Bendish's house, 398.
Hyde, Sir Edward (afterwards Earl of Clarendon), Chancellor of the Exchequer, 216, 218, et passim.
—— speech against the Earl Marshal's court, 197.
—— notes on the dissolution of Parliament, 211.
—— present of liquories cakes to, 217.
—— speech recommending the abolition of the Court at York, 219.
—— named one of those to try the Archbp. and Judges, 226.
—— minute of his being sworn a Privy-Councillor, 227.
—— receipt of Will. Barber to, 232.
—— receipt of money from, 243.
—— a trunk of his saved from plunder, 244.
—— bond of his to Sir G. Mompesson, ibid.
—— odious to the gentry of Devon, 263.
—— at Exeter, 264.
—— instructions to, 273.
—— instructions for him, as Chancellor of the Exchequer, 278.
—— Sir N. Crisp recommended to, 275.
—— order for provisions to be sent to him at Scilly, 308.

Hyde, Sir Edw., memorandum concerning the Prince's remove from Jersey, 321.
—— payments by, 331.
—— and Dr. Johnson, minutes of a conversation between, 338.
—— articles of association between him and others, for the defence of Jersey, ibid.
—— engages to repay Sir G. Carteret for repairing the fortifications of Jersey, 339.
—— his regular attendance at Church, 342.
—— C. Jones' account with, 345.
—— collections by him, on "Imposition," &c., 350.
—— memorandum on the States' ships, 445.
—— minutes relating to a conversation with Mr. Mowbray and Mr. M. Murray, 450.
—— Letters from him to :—
The Marq. of Antrim, 288.
Col. Arundell, 316.
Lord Ashburnham, 391.
John Ashburnham, 388.
William Ashburnham, ibid.
Sir J. Berkeley, 324, 328, 343, 351, 356, 359, 393, 415, 417, 429.
The Bishop of Londonderry, 349.
Mr. Bret, 319, 358.
Capt. Brett, 355.
Lord Bristol, 347, 353, 360.
Lady (Carnarvon ?), 208.
Sir F. Cornwallis, 403.
Dr. Creighton, 355, 360, 363.
Lord Treasurer Cottington, 342, 353, 359, 362, 387, 415.
Lord Culpeper, 354, 355, 373, 427, 431.
Lady Dalkeith, 339, 343, 348, 356, 364, 368, 376, 377, 379.
Sir Thos. Dayrell, 354.
Lord Digby, 316, 334, 347, 400, 448.
W. Edgeman, 304, 352, 358-360, 390, 394, 396, 399.
The Earl of —, 305.
Dr. John Earles, 354, 356, 361, 367, 384, 403.
R. Fanshawe, 409.
Mr. Gatford, 316.
Lord Goring, 263, 436.
The Governors of Penzance, St. Ives, and Pendennis, 275.
Richard Harding, 349, 375.
Lord Hatton, 368.
Lord H[olland?], 411.

Hyde, Sir Edward.
　Letters from him to:—
　　Lord Hopton, 306, 373, 374, 379, 404, 420.
　　Joseph Jane, 356, 362.
　　Lord Jermyn, 294, 318, 354, 355, 357, 374, 427, 448.
　　Cadw. Jones, 300.
　　Mr. Long, 297, 324.
　　The King, 324, 325, 343, 370, 385, 389, 391, 402.
　　The Lords of the Prince's Council, 444.
　　The Lords in the Downs, 437.
　　The Earl of Montrose, 409.
　　Sec. Nicholas, 268, 301, 319, 347, 352, 359, 361–363, 365, 367, 372, 375, 381.
　　The Earl of Norwich, 367.
　　The Marquis of Ormond, 335, 377.
　　Jeffrey Palmer, 448.
　　Mr. Pooley, 289.
　　The Prince of Wales, 370, 419, 427, 431, 433, 436.
　　The Queen, 303, 323, 419, 427, 438.
　　Prince Rupert, 410.
　　Capt. St. John, 355.
　　Lady St. Paull, 445.
　　Dr. Gilbert Sheldon, 385, 387, 391.
　　The Earl of Southampton, 371.
　　Dr. Stewart, 356.
　　Lady Isabella Thynne, 344.
　　Sir Baldwyn Wake, 347.
　　Lord Withrington, 326.
　—— letters written in behalf of his wife and children (1647), in case of his death, 370, 371.
　—— letter to ——, 324.
　—— letters of, mentioned, 216, 217.
　—— letters to him, 24, 33, 36, 70, 126, 160, et passim.
　—— petition to, 243.
　—— warrants to, 235, 269.
　—— warrants to Cadw. Jones, 273, 281.
　—— warrants of, to seize goods at Brixham, 276.
　—— warrant for payment to, 286.
　—— resolves to write the History of the Rebellion, has written sixty sheets (1646), 312; calls it a "Book of Martyrs," ibid.; writes it three hours a day, ibid.
　—— progress of his "History," 328, 403, 419, 462.

Hyde, Sir Edw., notices of his "History," 353, 355–357, 360, 382, 398.
　—— relations of military affairs communicated to him, for his "History of the Rebellion," 246.
　—— memoranda of events prepared for his "History," books 3–8; 503.
　—— his desires concerning his papers, 371.
　—— his last will and profession (1647), 371.
　—— his rents at Pyrton, 211.
　—— his wife and children, 370.
　—— his father-in-law, Sir G. Ayliffe, 209.
　—— his cousin, 221.
　—— his servant Parsons, 305.
　—— his cousin, Mrs. Lisle, 501.
　—— hand of J. Latche to, 502.
Hyde, Lady, 359.
　—— letter to, 371.
　—— message to, 319.
　—— Francis, 122.
　—— letters from to Edw. Hyde, 63, 160, 501.
　—— Henry, letter from to Nicholas Hyde, 30.
　—— —— letters to, 24, 33.
　—— Lawrence, 63, 126, 160.
　—— —— letter from to Henry Hyde, 33.
　—— Sir Nicholas, letters to, 30, 31.
　—— Serjeant, cousin of Sir Edw. Hyde, 371.
　—— Val., 63, 160.
　—— William, 390.
　—— —— expected from London, 372.
　—— —— factor at London for Sec. Nicholas, 352.
　—— —— letter enclosed for, 352.
　—— —— letter to Sir E. Hyde, signed "John Hopkins," 431.
Hyde Park, see London.
Hyeres, fleet at, 374.

L.

L., J., letter of intelligence to J. T., 387.
Jacintho, Father, a Capuchin, 22.
Jacob, instanced as a reformer, 320.
Jagendorf, Marquis of, 22.
James I., King of England, 18, 26, 27, 29, 322, 361, 365.
　—— Philip III. of Spain, and Albert and Isabella Clara Eugenia, of

INDEX. 561

Austria, treaty of alliance against Holland, 500.

James I., petition to, against Papistry, Puritanism, &c. (satirical), 500.
—— condolence on his illness, App. I. 6.
—— proclamation at Thetford, 172.
—— allowance made to Duke William, 214.
—— subscribed to the doctrine of the Church of Scotland, 320.
—— articles as agreed to by him, 1623; App. L. 1.
—— articles sworn to by him in favour of the Roman Catholics; App. L. 2.
—— articles sworn to by him concerning the Prince of Wales' match with the Infanta of Spain; App. L. 2.
—— and Louis XIII, articles of agreement between, for the marriage of Princess Henrietta Maria with the Prince of Wales, 501.
—— reports of his having been poisoned, 364.
—— account of his last illness and death, with proceedings against the Duke of Buckingham, 1647-8, 411.
—— the replies to Parliamentary proceedings concerning his death, 417.
—— warrants, letters, and public documents from, 6, 11, 24, 25, 26, 28.
—— letter from to the Committee of the House of Lords, 501.
—— —— to Queen Henrietta (when Princess), App. II. 9.
—— letters to, 27.
James, Duke of York, 290, 329, 414, 422, 433, 437, 446.
—— account of receipts and disbursements for his service, 443, 462.
—— account of moneys owing by him, 444.
—— a desire to make him King, 329.
—— his health and appearance (1647), 370.
—— his behaviour on hearing of his father's imprisonment, 408.
—— attempts to deliver a letter to the King, 411.
—— at Flushing, 420, 421.
—— account of his escape to Dort, 420-422.

James, Duke of York, visits the Queen of Bohemia, 421.
—— in Holland, 422.
—— order to the ships that signed the Kentish petition, 429.
—— list of servants to attend him at sea, 445.
—— a list of his servants which are dismissed, 445.
—— memorial concerning his going to Helvoetsluys, 449.
—— letters to, 445, 446.
James, Alex., his house in Jersey, 355.
Jane, John, letter to Mr. Edgeman, 229.
—— Joseph, 323.
—— —— letters to, 350, 362.
—— —— his cousin John Jane, 356.
Janetti, Guido, a servant of Henry VIII and Edward VI, imprisoned at Venice, 470.
J'anson, Dr. Henry, letter to Sir E. Hyde, 287.
Jardin, Edw. du, letter to Mr. Aylesbury, 441.
Jay, Thomas, his receipts for provisions for Prince Rupert's forces, 238.
Ibrahim, Sultan of Turkey, q. v.
Idiaquez, Don Alonso de, troops under him, 116.
Jeffery [Hudson], the Queen's dwarf, 116.
Jenkenson, or Jenkinson, Anthony, agent from Queen Elizabeth to the Emperor of Russia, 491, 496, 498.
—— letter in behalf of, 495.
—— letters recommending him to the Emperors of Russia and Persia, 476.
Jenkins, Judge David, information about, 364.
—— his answer to the Committee of Examinations, 371.
—— his printed declaration, 378.
—— is sent to Newgate, 395.
—— to be tried, 409.
—— his appearance at the bar of the House, 412.
—— particulars of, 413.
—— answer to his 'poysonous sedicious paper,' 416.
Jenkinson, Anthony, see Jenkenson.
Jenks, —, 280.
Jennings, Charles, 321.
—— Tho., 332.
Jephson, Col., his wife, 413.
Jermyn, Henry, M.P. for CorfeCastle,

4 O

INDEX

209, 310, 317, 323, 335, 338, 343, 353, 366, 387, 417.
Jermyn, Henry, Lord, agreement with Van Haesdonck, 215.
—— despatch to Sir D. Wyatt, 304.
—— his bill of credit, 311.
—— his supposed design to give up Jersey to the French, 338; and to buy Aurigny, ibid.
—— his rd. of "Tully," 354.
—— a judgment of, quoted, 362.
—— letter to Mr. Aylesbury, 428.
—— letters from to Lord Culpeper, 299, 303, 317, 319.
—— —— to Sir E. Hyde, 273, 274, 287, 288, 302, 310, 314, 318, 442.
—— —— to the King, 326, 333, 336, 346, 349.
—— letter from, 276.
—— letters to, 291, 318, 325, 327, 329, 330, 342, 343, 375, 331, 338, 350, 354–357, 374, 377, 427, 439, 448.
Jerome, Doge of Venice, q. v.
Jersey, Island of, 289, 305, 310, 311, 323–325, 340, 341, 343, 347, 348, 354, 356, 361, 365, 370, 372, 377, 385, 387, 391, 399, 402, 418, 449, 463.
—— merchants of, 141.
—— Mr. Gatford chaplain at, 272.
—— security of, 316.
—— the Prince sails for, and arrives in, 315, 316.
—— the Prince of Wales at, 319, 320.
—— residents in, 321, 342.
—— articles of association between Lord Capell and others, for its defence, 338.
—— engagement to repay Sir G. Carteret for repairing the fortifications, 339; certificate of Carteret for repayment, ibid.
—— is Episcopalian, 349.
—— proposed surrender of, 358.
—— "the best island in Christendom," 368.
—— prepared for any attempt on the island, 415.
—— Hyde leaves, 429.
—— militia of, 449.
—— letter received from, 314.
—— letters dated from, 287, 306, 315, 318, 322, 324, 326, 334, 335, 338, 341–343, 347, 352–364, 367, 368, 370–377, 379, 381, 387, 388, 390, 400, 403, 415, 419, 427.

Jersey, Castle Elizabeth, letters dated from, 345, 371, 376, 385, 419, 466.
Jesuits, 22, 50, 74, 103, 104, 107.
—— letter from to their Rector, 31.
Ilchester, 261.
Ilfracombe, prize ship at, 274.
Immaculate Conception, the, 228.
Imposition, 350.
Indemnity, Committee of, 412.
Independents, the, 254, 297, 298, 302, 313, 326, 340, 341, 342, 347, 352–355, 348, 312, 366, 369, 370, 375, 377, 380, 381, 383, 384, 395, 403, 405–407, 411, 415, 422, 458, 460, 461, 463–465.
—— treaty with, 325.
—— their petition, 370.
—— and Presbyterians, differences between, 377, 378, 394.
—— letter to a brother Independent, 448.
Indies, East, 66, 67, 69, 77, 86, 89, 91.
—— orders concerning the treaty of peace between England and Spain in the, 90.
—— expedition prepared for, 193.
—— East India Company, 66, 89, 177.
—— hope that the commerce of will be opened to all nations, 188.
Indies, West, 8, 29.
Indigo, account of some taken from the ship 'Danyell,' 441.
Infant and Infanta of Spain, q. v.
Inglefield, Mr., letter in behalf of, 497.
Ingram, ——, 446.
Innighfield, Gerard, of Dantzic, 475.
Innis, ——, 307.
Innocent X, Pope (Pamphilio), 296, 326, 361, 400, 402.
—— to pay to the Queen 100,000 crowns on certain conditions, 345.
—— his illness, 407.
—— holds a Consistory, 408.
—— the parentage and descendants of his younger brother, 402.
—— his nuncio in Ireland, see Rinuccini, J. B.
Innovations, 449.
Inquisition, the, 90, 117.
Inshivolaghan, letter dated from, 442.
Joachim, Marquis of Brandenburg, q. v.

INDEX. 563

Joachimi, Albert, commissioner for the alliance between England and the United Provinces, 29, 30.
—— letters of credence to him, 142.
Johnson, Mr., letter from to the Lord High Admiral, 4.
Jocasta and Alcibiades, their examples quoted, 356.
John, Count of East Friesland, q. v.
—— Duke of Finland, q. v.
—— "comes in Thenes capitaneus Rhohatinensis," letter to, 484.
John IV, King of Portugal, q. v.
John IV, Emperor of Russia, q. v.
John Frederick II, Duke of Saxony, q. v.
Johnson, Mr., i. e. G. Villiers, Duke of Buckingham, q. v.
Johnson, Mr., 297, 421, 431.
—— auditor, 321.
—— Dr. and Sir E. Hyde, conversation between, 318.
——, parson of Bishop's Wearmouth, recommended to Sir E. Hyde, 212.
—— Alderman John, of Chester, letter from to Arth. Annesley, 346.
—— Thomas, 441.
—— letter from to W. Edgeman, 360.
Jones, —, see Skidmore.
—— Capt., his impeachment, 391.
—— Mr., 356, 359, 372.
—— at Jersey, 415.
—— Cadwallader, Collector-General of Customs, 458.
—— —— warrant from Hyde to, 273.
—— —— warrants to, 281, 285.
—— —— letter to, on the ship 'Young Tobias,' at Fowey, 300; his decision, allowing the expenses of the master, &c., ibid.
—— —— order to him for an allowance to the Hamburg skipper, 302; certificate by him for the allowance, 304.
—— —— ordered to find candles at Foy (Fowey), ibid.
—— —— in danger of arrest, about the Hamburg ship, 306.
—— —— his account with Sir E. Hyde, 345.
—— —— his accounts, 353.
—— —— and Mr. Long, money matters between, 360.
—— —— letter from to W. Edgeman, 325.

Jones, Cadwallader, letters from to Sir E. Hyde, 282, 325, 328, 372.
—— Dr. Henry, letter to, 225.
—— Lewis, Bishop of Killaloe, commission appointed on his petition, 36.
—— Capt. Richard, of the 'Rose,' deposition touching the capture of the 'Francis,' 274.
Jordan, Capt., 400, 438, 444.
—— Richard, 492.
Joseph, Friar, 60.
—— Père, 57, 125.
—— and Card. Richelieu, 123.
Joyce, Thomas, letter from to W. Edgeman, 373.
—— disputes with the King, 382.
Ipswich, 358, 421.
Irasso, Don Francisco de, v. Hamuret.
Ireland, 1, 238, 251, 277, 285, 289, 290, 302, 303, 311, 318, 320, 325, 329, 333, 334, 336, 337, 348, 349, 351, 353, 356, 372, 373, 375, 377–379, 383, 400, 410, 413, 419, 420, 425, 426, 442, 459, 502.
—— pardons for, 2.
—— Mr. Treasurer of, 2.
—— grants of forts in, 8.
—— Lords Justices of (1615), letter to, 11.
—— ignorance of in England, a misfortune, ibid.
—— minutes relating to Lord Strafford's government, 36.
—— customs revenue, 75, 76.
—— attempted levy in for the Irish service, 144.
—— provision of Catholic Bishops in, 183.
—— discovery of a plot for an insurrection in, 184, 187.
—— how treated by England, 197.
—— designs upon, 224.
—— officers in, ibid.
—— Justices in, 222.
—— movements in, 225, 357.
—— a history of military operations in (Nov. 27 to March 31, 1642), 228.
—— the King's resolutions concerning, ibid.
—— letters on the King's intentions of visiting Ireland, 229.
—— letters from the Lords Justices to Secretary Nicholas, 234, 244.
—— petition to the King from the Catholics of, 234.
—— calculation of property in, belonging to the Protestants, 235.

4 C 2

INDEX.

Ireland, minutes of public letters, &c. relating to, in 1641-2; 235.
—— names of officers of the forces in, *ibid.*
—— property forfeited in the late Rebellion, *ibid.*
—— Lord Deputy of, his cypher, 215.
—— state of affairs in, 235, 362.
—— declaration of the officers, for payment and martial law, 236.
—— letter from the King, consenting to levy men for, *ibid.*
—— Protestants in, 237, 251.
—— —— their distress, 232, 253.
—— losses by the Rebellion in, 238.
—— arrears due from the Lord Lieutenancy to the Earl of Leicester, 247.
—— Catholics in, 248, 264.
—— of, their propositions to the King, on their remonstrance of grievances, 249; answer of the Protestants of Ireland to the same, *ibid.*; a summary of the seventeen propositions with other answers to them, *ibid.*
—— on the peace in, 249, 250, 254, 256-258, 261, 265, 269, 272, 276, 326, 334, 358.
—— letters on the Irish peace, 326-328.
—— English Roman Catholics in, 251.
—— proclamation concerning those employed in, 260.
—— Irish Papists, letter to the two Queens about, mentioned, 270.
—— Irish rebels and Lord Ormond, articles of peace between, 308.
—— the King and his Roman Catholic subjects, treaty between, *ibid.*
—— provisions from, 314.
—— report that the King is gone there, 316.
—— the Sergeant-at-arms, wounded, 329.
—— letter from the Nuncio and ecclesiastical congregation to the Marquis of Antrim, 330.
—— reasons offered by the congregation of the clergy for displacing Col. R. Butler, 331.
—— instructions of the congregation of the clergy, after the peace, *ibid.*
—— protestation of the clergy of, 332.
—— given up to Parliament, 341.
—— the chief offices of, to be in the hands of Catholics, 345.
—— collections relating to, 350.

Ireland, protestation of Irish clergy, 355.
—— certificate of expenses paid for the Lords Lieutenant of, 357.
—— Lord Lisle is appointed Lord Lieutenant of, 364.
—— reports from, 368.
—— advice on an accommodation between the Lord Lieutenant and the Confederate Catholics, 381.
—— standing army for, 390.
—— volunteers raised for, 414.
—— on the Rebellion in, 417.
—— the Catholic Committee in, 443.
—— alarm of Parliament at the proceedings in, 444.
—— nomination of great officers in, 449.
—— the King's and Commissioners' papers respecting, 451, 458.
—— letter from the Bishops of the Assembly to the officers of the army, 464.
—— eighteen letters to the lords and gentlemen of, 468.
—— the climate of, 502.
—— W. Brook's relation of his journey into, 503.
—— proceedings of the Committee [of Catholics in], 503.
—— the Lords and Confederate Council of Catholics in, letter to, 253.
—— letter from the Supreme Council of the Confederate Catholics to General Preston, 310.
—— protestation in behalf of the Confederate Catholics, 332.
—— assembly of the Confederate Catholics of, letter to, 363.
—— Confederate Catholics of, letter to the Lord Lieutenant, with replies, 365.
—— overtures for an accommodation from the general assembly of the Confederate Catholics (1646), 503; answer to, *ibid.*; propositions made to the Committee (1647), *ibid.*
—— Council of, letter from to Lord Mount-Norris, 136.
—— —— to the Lord Keeper (Lyttleton), 221.
—— —— letter to, 113.
—— Lords Justices of, letter to, 219.
—— Lords Justices and Privy Council of, letter from to the King, 229.
—— —— declaration to, 236.
—— a list of Irish Council, 258.

Ireland, letter from the Lord Lieut. and Council to Secretary Nicholas, 296.
—— the Supreme Council, 330.
—— instructions by the Lord Lieut. and Council, to be observed by the Lord Chief Justice of the Court of Common Pleas, &c., 332.
—— instructions agreed on by the Council, for Sir G. Lowther, 334.
—— letter of the Lord Lieutenant and Council, to the Speaker of the House of Lords, 334.
—— —— to the Lord Mayor of London, ibid.
—— Clerk of the Irish Council, see Davys, Sir Paul.
—— Irish Parliament, 204, 236, 345.
—— —— declaration on the impeachment of the Lord Chancellor, &c., 220.
—— —— requisite to be continued, 244.
—— House of Commons of, their remonstrance to the Lord Deputy, 211.
—— Lord Chief Justice of the Common Pleas, see Louther, Sir G.
—— Lord Deputy of (1614), answer to a charge, 5.
—— —— remonstrance to, 211.
—— Lord Lieutenant of, see Butler, James, Earl of Ormond.
—— the Pope's Nuncio in, see Rinuccini, Monsign.
—— Irish recruits, 101.
—— —— resident at Madrid, 144.
—— —— Customs, 148.
—— —— levies for Spain, 155-157, 159.
—— —— colony in the island of St. Christopher, 165.
—— —— soldiers to be exchanged for Spanish, 167, 170.
—— —— to be levied for service in Spain, 183, 185, 198.
—— —— —— serving in Spanish pay, 197.
—— —— friars, 219.
—— —— regiment cashiered, officers of, 222.
—— —— officers, tampering with, 223.
—— —— Manifest, the pretended, 226.
—— —— remonstrance to the Lords Justices, mentioned, 217.
—— —— war, 256.

Ireland, Irish cloths and lead, certificate of, sent to A. Higgs, 278.
—— —— rebels, propositions on prosecuting the war against, 334.
—— —— More, 367.
—— —— Commissioners, 422.
—— —— commanders, passes to, 503.
Ireton, Henry, 370, 373, 394-396, 398, 399.
—— his wife at Court, 392.
—— dispositions of his officers, 402.
—— declaration from the army penned by, 416.
—— Prynne attacked by, 439.
—— papers delivered to him, before the King's trial, 501.
Isabel, Queen of Spain, 102.
Isabella Clara Eugenia, Archduchess of Austria, q. v.
Isard, Count of Oldenburg, q. v.
Isarse, Don Diego de, military movements, 116.
Ispahan, 14.
Italy, 231, 425, 473.
—— forces raised in Spain and Germany for, 148.
—— state of affairs in (1638), 152.
—— Spaniards and French in, 154.
—— news from, 225.
—— the French King's generalissimo in, 275.
—— Princes of, in union against Spain, 402.
—— the Duke of Guise's movements in, 407.
—— successes over the Neapolitans in, App. L 6.
Ivan, or John IV, emperor of Russia, q. v.
Judah, Kings of, as reformers, 320.
Judges, 220.
—— censure of, 212.
—— proceedings against, 217.
—— on their trial, 226.
—— certificate of, concerning the customs of Waterford, 248.
—— of the High Court of Justice for trial of the King, list of their names, 466.
'Juliana,' the (ship), 491, 496.
Juliers, 133.
Jurisdictions, resolutions of the Committee of, on the Council of the Marches of Wales, 221.
Juxon, William, Bishop of London, Lord Treasurer, 94, 97, 384.
—— letter from to the King, 337.
—— letters to, 103, 335.

566   INDEX.

K.

Kintyre, or Kinlyre, Lord, see Campbell, James.
Keepers of the Seal, Lords, see Coventry, Thomas; Lane, Sir Rich.; Lyttleton, Edw.
Keblewhite, Francis, see Kibblewhite.
Keill, John, a safe conduct for, 400.
Kemp, Richard, 259.
—— letter from to the King, 258.
—— to Sir Will. and Sir John Berkeley, 258.
Kempe, George, 403.
Kennedy, Hugh, a commissioner for the Parliament and the Scots at Hampton Court, 388, 396.
Kensington, Lord, Le. Henry Rich, q. v.
Kent, disturbances in, 424.
—— gentlemen of, 414.
—— parsonage in, 216.
—— relation of the business of, in a letter to Lord Culpeper, 424.
Kent, Joseph, attestation to a document appointing him English Consul at Venice and Zante, 441.
—— petition from, 423 (bis), 428.
—— report from, 425, 426; account of the business of, ibid.
Kentish levies, 171.
—— Committee, 358.
—— gentry, their petition to the House of Commons in favour of Episcopacy, 227.
Kerr, Capt. James, letter from to the Captain of the garrison at Mount Edgecumbe, 271.
—— William, Earl of Lothian, 313.
Keynsham hundred, contributions from, 213.
Kibblewhite, Francis, letters from to Sir E. Hyde, 219, 244.
Kieffel, A., letter from to Secretary Windebank, 60.
Kildare, Earl of, 223.
Kilkenny, letter to the mayor and clergy of, 327.
—— return of burgesses to serve on the Supreme Council at, 348.
—— the Supreme Council at, letter to, 364.
—— meetings, 368.
—— letters dated from, 310, 329, 332, 349, 350, 464, 465.
Killeene, Baron of, E.

Killigrew, Dr., is to attend the Duke of York, 445.
—— H., 294, 316.
—— —— letter to the Prince of Wales, 323.
—— Sir P., 361, 323.
—— Tho., 445.
—— Sir W., 318.
Kilrush, account of Ormond's victory at, 230.
Kimbolton, Lord, see Montagu, Edward.
Kineeman, ——, or Kyneaman, q. v.
King, Capt., 19, 278.
—— General, 160.
—— ——, a vintner of Smithfield, 330.
—— Andrew, answer to Capt. J. Smith's complaint, 250.
—— —— receipt to, for bills of exchange, 302.
—— Richard, Dean of Tuam, 1.
Kingly government, discourse on, 360.
King's Bench, the, Lieut.-Col. Lilburne to be tried at, 409.
King's Evil, on touching for the, 375.
Kingsmill, Lady, 374.
Kingston, the Duke of Buckingham at, 430.
Kingston-upon-Hull, see Hull.
Kinigratz, see Koenigratz.
Kintyre, Lord, see Campbell, James.
Kirke, Geo., gentleman of the Bedchamber, grant to, 184.
—— his discharge of his jewels, 200.
Kirton, the Prince's forces to be quartered at, 270, 290.
Kirton, E., is committed for letters received from France, 369.
Knapp, Thomas, 488.
Knell, Dr., 490.
Knight, Capt., relations of the surrender of Donnington Castle and Winchester, 292.
Knighthood, new order of, in Poland, 228.
Knights, registration of, 27.
Knolles, Henry, letters of credence for, 480–482.
Knopper, Dr. Albert, Secretary to the King of Denmark 489, 491, 492, 494.
—— letters to, 487, 491, 492.
Koenigratz, capture of the city, 196.
Königsmark, General, his movements, 419.
Kynerman, or Kineeman, ——, ap-

INDEX. 567

pointed Auditor by Lord Treasurer Cottington, 363.
Kynesman, auditor, in Jersey, 312.
Kynesman, J., Cleric. Parliam., 370.
Kyrrie, John, 488.

L.

L., M., relation of the management of the fleet under the Prince, 138.
L., W., in the Downs, with commands from the King, 128.
La Bassée, the taking of, 386.
Lackham, letter dated from, 240.
Ladislaus, King of Poland, q. v.
Lambert, or Lambart, Charles, 382, 440, 462.
—— his signatures, 334, 362.
Lambert, Major-Gen., letter from to the officers in Pomfret Castle, inviting them to surrender, 415.
Lambeth, a fort to be built in, 110.
—— letter dated from, 210, 216.
Lamborne, Mr., 400.
Lammerman, Father, the Emperor's confessor, 100, 102, 111.
Lamplugh, ——, servant to the Earl Marshal, made away with, 502.
Lamport, garrison at, 206; insolence to it, 208, 209.
Lanark, *see* Lanerick.
Lancashire, 421, 466.
—— movements of the armies in, 435.
—— march of Cromwell's horse in, 440.
—— and Bucks, conduct of the sheriffs of, 417.
Lancaster, Duchy of, 213.
—— schedule of grants made in, 33.
Land, arable and pasture, 222.
Landrecy, 384.
—— siege of, 229.
Lane, Capt., commission for him, 500.
—— Sir Rich., King's Lord Keeper, 353, 371.
—— William, letter to, 238.
Lanerick, or Lanark, Earl of, *see* Hamilton, William.
—— Countess of, *see* Hamilton, Elizabeth.
Langdale, Sir Marmaduke, 282, 206, 323, 361, 378, 414, 422, 433, 448.
—— a reward offered for, 409.
—— in Lancashire, 421.
—— news from, 426.
—— his relation of the defeat of the Scots addressed to the Prince, 435.

Langdale, Sir Marmaduke, marches against Berwick and Carlisle, 440.
—— letter from to the King, 283.
Langen, Herbrand à, is commended to Queen Elizabeth, 172.
Langham, Alderman, his impeachment, 391.
—— Mayor of London, 410.
Langhorne, or Langherne, Col., 410, 460.
—— news sent from, 213.
—— his regiment seizes Swansea, 413.
—— escape of, 421.
—— his forces, 425.
Langrishe, Major or Col. Hercules, letters from to Col. N. Fiennes, 239, 241.
Languedoc, movements in, 361.
—— grant of money from, to the King, 375.
Lanreth, letter dated from, 252.
Lansdown, relation of the battle of, 246.
Lansford, Col. ——, letters on his exchange as prisoner for Col. Carr, 243.
Laredo, burnt by the French, 183.
Latche, John, bond to Edw. Hyde, 502.
Latin quotations, 373.
Latin verses, entitled, "In Causidicum nostrum," &c., 255.
Laud, William, Archbp. of Canterbury, 218, 356.
—— Irish Customs business referred to him, 148.
—— plot against, 175.
—— his trial, 226.
—— letter from to the University of Oxford, accompanying a gift of MSS. to the Bodleian Library, 210; reply of the University to, *ibid.*
—— letter from to Secretary Windebank, 158.
—— letters to, 49, 51, 73.
—— his Last Will and Testament, 256.
Lauderdale, Earl of, *see* Maitland, John.
Lauenburg, Duke of, *see* Saxony.
Launceston, 270, 280, 292, 295, 300.
—— march of troops to, 275.
—— Lords Wentworth and Culpeper at, 280.
—— the Lords of the Prince's Council at, 298.
—— letters dated from, 270-272, 274, 278, 280, 283, 298, 300.

Launsdale, William, affidavit concerning Sir J. Hotham, 272.
Lawrans, John, letters from to Secretary Nicholas, 458-461, 464-466.
Lawson, Capt. John, 459.
—— Philip, his deposition in the case of the 'Gideon,' 273.
Layton, Col. —, at Bristol, 264.
League and Covenant, confirmed by the King, 405.
—— explanation of the solemn, 425, 443.
Leander, Father, letters from to Secretary Windebank, 49, 53, 65, 57, 59, 61, 62, 71, 74.
—— to Cardinal Barberino, 55.
—— to Don Gregorio de Passani, 61.
—— letters to, 41, 52, 62-64, 66.
——, his cypher, 215.
Leather, report of an imposition on, 208.
Le Bassée, siege of, 229; its surrender, ibid.
Lechtenberg, Landgrave of, 20.
Ledbury, 305.
Lee, Bernard, letter from to Sir John Backhouse, 36.
Lee, Lady, of Ditchley, afterwards Countess of Rochester, letter to Sir E. Hyde, 211.
Leechland, Mr., 147.
Lee Road, fleets at, 438.
Leganes, Marquis de, 71, 74, 83.
—— troops under his command, 43, 69.
Leyard, Col. Chr., 459.
Legg, or Legge, Capt. William (afterwards Colonel), 399, 401.
—— instructions for him, 158.
—— letter from to Sec. Windebank, 161.
—— to survey the Holy Islands, 158.
—— is taken prisoner, 378.
—— warrant against, called in, 403.
—— is removed from the King, 407.
Leicester, 266, 361.
—— letter dated from, 8.
Leicester, Earls of, see Sydney, Robert; Dudley, Robert.
Leigh, —, M.P., 160.
—— Francis, see Chichester, Lord.
Leinster, Lord General of, see Preston, Gen.
Leitmeritz, 176, 178.
Lennox, Duke of, see Stuart, James.

Lent fast, dispensation from observing the, 463.
Lenthall, William, the Speaker of the House of Commons, 402, 417.
—— his sickness, 402.
—— documents signed by, 254, 428.
—— letter to, 363.
—— his return to the House with processions, 386.
—— warrant of, mentioned, 399.
Leominster's Ouze, bailiff of, 429.
Leopold, Archduke of Austria, q. v.
Lerida, 380; is invested, 378.
—— sortie from, 380.
—— siege of, raised by the Prince of Condé, 381.
Lernos, Condé de, late Vice-King of Naples, 129, 140.
Leskard, see Liskeard.
Lesley, Sir James, 316, 321, 325.
—— or Leslie, Robert, 328, 392.
—— Col. David, 166, 167, 207, 290, 305.
—— summoned to appear before the Council at York, 212.
Leslie, Col., 61, 85, 88, 94, 107, 116, 133, 135, 137, 138, 140.
—— misunderstanding between him and Sir Balthazar Gerbier, 190, 192.
—— letters from to Lord Arundel, Earl Marshal, 185.
—— to Lord Cottington, 92.
—— to Sir William Howard, 192.
—— to Mr. Taylor, 176, 178, 179, 184.
—— to Secr. Windebank, 101, 118, 135, 141, 170, 187, 192, 200.
—— letters to, 183.
—— Alexander, Earl of Leven, letter to, 278.
—— Gen. David, 206, 226, 357, 401.
—— occupies Newcastle and Tynemouth, 211.
—— Scotch army under him, 277.
—— Robert, see Lesley.
L'Estrange, Col. Sir Hamon, 382.
—— is near Exeter, 313.
Letters, anonymous, 377, 382, 384, 397, 421.
—— anonymous letters to Sir E. Hyde, 301, 429.
—— endorsed with the name of Sir R. Hopton, treating of the exchange of prisoners, 243.

INDEX. 569

Letter of an officer of the Parliamentary army, 283.
— from Scotland, 315.
— from Paris, extract from, 372.
— circular, sent to various States in behalf of the King (Jan. 23, 1648-9), 463.
Letters of news from England, 360, 385.
Letters of intelligence, 364, 366, 370, 375-380, 392-394, 398, 400-402, 404-428, 442, 444, 446, 447.
— extracts from, 357, 358, 360-362, 365, 368, 369, 373-375, 380, 381, 383, 391, 392, 395-398, 400-403, 415.
— from London, 318.
— from "13", 389, 390.
Levant Company, 19.
Levellers, the, 349, 399, 400, 460, 461.
Leven, Earl of, see Leslie, Alex.
Lever, Gen., favours the King, 311.
Levesey, or Levisey, Sir Michael, enters with 2000 men into Canterbury, 424.
Levesham, or Leviaham, Thomas, a London merchant, 483, 494.
Leverston, Sir W., 436.
Lewellyn, Mr., 406.
Lewes, letter dated from, 243.
Lewis V, Landgrave of *Darmstadt*, q. v.
Lewis, Sir T., rev. Tho. Bassett's answer to, 392.
— Sir W., M.P., 404, 460.
Lewkenor, Sir Christopher, 390.
Lewyer, Mr., letter to, 80.
Ley, James, Baron, a commissioner for the treaty with the United Provinces, 30.
Ley, James, Earl of Marlborough, ship fitted by him for the East Indies, 201.
— his account for victualling the King's fleet at Dartmouth, 249.
Leyden, letter dated from, 37.
Liege, 96.
— movements of the Duke of Lorraine at, 229.
— Gerard, Bishop of, letter to, 401.
Liégois forces, 206.
Lightfoot, or Lightfoote, Anthony, 441.
— letters from to W. Edgeman, 323, 360.

Lilburne, Col. John, 327, 349, 394, 397, 410, 411.
— seditious papers by, 179.
— his informations against Mr. Triplett, 212.
— evidence of his complicity in the plunder of a house, 216.
— his book, 372.
— his behaviour in the Tower, 390.
— ordered to the North, 399.
— mutiny in his regiment at Ware, 400.
— his imprisonment, 401.
— to be tried, 409.
— letter to Mr. Wollaston, 322.
Lille, or *Lisle*, q. v.
Limerick, 329.
— letter dated from, *ibid.*
Lincoln, 461.
— Bishops of, see Neile, Rich.; Williams, John.
— Earls of, see Clinton, Henry and Theophilus.
Lincoln's Inn, see London.
Lindhurst, 135.
— letter dated from, 68.
Lindsay, Mr., 78.
— John, Earl of Crawford, 338, 339, 340, 382, 415.
— letter to, 411.
— Ludovick, Earl of Crawford, recommended for the King's service, 161.
Lindsey, Earl of, see Bertie, Montago.
Lingen, Henry, is defeated on his way to North Wales, 440.
Linharew, Condé de, 121, 124, 129, 130, 138, 143.
Lints, letters dated from, 99-105.
— Prince Rupert at, 102.
'Lion's Whelp' (a ship), letter dated from, 5.
Lipstat, letter dated from, 219.
Liquorice cakes, presented to Sir E. Hyde, 217.
Lisbon, 3.
— ships at, 484.
— seizure of a ship near, 496.
— letter dated from, 401.
Liskeard, or Leakard, 283.
— letters dated from, 251, 270, 285, 292.
Lisle, or Lille, letter dated from, 200.
Lisle, or Lyle, Sir George, capture of 300 of his men, 264.
— his death, 417.
— Lord, see Sidney, Philip.

4 D

INDEX.

Lisle, Mrs., letter to her cousin, Edw. Hyde, 501.
Litchfield, 319.
Lithuania, 402.
'Little George,' the (ship), commander of, see Amy, Capt.
Littleton, Edw., Lord Keeper, see Lyttleton.
—— Sir Thomas, Chief Justice of the Common Pleas, 191.
Liturgy of Scotland, history of the, 247.
Liverpool, 321, 179.
Livingstone, James, Earl of Callender, 277, 305, 378.
—— letters to, 278, 431.
Livonia, 477.
Livy, read by Sir E. Hyde, 387.
Llanrwst, 440.
Llantrissant, Vicar of, see Bassett, Thos.
Lloyd, Dr., Fellow of All Souls' Coll., Oxford, his case, as to fees due from him to the University, 501.
—— Mr., to be impeached, 357.
—— Joshua, letter to Col. N. Fiennes, 241.
—— Sir Marmaduke, Judge of Assize, 392.
Lockhart, Col., 136.
Lodgings, a disputed debt for, 130.
Lodovisio, Cardinal, 27.
Loftus, Sir Adam, Vice-Treasurer of Ireland, 93, 258.
—— Chancellor, great suit of, 183.
—— Sir Edward, a summons served on, 126.
—— Sir Tho., Z.
—— letter from to the Lord Deputy, Z.
London, 285, 289, 301, 304, 309, 310, 314, 317, 325, 329, 330, 342, 346, 348, 349, 351-355, 357-360, 365, 377, 379-381, 384, 387, 389, 392-394, 396, 399, 402-405.
—— Lord Mayor and Aldermen, 203, 389.
—— disorderly election of the Lord Mayor, 207, 208; Ald. Wright chosen, 208.
—— the Mayor and City to be flattered, not threatened, 207.
—— Aldermen of, their petition mentioned, 211.
—— —— impeachment of, 415.
—— the Lord Mayor's house threatened to be pulled down, 222.

London, impeachment of the Lord Mayor and Aldermen, 391.
—— Recorder of, is freed from the Tower, 403.
—— the Mayor's feast for the General, 412.
—— complaints from French merchants in, 223.
—— merchants, 170, 486.
—— the President and Company of, letter to Princess Anne of East Friesland, 181.
—— —— letters on behalf of the society of, 189-191, 493.
—— petition from the City, alluded to, 205, 206.
—— petition of the City to the Commons, against bishops, 212.
—— petition of the poor of to the House of Commons, 222.
—— brewers of, their petition to Parliament, 222.
—— petition of the City against the Lords' propositions for peace, 244.
—— the City petition, alluded to, 353, 317, 309, 381, 425.
—— details of the City petition, 368.
—— petition from the Independents of, 390.
—— petition from the City to the Parliament, 424.
—— Independents, petition from against any personal treaty with the King, 130.
—— the King's propositions sent to, 291.
—— the King's safe conduct to, 314.
—— propositions, 325, 330, 333, 402, 403.
—— —— the King's answer to, mentioned, 337, 343, 350, 351.
—— proposition concerning the City of, 454.
—— and Oxford, on the trade between, 251, 252.
—— success of the money treaty with the City, 208.
—— treaty, 503; the King's approval of, 758.
—— powder promised by the City, 205.
—— proclamations inviting the apprentices to rise, ibid.
—— the vulgar look on the Scotch as redeemers, 207.
—— account of the loan from the City, 208.
—— Commissioners in, 211.
—— person summoned to, 212.

INDEX. 571

London, pass for the Duke of Richmond to, 253.
—— plan to march on, 277.
—— news, 314.
—— Presbyterians in, 320.
—— provincial Presbytery of, sits at St. Paul's, 375.
—— residents in, 330, 402.
—— plots, 356.
—— Common Council of, 363, 425.
—— banishment of the King's party from, 363.
—— money sent for the Scots from, 369.
—— prepares for war, 385.
—— the citizens protest against a violation of their liberties, 408.
—— affairs in, 410.
—— many of the King's party in, imprisoned, 412.
—— account of discourses at, 416.
—— bonfires in, 417, 418.
—— compliments between the City and the Parliament, 419.
—— apprentice riots in, ibid.
—— alarms on the army approaching it, 421.
—— militia of, 440.
—— the trade conference to be held in, 471.
—— agent from the Hanse Towns in, 491.
—— Charing Cross, 386.
—— Covent Garden, votes of the assembly at Kate's in, 369.
—— Eastcheap, scenes at a church in, 374.
—— House, ibid.
—— Hyde Park, general muster in, 318.
—— Leadenhall, the mint advised to be moved to, 206.
—— Newgate, 395.
—— Keeper of, see Wollaston, Mr.
—— two apprentices committed to, 222.
—— Queen St., the General in, 410.
—— St. James's, 399.
—— the King's children return to, 385.
—— St. James's Park, a case of homicide by a prisoner in, 247.
—— St. Martin's Church, disturbances in, 416, 418.
—— St. Paul's, legacy of Archbp. Laud to, 256.
—— soldiers to be quartered in, 410.

London, St. Paul's, sign of the King's Head, in the churchyard of, 416.
—— Dean of, see Stewart, Dr.
—— Smithfield, 320.
—— riots in, 361, 366.
—— Spring Garden, the, orders by the Ladies in Parliament at (satirical), 369.
—— the Tower of, q. v.
—— Westminster Hall and Scotland Yard fortified, 410.
—— Westminster Hall, soldiers in, 418.
—— ship of, see 'Danyell.'
—— Bishop of, see Juxon, William.
—— Commissioners of Scotland in, q. v.
—— letter to the City, 318.
—— letters to the Lord Mayor and Aldermen of the City, 334, 432.
—— letters dated from, 2, 3, 4, 6, 9, 11, 12, 14, 15, 38-40, 43, 54, 78, 87, 97-99, 101-103, 138, 150, 234, 236, 239, 285, 301-306, 318, 330, 357, 364, 370, 377-380, 382-384, 386-396, 398-400, 402-410, 412, 415, 417, 418, 420-426, 431, 437, 441, 444, 446, 467, 468, 474, 478, 481, 490, 492, 493, 496, 497, 499-501.
—— letters of intelligence from, 361, 397; see also Letters.
—— extracts of letters from, 392.
—— letter from merchants of, to Queen Elizabeth, 482.
—— Aldersgate St., letter dated from, 15, 19.
—— Cockpit, the, letter dated from, 233.
—— Covent Garden, letter dated from, 210.
—— Drury Lane, letters dated from, 15, 157, 158, 162, 164, 173, 175-178, 180-182, 184, 185, 196-198, 202-209.
—— Gray's Inn, letter dated from, 240.
—— Newgate, letter dated from the Cock-loft in, 222.
—— St. Martin's Lane, letters dated from, 18, 25.
—— St. James's, letters dated from, 2, 80, 478, 485, 488.
—— the Temple, letter dated from, 234.
—— Whitehall, 364, 379, 386, 459.

4 D 2

London, Whitehall, letters dated from, 5, 7, 8, 25, 26, 31–34, 36, 41, 75, 76, 121, 149, 150, 152, 155, 161, 162, 180, 187, 198, 219, 502, 503.
'London,' the (ship), letter dated from aboard, 252.
Londonderry, destruction of the plantation of, 211.
—— Bishop of, see Bramhall, John.
Long, Robert, warrant for payment of Ecclesiastical Tenths to, 289.
—— pass countersigned by, 131.
—— Sir Robert, letter to Hyde, 315.
—— Mr., 360.
—— letters to, 207, 324.
—— Secretary, 446.
Longcashell, William, a pirate, 3.
Longueville, Duke de, 125, 171, 369, 407.
—— Duchess of, 376.
Lord's Day, the, 374.
Lords Commissioners at Oxford, q. v.
—— House of, see Parliament.
—— made at Oxford, 317.
—— names of those summoned to wait on the Queen and Prince at the Louvre, 425.
—— on the impeachment of the seven, 403.
—— Lieutenant of counties, 203.
Lord Treasurer, the, see Treasurer.
Loring, William, letters to W. Edgeman, 336, 339, 360.
Lorraine, 75, 393.
—— difficulty about the restitution of, 168.
—— Duchy of, proposals for its restoration by France, 160.
—— forces, 296.
—— Charles III, Duke of, 50, 51, 77, 86, 92, 107, 108, 125, 131, 161, 167, 173, 178, 184, 196, 369, 431.
—— —— account of Mr. Taylor's interview with him, 162.
—— —— his movements at Liége, 229.
—— —— excommunicated, 230.
—— —— his excommunication suspended, 233.
—— —— communications held with, 408.
—— —— account of his levies and engagements, 418.
—— —— on the employment of his men in taking Guernsey, 449.

Lorraine, Charles III, Duke of, his Lieut.-General, see Montrose, Marquis of.
—— letters from to Charles I, 91, 152, 194, 196.
—— —— to Secretary Windebank, 196.
—— letter to, 200.
—— proclamation of, 193.
—— proposition to Charles I, 160.
Lorraine, Duchess of, 194.
—— Princess Henrietta of, letter from to Charles I, 94.
Lort, Roger, letter to Arthur Annesley, his brother-in-law, 223.
Lostwithiel, Cornwall, defeat of the Earl of Essex at, 306.
Lotherdale, Lord, or Lauderdale, q. v.
Lothian, Earl of, see Kerr, William.
Loudon, or Loudoun, Earl of, see Campbell, John.
Love, the (ship), 440.
Loveday, John, of Magdalen College, Oxford (1728), letters of the King copied by, 202, 203, 205, 206.
Loveiare, Mr., is committed, 424.
Lover, Thomas, of Newcastle, 473.
Loughborough, Lord, see Hastings, Henry.
Louis II, Prince of Condé, q. v.
Louis V, Landgrave of Darmstadt, q. v.
Louis XIII, King of France, App. I. 4–7; App. II. 10.
—— his respect for King James I, App. I. 6.
—— and King James I, articles of agreement between, 501.
—— instruction to English ambassador at his court, 71.
—— letters to, 13, 30.
—— treaty between him and Gustavus Adolphus, 30.
—— letter to Charles I, 502.
Louis XIV, King of France, 225, 394, 413, 420, 424, 429.
—— his birth, 140.
—— his absolute power, 218.
—— edict of, concerning English ships entering French ports, 213.
—— in Picardy, 316.
—— and Queen Regent, engagement with Charles I, 313.
—— his allowance to the Queen and Prince of Wales, 331.
—— gives to Prince Rupert the command of all English forces in France, 373.

INDEX. 573

Louis XIV, King of France, ordinance of July 10, 1643, alluded to, 376.
—— edict concerning English captains taking prizes into French ports, 378.
—— and the Queen-Mother, illness of, 402.
—— on the charge against Charles I, for assisting the French King against Rochelle, 407.
—— and Queen visit Chartres, 417.
Louvain, 220.
Low, Nich., 145, 160.
Low Countries, 165, 293, 373, App. L 7.
—— Magistrates of, propositions of the French ambassadors to, 12.
—— petition of merchants of, 32.
Lowden, Lord, i.e. John Campbell, Earl of Loudoun, q.v.
Lower, Humphrey, 265.
Lowtre, Laurence, case of, 146.
Lowther, Alex., letter from to Mr. Harriott, 3.
Lowther, or Louther, Sir Gerrard, Knight, Lord Chief Justice of the Common Pleas, 333.
—— is impeached, 220.
—— instructions by the Council of Ireland to, 334.
Lubeck, conference at, 178.
—— merchants trading at, 489.
—— ship of, 273.
—— treaty at, 156, 157.
—— letter dated from, 40.
—— letters to the civic authorities at, 470, 471.
—— letter to the Council and Senators of, 475.
Lucan Bridge, 341.
Lucas, Sir Charles, 428.
—— his death, 437.
—— Tho., his signature, 374.
Luce, St. Juan de, 110, 121.
Ludlow, —, 465.
—— Sir Henry, 209.
Luerre, John Vander, 472.
'Luke,' the, is wrecked, 196.
Lumley, Mr., letter to, 3.
Lumsden, Col., in Sweden, 207.
Luneburg, or Lunenburgh, deputies from, 155.
Luneburg, Duke of, see Brunswick.
Lunsford, Col., a royalist officer, 219.
Luquette, pictures by him, 66, 69, 76.
Lunatis, 131.
Lutherans, 152.
Lutos, 392.

Luxan, Don Diego de, 130.
Luxemburg, invasion of, 64.
Loyaa, Madre, a nun, 117.
Lydiard, letters dated from, 212, 216, 217, 218, 219, 220.
Lye Common, letter dated from the rendezvous at, 262.
Lyle, George, see Lisle, Sir Geo.
Lyme, relation of the siege of, 240.
—— forces of, 261.
Lynch, Dr. Walter, titular warden of the College of Galway, letters to the Bishops of Waterford and Ferns, 329, 331.
Lyne, Governor of, 296.
Lyon, ship of, 180.
—— a merchant of, 493, 496.
Lyons, 369.
—— the King of France at, 224.
—— letter dated from, 122.
Lyons, Cardinal of, 54, 112, 118.
—— at Rome, 224.
Lyttleton, or Littleton, Sir Edward, Lord-Keeper, 175, 217, 223.
—— warrant to bring him before the House of Lords, 231.
—— warrant to enforce the King's warrant issued at York, 259.
—— letters to, 221, 226.

M.

M., E., i.e. E. Massey, q.v.
MacCarthy, Donogh, Lord Muskerry, 250, 299.
M'Donald, James, 248.
Macdonell, Sir Randall, 8.
—— Randall, Earl and Marquis of Antrim, 169, 172, 358, 364.
—— instructions from the King to, 248.
—— military stores brought by him to Pendennis, 303.
—— his army, 465.
—— letters from to Sir E. Hyde, 287, 312.
—— letter to Mr. William, signed "Francis Chapman," 426.
—— his seal, ibid.
—— letter from the King to, 253.
—— letters to, 255, 288, 321, 325, 330, 340.
M'Donnell, Hen., his signature, 310.
Macdonnel, Captain Maurice, 180.
M'Guire, —, pardon of, 8.
—— Lady, pension granted to, 10.
Mackenzie, George, second Earl of Seaforth, 248, 312.

Mackinney, John, 445.
Mackmoiler, Captain Richard, 172.
Mackwell, Sir J., or *Mucknell*, q. v.
Mackworth, Sir Francis, 266, 289.
— letter from to Lord Goring, 262.
— letters from to Lord Hopton, 273, 300.
— — to Sir E. Hyde, 273, 288.
Madrid, water at, 2.
— Irish resident at, 144.
— character of the principal ministers at the court of (1639), 173.
— Doctors of, 202.
— letters dated from, 24, 27, 28, 33, 35, 42-44, 46-56, 58-70, 72-77, 83-87, 89-102, 104, 106-119, 121-130, 133, 134, 136-141, 143-145, 147-152, 155-157, 161, 165, 166, 168, 170-176, 178, 179, 181, 182-190, 192-196, 198, 199, 201-204, 206, 225.
— the Nuntio in, *see* Panzasoli, Monsign.
Maestro, Father, 22, 26.
Magdalen College, Oxford, *see* Oxford.
Magna Charta, 332, 378.
Mayne, Father, confessor to the King of Polonia, 114.
Maguire, —, to be hanged, 389.
Maguire, Redman, a footman to the Duke of York, 445.
Mahomet, Muley, 24.
Mahoney, or Mahun, Constantine, 'C. M. Hibernus,' *alias* F. Cornelius de Seto, Patritio, e Soc. Jesu, 401.
— orders in censure of his book, *ibid.*
Maidenhead, letter dated from, 234.
Maidstone, 466.
— particulars of the Lent Assizes at, 382.
— meeting of Dep.-Lieutenants at, 424.
Mails between France and England, 94.
Maismore, 305.
Maitland, John, second Earl of Lauderdale, 363, 375, 386, 388, 392, 450, 462.
— arrives in London, 370.
— is refused access to the King, 386.
— — his signature, 396.
— agreement at Carisbrook confirmed by, 405.
— letters from to the Prince of Wales, 433, 435; the Prince's replies to, 434, 435.
Maitland, John, second Earl of Lauderdale, letters to, 431, 460, 461.
Malaccas, the, 178.
Malachy, St., Archbishop of Armagh, 55.
Malaga, the plague at, 136, 137.
— wine, imposition on, 192, 193.
Malden, a ship of, 493.
Mallets, Justice, 382.
Malmesbury, 241, 388.
— disorder occasioned by sending men from, 240.
— letter dated from, 241.
Malo, St., *see* St. Malo.
Malaford, letter dated from, 17.
Malt, tax upon, 222.
Malta, Knights of, rupture between the States and, 438.
MaBravers. Lord, *see* Howard, Thos.
Malvezzi, Marquis Virgilio, 193, 197.
— letters of evidence for, *ibid.*
Man, Isle of, 206.
— Lord Digby's flight to, 289.
— escape of Col. Robinson to, 441.
Man, John, Dean of Gloucester, sent by Queen Elizabeth to the King of Denmark, 483.
— Sir W., 424.
Manbye, Thomas, letter from to Mr. A. Annesley, 122.
Mançera, Marquis de, 147, 168.
Manchester, Earls of, *see* Montagu, Henry and Edward.
Mandeville, Lord, *see* Montagu, Edward.
Manley, Laurence, 495, 496, 499.
— letter of safe conduct for, 495.
Manne, Hugh, 31.
Mannen, Fiart, 474.
Mannheim, siege of, 26.
Mansel, or Mansell, Sir Robert, 21, 23, 205.
— instructions to, 17.
— letter from to Mr. Aylesbury 18.
Mansfeldt, Count, General of the Elector Palatine, 21, 22, 23, 24; App. L. 5.
— recommended to the Prince of Wales (Charles I), App. L. 4.
— letter from to the forces of the Bishop of Bamberg, 20.
Mansfield, or Mansell, Fr., to be preferred to the Vice-Chancellorship, 233.
Mansfield, Count of, letter to, 483.

Mantua, assaulted, 122.
Mantua, dukedom of, 33.
—— Duchess of, 50, 142, 210, 231.
Manuscripts given to the Bodleian Library, 210.
—— see Satire.
Maqueda, Duke of, 63, 119, 128, 136, 140.
—— wounded in a duel with the Duke of Ciudad Royal, 202.
Maradas, Don Baltbasar de, 20.
Marcellus, Marcus, mould from a marble bead of, 164.
Marches of Wales, Council of the, 214.
Mareüill, Mons. de Fountenay, see Fountenay Mareüill.
Margaret, Princess of Parma, q. v.
'Margaret,' the (ship), of Minehead, attacked by Louis of Almeda, 188.
Margate Roads, letter dated from, 435.
Marie de Medici, Queen-Mother (1625), 137; App. L 2.
—— Lord Kensington's interview with, App. L 4; App. LL 10, 15, 16.
Marlborough, 393.
—— intended march of Lord Goring to, 264.
Marlborough, Earl of, see Ley, James.
Marler, Archdeacon, 371.
—— letters to Sir Edw. Hyde, 211, 212, 216-220.
Marlow, Little, rent-roll of, 41, 71.
Marquis House, letter dated from, 18.
Marrow, Captain, 361.
Marseilles, 108.
Marshall, Mr., 367.
—— appointed to preach on a thanksgiving day, 386.
—— returns from Scotland, 414.
Marshe, John, governor of the society of English merchants, letter to the Council of Hamburg, 493.
—— his signature, 484.
Marston Moor, battle of, see York.
Martelli, ——, ambassador, 178.
Marten, Sir Henry, letters from to the Lord High Admiral, 141; to the Lords of the Council, 15; to Mr. Aylesbury, 19.
Marten, or Martin, Henry, 106.
—— his scandalous book and disreputable behaviour, 412.
—— his remarks on touching for the King's Evil, 325.
Martin, H., 398.

Martin, H., laboured to impeach Cromwell, 399.
—— Hen., troubled with an evil spirit, 401.
——, ——, 411.
—— Dr., 353.
—— François, 466.
—— John, 487.
—— William, orders to the Council of Dantzic in his behalf, 487.
—— Richard, propositions tendered to the King, 80.
—— Thomas, letters on his case against persons of Dantzic, 479.
—— —— his son William seeks to recover money due to, 479, 480.
—— William, of Dantzic, his case, 485, 499.
—— —— edict granted to him respecting the Dantzic ships, revoked, 499.
Martyn, Harry, 390.
——, ——, abuse of, 416.
Martyr, Peter, 'Hist. of the Eight Decads of,' 500.
Mary, Princess Royal, proposed marriage with a Prince of Spain, 181, 194, 195, 196, 335, 421, 433.
—— with child, 341.
—— Queen, 171, 475.
—— —— charter granted by her, mentioned, 470.
—— —— letters to, mentioned, 467, 468, 471.
—— —— falcons presented to her, 467, 471.
—— Infanta of Spain, q. v.
—— Queen of Scots, letter to, mentioned, 478.
—— de Medici, see Marie de Medici.
Mary Ann, Duchess of Bavaria, q. v.
'Mary George,' the (ship), of London, 487.
Maskelyne, Nevill, papers signed by, 221.
Mason, Mr., a relation of Sir Humph. Bennet, 390.
—— Richard, letters to W. Edgeman, 310, 325.
Mass, two men dismissed for assisting at, 26.
—— proclamation against public attendance at, 41.
—— its legality in England questioned, 56.
Masaniello's fate at Naples, 400.
Massey, or Massie, Col. Edw., Governor of Gloucester for the Parliament, 278, 281, 421.

INDEX.

Massey, or Massie, Col. Edw., Governor of Gloucester for the Parliament, in Scotland, 414, 460.
— advance of, 269.
— his march to Taunton, 267.
— in the City, 379.
— his escape, 405.
— letter from to Col. Fiennes, 242.
——— to the Prince of Wales, 461.
Massey's "Reformadoes," 338.
Masson, Mr., 429.
— Richard, 427.
Massy, —, see Massey.
Master, the late Archdeacon, money transactions with, 211.
Masters of Requests, 417, 418.
Master of Requests Extraordinary, see Pierce, E.
Master of the Ward's Office, 269.
Matthew, or Matthews, Sir Toby, 342.
— opposes English religious orders, 62.
— his apprehension, 208.
Matthias, Emperor of Germany (predecessor to Ferdinand II), 20.
Maude, Arthur, 194.
Maule, Mr., 364.
———, a servant of the King's, 390.
Maurice, Prince of Orange, q. v.
Maximilian II, Emperor of Germany, letters from Queen Elizabeth to, 488, 490–492.
Maximilian, Duke of Bavaria, q. v.
— King of Bohemia, q. v.
— King of Hungary, q. v.
May, Baptist, 445.
— Charles, and two servants to attend the Duke of York, 445.
— Sir Humph., letters from to Mr. Annesley, 6–12, 16.
——— letter to, 6.
——— memoranda from the Lord-Deputy of Ireland, 8, 9.
— or Maye, John, letter to Sir F. Aylesbury, 410.
——— letter to the Duke of Buckingham, addressed to "Mr. Johnson," 137.
——— letter of, mentioned, 414.
Mayart, Mr., 421.
Maynard, Sir John, 447.
— is before the House, 411.
— William, Lord, his impeachment, 388, 389, 390, 391.
Mayo, Marquis of, 141.
— Sub-Sheriff of, 31.

Mayow, Thomas, 295.
Mazarin, Jules, Cardinal, 309, 313, 321, 326, 343, 364, 366, 424.
— at Rome, 224.
— advice from, 349.
— at Amiens, 378.
— extracts from a letter of, 320.
— orders from, mentioned, 346.
— his nieces, 380.
Mazarini, Michel, Archbishop of Aix, 378, 394.
— is to be viceroy in Catalonia, 393.
Meade, John, "Cl. Dom. Commun.," address signed by, 259.
Mecaw, Count of Merkan, or Meggan, 20.
Medina Sidonia, Duke of, 191.
— his confession, and the King of Spain's answer, 221.
— letter from to Lord Conington, 80.
— his death, 92.
Medina de las Torres, Duke de, 100.
Medmenham, rent-roll of, 41, 71.
Meggan, see Mecaw.
Meilleray, Marshal de la, 412.
— movements of, 423.
Melander, Otto, the Prince Elector with him, 152.
Melnick, 178.
Melo, Don Francisco de, Governor of Brussels, 49, 127, 142, 144, 173, 229, 232.
Melton-Mowbray, letter dated from, 283.
Menteleone, Duke of, 142.
Mentz, Bishop of, 80, 119.
— Elector of, 21, 54, 96, 106, 120.
Meppin, loss of, 153.
Merchants, English, complain of taxation in France, 176.
— insulted by the Dutch fleet, 181.
— wronged by impositions in Spain, 196, 199.
— in London, complaints of French, 223.
'Mercuries,' London and other, 415.
Mercurius, "Eleuticus," 419.
— Pragmaticus, 404.
Meredith, Sir Robert, 258.
Mericke, William, 498.
Mervyn, Captain, letter from to the Lords of the Council, 15.
Metcalf, Dr., 89.
Metropolitan, the, 217.
Metsham, letter dated from, 112.

INDEX. 577

Michael Federowitz, Emperor of Russia, q. v.
Micheldean, 303.
Middleborough, 228, 463.
—— ship from, 253.
—— residents at, 433.
—— letters dated from, 429, 433, 436, 437, 504.
Middlesex, Earl of, see Cranfield, James.
Middleton, George, agent of Queen Elizabeth in Russia, 496, 499.
Midhope, Edmund, 10.
Milan, 110, 155, 165.
—— Governor of, 231.
—— preparations for war in, 225.
—— Spanish forces of, 230.
Mildmay, Sir H., 412, 461.
—— abuse of, 416.
—— undertakes to keep the King's children (Jan. 1648-9), 463.
—— Lady, 426.
Milford, Anne, wife of a merchant of Newcastle, 473.
Milford Haven, letter dated from, 251.
Militia, 227, 258, 313, 318, 325, 326, 329, 333, 337, 339, 341, 346, 348, 351, 375, 377, 381, 383-385, 388, 389, 392, 403, 404, 406, 412, 414, 453, 503.
—— list of Lieutenants recommended to the King for, 224.
—— declaration against the new ordinance of, 232.
—— instructions for organizing the militia throughout the kingdom, 235.
—— settlement of, by Act of Parliament, 241.
—— the King's terms in the matter of the, 332.
—— given over to the Parliament, 346.
—— purged of "malignants," 395.
Miller, Hans, 498.
Milles, or Mylles, John, Advocate-General to Fairfax's army, letter to Dr. G. Morley, 286.
Mills, Mr., 10.
Milton, Col., 410.
—— John, his book on wedlock, 372.
Mince, Jack Mince's mind in the Bowling Green, 342.
Minehead, a ship of, 488.
Mines of gold in the West Indies, 29.
Minsterworth, 305.

Mint, the, 201, 203, 406.
Mint, the, charges of, 243.
—— in the Tower, 211.
—— seizure of money at, 202.
Miz, Don Juan, letter from to Don Carlos, 115.
Mirabel, Marquis de, 77, 93, 101, 102, 127.
Mirandula, Picus, quoted, 320.
Misserdean, Edward, letter from to Mr. Aylesbury, 20.
Mittenburg, Baron, see Swackovits, Adam.
Modena, 114.
—— ambassador of, 106.
—— castle of, 112.
—— Duke of, 112, 231.
Moldavia, 131.
Molesworth, Col., 260, 261.
—— Major-General, 295, 297.
Molcur, Abbé le, 152.
Mompesson, Sir Giles, 382.
—— bond of Hyde's to him, 244.
—— letter from to Philip Bassett, 213.
—— to Sir E. Hyde, 209, 211, 217.
—— petition to the King, 25.
Monaghan, 8.
—— letter dated from, ibid.
Monarchy and Episcopacy, 347, 350.
Money, brass, to be abolished in Spain, 193.
—— proposition for coining brass, 201; design of the copper money abandoned, 204.
Monk, General, his success over Monroe in Ireland, 412.
Monmouthshire, 238.
Monro, or Monroe, Gen., 248.
—— recalled from Ireland, 414.
—— Monk's success over, 412.
—— i. e. Montrose, Marquis of, q. v.
Monsigot, ——, secretary to Monsieur, 134, 159.
Monson, Sir W., letters from to the Lord High Admiral, 3, 4.
Montagu, Mr., 144.
—— Edward, Lord Kimbolton, afterwards Viscount Mandeville and Earl of Manchester, 226, 384.
—— —— Speaker of the House of Lords, letter to Lord Falkland, 233.
—— —— his signature, 428.
—— Henry, Earl of Manchester, letters from to the Lord Chief Justice, 31.
—— —— Lord Privy Seal, his con-

4 E

duct in the matter of the loan from the city, 209.
Montagu, J., letter from to the Earl of Newcastle, 210.
—— W., 200.
—— Walter, bearer of a letter from Princess Henrietta to the Prince of Wales (Charles I), App. II. 12.
—— —— commissioned to visit the Princess (afterwards Queen) Henrietta Maria, App. I. 6.
Montagu, S^r. de, i.e. Walter Montagu, q. v.
Monterey, Condé de, 100.
Montgomery, Earl of, see Herbert, Philip.
Montius, Dr. Christopher, see Mundt, C.
Montpellier, 357.
Montreuil, M. de, 307, 308, 321, 354.
—— conference with the Presbyterians, 336.
—— promises that the Scots army will receive the King as their sovereign, 309.
—— letters to, 297, 298, 299, 311-314.
—— letters from to the King, 298, 299, 301, 303, 313.
—— —— to Secr. Nicholas, 304, 306, 311, 312.
Montrose, Earl of, see Graham, Jas.
Montserrat, Dukedom of, 33.
Moore, Sir Garrett, 7, 289.
Moravia, 21.
Mordaunt, Henry, Earl of Peterborough, 130.
—— letters from to Hyde, 259, 433.
—— John, Earl of Peterborough, letter from to the Lord Chief Justice, 34.
More, Dr., letter from to Mr. Wilson, 61.
—— letter to, 60.
—— Mac Art', 468.
Moreton, Lord, see Douglas, W.
—— Thomas, Bishop of Durham (1636), certificate of, 98.
Morgan, Col., 121, 414.
—— Mr., 238.
—— —— his affidavit, 192.
Morlaix, letters dated from, 288, 289.
Morley, Dr. Geo., 31, 324, 371.
—— letter from to Hyde, 220.
—— letter to, at Exeter, 286.
—— Mr., 426.
—— James, a merchant of London, 483.
Morris, Col., a confidant of Overton, 461.

Morrison, Sir Rich. and Lady, 11.
Mors, Mr., at Jersey, 466.
Morse, Mr., arrested on suspicion of being a priest, 128.
Morton, Father, a Franciscan, at Naples, his threat to accuse Windebank, 217.
—— Lord, see Douglas, William.
—— Mr., the King's resident at Turin, 107, 227.
—— —— cypher with him (1635), 215.
—— —— letter to Lord Falkland, 227.
—— —— the King's agent with the Duchess of Savoy, his propositions, 449.
—— Sir Albert, 20, 20.
Moulins, the Prince Elector detained at, 182.
Moulton, Captain Robert, letter to, 271.
—— letter from to Ormond, 251.
Mounce, Thomas, letter from to Captain Moulton, 271.
Mounson, John, 134.
Mount Edgecumbe, letter to the Captain of the garrison at, 271.
—— the, see Cornwall.
Mountgarret, Lord, see Butler, Rich.
Mountjoy fort, 11.
Mount-Norris, 10, 11.
—— Lord, see Annesley, Francis.
Mowbray, Mr., Hyde's conversation with, 159.
Mucknell, or Mucknall, Sir John, and M. Schomacher, dispute between, 223.
—— petition to Prince Charles, 352.
—— —— to the Prince of Wales for a ship, 293.
Mullet, Edward, 463.
Mundt, Christopher, LL.D., envoy from Queen Elizabeth to the Prince Palatine, 469, 471.
—— his letters of credence from Queen Elizabeth to various German princes, 474, 479.
—— letters patent for, addressed to kings, &c., 467.
—— letters of credence for, 480, 481.
—— letters from Queen Elizabeth accrediting him to various German princes, 470.
Mucke, Col., at St. Malo, 308.
Munson, Sir J., his fine, 374.
Munster, condition of the Protestants in, 251.
—— Lord President of, 465.

INDEX. 579

Munster (Westphalia), peace negotiations at, 418.
Murray, Charles, 287, 364.
—— letter to Sir E. Hyde, 330.
—— Mungo, Sir E. Hyde's conversation with, 439.
—— Sir Robert, 290, 297, 313.
—— or Murrey, William, 290, 299, 303, 304, 335, 339.
—— William, Groom of the Bedchamber, his petition, 187.
—— —— imprisoned at Canterbury, 302.
—— —— in the Tower, 309.
—— —— his demands as to the Great Seal, 341.
—— —— bearer of a letter of the Prince's, 431.
—— —— his explanation of a passage in the Scotch Parliament's declaration, 433.
—— —— letters to, 337, 339.
Muscoso, Don Antonio, 44.
Muscovia Company Merchants, petition to the King, 32.
Muscovites, 40.
Muscovy, increasing power of, 472.
Musgrave, Sir Philip, 435.
—— his relation of the Scots engagement, *ibid.*
—— his march against Berwick and Carlisle, 440.
Mushry, or Muskerry, Lord, *see* MacCarthy, Donogh.
Mustapha Han, Sultan of Turkey, q. v.
Mylles, John, *see* Milles, J.
Mynde, letter dated from, 428.
'Mynion Oake,' the (ship), of Topsham, seized near Lisbon, 496.
Mytton, ——, defeated in Carnarvonshire by Sir J. Owen, 440.
—— Invades Anglesea and defeats Bulkeley and Col. Whiteley, *ibid.*

N.

N., A., i. e. *Nicholls*, q. v.
N., J., i. e. *Nicholls*, q. v.
Nantes, disturbances at, 375, 376.
Napier, Captain, 175.
Naples, 402, 417, 422, 423.
—— disorder at, 384.
—— account of affairs at, 400.
—— French affairs in, 418.
—— reverses at, 420.
—— residents at, 227.
—— letter dated from, L.
Narbonne, 143.

Narbonne, Duke Doria sent prisoner to, 224.
Naseby, battle of, 268, 319.
—— letter of the King seized at, 272.
Nassau, Duke John of, of Adenar, 169.
Navarre, 114, 127.
—— King of, 500.
Naunton, Sir Rob., letters to, 18.
—— commissioner for the alliance with the United Provinces, 30.
Navy (the English), 380, 424, 432.
—— details and estimates, 15, 105.
—— letter dated from, 432.
Nayler, Robert, a merchant of Hull, a letter on his behalf, 492.
Neale, Colonel, 169.
—— Mr., 146.
Neapolitans, successes over the, App. L 6.
Necolalde, Don Juan de, 38, 42–45, 47–49, 51, 52, 54, 59, 77, 79, 92–95, 100, 121, 138, 141, 146.
—— letters from to Charles I, 43.
—— to Lord Aston, 78, 87, 116, 128.
—— to Lord Cottington, 46, 122.
—— to Secretary Windebank, 40, 46, 48, 49, 65, 98, 99, 101–103, 123, 168.
—— paper by on the secret treaty, 47.
—— complaint of the seizure of ships, 120.
—— letters to, 41, 128.
Neda, George, has a commission to buy war supplies for Germany, 483.
Neile, Richard, Bishop of Lincoln, 1614, excuses his language in the House of Lords, 8.
—— Archbp. of York, letter from to Archbp. Laud, 51.
Nelson *versus* Nowell, a suit for debt, 146.
Nemours, Duke of, his illness and death, 366, 367.
Netherlands, details of military operations in, 200.
—— States-General of the United, treaty with, 413.
Nethersole, Sir Francis, memorials from to Charles I, 38; to Secretary Windebank, 39.
—— letter from to Charles I, 40. (No. 320, misprinted as Secretary Windebank to His Majesty.)

4 E 2

INDEX.

Nettersfield, Sir John, order to remove him from his command, 223.
Netterville, Mr., 8-10.
Nevinson, Capt. Roger, 459.
Neustadt, 161.
Newark, 202, 278, 279, 290, 296, 299, 307, 316.
—— Governor of, order for, burnt, 312.
—— letter dated from, 202.
Newburg, the Duchy of Juliers to be taken from, 133.
Newburg, or Newburgh, Wolfgang William, Duke of, 56, 85, 96, 152, 167.
Newburg, or Nieuburg, Duke of, is to marry the King of Polonia's sister, 228.
Newburgh, Lord, 89.
Newburn, account of the battle at, 213.
Newbury, 206.
—— account of the first battle of, 246.
—— the rebels in great force near, 265.
—— ; battle of, 403.
Newcastle, 202, 233, 293, 305, 321, 339, 388, 422.
—— affairs at, 410.
—— collieries, profits made of the, 207.
—— Mayor of, 98, 293.
—— merchants of, 473, 475, 484.
—— occupied by the Scots under Leslie, 204.
—— part of, 205.
—— on the propositions sent to the King, 328.
—— reinforced, 411.
—— ship of, 495.
—— letters dated from, 176, 318-323, 325-330, 332, 333, 335-339, 344, 345, 350, 351, 354-356, 358.
Newcastle, Earl and Marquis of, see Cavendish, William.
New Forest, 105, 247.
Newgate, see London.
Newman, —, charged with piracy, 41.
Newmarket, 225.
—— declaration of Parliament presented to the King at, 224.
—— the King to reside at, 364.
—— the King at, 380.
—— letters dated from, 14, 19, 25, 87.

Newport, papers delivered to the King by the Commissioners for the treaty at, 451, 452; the King's papers to the same, ibid.
—— letters dated from, 244, 443, 447, 448, 450-456, 458.
Newport, Earl of, see Blount, Mountjoy.
Newry, 362.
Newstead, letter dated from, 8.
Newton, —, 128.
Newton Bushell, 283.
Newtown by Evill, letter dated from, 232.
Nicasius, —, 488.
Nice, 230.
Nicholas's book, 372.
Nicholas, Secretary, 218, 224, 260, 348, 356, 463.
—— at Oxford, 252.
—— his brother, Dean of Bristol, 348.
—— money lent by, 371.
—— letters from to the King, 426.
—— —— to Lord Culpeper, 301.
—— —— to W. Edgeman, signed "Jo. Wilcocks," 386, 388, 394-397, 399, 404, 406-408, 411, 413.
—— —— to Sir E. Hyde, with the same signature, 167.
—— —— to Lord Falkland, 228.
—— —— to Sir E. Hyde, 345.
—— —— to M. Montreuil, 298, 312-314.
—— despatch to, 251.
—— letter of, 422.
—— letters to, 234, 244, 252, 257, 268, 272, 276, 296, 301, 304, 306, 311, 312, 319, 347, 352, 359, 361-363, 365, 367, 372, 375, 381, 382, 458-461, 464-466.
—— note to the King's letter of Jan. 10, 1645-6; 297.
—— papers of Sir R. Brown sent to, 413; letter from the same to, ibid.
—— warrant for printing the Proclamation of Dec. 28, 1641; 222.
Nicholls, Mr., 195, 355, 357, 367, 437.
—— secretary to Lord Dorchester, 362.
—— letters from to W. Edgeman, signed J. N. and A. N., 465, 466.
Nicholls, or Nicoll, Anthony, 295.
—— letter from to Col. N. Fiennes, 241.
—— document signed by, 244.
Nicholson, Thos., 216.
—— Thos. (a Scotchman), 178.

INDEX.   581

Nicolas, Capt. of Pendennis Castle, 229.
Nicolls, Mr., 374.
—— account of the conferences between Sir G. Carteret and Sir B. Wake for reducing Guernsey, 179.
Nieuburg, Duke of, see Newburg.
Nimeguen, 138, 139.
Nobility, proposition to reduce the estates of the, 393.
Noble, Captain, 141.
Nolan, Capt. James, 349.
'Nonsuch,' the (ship), letters dated from, 21.
Norfolk and Suffolk, discourses in various places in, 416.
Norfolk, Duke of, see Howard, Tho.
Nortlingen, letter dated from, 75.
Normandy, correspondence with, 343.
—— proposed English invasion of, 188.
North, Captain, 19.
North, Dudley, third Lord, 114, 459.
—— George, 184.
Northallerton, letter dated from, 203.
Northampton, 216.
Northampton House, letter dated from, 9.
Northampton, legacy to the poor of, 256.
—— Lord, see Compton, James.
—— Marchioness of, see Parr, Elizabeth.
—— Earl of, see Compton, Spencer.
North Petherwyn, troops quartered in, 284.
Northumberland, Earl of, see Percy, Algernon.
Norton, Mr., 17.
—— receiver of accounts for the King, letter from to Sir J. Colepeper, 238.
—— Sir Dudley, 12; letters from to Mr. Annesley, 9, 10.
—— Sir G., 461.
Norway, ill treatment from officials in, 178.
Norwich, 421.
—— letter dated from, 415.
Norwich, Earl of, see Goring, George.
Norwood, George, agent of John Gilbert, ill-treated by M. Swart, 194.
—— John, 33.
Nosticks, ——, 23.
Notbern, Duke of, 123, 124, 137, 140.
Notsweuf, James, 188.
Nottingham, 231.
—— Castle, Scotch officers in, 435.
—— Earl of, see Howard, Charles.

Nowell versus Nelson, a suit for debt, 146.
Nugent, Richard, Earl of Westmeath, his brother at Madrid, 1640; 192.
Nuntio, Papal, in England, see Panzani and Con.
—— Papal, in Ireland, see Rinuccini, John Bapt.
Nuremburgh, 472.
—— letters dated from, 97, 98, 117, 118.
Nye, [Philip], appointed to preach on a Thanksgiving-day, 386.
—— his prayer, 399.
Nyott, St., see St. Neots.

O.

Oath of allegiance in England, 30, 43, 49, 58, 62, 74, 130.
—— copies of, 55–57; two forms of, 128.
Oath, coronation, 319, 320.
Oath in the Canons of 1640, why it may not be sworn in the plain sense of the words, 214.
—— military, 363.
—— of a Privy Councillor, copy of, 58.
—— of simony, 220.
—— taken in Ireland, 252.
—— taken on composition, not to assist the King against the Parliament, 311.
Oaths, 205, 351, 392.
Oaths of allegiance and supremacy, 223, 346.
—— to be revoked, 345.
Oatlands, opposition to the King's coming to, 378.
—— letters dated from, 4, 187, 387.
Oblivion, act of, 447.
—— approved by the King, 346, 348, 351.
O'Brien, Murrough, Lord Inchiquin, 256, 418, 443, 447.
—— delivery of despatches from, 252.
—— his devotion to the Protestant religion, 252, 253.
—— the Queen's opinion of, 253.
—— his victory over Lord Taaffe, 402.
—— declares for the King, 419; his son, aged 9, sent to the Tower, ibid.
—— letter from to Col. Barry, 251.
—— letters from to the Marquis of Ormond, 251, 252, 442.
—— letters to, 245, 250.
O'Carroll's country, title of the Crown of England to, 6, 9.

INDEX.

O'Connor, —, chaplain to the Queen, committed for seditious words, 205.
O'Donnell, Earl of Tyrconnell, 140.
O'Driscol, —, Bishop of Brindisi, 189.
Ogle, Lord, see Cavendish, William.
Ogle, —, of the bishopric of Northumberland, imprisoned for holding intelligence with the Covenanters, 209.
—— Sir William, intercepts letters, 262.
O'Grady, Father Murtagh, a Franciscan Friar, 163.
O'Hartegan, Father, letter from to the Confederate Council of Catholics in Ireland, 253.
Okehampton, 274, 292, 295, 297.
O'Kelly, Lady, pension granted to, 10.
Olande, Henry, letter from to Col. Fiennes, 230.
Olave, Count of *Arro*, q. v.
Oldenburgh, deputies from, 153.
Oldenburg and Delovenhorst, Isard, Count of, letter to, 482.
—— Count Anthony of, letters to, 473, 482.
Oldenburgh, Princess of, see Friesland, East.
Oldsworth, or Oldisworth, Dr., 423.
—— his sermon on November 5th, 400.
Olivarez, Gaspar Gusman, Condé Duke de, 40, 42, 46, 47, 49, 50, 51, 54, 55, 59-61, 64-66, 76, 77, 80, 90, 93, 96, 100, 101, 107, 109, 111, 115, 117-119, 122, 126-128, 130, 133, 134, 136, 138-140, 145, 147, 148, 152, 154-156, 161, 165, 166, 168, 170, 171, 174, 178, 179, 181-184, 189, 190, 194-196, 199.
—— treaty articles agreed on with Lord Cottington, 35.
—— proposition for the transport of soldiers in English ships between Spain and Flanders, 188.
—— conference with, 201.
—— his incivility, *ibid.*
—— a pattern to favourites and ministers, 203.
—— is disliked, 210.
—— letters from to the Lord Treasurer, 62, 63, 105.
—— —— to Lord Aston, 70, 84, 85, 117, 140.
—— —— to Sir A. Hopton, 156.
—— letters to, 123-125.

Olivarez, Contessa de, 28, 117.
Oliver, Eustace, and John Walron, merchants of Exeter, their ship seized near Lisbon, 496.
—— John, letter from, 24.
—— Dr. John, letter from to Hyde, 216.
O'Meara, Dr. Dermot, 234.
Oñate, Condé de, 23, 41, 45, 72, 73, 79, 83-85, 89-91, 93-99, 102, 103, 106, 108, 109, 111, 113, 114, 121, 127-130, 136-140, 143, 145, 155, 162, 170.
—— is recalled, 148, 150.
—— made a grandee, 192.
—— letters from to Lord Aston, 125, 130.
—— —— to Windebank, 120, 131, 138.
O'Neale, or O'Neill, Brian, 249.
—— commended by the King to Ormond, 256.
—— Don Eugenio, his regiment, 164.
—— Hugh Boy, Drogheda besieged by the rebels under him, 227.
—— Serg.-Major, is killed at Newcastle, 204.
—— Sir Phelim, rumour of his death, 226.
—— Col., at Brussels, 229.
—— —, letter of, mentioned, 233.
O'Neile, —, 226, 231.
—— —, his designs upon Ireland, 224.
O'Neill, O'Neale, or O'Neil, Gen., 341, 366, 395, 442, 464.
—— letter from to the Marquis of Ormond, 340.
—— letter to, 340.
—— —, army under, 463.
O'Neill, Henry, Col. Tyrone, 165, 179.
O'Neill, John, Earl of Tyrone, 69, 176, 187, 189, 193, 195.
—— letter from to Sir A. Hopton, 204.
—— sentence against his father, *ibid.*
O'Niel, Dan., recommended by the King, 269.
Onuphrius, Cardinal, 53.
Oppenheim, 70.
Oquendo, Don Antonio de, 43, 128, 181.
Orandates and Aruscę (*pseudonyms*), 281.
Orange, Henry Frederick, Prince of, 45, 275, 296, 324, 343, 418.

Orange, Henry Frederick, Prince of, his daughter and the Prince of Wales, treaty for a match between, 285.
—— his daughter, 293.
—— his death, 1647; 369.
Orange, Maurice, Prince of, 18, 24, 284, 285.
—— letter from to the King of France, 13.
Orange, William I, young Prince of, 360.
—— meets the Duke of York, 421.
—— letter to, 131.
Orders, Holy, and Communion, 379.
Ordination of a Bishop, 62.
Ordnance, sent to Hull, 1638; 158.
—— department, abuses in administration of, 253.
—— Master-General of, see Hopton, Lord.
Oregones wine, 168.
Oristan, 125.
Orleans, Gaston John Baptist, Duke of, and Duke of Anjou, son of Henry IV of France, 51, 56, 361, 369, 370, 394.
—— his movements, 376, 378, 386.
—— his sickness, 391.
—— letter from to Charles I, 126.
—— Margaret, Duchess of, 370.
Ormond, Marquis of, see Butler, James.
Ormus, a pseudonym, 26.
Orumerus, Theobald, 172.
O'Rourke's country, 2.
Osborn, or Osborne, Sir Peter, 317, 373.
—— composition with, in the matter of Guernsey Castle, 318.
Osborn, Richard, letter from to the Prince of Wales, 462.
Osborne, Mr., bill of items due from, 314.
—— Edward, 185.
—— Lieut.-Col., 284, 285.
Oserlinsky, a Polonian ambassador, 105.
O'Shaughnessey, Sir Roger, propositions tendered by him to the King, 80.
Osnaburg, Bishop of, 119.
—— and Paderborn, John, Bishop of, letter to, 172.
Osmalt, Dr., his letters recommended to be read, 390.
Osnorius, ——, bearer of a letter to Queen Elizabeth, 500.

Ossory, R. C. Bishop of, see Rothe, David.
Ostend, 429, 431, 433.
—— letters dated from, 70.
Othen, Dr. Michael ab, physician to the King of Hungary, 481.
Ottery St. Mary, letter dated from, 270.
Otto, Prince, of Brunswick, q. v.
Oudart, Mr., 150.
Overbury, Mr., a Presbyterian, 408.
—— Sir Gil., brother of Sir T. Overbury, his son, 411.
Overton, ——, Governor of Pomfret Castle, 461.
Oughterlony, Sir James, App. L 5.
Owen, Sir J., defeats Mytton in Carnarvonshire, 440.
—— Sir Roger, 8.
Oxe, Peter, Danish Privy Councillor, letter to, 498.
Oxenstiern, Chancellor, 74.
—— letter from to Charles I, 95.
Oxford, 209, 231, 218, 257, 263, 266, 278-280, 290, 294, 299, 301, 304, 311, 313, 318, 319, 325, 361, 362, 368, 378, 387, 395, 399.
—— order of Parliament against carrying away the College plate, 233.
—— payment for powder supplied at, 235.
—— proclamation for adjournment of part of Hilary Term to, ibid.
—— the King's answer to the reasons of Parliament against the same, ibid.
—— persons captured on their way there, sent for examination, 239.
—— receipts and expenditure of the King's exchequer at, 241.
—— march of the enemy to, 242.
—— the revenues from, to be applied for the support of the King in the war, 245.
—— Mons. d'Harcourt at, 247.
—— names of inhabitants of, debtors of the King, ibid.
—— the Court at, 248.
—— on the trade between London and, 231, 252.
—— preparations to be made there for the King's service, 255.
—— legacy of Archbp. Laud to the poor of, 256.
—— on the siege of, 264.
—— hazard of the King's being taken at, 313.
—— blocked up with troops, 314.

Oxford, Fairfax and Cromwell at, 316.
— allies made from, 321.
— narrative of affairs at, from April 27 to May 30, 1646; 322.
— Savile imprisoned at, 353.
— Lords made at, 367.
— reports from, 379.
— reception of the ordinance of the two Houses at, 392.
— articles of sent to the Chancellor (1616), mentioned, 325, 311.
— articles, debates in the House on, 413.
— commissioners and Sir Thomas Fairfax's, treaty between, 322.
— commissioners ordered to press the Covenant on the University, 392.
Oxford, Univ. of, proceedings in Parliament for its reformation, 414.
— their appeal against the visitation, 390.
— delegates, summoned to attend the visitation commissioners, 399.
— visitors sent there made Heads of Houses, 409.
— Bodleian Library, the Archbp. of Canterbury's gift of MSS. to, 210.
— All Souls' College, letter dated from, 202.
— — Warden of, see Sheldon, Gilb.
— Christ Church, letter addressed to Edw. Hyde at, 50L
— Gloucester Hall, letter dated from, 3.
— Magdalen College, letter dated from, 24.
— Merton College, meeting of Commissioners at, 396.
— Oriel College, 359.
— — Hyde, Nicholas, and Cottington's meetings at, 341, 342.
— St. John's Coll., legacy of Abp. Laud to, 256.
— a professor of, see Baylie, W., M.D.
— Public Oratorship, a prebend of Ch. Ch. annexed to, 79, 92.
— scholars, 120.
— the Vice-Chancellorship of, 233, 234.
— Warden of Merton, see Brent, Sir N.
— Principal of Brasenose, see Radcliff, Dr.
— Master of Pembroke, see Clayton, Dr.

Oxford, Rector of Lincoln, see Hood, Dr.
— letter to, 210.
— order to the keeper of the University Library, 292.
— letter to a friend at, 236.
— letter from the King to the Lords Commissioners at, 231.
— letter of news from to Mr. Denman, 412.
— letters dated from, 210, 235–238, 240, 241, 243, 244, 247, 249, 253–260, 264, 286, 289, 297–300, 307, 309–311, 397.
— money paid from the diocese into the Exchequer, 248.
Oxfordshire, Papists in, 211.
— sums to be raised in, for the King, 234.
Oxon, letter dated from, 301.
Oyer and Terminer, commission of, 424.

P.

P—, D., a member of Parliament, letter of, 285.
P., II., i. e. II. Parker, q. v.
P., Lady, i. e. Lady Pawlet, q. v.
Paderborn, Bishop of, and Osnaburg, q. v.
Padstow, letter dated from, 273.
Paget, William, fifth Lord, 204.
— letter to the Parliament on his resolution to join the King's cause, 212.
Palatinate, the, 28, 72, 80, 82, 87, 90, 108, 109, 110, 112, 113, 116, 120, 122, 131, 132, 134, 138, 139, 140, 143, 148, 153, 155, 156, 157, 161, 162, 165, 169, 170, 172–175, 177–179, 183, 184, 187, 192, 200.
— letter on the negotiations with Spain for the restitution of, 801.
— restitution of, 203.
Palatine Belsko, q. v.
Palatine, Charles Louis, Prince, 54, 58, 59, 64, 66–68, 70, 72, 77, 79, 80, 82, 84–89, 91, 95, 97, 100, 110, 115, 119, 120, 124, 125, 127, 129, 131, 133, 135, 137, 140, 142, 145, 160, 178.
— Exchequer certificate to him, 129.
— letter from to Charles I, 154.
— of the Rhine, Frederic, Count, letter to, 489, 490.
— — Wolfgang, Count, letter to, 490.

INDEX. 583

Palatine of the Rhine, Anne, Countess, letter to, 489.
—— Frederick III, Count, letters to, 470, 471, 474, 479, 480, 482, 497.
—— Wolfgang, Count, letter to, 474.
—— the Princess, 140.
—— House, the King's exertions in behalf of, 219.
Palden, Captain, 444.
Palmer, Geoffry, or Jeffrey, of the Middle Temple, 371, 445.
—— letter to, 445.
—— Mr., a Presbyterian, his death, 389.
Palsgrave, the, will not be restored without Austria, 141.
Panfilio, Camillo, Card., conditions committed by him to J. B. Riniccini, the Papal nuncio in Ireland, 345.
Paulutius, Carolus, 118.
Panzani, Don Gregorio de, Papal nuncio in England, 121.
—— letter to, 61.
—— letter from to Secretary Windebank, 92.
—— Con, and Rosetti, entertainment of, 361.
Panzaoli, Monsignor, the Nuntio in Madrid, 225.
Papistry and Puritanism, petition against, 500.
Papists, 216, 361, 449.
—— notice of warrant to receive rents from, 218.
—— suspension of penal laws against, 258.
—— their mode of arguing, 320.
—— the King is ready to pass an Act of Parliament against, 377.
—— on the Queen's tampering with, 417.
—— and Cavaliers in London, new ordinances against, 424.
—— and Protestants, reconciliation of, 68.
Parcy, F., 443.
Parham, Lord Willoughby of, q. v.
Paris, 201, 335, 336, 338, 351, 354, 359, 362, 366, 420.
—— despatch from to Secr. Nicholas, 254.
—— extract of a letter from to a French general in Caen, 372.
—— letters dated from, 37, 40, 125, 126, 142, 150, 151, 153, 154, 213, 216–218, 222, 224, 225, 228, 232, 243, 247, 253, 280, 287, 299, 302,
304, 310, 311, 313–315, 325, 328, 329, 331, 336, 338, 340, 346, 356, 360, 361, 364, 366, 369, 370, 372–376, 378, 380, 383–385, 389, 393, 394, 402, 407, 408, 412, 417, 418, 420, 422–430, 442, 447, 448, 500, 503; App. L. 3–7.
Paris, news from, 356.
—— Parliament of, ibid.
—— —— proceedings in, 408.
—— Queen Henrietta in, 315.
—— —— and the Prince at the Louvre, 425.
—— residents at, 308, 351, 356, 380, 386, 463.
—— scarcity in, 467.
—— tradesmen, 367.
—— wedding at, 366.
—— agent from the English Parliament in, see Augier, M.
—— English ambassador at, see Browne, Sir Rich.
Park, T., bills of exchange payable by, in St. Malo, 302.
Parker, H., barrister of Lincoln's Inn, his "Answer to the seditious paper of David Jenkins, 1647," 416.
—— Mr., protestation denying his jurisdiction as judge of assize, 372.
Parks, proposed sale of, for payment of the King's debts, 247.
Parliament, 207, 211–213, 216, 221, 229, 231, 234, 243, 218, 251, 272, 284, 288, 298, 300, 302, 316, 320, 321, 326, 337, 340, 344, 346–349, 353, 357, 358, 364–366, 368, 371, 372, 374, 375, 378, 379, 381, 382, 384, 385, 389, 390, 395, 397, 398, 401, 403, 409, 414, 417, 419, 423, 464, 503; App. L. 2.
—— House of Commons, 224, 350, 403, 409.
—— —— articles of impeachment against the Earl of Strafford, 210.
—— —— petition of the City of London to, 212.
—— —— resolutions of, against ship-money, ibid.
—— —— petition to, 222, 227.
—— —— order of, to the Lord Lieutenant, 223.
—— —— lieutenants recommended to the King by, 224.
—— —— refuses to agree to the Lords' message to the King, 240.
—— —— order of, mentioned, 242.

4 F

586 INDEX.

Parliament, House of Commons, notes of their proceedings, Aug. 9, 1643, and a petition of the City to, 244.
—— —— Judges appointed by, to try the King, 266.
—— —— propositions of the Council of Ireland to, 331.
—— —— orders of, 341.
—— —— Presbyterian party in, 369.
—— —— speech of a member for the King, 392.
—— —— votes of Jan. 1st, 3rd, 5th, 1647-8; 407.
—— —— votes of mentioned, 410.
—— —— answer to their declaration against the King, 410.
—— —— sermon preached in, 425.
—— —— order to appoint a Committee to treat with the Common Council of the City, 430.
Parliament, House of Lords, 203-205, 209, 232, 322, 350, 359, 386, 398, 399, 405.
—— —— extracts from journals of 19.
—— —— summoned to York, 172.
—— —— their petition mentioned, 205.
—— —— petitions to, 211, 218.
—— —— their contemplated message to the King, 240.
—— —— petition of the City against their propositions for peace, 244.
—— —— letter to the Prince, 327.
—— —— letter to the Speaker of, 334.
—— —— letters addressed to the Speaker of, 337, 350, 451.
—— —— vote of, 361.
—— —— movements of Peers, 385.
—— —— letters to, 398, 400.
—— —— the bar of, 462.
—— —— on the powers and privileges of, ibid.
—— —— letter to the Committee of, 501.
—— notes on the mutual checks of the two Houses, 146.
—— elections for 1610; 191.
—— summoned to meet April 13, 1640; 190, 193.
—— speeches in 1640; 197, 198.
—— petition for summoning a, 201.
—— list of those who voted for a, 205.
—— promise of a, 208.
—— speech of the King at the opening of, 209.

Parliament, writs for, 209.
—— notes concerning the dissolutions of, 211.
—— their violent feeling against the clergy, 212.
—— a Committee of, 214.
—— journey, 215.
—— answer to a message from, to the Scots, 216.
—— Dr. Donne's petition to the Commons, ibid.
—— encouraged the persecution of orthodox clergy, 217.
—— English, conduct of, 218.
—— state of affairs in, and of the Bishops' seats, 220.
—— petition to, 222.
—— conference between the two Houses, about the proceedings of the Commissioners, ibid.
—— remonstrance by the Committee of, sitting at Grocers' Hall, 223.
—— declaration of, presented to the King at Newmarket, 224.
—— minutes of occurrences in, Aug. 1641 to May 1642; 230.
—— order against the King's demanding the attendance of any subject on his person, ibid.
—— order that the King's removal of the next Term to York is illegal (May 1642), ibid.
—— resolutions of, that the King intends to make war upon them, and their petition to the King to disband, 231.
—— warrant to their Gentleman-Usher to bring Lord Keeper Lyttelton before the House of Lords, ibid.
—— order against the King's disposing of the jewels of the Crown, 232.
—— order against carrying away the College plate at Oxford, 233.
—— reply of both Houses to the King's demands, ibid.
—— letter to the National Assembly of the Church of Scotland, and their petition of July 15, ibid.
—— Commissioners of, 233, 254, 258.
—— the King's answer to their reasons against the adjournment of Hilary Term to Oxford, 235.
—— legal treaties on their late orders made without the King's consent, 236.

INDEX. 587

Parliament, propositions received from, 237.
—— petition from Lord Mountnorris to, 238.
—— summons from the Parl. officers to the island of Portland to surrender, 239.
—— consignment of gunpowder on their account, 241.
—— busy with the discovery of a plot, 242.
—— Committee of, instructions for H. Peters to borrow money, 244.
—— notes concerning duration of Parliaments, 247.
—— history of the dispute between the King and, ibid.
—— fleet, 252.
—— ship at Cork, 252, 253.
—— at Westminster, order of the King to style it a Parliament, 253.
—— answer of the King to the propositions of, 254; reply of Parliament to the King's letter, ibid.
—— mission of the Duke of Richmond and Earl of Southampton to, 254.
—— breach of privilege of, 257.
—— powers of the Parl. Commissioners to treat with the King's, on religion, ibid.
—— Parl. protestation (1641), 271.
—— proposition to refer Church questions to, 276.
—— the Prince of Wales' request for passes to the Lords, 278.
—— forces, 281.
—— application to the Governor of Flanders to close the ports to the King's ships of war, 281.
—— instructions to their agent in Denmark, 286; letters to the King of Denmark and the States-General, ibid.
—— a treatise against the proceedings of, 295.
—— letter from the Speakers of both Houses to the Prince, 302.
—— oath not to assist the King against, 314.
—— orders of, 315.
—— and the Scots at defiance, 316.
—— letter to, 318.
—— debates in, on the disposal of the King, ibid.
—— design on the Prince of Wales, 320.

Parliament, Commissioners of the King's answer to their propositions, 325.
—— English, instructions to those who were to treat with the, after peace was rejected, 333.
—— the King's answers to the propositions of, 337, 351, 388.
—— the militia given over to, 340.
—— court of, 350.
—— pardons ordered by, 360.
—— orders by the ladies in (satirical), 369.
—— pretended plot against, 371.
—— the King's message to, or an answer to the propositions, 377.
—— members insulted by men of the City, 379.
—— eleven members suspend themselves, 382; news of their flight, 383.
—— the army's resolution and answer to the propositions of, 383.
—— Hertfordshire petition to, 385.
—— private resolutions of, 388.
—— army, proceedings of, from April 1645 till Sept. 6, 1647, 392; with the names of the colonels of horse and foot, ibid.
—— account of the reception of the ordinance of, at Oxford, 397.
—— the King's message to the two Houses of, 402.
—— answer of the Scots' commissioners on the four bills of, 401.
—— protestation against a clause in an ordinance of, 405.
—— a discourse on their vote excepting divers persons from pardon, 406.
—— message of the King to, ibid.
—— debate on the declaration against the King, 412.
—— proceedings of the Committee against the University of Oxford, 414.
—— pretended proclamation against, 417.
—— declaration presented in, 420.
—— news of, 423.
—— Dr. Isaac Dorislaus' credentials from, 428.
—— propositions of, 444.
—— proposition to revoke declarations, &c. against, 451.
—— the King's propositions to, 454, 456, 457; votes of both Houses concerning the same, 456.

4 F 7

INDEX

Parliament, propositions of, concerning Scotland, 157.
— Lord Coventry's speech to, 501.
— letters to, 272, 285, 311.
— letter from the King to, 236, 253.
— — from the Ambassadors of the States to, 250.
— proceedings in, 370, 380, 386, 387, 389-391, 394, 395, 397, 398, 400, 402, 403, 411-414, 417-421, 441, 458, 461.
— votes of, 381, 408, 409, 443, 454, 455, 456.
— army, use the Common Prayer-book, 370.
— forces, Commander-in-Chief of, see Bethell, Col. H.
— Parl. Generals, their address to the people of Cornwall, 276.
— ships of, 378, 385, 431.
— bound for Scilly, 317.
Parma, 228.
— Duke of, 114, 119, 122, 123, 125, 220, 230.
— Duchess of, 186.
— Prince of, his marriage, 188.
— Princess Margaret of, letter to, 472.
Parr, Elizabeth, Marchioness of Northampton, is attended by the physician, Dr. M. ab Othen, 186.
Parrott, Sir John, 81.
Parry, or Parrey, Sir George, 260, 273, 353.
Parsons, —, servant to Sir E. Hyde, his death, 305.
— Sir Will., 237, 258.
— Lord Justice of Ireland, letter to, 219.
Partington, Col., letter to, inviting him to surrender Pomfret Castle, 415.
Pasman, Cardinal, letter from to Cardinal Barberini, 34.
Passeaux, Baron of, 70.
Patrick, St., 332.
Pavelmnius, Adrian, of Hamburg, 485.
Pavier, Capt., 164.
— defended against a complaint of Sir W. Tresham, 167.
Pawlet, Lady, 287; letter to, 295.
Peace, articles of, 216.
— particulars of the petition for, 236.
— overtures made by the King for (1643), 246.
— proposals for, 318, 319.

Peace, articles of, concluded between Ormond and the Irish Roman Catholics (1648-9), 465.
Pecthius, Chancellor, 20.
Pedder, the (river), 283.
Pede, Frederic, 172.
Peers, list of, at York, 207.
— see also Parliament, House of Lords.
Peglia, Count of, see Pellegrino.
Pelham, or Pellam, D., 197.
Pellegrino, Andrea, Count of Peglia, papers relating to his case, 192.
Pembroke, 410, 425.
Pembroke Castle, 413, 414, 429.
— summons to surrender sent to, 417; details of the siege of, ibid.
Pembroke, Earls of, see Herbert, Philip and William.
Pembrokeshire, affairs in, 410.
Penal laws, 183.
— against Papists, 19.
— against recusants, repeal of, 261.
Pendennis and Prodennis Castle, 273, 278, 281, 284-286, 292, 294, 300, 301, 329, 334, 421.
— expenses of victualling it, 274.
— flax for making match for the fleet of, 276.
— receipt for tools and nails for, 288.
— proposal to erect a chapel in, 305.
— summons to the governor to surrender, 306.
— letter from the Council of War at, to the Prince, 310.
— and the Mount, 313.
— provisions designed for the garrison of, 314.
— relief of, 319.
— garrison of, 323.
— in great distress, 328.
— its surrender, 332.
— letters dated from, 278, 292, 302-305, 310, 312, 323.
— governor of, see Arundell, John.
Penhallows, John, 270.
Penmadock, Sir Jo., 463.
Pennington, Sir John, 182, 189.
— extract of a letter from, 15.
Penryo, or Penrbyn, 292.
— letter dated from, 270.
Penwith, list of parishes within the hundred of, with the names of the clergy, 293.
Penzance, letter to the Governor of, 275.

Penzance, vessel at, 290.
Peppard, Walter, 134.
Percival, Sir Philip, a witness against the Earl of Strafford, 221.
Percy, Mr., raises a troop of cuirassiers at his own expense, 202, 206.
Percy, Algernon, Earl of Northumberland, 339, 351, 353, 357, 384, 392.
—— his daughter, 392.
—— goes to Petworth, 409.
—— his goods stopped, 414.
—— two of his men employed at Paris, 420.
—— his signature to the Isle of Wight treaty, 451.
—— Henry, Lord, his agreement with J. van Heemdonck, 245.
—— —— committed to prison, 256.
—— —— is hated by the Queen, 362.
Pereira, John, delivers letters to Queen Elizabeth, 468.
—— his conduct of negotiations praised, 480.
Peretti, Prince, 57.
Perez, Gonsalo, chief secretary to the King of Spain, letter to, 491.
Pergamo, Capt. Fulvio, 44.
Periman, George, a merchant of Exeter, 492.
Perin, or Perran, letter dated from, 287.
Peronne, 428.
—— army at, 422.
Perpignan, 67, 181.
—— the Spaniards defeated in, 221.
—— the war about, 226.
Perriet, Jean de, letter to Lord Cottington, 195.
Perron, Cardinal, 390.
Persia, relation of Sir D. Cotton's embassy into, 52.
—— Tamasp I, Emperor of (1561), letter to, 476.
—— a commission, constituting Queen Elisabeth's agents in, 498.
Persians, defeat the Turks, 14.
Peru, the Franciscans in, 133.
Pesley, Fra., 265.
Peteck, Capt. Herman, and his ship detained, 195.
Peter, St., his primacy, 58.
Peter Port, Guernsey, letter dated from, 358.
Peterborough, an alms-house in, 227.
—— Earls of, see Mordaunt, John and Henry.
Peters, Captain, 81.
Peters, ——, 466.

Peters, Mr., with the King, 382.
Peters, Hugh, instructions for him to borrow money in Holland, 244.
—— letters to, 243, 264, 292, 301.
Peterson, Peter, 3, 463.
—— William, a merchant of London, 483, 489, 494.
Petitions from the counties mentioned, 404.
Petre, John, a merchant of Exeter, 492.
Pett, Peter, 18.
—— Phineas, 17.
Pettiplace, Mr., of Cartbagena, 128, 129.
Petworth, 409.
Phalsburg, Princess, 163, 167, 170–172, 174.
—— propositions made to Charles I, 156–160.
—— news about her treaty, 161.
—— letters to, 172, 191.
Philip, Landgrave of Hesse, q. v.
Philip II, King of Spain, 2, 475, 483, 499.
—— moneys due for corn supplied to his fleet, 172.
—— his chief secretary, see Perez, Gonzalo.
—— letters to, 468, 469, 470, 473, 476–478, 481, 483, 484, 486, 488–490, 494, 497, 498.
Philip III, King of Spain, 20.
—— treaty with James I against Holland, 500.
Philip IV, King of Spain, 22, 23, 24, 30, 35, 41, 43, 45, 46, 54, 60, 67, 77, 78, 94, 95, 102, 104, 124, 127, 140, 115, 178, 180, 225, 307, App. I, 1, 2, 7.
—— letter from to Lord Aston, 139.
—— complains against the decision of the English Admiralty, 145.
—— letter from to Charles I, 149.
—— levies raised for, 164.
—— and the Pope, 184.
—— memorial to, in behalf of Prince Rupert, 202.
—— business with, 208.
—— answer to the confession of the Duke of Medina, 221.
—— and the King of Holland, articles of peace between, 369.
—— despatch from, mentioned, 402.
—— letter of the English ambassadors to, 463.
—— letters from to Charles I, 59, 93, 170, 190, 194.
—— letters from on the Dowry, 78,

Philip IV, King of Spain, letters to, 77, 99, 121, 124, 133.
—— proclamation of, 27.
Philip, Phillips, or Philips, Father, Queen Henrietta Maria's confessor, 71, 168.
—— letter from to Secretary Windebank, 41.
—— his death, 357.
Philipeaux, —, document signed by, 375.
Phillips, Mr., (probably Father Philip), 54.
Piacenza, 117.
Picardy, 228.
Piccolomini, Condé, 71-74, 83, 85, 95, 107, 125, 131, 161, 166, 169, 190, 196.
—— recalled, 181.
—— letter from to Capt. Shaw, 196.
Piedmont, 228.
Piedmontese nobility and gentry, list of, 34.
Pierce, Edward, LL.D., is appointed Master of Requests extraordinary and knighted, 251.
Pierrepoint, Henry, Marquis of Dorchester, 318.
—— compounds, 368.
—— his fine, 370.
—— W., his signature, 451.
Pinaroh, 108.
Pinckney, Leonard, his receipts for provisions for Prince Rupert's forces, 238.
Pindar, Capt., 310.
Pinder, Col., at Bristol, 264.
Pinke, —, 234.
Pinnaces, building of, 18.
Pinner, Capt., 12.
Pinot, Col., accepts a company in Col. Colen's regiment, 223.
Piombino, 357.
—— French fleet embark from, 407.
Pipe, ancient revenue of the, 243.
Pirates, 10, 17.
Pirton, letters dated from, 30.
Pius IV, Pope, envoy of, 1560-1; 476.
Pius, Mons., the Danish ambassador, 159.
Plague, the, in Europe, 74, 108, 116, 121, 123, 130, 136, 137, 157.
Plaashington, —, 399.
Platt, Mr., Judge of Circuit, 231.
Playhouses, voted down, 410.
Pledwell, Mr., M. P., would have made a good Speaker, 211.
Plimpton, see Plympton.

Pliny, quoted, 306.
Ploughing with horses' tails, 11.
Plunket, Mr., letter from to Mr. Courtney, 45.
——, —, his designs upon Ireland, 224, 292.
—— Sir Nich., letter to, 464.
Plymouth, 269, 270, 282, 299, 410, 412.
—— Earl of Essex's success at, 251.
—— Customs of, 285.
—— Governor of, 304.
—— forces, 313.
—— and Gloucester, affairs at, 414.
—— letters dated from, 3, 4, 5, 153, 271.
Plympton, or Plimpton, Devonshire, 281.
—— letter dated from, 271.
Pocam, John, captain of the 'Mynion Gale,' 496.
Poetry, verses to the Prince, 301.
—— see Ballad.
Pogarvella, Frod., 497.
Poigny, 362.
Poingdexter, or Pointdexter, John, 363, 381.
—— letter from to Sir E. Hyde, 326.
Poins, Col., see Poyns.
Pointdexter, John, see Poingdexter.
Poland, 489.
—— threatened invasion by the Turks, 162.
—— Chancellor of, 229.
—— King of, 77, 114, 141, 156-160.
—— —— letter from to Charles I., 40.
—— —— his marriage, 61, 64, 74, 117.
—— —— confirms the resignation of the late Duke Frederic, 213.
—— —— his sister, 228.
—— Queen of, 131.
—— —— her marriage (1637), 137, 138.
—— Sigismund (II) Augustus, King of, letters to, 467, 475, 479, 485-487, 490, 493-495.
—— letter from to the Viceroy of the King, in Lithuania, 467.
—— order of "Sodales Beata Virginia," in, 228.
Poles, some Englishmen contract marriage with, 496.
Polish ambassadors in England from 1620 to 1637; 146.
Poleman, Gerard, 40.

Polkinhorpe, Roger, letter from to Sir E. Hyde, 278.
Pollard, Sir Hugh, 303, 324, 328.
—— letter from to Sir E. Hyde, 290.
Polonia, Cardinal of, 50.
—— King of, see Poland.
Poltimore, letter dated from, 281.
Pomerania, Duke of, letter to, 494.
Pomerland, or Pomerania, 133.
—— Imperialist army in, 144.
Pomeroy, John, 271.
Pomfret, defence of, 462.
—— Castle, letter of Major-General Lambert inviting the officers to surrender, 415.
—— Governor of, see Overton, —, and Cotterell, Major.
Ponderford, letters dated from, 268, 269.
Ponsonby, Col., his regiment, 413.
Pont, Mademoiselle de, enters a convent, 370.
Pont St. Esprit, 374.
Pontefract, 139.
—— a relation of the business of, 461.
—— Castle, is taken, 416.
Poole, forces landed at, 262.
—— Mr., 414.
Pooley, or Pooly, Mr., letter to, 282.
—— his journey, 320.
Pope, John, a merchant of Exeter, 402.
—— Thomas, 188.
—— Thomas, Earl of Downe, at Caen, 394.
Popes, better to submit to one than many, 333.
—— see Innocent X; Pius IV; Urban VIII.
Popham, Col. Alexander, letter from to Col. N. Fiennes, 239.
—— letter from to the Earl of Newcastle, 240.
—— letter to, 240.
—— his movements on the enemy, ibid.
—— Col. Edw., letter of, ibid.
—— —— letter from to Col. N. Fiennes, 241.
—— George, 200.
Popish Recusants, Statutes against affect Protestant dissenters, 117.
Pors, John, of Frankfort, 97, 98.
—— letter from to Secretary Windebank, 115.
Porter, Captain, 71, 72.
—— Mr., 362, 427.
—— Charles, is killed at Newcastle, 204.

Porter, Endymion, 148, 207.
—— letter from to W. Aylesbury, 434.
—— letter from to the Lord Chief Justice, 34; to Secretary Windebank, 105; instructions to, 53.
Porter, John, of Lynn, 490.
—— his ship the 'St. John Evangelist,' of Malden, 492.
Portland, Earls of, see Weston, Richard and Jerome.
Portland, island of, on the siege of, 239.
—— Castle, summons from the Parliamentary officers to surrender, ibid.
—— is taken by Col. Langrishe, ibid.
Portsmouth, 204, 234, 261, 426, 431, 503.
—— plan for strengthening it approved, 205.
—— fleet, 436.
Portugal, 210, 224, 225, 375.
—— the ports of closed (1637), 141.
—— commotions in, 143.
—— ministers in, 147, 150.
—— tumults in, 186.
—— John IV, King of, his orders in censure of Caru. Mahony's book, 401.
—— Sebastian, King of, letters to, 468, 478, 480, 484, 488, 494, 496.
—— Catherine, Queen of, letter to, 468.
Portuguese, English treaty with in the East Indies, 66.
—— one of their ports in the Indies taken, 129.
—— forces, 192.
Possoni, letter dated from, 143.
Post, allowance for a post between Madrid and London, 22.
Postmasters for foreign parts, proposed appointment of, 156.
Post-Office arrangements, 213.
—— committee, resolutions on the management of foreign posts, 217.
—— —— reconstitution of, to examine witnesses, 218.
Pou, Thomas, minute of a grant to, of the office of Master of the Prince's barriers, 229.
Potter, G., 273, 297.
—— payment to, 308.
—— ship of, 325.
—— letter to W. Edgeman, 315.
Potts, J., 151.
Poulett, Lady, see Pawlet.

Powder, &c., delivery of at the King's magazines, 257.
Powderham, letters dated from, 15.
Powell, —, 460.
—— charged with piracy, 41.
—— Col., declaration of, 418.
—— —— of Tenby Castle, 419.
Power, Lieut.-Col., 243.
Powerscourt, Viscount, account of moneys due to him, 40.
Poyer, —, 460.
Poyer, Col., and Col. Powell their declaration for restoring the King (1648), 418.
Poyer, Col., of Tenby Castle, 419.
Poyning's Act, 299.
—— suspension of, 258.
Poyning's law, 296.
Poyntington, Richard, 499.
Poyntz, Major-General, letter to, 281.
—— or Poins, Col., his indictment and sentence, 393.
—— Sir Robert, of Acton, letter to, 230.
—— —— warrant to seize his goods, 239.
Prague, letters dated from, 131, 133, 155-160, 178.
—— position of troops before, 170.
—— attack upon, 178, 179.
—— the leaguer by, letter dated from, 180.
Prayer, 362.
—— Book of Common, 444.
—— —— not admitted in Scotland, 431.
Preaching, 440.
—— anecdotes of, 330.
Presburg, letters dated from, 145, 148-150.
Presbyterians and Presbyterian Government, 302, 312, 320-322, 326, 327, 332, 333, 336-338, 341, 344, 345, 349, 350, 355, 362, 370, 375, 377, 379-382, 385, 397, 404-407, 422, 423, 425, 439, 459-461.
Presbyterians, English, 314.
—— in London, 320.
—— in Parliament, 369.
—— petition of, 365.
—— their party attempt to dissolve Parliament, 403.
—— discontent of, 421.
—— proposal to establish Presbyterianism in England, 297, 298.
Presbytery, the, 316.
—— the King's promises concerning, 305.

Presbytery, the, has possession of the churches, 391.
Preston, Mr., 45; letter from to Mr. William Haywood, 67.
—— Gen., 359, 368.
—— —— note dispensing with his observance of the oath, 328.
—— —— letter to the Bishop of Ferns, 330.
—— —— letter to the Marquis of Ormond, 340.
—— —— copies of his letters, 503.
—— —— letter to, 310.
—— Major T., 459.
—— Geoffry, imprisoned by Danish magistrates, 486.
—— —, his plot against the King of Denmark, 498.
Preymer, or Preyner, Baron Caspar, 470, 471.
Price, Howell, Custom-house officer, his affidavit concerning smuggled goods, 275; another, concerning goods seized at Brixham, ibid.; appraisement of, and warrants to seize the same, ibid.
—— William, 57, 74.
—— —— letter from to Secretary Windebank, 57.
Pride, Col., letter to, mentioned, 459.
Prideaux, Mr., 364.
—— Sir Richard, letter from to Sir E. Hyde, 275.
Priest, harlenring a, 81.
Priests, set free on bail, 73.
Priest, Simon, 291.
Primrose, Arch., Clerk of the Scots Privy Council, his signature, 229.
Prince of Wales, a Frenchman taken supposed to be the, 425.
—— see Charles, afterwards Charles II.
Princess, the, 373.
—— and her governess, Lady Dalkeith, at Exeter, 294.
—— Royal, the, see Mary.
Privy Council, the, 230, 261, 263, 265, 340, 356, 398.
—— orders to be observed in assemblies of, 31.
—— minutes of, 32, 33.
—— memoranda of business transacted at, 155.
—— Acts of, concerning the Scotch business, 206, 207.
—— copies for Acts of Council on the Scotch business, desired, 206.
—— at York, 207.
—— the hearing of Lords Bedford and Hertford by, 205.

INDEX.

Privy Council, at Oxford, order to style the two Houses at Westminster a Parliament, 253.
—— minute of, admitting Ed. Pierce as Master of Requests Extraordinary, 254.
—— Lords of, letter to the King, Queen, and Prince, 362.
—— of Scotland, q. v.
—— Oath of, q. v.
Privy Councillors, oath to be taken by, concerning the Prince's match, App. L 2.
Privy Seal, 281, 371.
—— clerks of, 260.
—— the Lord, see Montagu, Henry, Earl of Manchester.
Proclamation (printed) for registering Knights (1623), 27.
Proclamation for the contribution for foreign affairs (1633), 39, 40.
Proclamations mentioned, 223, 253.
Procter, Nicholas, 495, 496.
Progers, Mr., bearer of Lord Culpeper's letters, 314, 315.
Protestant allies of the French King (1637), 136, 137, 142.
—— Princes, alliance of, 482.
—— and Puritan doctrine, 191.
—— religion, 271.
Protestantism, 121.
Protestants, 334, 361.
—— practices against them, 2.
—— on the distribution of the rebels' lands among the plundered, 225.
—— and Papists, reconciliation of, 58.
Protestation against depriving the people of their free elections, 403.
Proud, Col., 398.
Proverb, 215.
—— Spanish, "In time medlars grow ripe," 224.
—— "Nullum bonum ex Aquilone," 421.
Provinces, ordinance of the allied, 189.
Provost Marshal, the, 415.
Prowsy, Hum., an officer at Exeter, 273.
Prussia, Prince Albert, Duke of, letters to, 467, 469, 471, 474, 479 (bis), 481, 488, 496, 497.
Pruyte, John, 498.
Prynne, Wm., 417, 460.
—— his book, 372.
—— report of his answer before the Lords, 146.
—— attacked by Ireton, 459.
Pucklechurch, resident at, 239.

Puebla, Condé de, his death, 141.
Pulford, Mr., 182.
—— John, letter to Mr. Denman, 413.
Pullen, Mr., letters of Secretary Nicholas sent by, 398.
Pullie, Mr., burglary at his house at Wootton, 239.
Punguy, Mons. de, 117.
Pupols, Baron de, 61.
Purbeck, Lady, see Villiers, Frances.
—— Viscount, see Villiers, John.
Puritan and Protestant doctrine, 191.
Purton, letter to Sir E. Hyde at, 275.
—— see Pyrton.
Putney, the head-quarters of the army at, 389, 392.
—— a Council of War held at, 395, 397.
—— letter dated from, 391.
Pye, Robert, letter from to Mr. Aylesbury, 18.
—— Sir R., the City horse under him defeated, 385.
—— Sir Walter, 227.
—— letter of, 428.
Pym, John, 203, 214.
—— his speech upon grievances, 209.
—— speech on the articles against Sir G. Ratcliffe, 213.
—— Jo., document signed by, 214.
—— letter of, 210.
—— letter of thanks to, 211.
Pyne, Hugh, 31.
Pyrton, Sir E. Hyde's rents at, 211.
—— rabbits there, 217.
—— accounts relative to the almshouses and poor's ground at, 231.

Q.

Quadra, Bishop Alvares de, q. v.
Quakers, 147.
—— in Southwark, 395, 397.
Queenborough, the fleet at, 438.
Quester, Matthew de, letter of safe-conduct for, 493.
Quinones, Don Seuro de, 66, 69, 75.
Quivoga, Fr. Antony de, 133.

R.

R., J., i. e. Jones J, q. v.
'R. Ad^{ll},' the (ship), 416.
Radcliffe, Sir George, see Ratcliffe.
Radolt, Clement (the Emperor's ablegate), 92, 127.
—— letter from to Secretary Windebank, 112.

Ragazzoni, James, a noble of Venice, letter to, 176.
Ragecourt, Sieur de, 93.
Ragland, letters dated from, 276, 277.
—— Castle, 332.
Rainsborough, Col., and Capt. Will., 130, 377, 378, 390, 398–400, 405, 406, 421, 446, 462.
—— instructions to treat with him, 314.
—— escapes being hanged, 421.
—— account of his death at Doncaster, 444.
—— , made Vice-Admiral by the Commons, 392.
—— Lord, proceedings in the House about him, 403.
Raleigh, Sir Walter, 17.
—— not to be made Earl of Pankeridge, 500.
—— letter from to Sir E. Hyde, 221.
—— letter to, 500.
Ramage, Thos., yeoman of the robes to the Duke of York, 445.
Ramsay, David, 98.
—— Sir James, 138, 139.
Ranezow, Sir Maurice, letter to, 481.
Rand, Thomas and William, their affidavits about drawing in the train bands to garrison Hull, 232.
Randall, Hannibal, 295.
—— or Randolph, Thomas, agent of Queen Elizabeth to the Emperor of Russia, 498, 499.
—— a commission to, 498.
Randolph, Thomas, i. e. Randall, q. v.
Ranelagh, Lady, see Boyle, —.
Rashleigh, Mr., 356.
Ratcliff, Dr., Principal of Brasenose, 253.
Ratcliffe, letter dated from, 17.
Ratcliffe, or Radcliffe, Sir George, Knight, letter to, 11.
—— speech against him for conspiring with the Earl of Strafford, 213.
—— at Rouen, 373.
—— Thomas, Earl of Sussex (1538), 468.
Rationalists, 305, 307.
Ratisbon, diet of, 94, 95, 97, 135, 136.
—— letters dated from, 103–116, 118, 119, 200, 502.
Ratisbonensis Pacificatio (1630), 33.
Ravenglass, embarkation at, 284.
Rawleigh, Sir Walter, see Raleigh.

Rawlins, Capt., 240.
—— his contempt for Sir W. Waller's warrant, 239.
Raynsborrow, Col., see Rainsborough.
Read, or Reade, Robert, 159.
—— letter from to Sir E. Hyde, 222.
Reade, or Read, Father, O. S. B. 49, 53, 71.
—— letters from to Father Leander, 52, 53.
—— Lieut.-Col., agent for the Catholics of Ireland, put to the torture of the rack, 234.
—— Mr., secretary to the English Commissioners in Scotland, relation of the Scots engagement in England, 462.
Reading, the Lord General at, 239.
—— account of the taking of, ibid.
—— Lord Craven's house near, letter dated from, 342.
—— sickness at, 386.
Rebellion, the, 362.
—— and treason, discovered by the laws of the land, 293.
Receiver-General, charges of, 243.
Reck, Baron de, President of the Aulic Council, 147.
—— minutes of Mr. Taylor's conversation with him, 159.
—— his character, 161.
Recorder, the, his trial, 388.
Recusants, their humble desires, 183.
—— in Berkshire, petition of, 175.
Redruth, letter dated from, 271.
Reeves, Judge, his charge to the jury, and death, 370.
Reformadoes, the Parliament's, 384.
Reformation, the, 320.
—— reverenced by the King, 319.
Regiomontana Rorusorum, letter dated from, 170.
Rehnen, letter dated from, 134.
Religion, 299, 300, 318, 319, 329, 330, 339, 340, 401, 469, 503, App. L Z.
—— Grand Committee of, evidence before, 212.
—— summons to Mr. Triplett, 219.
—— the penal statutes concerning, 236.
—— powers of Commissioners in the matter of, 237.
—— a proposition for settling, 335.
—— demands concerning, 354.
—— articles concerning (c. 1623), App. L L

INDEX. 595

Remington, T., letter from to Mr. Aylesbury, 430.
Renfrew, —, 451.
Renolledo, Capt., 120.
Requests, see Masters of Requests.
Revel, the Council of, letter to, 473.
Revenues, 221.
Reynardson, Guerret, his bill, 309.
Rhine, the, imperial forces under Beck and Melo on, 232.
Ribell, Robert, 271.
Ricaut, or Richaut, Mr., 150, 162, 172, 174, 179.
Rich, Mr. and Col., 444, 447.
—— Henry, Lord Kensington, afterwards Earl of Holland, 169, 224, 367, 430.
—— —— a Commissioner for the treaty against Spain, 30, 67.
—— —— to be Lord Deputy, 213.
—— —— is to be Lord Lieutenant, 218.
—— —— on the opening of his letters, 353.
—— —— letter to "Lord H.," 411.
—— —— two of his servants imprisoned, 412.
—— —— is taken prisoner, 430.
—— —— letters from to Charles I. App. L 2–7.
—— —— letters from the Prince to, App. L 3.
—— —— letter from to the Duke of Buckingham, App. L 6.
Rich, Robert, (twenty-second Earl of Warwick, 203, 384, 432, 435.
—— ship fitted by him for the East Indies, 201.
—— complaint against letters of Marque to, 214.
—— letter to, 376.
—— appointed Admiral, 424; refusal of the fleet to admit him as Admiral, ibid.; sent to Portsmouth, 426.
—— his fleet, 437, 438, 446.
—— the Vice-Admiral of his fleet, 438.
—— the Prince's answer to his summons, 438.
—— his first summons to the King's fleet, 439.
—— his excuse for leaving Gorée, 460.
'Richard and William,' appraisement of the (ship), 201, letter from the master, R. Simpson, 201.
Richards, Mr., of Mattingley, near Heckfield, Hants, 202, 322.

Richardson, John, Dean of Hereford (1632), letter from to Lord —, 38.
Richaut, Mr., see Ricaut.
Richelieu, Armand du Plessis, Cardinal and Duke of, 45, 62, 70, 111, 112, 127, 135–137, 155, 178, 188, 376.
—— and Père Joseph, 183.
—— at Avignon, 252.
—— young Duke of, is General of the Galleys, 369.
—— puts to sea (1647), 376.
Richmond, 381.
—— letters dated from, 1, 135, 488, 493.
—— or Greenwich, permission to the King to come to, 380.
Richmond Park, 227.
Richmond, Duke of, see Stuart, James.
Richards, —, papers signed by, 221.
Ridgeway, Lord, 12.
Rigby, in Lancashire, 440.
Rinuccini, John Baptist, the Pope's Nuncio in Ireland, 253, 328, 329, 334, 353, 395, 461.
—— particulars agreed on by, after disclaiming the peace, 331.
—— conditions committed to him by Cardinal Panfilio, 345.
—— letter from to the Bishop of Ferns and Sir R. Plunket, 461.
—— letter of, 464.
—— letter to, 327.
Ripon, instructions for Commissioners at, for payment of the forces, 207.
—— list of peers at, 207.
—— negotiation at, 208; information concerning the meeting at, ibid.
—— the Lords at, petition to, 218.
Risley, W., letter from to Lord Savile, 240.
Rithberg, Count de, troops under him, 86.
Rivers, John, a merchant of London, 482.
'Ro. Bu.,' the (ship), 446.
Robert, Mr., 426.
Robert, Prince, with the French Court, 303.
'Roberts,' the (ship), of Newcastle, seizure of, 195.
Roberts, Edmund, petition against, 402.
Roberts, Peter, letters from to W. Aylesbury, 420, 427, 429, 430, 479.

Robins, John, and John Cudling, their case, 402.
Robinson, Col., 440.
—— his house near Holyhead, ibid.;
escapes to the Isle of Man, 411.
—— Fr., a merchant of London, 493.
—— letter of credence for, ibid.
—— Luke, abuse of, 416.
Roças, or Rochas, Secretary, 77, 102, 116, 117, 120.
—— letter to Sir A. Hopton, 120.
—— letters from to Lord Aston, 70, 84, 108, 115, 124, 126.
—— letter from to "Champaign," 130.
Roobas, see Roças.
Rocheford, Lord, see Rochford.
Rochelle, 352, 417.
—— loss of, 83.
—— answer to the charge of Charles I's having assisted the King of France against, 407.
—— letter dated from, 241.
Rochester, 301.
—— a march to, 425.
—— Viscount, see Carr, Robert.
Rochford, Lord, see Carey, Henry.
Roebfort, Dr., 303.
Roe, Sir Thomas, 159, 162, 163, 171, 200.
—— failure of his negotiation, 157.
—— his cypher, 215.
—— ambassador to the Grand Signior, 502.
—— letter to, 25.
Roehampton, 43.
Roelans, Mons., 134.
Rogers, Humfrey, grant to him of the keepership of Hartleton Lodge, in Richmond Park, 227.
Rohan, Duke of, 37.
—— Madame de, 157.
Rolle, Sir Samuel, his woods, 291.
Rolls, Master of the, see Colepeper, Sir John.
Rolph, Major, his trial, 462.
Roman Catholic religion, free exercise of, 345.
Roman Catholics, articles agreed to by James I in favour of (1623), App. L 2.
—— toleration of, 26, 28, 35, 73, 71.
—— in the Palatinate, 112.
—— why they refuse communion with the Church of England, 198.
—— penal laws against, 220.
—— peace between the King's Lieutenant and, 465.
—— religion, ancient, 327.

"Romano Imperatori," letter to, 481.
Romans, King of the, election of, 107, 111, 119, 123, 124, 127.
Rome, 220, 223, 231, 299, 361, 369, 370, 378, 412, 417, 461.
—— the great number of English in, 501.
—— and Trent, Protestant alliance against, 182.
—— articles from, concerning religion (c. 1623), App. L L.
—— cardinals at, 224.
—— Castro and Monalto, the Pope's garrisons in, 226.
—— civil war among the Pope's forces in, 230.
—— Spanish troops in, 233.
—— Sir K. Digby leaves, 427.
—— letters dated from, 27, 30, 52, 53, 56, 62, 63, 70, 109, 117, 227, 274, 345, 460.
—— letter from, mentioned, 208.
Romish religion, oath against, 252.
—— parties of Scotland, Ireland, and England, L.
Roo, George, 483.
Rooks, destruction of, 31.
Roscarrock, Mr., letter from to the Lord High Admiral, 4.
Roscommon, Earl of, see Dillon, Wentworth.
"Roscommon, Canc.," signature of, 334.
Rose, the (ship), 274.
Rose, A., 463.
Rosetti, —, 361.
Ross, 305.
Rossacke, abbey of, Ireland, its owner Robt. Boyle's letter concerning, 305.
Rossiglione, defeat of the Spaniards at, 229.
Rossignano, 231.
Rossiter, engagement with, 462.
Rothe, David, R. C. Bishop of Ossory, letter to the officers of the army, 464.
Rotterdam, 433, 446, 464.
—— proposals to the company of merchants at, 435.
—— Admiralty at, 445.
—— provisions from, 463.
—— letters dated from, 45, 433.
Roucroix is surrendered, 500.
Rouen, 351, 362, 363, 367, 431.
—— residents at, 338, 342, 373, 387, 388, 390, 436.
—— ship of, 483, 484.

Rouen, letters dated from, 316, 321, 360, 379, 400, 411.
—— Laurence, letter to the Bishop of Ferns, 326.
Roundway Downs, 262.
Roundway, relation of the battle of, 216.
Rous, William, letter from to Lord Aston, 141.
—— case of, 148.
Rouse, Mr., chairman of the Committee of Lords and Commons, 414.
Roussillon, 224.
Rowle, William, an English merchant, 482.
Royalists, 321.
—— a difference between two, 370.
Roynon, Mr., his political opinions, 249.
Royston, M. Montreuil's interview with the Scotch deputies at, 311, 312.
Rosetti, Count, 191.
—— suggestion that he should retire into France, 205.
Ruban, letter dated from, 209.
Rudiard, Sir Benjamin, speech in Parliament (1640), 197.
Rufford, letter dated from, 105; App. I. 3.
Ruigraffe, Baron of, see Salvage, Philip.
Rumsey, Walter, Judge of Assize, at Cardiff, 302.
Rundell, Rich., 271.
Rupert, Prince, 160, 164, 167, 201, 253, 296, 341, 392, 409, 446.
—— at Neustadt, 161, 162.
—— ill treated in prison, 185, 186.
—— excellently treated at Lintz, 187, 192, 200.
—— memorial to the King of Spain in behalf of, 202.
—— receipts for provisions for his forces, 238.
—— Bristol taken by (1643), 246.
—— questions addressed to the Sheriff of Anglesea, on the protection of the island, 249.
—— his army, 264.
—— safe conduct granted by the Parliament to, 285.
—— his journal in England, from Sept. 5, 1642, to July 4, 1646; 324.
—— is chosen General of the English forces abroad, 316.

Rupert, Prince, memorials of his marches, mentioned, 419.
—— letter to Lord Goring, 267.
—— letter from the King to, desiring him to retire beyond seas, 277.
—— revocation by the King of all his commissions, ibid.
—— letter from to Major-General Poynts, 284.
—— —— to the Parliament, 285.
—— —— to the King, 289.
—— —— to an anonymous person in England, 323.
—— —— to Sir Wm. Batten, 449.
—— letter from the King to, 275.
—— letter to, 410.
—— letter to, mentioned, 335.
Rusdorf, Monsieur, 23, 88.
Rushworth, Jo., 383.
—— reply of Parliament brought by him to Beverley, 233.
Russell, —, letter to, 370.
Russell, Francis, Lord Bedford, 203.
—— his bearing at the Council, on his petition, 203.
—— to be Treasurer, 212.
—— Robert, letter to Sir B. Wake, 358.
—— —— letter to, ibid.
—— Sir W., ill-used, 118.
Russia, 487.
—— commission to Queen Elizabeth's agents in, 498.
—— merchants, letter to the governors of the company of, 499.
—— ports of, navigation to, 481.
Russia, Michael Federowitz, Emperor of, 32.
—— —— rumour that he will retire into a monastery, 228.
—— Alexis, Emperor of, English merchants seized by, 412.
—— John IV, Emperor of, letters to, 476, 485, 491, 495-490.
Ruthin, Lord Henry Grey of, q. v.
Ruthyn, or Ruthven, Patrick, Earl of Brentford, 270, 296, 315, 346, 438.
—— letter from to the Marquis of Montrose, 408.
—— letter to, 415.
—— letter from the King to, promising to make him Master of the Ordnance, 248.
—— his services to the King, 257.
—— letter from the King to, 247.
—— letters to, 237, 248.
Ruter, Ralph, 491.
Ryder, Captain, 26.
Ryman, Captain, 14.

S.

Sabbath, 374.
—— breaking, innovations, and pluralities, 351.
Sackville, Edward, Earl of Dorset, 359.
—— engagement on behalf of the King, 404.
—— Thomas, Lord Buckhurst (Lord Treasurer), letter to, 3.
Sacraments, 330.
Sadler, —, 466.
Sadler's condemnation, 288.
Saffron Walden, the army at, 377.
St. Albans, 380.
—— the army at, 380.
St. Albans, Lord, see Burgh, Ulick de.
St. Amour, in Franche-Comté, 125.
St. Bees, troops for, 169.
St. Buryan's, Dean of Cornwall, i.e. Dr. Creighton, q. v.
St. Christopher, an Irish colony in the island, 165.
St. Cruz, Marquis de, 81.
Saintterre, Mons. de, 117.
'St. George,' the (ship), of Dartmouth, purchase of, 245.
—— warrant to go on board her, and the valuation made, ibid.
—— agreement concerning, 250.
—— papers relating to the expenses of, in conveying the Queen to France, ibid.
—— disbursements of, during 1640-45, 294.
St. George's Channel, letter dated from, 2.
St. George's, near Brussels, letter dated from, 198.
St. Germains, 273, 315, 329, 342, 347, 387, 388, 390, 397, 418, 425, 427, 441, 467.
—— Queen Henrietta at, 336.
—— Scotch messengers at, 423.
—— letters dated from, 273, 287, 288, 316–321, 326, 328, 330, 391, 333, 335, 339, 340, 343, 341, 406, 418, 421, 422, 424, 426–429; App. L. 4.
St. Helen's Point, 503.
Sainthill, Peter, an officer at Exeter, 273.
St. Honorato, island of, 130.
St. Isidore, relic of, 130.
St. Ives, Cornwall, letter to the Governor of, 275.

St. Ives, garrison at, and execution there, 277.
St. James's, see London.
St. John, —, 383.
St. John, Captain, letter to, 355.
St. John, Mr., his will mentioned, 445.
—— Sir John, letters to Edw. Hyde, 211, 212, 216.
—— —— petition of, 44.
—— Sir Oliver, 6.
—— —— letter from to the Lord High Admiral, 4.
—— Sir William, letters from to the Lord High Admiral, 5.
—— —— to the Lords of the Council, 18.
'St. John the Evangelist,' the (ship), of Malden, 493.
St. Johnston's, letter dated from, 226.
St. Legrr, Mr., letter to Lord Falkland, 234.
—— Sir William, 301.
—— bearer of a letter of the King, 237.
St. Loe, Laurence, letters to Edw. Hyde, 212, 217.
St. Lucar de Barameda, English residents at, 93.
St. Malo, 302, 315, 321, 347, 353, 358, 376, 427, 461.
—— Irish officers and Bretons at, 223, 225.
—— letters dated from, 308, 315, 325, 329, 332.
St. Martin's Lane, see London.
St. Mawes, informations of soldiers of the garrison of, against the governor, 277.
—— Governor of the Castle of, see Bonithon, Major H.
St. Neots, or St. Nyott, 430.
—— tin blown there, 268.
St. Paul, Lady, letter to, 443.
St. Paul's, see London.
St. Pol, Spanish garrison of, 123.
—— the army near it, 70.
St. Quintin, Mr., grant of a baronetcy to, 227.
St. Vallery, the Prince of Condé at, 356.
St. Vet, 396.
St. Ursane, captured by the French, 125.
St. Ursula's field, 342.
Salamanca, Don Miguel de, 231.
—— letter to Col. Gage, 190.
Salcedo, or Salyedo, Don Geronimo

de, agent to the ambassador in Spain, 104.
Salcedo, or Salyedo, Don Geron. de, letter from to Lord Cottington, 63.
Salisbury, 301.
—— letters dated from, 67.
—— gaol, letter dated from, 5.
Salisbury, Captain, 15.
—— Bishop of, see Duppa, Brian.
—— Earls of, see Cecil, Robert and William.
—— see Sarum.
Salisden, alias Bedingfield, 100.
Sallee, pirates of, 121, 124, 125.
—— taken, 136.
Sallowy, Mr., 340.
Sallinos, Capt., 28.
Salop, see Shropshire.
Salsee, besieged, 181, 184–186, 188–190, 192.
—— recovered, 193.
—— fortified by the French, 183.
Saltmarsh, Mr., his rebuke to Sir T. Fairfax, and his death, 404, 407.
—— his ghost appears to the General (Fairfax), 408, 411.
Saltpetre mines, and supply of, 19.
Salvage, Philip, Baron of Ruigraffe, joins the Christian forces against the Turks, 191.
Samborne, John, 289.
Sampson, Capt., recommended by his kinsman, J. Ashe, 241.
Samuel, William, 17.
Sancto Patritio, P. Corn. de, l. e. C. Mahoney, q. v.
Sanderson, Mr., 142.
Sandowne, Kent, 428.
Sandringham, 61.
Sandwich, 423, 428.
—— Mayor of, reports by, 423.
—— a march towards, 424.
Sandys, Mr., 362, 367.
—— Thomas, concerned in a duel, 355.
San Lucar, Duke of, 33.
—— the port of closed, 141.
San Sebastian, 141.
—— squadron, the, 52.
—— letter dated from, 94.
Santa Clara, Franciscus a, see Damport.
Santa Margareta, island of, 130.
Saragossa, 204.
Sardinia, French troops in, 125.
Saria, Marquis of, see Castro, Don Ferd. de.
Sarrasin, —, made a song upon the Prince of Condé, 384.

Sarsfield, Sir Dominick, 11.
Sarum, Chapter and Prebendaries of, 238.
Satire, "the Scots Apostacy," 369.
'Satisfaction,' the (ship), 446.
Savage, Dorothy, 99.
—— Thomas, Viscount, his death, 76.
Savile, Thomas, Lord, Earl of Sussex, 241, 272, 282.
—— his answer to the charges against him, 240.
—— informations against him, for corresponding with the rebels, while Governor of York, 240.
—— letter from the King, commanding his release, ibid.
—— is imprisoned at Oxford, 353.
—— declaration of the King, committing him to prison, 256.
—— charges against him, 257; reply to the charges brought against him by the King, ibid.
Savin, Alderman, 424.
Savionets, —, 125.
'Saviour,' the (ship), of London, 487.
Saunders, —, 463.
Savoy, App. L 8.
—— and Venice, ambassadors of, 191.
—— the resident of in England, applies for leave to levy troops, 97.
—— Cardinal of, 118, 147.
—— Charles Emmanuel, Duke of, his success in Italy, App. L 6.
—— the French King's generalissimo in Italy, 275.
—— letter to, 192.
—— Duchess of, 154, 156, 412.
—— Duchess and Prince of, heads of accord between, 233.
—— the Princes of, receive 20,000 crowns from the Spaniards, 228.
—— house of, 225.
—— Prince Thomas of, 45, 48, 225, 231.
—— letters from to Charles I, 44, 61.
—— representation of, 56.
—— commanders of regiments serving with him, 164.
—— is inclined to exchange certain soldiers, 167.
—— is offered the command of the army against the Catalans, 210.
—— Victor Amadeus, Duke of, his death, 107, 142.
—— letter from to Charles I, 61.
Saunas, Andrew, 172.
Sauvage, Anthony, a London merchant, 494.

INDEX.

Sawyer, Sir Edmund, auditor, warrant to, concerning the King's revenue, 243.
Saxe, Duke of, 22, 23, 113, 153, 156.
Saxey, Henry, and William Hudson, dispute between, 471.
Saxony, 485.
—— peace with, 67.
—— Duke of, 67, 68, 74, 77, 78, 83, 85, 106, 142.
—— letters from to Charles I, 61.
Saxony and Lauenburg, Francis, Duke of, letter to, 477.
Saxony and Weimar, Bernard, Duke of, movements of his troops, 137-140, 150, 153, 154, 156, 157.
—— his death, 162.
—— Catherine, relict of the Duke of, letter to, 475.
—— John Frederic II, Duke of, letters to, 469, 472, 474, 480, 490.
—— Augustus, Duke and Elector of, letters to, 469, 470, 472, 474, 480, 490, 498.
—— Duke Ernest of, mediates between Hesse Cassel and Darmstadt, 419.
Say and Sele, Viscount, see Fiennes, William.
Scaglia, Abbot de, 42, 45, 53, 70.
Scarborough, 436.
—— memorials concerning its surrender to the Queen, 238.
—— taken by Cromwell's men, 439.
—— Castle, orders of the Council of War in, on the summons to surrender, 458.
—— —— articles agreed upon between the Officers of the Parliament forces and the Governor and Officers of Scarborough Castle, 459.
Seawen, W., 274.
—— Lieut.-Col., Judge of the Vice-Admiralty, answer to his petition, 293.
Schentedt, Lord Hannibal, Counsellor of State to the King of Denmark, acknowledgment of debt to, 351.
Schimbell, Peter, of Lubeck, agent in England, 491.
Schomacher, Martin, master of the ship 'Gideon,' petition to the Prince of Wales, 273; his affidavit, *ibid.*; report in favour of restoring his ship to him, *ibid.*
Schomberg, Count, 51, 59, 65, 168, 171.
—— Duke of, Viceroy of Catalonia, 422.

Scilly, 3, 290, 293, 309, 310, 315, 316, 317, 320, 322, 335, 466.
—— warrant for committal of the Duke of Hamilton to, 273.
—— order for provisions to be sent to, 308.
—— fleet designed for, 314.
—— Lords Hopton and Capell at, 316.
—— garrison of, 323.
—— articles of, upon its surrender to the Parliamentary fleet, 332.
—— engagement near, 352.
—— taken by some French, 439.
—— St. Mary, commander of the fort of, see Bassett, Sir T.
Scot, Mrs. Katharine, receipt of money from Hyde for her use, 243.
—— Mary, Lady Dalkeith, 294, 321, 356, 359, 367.
—— —— settlement on her, 105.
—— —— her illness, 291.
—— —— governess to the Princess, 294.
—— —— the Queen's resentment against, 303.
—— —— letter from to Sir E. Hyde, 214.
—— —— letters to, 339, 343, 349, 356, 364, 368, 376, 377, 379.
—— —— letter to, mentioned, 421.
Scotland, Scotch, Scotchmen, Scots, 1, 157, 201, 218, 276, 277, 325, 326, 347, 381, 388, 397, 413, 419, 421, 429, 461.
—— French and Hollanders' designs on, 167.
—— her troubles discussed (1638-9), 168.
—— affairs in, 337, 406.
—— minutes relating to the preparation of forces for, 161, 162.
—— Montrose's victories in, 228.
—— payment of Scotch forces, 207.
—— Earl of Antrim and Col. Steward's services in, 255.
—— army of, 218, 311, 314.
—— —— movements of, in 1644, 255.
—— —— the King agrees to join, 313.
—— —— to be disbanded, 393.
—— —— appointment of officers to, 421.
—— —— movements of, in Lancashire, 410.
—— business, the, copies desired of Acts of Council on, 206; the same enclosed in a letter, 207.

INDEX.

Scotland, Church of, 320, 420.
—— National Assembly of the Church of, letter from the Houses of Parliament to, 233.
—— Liturgy of, 247.
—— Presbyterian government, the Directory, and Assembly of Divines confirmed by the King, 405.
—— impetuosity of Scotch clergy, 375.
—— letter to the Commissioners of the General Assembly of the Kirk of, 462.
—— Commissioners of the Parliament of, the King's answers to the propositions of, 337, 351.
—— Estates of, 410.
—— letter from the committee of Estates of, to the King, 391.
—— Committee of Estates of the Parliament of, letter on behalf of, to the Prince of Wales, 433; the Prince's replies to, 434.
—— extracts from Scotch Acts of Parliament, passed 1640–41; 502.
—— Committee of Estates in, letter from to the Prince, 441.
—— Commissioners of the General Assembly in, letter from to the Prince, *ibid.*
—— Commissioners of, 254, 290, 350, 357, 389, 397, 399, 431, 445.
—— letters from to the House of Lords, 398, 400.
—— in London, appointment of Commissioners to treat with, 211.
—— appointment of, to make a treaty in England, 250.
—— their answer to the Parliament, 372.
—— letter from to the King, 392.
—— in London, 395, 396; letters to, 307–309; supplement and postscript, 307.
—— their address to the King on his removal from Holdenby, 396.
—— the King's answer to their paper, 401.
—— answer to the four Bills, 404.
—— the King's answer to their propositions, 502.
—— reports of the Scotch Convention, 112.
—— covenanters, 179, 181.
—— proceedings in Parliament, 419.
—— on bribing the Scots, 409, 415.

Scotland, propositions of Parliament concerning, 457; the King's answer to, 458.
—— relation of the Scots' engagement in England, 162.
—— Scotch Government, 278.
—— Scotch guards for the French King, 151.
—— forces landed in the Highlands, 251.
—— the Highlanders' good-will towards Montrose to be encouraged, 408.
—— Scotch levied for the French service, 166.
—— examinations of Scotch mariners touching prizes taken by Haesdonck, 278.
—— Scotch officers in Gottenburg, to be intercepted in their voyage to Scotland, 207.
—— Parliament of, 304, 341; their thanks to the City of London, 301.
—— the King's message to, 402.
—— explanation of a passage in their declaration, 113.
—— petition to the King, with his answer, 205.
—— proclamation for suppressed, 175.
—— proposition of, 418.
—— Scotch rebels, 258.
—— Scotch regiment of guards to be formed, 226.
—— ships of detained, 171.
—— captured, 200.
—— arrested, on the sale of, 206.
—— commissions given by the King to Scotchmen, 417.
—— Scotchmen at Wespend Island, 478.
—— a letter from, Sept. 1616; 335.
—— army of, 277.
—— Earl Marshal of, 203, 212.
—— Lord Chancellor of, *see* Campbell, John, Earl of Loudoun.
—— the Scots, 220, 281, 285, 297, 298, 301, 304, 305, 309, 311, 315, 327, 329, 330, 333, 336, 338, 343–345, 349, 350, 352–355, 358, 360, 361, 368, 369, 377, 380, 389, 392, 394, 395, 398, 401, 403, 407, 408, 409, 411, 417, 418, 423, 432.
—— and the English Parliament, proposed treaty between, 411.
—— answer to a message from the Parliament to, 216.

662

INDEX.

Scotland, the Scots' apostacy, a satire, 362.
— the Scots, are excluded from all business of design and policy, 407.
— — as executioners of Papists, 218.
— — declaration being framed by Parliament against, 406.
— — their declaration mentioned, 410, 421; a paper in explanation of, 425.
— — their engagement, Sir P. Musgrave's relation of, 135.
— — in London, money paid to, 309.
— — letter from to Lord Lanerick, 207.
— — petition against re-engaging them, 385.
— — plunder of a house by, 216.
— Privy Council, their opinion against the King's visiting Ireland, 229; letter to the Lords of, ibid.
— — success of, 207; their intention to conquer England, ibid.
— — take grass, hay, &c. without payment, 213.
— — their purposes gathered from their Propositions, 430.
— — the King's answer to the London Propositions rejected by, 331.
— — the King's journey to, 318.
— — the King's reception by, 319.
— — treaty with, 346.
— — wait to be bribed, 404, 405.
— and England, negotiations between, 421.
— — negotiations of Scotch and English Commissioners, 414.
— Scotch and Dutch Commissioners, 466.
Scots, Mary, Queen of, see Mary.
Scott, Major, 380.
— is suspended the House, 400.
— —, the Leveller, his death, 408.
Scotten, Capt. Edw., letter to Col. Fiennes, 239.
Scripture, private interpretation of, 321–323.
— verses of, interpreted, 316.
— places of Holy Scripture applied by the rebels to their purpose, 416.
Scrope, Mr., at Havre, 306.
Scudamore, Mr., 64.
— John, Lord, ambassador at the French court, 71, 99.

Scudamore, John, Lord, ambassador at the French court, Instructions to, 75.
— letters from to Sec. Windebank, 125.
Seaforth, Earl of, see Mackenzie, Geo.
Seal, the Great, 260, 337, 344, 358, 362, 375, 377, 397, 450.
— — (1624), 501.
— the new, 464.
Seaman, Captain, 252.
— letter from to the Marquis of Ormond, ibid.
— letters dated from aboard his ship, ibid.
Sebastian, King of Portugal, q. v.
Sedan, 125.
— the lands about there to be valued, 369.
Sedan, Muley, 24.
Sedgewick, —, his revelations, 370.
Seeds sent from Spain to England, 189.
Selbye, Father, letters from to Father Leander, 53, 71.
— — to Secr. Windebank, 56.
Selden, Mr., 412, 414.
— abuse of, 416.
Semple, Father Hugh, 161, 163, 165, 166, 168, 170, 174.
— his mission to England, 201–203.
Seneca, 217.
Senneterre, —, French ambassador, 79, 134.
Sequestrations, petition to Committee of, 265.
Seralbo, Marquis de, 174.
Serjeant-at-Arms, 233.
Sermon, a, 32.
Servient, M, 361.
Seton, Mr., 142.
Severn, the (river), report of the enemy's troops coming it, 242.
Seville, Archbishopric of, 102, 104.
— Spanish commissary it, 144.
Sewill, Hugo, an astrologer, 33.
Seymour, Mr., 303, 410.
— Sir E., letter from to the Lord High Admiral, 15.
— Edward, Lord Beauchamp and Earl of Hertford, a letter recommending him to the Duke of Florence (1562), 478.
— Sir Francis, 177.
— Francis, Lord, 224, 353, 371.
— — warrant signed by, 245.
— Sir J., message from Hyde sent by, 316.

INDEX.   603

Seymour, Jo., royalist, letters signed by, 239.
—— William, Marquis of Hertford, 203, 244, 358, 360, 393.
—— his hearing at the Council, on his petition, 205.
—— interview with, ibid.
—— engagement on behalf of the King, 464.
Seynwhin, John, 332.
Shaftesbury, Parliamentary forces approaching, 240.
—— Waller's forces at, 263.
Shafton, letters dated from, 261 (four).
Shaw, Captain, letter from to Lord Cottington, 200.
—— letters from to Secr. Windebank, 71-73, 83, 186, 190.
Sheldon, Dr. Gilbert, Warden of All Souls', Oxford, 335, 371, 384, 391, 402.
—— letter from to Sir E. Hyde, 209.
—— the King's first vow preserved under ground by, 311.
—— letters to, 385, 387, 391.
—— with the King, 382, 383.
Shelford, slaughter of the whole garrison of, 289.
Shelley, Henry, 321.
Shepard, Thos., letter to Hugh Peters, 292.
Sherborne, 282, 284.
—— Lord Digby's defeat at, 285.
—— letters dated from, 253, 261.
Sherbrook, i. e. Cherbourg, q. v.
Sheriffs, rescue from, 222.
Sherley, Sir Tho., letter from to the Lord High Admiral, 5.
Sherwood Forest and Park, 247.
Sherwood, Capt., 439.
—— Dr., sermon by, 371.
Shipman, or Shippman, Sir Abraham, 244.
—— his signature, 310.
—— letter to the Prince, 323.
Shippon, or Skippon, —, 259, 330.
Ship, instructions for the redemption of a, 281.
Ship-money (City), 32; (Royal), 106.
—— note of money levied and paid for shipping business, 105.
—— of 1639, 101.
—— resolutions against and speeches on, 212.
—— efforts to abolish it, ibid.
Ships, 201, 252, 253, 259, 279, 354, 355, 478.

Ships, edict on prizes taken by, 376.
—— a list of English merchant vessels, 493.
—— letters on behalf of the Society of London merchants, ibid.
—— list of, in the Thames, 13.
—— under Gen. Van Haesdonck's command, 270.
—— lists of, 284.
—— names of, 2-5, 17-19, 23, 25, 40, 70, 94, 96, 102.
Ships, names of:—
  Admiral, 116.
  Advantage, 4.
  Adventure, 5.
  Bl. Lady, 446.
  Bonaventure, 233, 373, 503.
  Brownfish, 23.
  Char., 446.
  Christ, of Newcastle, 487.
  Christophera, of Lynn, 480.
  Convert, 446.
  Danyell, of London, 441.
  Discovery, 40.
  Eagle, 279.
  Elizabeth and Francis, of London, 94.
  Elizabeth Bonaventure, 2.
  Fame, of London, 282.
  Francis, 271.
  Gideon, of Lubeck, 271.
  Gray, of London, 487.
  Hercules, 120.
  Hind, 446.
  Juliana, 491.
  Lion, 2, 70.
  Little George, 322.
  London, 252.
  Lord Thomas, 19.
  Love, 446.
  Luke, 496.
  Margaret, of Minehead, 488.
  Mary George, 487.
  Mary Rose, 18, 23.
  Mynion Gale, of Topsham, 496.
  Newcastle, 285.
  Penelope, 4, 5.
  Priscilla, 17.
  Prosper, of London, 94.
  R. Admiral, 446.
  Richard and William, 291.
  Roberta, of Newcastle, 493.
  Ro. Bu., 446.
  Rose, 271.
  St. Andrew, 70.
  St. George, 291.
  St. John the Evangelist, 493.
  Sampson, of Plymouth, 25.
  Satisfact., 446.

Ships, names of, *continued*:—
  Saviour, of London, 487.
  Speedwell, 5.
  Spread Eagle, 307.
  Tenth Whelp, 274.
  Tho., 446.
  V. Admirall, 446.
  Vanguard, 3.
  Ulysses, 4.
  Young Tobias, of Hamburg, 300, 302–304.
  Zulphen, 141.

Shipton, Edw., claim made on, 236.
Shirley, Sir Harry, a bequest of, 81.
—— Lord, in Persia, 32.
Shrewsbury, riots in, against Excise officers, 412.
Shropshire, 214, 410.
—— list of gentlemen of that county, 463.
Shuttleworth, —, a Presbyterian, 431.
Siburg, 74.
Sicily, 381.
Sidney, Robert and Philip, see Sydney.
Sienna, 111.
Sigfried, —, 498.
—— his plot against the King of Denmark, *ibid.*
Sigismund Augustus, or Sigismund II, King of Poland, q. v.
Signet, clerks of the, 260.
Silesia, 21, 232.
Silva, Don Francisco de, 39.
—— Don Philip de, 47, 63, 69.
Silverton, 286.
Simeren, Duke of, 160.
Simony, oath of, 220.
Simpson, Richard, master of the 'Richard and William,' letter of, 291.
Sinclair, Col., in Sweden, 207.
Sinclair, John, Lord, 280.
—— and David Lealey, a difference between, 401.
Skidmore, John, *alias* Leander, 41.
Skillinge, —, papers signed by, 221.
Skipton, —, articles against him, 431.
Skipton, —, his relation of the siege of Lyme, 216.
Skipton, letter dated from, 282.
—— the loss of, 280.
Slaney, or Slanie, Humphrey, 18, 92.

Slaughter, Col., 136.
—— Will., 321.
Sleek, Count, President of the Council of War, 131, 133, 139.
—— minutes of Mr. Taylor's conversations with, 138, 159.
Sligo, Lord, 352.
Slingsby, Col. Richard, paymaster at Bristol, 374.
—— his relation of the battles of Lansdown and Roundway, 246; of the siege of Bristol, *ibid.*; of the battle of Alresford, *ibid.*
—— narrates the doings of a Yorkshire fanatic, 408.
—— letters to Sir E. Hyde, 279, 292.
—— Walter, 323.
Sluce, Robert, 18, 23.
Smith, Mr., 93.
—— fined for conspiracy, 168.
—— at the Hague, 432.
—— Captain, 70.
—— Lieut., success over Sir Arch. Douglas, 207.
—— Capt. John, 215.
—— —— receipt to Sir N. Crisp, 250.
—— —— agreement with Crisp concerning the 'St. George,' *ibid.*
—— —— his complaint against Crisp concerning the 'St. George,' *ibid.*
—— —— account of sums spent as between him and Crisp, *ibid.*
—— —— agreement with Sir N. Crisp for prize-money, 258.
—— —— his complaint against Sir N. Crisp, 212.
—— John, 466.
—— Hans, a Dunkirker, 30.
—— Sir James, his disobedience, 279.
—— —— Goring's complaint against him, 280.
—— —— letter to, *ibid.*
—— Richard, Bishop of Chalcedon, 40.
—— —— receipt to Mr. Fanshawe, 315.
—— W., Sir E. Hyde returns a letter for, 341.
—— William, one of the King's trumpeters, his death, 502.
—— William, an English merchant at Weypend island, 478.
Smithfield, *see* London.
Smolensk, letter dated from, 40.
Smyrna, Sir S. Crow sent there, 308.
Smyth, Col., Sir Alex. Denton's son-in-law, his proceedings in Jersey, 317.

INDEX.

'Smyth, Thomas,' letter of intelligence from, 421.
Smyth or Smythe, Sir Thomas, letters from to the Lords of the Council, 14, 15.
Smythe, ——, 422.
Soame, Alderman, supersedes Acton in the election of Lord Mayor, 207.
Soames, see Somes.
Sobre, Condé de, 74.
Socinians, 392.
Soissons, Count de, his jealousy of his rival, the Prince of Wales, (Charles I.) App. L 3.
Soldiers, a plan for payment of, 246.
Solicitor-General, place of, 372.
Somerset, 259, 262, 264, 265, 267.
—— insolence of the club-men of, 268, 269.
—— levies, 283.
Somerset, Edward, Earl of Glamorgan, afterwards Marquis of Worcester, 301, 306, 371, 503.
—— warrant given by the King to, 296.
—— letter to Sir E. Hyde (1660); ibid.
—— his dealings with the confederate Catholics, ibid.
—— letter of the King directing Ormond to prosecute Glamorgan, 300.
—— letter from to Lord Culpeper, 304.
—— concludes peace in Ireland, and is imprisoned, 332.
—— is much misunderstood, 358.
—— instruction for, 361.
—— letter from to the Bishop of Ferns, 305.
—— news sent from Langherne to, 423.
Somerton, letter dated from, 263.
Somes, or Soames, Dr., sermon by, 374.
Sorherka, Simon, merchant of Westpond island, 478.
Sorbonne, Doctors of the, 54.
Soubize, Mons. de, 157.
Southam, Thomas, 489.
Southampton, letter dated from, 30.
Southampton, Earl of, see Wriothesley, Thomas.
Southenorthe, Edward, merchant of London, a letter concerning him, 482.
Southwark, 207.
Southwark, Quakers at, 395.
—— the army's proposals agreed to at, 386.
—— affairs in the City and, 386.
Southwell, letter dated from, 311.
Southwell, Sir Richard, L.
Southworth, John, petition to Charles I, 147.
Spa, the, 412.
Spada, Cardinal, 30.
Spahan, see Ispahan.
Spain, 42, 44, 96, 104, 225, 273, 340, 346, 366, 376, 378, 400, 402, 485, 502.
—— ambassadors to, 204.
—— Spanish ambassador (1620), 19.
—— —— (1563), his speech, L.
—— —— his infamous conduct (1624); App. L 3.
—— Spanish ambassadors (1640), 198.
—— —— result of conference with, 199.
—— —— a loan promised by, 211.
—— Spaniards' power by sea, 13.
—— Spanish match, negotiations on, 20, seqq.
—— —— finance, 126.
—— —— ports, embargo on, 141, 144.
—— —— rank of grandee, 148.
—— —— foreign ministers, four degrees of, 149.
—— Spaniards' aims in Germany, Italy, and Brazil, 150.
—— Spanish fleet defeated by the Dutch, 168.
—— —— defeated in English waters, 187, 188, 189, 194.
—— —— in the Groyne, 183; in the Downs, 185.
—— —— offer of English protection to, 184-186.
—— Spanish navigation, decay, 188.
—— —— shipping, state of, 175, 198.
—— defeat of Spaniards at Bouzy and elsewhere, 170.
—— prosperity of, 171.
—— Spaniards taken by Hollanders out of English ships, 177, 180.
—— Spanish troops transported in English merchant ships, 182.
—— Spanish trade to Flanders, 182.
—— narrow escape of the King and Queen from fire, 195.
—— merchants' complaints in, 201.
—— passage of Irish from, 219.
—— defeat of Spaniards, 221.

Spain, receipt of money from Spaniards, 228.
— defeat of Spaniards by the French at Rossiglione, 229.
— victory of Spaniards over the French near Cambray, 231.
— troops of, admitted into Rome, 213.
— Spanish army, 380.
— news of the Spanish army in Flanders, 383.
— Spanish armada, 417.
— a French convoy taken by Spaniards, 123.
— Lord Goring's training in the Spanish army, 136.
— disturbances between Spanish and English merchants, 186.
— English ships detained in, 190.
— Ferdinand, Infant Cardinal of, his jealousy, 210.
— his death, 231.
— the Infant Don Carlos; App. l. 3.
— letter to, 115.
— Mary, Infanta of, articles agreed on in the match of the Prince of Wales (Charles I); App. L 1, 2.
— Kings of, see Philip II, III, and IV.
— Queen of, see Isabel.
— and England against Holland and Sweden, negotiations for alliance with, 210.
— and France, 418.
— peace between attempted, 127.
— strength of the latter, 166.
— secret treaty between, 198.
— peace between, 347.
— war between, 374.
— and Holland, peace between, 372.
— treaty between, in suspense, 366, 368.
— and the Empire (1638), 147.
Spanish proverb, 224.
Speaker of the House of Commons, the, see Lenthall, W.
— the new Speaker (1627-8), see Finch, Sir John.
Spencer, or Spenser, James. 478.
— letters in behalf of, 497.
— his letters commendatory to the Magistrates of Dantsic, 498.
— Lieut.-Col. W., 159.
Spernou, —, at Caen, 322.
Spinola, Marquis, 21, 22.
— with the Spanish army, 183.

Spires, 22, 23.
— Bishop of, 21.
— letters dated from, 61.
Spithovius, or Spithoneus, John, prebend of Gillingham Major, his credentials to the King of Denmark, 471. 472.
— letters patent granting him leave of absence to travel, 476.
'Spread Eagle,' account of sails and ropes put on board the (ship), 307.
— receipt for the same, ibid.
Spring Garden, the, see London.
Spruson, Mr., commission to, to apprehend pirates, 8.
Squibb, Mr., is taken with Parliament letters, 422.
— letter to, mentioned, 463.
Stackpool, letter dated from, 223.
Stafford, 249, 440.
Stafford, Viscount, see Howard, William.
Stannes, or Staynes, Doctor, 287, 418.
Stamford, Earl of, see Grey, Henry.
Stanley, James, Earl of Derby, 296, 375.
— Charlotte, Countess of Derby, 296.
— William, Earl of Derby, letters from to the Lords of the Council, 14, 15.
Stanton, Capt., 437, 452.
Stapleton, —, M.P., 336.
Star Chamber, the, 243, 350.
— a suit in, 148.
— Judges' opinions published in, 212.
— examinations, reports of, about the poisoning of James I, 364.
State, Secretary of, 244.
— letters from to Dr. Knopper, Secretary to the King of Denmark, 487, 491, 492.
— to the Mayor, &c. of Dunkirk, 488.
— see Falkland, Lord.
State reasons against the proceeding to try the King, 504.
States, the, French and Portuguese deputies welcome the Duke of York, 421.
— letter from the Ambassador of, to the Parliament, 250.
— Dr. Isaac Dorislaus' credentials addressed to, 428.
— and the Knights of Malta, rupture between, 438.

INDEX. 607

States-General of the United Provinces, warrant for conveyance of Duke of Buckingham's pictures from Amsterdam, 114.
— credentials of W. Strickland to, 363.
— act of, L.
— treaty negotiations, 29, 30, 42.
— letters to, 286.
— agent resident with, see Boswell, J.
— ships of, 415.
— and the Prince of Orange, 418.
— their allowance to the Prince of Wales, 438.
Statute 28 Hen. VI, de Resump. in Turri Lond., 350.
Stawell, Sir E., see Stowell.
— Sir John, letter to, 31.
— — to be tried, 409.
Staynes, Dr., see Staines.
Stephens, — 242.
— Edw., M.P., royalist, 160.
— letters signed by, 239.
Stopkins, Col., is betrayed and killed, 440.
Sterrene, Henry, Captain, and his ship, detained, 195.
Stettin, 136, 137, 155.
Steuart, Mr., letter from to Secretary Windebank, 118.
Stevenston, letters dated from, 270-272.
Steward, or Stewart, Capt., 138, 149, 150.
Steward, Capt., his business with the Spanish King, 208.
— Col., employed by the King on the Scotch business, 255.
— Dr., 380.
— grant of the Deanery to, 227.
— — is appointed Dean of the Prince's chapel, 329.
— — recommended by the King, 333.
— — his relation of the management of the fleet under the Prince of Wales, 437.
— — letter to, 350.
— John, Earl of Traquaire, 183, 404, 435.
— Capt., letter from to Mr. Aylesbury, 23.
— Capt. Robert, 95, 98, 102-104, 114, 121.
Stickhem, letter dated from, 184.
Stirling, the King at, 335.

Stirling, treaty of, 160.
Stockholm, Swedish fleet at, 272.
Stoke, the King at, 287.
— letter dated from, 386.
Stokes, Da., his signature, 502.
Stone, Henry, 19.
Stookhem, see Stickhem.
Stowell, Sir Edw., 342, 371, 390.
— letter to W. Edgeman (signed Stawell), 376.
— Sir John, see Stawell.
Stradling, Capt. Sir J., of the ship 'Bonaventure,' 119.
— orders from the King to, 233, 371.
— order to, to take his ship to Portsmouth, 503.
Strafford, Earl of, see Wentworth, Thomas.
Stralendorff, Baron, Vice-Chancellor, 21, 23, 83, 93, 100, 101.
Stralsund, 130.
— letter to the Council of the city of, 494.
— letter dated from, 95.
Strangways, Giles, 389.
— Sir John, has compounded, 417.
Strasburg, letter dated from, 468.
Stratton, 303.
Straubing, 104.
— letter dated from, 20.
Straughan, Capt., concerned in a duel, 360.
Strickland, Walter, Parl. agent in Denmark, 286.
— resident at the Hague, 244.
— his credentials to the States-General, 363.
— instructions for, mentioned, ibid.
— sent to treat with the States-General, 413.
Strode, Sir G., letter to Secretary Nicholas, 382.
— Sir Richard, a suit of his, 118.
— Col., sends 100 men from Malmesbury, 240.
Stroud, —, 242.
Strowd, Col. W., 460.
Stuart, Alex., 40.
— Henry, Earl of Darnley, his death (1568), 497.
— James, fourth Duke of Leonox, 208.
— — letters from to Secretary Windebank, 106, 116.
— James, Duke of Richmond, 383, 384, 391.

Stuart, James, Duke of Richmond, application of a pass for, 253.
—— instructions to, on his mission to the Parliament, 254.
—— confers with the Independents on behalf of the King, 464.
—— letter to, 321.
Stuckley, Sir Lewis, 15.
Sturmius, John, letters of commendation from, 468.
Subrao, Prince of, 50.
Suet, near Stettin, 113.
Suffolk, county, Admiralty suits in, 17.
—— news from, 423.
Suffolk, Lady, letter for her, 497.
—— Earls of, see Howard, Thomas and James.
Sugars, 4.
Summer, a hot, 3.
Supremacy, Royal and Papal, 56.
Surrey and Kent, petition from, to be presented, 423.
—— Owen, receipt from, 315.
Surrey, Parliament apologizes to the County of, 424.
—— petitioners, eleven killed, 425.
Surrey, Earl of, see Howard, Thos., Earl of Arundel and Surrey.
Sussex, 416.
—— letter from the Commissioners of, to Hugh Peters, 243.
Sussex, Earl of (1558), see Ratcliffe, Thomas.
—— —— see Savile, Thomas.
Sutton's Hospital, 421.
Swansea, 291.
—— seized by Langborne's regiment, 413.
Swart, Martin, ill-treats G. Norwood, 491.
Swartenburg, Count of (ambassador of Brandenburg), 119.
Sweckovitz, Adam, Baron Mittenburg, ambassador from the Emperor, 488.
Sweden, 74, 75, 77, 78, 104, 116, 157, 210, 336, 361, 383, 487.
—— Scottish officers who have served in, 207.
—— Cecilia, Princess of, 484, 488, 489.
—— —— letter to, 481.
—— —— visits England, 489.
—— —— her husband, see Baden, Prince of.
—— Eric, Prince (afterwards King of), letters to, 470, 473, 474, 476, 479, 481, 484, 486–491, 493, 496.

Sweden, Eric, King of, agents to, 485.
—— Gustavus, King of, his death, 473.
—— —— letters to, 470, 473.
Sweden and Denmark, peace between, 276.
—— and Poland, 141.
—— and France, league between, 142.
Swedes, the, 369, 410.
—— are beaten in Germany, 422.
—— and Danes, expected to assist the Scots, 408.
—— and Imperialists, treaty between, 143, 144, 145, 146, 152, 160.
—— —— in Silesia, movements of, 232.
Swedish fleet at Stockholm, 232.
—— ships, 377.
Swinnen, ——, M.P., 460.
Sydney, Algernon, letter to W. Aylesbury, 441.
—— Philip, Lord Lisle, his departure from Belfast, 345.
—— —— at Bristol, 361.
—— —— is appointed Lord Lieut. of Ireland, 361.
—— —— arrears due to, 247.
—— Robert, second Earl of Leicester (1656), 92, 96, 100, 114, 148, 149, 157, 176, 212, 326.
—— —— difference between him and Lord Scudamore, 92.
—— —— cypher with, sent to him in France (1637), 216.
—— —— as ambassador at Paris, 413.
Sydney, ——, Lady Leicester, 218.
Sydney, R., letter from to Mr. Aylesbury, 429.
Sydon Lane, letters dated from, 216, 220.
Symkis, or Simkis, Capt., 440.
Symmachus quoted, 320.
Synod, the, 464.

T.

T., J., letter of intelligence to, 387.
Taaffe, Theobald, Viscount, 442.
—— Lord Inchiquin's victory over him, 402.
—— declares for the King, 419.
—— letter from to Sir E. Hyde, 311.
Tabor, 23.
Tacitus, 387.

INDEX.

Talbot, Mr., consul at Seville, letter from to Mr. Hopton, 72.
—— Sir Gilbert, letters from to Lord Falkland, 224–226, 228–231, 233.
—— Henry, 234.
—— John, 163.
—— Sir R., 442.
—— T., letter from to R. Hunt, 66.
Talmont, Prince of, proposed marriage with the sister of the Landgrave of Hesse, 394.
Tamasp I, Emperor of *Persia*, q. v.
Tarragona, 386.
Tartars, in Moldavia, 131.
Tartary, the Great Cham of, 82.
Tate, Mr., 447.
Taverner, E., letter from, 34.
Tavistock, 200, 295.
—— letters dated from, 3, 25, 297, 300.
Taunton, the capture of, 241.
—— proposal to burn, 261, 262.
—— the siege of, 261, 263–265, 267, 268.
—— defeat of the forces of, 261.
Tayler, —, paymaster at Berwick, requires money to pay the garrison, 207.
Tayller, Henry, 186.
—— letters from to Secr. Windebank, 101, 171, 193.
—— letter from to Mr. J. Taylor, 178.
Taylor, Mr., account of his interviews with Count Trautmansdorf and the Duke of Lorraine, 162.
—— and Secretary Windebank, 173.
Taylor, Mr., English agent at Vienna, is recalled, 170, 174, 197.
—— letters from to Sir Wm. Howard, 167.
—— John, 48, 62, 63, 99, 101, 110, 114, 118.
—— relation of his negotiation in Germany, to 1630; 172.
—— committed to the Tower, 185.
—— his innocence asserted, 186.
—— his cypher, 215.
—— letters from to Lord Cottington, 57, 60, 71, 86, 89, 94, 116.
—— letters from to the Emperor Ferdinand II, 82, 88, 89.
—— letters from to the Emperor Ferdinand III, 145, 149.
—— letters from to Secr. Windebank, 49, 51, 52, 56, 70, 71, 75,

77, 78, 80, 82, 83, 85, 87, 88, 90–94, 95, 96, 98, 100, 102–107, 109, 111–113, 118, 119, 131, 133–145, 147–167, 169, 170, 172.
Taylor, John, instructions for, 68.
—— letters to, 82, 85–87, 89, 94, 112, 151, 176, 178, 180, 184.
—— arrives at Middleborough, 436.
Taynton, 305.
Temple, the, letters dated from, 33.
Temple, Sir Peter, 257.
—— Lady, her friendships, *ibid.*
Tenby, blockaded by Horton, 425.
—— Castle, report that it joins Pembroke against the Parliament, 418.
—— officers of, 419.
'Tenth Whelp,' the (ship), 271.
Tenyson, Mrs. Margaret, 150.
Teracusa, Marquis de, 171.
Terçeras, merchants in the, 174.
Testament, Greek, 355.
Tetuan, Moorish governor of, letter from to Mr. John Dupps, 23.
Tewkesbury, 303.
Texts quoted, 416.
Thatcham, 265.
Thestepians, Bay of, Virginia, 500.
Thetford, proclamation at, 1604; 177.
Thinn, Sir James, 209.
'Tho.,' the (ship), 146.
Thomas, Prince of Savoy, q. v.
—— Hugh, 293.
Thompson, T., letter from to the Lord High Admiral, 2.
Thraciger, Adam, chancellor to the Duke of Holstein, 470.
Threcius, Christopher, and his pupil, 468.
Throckmorton, Th., letter from to Col. Fiennes, 242.
Thrupp, or Thruppe, 394.
Thruppe, John, letter from to W. Edgeman, 383.
Thuringia, 131.
Thurles, Viscount, 20.
Thynne, Charles, his acquirements praised, 500.
—— Clement, document signed by, 213.
—— Lady Isabella, letter to, 344.
Tier, —, (*a pseudonym*), 352.
Tichborne, *see* Titchborne.
Tilbury and Gravesend held by the army, 385.
Tildesley, Sir T., 436.
Tillingham, Essex, the living of, 216.
Tin, blown at St. Neot's, 268.
Tintoretto, Giac. Robusti, II, 60.
Tirlemont, 66.

Titchborne, Col., made Lieutenant of the Tower, 387.
Titchborne, or Tichborne, Sir Henry, Governor of Drogheda, 227.
—— his signature, 334.
Tithes, petitions against, 330.
Tiverton, 271.
Tobacco, 3, 4.
—— monopoly of, 211.
Tod (of Sweden) revolts, 104.
Toledo, Don Frederick de, 47; his death, 55, 60.
Tomasillo, i. e. Thomas Cary, q. v.
Tomline, Jeremy, 305.
—— Major, addresses the King at Holmby, 382.
Tomlinson, William, letter to Mr. Triplett, 212.
Tomson, Thomas, of London, 469.
Tonnage and Poundage, commission to sign the Bill of, 227.
Topsham, ship of, 196.
Toralts, Prince, and his son, death of, 400.
Torgau, 131.
Torre, La, letter dated from, 227.
Torrington, 300.
—— letter dated from, 301.
—— Lord Goring at, 268.
—— Lords Hopton and Capell at, 303.
Tortosa, 376.
Totnes, 297.
—— letter dated from, 283.
Touchet, Mervyn, Lord Audley, Earl of Castlehaven, 382.
—— his capital sentence alluded to, 351.
—— his trial, 34.
Toulon, 378.
Tower of London, the, 309, 389, 390, 403, 409, 422.
—— prisoners there, 206, 207, 212, 358, 419.
—— the Mint in, advised to be moved to Leadenhall, 206.
—— the strengthening of, 205.
—— Mr. Palmer sent there, 221.
—— Col. Copley condemned to, 389.
—— delivered to West, 424.
—— letters dated from, 15, 219.
—— Constables of, see Cottington, Lord; Fairfax, Sir T.
—— Lieutenants of, see Conyers, Sir J.; Titchborne, Col.
Towerson, Captain, 79.
Tracy, Mons. de, 374.
Trade, decay of East-country merchants, 1620; 19.
Trade, letters on, 477.

Traill, Lieut.-Col., letter to Arthur Annesley, 339.
Trainbands, list of for thirteen northern counties, 163, 164.
—— instructions for summoning, 235.
Transylvania, invaded by the Turks, 111.
Traquhair, Earl of, see Stewart, John.
Trautmansdorf, Count, 131, 142, 148, 151, 161.
—— account of Mr. Taylor's interview with him, 162.
—— a story of, 164.
Trayle, John, 426, 427, 430.
Treasurer, Lord Hiyh, see Cottington, Francis, Lord.
—— Vice, office of, 200.
Treasury Commissioners (1638), 73.
—— warrant from, 221.
Treaty of Cologne, 113, 114, 118, 131, 133.
—— between England, France, and the United Provinces, project of, 58, 127.
—— between England and France, project of, 129, 131, 134.
—— between France, England, Spain, and Austria, project of, 77, 78.
—— between the English and Portuguese, 66.
—— proposed between France, Spain, and the Empire (1636), 109; (1637), 132.
—— of Prague, 116, 121, 137.
—— of Uxbridge, 443.
—— secret, between Spain and England, 46–51, 53, 59, 68.
—— of the Isle of Wight, 443.
—— —— heads of, 449.
—— see also under the names of Countries.
Tredeban, Sieur de, of St. Malo, 465, 466.
Tregarden, letter dated from, 275.
Trelawny, ——, 316.
Tremayne, Lewis, 323.
Tremellius, Emanuel, 497.
Trent, Council of, 482.
Tresham, or Tresam, Col. Sir Will., 98, 101.
—— answer to complaints brought by him, 164, 167.
—— quarrel between him and Col. Gage, 165.
Treswell, Serjt., 424.
Trethewy, or Trethewey, Mr., 376, 379, 387, 389, 396.
—— at Caen, 322.

INDEX.   611

Trethewy, Mr., his brother L., 100.
—— letter of, 383.
—— letter to W. Edgeman, 400.
Trevanion, Sir Charles, Vice-Admiral of the South of Cornwall, 278, 295.
—— tenths of prizes to be paid to, 274.
—— answer of Sir Nich. Crisp to his petition, 293.
Treeware, letters dated from, 433.
Treves, Bishop of, 80, 137, 138.
Treves, or Triers, Philip Christopher, Elector of, 21, 106, 110, 111.
—— imprisoned, 64, 110.
Trevise, 292.
Trevor, Arthur, 410.
—— Capt. Edw., letter to, 11.
—— Sir John, letter from to the Lord High Admiral, 4.
—— Thomas, 127.
Trim, 362.
Trinity House brethren, letters from to the Lord High Admiral, 16-18.
Trinity House, Ratcliff, letters dated from, 16-18.
Triplett, Thomas, 367.
—— hardships of his case, 215, 216.
—— his joy at receiving Hyde's letters, 217.
—— petition to the Lords at Ripon, 218.
—— summons to, to appear before the Grand Committee of Religion, 219.
—— letters from to Sir E. Hyde, 212, 215-221, 282.
—— —— to W. Edgeman, 288.
—— letter to, 212.
Tromp, Admiral Van, 185.
Troughton, Captain John, commission to, to suppress piracy, 2.
Trowbridge, division of lands at, 30.
Trumbull, Mr., 18.
Trump, Admiral, made a Knight of the Garter, 226.
Truro, 277, 287, 303, 304.
—— execution at, 277.
—— letters dated from, 270, 277, 278, 285, 288, 289, 292.
Tuam, 311.
—— letter dated from, ibid.
—— Dean of, see King, Richard.
—— John, Archbishop of, 191.
—— letter from to the officers of the army, 464.
Tule, Bernard, of Dantzic, 479.
Tunbridge, Lord, see Burgh, Richard.
Turberville, Humphry, a prisoner for religion, 53.
Turenne, Marshal de, 378, 383, 384, 393, 394, 407, 419.

Turenne, Marshal de, his movements, 380.
Turin, letters dated from, 61.
—— the King's resident at, 1635, see Morton, ——.
Turkey, Amurath IV, Emperor of, 37.
—— petition for employment in, 255.
—— Turkish galleys defeated, 381.
—— Ibraim, Sultan of, drawn out of his seraglio, 118.
—— Mustapha, Sultan of, makes a treaty of commerce with England, 502.
—— ambassador to the Grand Signior, see Rose, Sir Thos.
Turks, the, invade Transylvania, 111; are defeated, 114.
—— at sea, 120, 491.
—— threaten Christendom, 131.
—— their impending descent on Christendom, 174.
—— said to be negotiating with the French, 184.
—— threaten an invasion of Poland, 162; of Hungary, 193.
—— and the Venetian republic, peace with, 361.
Tuscany, Ferdinand II, Duke of, 99.
—— —— agent for, 118.
Tutbury, letters dated from, 47, 266.
Tweed, the, a story of rats crossing it, 389.
Twerdie, Stephen, 497.
Twisden, or Twysden, Sir Roger, 382.
Tynemouth, occupied by Leslie, 204.
Tyrconnell, Colonel, 165, 170, 180.
Tyrone, ploughing fines in, 5.
—— Col., 165, 169.
—— Earl of, see O'Neill, John.
Tyrrel, Dr., 364.

V. W.

Vachan, Cuthbert, is illtreated by officials in Norway, 478.
Valentia, Viscount, see Annesley, Francis.
Valentin, John, 486.
Valentine, Thomas, detained at Copenhagen, 485.
Valenza sul Po, assault on, 71.
—— siege of, 160.
Valette, Cardinal de la, 66, 71.
—— Duke of, 124.
—— —— condemned for treason, 171.
Vallois, Mons., letters of, 431, 432.
Valparaiso, Marquis de, 116, 123.
Valteline, the, 108.
Vandale, Arnold, 480.

4 I 2

612 INDEX.

Vanderpal, —, 130.
Vandyke, Sir Anthony, 92.
Vane, Sir Henry, letter from to Charles I., 37, 392.
— letter to, ibid.
— succeeds Secretary Coke, 194.
— letter from to Secretary Windebank, 204.
— Treasurer, letter to Windebank, 208.
— Secretary, letter from to the Lords Justices of Ireland, 219.
Vane, Sir H., jun., 357, 412, 451.
— document signed by, 413.
— his report to the King's prejudice, 458.
— letters to, 305, 306.
'Vanguard' (a ship), letter dated from, 1.
Van Tromp, Admiral, see Tromp.
Vavasour, Sir W., 437.
— his journal of military motions, 305.
Vaud, or Vawdye, Giles, 401.
— letter of safe-conduct for, 495.
Vaughan, Capt., 219.
— Roger, 415.
Veale, Capt., of Alvaston, warrant to seize his goods, 239.
Velada, Marquis de, 193-195, 197.
— letter of credence for, 180.
Velasquez, —, painter, 201.
Velez, Marquis de los, 173.
Vendôme, Duke of, 393.
— escape of his son from Vincennes, 425.
Venetian ambassador, 361.
— declaration of, 412.
— ambassadors, their precedence, 100.
— — in England and Holland, 123.
— — make peace with the Turks, 181.
— fleet, defeat fifty Turkish galleys, 381.
Venetians, 228, 233.
Venice, 275.
— oppresses the English, 126.
— and Savoy, ambassadors of, 191.
— English consulship at, 192.
— embassy to, 227.
Venice, Jerome, the Doge and Council of, letters to, 476, 480, 492.
— Pope Urban VIII's quarrel with, 501.
— letters dated from, 63, 70, 112, 126, 160, 223-226, 228-231, 233, 275, 501.

Venice, English consul at, see Kent, Joseph.
Venn, Alderman, letter to, 43.
— Capt., evidence against, 221.
Verdeman, —, Ablegate, commissioned to England, 88.
Vere, Sir Horace, invades Spires, 22, 23.
Veruge, John, serjeant, 121.
Veulo, on the Mass, 186.
Ufford, Northamptonshire, the living of, 216.
Vibert, Capt., sent to Amsterdam, 410.
Vic, Sir Henry de, afterwards Chancellor of the Garter, 112, 163, 427, 436.
— is recalled from Brussels, 362.
— his successor, Sandys, 367.
— letter sent by, 427.
— letter to, 433.
— letters from to Lord Falkland, 223, 224, 226, 231-233.
'Vice-Admiral,' the (ship), 116.
Victor Amadeus, Duke of Savoy, q. v.
Vielart, Captain Peter, 103.
Vienna, 471.
— letters dated from, 20-22, 77, 78, 80, 82, 83, 85-96, 134-145, 147, 149, 151-155, 160-167, 169, 170, 176, 178, 179, 192, 197.
— Bishop of, see Villars, Pierre VI de.
Vieuville, Marquis de la, 156, 157.
Villada, Marquis de, 196.
Villa-franca, Marquis of, 104, 110, 114.
Villa Mediana, Condé de, 131, 141.
— letter from to Lord Aston, 125.
— — to Secretary Windebank, 131, 138.
— v. Oñate.
Villars, Pierre VI de, Bp. of Vienna, 100, 101, 103, 105, 107.
Ville, Marquis de, envoy of the Duke of Lorraine, 195, 198.
Villena, Marquis of, 166.
Villiers, Lady Barbara, letter from to Edward Hyde, 36.
— George, Lord High Admiral, Marquis and first Duke of Buckingham, 13, 31, 32; App. I. 5, 6; App. II. 15.
— account of gold mines related to, 29.
— letter from Lords Carlisle and Holland to, App. I. 6.
— letters from to the King; App. I. 7, 8.
— letter in praise of him, App. I. 7.

Villiers, George, first Duke of Buckingham, letter from to the Earl of Bristol, on the negotiations with Spain, 501.
—— letter from to the Vice-Admiral of North Wales, 19.
—— treaty with Gustavus Adolphus, 29.
—— order from to the London Custom Officers, 30.
—— speech at the Council, 32.
—— grievous wrongs done by him to Lady Purbeck, 218.
—— proceedings against him, 411.
—— letters to, 14–17, 20, 22, 24, 25.
Villiers, George, second Duke of Buckingham, and his brother, in London, 309; is to marry the Earl of Northumberland's daughter, *ibid*.
—— warrant for conveyance of his pictures to Amsterdam, 414.
—— at Kingston, 130.
Villiers, John, Viscount Purbeck, proofs that a patent was passed for him, 17 James I, 218.
—— Frances, Lady Purbeck, daughter of Sir Edw. Coke, petition to the House of Lords, 218.
—— Mary, Duchess of Buckingham, legacy of Archbishop Laud to, 256.
Vincennes, escape from, 125.
Vintners and merchants, settlement of the dispute between, 116.
Violett, ——, prohibition against, 14.
Virginia, claim made by the King of Spain to, 174.
—— not included in the articles of peace (1647), 144.
—— R. II.'s enterprise in, 500.
—— Bay of the Thesteplane, *ibid*.
Visitation, appeal against, 380.
Vitry, Marshal, 125.
Vivian, Sir Rich., *see* Vyvyan.
Vladislaus VI, King of Poland, *see* Poland.
Ulster, ploughing fines in, 5.
—— customs in, 7.
—— President of, 11.
—— Lord General of, *see* O'Neil, Owen.
Ulyssipone, book printed at, 101.
United Provinces, *see* States-General.
Universities, 337.
—— on regulating the two, 449.
Vosbergen, Sieur, 13.
Uplendon, 305.
Upton, E., letter to Mr. Edwards, 390.

Urban VIII, Pope [Maffeo Barberini], permits 600,000 ducats to be raised for the King, 126.
—— report of his death, 130.
—— instructions to his Nuncio in England, 101.
—— his illness, 224.
—— and the Duke of Parma, quarrel between, 226, 230, 231.
—— his ministers, 227.
—— suspends the Duke of Lorraine's excommunication, 233.
—— his quarrel with Venice, 501.
—— letter from to the King of France (Louis XIII.), 30.
—— letters to, 53, 58.
Uscome, Richard, 499.
Utrecht, letter dated from, 98.
Uttoxeter, the Duke of Hamilton taken by Lord Grey at, 440.
Uvedale or Uvedall, Sir W., 7, 10, 203.
Uxbridge, 307.
—— Conference, 257.
—— Commissioners, warrant to, 258.
—— treaty of, 352, 356, 373, 381, 382, 413.
Vyvyan, Sir Richard, warrant to deliver him a ton of flax for the Pendennis fleet, 276.

W.

W., A., i.e. *Woodhead*, A.
Wade, Sir Will., ambassador to the Duke S. Adolphus, 468.
Wagh, Mrs. Susan, letter of, mentioned, 427.
Wagstaff, Serj.-Major, 222.
Wagstaffe, Sir Joseph, 263, 271, 290.
Wake, Sir Baldwin, 327, 347, 353, 373, 417.
—— ammunition taken from the 'Eagle' by, 279.
—— note by, 307.
—— note of expenses, 315.
—— and Sir G. Carteret, conferences between, for the reduction of Guernsey, 439.
—— account of twelve barrels of indigo delivered to, 441.
—— letter from to Robert Russell, 358.
—— to W. Edgeman, 370.
—— letters to, 347, 358.
—— is dispensed from observing the Lent fast, 462.
Walden, Geo., owner of a ship, 180.

Wales, 256, 381, 388, 421, 422, 426.
—— Council of the Marches of, 213.
—— —— why the four English counties ought to be under their jurisdiction, 214.
—— —— resolutions on, 220.
—— —— its jurisdiction a grievance, 221.
—— Welsh, the, opposed to Cromwell, 378.
—— affray between some Welshmen and soldiers, 411.
—— military movements in, 393, 418, 420—425.
—— defeat in, 423; affairs in, *ibid.*
—— militia of, 449.
—— North, 419, 440.
—— South, judge of circuit in, 234.
—— —— favourable for the King, 416.
Wales, Prince of, see Charles (II).
—— a counterfeit Prince of, see Evans, Corn.
Walgrave, Charles, 121:
Walker, Mr., M.P., 460.
—— Col., 272.
—— Mr. (Blanch Lyon), letter from to Lord Maltravers, 115.
—— C., letter from to Col. Fiennes, 242.
—— Sir Edward, 353, 355.
—— —— Garter King at Arms, warrant from the King to, 264.
—— —— in France, 348.
—— —— his journal, mentioned, 398.
—— —— "Historical Discourses" (1705), 450.
—— Thomas, a London merchant, 491.
Wallace, Mr., 116.
—— letters from to Charles I., 117, 120.
—— —— to Secretary Windebank, 119.
Waller, Mr., M.P., 394, 460.
—— David, 231.
—— Sir Hardress, particulars for him to relate on Irish affairs, 235.
—— —— letter from to the Marquis of Ormond, 251.
—— —— is imprisoned, 419.
—— —— is repulsed by Fortescue, 420.
—— —— supersedes Cromwell in his command, 422.

Waller, Sir William, 234, 241, 259-263, 370.
—— draws his forces to Bath, 240.
—— request for 500 men, 242.
—— a report that he is to take Jersey, 365.
—— letters attributed to, 243.
—— letter from to Capt. Thomas Counsell, 239.
—— —— to Col. Fiennes, 242.
Wallingford, names of persons in, debtors of the King, 247.
—— alleged abuses in the non-payment of the garrison at, 251.
—— is taken, 328.
—— House, letters dated from, 33, 53.
Walpole, Thomas, barber, to attend the Duke of York, 445.
Walron, John, of Exeter, 496.
Walrond, Mr., letter from to Sir John Stawell, 31.
—— Capt., warrant to, 286.
Walsh, J., 442
—— Sir Robert, see Welsh.
—— Thomas, R. C. Bp. of Cashel, letter from to the officers of the army, 464.
—— William, L
Walsingham, —, 309.
Walwick, Arnold, 187.
Wanderford, Christopher, Master of the Rolls, letter to, 11.
Wandesforde, or Wansford, John, 136, 137.
—— —— letters from to Sir E. Hyde, 445, 446.
Wandsworth, murder of the miller of, 423.
Wansford, John, see Wandesforde, John.
War, Council of, 282, 314, 370, 385, 390, 395, 397, 399, 401.
—— resolutions passed at, tendered to Parliament, 384.
—— resolution of, 408.
—— their declaration disavowed by the army, 411.
—— resolutions for the campaign settled at a, 418.
—— in Scarborough Castle, orders of, 458.
—— letter to, 465.
War, Secretary of, see Fanshawe, Mr.
Wards, Court of, order to the Master and Council of, 35.
—— and Liveries, Court of, 450.
—— —— papers respecting, 454, 455.

INDEX. 615

Ware, the head quarters of the army, 399.
—— rendezvous at, 400.
Ware, Sir James, a witness against the Earl of Strafford, 221.
—— his signatures, 334, 362.
Wareham, the taking of, 305.
Wariston, Lord, 461.
Warminster, its capture mentioned, 240.
Warneford, ——, 365.
Warren, Serg.-Major, 236, 237.
—— Capt., bill for sailing tackle to, 307.
—— —— his receipts for the sails and ropes, ibid.
—— Henry, letter to Dr. Henry Jones, 225.
Warrington, 439.
—— Col. Booth taken there, 440.
—— letter dated from, 293.
Warwick, Earl of, see Rich, Robert.
Washington, Capt., 219, 433.
Waterford, disputed right to the customs of, 248.
—— Congregation at, letter from to Piers Fitz-Gerald, 329.
—— —— "decretum perjurii," ibid.
—— letters dated from, 304, 311, 312, 327, 328, 330, 332.
—— R. C. Bishop of, see Comerford, Patrick.
Watford, rendezvous appointed at, 400.
Watson, ——, 400.
—— James, 492.
—— Rev. Richard, letter from to W. Edgeman, 400.
—— Roger, 475.
—— Scout-Master, letter from to a brother Independent, 448.
—— William, 476.
Webb, or Webbe, General, 282, 283.
—— postscript to a letter from the Prince of Wales to, 298.
Webster, John, of Amsterdam, provisions ordered of, 420, 427.
—— letter to John Aylesbury, 432.
—— supplies match and shot, 446.
Weedon, Messrs., 61.
Weemes, or Wemyss, Capt., instructions to be sent to, 502.
Welbeck, 296.
—— letter dated from, 150.
Welch, Sir Robert, 445.
—— or Walsh, Sir Robert, the Prince's judgment on, 444.
—— judgment upon him for his attempt on the person of Lord Culpeper, 438; is forbidden the Court, ibid.
Welden, Col., 414, 444.
Welford, Father, or Wilford, q. v.
Welles, Mr., letter from to Sir Tho. Aylesbury, 35.
Wellington, 261, 263.
—— letter dated from, 234.
Wells, petition to the Prince of Wales at, 267.
—— letters dated from, 241, 263, 264.
Welsene, letter dated from, 180.
Wemyss, or Weemes, Patrick, the King recommends severity against, 258.
Wenman, Sir F., 294.
—— lady, debt of 100l. to Sir E. Hyde, 319.
—— Thomas, his signature, 451.
Wentworth, John, petition to the King, 147.
Wentworth, Thomas, Visc., afterwards Earl of Strafford, Lord Deputy of Ireland, 117, 202, 213, 217, 233.
—— propositions concerning the government of Ireland, 31.
—— articles of impeachment against for high treason, 210.
—— petition to the Lords, on the examination of witnesses in his case, 211; another, to be heard by counsel, ibid.
—— in the Tower, 212.
—— his answers to the articles of indictment, 212.
—— his last letter to the King, 219.
—— the wrongs done by him to Lord Mountnorris, 220.
—— witnesses against him, 221.
—— order of the House of Commons to, 221.
—— his death, 344.
—— his impeachment, mentioned, 382.
—— minutes of papers relating to Ireland on his going there, 36.
—— letter to, 87.
—— letter of thanks to him, 143.
—— letters from to Lord Mountnorris, 44, 136.
—— —— to Secretary Windebank, 89, 168.
Wentworth, Thomas, Lord, afterwards Earl of Cleveland, 269, 280, 281, 287, 291, 298, 321.

Wentworth, Thomas, Lord, afterwards Earl of Cleveland, at Launceston, 280.
—— letter from to Lord Goring, 263.
—— —— to Lord Culpeper, 240.
Werchten, letter dated from, 186.
Westpend island, English merchants at, 478.
Wesenn, see Wehene.
West, —, the Tower delivered to, 421.
—— Nicholas, letter from to Mr. Huly, 226.
Westbury, letter dated from, 210.
West House, letter dated from the rendezvous at, 260.
West Indies, ships fitted for, 201.
Westmeath, Earl of, see Nugent, Richard.
Westminster, 315, 343, 349, 401.
—— armed mob raised in, 221.
—— prayers desired for the destruction of the taskmasters that sit at, 401.
—— letters dated from, 4, 9, 10, 25, 28, 32, 36, 39, 44, 69, 75, 79, 86, 89, 92-94, 97, 122, 127, 129, 131, 133, 134, 140-142, 145, 146, 150-152, 156, 184, 243, 251, 309, 367, 468-482, 486-489, 491-497.
—— the Parliament at, q. v.
Westminster Hall, 358.
Weston, Jerome, second Earl of Portland, 359.
—— instance of his opening Lord Holland's letters, 353.
Weston, Richard, a Baron of the Exchequer and Chancellor of the Exchequer, afterwards Lord Treasurer and first Earl of Portland, 129.
—— argument in John Hampden's case, 116.
—— commission for the treaty against Spain, 29, 30.
—— letter from to Lord Chief Justice Hyde and Sir F. Harvey, 31.
—— letters to, 44, 50, 51, 59-61, 92.
—— his death, 73.
—— moneys allowed to his use, 52.
Westmoreland, 110.
Westrow, Mr., 418.
Wexford, 221.
—— new plantation of, 2.
—— Mayor and Council of, 327.
—— is harassed by —— Dalton, 342.
—— letter dated from, 727.
Weymouth, 330.

Weymouth, arms and ammunition to be delivered there, 215.
—— forces landed at, 242.
—— a ship of, 425.
—— letters dated from, 86, 239, 245.
Whaley, Col., conversation with the King, 340.
—— his wife at Court, 307.
Wharton, Philip, Lord, letter to, mentioned, 462.
—— Sir Tho., 251, 310.
—— letters from to the Marq. of Ormond, 251.
Wheatley Bridge, the Lord General's army there, 242.
Wheatley, Col., letter to, 415.
Wheeler, —, M. P., 460.
—— murdered, 176, 178.
Whetham[stead], letter dated from, 34.
Whitchurch, Marmaduke, letter to, 11.
White, —, 362.
—— Dr., 320.
—— Major, his regiment, 392.
—— John, a merchant of London, letter from to Queen Elizabeth, 483.
Whitehall, see London.
Whitelock, Mr., 414.
—— on the Committee against the King, 400.
—— Bulstrode, letter from to Sir E. Hyde, 234.
—— his uncle, ibid.
Whitely, Col. Roger, at a rendezvous in Dellamour Forest, 410.
—— defeated in Anglesea, ibid.
Whiting, John, 332.
Whitman, Mr., 427, 430.
Whitmore, Sir Walter, theft from his house at Pucklechurch, 239.
Whitney, letter dated from, L.
Wist, i. e. Wyatt, Sir Tho., his rising mentioned, L.
Wiatt, Dudley, bearer of a letter from the Queen, 317.
Widdrington or Withrington, William, afterwards Lord, 45, 323, 438.
—— letter to, 326.
Widdrington, General, 460.
Wieluo, military prefect of, 468.
Wight, Isle of, 388, 401, 402, 405, 410, 416, 426, 434, 450.
—— Spaniards take refuge in, 177.
—— a sea-fight near, 377.
—— the King in, 399, 400, 402, 403.
—— the King's message from, mentioned, 404.

INDEX. 617

Wight, Isle of, English and Scotch Commissioners in, 405.
—— on the Treaty of, 411, 413, 417, 418.
—— the King's account of the Treaty, 458.
—— heads of the Treaty, 449.
—— papers which passed in the Treaty of, 450.
—— letters dated from, 442, 449–456.
—— Governor of, see Hammond, Col.
Wilcocks, Jo., i.e. Secretary Nicholas, q. v.
Wild, Serjt., 424.
Wilde, Edward, of Limehouse, 17.
Wilford, Mr., 114.
Wilford or Welford, Father, his cypher, 215.
—— letters from to Father Leander, 52, 62-64.
Wilford, Thomas, 498.
Wilkins, Capt. T., 459.
William, Duke, allowance made to him by James I, 214.
William, Duke of Cleves, q. v.
William I, Prince of Orange, q. v.
William V, Landgrave of Hesse, q. v.
William, Mr., letter to, 426.
Williams, Captain, letter from to the Lord High Admiral, 2.
Williams, Sir Abraham, 39.
—— John, Bishop of Lincoln, afterwards Archbishop of York, 134, 137, 241, 410, 417.
—— speech on the Spanish negotiations, 29.
—— a prisoner in the Tower, 206.
—— holds places in North Wales for the King, 119.
—— Thomas, deposition in the case of the 'Gideon,' 273.
—— letter from to Archbishop Laud, 49.
—— Walt., petition from to Charles I, 81.
Willis, Sir Richard, 284, 285.
Willmot, or Willmott, Lord, see Wilmot, Henry, Lord.
Willoughby, Col., formerly a carpenter, 443.
—— Sir Francis, Knight, Sergeant-Major-Gen. of the army, 333, 339.
—— letter from to Lord Deputy Wentworth, 144.
—— is despatched from London, 340.

Willoughby of Parham, Francis, Lord, 411, 412, 414, 421, 428, 429.
—— is impeached, 343, 330.
—— his signature, 412.
—— Lord Treasurer, 411.
—— Philip, a notorious libeller, 359.
—— letter to William Lane, 238.
Wilmot, Henry, Lord, 359, 364, 366.
—— is taken prisoner, 204.
—— and his Lady, 324.
—— wounded in a duel, 395.
—— letter from to Sir Edw. Hyde, 223.
Wilson, Matthew, letter from to Dr. More, 60.
—— letter to, 61.
—— Dr. Tho., agent from Queen Elizabeth to the King of Portugal, 494.
Wilton, 209.
Wilton House, part of it burnt down, 369.
Wiltshire, 260, 264, 288.
Wimbledon, or Wimbleton, 420, 466.
Wimbleton, Lord, see Cecil, Edw.
Wincanton, 262.
Winchester, account of its siege and surrender by Lord Ogle to Cromwell, 292.
—— trial at, 402.
Winchester House, letter dated from, 51.
Windebank, Christopher, 60, 73, 76, 123, 131, 141-143, 154, 157, 162, 166, 178, 181, 182.
—— letter from to Secr. (Francis) Windebank, 130.
Windebank, Sir Francis, Secretary of State, 25, 27, 35, 36 et passim.
—— minutes of an interview with Necolalde, 38.
—— memorandum on Gage's employment, 166.
—— and Mr. Taylor, 173.
—— memoranda of an interview with Cardenas, 177.
—— reaches Calais in safety, 212.
—— his character, 216.
—— a threat to accuse him of great matters, 227.
—— document in his handwriting, 243.
—— letters from to the Earl Marshal, (Arundel and Surrey), 101.
—— —— to Lord Aston, 79, 83, 94, 121, 127, 129, 131, 133, 134, 138, 140-142, 145, 149, 150.
—— —— to Abbot Cavarell, 59.

4 K

Windebank, Sir F., Secretary of State, letters from to the King, 38, 39, 47, 48, 52, 60, 71, 73, 86, 97, 105, 107, 109, 122, 134, 137, 148, 149, 150, 157, 158, 172, 173, 175-182, 202-209.
—— —— to Lord Cottington, 103.
—— —— to Col. Gage, 184.
—— —— to Mons. Gerbier, 160.
—— —— to Mr. Hopton, afterwards Sir A. and Lord Hopton, 41, 42, 45, 51, 89, 159, 162, 163, 165, 170, 171, 176, 178, 180-182, 185-187, 190, 194-198, 200, 201, 204, 207, 208.
—— —— to Father Leander, 41.
—— —— to Count Leslie, 185.
—— —— to the Lord Mayor of London, 180.
—— —— to the Earl of Newcastle, 150.
—— —— to Princess Phalsburg, 191.
—— —— to Mr. Taylor, 82, 85, 87, 89, 92, 112, 151, 161.
—— —— to the Lord Treasurer (Portland), 41; (Juxon), 103.
—— letters to, 39, 40, 42, 43, 46-83, 85-119, 121-131, 133-145, 147-172, 174-176, 178, 179, 181-185, 187-190, 192-202, 205, 208, 209, 502.
Windebank, Francis, jun., 111-115.
—— letters from to ——, 112.
—— Thomas, 91, 111, 113, 115, 123, 159.
—— letter from to the Earl Marshal, 102.
—— letters to, 123.
Windham, Mr., report of his being killed, 402.
Windsor, 397, 460.
—— head-quarters at, 447.
—— the King at, 461.
—— the Bishop of Hereford's case with the Chapter of, about the dividing of rents and tithes, 502.
—— letters dated from, 9, 27, 482-485, 493, 499-501.
Windsor Castle, constable and ranger at, 460.
—— prisoners in, 378, 437.
Wines, settlement of the monopoly of, 146.
—— imposition on, 417.
Winston, Dr., accident to, 463.
Winter, Sir John, 287.
—— William and George, and their ships, letters in behalf of, 494.
—— —— their petition, ibid.

Winterborne, letter dated from, 239.
Wiotour, Sir John, 305.
—— letter to Sir E. Hyde, 287.
Wirtemburg, see Wurtemburg.
Wirtsburgh, see Wurtzburgh.
Wise, Richard, case in Chancery between his wife Lucy and Sir C. Egerton, 255.
Wiseman, R., letter to Mr. Edgeman, 441.
Withering, Mr., complaints against him concerning the Post-Office, 213.
—— resolutions to restore him to the management of the foreign Posts, 217.
Witherington, Lord, see Widdrington, William, Lord.
Withipoole, Sir William, fined 500l., 52.
Witney, see Whitney.
Witte, Nicholas de, justice demanded against, for plundering vessels of Hull, 286.
Wittingau, to be restored, 23.
Wittipoole, see Withipoole.
Woburn, the King and army go there, 386.
Wogan, E., proceedings of the Parliament army drawn up by, 392.
Wolfgang, Count Palatine of the Rhine, q. v.
Wolgast, storming of, 145.
Wollaston, Mr., Keeper of Newgate, 322.
Wolley, Dr., 106.
Wollnode, Benjamin, letter from to Lord Aston, 144.
—— case of, 148.
Wolstenholme, Sir John, letters from to Sir Edw. Hyde, 216, 220.
—— his daughter, Lady Lee, q. v.
Wolverhampton, letter dated from, 287.
Wood, Captain, letters from to the Lord High Admiral, 3, 4.
Woodhead, A., fellow of —— Coll., Oxford, letters from to W. Denman, 430, 431, 442.
—— letter of, 439.
Woodstock, letters dated from, 289, 500.
Wool, order to grant licences for transportation of, 301.
Wootton, resident at, 239.
Worcester, 284, 290, 305.
—— the King's victory near, 287.
—— is taken, 328.
Worcester, Marq. of, see Somerset, Edward.

Worcestershire, 214.
—— disturbance in, 417.
Worington, letters dated from, 297-299.
Worlam, letter dated from, 36.
Wormeley, Capt. Raph., his gallantry commended, 259.
Worton, its surrender to the rebels, 290.
Wotton, Nich., Dean of Canterbury, letters of credence for, as agent to the King of Spain, 468.
Wrangel, General, movements of his troops, 133, 135-137, 419.
Wrathe, Mr., letter from to Colonel Fiennes, 240.
Wren, Christopher, 64.
Wright, Alderman, chosen Lord Mayor, 208.
—— Benjamin, 122.
—— Captain, 358.
—— Hirke, 31.
Wriothesley, Henry, Earl of Southampton, letter from to the Lord High Admiral, 5.
—— Thomas, Earl of Southampton, 253, 319, 366, 393, 404.
—— instructions to, on his mission to the Parliament, 254, 314.
—— and other Lords, solicited to make a treaty with the King, 419.
—— letter to, 371.
Wurtemburg, Christopher, Duke of, letters to, 471, 474, 479, 480, 482, 490.
Wurtemburg, Frederic, Duke of, commission for the delivery of the Garter to, 500.
—— submission of the Duke, and division of his country, 152.
Wurtsburg, Bishop of, 20.
—— deputies from, 155.
Wyatt, Sir Dudley, 294, 304, 321.
—— despatch of, mentioned, 303.
—— Sir Tho., see Wiat.
Wynne, Lady, burglary at her house at Wimbledon, 420.
—— Capt. Owen, letter from to the Lord High Admiral, 5.
Wyse, Math., 323.
Wyverton, letter dated from, 285.

Y.

Yarde, Gilbert, an officer at Exeter, 273.
Yarmouth, Great, complaints of the Aldermen, 123.
Yarmouth, Great, its loyalty, 128.
—— merchants of, 496.
—— letters dated from, 5, 18.
Yeddon, Richard, a soldier of Hull, his affidavit concerning Sir J. Hotham, 232.
Yew, certificate for its importation into England, 485.
Yllan, Garcia de, Licentiate of law, 123.
Yonge, Mr. J., letter from to the Lord High Admiral, 2.
York, 203, 205-209, 225, 231, 232, 462.
—— on certain manors in the county of, 146.
—— the House of Lords summoned to, 172.
—— the King's forces near, 204.
—— petition to the King from the gentry of, 206.
—— privilege granted to, 206.
—— list of Peers assembled for the great Council at, 207.
—— speech of the King at, mentioned, 208.
—— Council at, 213.
—— jurisdictions of the county of, ibid.
—— Prebendary of, 214.
—— Yorkshire, suffers from both armies, 217.
—— speech on the abolition of the Court of, 219.
—— resolutions of the Committee on the Court of, 220.
—— order of Parliament that the King's removal of the next term to York is illegal, May, 1642; 230.
—— the King at, 231.
—— the declaration of the Lords at against the new militia ordinance, 232.
—— account of the battle of 'Marston Moor,' 250.
—— warrant of the King issued at, 260.
—— the forces in Yorkshire, 321.
—— particulars of the doings of a Yorkshire fanatic, 408.
—— militia of Yorkshire, 466.
—— letters dated from, 126, 175, 202-206, 208, 215-220, 226-228, 231, 233, 258.
—— Archbishops of, see Neile, Richard; Williams, John.
—— Governor of, see Savile, Thos., Lord.
Youghal, town of, 252.

'Young Tobias,' the (ship), of Hamburg, 300.
—— order to Joachim Hardwick, skipper of, 302.
—— expenses of, 303; certificate, 304.

Z.

Zabern, loss of, 103-105.

Zaneti, Cardinal, legate, 72.
Zante, English consul at, *see* Kent, Joseph.
Zealand, island of, 35.
Zenck, Adolphus, his petition against Edmund Roberts, 497.
Zulestein, Herr, 421.

MISTAKES AND MISPRINTS.

No. 91, *for* Sept. 17, *read* Sept. 7.
„ 98, *for* Jan. 13, *read* Jan. 30.
„ 118, *for* 1619, Ap. 14, *read* 1618, Ap. 24.
„ 154, *for* Nov. 7, *read* 1618, Nov. 7.
„ — *for* Draught, *read* Original.
„ 238, *for* Best, *read* Best.
„ 265, *for* No date, *read* March 24.
„ 320, *for* Rec. Winlebank, *read* Sir F. Netherole.
„ 468, *for* Fernambuco, *read* Pernambuco.
„ 470, *for* Pansana, *read* Panzani.
„ 636, *for* Henacides, *read* Heraclides.
„ 551, *for* Infanta, *read* Infant.
„ 578, *for* 12,000, *read* 11,000.
„ — *add* Endorsed Jan. 21, 1635-6.
„ 580, *for* yade, *read* jade.
„ 638, *for* Lord Aston, *read* Lord Cottington.
„ 710, *for* Cologne, *read* Madrid.
„ — *for* The same, *read* Lord Aston.
„ 1015, *for* Lord Aston, *read* Mr. Taylor.
„ 1016, *for* The same, *read* Lord Aston.
„ 1029, *for* No date, *read* 4 Aug. 11 Car.
„ 1054, *this letter should be followed by* 1202.
„ 1130, 34, 37, 38, *for* Mr. Gerbier, *read* Sir Balthazar G.
„ 1184, *for* arundincow, *read* arundineus.
„ 1191, *for* Brussels, *read* Dunkirk.
„ 1202 *should follow* 1054.
„ 1267, *for* June 19, *read* June 27.
„ 1305, *for* No date, *read* Oct. 16.
„ 1357, *for* Athenry, *read* Athenry.
„ 1342, *for* English, *read* English trade.

No. 1342, *iv, for* Charles II, *read* Charles I.
„ 1393, *for* Gahier, *read* Gerbier.
„ 1395, *for* Charles IV, *read* Charles III.
„ 1412, *for* Hambden, *read* Hampden.
„ 1437, 8, *for* Rippon, *read* Ripon.
„ 1167, *for* Clarendon, *read* Windebank.
„ 1577, *for* Dockley, *read* Berkeley.
„ 1886 and 1812, *for* Mr. Browne, *read* Sir R. Browne.
„ 1958, *for* Parliamernt, *read* Parliament.
„ 1966, *for* Highe, Sheriff, *read* High Sheriff.
„ 1971, *for* 3,000l, *read* 35,000l.
„ 2074, *for* Sir Joseph Fane, *read* Joseph Jane.
„ 2303, 4, *the reference to Hoskins is to* No. 2301.
„ 2325, *for* St. Germains, Oct. 9, *read* Newcastle, Oct. 3.
„ 2330, *for* Long, *read* Loring.
„ 2394 note, *for* on, *read* an.
„ 2605, *for* Hyde, *read* Forde.
Page 396, *for* No. 2362, *read* 2612.
No. 2703, *for* Saltmarshe's, *read* Saltmarsh's.
„ 2726, *for* Meilonay, *read* Meilleray.
„ 2669, *for* Newport, *read* Norwich.
„ 2882, *for* cause, *read* causes.
„ 2933, *for* Cl. S. P. vol. S. p. 432, *read* p. 443.
„ 2934, 5, *for* Denzall, *read* Denzell.
„ 3007, *for* Francois, *read* François.
Addenda, No. 13, *for* crown, *read* count.
Page 497, *for* p. 479, *read* 497.
Index, p. 513, Fane, *see* Jane.
„ p. 561, Jane, Joseph, 194.

END OF VOLUME L

APPENDIX No. I.

The MS. papers described in this Appendix are all contained in one thin volume, bound in vellum, wherein they were placed by King Charles I. It has been thought fit to retain them as he placed them, and to describe their contents in a separate Appendix. The volume commences with an entry in his hand, "Dispaches concerning Germanie and the Spanishe mache in the year 1611." All these papers have been removed and are probably those among the Papers on the subject printed in the "Cl. S. Papers." The following papers are preceded by an entry of the King, "Here followes the Articles that were drawen concerning the Matche with Spaine."

                1623.
(1.) *The Articles as agreed to by His Majesty*, with the No date. securities for their observance to be given by him.—Latin.
                 Copy.
   This is an early copy of the Articles before the arrival of the Dispensation, and differs in many respects from those finally sworn to by
   His Majesty.

(2.) *The Articles concerning Religion.* The paper is headed No date. thus, "All those Articles which came from Rome to which His Majesty took no exceptions in his directions to the Earl of Bristol under his hand of the 9 of September passed as not disallowed by His Majesty. Those wherein remained any difference are accommodated in the form following."
           Amended Copy.

(3.) *The Heads of such temporal Articles as are hitherto agreed* No date. *on in the Match for His Highness.* This also is before the arrival of the Dispensation, and fixes the day for the Infanta to start for England, "on the last of March, 1624." The King of Spain is herein bound to give the Infanta two million crowns of twelve reals each.   *Copy.*

(4.) *Instrumentum acceptationis, approbationis ratificationis* No date. *et confirmationis matrimonialis conventus habiti inter Serenissi- mum Walliæ Principem et Serenissimam Infantem et communes*

APPENDIX I.

1623. *eorundem commissarios.*—Latin. Copy of the Articles as sworn to by His Majesty and the Prince, with their oath annexed.—Latin. *Copy.*

> English copy in Rushworth, vol. I. p. 86, with some few and immaterial variations.

No date. (5.) [*Instrumentum, quo*] *continentur omnia quæ a Serenissimo Magnæ Britanniæ Rege jurejurando privatim confirmanda sunt.*—Latin. Copy of the four private Articles sworn to by His Majesty in favour of the Roman Catholics.—Latin. *Copy.*

> English copy printed in Rushworth, vol. I. p. 89, but this is without the Prince's special engagement there annexed.

No date. (6.) [*Instrumentum, quo*] *continentur omnia quæ a Serenissimo Magnæ Britanniæ Rege privatim verbo et scripto promittenda sunt,* whereby he undertakes that the abrogation of the penal laws against the Roman Catholics shall be effected within three years, and gives permission to his Privy-Councillors to swear to the Treaty.—Latin. *Copy.*

No date. (7.) [*Instrumentum, quo*] *continentur omnia quæ a Serenissimo Walliæ Principe jurejurando privatim confirmanda sunt.* An undertaking in favour of religious toleration, and the prolongation of the mother's care of the children of the marriage from the 10th to the 12th year of their age.—Latin. *Copy.*

> N.B. This differs materially from the English copy printed in Rushworth, vol. I. p. 89, which contains parts of the substance of this and the next paper.

No date. (8.) [*Instrumentum, quo*] *continentur omnia, quæ a Serenissimo Walliæ Principe privatim verbo et scripto promittenda sunt.* A promise to connive at the attendance of Roman Catholics at the Infanta's chapel, and to listen to the arguments of Roman divines.—Latin. *Copy.*

No date. (9.) *Formula juramenti a consiliariis præstandi.*—Latin. *Copy.*

> An English copy, literally translated, printed in Rushworth, vol. I. p. 90.

> N.B. The last six papers are all in the same hand, and endorsed as given above, and also with a summary of the contents. The following papers are preceded by an entry in Charles I.'s hand, "Heere beginnes the dispatches concerning the Frenche Mariage."

1623-4.
March 23. (10.) *(Henry Rich) Lord Kensington to the Prince of Wales,* expressing hopes of a comfortable conclusion of Parliament.

> Endorsed by the Prince. Cl. S. P. vol. II. App. p. ii.

APPENDIX I.

(11.) *Lord Kensington to the Prince of Wales.* A letter of thanks and professions. — 1624. April 6.
      Endorsed by the Prince. Cl. S. P. vol. ii. App. p. ii.

(12.) *The same to the same.* Madame's picture shall be despatched within four days. Expresses in the strongest terms his sense of the infamous conduct of the Spanish Ambassador (apparently in spreading reports to break the match). — May 1⁵/₁₅.

(13.) *The same to the same.* Of the beauties of Madame and the jealousy of his rival the Count de Soissons. — May 21.
      Endorsed by the Prince. Cl. S. P. vol. ii. App. p. iii.,
      (with the exception of an immaterial postscript).

(14.) *The same to the same.* Forwards the pictures and entreats for letters to allay the alarm raised by the Spanish intrigues. The Infant Don Carlos is proposed for Madame. — Compiègne, [Whitsunday].
      Endorsed by the Prince. Cl. S. P. vol. ii. App. p. iv.

(15.) *The same to the same,* expressing his joy at the arrival of Lord Carlisle. — Compiègne, May 26.
      Cl. S. P. vol. ii. App. p. v.

(16.) *The same to the same,* forwarding the articles as propounded by France. — Compiègne, June 14.
      Cl. S. P. vol. ii. App. p. v.

(17.) (*James Hay*) *Lord Carlisle to the same.* Of his reception at Court. — Compiègne, June 14.
      Endorsed by the Prince. Cl. S. P. vol. ii. App. p. vi.

(18.) *Lord Kensington to the same,* forwarding letters to be written by the Prince and returned. — July 21.
      Endorsed by the Prince. Cl. S. P. vol. ii. App. p. vii.

(19.) *The Prince of Wales to Lord Carlisle,* peremptorily ordering him to break off the Treaty if the French persist as they have begun. — Rufford, August 13.
      Copy in his own hand and endorsed by him. Cl. S. P. vol. ii. App. p. ix.

(20.) *The same to Lord Kensington.* A short and peremptory note, to the same effect as the last. — Rufford, August 13.
      Copy in his own hand and endorsed by him. Cl. S. P. vol. ii. App. p. x.

(21.) *Lord Carlisle to the Prince of Wales.* A short note of acknowledgment. — Paris, August 23.
      Endorsed by the Prince. Cl. S. P. vol. ii. App. p. x.

APPENDIX I.

1624.
Paris,
August 31.
(22.) *Lord Kensington to the Prince of Wales.* Recounts an interview with the Queen-Mother, and with Madame.
Endorsed by the Prince.   Cl. S. P. vol. ii. App. p. viii.

Sept. 9.
(23.) *The same to the same.* Announces the favourable alteration of the Articles and the great joy in France at the prosperous issue of the negotiation.
Endorsed by the Prince.   Cl. S. P. vol. ii. App. p. x.

No date.
(24.) *The same to the same.* Recounts the great rejoicings of the Court, and especially of Monsieur and Madame.
Endorsed by the Prince with the date Sept. 3 (13).

St. Germain,
Sept. 3/13.
(25.) *Lord Carlisle to the same,* recommending a noble usage of Count Mansfeldt.
Endorsed by the Prince.   Cl. S. P. vol. ii. App. p. xii.

St. Germain,
Sept. 3/13.
(26.) *Lord Kensington to the same.* Of Madame's exquisite singing.   Endorsed by the Prince.   Cl. S. P. vol. ii. App. p. xii.

Sept. 4/14.
(27.) *Lord Carlisle to the same.* Recommends a present to be sent to Madame by "sweet Tomasillo," who will be the meetest messenger.   Endorsed by the Prince.

Sept. 4/14.
(28.) *Lord Kensington to the same.* Tom Cary (to whom probably is the allusion in the last) is recommended as the bearer of the present.
Endorsed by the Prince.   Cl. S. P. vol. ii. App. p. xiii.

Paris,
Sept. 24.
(29.) *Lord Carlisle to the same.* Expresses his thankfulness at the Prince's escape from danger in a fall from his horse.
Endorsed by the Prince.   Cl. S. P. vol. ii. App. p. xiv.

Paris,
Sept. 24.
(30.) *Lord Holland* to the same.* The King will send to congratulate him on his escape. Expresses his gratitude for his new honour.
Endorsed by the Prince.

Paris,
Oct. 10.
(31.) *The same to the same.* Great affliction is caused in France by the English delay in acceding to the Articles.
Endorsed by the Prince.   Cl. S. P. vol. ii. App. p. xv.

Oct. 29.
(32.) *Lord Carlisle to the same.* The obstacle is in the French Ministers, not in the Court or Madame.
Endorsed by the Prince.   Cl. S. P. vol. ii. App. p. xv.

---

* Lord Kensington was created Earl of Holland on this day.

APPENDIX I.

(33.) *Lord Holland to the Prince of Wales.* The alteration of a few words is all that is now in dispute.   1624. Oct. 29.
        Endorsed by the Prince.   Cl. S. P. vol. ii. App. p. xvi.

(34.) *Lords Carlisle and Holland to the same.* The French are inclined to concede what is required of them.   Paris, Nov. 6.
        Endorsed by the Prince.   Cl. S. P. vol. ii. App. p. xvi.

(35.) *The same to the same.* The Articles are to be signed and the bonfires lighted to-night. Will send more particular account by Sir James Oughterlony.   Paris, Nov. 9.
        Endorsed by the Prince.

(36.) *Lord Carlisle to the same.* They have now made sure of Madame, and assistance to Mansfeldt for six months. Encloses a draught of a letter to be written to the Princess.   Paris, Nov. 11.
        Endorsed by the Prince.   Cl. S. P. vol. ii. App. p. xvi.
(with the exception of a paragraph at the end strongly recommending the bearer. The words "some time," in the fourteenth line of p. xvii., are inserted in the Prince's hand.)

(37.) *Lord Holland to the same.* Announces, by Sir J. Oughterlony, the joy of Madame, who is to be in England by Jan. 15th, and who has begun to study an English grammar. Desires a letter to be sent by Tom Cary.   Paris, Nov. 11.
        Endorsed by the Prince.

(38.) *The same to the same.* His letters have been delivered by "sweet Tom Cary." Desires that the Duke of Buckingham be despatched directly the Dispensation comes. Madame insists on signing to the Prince "tres humble," instead of formally "bien humble," as some advise her.   Paris, Dec. 1/11.
        Endorsed by the Prince.

(39.) *Lords Carlisle and Holland to the same.* They have determined, if the Prince shall come to France, not to place him on the King's right hand, as precedence has never been given except to a crowned head.   Paris, Dec. 18.
        Endorsed by the Prince.   Cl. S. P. vol. ii. App. p. xviii.

(40.) *Lord Holland to the same.* Has discussed with Madame the question of the Prince's reception. The Dispensation is daily expected, having been despatched from Rome a fortnight since.   Paris, Dec. 18.
        Endorsed by the Prince.

(41.) *Lords Carlisle and Holland to the same.* Recommend preparations at Dover and London for the reception of the Princess.   1624-5. Paris, Jan. 1/4.
        Endorsed by the Prince.   Cl. S. P. vol. ii. App. p. xix.

APPENDIX I.

1624–5.
Paris,
Jan. 1/11.
(42.) *Lord Holland to the Prince of Wales.* Is anxiously expecting Cary with the present, and the Duke of Buckingham.
Endorsed by the Prince.

Paris,
Feb. 16.
(43.) *Lord Carlisle to the same.* No ear should be given to the encroachment of any new conditions.
Endorsed by the Prince.   Cl. S. P. vol. ii. App. p. xx.

[Feb.]
(44.) *Lord Holland to the same.* Madame sends her colours, which he has promised her shall be displayed by the Prince in the noise and breach of lances.
Endorsed by the Prince, with the date Feb.

March 3.
(45.) *Lord Carlisle to the same.* He should relax in nothing, but disdainfully reject the whole, which will bring them to a speedy conclusion.
Endorsed by the Prince.   Cl. S. P. vol. ii. App. p. xx.

March 1/5.
(46.) *Lord Holland to the same,* of Madame's grief and fear that something is amiss.
Endorsed by the Prince.   Cl. S. P. vol. ii. App. p. xxi.

Paris,
March 21/11.
(47.) *Lord Carlisle to the same.* Recommends absolute rejection of the new conditions.
Endorsed by the Prince.   Cl. S. P. vol. ii. App. p. xxi.

Paris,
March 21/11.
(48.) *Lord Holland to the same.* In his joy at the happy conclusion of affairs, is willing to forgive the Monsieurs their little arts.
Endorsed by the Prince.

1625.
Paris,
March 25.
(49.) *Lords Carlisle and Holland to the Duke of Buckingham,* by a French messenger sent with condolences on His Majesty's illness. The King will welcome Buckingham gladly. News has come of the successes in Italy of the Count d'Alay, the Duke of Savoy, and the Constable, over the Neapolitans.
Endorsed by the Prince.

Paris,
March 29.
(50.) *Lord Carlisle to the Prince of Wales (Charles I*).* Defends himself against imputations of having caused the delay.
Endorsed by the Prince.   Cl. S. P. vol. ii. App. p. xxii.

Paris,
April 9.
(51.) *Lords Carlisle and Holland to His Majesty (Charles I).* Recommend that Mr. Walter Montagu be commissioned to visit Madame, who is somewhat indisposed; and that, to mark Monsieur's singular respect to his late Majesty, His Majesty write to him with the title of 'frere.'
Endorsed by His Majesty.

---

* James I. died March 27th, 1625.

APPENDIX I.

(52.) *Lord Carlisle to His Majesty.* The expectations of all men look to His Majesty as arbiter of the Christian world. — 1625. Paris, April 9.
Endorsed by His Majesty.

(53.) *Lord Holland to the same.* Renews professions of loyal attachment. — Paris, April 9.
Endorsed by His Majesty.

(54.) *Lord Carlisle to the same.* Has sounded the King and Cardinal as to His Majesty's intervention between them and those of the Religion. Advises that the thorns of his only two rivals, the Kings of Spain and France, viz. the Low Countries wars and those of the Religion, be not rooted out. — April 11.
Endorsed by His Majesty. Cl. S. P. vol. II. App. p. xxii.

(55.) *The same to the same.* The marriage will be solemnized next Sunday. — Paris, April 14.
Endorsed by His Majesty.

(56.) *The same to the same.* Madame will start on May 9th, and reach Boulogne in a week, accompanied by the two Queens and Monsieur. — April 28.
Endorsed by His Majesty.

(57.) *The same to the same.* The marriage is this day concluded. — May 1.
Endorsed by His Majesty. Cl. S. P. vol. II. App. p. xxiii.

(58.) *Lord Holland to the same.* Expresses his joy at not having fallen, as he feared, from favour. — May 1.
Endorsed by His Majesty.

(59.) *Lord Carlisle to the same.* Remonstrates concerning his design of coming to Boulogne, and advises that, while he publically proclaims his intention of so doing, he yield to a petition of Council not to imperil his person. — Paris, May 12.
Endorsed by His Majesty. Cl. S. P. vol. II. App. p. xxiv.

(60.) *(George Villiers) Duke of Buckingham to the same.* If the King be well enough, they will start on Wednesday: otherwise the Queen-Mother, himself, and Doncaster (Lord Carlisle) remain behind. — May 15.
Endorsed by His Majesty. Cl. S. P. vol. II. App. p. xxv.

(61.) *Lord Carlisle to the same*, in praise of the Duke of Buckingham. — May 15.
Endorsed by His Majesty.

(62.) *The same to the same.* The Queen has departed from this town. — Paris, May 23.
Endorsed by His Majesty.

1628.
[Amiens.]
May 30.

(63.) *The Duke of Buckingham to His Majesty.* Relates the promises he has obtained from France, Savoy, and the Duke de Chevereux, regarding the wars.

Endorsed by His Majesty.   Cl. S. P. vol. II. App. p. xiv.

[Amiens,]
May 30.

(64.) *Lord Carlisle to the same.* The Queen desires to be informed what ladies she is to kiss, and who are to kiss her hand.

Endorsed by His Majesty.

APPENDIX No. II.

The MSS. of the letters contained in this Appendix are pasted in a separate volume. As they are such as cannot well be analysed, and owe their interest more to their manner than their matter, it has been thought proper to print them in full in a separate Appendix. Four of them are printed as specimens in the Appendix to the second volume of the Cl. S. Papers. The letters of Madame to the Prince are all originals; those of the Prince to Madame are rough draughts in his own hand.

I. Madame ma treschere fille chasque jour qui s'est passé, depuis que mon fils vous escriuit sa derniere Lettre, n'a que redoublé son ennuy dont il est forcé ne pouant trouuer aucun repos en son ame, sans qu'il vous puisse faire seruice d'escrire derechef par le messager que vous aues desja veu pour vous tesmoigner sa langeur jusques a tant qu'il puisse auoir l'honneur et l'heur de jouir de vostre presence neantmoins je vous prieray de croire qu'en cest langeur ne luy cedera jammais,

Vostre tresaffectionné Pere,

J. R.

II. Je nay osé prendre la hardiesse de vous tesmoigner par un mot de lettre l'impatience dont mon ame a esté gehenné durant ma long attente pour l'hereus l'accorde des ces treté, jusque a tant que j'en eus receu les bonnes nouelles, vous priant de vous asseurer qu'outre la renummé de vos vertus ces perfectionns qui s'eclatte par tout, je le tien pour comble de mon bonheur, que j'eu l'honneur d'auoyr deja veu vostre personne, bien qu'incognu de vous qui ma rendu infinement satisfait que l'exterieur de vostre personne ne demente rien au lustre de vos verteus, mais je ne puisse exprimer par escrit a passion de mon ame pour auoir l'eur d'estre estimé vostre, &c.

Cl. S. P. vol. II. App. p. xvii.

III. Monsieur,

Impatiense que vous me temoygnes avoir eue durant le temps qui sest passe sur le sujet du traite et le contantement que vous me faites paroistre avoir receu de la nouuelle de ce qui a esté acordo par deca me donnent certaine connoissance de vr̄e bonne voulonté envers moy telle que vous me la representes par vr̄e Letre. Le Roy Monsieur Monfrero et La Royne Madame Mamero ayant eu agreable que je resceuse ces temoynages de vr̄e affection je ne sçay vous dire que si elle n'a pas pour asseuré fondement tout le bien quelle vous fait remarquer en moy du moins je reconnoistres vous vue franche voulonté de vous faire voir que vous n'en obligeres point vue personne ingrate et que je suis et seray tousjours,

Monsieur,
    Vr̄e treshumble et tres
     afectionnee seruente
      HENRIETTE MARIE.

(L. S. P. vol. II. App. p. xvii.)

IV. Je ne me suis jamais estime si heureux qu'alors que je receu l'honneur de vostre lettre par la quelle jay eu le contentement de voir que vous auez accepté benignement l'offre de mes treshumbles seruices a V: A: ce que je tacheray toujours de meriter par toutes les vois qui me sera possible vous priant de croire que vous ne pouuie jamais obliger person qui vous honnerera aimera et seruira si je ne dis plus mais si fidelement que moy qui ne pourray jamais auoir de contentement qu'alors que vous m'estimeres.

V. Ayant entendu de vostre indisposition, quoy qu'on me mende qu'il n'i a pas grand denger toutesfoyse, le moindre mal qu'il vous peule arriue m'estant vne extreme dolleur, j'ay enuoyé ce gentilhomme mon seruiteur le Sr. Goring pour vous baiser les mains de ma part, est de sçauoyr comme j'espere de vostre bon portement, car j'espero que Dieu ne me donnera pas des afflictions plus qu'insupportables, cependent, je seray tousjours en inquietude jusques a ce que j'entendray de vostre parfaite santé vous priant de croire que person ne vous souhaite plus de prosperité que.

VI. Monsieur,

Jay eu dautant plus agreable les sentimens de la continuation de l'honneur de vr̄e amitie quil vous a pleu me temoigner par vr̄e derniere que je les ay trouues samblables aux miens vous assurant que jauray tousjours vne tres particuliere Inclination de satisfaire aux choses que je reconois-

tray vous agreer ne soutraytant rien tant que les succations
de vous en pouuoir donner de plus particulieres preuues mais
parce que j'ay donné charge au S`r`. gorin de vous en assurer
je me contenteray de vous faire connoistre que je conseruerey
tousjours la voulonte que j'ay de demeurer toute Ma vie,
 Monsieur, V̄r̄e treshumble et tresobeissante
       seruente
         . Henriette Marie.

VII. Madame,
 Vos faueurs m'ont fait prendre la hardiesse de vous
supplier de me faire l'honneur l'accepter ce petit present que
ce Gen: mon seruiteur vous donnera de ma part, quoy que
ce soit grandement indigne de vous, toutefois j'espere vous
le prendres en bonne part come venant de luy qui sera bien
ayse de hazarder sa vie a uous faire seruice souhaitant rien
plus que d'estre honoré par vos commandements, & d'auoir
quelque occasion de me monstrer par effects combien je suis,
 Madame,   Vo:
       Cl. S. P. vol. II. App. p. xviii.

VIII. Monsieur,
 Ne pouuant asés dignement louer les presens quil
vous a pleu menuoyer ny vous en remercier je remets au S`r`.
Cayrry de vous faire conoistre lestime que jeu fais comme
aussi conbien je cheris lhonneur de v̄r̄e amitie dont la continuation me sera tousjours aussi agreable que les succations
de vous pouuoir faire paroistre que je suis,
 Monsieur, V̄r̄e tres humble et
      tres obeisante seruonte
        Henriette Marie.
       Cl. S. P. vol. II. App. p. xviii.

IX. Je ne me puis pas tarder d'auentage de vous donner
mes tres humbles remerciments de ce que vous m'auez hon-
noré tant que de m'enuoyer vos couleurs, ou quoy je marque
que vos dernier fauers sont tousjours les plus grants aug-
mentant s'il estoit possible l'obligation que j'ay a vous seruire,
mais puis que je me suis desja donné tout a vous, je ne çay
comment de vous remercier, pour l'infinite de vos fauers,
otrement que le vous asseurer que je suis Eternellement.

X. Monsieur,
 Je cheris tellement les occations de vous pouuoir
temoygner le resentiment que jay de lhonneur de v̄r̄e souuenir

que je nay voulu laisser partir le S^r. de Montegu sans vous en donner des preuues et aussi pour vous assurer de la continuation de mon entiere affection en attendant que le temps me donne plus de moyen de vous pouuoir faire connoistre que je suis veritablement,

Monsieur, V^re tres humble et tres
obeissante seruante
HENRIETTE MARIE.

XI. Madame,

Voyant, par la lettre que m'a rendu M^r. Montague de vostre part, la Constance de vostre bienueillance, tousjours augmente vos faueurs enuers moy: Comme aussi au mesme temps, entendant l'heureuse nouuelle du finall accord du trotté du Marriage entre vous et moy: je creueroys si je me laissoys plus long temps sans vous exprimer l'extreame joy & contentement que j'ay en la continuation de vos faueurs, & d'estre si heureux que d'auoir l'occasion de vous pouuoir rendre les treshumbles seruices que je vous ay voué: A cet heure je ne songeray a austre chose, que de haster par tous moyens le jour au quel j'auray l'honneur de vous baiser les mains comme.

XII. Monsieur,

Encores que mes sentimens soient tardifs a temoigner a v^re Majesté ce que je dois a la memoire tres glorieuse du feu roy son pere, neanmoins je la suplie de croyre qu'ils sont tels que v^re Majesté les peut souhaiter, l'assurant que je prendray tousjours vne tres particuliere part aux choses qui luy toucheront n'ayant autre desir que de luy pouuoir faire connoistres en toutes sortes d'occations que je suis,

Monsieur, V^re treshumble et tres
obeissante seruante
HENRIETTE MARIE.

XIII. Je n'ay jamais aperçeu si euidemment le pouuoir que vous aues sur moy qu'a cest heure, car je n'usse pas prinse estre possible qu'aucune chose du Monde m'ust peu tant soulager, apres une si grande perte que j'ay soufert, como je esté soulagé par vostre derniere, en quoy jay veu la continuation de vos faueurs si benignement exprimé, que c'a esté le mellour cordial que jamais homme ayt eu en un temps de si grande tristesse pour laquelle, et toutes les austres obligacions que vous aues comblé sur moy, je ne sçay comment je les pourray meriter, si non de viure et mourir.

XIV. Monsieur,

Je tiens si chers les temoygnages quil a pleu A vr̄e Majeste me faire connoistre de sa bonne volonté par le S^r. Gorin que je rechercheray toute ma vie les ocations de luy faire paroytre le ressentyment que j'en ay, je remets a son fils de faire entendre a vr̄e Majeste comme je suis en parfait sante, la quelle j'esmiray de conseruer, a fin de luy pouuoir rendre le seruice que je luy dois lorsquelle m'honnorera de ses commendes ce quattendant je de meureray,

Monsieur,   V<del>r</del>e treshumble et tres
            obeisante seruente
                HENRIETTE MARIE.

XV. Vous ne m'aues jamais honoré auec une lettre qui m'a plus contente & rejoui que la derniere qui n'a esté rendu par le june Goring, la quelle me donnant asseurance de vostre bienveillance anuers moy m'a ausi asseuré de vostre parfaite santé, tellement qu'il ne me rest plus a souhaiter que d'auoire bien tost l'honneur de vous baiser les mains en atendent je demoure impatiamant mais constamant.

XVI. Monsieur,

le resentiment que jay de lindisposition de vr̄e Majeste ne me permet pas destre plus long tens sans luy faire scauoir linpatiance que jay den aprendre des nouuelles cest pour quoy ayant donne charge au s^r Gorrin de luy faire connoistre le deplaysir que jeu resois je supleray tres humblement vr̄e Majeste de croyre que je nay rien de si cher que sa sante la quelle je prie Dieu luy vouloir donner aussi entierre que je suis,

Monsieur,   V<del>r</del>e treshumble et tres
            obeisante seruente
                HENRIETTE MARIE.

XVII. Monsieur,

Je croirois manquer a l'affection que l'honneur de la bienueillance de vr̄e Majeste m'oblige d'auoir, si je ne luy tesmoignois le ressentiment que j'ay de son indisposition et l'impatience que jay d'en aprendre des nouuelles, cest pour quoy je suplie tres humblement vr̄e Majesté de croyre que je seray toujours en inquietude jusque asequo je sache que le recouurement de la sante de vr̄e Majeste soit aussi parfait que je suis parfaitement,

Monsieur,   V<del>r</del>e treshumble et
            tresobeisante seruante
                HENRIETTE MARIE.

XVIII. Monsieur,

Je cheris tellement les occasions de pouuoir tesmoigner a vr̄e Majeste conbien je desire la continuation de lhonneur de sa bienueillance que je nay voulu laisor passer celle cy afin quen lasurant de mon entiere disposition je peusse aussy confirmer a vr̄e Majeste les veux de ma tres humble obeissance que je la suplie [...] aussi agreables que la voulonte que je de dimeurer toute Ma vie,

Monsieur, Vr̄e treshumble et tres
obeisante seruante
HENRIETTE MARIE.

XIX. Monsieur,

Je souhaite si passionnement la continuation de lhonneur de la bienueillance de vr̄e Majeste que je cheriray tousjours les occasions de luy en pouuoir renouueller le ressouuenir comme je fais maintenant par le s' Gorin afin de faire connoistre a vr̄e Majeste que je nauray jamais plus de sattysfaction que lors que je pouray luy donner de tres particulierres preuues de mon entiere afection le supliant de croyre que je suis,

Monsieur, Vr̄e treshumble et tres
obeisante seruante
HENRIETTE MARIE R.

XX. Vous comblés tellement en toutes occasions vos obligations sur moy que je ne sçay comment l'exprimer la joy et le contentement que j'ay de voir que les veus que j'ay fait a vous seruir sont si bien acceptés comme je troue per le contentement que vous tesmoignes auoir par la conclusion de notre Mariage rien ne mestant si cher que l'asseurance que j'ay que vous me croyés eternellement.

XXI. Monsieur,

Sil ce pouuoit augmenter quelque chose au ressantiment que j'ay de l'honneur que vr̄e Majesté me fait, je la puis assurer que la continuation de sa bien-veilance auroit ce pouuoir, mais je la suplie de croire que mon affection ne se peut augmenter ny jamais alterer, puis qu'elle est au comble de toutes perfections, je remés au s' Gourdon de faire entendre a vr̄e Majesto les particullarités de l'action qui se vient de passer, comme aussi le contentement que j'en resois esperant quelle me donnera bien tost lhonneur que je souhayte et le moyen de pouoir faire connoistre a vr̄e Majeste que je suis,

Monsieur, Vr̄e treshumble et tresobeisante
seruante
HENRIETTE MARIE R.

XXII. Madame,

Je me sens si infinement obligé a vos fauours, que quand j'auois l'enuie de l'exprimer, je troue que lo contentement de l'ame ne scauroit estre exprimé par parolls; ce pourquoy ne schassant commët je me puise satisfair, je remets au S' Gordon tout ce qui se poura dire de la joy et le contentement que j'ay en vostre affection, & l'impatience que j'ay & j'aurny jusques a ce que je vous puis baiser les mains como.

Madame,   Vostre treshûble tresaffectionne
                             & tresfidell seruiter
                                        CHARLES R.

XXIII. Monseigneur,

Jay receu par le retour du s' gordon le contantement que j'esperois 'puis quil m'a asuré de la continuation de l'amitie de v̄r̄e Majesté que je cheris plus que toutes les choses dumonde ne souhaitant rien dauantage que quelque occasion luy en donne de plus particulieres prouues afin quelle me face lhonneur de me croyre,

Monseigneur,   V̄r̄e treshumble et tres
                             obeisante seruante
                                   HENRIETTE MARIE R.

XXIV. L'impatient desir que j'ay de vous voir m'a fait enuoier Buckingham pour accourcir le temps de ma langueur que j'auray tousjours jusques a ce que je vous puise baiser le mains. Je ne veus vous importuner dauantage a cest heur auec ce lettre, esperant dedans peu de temps d'auoir l'honneur de vous dir par bouche combien je suis.

Encor que je vins d'escrir par Bu: qui jespere sera long temps auec vous deuant celle ci, si ce que je ne puis permetre personne de partir vers vous sans porter un tesmoignage de mon afection, mais de peur de tardor trope sur le chomin la chose que j'estime le plus je me contenteray pour lo present de dire que je suis & ne puis jamais estre otre que,

       Vostre tres affectione seruiteur et MARIE.

XXV. Monseigneur,

Me voyant arestee en ce lieu pour quelque jours acause deun peu dindisposition suruenue à la Royne Madame mamore je me trouue conbatue dun double de plaisir pour voir du mal a vne personne qui mest si chera et pour me voir plus eloynee de lesperance que je veys da voir lhonneur de voir bien tost v̄r̄e Majesté jespere aveo layde de Dieu que le mal sesant je me trouuayray dans peu de jours avec le conianionxont que jatans de la vue de v̄r̄e Majeste ce que je souhaite avec la mes afection que je suis,

 Monsiegneur, V̄r̄e treshumble et tres
        obeisante seruante
         Henriette Marie R.

XXVI. Monseigneur,

 Le s' conte de Carlil sannalant trouuer v̄r̄e Majeste manpechern de vous faire longue letre sachant que vous pranderes toute creance en ce quil vous dira de ma part et ce que je a vous temoygner par ces lignes est mon desir et mon inpatience de me voir aupres de v̄r̄e Majeste afin quelle entande par ma bouche plus tost que par mes lottres conbien je suis,

 Monsiegneur, V̄r̄e treshumble et tres
        obeisant servante
         Henriette Marie R.

XXVII. Monseigneur,

 Le s' conte de Mongoumori represantera A v̄r̄e Majeste ce qui est du desir de la Royne Madame mamere et du mien sur lavancement de mon voyage et que le retardement qui ne sera que jusque a Lundi ne procede que de son indisposition ce pandant je vous suplie a voir agreable ce quil vous presentera de ma part afin que vous me fasies lhonneur de vous souuenir de celle qui est,

 Monseigneur, V̄r̄e treshumble et tres
        obeisante seruante
         Henriette Marie R.

www.ingramcontent.com/pod-product-compliance
Lightning Source LLC
Chambersburg PA
CBHW021223300426
44111CB00007B/409